W9-CIK-964

Contents

NINTH BOOK *of* JUNIOR AUTHORS AND ILLUSTRATORS

Edited by

Connie C. Rockman

The H.W. Wilson Company
New York • Dublin
2004

Biographical Reference Books and Databases from The H. W. Wilson Company

Junior Authors Electronic Edition
The Junior Book of Authors
More Junior Authors
Third Book of Junior Authors
Fourth Book of Junior Authors and Illustrators
Fifth Book of Junior Authors and Illustrators
Sixth Book of Junior Authors and Illustrators
Seventh Book of Junior Authors and Illustrators
Eighth Book of Junior Authors and Illustrators

Wilson Biographies Plus Illustrated

American Reformers

Greek and Latin Authors 800 B.C.–A.D. 1000
European Authors 1000–1900
British Authors Before 1800
British Authors of the Nineteenth Century
American Authors 1600–1900
World Authors 1900–1950
World Authors 1950–1970
World Authors 1970–1975
World Authors 1975–1980
World Authors 1980–1985
World Authors 1985–1990
World Authors 1990–1995
World Authors 1995–2000
Spanish American Authors of the Twentieth Century

Old Worlds to New

Great Composers: 1300–1900
Composers Since 1900
Composers Since 1900: First Supplement
Musicians Since 1900
American Songwriters
World Musicians

Nobel Prize Winners
Nobel Prize Winners: Supplements I, II, & III

World Artists 1950–1980
World Artists 1980–1990

Leaders of the Information Age

World Film Directors: Volumes I & II

To Elena and Jon,
for sharing so many reading adventures.

International Standard Book Number 0-8242-1043-3

Library of Congress Cataloging-in-Publication Data

The ninth book of junior authors and illustrators / edited by Connie C. Rockman.
　　p. cm.
　Includes biblographical references and index.
　ISBN 0-8242-1043-3
　1. Children's literature—Bio-bibliography—Dictionaries. 2. Children's literature—Illustrations—Bio-bibliography—Dictionaries. 3. Children—Books and reading—Dictionaries. I. Rockman, Connie.

PN1009.A1N58 2004
809'.89282'03—dc22
[B]

2004061627

Printed in the United States of America

Visit H. W. Wilson's Web site: *www.hwwilson.com*

List of Authors and Illustrators

(Updated profiles from earlier volumes are preceded by an asterisk.)

Preface

The Junior Authors and Illustrators series celebrates the imaginative people who believe that creating books for young people is work of the highest calling. Within these pages you will meet authors and illustrators of picture books, novels, poetry, and informational books of all kinds. These authors and illustrators come from a variety of ethnic and cultural backgrounds; they live in the United States and around the world. But they all have one thing in common: Through their artistry they share deeply held beliefs and dreams with young readers. As you read through these profiles, you will meet people whose life experiences have expanded their view of the world and who are dedicated to passing on what they have learned about joy, sadness, courage, humor, compassion, and hope through the magic of books.

This series has provided access to creators of books for children and young adults for many years. *The Junior Book of Authors*, published in 1934, was the first compilation of its kind, containing short sketches of writers, often autobiographical, and written in a conversational style that gave the impression of a virtual visit with the author. Subsequent volumes have maintained this immediacy while adding to the articles—editorial comments about each person's work, awards and prizes received, representative bibliographies, and suggested lists of articles for further research. The 1934 volume underwent a major revision in 1951, adding many newcomers and dropping some well-known early figures, such as Louisa May Alcott, whose biographies could readily be found in other sources. Since that time, volumes have been added to the series with increasing frequency. While the focus is still on new contributors, the *Eighth Book of Junior Authors and Illustrators* began a process of updating older profiles of prominent people in the field. The *Ninth Book* continues this process, with 17 updated entries that celebrate the long careers of award-winning authors and artists.

Many changes have occurred in literature for young people in the years since this series began. The number of books published each year has grown enormously. Other biographical dictionaries about authors and illustrators have appeared, and a large body of research and critical writing has accumulated, validating the concept of a distinctive literature for children. Cultural diversity has greatly enriched the field. The Internet has created a new venue for research. Information on authors and illustrators is often accessible through online searching, and now this series is also available in an electronic version.

The Junior Authors and Illustrators series provides a unique approach to biographical information. Every attempt is made to obtain a statement in the author's or artist's own words, so that readers can feel they are getting to know each subject in a personal, informal way. The editorial piece in each profile points out information about the life and work that was not mentioned in the autobiography. The bibliographies are not comprehensive lists but are meant to give a representative sampling of each person's work. They include books that are out of print as well as current titles. A list of suggested reading accompanies most of the sketches. This volume, used in conjunction with earlier books in the series or with the *Junior Authors Electronic Edition* offers an excellent point of entry for young readers who want information about their favorite writers and illustrators and provides insights for adult researchers, teachers, librarians, and parents as well.

Like each of the preceding volumes in the series, this one was carefully constructed. The editor compiled a voting list of names gleaned from annual lists of "Best Books," awards in the field, and core lists developed by booksellers and librarians. The list was sent to experts in children's literature, chosen to represent different geographical areas of the country; they were asked to vote for the subjects they felt were most prominent today and to add others they felt should be included. They also voted on a list of articles from earlier volumes to be updated. The expertise of this advisory committee and their collective years of dedicated work in the field of children's books helped ensure the best possible selection of subjects for this volume. Members of the advisory committee for the *Ninth Book of Junior Authors and Illustrators* were: Ellen Fader, youth services coordinator, Multnomah County Library, Oregon; Ginny Moore Kruse, former director, Cooperative Children's Book Center, University of Wisconsin-Madison; Martha V. Parravano, executive editor, *The Horn Book* magazine, Boston, Massachusetts; Grace Ruth, children's materials selection specialist, San Francisco Public Library, California; and Pat Scales, South Carolina Governor's School for the Arts, Greenville, South Carolina.

After the votes were tallied, the authors and illustrators on the final list were contacted through their most recent publisher and asked to contribute an autobiographical sketch. The paragraphs after each autobiography were written either by myself or a freelance researcher. Contributing editors for this volume were Catherine Balkin, Tess Beck, Julie Cummins, Suzanne Hawley, Sara Miller, and Gail Ostrow, and I am deeply grateful for their dedication to tracking down information, verifying facts, and searching out awards, as well as crafting enlightening articles. After the editorial pieces were written, the completed articles were sent to each author and artist for a final verification of facts.

The 17 updated entries for persons who appeared in earlier volumes often include new or substantially revised autobiographical statements and an expanded editorial essay that emphasizes lifetime achievement awards more than prizes won by individual titles. They also have much more substantial representative bibliographies, which include both familiar and lesser-known works, out of print or still available, across the span of a long career.

In recent years many authors and illustrators have created their own Web pages; others have had Web sites created for them by devoted fans; still others have a minimal Internet presence or none at all. To accommodate these developments, we have provided Web site addresses when they seemed substantial and reliable. (E-mail addresses are not included because they tend to be more changeable.) Many authors and artists may be contacted through their Web sites or through the marketing department of their most recent publisher, whose name can easily be discovered through online searching or a visit to the local library.

No work of this magnitude exists without the support and encouragement of many people behind the scenes. I am grateful to Judy O'Malley, now editor at Charlesbridge Publishing, for involving me as a consultant on the Junior Authors series when she was an editor at the H. W. Wilson Company and to Sally Holmes Holtze, editor of the fifth, sixth, and seventh books in the series, who offered much good advice when I began work on the eighth. To Michael Schulze, who hired a "green" editor for the *Eighth Book of Junior Authors and Illustrators* and who has done so much to keep this current project moving along, my heartfelt gratitude for his continuing support. Special thanks to Lynn Messina, editor in the General Reference department, for her attention to detail and her patience as I gathered those details; to Rich Stein and Gray Young for their technical expertise and interest in the project; and to Norris Smith, the very best copy editor, for her meticulous work, her store of literary knowledge, and her sly sense of humor. Thanks to all the members of my New York–based book discussion group for their continued friendship, support, and stimulation. To Paula Quint and Michelle Bayuk of the Children's Book Council, much appreciation for allowing me to preview their new and excellent electronic resource file, Awards and Prizes. For clerical help, kudos go to my ever-dependable assistant, Brie O'Keefe, who graduated from high school as this book graduated from my office. She spent countless hours tracking down titles for the bibliographies, organizing award lists, and completing many other tedious chores. And for his support, patience, and understanding during the long process from start to finish, my husband, Joe Witkavitch, takes the grand prize.

I can never express adequately my gratitude for the help and support that the other editors and I received from marketing and editorial departments in the publishing houses. They contacted authors, provided bibliographic information and biographical pamphlets, answered dozens of questions, and rounded up book jackets to illustrate the articles. The people who publish and market children's books are a community of spirited, dedicated professionals. Their cheerful assistance made this book what it is today. And, finally, I want to thank all the contributors to the *Ninth Book of Junior Authors and Illustrators* who took time away from their own creative lives and livelihoods to write the wonderful autobiographical statements you will enjoy in this volume. They willingly answered questions and verified facts so this volume could be as vibrant and accurate as possible. They have shared their talents with us in remarkable books of all kinds, and now each one also shares a window into his or her own life so that we may know their work a little better than before.

Connie Rockman
Stratford, Connecticut
December 2004

"**I** have always loved to read. Before I could read, I loved to be read to. I memorized all the books my mother read me and corrected her if she turned the page at the wrong word. We quoted lines from books to each other. 'We all have faults,' she would say. 'And mine is being wicked,' I would quote back to her in lines from one of our favorite books, *The Thirteen Clocks*, by James Thurber.

"I never thought much about reading. It was just something I did. I never thought about the person who wrote the book. I never thought about how books were created. It was the book and the people *in* the book that I loved. It wasn't until I was in college that it occurred to me that books were actually written by people, that someone sat down and wrote those books, made up those characters that I loved. In my freshman English class, my wonderful teacher, Miss Rosenberg, gave us the assignment of verifying 25 footnotes in a book called *Shakespeare's Audience*. The book had thousands of footnotes, and I thought the assignment was dumb until I started to do it and found that the author had made incredible mistakes: citing the wrong page, incorrectly quoting, including sentences lifted directly from the source without quotation marks. I never knew whether Miss Rosenberg had selected that book because she found all those errors herself, or whether she knew that no matter what book she chose, it would be replete with mistakes. Whatever her reasons were, the assignment provided me with a completely new perspective on my beloved books. People had created them. Funny that it was the errors in books that made them human to me.

"I did write a few short stories as a kid; one was entitled *The King* and was about a king who had 267 children. The only other one I remember was about a garden hose named Huey, who went traveling around the world. Maybe he was a prince who was turned into a hose. But I only wrote when I was home sick from

Courtesy of Steve Hoffman

Joan Abelove

January 14, 1945–

school and got tired of playing with my paper dolls. Once I got to college, I decided to major in English literature because I loved to read. But I never took a creative writing course. I never felt that I had a creative bone in my body. I simply loved reading.

"When I graduated from college, I had to figure out what to do with my life. I had done everything my parents expected up until then, but now—what was I to do? I didn't have a boyfriend, so I wasn't about to get married. I quickly went out and got a job teaching emotionally disturbed boys at a state hospital. I was supposed to teach them Language Arts, although I didn't know what that was. It turned out I was supposed to teach them how to read. The boys ranged in age from 6 to 16, and most of them couldn't read at all. So I did the only thing I could think of—I read to them. I read them books I had loved as a child, and by the end of the year, they had all learned to read.

"Many years after that, I had the opportunity to go to the Amazonian jungle to do anthropological fieldwork. I lived in an Indian village for two years. When I came back to New York, I got a Ph.D. and started to teach anthropology to undergraduates. But in the back of my mind was a yearning to write a book about that experience. I started and stopped and started and stopped many, many times. Finally, in 1991, I began to take a wonderful class in writing for children, thinking maybe I could get somewhere with my jungle book. But instead I started writing the book that turned out to be my second novel, *Saying It Out Loud*. About three years into writing that book, a voice whispered in my ear, 'Two old white ladies moved into my village today.' And I knew that was it—that was the voice I had been searching for to write my book about the jungle. And so I wrote *Go and Come Back*."

> *"I memorized all the books my mother read me and corrected her if she turned the page at the wrong word."*

❀ ❀ ❀

Born and raised in upstate New York, Joan Abelove received a B.A. degree from Barnard College in New York City in 1966 and a Ph.D. in Anthropology from the City University of New York in 1978. While doing research for her doctoral program in clinical psychology, she spent two years in the Amazon jungle of Peru from 1972 to 1974, living in a village very much like the one that is the setting for her remarkable first novel, *Go and Come Back*. The experience changed her doctoral focus from clinical psychology to cultural anthropology and gave her the raw material for writing a book about the fictional village of Isabo. Once she found the voice of her main character—a young girl in the village who is fascinated by the outsiders who come to study her tribe—the book was on its way to appearing on every one of the year's "best books" lists. It was named both an ALA Notable Children's Book and a Best Book for Young Adults. *Publishers Weekly, Booklist, School Library Journal, The Bulletin of the Center for Children's Books, The Horn Book,* and *Book Links* all praised the book resoundingly for its insightful and respectful look at a completely unfamiliar way of life. More than the differences between cultures, it is the similarities among people the world over that impressed Abelove in the time she spent in the Amazon. While the story is based on real events and the characters on actual people, Abelove has said that writing a fictional account freed her to communicate her experience rather than just report the facts. *Go and Come Back* was also a finalist for the prestigious *Los Angeles Times* Young Adult Book Award.

Abelove's second novel was named to the ALA Best Books for Young Adults list and cited in the New York Public Library's Books for the Teen Age roster. *Saying It Out Loud* was actually the first novel she started to write, while taking a writing workshop with Margaret Gabel at the New School in New York. This poignant story of a high school girl dealing with her mother's death from a brain tumor is based on the author's own experience while she was in her senior year of high school. "Writing about it was therapeutic; it helped me make sense of my life and my feelings," Abelove said in an interview with *Publishers Weekly*, which named the book one of its Best of the Year for 1999.

Joan Abelove married Steve Hoffman in 1987. She lives with her husband, their son Andrew, and two cats in New York City. She works in downtown Manhattan as a technical writer but writes fiction in her free time. In addition to her novels, she has published short stories in anthologies.

Courtesy of DK Publishing

SELECTED WORKS: *Go and Come Back*, 1998; *Saying It Out Loud*, 1999; "Sproing," in *Lost and Found: Award-Winning Authors Sharing Real-Life Experiences Through Fiction*, ed. by M. Jerry and Helen S. Weiss, 2000; "The Best Parts," in *In My Grandmother's House*, ed. by Bonnie Christensen, 2003.

SUGGESTED READING: *Something About the Author*, vol. 110, 2000. Periodicals—Brown, Jennifer, "Joan Abelove," *Publishers Weekly*, June 29, 1998. Online—Interview with Joan Abelove, *www.downhomebooks.com*, August 2003.

"I was born (left-handed) in the United States, in 1958, one of four brothers, the third son of devoted parents: my mother, a talented musician, and my father, the celebrated designer John Alcorn (1935–1992). Together they instilled in all four children a profound respect and love for the arts. My father made a point to work at home. As a result, I had the good fortune

Stephen Alcorn

September 28, 1958–

to be exposed, at a very tender age, to the creative processes that enabled my father, day in and day out, to give tangible shape and form to his unique vision—a vision in which a truly profound appreciation for the marvels of previous epochs converged brilliantly with the unfolding of the future to form a fresh, new language. In my humble opinion, my father's prolific output constitutes one of the most eloquent dialogues between the past and the present, the old and the new, ever to be conducted by a 20th century graphic artist.

"This appreciation for both the old and the new was further nurtured by my having spent a part of my formative years in Florence, Italy, famed as the 'cradle of the Renaissance,' where I met my future wife, botanical artist Sabina Fascione, a native

of Pisa, Italy. In Florence my family and I lived in the bustling quarters of Porta Romana, a district rich in history and populated by industrious artisans of the highest order; there I attended the fabled Istituto Statale d'Arte, an experience that left an indelible impression upon me and infused my work not just with a passion for the history of art, but also with a passion for bold technical experimentation. To this day I continue to work in a wide range of mediums, including (but not limited to) etching, relief-block printmaking, lithography, painting (in oils, watercolor, and casein), and sculpture. This technical versatility, in turn, is echoed by my compulsion to employ, depending on the task at hand, varying degrees of abstraction and/or realism—a direct result, I suspect, of my having had to

Photo by Sabina Fascione Alcorn

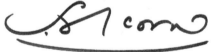

learn a second language (Italian) as a young boy, and of my having experienced, within the confines of the ancient city walls of Florence, not only the inherent modernity of my father's design work, but the discovery of Picasso as well—a curious and immensely stimulating paradox that would forever shape my view of the world. For that contemporaneous absorption of ancient splendor and audacious modernity I shall remain forever grateful, for it taught me, at an impressionable age, to perceive the world from shifting perspectives, and, ultimately, to feel at home working in a modern vernacular as well as a traditional one.

"For as long as I can remember I have felt inclined to employ a variety of styles and techniques; perhaps it is this restless curiosity that has led me to embrace a wide variety of themes in my work, ranging from the interpretation of adult literary classics to the art of the children's picture book. It was my passion for the relief-block print that first drew me, while still a teenager, to publishing, a field inextricably linked to the history of printmaking. Since then the realms of adult and children's literature alike have consistently allowed me to indulge my fondness for whimsical formal invention, a defiance of the laws of gravity, a spirited inversion of scale, and perhaps most significant of all, a revealing marriage of seemingly disparate (but nonetheless compatible) folk and fine art elements. I am fascinated by the juxtaposition of things seen and things dreamed, and I have found that these qualities lend themselves to the interpretation of poetry. This has led to the many poetry-related projects I've embraced, most notably with Lee Bennett Hopkins and Catherine Clinton.

"Since 1986 I have lived and worked with my wife and our two daughters in the village of Cambridge, New York. The year 1993 marked the opening to the general public of the Alcorn Studio & Gallery, a multifaceted workshop featuring rotating exhibits of our painting, printmaking, and art-of-the-book activities. When I am not drawing, making prints, and/or painting, I may be found composing and performing odes to my wife on my beloved Gibson guitar."

"I am fascinated by the juxtaposition of things seen and things dreamed, and I have found that these qualities lend themselves to the interpretation of poetry."

✲ ✲ ✲

Multifaceted artist Stephen Alcorn was born in New York City but moved to Italy with his family when he was a teenager. In 1975, at the age of 17, he illustrated his first book, *Il Naso* (*The Nose*, an absurdist story by Nicholai Gogol), for an Italian publisher. He returned to the United States in 1977 to study at the Cooper Union in New York City but transferred the next year to the State University of New York in Purchase, where he majored in printmaking and painting, graduating with honors in 1980. On his return to Italy in 1981, he married Sabina Fascione, a classmate from Florence and a native of Pisa. Besides being a botanical artist, Sabina is a textile designer and has worked for textile design firms in both Como, Italy, and New York City. During the five years the couple lived in Italy, Stephen continued his work in book illustration (including portraits of 20th century authors for a series of literary works) in addition to his oil painting—Tuscan landscapes, still-lifes, and portraits. His first one-man show was held in Siena in 1982. During this time he was also commissioned by Random House to design a series of interpretive black-and-white linocut prints for the dust jackets and frontispieces of the Modern Library series of classic texts, ranging from Plato to Dostoyevsky.

In 1986 Stephen and Sabina moved to the United States to settle in Cambridge, a small historic town in upstate New York, where they have raised their two daughters, Lucrezia and Ludovica. While continuing to pursue book illustration, Stephen devoted himself at this point to printmaking, experimenting with form and color in his work. An art historian writing in the Italian

ANDREA DAVIS PINKNEY

Let It Shine

Stories of Black Women Freedom Fighters

Illustrated by STEPHEN ALCORN

Courtesy of Gulliver Books, Harcourt, Inc.

publication *Linea Grafica* has said: "Not since the Belgian master Frans Masareel (1889–1972) has an artist reached such elevated heights in the art of printmaking." Stephen's illustrations for *Rembrandt's Beret*, an art history fantasy composed by his brother Johnny, were generally admired, and after the opening of the Alcorn Studio and Gallery to the general public in 1993, his work in children's book illustration increased. His art has enhanced many nonfiction titles about people who have fought for social justice, as well as poetry volumes that express the emotions and convictions of America's multicultural population.

For books in collaboration with writer Milton Meltzer about Abraham Lincoln, Frederick Douglass, and Langston Hughes, Stephen Alcorn created vigorous linoleum blockprints to help earn those volumes a place on the Notable Trade Books in the Field of Social Studies lists. *Frederick Douglass, in His Own Words* was also a Parents' Choice Honor Book and was featured in the New York radio station WBAI's Fourth of July celebration, including a live interview with the artist. *I, Too, Sing America*, a collection of African American poems selected by Catherine Clinton, was named to New York Public Library's list, 100 Titles for Reading and Sharing. Alcorn's new illustrations for Meltzer's revised biography of Langston Hughes, executed in black and white with tones of sepia and blue, perfectly capture the sense of Hughes's work during the Harlem Renaissance and throughout his career, and the book earned a Carter G. Woodson Award. *Let It Shine: Stories of Black Women Freedom Fighters*, written by Andrea Davis Pinkney and illustrated with Alcorn's colorful, intensely evocative oil paintings, was designated an ALA Notable Children's Book and a *Smithsonian* notable book, and recommended by the Bank Street College of Education's Children's Book Committee. Stephen Alcorn's fine craftsmanship and juxtaposition of images that express the unique sense and feeling of each volume have earned him the highest praise from readers and critics alike. In addition to book illustration, his work has appeared in a wide variety of newspapers and magazines, graced CD covers and annual reports, and can be found in galleries, museums, and private collections throughout the United States and Europe.

SELECTED WORKS ILLUSTRATED: *John Brown's Body*, by Stephen Vincent Benét, 1985; *Owl, a Story for Children*, by David Mamet and Lindsay Crouse, 1987; *Rembrandt's Beret, or, The Painter's Crown*, by Johnny Alcorn, 1991; *Lincoln, in His*

Own Words, ed. by Milton Meltzer, 1993; *Frederick Douglass, in His Own Words*, ed. by Milton Meltzer, 1995; *Langston Hughes*, by Milton Meltzer, 1997; *I, Too, Sing America: Three Centuries of African-American Poetry*, sel. by Catherine Clinton, 1998; *My America: A Poetry Atlas of the United States*, sel. by Lee Bennett Hopkins, 2000; *Nazi Germany: The Face of Tyranny*, by Ted Gottfried, 2000; *Let It Shine: Stories of Black Women Freedom Fighters*, by Andrea Davis Pinkney, 2000; *Year of the Paper Menorahs*, by Doreen Rappaport, 2000; *Children of the Slaughter: Young People of the Holocaust*, by Ted Gottfried, 2001; *Deniers of the Holocaust: Who They Are, What They Do, Why They Do It*, by Ted Gottfried, 2001; *Displaced Persons: The Liberation and Abuse of Holocaust Survivors*, by Ted Gottfried, 2001; *Heroes of the Holocaust*, by Ted Gottfried, 2001; *Home to Me: Poems Across America*, sel. by Lee Bennett Hopkins, 2002; *Broken Feather*, by Verla Kay, 2002; *Hoofbeats, Claws & Rippled Fins: Creature Poems*, sel. by Lee Bennett Hopkins, 2002; *Poems of Her Own: Voices of American Women Yesterday and Today*, ed. by Catherine Clinton, 2003; *The Book of Rock Stars: 24 Musical Icons That Shine Through History*, by Kathleen Krull, 2003.

SUGGESTED READING: Fischer, Mary Pat, and Paul Zelanski. *The Art of Seeing*, 2nd ed., 2000. Periodicals—Baroni, Daniele, "L'Illustrazione di Stephen Alcorn," *Linea Grafica*, no. 296, Milano, Italy, 1995 (cover story); Brower, Steven, "I Know It's Only Rock 'n' Roll . . .: Stephen Alcorn's Music Masters Series Gives New Life and Luster to Pop Icons," *Print*, January 2003; Croop, Patti, "The Texture of Life: Cambridge Artist Stephen Alcorn Uses Variety of Media to Create Striking Images," *Glens Falls Journal*, April 2001; Stevens, Carol, "Choice Cuts: Linocut Portraits by Stephen Alcorn," *Print*, January/February 1994.

WEB SITE: *www.alcorngallery.com*

Sally Hobart Alexander

October 17, 1943–

"Recently a writing friend told me, 'a consistent motif in your books is water as a healing force.'

"'No kidding!' I replied, but I shouldn't have been surprised. "Poet Kathleen Norris speaks of our 'emotional geography' as the setting in which we feel most comfortable and at home. Water is surely that for me, whether lake or creek or pool or ocean.

"During most of the first half of my life, the sighted part, I lived in rural Pennsylvania, tramping through creeks in woods and mill streams. My favorite spot in all the world was Greenwood Lake, the setting for *Maggie's Whopper*. I canoed and rowed boats and caught salamanders there. At the age of four, I learned to swim there. I still remember the wondrous experience of mastering the concept of breathing under water, blowing out the air slowly in an effortless oneness with the water. This skill served me well later in high school and college water ballet shows. My friends and I linked our feet to each other's neck and chin for chain back dolphins, then disappeared for a minute or two beneath the surface.

"Greenwood Lake is still 'clean enough to drink,' as my daughter puts it. Sand covers the bottom and the beach. Woods surround it, and only three cabins occupy it, so it is quiet and private and no different today than it was in 1947. I caught my first fish at Greenwood and at 16 had my first boyfriends there.

"After college, I left northeastern Pennsylvania for a teaching job in southern California. I snagged an apartment between the ocean and the bay. I swam in that bay, sailed, played beach volleyball, and always strolled the beach. *Taking Hold: My Journey into Blindness* begins on that beach: 'I walk barefoot on the beach, sliding my feet through the warm sand, not knowing that something is about to happen that will change my whole way of life forever.' The book ends at Greenwood when I, blind now, make a final decision about an ex-fiancé and launch a new beginning.

Courtesy of Sally Hobart Alexander

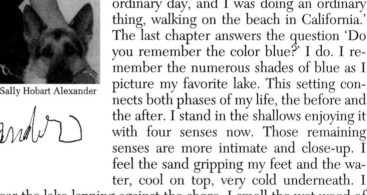

"Unintentionally, my question-and-answer book, *Do You Remember the Color Blue?* begins and ends the same way. Chapter one of the book answers the question how I became blind: 'I still remember everything about the day it began. It was an ordinary day, and I was doing an ordinary thing, walking on the beach in California.' The last chapter answers the question 'Do you remember the color blue?' I do. I remember the numerous shades of blue as I picture my favorite lake. This setting connects both phases of my life, the before and the after. I stand in the shallows enjoying it with four senses now. Those remaining senses are more intimate and close-up. I feel the sand gripping my feet and the water, cool on top, very cold underneath. I hear the lake lapping against the shore. I smell the wet wood of the pines.

"The books set in the second half of my life, *Mom Can't See Me* and *Mom's Best Friend*, take place in the city, the emotional geography of my children, who claim to 'love concrete.' The city is the venue for my everyday life as wife, mother, and writer. Errands to the grocery, book, video, and drug stores highlight the feel of the hard edge of sidewalk curbs, the noise of traffic, the echo of my footsteps bouncing off the telephone poles. In both phases of life, the sighted and the blind, my goal is to be outside, not confined within a safe house, safe from injury, safe from embarrassment. Inside is easy for a blind person; the challenge and difficulty is outside, but that is where the triumph is, too.

"When the photographer came to shoot *Mom Can't See Me*, he had planned all the shots to be indoors. He was responding to the stereotype that blind people should be inside where the risks are few. But I wanted the book to reflect my life, and that is outdoors, as it's always been.

"I still love the setting of my younger life with its sounds of ocean waves and lakes lapping, but I've also psychically absorbed this urban setting. The roar of buses and cars and all the traffic sounds have become friends, too. Their noises guide me and help orient me for my independent life. And the city of Pittsburgh, where I live, has water. We have parks with ponds and streams and three huge rivers. All those waterways lap against the shore and offer calm to a busy, vibrant city life."

Courtesy of Viking Children's Books

❊ ❊ ❊

Sally Hobart Alexander was born in Owensboro, Kentucky, but her family moved to Pennsylvania very early in her life, and she grew up in the small rural town of Conyngham. She received her B.S. degree from Bucknell University and taught in Long Beach, California, from 1965 until 1969. Returning to western Pennsylvania after her blindness, she enrolled in an excellent training program for newly blinded adults at the Pittsburgh Guild for the Blind and also taught there for a year. After attaining a master's degree in social work from the University of Pittsburgh, Alexander was a child therapist at St. Francis Hospital of Pittsburgh from 1973 till 1976.

In June of 1974, Sally Hobart married Robert Alexander and left her job in child therapy when her son was born. She and Robert have two grown children, Joel and Leslie. When Sally realized how much she enjoyed concocting stories for her young children, she joined a writing workshop and began to write seriously. Her greatest contribution to the field has been the books that explain to children what life is like for a person without sight. *Mom Can't See Me*, a picture book for young readers, was cited by the National Council of Teachers of English and placed on *Booklist* magazine's Editors' Choice list as an outstanding nonfiction work. *Mom's Best Friend* explains for children the special relationship between a Seeing Eye guide dog and its owner. Sally Alexander's autobiographical books, *Taking Hold* and *On My Own*, follow the course of her life from the sudden onset of blindness when she was 24 years old through her growth in independent living without sight. *Taking Hold* received a Christopher Medal in 1995 and was named one of the New York Public Library's Books for the Teen Age. *Do You Remember the Color Blue?*, answering the many questions children often ask about blindness, was cited as a Notable Social Studies Trade Book for Young People.

Sally Alexander currently lives in Pittsburgh with her husband.

SELECTED WORKS: *Mom Can't See Me*, photos by George Ancona, 1990; *Sarah's Surprise*, illus. by Jill Kastner, 1990; *Mom's Best Friend*, photos by George Ancona, 1992; *Maggie's Whopper*, illus. by Deborah Kogan Ray, 1992; *Taking Hold: My Journey into Blindness*, 1994; *On My Own: The Journey Continues*, 1997; *Do You Remember the Color Blue?: And Other Questions Kids Ask About Blindness*, 2000.

SUGGESTED READING: *Contemporary Authors*, vol. 150, 1996; *Something About the Author*, vol. 84, 1996.

Courtesy of Bill Eichner

Julia Alvarez

March 27, 1950–

"I always say that I would never have become a writer unless I had come to the United States at the age of ten. Oddly enough, I was born in New York City during my parents' first and failed emigration to the States. They returned to their homeland when I was three months old. I grew up in the Dominican Republic in the 1950s during a dangerous and bloody dictatorship. My family didn't own many books. In fact, I hardly ever saw anyone reading. Books were not only ignored, they were considered dangerous. In a dictatorship where every word was censored, people were careful not to give the wrong impression. To be caught reading was to be branded an intellectual, a troublemaker. Although I did not grow up among books or readers, I did grow up in an oral culture where storytelling was a high art. My family was full of great storytellers, vying for the limelight at the big, midday meal where the extended family came together to nurture each other with food and stories.

"My exposure to books did not happen until our immigration to New York City. In August 1960, my father's participation in an underground group of freedom fighters was discovered and we were forced to flee. Overnight, we lost everything—our country, our home, our extended family structure, our economic security, our language.

We became 'spics' with no money or prospects. We arrived in this country at a time in history that was not very welcoming to people who were different, whose skins were a different color, whose language didn't sound like English. I struggled with a language and a culture I didn't understand.

"Homesick and lonely, I soon discovered a refuge. Between the covers of books, I found what I had been looking for on the streets and playgrounds of the U.S.A. A portable homeland where I belonged, where my spirit was free to soar. I became a reader. Soon, I began to dream that maybe I, too, could create worlds where no one would be barred. But that dream of becoming a writer required hard work. When I started writing, none of the great classics I read in school were written by anyone like me. How could a Dominican girl with Spanish as her first language ever become an American writer?

"But I was forgetting something. We had arrived with only four suitcases, but there were hundreds of stories in my head and a passion for storytelling in my heart. And so I kept writing. The books I read encouraged me. 'I'm nobody. Who are you? Are you nobody, too? Then there's a pair of us.' (Emily Dickinson) Another message read: 'I, too sing America. I am the darker brother.' (Langston Hughes) These words were secret handshakes being passed around an underground of book- and freedom-lovers: *We are free spirits. Please pass on this important message!* Finally, in 1991, when I was 41 years old, after over 20 years of writing with no success, my first novel, *How the García Girls Lost Their Accents*, was published. My bottle had finally been found on the shore! I had passed on my own words to others.

"As for writing for younger readers? I became interested in children's literature when my husband and I started a sustainable farming project in the mountains of the Dominican Republic. When we discovered that over 95 percent of our neighbors did not know how to read or write, we decided to open a school and a small library on the farm. At Alta Gracia (as we named the farm and literacy center), we used children's books to teach literacy. I began to read a lot of literature for young readers. I discovered a dearth of books dealing with the stories I had heard as a young girl in the Dominican Republic and with the histories, tragedies, and triumphs of our countries south of the U.S.A. border. My first picture book, *The Secret Footprints*, was based on the legend of the *ciguapas*, which my mountain neighbors at Alta Gracia all know by heart.

"Knowing by heart is always my first step as a writer. But the message has to be put down on paper and inserted in a capsule that can weather the seas of time. My hope is that the books I write will reach readers with that important, implicit message of the best literature: *We all belong.*"

"We had arrived with only four suitcases, but there were hundreds of stories in my head and a passion for storytelling in my heart."

❋   ❋   ❋

Although Julia Alvarez was born in New York City, her physician father moved the family to the Dominican Republic shortly after her birth. Ties to the United States, however, remained strong in a family where all her uncles had attended Ivy League colleges and her grandfather was a cultural attaché at the United Nations. Even while she lived in the Dominican Republic, Alvarez dressed like an American, went to an American school, and spent much of her day speaking and reading English. In 1960, her father's involvement with an unsuccessful attempt to overthrow the Trujillo dictatorship forced the family to emigrate back to New York, though by the time she was fifteen, Alvarez and her sisters were returning to the Dominican Republic every summer.

After her move to the United States, Alvarez attended private school and, in 1967, enrolled at Connecticut College. After two years she transferred to Middlebury College, where she was elected to Phi Beta Kappa and received her B.A. in 1971. Her M.A. in creative writing was granted by Syracuse University in 1975. Pursuing an academic career in conjunction with her writing, Alvarez has taught English and writing at Phillips Andover Academy, the University of Vermont, George Washington University, the University of Illinois, and at Middlebury, where she became a tenured professor in 1991. She resigned her professorship in 1998 to teach part-time as a writer-in-residence.

Alvarez's first adult novel, *How the García Girls Lost Their Accents*, tells the story of four sisters who, like the author and her family, emigrated to New York from the Dominican Republic and struggled to find an identity between two disparate cultures. The same characters appear in her 1997 novel *¡Yo!. In the Time of the Butterflies*, which also draws on her Latina roots as well as her father's revolutionary involvement, was named an American Library Association Notable Book and a National Book Critics Circle Award finalist. Alvarez writes in a variety of genres and has published essays, stories, and poems in the *New York Times Magazine*, *Allure*, the *New Yorker*, *Hispanic Magazine*, *Latina*, *USA Weekend*, the *Washington Post Magazine*, and the *American Scholar*, among others.

All three of Alvarez's children's books have been cited by the New York Public Library on its annual list, 100 Titles for Reading and Sharing. *How Tía Lola Came to (Visit) Stay* was named a *Child Magazine* Best Children's Book and a *Parent's Guide to*

Children's Media Outstanding Book for 2001. *Before We Were Free*, a novel that tells the story from a child's point of view of a family's involvement in the plot to overthrow Trujillo, was designated an ALA Notable Children's Book as well as an ALA Best Book for Young Adults. In 2004 *Before We Were Free* won Julia Alvarez the Pura Belpré Award, which honors Latino authors and illustrators whose work "best portrays, affirms and celebrates the Latino cultural experience in a children's book."

SELECTED WORKS FOR YOUNG READERS: *The Secret Footprints*, illus. by Fabian Negrin, 2000; *How Tía Lola Came to (Visit) Stay*, 2001; *Before We Were Free*, 2002.

SELECTED WORKS FOR ADULTS: *Homecoming: Poems*, 1984; *How the García Girls Lost Their Accents*, 1991; *In the Time of the Butterflies*, 1994; *The Other Side: El Otro Lado*, 1995; *Homecoming: New and Collected Poems*, 1996; *¡Yo!*, 1997; *Something to Declare: Essays*, 1998; *Seven Trees*, 1999; *In the Name of Salomé*, 2000; *A Cafecito Story*, 2001.

SUGGESTED READING: *Contemporary Authors*, New Revision Series, vol. 101, 2002; *Dictionary of Hispanic Biography*, 1995; *Notable Hispanic American Women*, 1998; *Something About the Author*, vol. 129, 2002; *World Authors 1990–1995*, 1999. Periodicals—Alvarez, Julia, "Place of a Lifetime: Dominican Republic," *National Geographic Traveler*, October 2002; Bing, Jonathan, "Julia Alvarez: Books That Cross Borders," *Publishers Weekly*, December 16, 1996; Jacques, Ben, "Julia Alvarez: Real Flights of Imagination," *Americas*, January 2001; Prescott, Stephanie, "Julia Alvarez: Dominican American Storyteller," *Faces: People, Places, and Cultures*, February 1999.

Rudolfo Anaya
October 30, 1937–

"When I was a student at the University of New Mexico in the early 1960s I felt a desire to write. I felt I had a story to tell, my story. At first I wrote poems, short stories, adventure novels, but none seemed to tell the story I really needed to tell. When I started to write my first novel, *Bless Me, Ultima*, a fictional account about growing up in my hometown of Santa Rosa, New Mexico, I knew I had found a story worth telling.

"As a child growing up in that small town in New Mexico, on the banks of the Pecos River, I loved to listen to the stories of the elders. The Hispanic/Mexican-American population has a rich storehouse of folktales. Storytelling was a natural pastime in our home, and so the oral tradition was a great influence on me. Later, when I started public school, I learned I loved to read.

"These simple lessons have served me well as a writer. First, one must write a story that really needs to be told. Secondly, you listen to the stories people tell about their lives. Finally, you read as much as you can.

"I was born in 1937 on the eastern plains of New Mexico. My Spanish-speaking ancestors settled there long before New Mexico was a state. My parents were hard-working farmers and ranchers, so they had no public school education. We spoke only Spanish at home; when I started school it was quite a shock to have to learn English.

"Our family was large, and all of us children attended school because my parents realized the value of a good education. My mother, especially, encouraged us to learn. It wasn't easy to go from a Spanish-speaking family and community to one that spoke English, but I survived. When I look back I realize how much my family upheld us. As did our friends, neighbors, and the teachers who knew we needed extra help if we were going to stay in school.

Courtesy of Mimi

"The small-town influence helped also; we knew everyone, and if we stepped out of line neighbors were sure to tell our parents. I have fond memories of playing at the river all summer long, starting school, going to my grandfather's farm in autumn to pick vegetables and fruit. During harvest time neighbors would help neighbors, and there was always a good storyteller to entertain us. Since then I have translated from Spanish to English many of those folktales from our community.

"During my sophomore year in high school I had a swimming accident. I suffered fractured vertebrae and had to convalesce in a hospital that summer. Traumatic accidents do tend to affect and shape one's entire life. I regained my health and was able to graduate from high school, and a few years later I enrolled at the University of New Mexico. That's where I really fell in love with reading. University classes were difficult; I was poorly prepared for the rigors of academic life. But my family and friends stood by me, and so did my love for literature.

"I never thought I would be a published author, but I loved to write. When you love something you have to stick to it. After I graduated from the university I was a teacher in the Albuquerque public schools. I loved teaching. I met and married Patricia. Since she also loves books we have a wonderful life together.

"When my granddaughter Kristan came along, I told her bedtime stories. She especially loved the scary stories I composed. I thought of writing the stories and sending them to a publisher. That's how I got started writing for young people. I love to go to elementary and middle schools and tell stories to students.

"Being a teacher and an author has been a wonderful career, and it is a very important part of my life. I encourage young people to read. I know a lot of the new technology is enticing, but there's nothing like a good book. Nothing like a good story."

❁ ❁ ❁

Born in Pastura, New Mexico, the prize-winning Chicano novelist, poet, social historian, and teacher Rudolfo Anaya is widely known for his work for adults. A passionate exponent of Hispanics' discovering—and taking pride in—their own rich heritage, he has imbued his writing with a combination of folklore, mystical experience, and realism. After spending his childhood in the village of Santa Rosa, he moved with his family to Albuquerque as a teenager, entering high school there. The swimming accident he suffered in high school was fictionalized years later in his novel *Tortuga*. He recovered from the paralysis caused by his spinal injury, made good grades, and was determined to have an active, exciting life that would include travel and mountain climbing. First, though, he went to business school to become an accountant. Finding that such a career didn't suit him, Anaya returned to school, working his way through the University of New Mexico, earning a B.A. in 1963, an M.A. in English in 1968, and returning for a second M.A. in guidance and counseling in 1972. He continued to struggle with formal English, wrote poetry, and taught in junior high and high school. During that time he met and married Patricia Lawless, a writer. Believing in Anaya's creative gifts, Patricia encouraged him to keep writing. He did so, after school hours, and began the book that would become *Bless Me, Ultima*.

Critics and reviewers praised *Bless Me, Ultima* as an extraordinary work, one that burst upon the American literary scene filled with Mexican American character, life, and feeling. In the novel, Anaya introduces an old woman known as a healer, a *curandera*. She represents beauty and connection to a traditional way of life to the young protagonist, who tries to merge that life with modern, urban ways. Winning the Premio Quinto Sol Award for the best Chicano novel of 1972, the book made Anaya a prominent author, and he moved to a position in the English Department at the University to teach creative writing. *Heart of Aztlan* and *Tortuga*, both award-winning and much discussed novels, continued Anaya's exploration of old and new ways, faith and modern life. He wrote four mystery thrillers in the 1990s, beginning with *Albuquerque,* and has published poetry, short stories, political essays, and plays as well. In 2001 Rudolfo Anaya received a National Medal of Arts, one of this country's highest honors available to a writer.

Entering the field of children's books in 1995 with a picture book, *The Farolitos of Christmas*, Anaya won the very first Tomás Rivera Mexican American Children's Book Award, given by Southwest Texas State University. *Farolitos for Abuelo*, a gentle

"As a child growing up in that small town in New Mexico, on the banks of the Pecos River, I loved to listen to the stories of the elders."

ILLUSTRATED BY AMY CÓRDOVA

Courtesy of HarperCollins Children's Books

story about the death of a young girl's beloved grandfather and her remembrance of him, was named a Notable Trade Book in the Field of Social Studies. *My Land Sings: Stories from the Rio Grande*, a collection of 10 short stories for young adults reflecting Hispanic and Native American heritage in the Southwest, received the 1999 Tomás Rivera Mexican American Children's Book Award. The author has adapted *The Farolitas of Christmas* as a play and seen it first produced by the Menaul High School Theater in Albuquerque. In 1993, with his wife, Patricia, Rudolfo Anaya established the Premio Aztlán Literary Prize to reward and encourage new Chicano/Chicana writers. Over the years this award has helped many now-established writers to begin their careers.

SELECTED WORKS WRITTEN FOR CHILDREN: *The Farolitos of Christmas*, illus. by Edward Gonzales, 1995; *Maya's Children*, illus. by Maria Baca, 1997; *My Land Sings: Stories from the Rio Grande*, illus. by Amy Cordova, 1999; *Farolitos for Abuelo*, illus. by Edward Gonzales, 1999; *Elegy on the Death of Cesar Chavez*, illus. by Gaspar Enriquez, 2000; *Roadrunner's Dance*, illus. by David Diaz, 2000.

SELECTED WORKS WRITTEN FOR ADULTS: *Bless Me, Ultima*, 1972; *Heart of Aztlan*, 1976; *Tortuga*, 1979; *Albuquerque*, 1992; *Zia Summer*, 1995; *Shaman Winter*, 1999.

SUGGESTED READING: *Authors and Artists for Young Adults*, vol. 20, 1997; *Beacham's Guide to Literature for Young Adults*, vol. 13, 2001; *Chicano Authors: Inquiry by Interview*, 1980; *Contemporary Authors*, New Revision Series, vol. 51, 1996; *Contemporary Authors*, New Revision Series, vol. 124, 2002; *Contemporary Authors Autobiography Series*, vol. 4, 1986; *World Authors 1985–1990*, 1995.

M. T. Anderson

November 4, 1968–

"People write for children for two reasons: Either they have children, or they are children. I'm in the latter category. I loved my childhood, and I write for children so that I can recall it.

"I grew up in a small town surrounded by apple orchards and woods that had grown up where fields once stood. My town was one of the first to oppose the British during the Revolution. I spent my childhood playing in the forest, naming the streams and the valleys formed by quarries. I was not the only one to wander in those woods, and I was always stumbling across weird assemblages of refuse in glades and on hidden paths: automobile chassis overgrown with sweet-fern; bizarre curtains of unspooled cassette tape hanging across ravines; a window leaning on an old, burnt washing machine festooned with yarn. These artifacts arose naturally out of the landscape like story itself. The forest seemed to be bursting with fantasy. The wood led right up to our back door like George MacDonald's *Fairy-Land*, but with bikers, keggers, and free-range junkies.

"I didn't live near many kids and I was socially inept anyway, so my fantasy world was very involved and quite internal. I apparently became a little too dreamy and distracted—so much so that in fifth grade, my teachers became concerned that I was borderline autistic or had some serious learning disability; and my grandmother, seeing me whisper to some imaginary androids in the woods, became convinced that I was possessed by evil spirits. For the next 10 years or so, she would regularly exorcise me.

Courtesy of Candlewick Press

"My love of fantasy became a love of literature. I began to write plays for my friends to put on. When I was about eleven, we did a dramatic version of *Beowulf* with a giant foam-rubber dragon puppet and lots of gruesome alliteration that was supposed to be Anglo-Saxon. Around the same time, we did *A Midsummer Night's Fever*, which was supposed to be *A Midsummer Night's Dream* recast with John Travolta. I don't remember much about it except that Puck sang in a high-pitched voice like the BeeGees.

"There's not much more to tell. The important thing to do if you want to be a writer is first of all to read—read everything— romance novels, 19th-century novels, Sanskrit prayers, Greek epics, Chinese poetry, installation instructions for plumbing, trade magazines for petshop owners—everything—and second of all, to write. Staring into the woods dreaming, after all, will only get you so far."

✢ ✢ ✢

Born in Cambridge, Massachusetts, Matthew Tobin Anderson—who goes by the name Tobin—grew up in the nearby town of Stow, though his family lived in Italy for two years when he was a small child. Tobin attended Stow's public school until he was 13 and then St. Mark's School in Southborough, Massachusetts. At age 17 he attended Winchester College in England, then (briefly) Harvard University in 1987, completing his B.A. degree at Peterhouse College, Cambridge University, England, in 1991. He worked as an intern at the *Boston Review*, a magazine that combines political, cultural, and literary material, for a semester immediately after college. Then for several years he was an editorial assistant at Candlewick Press in Cambridge, Massachusetts. During that time he also worked as a disc jockey at WCUW, a public radio station in Worcester, and reviewed classical music for *The Improper Bostonian*. In 1996 he left Candlewick to pursue a graduate degree and concentrate on his own writing, and in 1998 he earned an M.F.A. in creative writing at Syracuse University.

On the publication of his first novel for young adults, *Thirsty*, Tobin Anderson was hailed as a fresh new voice in the field; the book received a Blue Ribbon citation from the *Bulletin of the Center for Children's Books* and was named a Quick Pick for Reluctant YA Readers by the American Library Association. This debut novel combines social commentary and adolescent psychology with gothic horror to create a vampire story with an original ironic twist. His second novel, *Burger Wuss*, a New York Public Library Book for the Teen Age selection, showcases Anderson's wickedly incisive humor. A story of young love and the revenge of the underdog, it is also a witty take on the fast-food industry, owing much to the author's own brief experience as a teenage employee of McDonald's.

> *"I loved my childhood, and I write for children so that I can recall it."*

Anderson's unerring ear for contemporary teen language patterns and his skill in satirical writing combined in a tour-de-force novel, *Feed*, which became a finalist for the National Book Award, winner of the *Los Angeles Times* young adult prize, and a *Boston Globe–Horn Book* Honor Book in the fiction category. In addition to being cited by many journals in the "best" lists for 2002, *Feed* was a *Publishers Weekly* Cuffie Award winner for Favorite Novel of the Year and Best Opening Line. Original and outrageous, *Feed* takes the reader into the garbled minds of teenagers of the future, who casually accept spring break trips to the moon, sexual promiscuity, and the ever-present "feed" that is implanted in their brains—a combination of MTV, instant-messaging, advertisements, round-the-clock news, and every other simultaneous distraction you can imagine without being able to turn it off. This tragicomic, over-the-top satire of a wired consumer society rewards its readers with much food for thought.

Employing the same humorous wit that enlivens his young adult novels, Anderson's short biographies of musicians, both classical and contemporary, breathe new life into these historic figures. *Handel, Who Knew What He Liked*, with illustrations by Kevin Hawkes, was an ALA Notable Children's Book and a *Boston Globe–Horn Book* Honor Book in the nonfiction category as well as a Notable Children's Trade Book in the Field of Social Studies. Emphasizing childhood pranks and humorous incidents, Anderson makes the master of Baroque seem remarkably human. He does the same for a very different musical icon in *Strange Mr. Satie*, wittily illustrated by Petra Mathers. His most recent book is a middle-grade adventure story, *The Game of Sunken Places*, with a fast-moving plot and a mysterious forest reminiscent of the one he explored as a child.

Tobin Anderson currently lives in Cambridge, Massachusetts, and serves as faculty chair of the Vermont College M.F.A. program in Writing for Children and Young Adults. He has published a number of short stories in various journals and is the fiction editor for *3rd bed*, a literary journal devoted to surreal and absurdist writing.

SELECTED WORKS: *Thirsty*, 1997; *Burger Wuss*, 1999; *Handel, Who Knew What He Liked*, illus. by Kevin Hawkes, 2001; *Feed*, 2002; *Strange Mr. Satie*, illus. by Petra Mathers, 2003; *The Game of Sunken Places*, 2004.

SUGGESTED READING: Anderson, M. T., "A Brief Guide to the Ghosts of Great Britain" (memoir), in *Open Your Eyes: Extraordinary Experiences in Faraway Places*, ed. by Jill Davis, 2003; *Something About the Author*, vol. 146, 2004. Periodicals—Anderson, M. T., "The Writer's Page Not a Vaudeville Routine: How to Write Comic Dialogue," *The Horn Book*, March 2001.

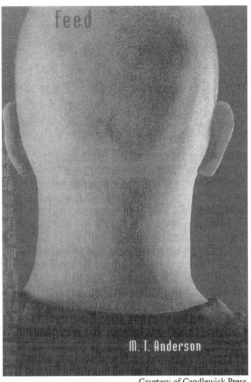

Courtesy of Candlewick Press

Catherine and Laurence Anholt

Catherine Anholt: January 18, 1958–

Laurence Anholt: August 4, 1959–

Laurence Anholt writes: "If there's one thing I feel most grateful for in my upbringing, it is that my parents had extremely eclectic tastes. I was taught to value diversity above all else. My father—a kindly, frustrated, complicated man with strong artistic leanings—taught me to appreciate artists from Caravaggio to Robert Crumb. My mother, an English teacher, helped me to realise that it is safe to experiment with a mixed dose of Tintin and Tolstoy. My childhood was punctuated by fiery debates in which nothing was taboo; my father gleefully playing 'devil's advocate' to stir things up.

"My three siblings and I spent those early years in Amsterdam, a delightfully cosmopolitan place to which I often return. Our ancestry is a strange mixture of Dutch, English, Scottish, and Eastern European (my three children have all that, with a liberal dash of Irish too!). I have always believed that—unlike an artist's pigments—blood does not turn muddy-grey when mixed and mixed again; on the contrary, it grows thicker and redder and more full of Life.

"The trouble with all this free thinking and continual immersion in the world of the imagination is that a child can develop a mind like a butterfly—full of colourful ideas, but with a morbid fear of closed boxes! If the said child is sent to an old-fashioned English boarding school, trouble will be sure to follow. My school days were an unmitigated disaster; I left with few qualifications and a thirst for freedom. However, I loved to write and draw and I also had a remarkable repertoire of silly voices! At sixteen, I was fortunate enough to stumble into art school, where I felt immediately at home and spent the next eight years of my life. Again, I frustrated my tutors with a reluctance to settle to a particular 'style,' preferring instead to flit from tiny realistic drawings to huge abstract paintings to peculiar three-dimensional constructions. I tried animation and printmaking and began to write a few poems and short stories. I graduated, eventually, with a master's degree from the Royal Academy of Art in London and met Catherine, my friend, co-worker and, later, mother of our three children, Claire and twins Tom and Maddy.

Courtesy of Sherina Cadnum

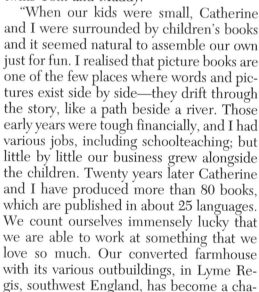

"When our kids were small, Catherine and I were surrounded by children's books and it seemed natural to assemble our own just for fun. I realised that picture books are one of the few places where words and pictures exist side by side—they drift through the story, like a path beside a river. Those early years were tough financially, and I had various jobs, including schoolteaching; but little by little our business grew alongside the children. Twenty years later Catherine and I have produced more than 80 books, which are published in about 25 languages. We count ourselves immensely lucky that we are able to work at something that we love so much. Our converted farmhouse with its various outbuildings, in Lyme Regis, southwest England, has become a chaotic but surprisingly effective environment in which family and business life are intertwined. Catherine is one of eight siblings, so our children have dozens of small cousins who constantly 'road test' our books. We also own a store in Lyme Regis, which is stocked with our books, cards, and prints. There is a small children's museum upstairs, showing how a book is made.

"Through the work, we have met many extraordinary people and visited some amazing places. For example, as I write this I have just returned from a five-week author tour of the Far East, where I found myself in huge schools in Jakarta and Singapore and remote villages in the forests of Bali and Java. More than anything else, it is the variety that I enjoy so much. At any one time, I have several widely different projects 'on the go.' For example, I have just completed the latest in my self-illustrated series about Great Artists and the real children who knew them—this time the focus was on Monet. At the same time I am involved with the animated adaptation of my Seriously Silly Stories (called Funny Fairy Tales in the United States). Meanwhile, Catherine and I are immersed in the latest adventures of Chimp and Zee, our character series for the very young. All we need is a few more hours in the day!"

Catherine Anholt continues:

"My parents are from Kerry in Southern Ireland, but I grew up in a tiny village in the Cotswold Hills in England, in fact the very part of the world where Laurie Lee's *Cider with Rosie* takes place. I was one of eight children, so have always retained a strong image of childhood. My father was a potter and artist, and part of our old cottage was given over to this. My mother was a children's nurse at a nearby hospital.

"I have vivid memories of being brought up in a creative household—drawing and making things with clay. For a few years I worked as a nurse myself, before turning to a career in art, which seemed better suited to my temperament. At art school I rediscovered a whole part of myself and a passion for colour, marks, and images. After the birth of our first child, Claire, which coincided with finishing an M.A. at the Royal College of Art, I decided to try to find some way of continuing my interest in art whilst being around to see our new family grow up. Although I had been trained in fine art, illustration was new to me and at first came very slowly. All my drawings are from memory, although I have always intended to work from life. Other people observe that I absorb the environment I live in subliminally and references pop up in my work without my realising it.

"I work very closely with my husband, Laurence, who writes the text for our books as well as illustrating his own stories. Our first ideas were developed on the kitchen table, surrounded by highchairs and soggy cookies. Working with a partner can be incredibly effective because there is a kind of shorthand in place, so that we are able to focus in on ideas very quickly and we have exactly the same vested interest in getting the thing to work. I think Laurence and I share visual sensibilities—we are equally responsive to colour and have collected numerous paintings over the years. Our house, near the sea in Lyme Regis, southwest England, is crammed with books and colourful objects, which we have collected from around the world and from artist friends. The downside of a family business is that it is difficult to switch off, and whenever we take a walk or a holiday, we inevitably end up talking about our latest project. Sometimes we push an idea around for months on end, pushing it backward and forward until it takes shape. Children's books are minimal constructions,

"I realised that picture books are one of the few places where words and pictures exist side by side—they drift through the story, like a path beside a river."

but that doesn't make it easier; on the contrary, every word and every detail has to be exactly right.

"Our business has grown with our three children and now they are independent teenagers; for them, the sky is the limit. I am really pleased to say that for Laurence and me, the same thing is true of our work—we are as excited by it now as when we began, and we have many ideas for the future. We are currently involved with all kinds of subsidiary projects, such as animation and merchandising. My biggest project at the moment is Chimp and Zee—stories based on memories of our twins, Tom and Maddy, when they were very young. We are always looking for universal themes—the daily ups and downs of family life and the development of young children. We want children to identify with our characters and themes and we want them to laugh. Our ultimate aim is to produce that elusive thing: a timeless classic children's story. I never forget how fortunate I am to be able to work from home at something I really enjoy."

❀   ❀   ❀

> "We want children to identify with our characters and themes and we want them to laugh."

A popular and critically acclaimed author/illustrator team in Great Britain, Laurence and Catherine Anholt create books together that reflect their own close family life and the stages they have observed in the lives of their three children. Laurence has written all of their books that Catherine has illustrated. In addition, he has illustrated some of his own stories and has written a number of books illustrated by other artists. With over 80 books in print, and translated into 25 languages, including Cantonese, Hebrew, Icelandic, and Welsh, the Anholts are truly making an impact on children's books in the world at large.

One reason the Anholts' books appeal to an international audience is that Catherine's illustrations often feature toddlers in multi-ethnic variety. *What I Like*, designated a Children's Book Foundation Book of the Year in 1991, is an example of this approach, showing six different preschool children expressing their likes and dislikes about a wide range of objects and situations. The satisfying conclusion is that all the children like making friends and playing with each other. With their rhyming texts and cheerful, bouncy cartoon-style watercolor illustrations, the Anholts' stories of toddlers and preschoolers involved with the world around them invite participation when they are read aloud. Situations faced by children in everyday life, such as concerns over starting school, provide the Anholts with plenty of grist for their story mill, as in *Billy and the Big New School*, which was named a top book of the year by *Smithsonian* magazine in 1999. *Harry's Home*, about a boy who learns the importance of home wherever it is, won an Oppenheim Toy Portfolio Gold Award and was included in the CCBC Choices list. *Sophie and the New Baby* perfectly presents a child's point of view about a universally familiar situation and was also cited by CCBC Choices.

Courtesy of Candlewick Press

After many individual titles, Catherine and Laurence Anholt felt inspired to start a series of books that would follow the adventures of characters patterned on their own twins. An incident that had occurred on a seaside holiday 10 years earlier blossomed into the monkey characters Chimp and Zee, who wander off on an adventure in the midst of a perfectly normal excursion with their mother, Mumkey. Catherine illustrated the story with pencil, ink, and watercolor pictures that were cut out and pasted onto bright-colored paper. An oversize format and a rollicking refrain completed the highly successful package of Chimp and Zee, which captured the 2001 Nestlé Smarties Gold Award in the under 5 category as well as the hearts of picture book readers around the world. Two board book adaptations of the pair's adventures followed—*Chimp and Zee's Noisy Book* and *Monkey Around with Chimp and Zee*—as well as a second storybook, *Chimp and Zee and the Big Storm*.

Laurence also received a Nestlé Smarties Gold Award in the ages 6 to 8 category two years earlier for one of his Seriously Silly Stories—*Snow White and the Seven Aliens*, illustrated by Arthur Robins. In this upbeat reworking of the old story, the Mean Queen refuses to be upstaged when Snow White tries to become a pop star. Adept at satire and wordplay, Anholt has created a dozen "fractured fairy tales" in this series, all illustrated with equally raucous abandon by Robins, and work is in progress to turn the stories into an animated series. In a more serious vein, Anholt's self-illustrated stories of children interacting with famous artists—launched in 1994 with *Camille and the Sunflowers: A Story About Vincent Van Gogh*—has been hailed as an excellent introduction for young children to the work of the masters.

Catherine and Laurence Anholt have created a unique niche for their work in the children's book field by exploring their love of art, their joy in family, and their optimistic worldview. They live and work in Lyme Regis, in the southwest of England.

SELECTED WORKS WRITTEN AND ILLUSTRATED BY LAURENCE ANHOLT: *The Forgotten Forest*, 1992; *Camille and the Sunflowers: A Story About Vincent Van Gogh*, 1994; *Degas and the Little Dancer: A Story About Edgar Degas*, 1996; *Picasso and the Girl with a Ponytail: A Story About Pablo Picasso*, 1998; *Leonardo and the Flying Boy: A Story About Leonardo da Vinci*, 2001; *The Magical Garden of Claude Monet*, 2003.

SELECTED WORKS WRITTEN BY LAURENCE ANHOLT: *Knee-High Norman*, illus. by Arthur Robins, 1996; *The Rather Small Turnip*, illus. by Arthur Robins, 1996; *Rumply Crumply Stinky Pin*, illus. by Arthur Robins, 1996; *Billy Beast*, illus. by Arthur Robins, 1996; *Cinderboy*, illus. by Arthur Robins, 1996; *Little Red Riding Wolf*, illus. by Arthur Robins, 1998; *The Fried Piper of Hamstring*, illus. by Arthur Robins, 1998; *Shampoozel*, illus. by Arthur Robins, 1998; *Snow White and the Seven Aliens*, illus. by Arthur Robins, 1998; *Stone Girl, Bone Girl: A Story about Mary Anning*, illus. by Sheila Moxley, 1999; *Summerhouse*, illus. by Lynne Russell, 1999; *The Emperor's New Underwear*, illus. by Arthur Robins, 1999; *Silly Jack and the Bean Stack*, illus. by Arthur Robins, 1999; *Seriously Silly Stories: The Collection*, illus. by Arthur Robins, 1999; *I Like Me, I Like You*, illus. by Adriano Gon, 2001; *Ghostyshocks and the Three Scares*, illus. by Arthur Robins, 2002; *Eco-Wolf and the Three Pigs*, illus. by Arthur Robins, 2002; *Jack and the Dreamsack*, illus. by Ross Collins, 2003.

Courtesy of Penguin Putnam Books for Young Readers

SELECTED WORKS WRITTEN BY LAURENCE AND ILLUSTRATED BY CATHERINE ANHOLT: *Truffles Is Sick*, 1987; *Truffles in Trouble*, 1987; *Tom's Rainbow Walk*, 1990; *When I Was a Baby*, 1991; *Good Days, Bad Days*, 1991; *What I Like*, 1991, 1998; *All About You*, 1992; *The Twins Two by Two*, 1992; *Bear and Baby*, 1993; *Toddlers*, 1993; *Come Back, Jack!*, 1994; *One, Two, Three, Count With Me*, 1994; *Here Come the Babies*, 1995; *What Makes Me Happy?*, 1995; *Sun, Snow, Stars, Sky*, 1995; *First Words and Pictures*, 1996; *Catherine and Laurence Anholt's Big Book of Families*, 1998; *Billy and the Big New School*, 1999; *Sophie and the New Baby*, 2000; *Harry's Home*, 2000; *Chimp and Zee*, 2001; *Chimp and Zee's Noisy Book*, 2002; *Monkey Around With Chimp and Zee*, 2002; *Chimp and Zee and the Big Storm*, 2002; *Catherine and Laurence Anholt's Big Book of Little Children*, 2003.

SUGGESTED READING: *Something About the Author*, vol. 131, 2002. Periodicals—Carden, Karen, "Life Stories for the Littlest Readers," *Christian Science Monitor*, March 25, 1999.

WEB SITE: *www.anholt.co.uk*

"When I was in the first grade I learned how to spell the word 'architect.' It was powerful—the spelling of it. My parents paraded me in front of my relatives for this display of phonemic greatness. I spelled it at family gatherings. I spelled it at church. I even spelled it to my aunt over the phone, long distance! But best of all, when I recited it during show-and-tell in my first grade classroom, my teacher, Mrs. Beall with her black bouffant hair, looked at me with amazement and said, 'Kathi, I think you're going to grow up to be a writer!'

"Somehow, at that very early age, I believed her. I believed Mrs. Beall.

"I was born in Fayetteville, North Carolina, en route to the Army Hospital, in the front seat of my father's Ford, on the hot night of July 6, 1954. I was the first of three daughters. When my father finished his tour of duty in the service, he moved us back to my parents' hometown of Houston, where I grew up amidst a bevy of grandparents, cousins, aunts, and uncles. My dad was a heavy equipment operator. He loved forklifts and cranes and oil derricks and spent most of his life in the oil patch.

"It doesn't seem that a man like my father would have been much of a reader, but in fact he was rarely without a book. And when I was very small, he read Rudyard Kipling to me almost every night. Those times together with my father are among the most treasured memories of my childhood, when it was just my dad and me and the book. My mother, too, loved books, and on my sixth birthday, she and my dad gave me a bookcase of my very own! It is my mother, above all people, who has been my steadfast champion. At all points in my life, especially when I was 11 and my father left us and started another family, my mother has always been supportive. She has encouraged me, believing, even when I did not, that I could become an author.

"My parents' divorce was a very painful episode in my life. One of the places I turned to for solace was my journal. All these years later, I'm still an avid journalist, pouring my thoughts and worries, my joys and consolations onto the blank white pages. I

Courtesy of John Stevens

Kathi Appelt
July 6, 1954–

have written my own stories there and I have found stories that seemed to come from nowhere; I'm constantly surprised by what shows up in my journal. In the late 1970s, having spent several years in and out of college, I met a quiet man who loved to play guitar and sing. Ken brought a sweetness into my life, and that sweetness continues almost 24 years after our wedding date. We are the parents of two sons, Jacob and Cooper.

"When Jacob was born, Ken and I were graduate students at the University of Iowa. Parenthood caught me off guard. Despite my education, I was not prepared to be a mother; I felt desperately incompetent. So, out of self-defense really, I did the only thing I knew was the right thing to do—read to him. Thanks to Jacob, and later his brother, Cooper, I began a love affair with children's books that remains to this day. The stories that we read together created an incredible special bond between us. The boys are all grown up now, but those books are like old family members, and like other family members, they inspired me to try my hand at writing my own.

"There's a certain kind of rapture that comes from the act of shared reading. Whether it's *The Jungle Book* or *Peter Rabbit*, the book itself doesn't matter so much as the being together, when the rest of the world evaporates and there's only the people you love and a story. I think of it as a magic circle.

"And if one of my books can be part of a magic circle between another little girl and her dad or a little boy and his mother, how great is that?"

"Those times together with my father are among the most treasured memories of my childhood, when it was just my dad and me and the book."

❁ ❁ ❁

Kathi Appelt was born in Fayetteville, North Carolina, where her father, Bill Cowgill, was stationed with the 82nd Airborne. Not long after Kathi's birth, her parents moved to El Paso, Texas, and finally to Houston, where most of her relatives lived. Patricia, Kathi's mother, made it easy for Kathi and her two sisters to express themselves in writing. In the garage she made three sections on one of the unfinished sheetrock walls. Each Cowgill daughter had her own section on which to write, draw, and scribble at will. Kathi looks upon this as her first journal. The wall was a testament to the girls' writing progress—from early scribbles to attempts at poetry.

Kathi earned a B.A. from Texas A&M University in 1979 and married Kenneth Appelt the same year. Their sons were born in 1982 and 1984. It was *Elephants Aloft*, published in 1993, that established Kathi Appelt as a serious writer of children's literature. A concept book that tells the story of two Indian elephants who take a balloon journey to visit their aunt in Africa, it was chosen by the American Booksellers Association as a Pick of the Lists. Appelt began writing about bats to overcome her fear of them, and her first bat book, *Bat Jamboree*, published in 1996, became an American Booksellers Pick of the Lists for that year. Another bat book, *Bats Around the Clock*, received an IRA/CBC

Children's Choice award. *Bayou Lullaby* and *Bubba and Beau, Best Friends* received the Irma S. and James H. Black Award from Bank Street College of Education and were both named *School Library Journal* Best Books of the Year.

Appelt's first book for teenagers, *Kissing Tennessee, and Other Stories from the Stardust Dance*, was included on ALA's Best Books for Young Adults list and was also an ALA Quick Pick for Reluctant Readers. In 2001, Appelt published her first book of nonfiction. Co-authored with Jeanne Cannela Schmitzer, *Down Cut Shin Creek: The Pack Horse Librarians of Kentucky* is a fascinating account of the way the government recruited and trained riders to navigate the Appalachian trails to deliver reading materials to the poor and needy during the Great Depression. The book was chosen as an American Booksellers Association Pick of the Lists.

Ideas for Appelt's poems and stories often come to her as she writes in her journals. She also gets ideas while taking long, leisurely walks in College Station, Texas,

Courtesy of Henry Holt & Co.

where she lives with her husband, a high school English teacher and musician. The two collaborated on *Just People and Paper/Pen/Poem: A Young Writer's Way to Begin*, which was named an ALA Best Book for Young Adults. Kathi Appelt teaches creative writing at Texas A&M University and is also on the faculty of the M.F.A. Program in Writing for Children and Young Adults at Vermont College.

SELECTED WORKS: *Elephants Aloft*, illus. by Keith Baker, 1993; *Bayou Lullaby*, illus. by Neil Waldman, 1995; *The Bat Jamboree*, illus. by Melissa Sweet, 1996; *The Thunderherd*, illus. by Elizabeth Sayles, 1996; *Watermelon Day*, illus. by Dale Gottlieb, 1996; *A Red Wagon Year*, illus. by Laura McGee Kvasnosky, 1996; *Just People and Paper/Pen/Poem: A Young Writer's Way to Begin*, photos. by Ken Appelt, 1996; *I See the Moon*, illus. by Debra Reid Jenkins, 1997; *Cowboy Dreams*, illus. by Barry Root, 1999; *Someone's Come to Our House*, illus. by Nancy Carpenter, 1999; *Bats on Parade*, illus. by Melissa Sweet, 1999; *Bats Around the Clock*, illus. by Melissa Sweet, 2000; *Kissing Tennessee, and Other Stories from the Stardust Dance*, 2000; *Hushabye, Baby Blue*, illus. by Dale Gottlieb, 2000; *Oh My Baby, Little One*, illus. by Jane Dyer, 2000; *Toddler Two-Step*, illus. by Ward Schumaker, 2000; *Down Cut Shin Creek: The Pack Horse Librarians of Kentucky*, with Jeanne Cannella Schmitzer,

2001; *Rain Dance*, illus. by Emilie Chollat, 2001; *The Alley Cat's Meow*, illus. by Jon Goodell, 2002; *Bubba and Beau, Best Friends*, illus. by Arthur Howard, 2002; *Where, Where Is Swamp Bear?*, illus. by Megan Halsey, 2002; *Poems from Homeroom: A Writer's Place to Start*, 2002; *Bubba and Beau Go Night-Night*, illus. by Arthur Howard, 2003; *My Father's Summers: A Daughter's Memoir*, 2004; *Bubba and Beau Meet the Relatives*, illus. by Arthur Howard, 2004.

SUGGESTED READING: *Contemporary Authors*, vol. 150, 1996; *Something About the Author*, vol. 129, 2002.

WEB SITE: *www.kathiappelt.com*

Courtesy of Michael Reynolds

K. A. Applegate

October 9, 1956–

"I grew up with a menagerie of dogs, cats, and gerbils, not to mention three younger siblings. I spent most of my childhood in East Grand Rapids, Michigan; Cary, Illinois; and Nassau Bay, Texas. I liked animals but disliked school. During high school, I worked for a veterinarian, doing everything from cleaning cages to assisting in surgery.

"Although I always expected that I'd end up being a writer, for a long time I did little to pursue that goal. I graduated from the University of Texas at Austin, but refused to settle down, stay put, and focus on a career. Instead I worked at a variety of jobs, from waiting tables to caring for plants. Only when I reached my early thirties did I decide to get serious about writing. By then my desire to put words on paper won out over my desire not to make a fool of myself. Also, I needed to pay the rent. Then I got very serious indeed, writing 150 books in the next 12 years.

"With my husband and co-author, Michael, I ghostwrote books for Sweet Valley Twins and several other series. I wrote numerous books for Disney Press, including various Aladdin, Little Mermaid, and Mickey Mouse books. Ghosting is great practice for writing your own books. In trying to mimic someone else's voice and style, you learn a lot about your own; on the other hand, when you write the books yourself, there's no one else to blame. But I decided to take the blame—or praise—or whatever came, and soon I was writing my own books and doing so at such a rate that I was compelled to use numerous pseudonyms to avoid confusion. In addition to being Katherine Applegate and K. A. Applegate (K. A. was chosen because it's a neutral gender), I've written as C. Archer (the Christy series), Beth Kincaid (the

Silver Creek Riders series), A. R. Plumb (Disney's Aladdin books), Pat Pollari (the Barf-O-Rama series), and several other names.

"My first major hit came five years after I started writing, when I created the Animorphs series. Born out of my love of animals as a kid and my desire to get kids into the heads of various species, this science fiction series about young people who can 'morph' into a variety of animals sat atop the children's bestseller lists for several years and spawned a television show and a line of toys and games. When I was doing research for Animorphs, I did a lot of reading and talked to zoologists and zoo curators because they observe animals all day long. But after a certain point, it's just guessing. Climbing into the head of an animal is like climbing into the head of another human being. It becomes pure imagination. Other series followed: Everworld—a parallel universe created by ancient immortals that four modern high school students find themselves in—and Remnants, about people who manage to escape a catastrophic destruction of the Earth and their eventual return.

"Finally, after more than 20,000 pages, I decided it was time to call a temporary halt. It was just too hard to write and chase toddlers around at the same time, so I took a few years off to raise my son, Jake, and my daughter, Julia. We moved from Illinois to North Carolina because the weather was better than Chicago, the real estate was cheaper in Chapel Hill, and because we found a school we liked for our kids in Durham. Then, in 2004, once we were settled in North Carolina, I put pen to paper (or finger to keyboard) and began writing again. My first new book after the hiatus will be something entirely new—a picture book called *The Buffalo Storm*. In typical hyperactive style, I'm also at work on three other projects."

> *"Climbing into the head of an animal is like climbing into the head of another human being. It becomes pure imagination."*

Katherine Alice Applegate's bestselling young adult series, Animorphs, has sold about 40 million copies and has been translated into over 20 languages. Initially called the Changelings, the Animorphs series first appeared in 1996 and the last book was published in 2001. Applegate wrote 65 books altogether for the series and its spin-offs, the Megamorphs and Alternamorphs titles. The first book in the Animorphs, titled *The Invasion*, set the stage and outlined the basic rules. Jake and his friends learn the human race is under attack, and they are given the power to fight the evil "yeerks" by morphing into any animal they choose. They accomplish this by touching and concentrating on that animal, but they can't retain their animal form for more than two hours or the metamorphosis becomes permanent, which does indeed happen to one character. Nickelodeon adapted the Animorphs stories into a live-action TV show, airing it in the United States, Latin America, and Australia.

Courtesy of Scholastic Press

Applegate's first series was written for readers who prefer realism to fantasy and want to read about relationships. Dubbed the Boyfriends and Girlfriends series, it was later reissued as the Making Out series. In *Zoey Fools Around*, Zoey has been dating a boy named Jake for a long time, but her relationship with him is thrown off balance when the boy responsible for the drunk-driving accident that killed Jake's brother returns home after spending two years in a reform school. As other characters struggle with romantic difficulties, the book sets a gossipy yet enticing tone for the beginning of this series.

Applegate claims the Everworld series was more challenging to write because the conflict kept changing. In the first title, *Search for Senna*, David and his friends end up in a frightening but thrilling land populated by trolls, unicorns, winged creatures, and a Viking colony battling an Aztec god's army. The author enjoyed taking contemporary teenagers and placing them in this extraordinary fantasy environment. In the gripping and fast-paced *Mayflower Project*, the first of the Remnants series, four teens are among the 80 chosen to leave Earth on a shuttle because Earth is about to be destroyed by an asteroid. In this first book the teens struggle to get their ship off the ground, fighting with old and new technology as well as terrorists who are trying to get on board. In *Sharing Sam*, which was part of the Love Stories series penned by various authors, two best friends like the same boy, but one of the girls is dying of brain cancer. The question of who gets the guy becomes a question of how far one should go to bring happiness to another. *Sharing Sam* explored themes of love, honesty, personal sacrifice, and inevitable loss, and it was named an ALA Quick Pick for Reluctant Young Adult Readers.

Asked which of her books were her favorites, Katherine Applegate answered, "I have found that I end up feeling the most affection for the ones that gave me the most trouble." She is the author of over 150 books, both for children and adults. She lives in Chapel Hill, North Carolina, with her husband and two children.

SELECTED WORKS (written as K. A. Applegate): The Animorphs series—*The Invasion*, 1996; *The Encounter*, 1996; *The Message*, 1996; *The Forgotten*, 1997; *The Reaction*, 1997; *The Decision*, 1998; *The Departure*, 1998; *The Illusion*, 1999; *The Mutation*, 1999; *The Other*, 2000; *The Test*, 2000; *The Sacrifice*, 2001; *The Answer*, 2001; *The Beginning*, 2001. The

Animorphs Megamorphs series—*The Andalite's Gift*, 1997;
Elfangor's Secret, 1999. The Animorphs Alternamorphs
series—*The First Journey*, 1999; *Next Passage*, 2000. The
Everworld series—*Search for Senna*, 1999; *Enter the
Enchanted*, 1999; *Fear the Fantastic*, 2000; *Understand the
Unknown*, 2000; *Entertain the End*, 2001. The Remnants
series—*The Mayflower Project*, 2001; *Nowhere Land*, 2001;
No Place Like Home, 2002; *Begin Again*, 2003.

SELECTED WORKS (written as Katherine Applegate): The
Boyfriends and Girlfriends series, reissued as the Making Out
series—*Zoey Fools Around*, 1994; *Jake Finds Out*, 1994; *Nina
Won't Tell*, 1994; *What Zoey Saw*, 1994; *Ben Takes a Chance*,
1999; *Don't Tell Zoey*, 1999; *Zoey Speaks Out*, 1999. Love
Stories series—*Listen to My Heart*, 1996; *Sharing Sam*, 1996.
Summer series—*June Dreams*, 1995; *July's Promise*, 1995;
August Magic, 1995; *Sand, Surf, and Secrets*, 1996; *Rays,
Romance, and Rivalry*, 1996; *Christmas Special Edition*, 1996;
Spring Break Reunion, 1996.

SELECTED WORKS (written as C. Archer): The Christy Series—
The Bridge to Cutter Gap, 1995; *Silent Superstitions*, 1995;
The Angry Intruder, 1995; *Midnight Rescue*, 1995; *Christy's
Choice*, 1996; *The Proposal*, 1996; *The Princess Club*, 1996;
Family Secrets, 1996; *Mountain Madness*, 1997; *Stage Fright*,
1997; *GoodBye, Sweet Prince*, 1997; *Brotherly Love*, 1997.

SELECTED WORKS (written as Beth Kincaid): The Silver Creek
Riders Series—*Back in the Saddle*, 1994; *True Romance*,
1994; *Winning*, 1995.

SELECTED WORKS (written as A. R. Plumb): The Further
Adventures of Aladdin Series—*A Thief in the Night*, 1994;
Birds of a Feather, 1994; *A Small Problem*, 1995; *Iago's
Promise*, 1995.

SELECTED WORKS (written as Pat Pollari): The Barf-O-Rama
series—*The Great Puke-Off*, 1996; *The Legend of Bigfart*,
1996; *Mucus Mansion*, 1996; *Garbage Time*, 1996; *Scab Pie*,
1996; *Party Pooper*, 1996; *Pig Breath*, 1996; *The Splat in the
Hat*, 1997; *Forest Dump*, 1997; *Hambooger and French Flies*,
1997; *Jurassic Fart*, 1997; *Shoe Chew*, 1997; *Grossest Gross
Jokes*, 1997.

SUGGESTED READING: *Children's Literature Review*, vol. 90,
2004; *Something About the Author*, vol. 109, 2000.
Periodicals—Heppermann, Christine, "Invasion of the
Animorphs," *The Horn Book*, January/February 1998; Lodge,
Sally, "Scholastic's Animorphs Series Has Legs," *Publishers
Weekly*, November 3, 1997. Online—
www.scholastic.com/animorphs/index.htm.

Courtesy of Marina Budhos

Marc Aronson

October 19, 1960–

"I have always loved reading nonfiction; in fact, that is how I became a reader. I was very bored with early readers, and my parents grew concerned because I didn't seem to like books. A reading specialist suggested that I just didn't care if Spot ran or whether Jack or Jill made it up the hill. I remember the summer it all changed, when I was six and read *The First Book of George Washington*. This was interesting! I could not get enough of the First Book series. And while I eventually came to enjoy fiction and poetry, it was the Land and People books, the Landmark books, which I eagerly looked for on the shelves as I was growing up.

"As an undergraduate I was a history major, and had a marvelous professor named Norman Cantor in a medieval history seminar who had us read through Anglo-Saxon laws and build historical explanations out of those primary sources and guided secondary reading. I did not pursue history immediately after getting my degree, but at a point I noticed that I was eagerly reading reviews of new history books and endlessly browsing library shelves. I returned to graduate school, thinking my focus was going to be medieval heresy. Professor Cantor was now at NYU, and I went to study with him. While I eventually shifted over to American history, I was once again immersed in the study of the past.

"In the first years of graduate school I was working at Facts on File, editing reference books. One day I saw an ad for a new editor of the revised Land and People series. This was a dream come true for me, and working on those books was my re-introduction to children's books. I had recently edited an adult encyclopedia (*The World Encyclopedia of Political Systems and Parties*) that put me in touch with many experts on the peoples and nations of the world. The Land and People books were outdated, both in their information and in their tone. I decided to work with academics who really knew the countries and help them to write for younger readers, rather than to approach children's writers to research foreign countries. This yielded some excellent books in which even late-breaking events proved how astute the authors were. The book on China was late in production as the Tiananmen Square demonstrations took place. We managed to add in a box with a wire-service photo of the Statue of Liberty being carried during the protests, and it fit perfectly. Similarly, the book on the Soviet Union was a forecast of the fate of that empire, even as it crumbled.

"There is something of a twist in this story, because while I love nonfiction, one of the topics I most like reading about is cultural history in its many meanings: the history of ideas, civilizations, peoples, but also the history of the arts. The Edge series I edited at Holt was meant to bring books that dealt with cultural borderlines to teenagers, crossing their own boundaries. As I edited books for young people on culture and history I began to want to write one myself, and I returned to a subject that had been a passion of mine as a teenager and into my twenties: the artistic avant-garde. My parents were set designers, and I grew up in Manhattan in a very pro–Civil Rights environment, surrounded by discussions of art and politics, modernism and tradition. The book became *Art Attack*. I took it to Dorothy Briley at Clarion because I knew her to be an excellent nonfiction editor with her own strong taste, and she agreed to publish it.

"I was motivated to write about Sir Walter Ralegh because of my experience being an editor in 1992. Children's publishers had great difficulty deciding how to approach the 500th anniversary of Columbus arriving in the New World. We couldn't follow the old European 'discovery' model, and the revisionist 'genocide' approach seemed too harsh. I wanted to write a book that captured the complexity of the first meetings of different peoples in this hemisphere. Ralegh, his circle, and their writings gave me the chance to do that.

"Encouraged by the response to the Ralegh book, I decided to expand it into a trilogy on the colonial American period, on the three ideas or concepts Europeans had of the New World: Ralegh's El Dorado; the Puritans' Land of Promise; and the nation of self-interest and law that is the basis of Madison's Constitution. I hope to keep writing books that capture moments of change for young readers and to pass on to them my fascination with the endless effort of intelligence and creativity that takes place as we seek to understand who we are and how we came to be that way."

✿　✿　✿

"I wanted to write a book that captured the complexity of the first meetings of different peoples in this hemisphere. Ralegh, his circle, and their writings gave me the chance to do that."

It is easy to understand the unique quality of Marc Aronson's nonfiction books when you read about his passionate interest in his subjects. Aronson's writing is enlivened by his fresh approaches to source material and his insight into the details that can bring a historical period to life. He clearly stated his approach to writing informational books in his acceptance speech for the *Boston Globe–Horn Book* Award in 2000: "I urge authors of nonfiction for young readers to experiment, take risks, try out all sorts of new narrative forms—none of which require any kind of invented dialogue or made-up interior monologues. And they should purchase that license, that freedom, by laying a clear foundation showing their own research and thought processes. That way we trust readers and invite them to share with us in the joy of discovery . . ." (*The Horn Book*, January/February 2001).

Courtesy of Clarion Books

Art Attack was named a *Publishers Weekly* Best Book of the Year and a *New York Times* Notable Book for 1998. *Sir Walter Ralegh and the Quest for El Dorado* received the *Boston Globe–Horn Book* Award for nonfiction in 2000 and was the winner of the first Robert F. Sibert Award for the most distinguished informational book of the year, presented by the American Library Association. *Ralegh* was also named an ALA Notable Children's Book, a *School Library Journal* Best Book of the Year, and a *Bulletin of the Center for Children's Books* Blue Ribbon Book.

Aronson attended Brandeis University for two years, where he first studied with his mentor, Professor Cantor, and he graduated from New York University in 1982 with a degree in history. He received his Ph.D. in history from New York University in 1995. He has worked as an editor of books for young people at HarperCollins; at Henry Holt, where he helped to inaugurate the Edge imprint for young adults; and at Carus Publishing, where he was editorial director and vice president of nonfiction development. Currently, he acquires YA fiction and other types of books in a special relationship with Candlewick Press, while developing nonfiction projects for a variety of publishers. He lives with his wife, Marina Budhos, a writer, and two sons in Maplewood, New Jersey.

SELECTED WORKS WRITTEN: *Day by Day: The Seventies*, with Thomas Leonard and Cynthia Crippen, 1988; *Day by Day: The Eighties*, with Ellen Meltzer, 1995; *Art Attack: A Short Cultural History of the Avant-Garde*, 1998; *Sir Walter Ralegh and the Quest for El Dorado*, 2000; *Exploding the Myths: The Truth About Teens and Reading*, 2000; *911: The Book of Help*, edited with Michael Cart and Marianne Carus, 2002; *Witch-Hunt: Mysteries of the Salem Witch Trials*, 2003; *John Winthrop, Oliver Cromwell, and the Land of Promise*, 2004.

SUGGESTED READING: *Contemporary Authors*, vol. 196, 2002; *Something About the Author*, vol. 126, 2002. Periodicals— Aronson, Marc, "Image Quests," *School Library Journal*, February 2004; "Coming of Age: One Editor's View of How Young Adult Publishing Developed in America," *Publishers Weekly*, February 11, 2002; "The Myths of Teenage Readers," *Publishing Research Quarterly*, Fall 2000; "Slippery Slopes and Proliferating Prizes," *The Horn Book*, May 2001; "2000 Boston Globe–Horn Book Awards: Nonfiction Award Winner," *The Horn Book*, January/February 2001; "Unholy Wars: How Does History Help Us Understand Our Enemies and Ourselves?" *School Library Journal*, November 2001.

"I was born and raised along with my two sisters and brother in Maine, where we spent a lot of time outdoors. Wildlife and nature, the rhythm of the seasons, were a big part of growing up and learning about life. Books were too. My parents were avid readers and shared that joy with us through bedtime stories and trips to the library. Our house was filled with books, and reading, which began as a habit, quickly became a pleasure. I read crouched in the branches of trees, in the back of my closet with a light, in the gaps in the hedges that surrounded our house, anywhere I could create a space of my own. Books were a refuge, somewhere to escape to after a disappointment, a place to meet new people or to have a laugh or a cry. I met all sorts of people I liked in books and some that I didn't like. As I grew up, I found books helped me to sort out life. They were a good place to become familiar with emotions—confusion, sadness, anger, grief, humiliation, and love. I especially liked picture books, and the way in which words and illustrations could create a whole new world in which sometimes real and other times magical and unexpected things could happen.

"As a child I had a big imagination, which I channeled into games of make-believe. I liked inventing—lying, as my siblings termed it. When I got too old for make-believe, sports and dance provided outlets for my creative energy. In the few quiet moments left, I read. But for me, a book never ended with that last page. I spent hours imagining sequels, rewriting characters, pondering plots. I thought everyone did this. And I began revisiting and collecting picture books, examining how they were made, discovering things I'd missed as a child. At university I studied history, which proved a worthy topic for invention. I chose childhood and children's literature as an honors topic, and I began to look at children's books from yet another perspective.

"As for being an author, I never told anyone I wanted to be a writer—except myself. Even then, I was not convinced that writing was a wise career choice. Ghosts of poverty, failure, writer's block, and rejection slips loomed large. Any alternative suddenly seemed very appealing, if boring. My sister wanted to be a doctor and my brother was a mathematics whiz. My college classmates were heading for careers in business, medicine, or law. I knew I could probably be a good lawyer or professor, but I wasn't sure I could be a good writer. When I finished college, I took the law school entrance exams and filled out a dozen of

Courtesy of Amy Gould

Kate Banks

Kate Banks

February 13, 1960–

applications to law school. Days before they were due, I tossed them into the garbage and sent around resumes for jobs in publishing. There were none, and so I did freelance research for six months, regretting that I wasn't in law school. Then, by lucky chance, I was offered a job by a children's book editor, Frances Foster. Suddenly, I found myself where I'd always wanted to be. I worked in the editorial department and loved everything about it. I was happy making books, and I acquired the know-how and courage to start writing. My first book, *Alphabet Soup*, was written during a vacation in Europe with my Italian boyfriend, who was sick in bed. He later became my husband, and we moved to Rome, where we lived for nine years. That's where both of my sons were born. We moved to France five years ago. But no matter where I've been or am, I wake up every day thankful that I am able to do something I really love and have always wanted to do.

"When I'm not thinking about books, I love playing the piano, doing pottery, puttering around outdoors, and cooking. I especially like making birthday cakes, but I hate cleaning up. And I love being with children. I love listening to them, watching them, and of course I like writing for them."

> "As I grew up, I found books helped me to sort out life. They were a good place to become familiar with emotions—confusion, sadness, anger, grief, humiliation, and love."

❈   ❈   ❈

A writer with an uncanny gift for tuning in to the emotional needs and interests of children, Kate Banks received her B.A. from Wellesley College in 1982 and her M.A. in history from Columbia University in 1986. While in graduate school, she met her future husband, Pierluigi, who was studying at the Columbia Business School; they were introduced just before he returned to his home in Rome. Banks had accepted a job with a family in Rome the following summer, met him again there quite by chance, and the romance began to bloom through three years of weekly correspondence and meeting every three months in America or in Europe. In 1988 they decided to marry and live in Italy. Her first years there were difficult as she struggled with learning the language. She remembers asking for "basilica" once in a vegetable market, rather than "basilico"—the equivalent of asking for a cathedral to put on your pasta instead of the herb basil. In the course of the nine years the couple spent in Rome, Kate Banks eventually did learn to speak Italian and their two sons were born, Peter in 1991 and Max in 1996. In 1997 Pierluigi moved his business to the South of France, where the family make their home today.

While living in Rome, Kate met illustrator Georg Hallensleben, a German artist whose work she admired and with whom she collaborated to create *Baboon*, a 1997 *Horn Book* Fanfare title, and *And If the Moon Could Talk*, which received the 1998 *Boston Globe–Horn Book* Award for Picture Books as well as being named an ALA Notable Children's Book. Gallimard Books, a publishing house in France, has been supportive of the collaboration between these two, and most of their titles have been published both in France and in the United States. During the early years of working together, when they both lived in Rome, Hallensleben built himself a portable studio in a van and parked it by Banks's house while they worked on a book. Just before her move to the South of France, he had relocated to Paris, and their work has continued to garner awards over the years. *The Night Worker* was an ALA Notable Children's Book, and Banks received the 2001 Charlotte Zolotow Award for her text. *Close Your Eyes*, another collaboration with Hallensleben, was named a *School Library Journal* Best Book. Working with other illustrators,

Courtesy of Farrar, Straus and Giroux

Kate Banks has produced a variety of other picture books as well as a series of chapter books for young readers featuring a boy named Howie Bowles.

Recently, Banks has turned to writing novels for older children that deal with sensitive life issues. For the setting in *Dillon, Dillon*, about a 10-year-old boy's need to come to terms with a long-held family secret, she returned to the Maine of her childhood. She grew up in Bangor, but the family spent all of their summers on a lake in Camden, her parents' hometown. A room at the Camden library and a special collection of books there are dedicated to the memory of her father, who was one of the foremost authorities on Maine history. *Dillon, Dillon* is set on the lake where the family spent many long summers and, though she can't return as often as her siblings, Kate Banks said in a recent interview, "my heart and roots are still there."

SELECTED WORKS: *Alphabet Soup*, illus. by Peter Sís, 1988; *Big, Bigger, Biggest Adventure*, illus. by Paul Yalowitz, 1990; *The Bunnysitters* (Stepping Stone Books), illus. by Blanche Sims, 1991; *Peter and the Talking Shoes*, illus. by Marc Rosenthal, 1994; *Baboon*, illus. by Georg Hallensleben, 1997; *Spider, Spider*, illus. by Georg Hallensleben, 1997; *And If the Moon Could Talk*, illus. by Georg Hallensleben, 1998; *The Bird, the Monkey, and the Snake in the Jungle*, illus. by Tomek Bogacki, 1999; *Howie Bowles, Secret Agent*, illus. by Isaac Millman, 1999; *The Night Worker*, illus. by Georg Hallensleben, 2000; *Howie Bowles and Uncle Sam*, illus. by Isaac Millman, 2000; *A Gift from the Sea*, illus. by Georg Hallensleben, 2001; *Mama's Little Baby*, illus. by Karin Littlewood, 2001; *The Turtle and the Hippopotamus*, illus. by Tomek Bogacki, 2002; *Dillon, Dillon*, 2002; *Close Your Eyes*, illus. by Georg Hallensleben, 2002; *Walk Softly, Rachel*, 2003;

Mama's Coming Home, illus. by Tomek Bogacki, 2003; *The Cat Who Walked Across France*, illus. by Georg Hallensleben, 2004.

SUGGESTED READING: *Something About the Author*, vol. 134, 2003. Online—Elias, Tana, "The World Is Big: An Interview with Kate Banks," January 8, 2002, Cooperative Children's Book Center, University of Wisconsin, Madison: *www.education.wisc.edu/ccbc/friends/banks.htm*.

Courtesy of Stephanie Klein-Davis

Susan Campbell Bartoletti

November 18, 1958–

"I don't ever remember wanting to be a writer. As a child, I loved to read and to draw and to paint. In school, I liked art class best, and I won several ribbons—and money once—in art contests. My high school art teacher encouraged me. After my junior year, I left high school to start college. I declared myself an art major right away and signed up for studio workshops in drawing and painting. I bought all the right tools: charcoal, pencils, paints, a palette, canvas, sketchpad, and portfolio case.

"The classes met early—eight o'clock— and I was usually the first one there. Each day, I perched on the tall stool in front of the easel, surrounded by classmates who had also won art contests, and I sketched and painted, happier than I ever remember. Sometime during the second semester a gap appeared between the pictures I saw in my head and the art I made on canvas. I compared my work to the other students, and I didn't think that my work was as good as theirs. The gap widened, until one day I put away my pencils and paints. I felt frustrated and frightened. If I wasn't an artist, I wondered, what was I?

"About this time, my English professor was praising my writing, often using it as an example in class. This astonished me. Even though I had always earned good grades, no English teacher had ever told me I was a good writer. The praise embarrassed me on the outside, but on the inside it felt very good.

"The next year I transferred colleges and loaded my schedule with literature classes, where I wrote research papers. I took a creative writing class and wrote short stories and poetry for the first time. I interned as a journalist at a local newspaper, writing features and other articles. I didn't know that these experiences were revealing anything to me. I just knew that I grinned at each research assignment and ran to the library to get started. I stayed up all hours, writing stories and poetry, often combining words and pictures in some way.

"At the end of my sophomore year, I married. My husband, who is a history teacher, suggested that I earn education credits. I did, and I landed a teaching position as soon as I graduated. For the next 18 years, I taught eighth-grade English. I never intended to teach, but kids are easy to get hooked on. Even junior high kids.

"My students kept journals. They wrote poems, stories, and essays. They researched, wrote, and illustrated their own nonfiction picture books. They held poetry readings. They published their work in the school's award-winning literary magazine, which I co-advised for 15 years. Some even had their work accepted for national publication in anthologies.

"During these years, our daughter and then a son came along. For many years our house seemed filled with kids, pets, stories, books, music, and sports. Most vacations, we tent-camped. Up and down the East Coast, we explored our nation's history in national parks, battlegrounds, forts, and museums.

"Though I loved teaching and felt immense satisfaction in watching my students grow as writers and readers, something was missing. At night I often spread out the newspaper and pored over the want ads, looking for something but not knowing what. Then I joined a writers group and began to write stories for children. For the first time something felt terribly right. I stopped reading the want ads: At last I knew what I wanted to do. Write. When I sold my first picture book, my students cheered me, just as I had cheered them. For the next several years, I got up at 4 A.M., in order to have time to write before I left for school.

"I didn't know that these experiences were revealing anything to me. I just knew that I grinned at each research assignment and ran to the library to get started."

"In 1997 I was offered my sixth book contract, and I knew the time had come for a difficult decision: either teach full time or write full time. I had already had one career that I loved. Could I make it as a full-time writer? 'Leap and the net will appear,' a friend told me. I leaped."

☼　☼　☼

Born in Harrisburg, Pennsylvania, Susan Campbell Bartoletti received her B.A. from Marywood College in 1979 and graduated with an M.A. in English from the University of Scranton in 1982. In 2001 she completed a Ph.D. in creative writing at the State University of New York at Binghamton. Married to Joseph Bartoletti, a history teacher, since 1977, she has two children, Brandy and Joey. For 18 years she taught English at the North Pocono Middle School in Moscow, Pennsylvania, writing numerous textbooks and articles as well as two screenplays during that time. Starting in 1997, she has taught children's literature and creative writing at the State University of New York at Binghamton, and is currently a visiting associate professor in creative writing at Hollins University in Roanoke, Virginia.

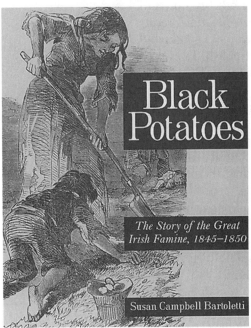

The Story of the Great Irish Famine, 1845–1850

Susan Campbell Bartoletti

Courtesy of Houghton Mifflin, Inc.

History comes alive in Susan Bartoletti's award-winning books, whether fiction or nonfiction. Known as an impeccable researcher with a passion for filling in the gaps in history for young people, she chooses whichever form best suits the characters she presents. Her first picture book, *Silver at Night*, was based on her husband's grandfather's tales of life in the coal mines of Pennsylvania. Fascinated by what she learned about the coal industry, she followed with a longer work of nonfiction about children in the mines, *Growing Up in Coal Country*, which was a Golden Kite Honor Book for Nonfiction, an ALA Notable Children's Book, an ALA Best Book for Young Adults, and a Notable Children's Trade Book in the Field of Social Studies.

Bartoletti's further research led to *Kids on Strike!*, about children hired to work in 18th and 19th century mills and surviving on city streets as bootblacks, as well as working in the mines. *Kids on Strike!* was named an ALA Notable Children's Book, an ALA Best Book for Young Adults, a *School Library Journal* Best Book, a Notable Children's Trade Book in the Field of Social Studies, and was included in the New York Public Library's Books for the Teen Age. *No Man's Land: A Young Soldier's Story*, was also named a Notable Children's Trade Book in the Field of Social Studies. In *A Coal Miner's Bride: The Diary of Anetka Kaminska, 1896*, Bartoletti returned to the harsh conditions of coal mining life in Pennsylvania, telling the first-person story of a 13-year-old Polish girl's voyage to America and her arranged marriage to a stranger. Bartoletti's greatest success to date came when *Black Potatoes: The Story of the Great Irish Famine, 1845–1850* received the Robert F. Sibert award as "the most distinguished informational book for children published in 2001," as well as the Golden Kite Award for Nonfiction and the Orbis Pictus Award. Susan Bartoletti was named the 2001 Outstanding Pennsylvania Author of the Year.

SELECTED WORKS: *Silver at Night*, illus. by David Ray, 1994; *Growing Up in Coal Country*, 1996; *Dancing with Dziadziu*, illus. by Anika Nelson, 1997; *Kids on Strike!*, 1999; *No Man's Land: A Young Soldier's Story*, 1999; *A Coal Miner's Bride: The Diary of Anetka Kaminska, 1896*, 2000; *Black Potatoes: The Story of the Great Irish Famine, 1845–1850*, 2001; *The Christmas Promise*, illus. by David Christiana, 2001; *Finn Reardon, A Newsie: New York City, 1899*, 2003; *Nobody's Nosier than a Cat*, illus. by Beppe Giacobbe, 2003; *The Flag Maker*, illus. by Claire A. Nivola, 2004.

SUGGESTED READING: *Authors and Artists for Young Adults*, vol. 44, 2002; *Beacham's Guide to Literature for Young Adults*, vol. 10, 2000; *Contemporary Authors*, vol. 152, 1997; *Something About the Author*, vol. 135, 2003. Periodicals—"Exploring the Gaps," *Book Links*, August/September 2000.

"Despite the fact that I grew up wearing other kids' clothes—most notably our neighbor Ellen Katz's underwear, blouses, shorts, and dresses—I had a strong sense of who I was and what I could and couldn't do. I knew that I liked the color red and not the color green, hot dogs and not hamburgers, and stories about families as opposed to stories about monsters. I knew that if I wanted to, I could make myself run fast in a race, spell all the words correctly on a spelling test, and not eat one more bite of liver—or I would burst.

"As a child growing up in New York City in the 1950s, I had no idea that one day I would be a writer. In fact, whenever I was asked what I wanted to be, I invariably answered 'a ballplayer.' In those days, every city kid played with a small pink rubber ball that was easy to lose because of its innate property of bouncing high. The ball, of course, was the legendary 'spaldeen' adapted by the Spalding Sporting Goods Company from the core of its tennis balls.

"In time, my ball came to be a natural extension of myself—like my foot or my finger or my ear or my nose. I didn't go anywhere without it. Playing ball made me—a painfully shy, self-conscious kid—feel at best every bit as confident, uninhibited, and fulfilled as the best-adjusted kid in the neighborhood. Remarkably, no one ever had to make me practice. I wanted to be the best ballplayer I could be. 'So what if I was a girl?' I asked myself. I played ball outside with friends and inside alone, much to the horror of my mother, who tried very hard to get me to be a ballerina. But like all good mothers, mine realized early on that my heart was not in first and second position but on first and second base. Anna Pavlova would have thanked her from the bottom of her toe shoes.

"I began writing for many of the same reasons that I played ball. I didn't have to talk. I found that I was able to carry my writing around with me like I carried that ball. My pencil and paper became natural extensions of myself like my feet or my fingers, my ears or my nose. And no one ever had to make me practice. Sometimes I wrote for hours. I went on record as having the

Courtesy of M. Schindel

Cari Best

May 30, 1951–

longest journal in my high school's history. As a painfully shy, self-conscious young adult, writing made me feel confident, uninhibited, and fulfilled. Teachers and friends and even my mother encouraged me to write. How marvelous that I could convey my passions without ever having to utter a word. And when an English professor at Queens College read my paper about Charles Dickens's *Nicholas Nickelby* and proclaimed, 'You are a born writer,' I thought for the first time in a long time that I might want to do something else besides play ball.

"Being in touch with what I felt as a child has never been difficult. The challenge has always been to convert those feelings—however ill and negative—into something that might help a child deal with a similar situation in his or her life today. I continue to hope that readers will care as much as I do even if the story is about my grandmother and not theirs and how much I loved her knees and her cheeks and the sound of her Russian language. I try to awaken in each of them a passion—whether it's for playing ball, a ride in a taxi, or an animal that's been hurt. And of course when the reader then feels inclined to indulge the passion in himself, I am rewarded. There goes a child, I hope, who will one day grow up to be a caring adult.

"One of the joys (and there are many for me) of being a writer is to hear the voices of the hundreds of kids that I visit in inner cities each year. I make a point of answering every letter that I receive. 'I like your books so much that I could eat them up like candies!' says one. Or 'You made me think that I could be an author someday too.' How much better could life be!"

"I began writing for many of the same reasons that I played ball. I didn't have to talk."

✿　✿　✿

Cari Best grew up in New York City, as she says, "in an extended European family dominated by confident, beautiful women who loved to talk." One of the highlights of her childhood was winning an elementary school spelling bee with the words "aurora borealis." One of the highlights of her adulthood was being invited to the Baseball Hall of Fame to talk about her childhood.

A graduate of Queens College of the City University of New York, she also received a master's degree in library science from Drexel University in 1975. She served as the first librarian at the International Reading Association headquarters in Newark, Delaware, as well as children's librarian at a public library. Later, she was editorial director for Weston Woods Studios. She has three children, two of whom are teachers and all of whom are avid baseball fans, and currently lives with her husband in Weston, Connecticut. She loves to grow things like flowers, vegetables, and dogs.

Cari Best's picture books depict real life problems that children encounter—divorce, disappointment, bullying, shyness—and show a realistic and satisfying outcome in each case, creating in her young readers a sense of hope. Her first picture book,

Taxi! Taxi!, relates Tina's joy in a Sunday spent with her father, a taxi driver who "lives someplace else" and sometimes disappoints her. The story describes one wonderful Sunday that they do spend together. For this book, Best won the Ezra Jack Keats New Writer's Award in 1995. She has continued to have great success with her picture book writing. *Shrinking Violet* was designated a *School Library Journal* Best Book of the Year.

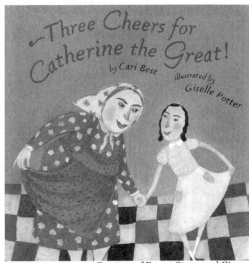

Courtesy of Farrar, Straus and Giroux

Three Cheers for Catherine the Great!, a story about Best's Russian grandmother and a very special birthday party, won a Charlotte Zolotow Honor Book Award for picture book writing and was also an ALA Notable Children's Book. The Swedish edition, *Hipp, Hurra för Mormor!*, received the Peter Pan Award in Sweden, and Best's reward, along with illustrator Giselle Potter, was to be a trip to the Göteborg International Book Fair to present a seminar on September 14, 2001. Unfortunately, the disruption of air travel after September 11 that year prevented her from making the trip. Cari Best's picture books continue to provide strong characterizations and satisfying stories for children and the adults in their lives.

SELECTED WORKS: *Taxi! Taxi!*, illus. by Dale Gottlieb, 1994; *Red Light, Green Light, Mama and Me*, illus. by Niki Daly, 1995; *Getting Used to Harry*, illus. by Diane Palmisciano, 1996; *Top Banana*, illus. by Erika Oller, 1997; *Last Licks: A Spaldeen Story*, illus. by Diane Palmisciano, 1999; *Montezuma's Revenge*, illus. by Diane Palmisciano, 1999; *Three Cheers for Catherine the Great!*, illus. by Giselle Potter, 1999; *Shrinking Violet*, illus. by Giselle Potter, 2001; *Goose's Story*, illus. by Holly Meade, 2002; *When Catherine the Great and I Were Eight*, illus. by Giselle Potter, 2003.

SUGGESTED READING: *Something About the Author*, vol. 149, 2004. Periodicals—"Women on the Job," *Book Links*, September/October 1997.

"I loved going to bed when I was a child, but not because I had any intention of going to sleep. Bedtime was a precious private space, away from the hubbub of my large family, where I could spin out one of the stories always simmering in my mind. But I never thought I'd be an author. In fact, I never thought I'd be much of anything, because I was such a lousy student. I daydreamed instead of listening to the teacher; I read instead of doing my homework. Reading was the only thing I was any good

Franny Billingsley

July 3, 1953–

at. I was rather shy and solitary, but never lonely, for I had a universe of friends inside my head.

"I was most truly myself outside school, which is perhaps why I loved the year I left the American school system to spend fifth grade in Denmark. Denmark was a fairy-tale place for me, home of the great fairy-tale writer, Hans Christian Andersen. I read his stories over and over, especially *The Snow Queen* and *The Little Mermaid*. My memories of that year come to me now as if through a magical lens: the statue of the Little Mermaid rising from the gray waves of the Copenhagen harbor; myself at Christmas, wearing a crown of lighted candles; the Snow Queen's palace, present everywhere in the dark afternoons, the drifts of snow, the moon-shot ice.

Courtesy of Richard Pettingill

"In my mid-teens, however, I became self-conscious about being the outsider, the oddball, and I began making an effort to fit in. I became so determined to join the crowd that I consciously set aside my nighttime imaginings. I spent years pretending to be like the others—pretending even to myself—and after college I went to law school, just like everyone else. Law school was miserable, and practicing law even more so. I understand now why—I was like a square peg squeezed into a round hole. A lawyer's mind works entirely differently from the way mine does. A lawyer collects information from the outside (research and interview) and uses it to convince you that something in the real world is true. My strength is gathering information from the inside (imagination and memory) and using it to convince you that something imaginary is true.

"I'd been a lawyer for five years when my life turned around. I took a vacation to visit my sister, who was then living in Barcelona teaching English. How I envied her life! She had very little money, but her life was rich in the ways that mine was poor. She had time to dwell in the world of ideas and imagination; she had a community of friends with common interests and values. That trip to Barcelona jolted me out of my misery and boredom. I saw clearly that I had chosen a false life for myself, and within two weeks I had decided to quit my job and live in Spain. I intended to do nothing in Spain but luxuriate in stories, so I brought with me many of my favorite children's books. Once I began reading, I came round, full circle, to my oldest passion. *This is what I really love,* I thought. *How could I have gotten so far from the world of children's books?* From there, it was just a small step to writing them myself. It was a big step, however, to getting published. That took 14 years. After a couple of years in Barcelona, I ran out of money, and I returned to my hometown of Chicago to manage the children's section of a bookstore. But however busy I was, I always made time for writing.

"Let us return now to my memories from fifth grade: *The Snow Queen*, *The Little Mermaid*, the crown of lighted candles. I am fascinated by the way childhood details creep into my novels without conscious effort. The heroine of my first novel, *Well Wished*, puts on a play of *The Snow Queen*; she wears a crown of lighted candles. The heroine of my second novel, *The Folk Keeper*, is much like the Little Mermaid: She is half human, half sea-creature; she has to choose between land and sea.

"I now live in my childhood home with my husband and two children, but I no longer have to reserve my story-spinning for bedtime. I am wonderfully lucky that I can now spend my days dwelling in the world of imagination and setting down what I see there for others to read."

✲ ✲ ✲

The refreshingly original fantasy of Franny Billingsley has been highly praised in reviews of her first two novels for young readers. *Well Wished* was a *School Library Journal* Best Book and named one of the *Booklist*'s Top 10 First Novels for Youth, in addition to being cited as an honor book for the Anne Spencer Lindbergh Prize for the best fantasy written in the English language in 1997–1998. *The Folk Keeper* won the coveted *Boston Globe–Horn Book* award for fiction as well as being a *Booklist* Editors' Choice, a *School Library Journal* Best Book, a Blue Ribbon book in the *Bulletin of the Center for Children's Books*, and an ALA Notable Children's Book. In 2003 Franny Billingsley won the PEN/Phyllis Reynolds Naylor Working Writer Fellowship, which is presented annually to a children's or young adult author who has written at least two but no more than three books, and whose work has been "well reviewed and warmly received by literary critics."

"I saw clearly that I had chosen a false life for myself, and within two weeks I had decided to quit my job and live in Spain."

The theme of transformation that runs through these first two novels may well parallel Billingsley's own life and her metamorphosis from dreamy child into lawyer and then into a writer who relies on her imagination and wit. Her father was a probability theorist at the University of Chicago, but he is also very active in the arts. He paints and has appeared in theater productions as well as a few small film roles. Franny traces her interest in Celtic folklore to her father's singing of Scottish ballads when she was growing up. Her mother was a reporter for Time-Life for a number of years, so writing was also part of the family background. Graduating with a B.A. from Tufts University in 1976, Franny went on to earn her law degree from Boston University in 1979. After quitting her position in law in 1983 and living for several years in Spain, she returned to her hometown to work in a bookstore.

Courtesy of Atheneum Books for Young Readers

Soon after returning to Chicago, she was introduced to Richard Pettengill, who was then working as dramaturge for the Court Theater, where her father was acting in a production of *Heartbreak House*. Franny Billingsley and Pettengill married and now have two children: Miranda, born in 1990, and Nathaniel, born in 1994. Franny continued working as a buyer and manager in the children's book section of the bookstore and led several storytimes a week from 1987 to 1999. Since 1998, she has taught fiction writing at Columbia College and the University of Chicago's Graham School and has spoken at many schools, libraries, and teacher conferences on the writing process and the importance of reading. Her husband, after many years as dramaturge and arts educator in Chicago theaters, received his Ph.D. in English from the University of Chicago and is now teaching at Lake Forest College in the English and theater departments.

SELECTED WORKS: *Well Wished*, 1997; *The Folk Keeper*, 1999.

SUGGESTED READING: Martin, Philip, ed., *The Writer's Guide to Fantasy Literature*, Writer Books, 2002. Periodicals—"*Boston Globe–Horn Book* Award Acceptance Speech," *The Horn Book*, January/February 2001. Online—Interview with Franny Billingsley, *www.cynthialeitichsmith.com/auth-illFrannyBillingsley.htm*.

WEB SITE: *www.frannybillingsley.com*

Christopher Bing

March 2, 1959–

"My two earliest memories from childhood (when I was around 3–4 years old) are: 1) the excitement of my grandfather reading to me at bedtime and 2) drawing with my grandmother for hours. This was before there were cartoon cable channels, movies on videotapes or DVDs, video games, home computers, or huge warehouse toy stores. While I was growing up my passions were reading comic books and the adventure strips on the comic pages in the newspaper, and spending hours trying to imitate the art. When I was old enough I had a paper route and would ask some of my customers who read the other local paper, which ran different comics, to cut them out and save them for me. At the end of each week when I collected the pay envelopes I also collected the strips they saved for me.

"I spent all the money I earned on comic books, books, pens, pencils, and drawing paper. When I was around 11 or 12 a local museum had a night class in 'comic book' and 'comic strip' art, and my mother signed me up. I lived for that class. I was the only kid in the class; everyone else was 18 or older. It made my dreams of becoming an artist seem more attainable. These people also introduced me to alternative comics, and how comics could be about social issues, not just adventure and superheroes. So I started looking at the political cartoons on the editorial pages and discovered the art of editorial illustration (a cartoon uses words to help convey its idea, but an illustration makes its point through the image alone). I had found a way of saying things, powerful things, through images alone. I had found my place in the world, the place I wanted to be.

"As I got older, I was somewhat solitary. I think this was because, in part, I was not a very good student. I loved to read but couldn't write or spell well, and found school very hard—even the art classes, because I didn't get to draw what I wanted, comics. I spent most of my time in class daydreaming and drawing, and I got into a lot of trouble for doing that. Drawing was my way of communicating with the world, but it was unacceptable as a way to do English papers. Even as an adult I find it embarrassing and hard to write unless I can do it on a computer where I have tools like spell-check and grammar-check.

Courtesy of HandPrint Books

"My favorite time of the week was Saturday, when I would draw while watching cartoons; then after I finished my Saturday chores the local UHF channel would show a sci-fi or monster movie, and I would sit and draw some more. I also loved climbing trees, going exploring in the nearby woods, and doing all the stuff kids like to do. But when sitting quietly alone, my fingers would itch to hold a pencil and draw all the visions that endlessly raced through my head. When I graduated high school I took a year off before going on to college. Actually, I wasn't sure that I could get into college with my grades from high school. Thanks to the efforts of a family friend, who applied for me, and has remained unidentified to this day, I found myself the next year at the Rhode Island School of Design.

"Today I consider myself a conceptual editorial and political illustrator (I do drawings for the editorial pages of newspapers and magazines) who has joyously stumbled into the world of children's books. I have over 50 ideas (and still counting) for books I am currently working on plus at least 30 public-domain works that I would like to do. The kind of children's books I love best are not only well illustrated but have a good idea with a little

Twilight Zone–style twist to it. One of my daughters saw the list of book ideas I have typed up and asked me how long will it take to complete all of them. After a little calculating we found that if I do only one a year I will need to live to be over 110 years old—and that's only the books I have in my head at the moment. Something tells me that I'm going to have more ideas.

"So, in the future, if you come across one of my books or political illustrations, and you have any questions or something to say about it, send me a letter via my publisher. I would love to hear from you! May you have many wonderful imaginative visions and dreams and find your own place in the world to share them with the rest of us."

❄ ❄ ❄

The story of how Christopher Bing, a political and editorial illustrator, came to illustrate books for children is a fascinating one. After graduating from the Rhode Island School of Design in 1983, he immediately began work as a freelance artist; his first published illustration appeared in the *Boston Globe* in the spring of his senior year. Looking for a personal art project, one to stretch his own perceptions beyond the confines of the editorial page, Bing started working—with no thought of publication—on illustrations for his favorite childhood story, Helen Bannerman's *Little Black Sambo*, which had been read aloud to him many times by his grandfather. Receiving positive feedback on the drawings from friends and fellow artists, and notably from Henry Louis Gates, Jr., Bing encountered editor and publisher Christopher Franceschelli, who agreed to publish his illustrated version of the old story on one condition: that he publish two other books first. Bannerman's story seemed too controversial for a first book because of the many versions that had appeared over the years with racist and derogatory images.

> "I had found a way of saying things, powerful things, through images alone. I had found my place in the world, the place I wanted to be."

Casting about for another illustration idea for a children's book, Bing remembered a gift his parents had given him when he was in high school—Wallace Tripp's newly illustrated version of "Casey at the Bat." At the time he was most interested in a note in the back of the book stating that the poem had originally appeared in the *San Francisco Examiner* in 1888. He wondered why no one had ever illustrated the poem as if they were reading it in a newspaper, but the idea seemed so obvious he assumed it had been done. Over time, he would look up different versions of "Casey at the Bat" in various libraries, but never did find one that matched his vision. When asked by Franceschelli to come up with another idea, he says that his own version of Casey "sprang to the front of the line and started knocking on the inside of my skull shouting, 'Let me out.'" Seven years later, the book was finished and met with instant success. It was named a Blue Ribbon book by the *Bulletin of the Center for Children's Books* and an ALA Notable Children's Book and captured a Caldecott Honor Award, a remarkable achievement for a first book. The intricate illustrations—created in pen and ink on scratchboard and overlaid with baseball memorabilia, newspaper ads, box scores, and vintage photographs—create the sensation of reading clippings in an old scrapbook found in a family attic. With its startling perspectives and historically accurate settings and clothing, the book appeared both innovative and "classic."

For Bing's second book, he illustrated Henry Wadsworth Longfellow's poem "The Midnight Ride of Paul Revere," again including layered images that enhance understanding of this famous episode in the early years of our country and reflect the meticulous research in Bing's artwork. This book was also named an ALA Notable Children's Book as well as a *School Library Journal* Best Book of the Year. And that paved the way, after a 20-year labor of love, for the publication in 2003 of *Little Black Sambo*. Creating a vibrant black child wandering through a mythic Indian landscape, Bing gave his protagonist a larger-than-life feel in a book that has an unusually large trim size. The boy seems to be leaping off the pages as he confronts the bullying tigers and eventually triumphs over them, winning back his elegant clothes. Bing has called *Little Black Sambo* the "perfect story for pre-school age boys: a brave, smart hero who is loved and has the independence to explore the world alone."

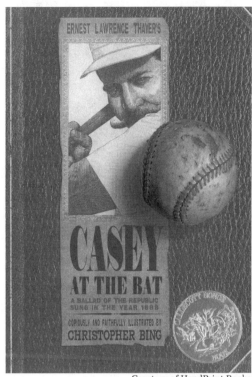

Courtesy of HandPrint Books

Ever mindful of the importance of friends, mentors, and teachers in his life, Bing includes their names in his books where an old-time engraver's signature would appear. The illustrator Chris Van Allsburg's name appears in *Casey* because as a teacher at RISD, Van Allsburg introduced Bing to the scratchboard technique, which has given depth and texture to his pen-and-ink work. Christopher Bing lives today in Lexington, Massachusetts, with his wife, Wendy, and their three children.

SELECTED WORKS ILLUSTRATED: *Casey at the Bat: A Ballad of the Republic Sung in the Year 1888*, by Ernest Lawrence Thayer, 2000; *The Midnight Ride of Paul Revere*, by Henry Wadsworth Longfellow, 2001; *The Story of Little Black Sambo*, by Helen Bannerman, 2003.

SUGGESTED READING: Brown, Jennifer, "The Journey of Little Black Sambo: Caldecott Honor Artist Offers a New Interpretation of a Controversial Tale," *Publishers Weekly*, December 15, 2003; Vogel, Heather Frederick, "Christopher Bing," *Publishers Weekly*, December 18, 2000.

Courtesy of Susan Henry

Ann Blades

Ann Blades

November 16, 1947–

"I began painting with watercolours at a school in England when I was 11 years old. I won a self-portrait contest and discovered that I loved to paint. We lived there for only a year while my father took some courses at Oxford. My family moved frequently, and I attended seven schools. As a result, I didn't have a lot of friends and spent much of my free time during high school painting with watercolours.

"After two years at a university, I began teaching in 1967 at Mile 18, a remote community in northern British Columbia. Here I began my first book, the story of a little girl who longs to keep a wolf pup she has found. Several factors prompted me to write and illustrate *Mary of Mile 18*. One was the isolation; there was absolutely nothing to do. Another was the fact that a lot of books available to the children in this isolated two-room school were not relevant to children living in rural communities. Inspired by Harald Wiberg's illustrations in *The Tomten and the Fox*, I began working on a book about a little girl in my class called Mary.

"I continued to teach for a few more years, in the isolated Native community at Taché in central British Columbia and in Surrey, just outside Vancouver. I wrote and illustrated another book, *A Boy of Taché*.

"Between 1972 and 1974 I trained as a registered nurse and worked four months every summer until 1980 on a men's surgical ward in a small Vancouver hospital. During this time I wrote and illustrated one more book and then made the decision to concentrate on the illustration of picture books. A number of these books were set either on the coast or in the interior of British Columbia. In 1982 I began showing watercolour paintings at the Bau Xi Gallery in Vancouver, and during the next 15 years I had 10 shows at this gallery. These watercolours were larger than my book illustrations, but similar in subject and setting. After my sons were born in 1984 and 1987, I continued to work on book illustrations one year and paintings for a show at the Bau Xi the next year. I temporarily gave up book tours.

"By the mid-1990s I was divorced and supporting two children on my own, so I resumed school and library visits to supplement my income. I did hundreds of presentations and discovered that I enjoyed talking to children about picture books more than I enjoyed creating picture books. Income from selling paintings was unpredictable and my royalties were dwindling. I decided to return to teaching. In the fall of 2000 I began two years of university courses to re-certify as a teacher and complete a degree. In the midst of this retraining, a special 30th anniversary edition of *Mary of Mile 18* was published, in the fall of 2001. It felt as if I had gone a full circle. Thirty years as a writer and illustrator of picture books began when I was a young teacher in a two-room school at Mile 18. Now, on the 30th anniversary of the publication of *Mary of Mile 18*, my career as a teacher was beginning again, after a long time away.

"I am now enjoying teaching kindergarten in Surrey, British Columbia. I feel fortunate to have been able to return to a career that I had always regretted leaving. Since 2000 I haven't done a single painting or book illustration and I don't miss it. I plan to teach for about 10 years, work in my garden, and spend as much time as I can at my little log cabin on Bridge Lake in the interior of British Columbia."

❈ ❈ ❈

Ann Blades's first book, *Mary of Mile 18*, appeared to great acclaim when it was first published in 1971. The author was only 19 years old when she went to teach in the remote community of Mile 18. Mary, a character based on a young Mennonite girl that Blades taught, befriends a wolf pup in the story. Her father tells Mary she cannot keep the wolf as a pet and must return it to the wild, but the pup soon proves its importance to the family. The emotional depth shown in Ann Blades's naive, folk-primitive-style paintings won the book many fans throughout her native Canada, and it was named Book of the Year by the Canadian Library Association. The story was also very popular in the United States and England, and appeared in translation in Europe as well. The National Film Board of Canada created a film version in 1981.

"I began painting with watercolours at a school in England when I was eleven years old."

Similar sensitivity of style was apparent in Blades's second book, *A Boy of Taché*, an adventure/survival story, and in her illustrations for Betty Waterton's *A Salmon for Simon*. In the latter, a young Native boy wishes all summer to catch a salmon, but when he has his chance the wonder and beauty of the wild thing overtake his own longing, and he decides to set the fish free to swim the ocean. *A Salmon for Simon* was named the best illustrated book of the year by the Canadian Library Association and won the Canada Council Children's Literature Award (now known as the Governor General's Award) for Illustration. Blades was equally successful when she created the highly praised illustrations for *A Dog Came, Too: A True Story*. Based on the journals of explorer Alexander Mackenzie, who in 1793 became the first European to have crossed the continent, Ainslie Manson's story tells of the stray dog that accompanied Mackenzie's party of voyageurs and Native guides on their trans-Canadian adventure. The dog, known only as "Our Dog," followed alongshore when the group traveled by canoe because there was no room in the boats for him; he guarded the camps at night, warning of

MARY OF MILE 18

STORY AND PICTURES BY ANN BLADES

Courtesy of Tundra Books

approaching bears and wolves. When the dog disappeared, all members of the team mourned his loss, but he found them again on their return trip. Blades's pictures were carefully researched to depict historically accurate clothing and equipment the voyageurs used, setting the story firmly in its time period.

The simplicity and childlike perspectives in Ann Blades's work seem perfectly adapted to books for the very young. Her board books on the seasons of the year were popular in both Canada and the United States, and her alphabet book *By the Sea* won the first Elizabeth Mrazik-Cleaver Canadian Picture Book Award in 1986. Her own experience with her two children undoubtedly inspired her retelling of an old folk tale that she entitled *Too Small*. Blades has created lasting images for young readers of the Canadian landscape, in remote places as well as more populated areas. Original drawings and background materials for several of her books are available at the National Library of Canada.

SELECTED WORKS WRITTEN AND ILLUSTRATED (Dates are for Canadian editions; U.S. publication dates are shown in parentheses): *Mary of Mile 18*, 1971 (1976); *A Boy of Taché*, 1973 (1976); *The Cottage at Crescent Beach*, 1977; *By the Sea: An Alphabet Book*, 1985; *Summer*, 1989 (1990); *Fall*, 1989 (1990); *Winter*, 1989 (1990); *Spring*, 1989 (1990); *Back to the Cabin*, 1996; *Wolf and the Seven Little Kids*, based on a tale from the Brothers Grimm, 1999; *Too Small*, 2000.

SELECTED WORKS ILLUSTRATED (Dates are for Canadian editions; U.S. publication dates are shown in parentheses): *Jacques the Woodcutter*, by Michael Macklem, 1977; *A Salmon for Simon*, by Betty Waterton, 1978 (1980); *Six Darn Cows*, by Margaret Laurence, 1979; *Anna's Pet*, by Margaret Atwood and Joyce Barkhouse, 1979; *Pettranella*, by Betty Waterton, 1980 (1980); *A Candle for Christmas*, by Jean Speare, 1986 (1987); *Ida and the Wool Smugglers*, by Sue Ann Alderson, 1987 (1987); *The Singing Basket*, by Kit Pearson, 1990; *A Dog Came, Too*, by Ainslie Manson, 1992 (1992); *A Ride for Martha*, by Sue Ann Alderson, 1993; *Pond Seasons*, by Sue Ann Alderson, 1997.

SUGGESTED READING: *Something About the Author*, vol. 69, 1992. Periodicals—"The Art of the Children's Book Illustrator," *Quill and Quire*, October 1985. Online— *www.collectionscanada.ca/3/10/t10-401-e.html*.

"I stumbled into the role of biographer quite by accident. Early in the spring of 1972, I developed a problem which ultimately kept me off my feet for six months. It was then that I chanced upon an article in *Writer Magazine* about writing biographies for teenagers. My husband challenged me to try. 'You have always wanted to write,' he said. 'Besides, it will keep you sane.' Never one to ignore a challenge, I decided to take him up on it. I had always wanted to write, but I had never had the nerve to try. I was shy and introverted as a child, and I never thought I could write. When I followed my mother's suggestion that I get a teaching degree, I discovered that I loved teaching. I enjoyed helping students to write well, but I didn't attempt any writing myself.

"Now, following the step-by-step suggestions in the article, I produced *William Wordsworth: The Wandering Poet*. When it was named to the Child Study Association list of Best Books of the Year 1975, I was off and running, figuratively and literally! Since then, writing lives has been an exciting adventure because I never know where my research will lead me. It has taken my husband and me to many parts of the world, and even to an extraordinary evening at the White House. And it has introduced us to some remarkable people. As I read, interview, travel, study the work my subjects produced (whether it be paintings or poetry, personal letters and diaries, or historical

Courtesy of Lawrence H. Bober

Natalie S. Bober

Natalie Bober

December 27, 1930–

documents such as the Declaration of Independence) trying to get inside their minds and their hearts—to see and hear and feel what they did, I must lift the curtain of time that shuts away the centuries, and find the details that give the past a pulse. The excitement comes from search and discovery, re-creating a life from details, and making a story out of the chaos of reality. This is the challenge of biography that has kept me on a perpetual treasure hunt since 1972. I can think of few pursuits that would afford me more pure pleasure.

"As I reflect on the 30 years that my career as a writer has spanned, and search for the greatest influence on that career, it immediately becomes apparent that it was my mother who deserves much of the credit. The hours she sat with me as a child, patiently helping me with homework and teaching me to do the same kind of careful, meticulous research and writing that she did in her profession, have been the cornerstone on which my life as a biographer has been founded. (In her first job, she served as an editor of the *Readers' Guide to Periodical Literature* with the H. W. Wilson Company, publishers of this very book!) She set a wonderful example for me, and passed on to me a legacy of research and writing that has now been passed down to my children and my children's children. In fact, two of my granddaughters have worked closely with me, giving me the benefit of their perspectives and contributing significantly to my research. And it was my son who, while reading the manuscript of my first biography of Thomas Jefferson, recognized before I did that I was falling in love with Abigail Adams and encouraged me to tell her story. *Abigail Adams: Witness to a Revolution* went on to win the *Boston Globe–Horn Book* Award for Nonfiction, the Golden Kite Award from the Society of Children's Book Writers and Illustrators, and numerous others.

"Yet when I graduated from college in 1951, I had no sense at all of where I would be today. What I did know was that I had a husband who valued my education as much as I did, and who would do everything in his power to make it possible for me to continue that education, and to pursue whatever dreams I had. And that was in the days when many husbands didn't do that!

"In addition to writing, I have taught, edited, conducted workshops, lectured, and even been a part of a television documentary on Thomas Jefferson. But what provided me with the most happiness were the 10 years that my daughter and I owned and operated a children's book store—even though all of our friends said a mother and daughter could never work together. If anything, it brought us even closer. And it gave me greater insight into the wonderful literature being written for young people.

"Over the years my life has taken many unexpected turns, and I have often found myself torn between conflicting loyalties. I have had to deal with sometimes painful choices and interruptions that made it necessary for me to creatively reassemble the pieces, to shift gears, and to move in a slightly different direction

"I have had to deal with sometimes painful choices and interruptions that made it necessary for me to creatively reassemble the pieces, to shift gears, and to move in a slightly different direction from the path I had been traveling."

from the path I had been traveling. I liken it to the frequent need to tack back and forth in our sailboat in order to reach a destination. The ability that I have discovered within myself to communicate with young people—to enrich their lives with my books—to help them to sympathize and connect with history, and then to search for the greatness within themselves—has brought much happiness.

"But it didn't start there. It began with my first summer job—at age 16—just after I had graduated from Hunter College High School—working in the stacks at the main branch of the New York Public Library. How I loved the smell and the feel of the old books! I never even minded the dust that seemed to be a permanent part of them. From then on, I was certain that books would always be a thread that was tightly woven into the fabric of my life. Little did I know then that I would one day be *writing* books that would have a special niche on those shelves!"

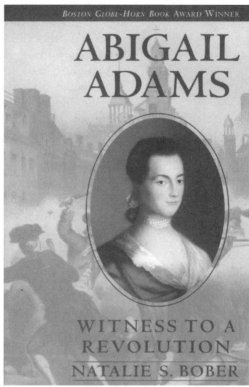

Courtesy of Atheneum Books for Young Readers

Natalie Bober was born and raised in New York City and received her B.A. degree in English from Hunter College in 1951. While studying at Hunter, she received the strong background in English and American literature and history that would inform her later career of writing remarkably readable and well-researched biographies of politicians, poets, and artists. She went on to receive a Master of Science degree in reading from Hofstra University in 1966, taking additional graduate courses at C. W. Post University, New York University, and the City University of New York through the years. In addition to teaching and serving as a consultant on the secondary school and graduate college level, Natalie has been a guest lecturer at several American universities, led numerous biography workshop sessions at various institutions, and lectured at Oxford University in England in 2001 at a symposium entitled "The Unpleasantness in the Colonies: The American Revolution." In May 2001 she was elected to the Hunter College Alumnae Hall of Fame.

Bober's books have garnered many awards. Most of them have been included on New York Public Library's annual Books for the Teen Age list and several have been named as Notable Trade Books in the Field of Social Studies. *A Restless Spirit: The Story of Robert Frost* also won a Dorothy Canfield Fisher Award in the state of Vermont. *Abigail Adams: Witness to a Revolution* received the prestigious *Boston Globe–Horn Book* Award for the most distinguished nonfiction book of the year as well as the Golden Kite Award for nonfiction from the Society of Children's Book Writers and Illustrators. This title was also cited as a *School Library Journal* Best Book, a *Booklist* Editors' Choice, and an ALA Best Book for Young Adults, among other accolades.

Natalie Bober's writing has led to unexpected ventures into other media. Because her biography of Thomas Jefferson, *Thomas Jefferson: Man on a Mountain*, presented the early patriot and president in such "accessible human terms," she was asked to serve as a consultant and a "talking head" on the Ken Burns PBS documentary that was initially aired in February 1997. In a letter to the author after the show was completed, the co-producer stated that her presentation of Jefferson ". . . will extend to our audience an emotional connection that will reverberate for them long after viewing." Previously, in 1993, she had delivered a speech in Charlottesville, Virginia, as part of the celebration of the 250th anniversary of Jefferson's birth, and she has conducted all-day workshops at Monticello for students and teachers. In 2002 she was a member of the faculty at a symposium held at the University of Virginia entitled "Writing the Life of Thomas Jefferson," and in 2003 she was awarded a fellowship by the International Center for Jefferson Studies. She is a member of the board of directors of the Jefferson Legacy Foundation.

Married since 1950 to her husband, Lawrence, Natalie Bober has three grown children, four grandchildren, and three great-grandchildren. She lives in White Plains, New York.

SELECTED WORKS: *William Wordsworth: The Wandering Poet*, 1975; *A Restless Spirit: The Story of Robert Frost*, 1981; *Breaking Tradition: The Story of Louise Nevelson*, 1984; *Let's Pretend: Poems of Flight and Fancy*, 1986; *Thomas Jefferson: Man on a Mountain*, 1988; *Marc Chagall: Painter of Dreams*, 1991; *Abigail Adams: Witness to a Revolution*, 1995; *Countdown to Independence: A Revolution of Ideas in England and Her American Colonies: 1760–1776*, 2001.

SUGGESTED READING: *Something About the Author*, vol. 87, 1996; *Something About the Author Autobiography Series*, vol. 23, 1997. Periodicals—Bober, Natalie S., "Writing Lives," *The Lion and the Unicorn*, December 1991; Bober, Natalie, "Acceptance Speech for the *Boston Globe–Horn Book* Award," *The Horn Book*, January/February 1996.

Louise Borden

October 30, 1949–

"There were already two Louises in my family when I was born: my mother and my grandmother, Nana, who lived with us when I was growing up. Years later, my niece was born and also named Louise. Then there were four of us with the same name.

"I grew up in a house at the top of a steep street in Cincinnati, Ohio, the kind of street that is a challenge when you are pedaling uphill on your bicycle. My two sisters and I used to ride our bikes down, down our street, and then to the local dime store to buy candy bars or meet our friends. But coming home, we had to pedal up our long hill. Pedaling slowly up my street may be where I learned perseverance, something all writers need when they are working alone at their desks.

"Another part of my childhood was going to watch the Cincinnati Reds play at old Crosley Field. Tony Perez is still one of my all-time baseball heroes. I attended a small elementary school named Lotspeich, and that is where I became a lifelong reader. I loved our school library and those shelves of books. I didn't know then that I would someday become a writer. When I was in third grade, I wanted to be a composer. I was taking piano lessons, and my teacher was Miss Cornn, the music teacher in our school. Everyone loved Miss Cornn, and I loved her especially because we shared a name. Her name was Louise, too. My idea about being a composer was short-lived and after a few years, I gave up taking piano lessons. But Louise Cornn remains a key person in my early school memories.

"Writing picture books came later—after studying history in college, getting married, and raising three children. I like to think that my picture books are almost songs—because the sound of words and the poetry of my style are so important in the texts that I write. Spending over 50 summers in Leland, Michigan, with my family in a landscape of sky and water has instilled in me a true sense of place—as well as an eye for visual images. Now, in the settings of my books, I work very hard to take the reader to those places through my words.

Courtesy of Robert Flischel

"Ordinary children are the characters in my fiction. They are kids like I was years ago, and they have the same universal feelings that we all share. Parts of my books are made up, and other parts come from personal experience. A few of my books are biographies. All of my writing comes from within: I care deeply about the people, the places, and the events that I write about. One additional aspect of my work that has been wonderful and rewarding: the collaboration of writing two books with Mary Kay Kroeger and one nonfiction book with Trish Marx. I also know other fine writers and illustrators, and these friendships have been an essential part in my growth as a writer.

"I have spoken in hundreds of schools and met many students, teachers, and librarians. Often I am in my car, driving to new places to talk about my writing. I have a lot of thinking time in those miles. Thinking time—it's so very important for a writer.

I think about ideas for books and new ways to write them. I think about what is important to me. I think about visual images. I think about the books I read as a child—and the books I am reading today. I think about my husband and our children and my friends—my great encouragers! And my wonderful editors who understand, in just the right way, my creative vision for each new book. These thoughts inspire me to return to my desk and begin working on a manuscript. I feel very lucky because I love what I do. I type my name on the first page, then pause for a moment to look at it: Louise Borden. That's me, one of many Louises. Now I'm a writer."

❊ ❊ ❊

Louise Borden was born Louise Walker in Cincinnati, Ohio, and she has lived most of her life in Ohio. The interest in history that is evident in her books began early in life with the influence of a grandmother who loved history. When she was in sixth grade, Louise's teacher wrote on her report card: "Her work in Social Studies is really outstanding and I think she will enjoy research all her life." That interest continued in college, where Louise majored in history at Denison University, receiving her B.A. in 1971. That same year she married Peter Borden, who is in the machine tool business. For several years she taught school, first as an assistant first grade teacher at the Meadowbrook School in Weston, Massachusetts and then for a year as a pre-primary teacher at Cincinnati Country Day School, before concentrating on raising three children—Cate, Ayars, and Ted—who are now all in their twenties.

From 1986 to 1991, Louise Borden was part-owner of The Bookshelf, an independent bookstore in Cincinnati, and it was during this time that she had her first book accepted for publication. Since 1991, her time has been devoted to researching and writing books and speaking in schools and libraries. Leisure activities of skiing, skating, boating, biking, travel, and gardening provide a rich balance to the solitary craft of writing. In fact, she signed her first book contract several days after breaking both wrists while ice-skating. Watching baseball, especially her beloved Cincinnati Reds, is another passionate interest for this writer.

Louise Borden's books are all written from strong feelings—either remembered emotions and experiences from her own childhood or stories she has encountered through life experience and research. She has always been interested in viewing historic events through the eyes of ordinary people, as is evident in two of her books that have been named Notable Children's Trade Books in the Field of Social Studies—*Good-Bye, Charles Lindbergh* and *The Little Ships*. Her curiosity was piqued one day by a "Dear Abby" letter in the newspaper in which a man spoke of his childhood meeting with Charles Lindbergh. The image of that young boy on his horse in a farm field looking up to see

"Ordinary children are the characters in my fiction. They are kids like I was years ago, and they have the same universal feelings that we all share."

Lindbergh's biplane stayed with Borden until she tracked down the letter-writer, contacted him, and eventually flew to Arkansas to meet him, resulting in her telling of his story in *Good-Bye, Charles Lindbergh*. A longtime fascination with the civilian rescue of Allied soldiers from the beach at Dunkirk in June 1940 led her to ask an older British man whom she met on vacation if he had been there. He connected her with a man from his village who had been involved in that enormous rescue effort over 50 years before. As part of her research for *The Little Ships*, Borden traveled to England to take part in the reunion sail from Dover to Dunkirk in 1995, the 55th anniversary of the rescue. She also tells stories gathered from experiences closer to home. *Good Luck, Mrs. K.!*, the touching story of a third-grade class dealing with the news that their beloved teacher has developed cancer, was awarded a Christopher Medal in 2000.

Courtesy of Margeret K. McElderry Books

SELECTED WORKS: *Caps, Hats, Socks, and Mittens: A Book About the Four Seasons*, illus. by Lillian Hoban, 1989; *Neighborhood Trucker*, illus. by Sandra Speidel, 1990; *The Watching Game*, illus. by Teri Weidner, 1991; *Albie the Lifeguard*, illus. by Elizabeth Sayles, 1993; *Just in Time for Christmas*, illus. by Ted Lewin, 1994; *Paperboy*, with Mary Kay Kroeger, illus. by Ted Lewin, 1996; *Thanksgiving Is*, illus. by Steve Bjorkman, 1997; *The Little Ships: The Heroic Rescue at Dunkirk in World War II*, illus. by Michael Foreman, 1997; *Good-Bye, Charles Lindbergh: Based on a True Story*, illus. by Thomas B. Allen, 1998; *A. Lincoln and Me*, illus. by Ted Lewin, 1999; *Good Luck, Mrs. K.!*, illus. by Adam Gustavson, 1999; *Sleds on Boston Common: A Story from the American Revolution*, illus. by Robert Andrew Parker, 2000; *Fly High! The Story of Bessie Coleman*, with Mary Kay Kroeger, illus. by Teresa Flavin, 2001; *The Day Eddie Met the Author*, illus. by Adam Gustavson, 2001; *America Is . . .*, illus. by Stacey Schuett, 2002; *Touching the Sky: Flying Adventures of Wilbur and Orville Wright*, with Trish Marx, illus. by Peter Fiore, 2003; *Sea Clocks: The Story of Longitude*, illus. by Erik Blegvad, 2004; *The A+ Custodian*, illus. by Adam Gustavson, 2004; *The Greatest Skating Race: A WWII Story from the Netherlands*, illus. by Niki Daly, 2004.

SUGGESTED READING: *Something About the Author*, vol. 104, 1999.

WEB SITE: *www.louiseborden.com*

Courtesy of Betsy Bowen

Betsy Bowen

Betsy Bowen

January 1, 1947–

"Here is my first memory, my first story: When I was little, I had a special treasure, the bottom half of a flat crayon box, the kind the big fat ones come in. I thought the cardboard was so beautiful with all the specks of color from each time a crayon bumped. I had put the box under the couch in a safe shadowy place. One evening when I was about two, my mom and dad and little me were in the living room by the fireplace. My mother was straightening up the room, and scooped up my little yellow box and tossed it in the fire. I yelled and wanted to get it out, and couldn't, and watched it go.

"When I remembered this story as an adult, after I had become an artist, I thought, 'Well just look, those colors, and the magic of a line coming out of a crayon when it is pulled across the paper, have always been important to me. That's just the way I was made. How fortunate then that I can be an artist.'

"I had art lessons as a child from Mrs. Test, in her home that was full of interesting folk art and objects from all over the world. Instead of Christmas cards, she sent us postcards from her travels. I think that she is the reason that I knew a wider world existed beyond my little hometown near Chicago. My parents died near the time I finished high school and went off to college. Since then I have looked for the people around me to be my 'family.' At age 19 I got married and had a family of three boys, and moved to my original family's vacation place on an old homestead in northern Minnesota.

"I had sporadic art school training, but did learn to make a woodcut. When all the boys were nearly grown up, I began to make a lot of woodcuts of the things I saw around me in the northwoods. I met Ann Rider, a children's book editor, who helped me put together *Antler, Bear, Canoe: A Northwoods Alphabet Year*, and that became my chance to tell part of my own story, and make pictures of family activities that I like. I love the woodcuts, as they have a rugged, edgy character that echoes my view of life; it is not always romantic and soft, but has beautiful rough places, too.

"As a young college student I spent a number of weeks in a small village in Guatemala, learning how families have lived there for hundreds of years, farming and weaving. I wanted something from that experience to be part of my life, and worked as a weaver before I was a printmaker. I loved, as Mrs. Test had, the stories of the different places in the world and have illustrated troll stories from Norway and an Ojibwe story from native people that live near my town.

"Finally, at age 50, in 1997, I finished college. During these later life studies I learned more about my interests in dance, puppetry, and performance. Now I help produce community pageants for celebrating the summer and winter solstices, and even weddings and funerals. I crave the artistic expression of the community, feelings about the mysteries of the natural world and the human world. Leo Tolstoy said that 'The aim of an artist is to make people love life,' and I agree."

☼ ☼ ☼

Best known in the children's book world for her lovely colored woodcuts, artist and writer Betsy Bowen was born in Chicago and raised in Hinsdale, Illinois. Her parents were Betty Lovejoy Olsen and Ernest H. Olsen. After what she calls "an eclectic series of educational experiences," she received a B.A. in creative expression at Vermont College in 1997. Bowen has spent much of her adult life on an old homestead at the edge of the wilderness near Lake Superior's north shore, where she raised her three sons, Eric, Jeremy, and Philip. All of her sons, now grown, are involved in some way with her studio and/or with outdoor life. Eric is the studio's Web master. Jeremy is a printmaker and sailboat racer. Philip helps with the prints, does fine woodworking, and has trained for competitive cross-country skiing.

Courtesy of Houghton Mifflin, Inc.

Bowen's first picture book, *Antler, Bear, Canoe: A Northwoods Alphabet Year*, came out in 1991 and is a fine companion to the later *Gathering: A Northwoods Counting Book*, both of them portraying nature and seasonal activities in the outdoors through loving prose and glowing woodcuts.

Shingebiss: An Ojibwe Legend retold by Nancy Van Laan and illustrated by Bowen was named a Notable Children's Trade Book in the Field of Social Studies in 1998. *The Troll with No Heart in His Body,* by Lise Lunge-Larson, has also won special attention for its graceful combination of folklore and woodcuts. It was a Notable Trade Book in the Field of Social Studies, an ALA Notable Children's Book, and a *Horn Book* Fanfare title.

SELECTED WORKS WRITTEN AND ILLUSTRATED: *Antler, Bear, Canoe: A Northwoods Alphabet Year*, 1991, reissued 2002; *Gathering: A Northwoods Counting Book*, 1995, 1999; *Tracks in the Wild*, 1999.

SELECTED WORKS ILLUSTRATED: *Heart Talks with Mother God*, by Bridget Mary Meehan, 1995; *Shingebiss: An Ojibwe Legend*, by Nancy Van Laan, 1997; *The Troll with No Heart in His Body*, by Lise Lunge-Larsen, 1999; *Borealis*, by Jeff Humphries, 2002.

SUGGESTED READING: *Duluth News Tribune*, September 18, 1998.

WEB SITE: *www.woodcut.com*

Courtesy of HarperCollins Publishers

Jeff Brown

1926–December 3, 2003

Jeff Brown was born in New York City. His name was not originally Jeff, but Richard Chester Brown. As a child he was so interested in acting that his parents sent him to the Professional Children's School and moved to Hollywood so that he could become a child actor. But when he joined Actors' Equity they already had a Richard Brown as a member, so the guild gave him the name Jeff, and he kept it. His brother's name, Robert, did not get changed.

Brown's voice was used in a radio drama, and he also appeared onstage. When he grew up, he stayed in the entertainment business, working as an assistant film producer for Samuel Goldwyn Jr. and as a story consultant with Pennebaker Productions and Marlon Brando at Paramount Pictures. But he found that he preferred the literary world and turned to work on the editorial staffs of the *New Yorker* and the *Saturday Evening Post*. He then began to sell fiction to national magazines, those where he worked as an editor and also *Life*, *Esquire*, *Saturday Review*, and *Holiday*. Eventually he took a job as a senior editor at Warner Books, where he stayed until 1980. He did not write for children until his own sons, Anthony (known as Tony) and Jeffrey (known as J.C.) were young. One night they were stalling their bedtime and J.C. claimed that he was afraid that the large bulletin board above his bed would fall on him during the night and squash him flat. This led to a discussion of what life would be like for a person who was flat, and Stanley Lambchop was born. For a long time he was known and loved only as the subject of amusing stories told to Jeff Brown's sons. Many months later, a friend who was in the children's book business heard Jeff telling one of the stories to J.C. and Tony and suggested that he write them down and publish them. *Flat Stanley* was welcomed by readers and critics alike. He is a generous, friendly fellow, always willing to help out in whatever way he can. In the last book about him,

Stanley, Flat Again!, he becomes a sail so that a friend can win a boating race, and he rescues a nasty little girl who has been trapped underneath a collapsed building. Stanley does not always remain flat, and along with his brother Arthur and his parents, he has many adventures.

By 1983, over 1 million copies of the Flat Stanley books had been sold, and children all over the world now know and enjoy the stories. They send "Flat Stanleys" on journeys to one another in envelopes, just as the original character went by mail to visit his friends in the first book, *Flat Stanley*, published by Harper & Row Junior Books in 1964. An enterprising teacher in Canada, Dale Hubert, devised the Flat Stanley Project, to encourage children around the world to interact with each other through Flat Stanley interchanges. Teachers can log on to *www.flatstanleyproject.com* to partic-ipate in sending "Stanleys" around the world; many also create their own Flat Stanley pen pal projects and track his trav-els in their classrooms. Stanley is known in France as "Clement Aplati"; in other translations he has traveled through Spain, Italy, Japan, Israel, Germany, and various other countries; he has also been published in braille. He has visited Mount Everest and the Taj Mahal, appeared on network television shows, and even orbited Earth with the *Discovery* astronauts.

Courtesy of HarperCollins Children's Books

Jeff Brown never tired of sharing his love of writing with children in schools. He trav-eled himself, not by envelope, but by more conventional means, to Texas, Florida, Oklahoma, Tennessee, New Hampshire, and other states, talking about his books and encouraging children to write stories themselves. He was first married to Alisa Littel Storrow, the mother of Tony and J.C. At the time of his death, he had been mar-ried for 15 years to his second wife, Elisa-beth Tobin, with whom he had another son, Duncan. Jeff Brown died unexpectedly of a heart attack in December of 2003. He had homes on the Upper East Side of New York City and in Connecticut. Playful and imaginative, creative and inventive, Jeff Brown will always be re-membered as the creator of the international flat boy with a well-rounded heart.

SELECTED WORKS: *Flat Stanley*, illus. by Tomi Ungerer, 1964 (reissued with illus. by Scott Nash, 2003); *A Lamp for the Lambchops*, illus. by Lynn Wheeling, 1983 (reissued as *Stanley and the Magic Lamp* with illus. by Scott Nash, 2003); *Stanley in Space*, 1990 (reissued with illus. by Scott Nash,

2003); *Invisible Stanley*, illus. by Steve Bjorkman, 1996; *Stanley's Christmas Adventure*, illus. by Scott Nash, 2003; *Stanley, Flat Again!*, illus. by Scott Nash, 2003.

SUGGESTED READING: *New York Times*, December 6, 2003 (obituary). Online—*www.flatstanleyproject.net*

Courtesy of Marcia Brown

Marcia Brown

July 13, 1918–

"**F**rom my earliest memory, which is of myself running early one morning to get a picture book and asking my mother to read it to me, books and pictures have been very important in my life.

"I was born in Rochester, New York, where my parents had both grown up, on the 13th of July, just in time to celebrate Bastille Day. My father was a minister, and we lived in a succession of small towns in New York State with the freedom to roam freely—first the woods behind our house in Clifton Springs, then the woods and fields around Otsego Lake near Cooperstown, and then the shores of the Husdon River near Catskill. Water was always important to me, whether vast Lake Ontario, Otsego Lake, or the beautiful and busy Hudson, where I learned to swim and loved to watch the constant river traffic—sidewheeler day boats that threw up huge swells, night boats like silver fish, tugs and heavy barges so sluggish they would be in sight all day long, tankers, freighters from all over the world, and our own boats, of course, for my sister and I made many of our toys. Now the sea—whether the Atlantic off Cape Cod or the Caribbean, the Mediterranean, or the Pacific where I live today—has the same fascination for me.

"Reading was the main entertainment of our family, the public library being a second home. Fairy tales—Andersen, Perrault, Grimm, and *The Arabian Nights*—were favorites and still are. Of course we drew—when we were very small on the 'empty pages' of old magazines and then on large pads of drawing paper that appeared on Christmas and special days. My father painted one of our kitchen walls for me to use as a blackboard, where I drew by the hour. My favorite subjects were our cat Midnight and comfortable red barns with benign fairies hovering overhead like angels. When I was about twelve, I decided I would like to make pictures in books someday.

"After graduating from Kingston High School, I went to New York State College in Albany. In the summers I learned to paint under Judson Smith in Woodstock. After college, I taught English for three years in Cornwall (New York) High School but decided I really wanted to paint and make books for young children. So I came to New York to live on the same Sullivan Street that is in *The Little Carousel*, to study painting under Yasuo Kuniyoshi and Stuart Davis at the New School, and to work in the New York Public Library. While working in the library for five years, I told stories from all over the world to children who came from almost all over the world—Polish, Italian, West Indian, Czechoslovakian, Finnish, Chinese. I worked in the Tompkins Square Branch, on the Bookmobile, and in the Central Children's Room behind the lions on Fifth Avenue. The large collection with books in 46 languages was a refuge during World War II to many displaced children, who often had astounding personal stories of courage and escape. Telling stories at the special story hours on Saturday afternoons or traveling around with a satchel of sure-fire picture books like *Andy and the Lion*, *Millions of Cats*, and *Horton Hatches the Egg* on the Library Bookmobile, stopping where the audience would often be in a tree overhead, was both fun and invaluable exposure to the rhythmic prose of good picture books.

"I was able to meet many of the distinguished illustrators of the books I loved and handle their rough drafts and final originals. It was a truly unique opportunity to learn what had gone into those books and to feel both joy and humility. A big reference library is a veritable feast for the eyes and the mind, and I took full advantage of what it offered—from the beautiful picture books of the Russian tales that Bilibin made for the children of the last tsar to the innovative lithographic books of Felix Rojankovsky and Nathalie Parain to the tiny chapbooks from pedlars' trays in early 19th century England. With these rich resources, I was able to immerse myself in the research for *Dick Whittington and His Cat*, *Cinderella*, and *Puss in Boots*.

"Travel helped me create the settings for most of my books. Having grown up in the homogenous atmosphere of small towns in New York State, I was drawn to the exotic. New York City itself was exotic to me. In those years during and right after the war, New York was a wonderfully stimulating place. Concerts, art exhibitions, dance performances were affordable on modest salaries. Summer vacations in Provincetown, Cape Cod, produced *Skipper John's Cook*, and after a trip to the Virgin Islands, *Henry-Fisherman* gave me a way to capture the color of the islands, the brilliant fish, and the vibrant people. A poem I recited in the fourth grade about Venice initiated a yearning that was finally satisfied many years later—I was able to spend almost four years in Venice between 1956 and 1962, traveling to see ballet performances in England, France, Italy, and Vienna. My story *Felice*, set in Venice, was published during that time. In 1962 I was invited to be a guest of the Second Hawaiian Book Fair in Honolulu and to remain for a month that expanded into three years. In the midst of that astonishing beauty I illustrated *Back-*

"Each of my books has come out of a deep personal interest in the subject and a desire to share it with children or anyone who will look with intensity."

bone of the King, told in Anglo-Saxon simplicity from the literally translated notes of Dorothy Kahananui, who taught Hawaiian at the University of Hawaii. Moses Nakuina had written down the legend from oral history, not too many years after orthography into Roman letters was first introduced into the islands. Having the freedom to stay in a place long enough to absorb the atmosphere was again invaluable.

"In 1979 I had a chance given to me by a dear friend and editor, Janet Loranger, to go to China. Ever greedy, I took too much camera equipment. By that time I was deeply interested in Oriental painting. The trip whetted a desire for more. I went again with a group from the University of Minnesota at Duluth to travel and study for two months in Hanghou, at the Zhejiang Academy of Fine Arts. I met some of the teachers in 1986 in Duluth, was able to arrange workshops for them in different parts of the country, and was incredibly fortunate in being invited to return for private study in 1987. Janet and I were later able to hold workshops in my good-sized studio in California with visiting Chinese professors of landscape painting and calligraphy.

"Each of my books has come out of a deep personal interest in the subject and a desire to share it with children or anyone who will look with intensity. Artists and illustrators are lucky. They can work anyplace that interests them. Our whole life is the source of our material. Art is communication—sharing feelings, humor, and imaginative visions with others."

"Art is communication— sharing feelings, humor, and imaginative visions with others."

❄ ❄ ❄

Raised in a minister's family as one of three daughters during the Depression years, Marcia Brown graduated from the New York State College for Teachers in 1940, expecting to pursue a practical career goal in teaching school. She worked on the art staff for college publications and majored in English and theater, subjects that she taught during her brief career at Cornwall High School. But art had become her first love, and in 1943, at the age of 25, she moved to New York City. Working as a children's librarian at the New York Public Library for the next five years, she pursued her art education and published her first books, which were received with great acclaim. Her second book, *Stone Soup*, which has become a modern classic, was a runner-up for the Caldecott Medal in 1948, a designation now referred to as an Honor Book. From 1950 to 1954, every book she published received a Caldecott Honor Book award—*Henry-Fisherman, Dick Whittington and His Cat, Skipper John's Cook, Puss in Boots*, and *The Steadfast Tin Soldier*—and in 1955 she won the Caldecott Medal for *Cinderella, or The Little Glass Slipper*.

She went on to win the award two more times—for *Once a Mouse* in 1962 and for *Shadow* in 1983. To date she is the only illustrator to have the distinction of winning three Caldecott Medals. What is most remarkable is that all three of her winning titles were created in totally different styles and techniques. Her hallmark is the originality she brings to her art: wispy watercolors for *Cinderella*; rustic, hewn woodcuts for *Once a Mouse*; and silky silhouettes and dramatic collage for *Shadow*.

Marcia Brown has brought to each of her stories her own special vision and vitality. She has said, "I think of the illustrator as the performer of the spirit of the book. The illustrator must feel the rhythm of the story to interpret and intensify its meaning. The vigor, the delicacy, the mood, the setting, and especially the atmosphere, all determine the look. Freshness lies in the intensity of expression, not the novelty of technique." The many techniques and styles she has employed astound the reader; from woodcut to watercolor, from collage to photography, it seems she has explored every medium available to the artist, and all with great distinction.

Travel has been an influence and stimulus in Brown's life and books, reflected in her love for folklore and fairy tales. "Fairy

Courtesy of Atheneum Books for Young Readers

tales are the abiding dreams and realities of the human soul," she has said. Her re-creations of the tales are enhanced by the storytelling expertise she gained from working as a children's librarian. Her belief in the power of story for building personality and achieving self-definition is exemplified in this statement: "A child needs the stimulus of books that are focused on individuality in personality and character if he or she is to find his or her own. A child is an individual, a book is an individual. Each should be served according to its needs." A love of music—opera, chamber music, and playing the flute—also permeates her books and the rhythm of her storytelling. Her collaborations with Violette Verdy of the New York City Ballet resulted in books that express the language of dance in text and illustrations.

Marcia Brown's work has been honored with many significant awards. She received the University of Southern Mississippi Medallion in 1972, the Regina Medal in 1977, and in 1992 the Laura Ingalls Wilder Award, all for her body of work. Twice she has been nominated for the Hans Christian Andersen Award. She received the Distinguished Alumni Award in 1969 and an honorary doctorate of letters in 1996, both from the State University of New York in Albany (which had grown out of her alma mater, New York State College for Teachers). After living and working for many years in a studio in West Redding, Connecticut, Marcia Brown moved to Southern California in 1993. When she moved, she donated a significant collection of her papers and original art to the State University of New York in Albany, where it is now housed in the M. E. Grenander Department of Special Collections and Archives. Another important collection of her work resides in the deGrummond Collection at the University of Southern Mississippi.

With amazing versatility, Marcia Brown has created children's books of visual beauty and perceptive insight. Crafted with care and precision, her books inspire joy and wonderment in her readers.

SELECTED WORKS WRITTEN AND ILLUSTRATED: *The Little Carousel*, 1946; *Stone Soup*, 1947; *Henry-Fisherman: A Story of the Virgin Islands*, 1949; *Dick Whittington and His Cat*, 1950; *Skipper John's Cook*, 1951; *The Flying Carpet*, 1956; *Felice*, 1958; *Tamarindo!*, 1960; *Neighbors*, 1967; *How, Hippo!*, 1969; *The Bun: A Tale from Russia*, 1972; *All Butterflies: An ABC*, 1974; *The Blue Jackal*, 1977; *Listen to a Shape*, 1979; *Touch Will Tell*, 1979; *Walk with Your Eyes*, 1979.

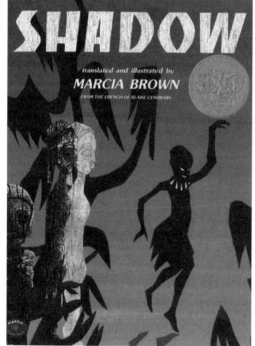

Courtesy of Atheneum Books for Young Readers

SELECTED WORKS ILLUSTRATED: *Puss in Boots*, by Charles Perrault, 1952; *The Steadfast Tin Soldier*, by Hans Christian Andersen, trans. by M. R. James, 1953; *Cinderella, or The Little Glass Slipper*, by Charles Perrault, 1955; *The Three Billy Goats Gruff*, by P. C. Asbjørnsen and J. E. Moe, 1957; *The Wild Swans*, by Hans Christian Andersen, trans. by M. R. James, 1963; *Giselle, or The Wilis*, adapt. from Théophile Gautier by Violette Verdy, 1970; *The Snow Queen*, by Hans Christian Andersen, trans. by R. P. Keigwin, 1972; *Shadow*, by Blaise Cendrars, 1982; *Of Swans, Sugarplums, and Satin Slippers: Ballet Stories for Children*, by Violette Verdy, 1991; *How the Ostrich Got Its Long Neck: A Tale from the Akamba of Kenya*, retold by Verna Aardema, 1995.

SUGGESTED READING: Brown, Marcia, *Lotus Seeds: Children, Pictures, and Books*, 1986; Cullinan, Bernice, and Diane Person, eds. *The Continuum Encyclopedia of Children's Literature*, 2001; Silvey, Anita, ed. *Children's Books and Their Creators*, 1995; *Something About the Author*, vol. 47, 1987. Periodicals—Brown, Marcia, "Caldecott Acceptance Speeches," *The Horn Book*, August 1955, August 1962, August 1983. Online—*www.albany.edu/feature/marcia_brown*.

An earlier profile of Marcia Brown appeared in *More Junior Authors* (1963).

"As a child, I was extremely dreamy and shy. I used to wander around muttering to myself and playing games with imaginary friends. My parents had to shout, 'He's in the land!' to explain to people why I apparently couldn't hear what they were saying to me. I did very badly at school; I was daydreaming too much to concentrate on anything, and it wasn't until I was pretty nearly grown up that I started to think that the world around me might be at least as interesting as what was going on in my own head.

"As a result I did poorly at school, although occasionally teachers would think I had a lot of promise. In those days we had an exam called the 'eleven plus,' which you did just before you went to High School. If you were a kid with a brain, you passed and went to Grammar School to learn brainy things, but if you were a kid with no brain, you failed and went to Secondary Modern School and learnt how to do things with your hands. I was a kid with hands.

"I hated that school. I remember my English teacher there bawling me out for doing a story in a way she hadn't told us to—I'd done it as a diary. She was furious! She called me out in front of the whole class and made a fool of me. I got nowhere with her. But my parents moved again, to Reading in Berkshire. This new school was going comprehensive, for children of all abilities. I got on much better there, due to one or two very good teachers who helped me along. I remember in particular Mrs. Stafford, who was so enthusiastic about my stories. She set me on the road to writing, I think. But I was still a poor worker, and came away with two very bad A levels. Mine was only the second year to do A levels, I'm sure. If they hadn't been just gagging to let anyone do them, no one would have let me near the exams at all.

"Life got rapidly better for me after I left school, but for the first few months I hadn't got a clue what to do. My dad eventually filled in an application form for a job as a journalist with the local newspaper. Somehow I got the job and went off to do a six months' training course.

"The course was great—it was my only real time as a student—but by the end of it I had decided that I really wanted to write and that no other career would do. I packed in the job as soon as I got back home, much to the editor's disgust. 'I think the saddest thing, Melvin, is that you have deprived someone else of a career opportunity,' he intoned.

"Then I got on with writing my first book, which, of course, no one wanted to publish.

© Michael Dyer Associates, Ltd.

Melvin Burgess
April 25, 1954–

"For the next 15 years, I wrote on and off, had casual jobs here and there, spent a lot of time out of work with not much to do, and I enjoyed myself enormously. I moved to Bristol after a couple of years, where I lived until I was 30. Inner-city Bristol was a great place to live, with a big racial and cultural mix. I learned a lot there and got my feeling for life. My book *Smack* is based on Bristol in those years, and although it is not autobiographical, you can pick up a lot of the atmosphere and meet a few of the people in its pages.

"I was living in London aged about 35 when I began to think it was time for me to really try hard to see if I could make writing work for me. I'd written a great deal off and on for years, a lot of it experimental, but I'd never really put getting published over writing what I felt like writing. So I had a go. I did short stories, radio drama, and children's fiction. I had some success in all three, but the children's book, *The Cry of the Wolf*, was shortlisted for the Carnegie Medal. So that's what I've been doing ever since.

"I now live in Manchester, with my wife, Judith, my son, Oliver, and my stepson, Sam. I have a daughter, Pearl, who lives with her mother in Odessa, Ukraine."

A writer well known for his frank, realistic novels—realistic even when involving fantasy elements—Melvin Burgess was born in Twickenham, Surrey, the son of educational writer Christopher Burgess and his wife, Helen. Though Burgess found school uninteresting, he was an imaginative child who grew up to become an author willing to look a great many difficult subjects in the eye and write creatively about them. His first novel, *The Cry of the Wolf*, was a Carnegie Medal runner-up in 1991 and relates the stark tragedy of the extermination of a pack of wolves by a human interested only in being famous. An endangered animal takes center stage in a later novel as well. *Tiger, Tiger* is about a rare Siberian tiger named Lila who escapes and meets a group of children who meld with her to become something mythic and feared.

From man's cruelty to animals, Burgess moved to man's inhumanity to children who are different in *Burning Issy*, which deals with witch-burning, and *An Angel for May*, a time-slip fantasy which was also a runner-up for the Carnegie Medal. His futuristic novel, *The Baby and Fly Pie* deals with homeless children on the streets of London and the hard choices they must make in order to survive.

MELVIN BURGESS

THE COPPER TREASURE

ILLUSTRATIONS BY RICHARD WILLIAMS
Courtesy of Henry Holt & Co.

Burgess's Carnegie Medal winner, *Junk*, narrates the descent of two teens who leave harsh home conditions for the even more desperate life of runaways as they move into a world of stealing, prostitution, and drugs. Winner of the Guardian Fiction Award as well, *Junk* was re-titled *Smack* when published in the United States and was a 1998 *School Library Journal* Best Book. This uncompromising look at the deadly effects of drug addiction earned Burgess a firm place in the world of contemporary young adult literature.

SELECTED WORKS (Dates are for British editions; American publishing dates are in parentheses): *The Cry of the Wolf*, 1990 (1992); *Burning Issy*, 1992 (1994); *An Angel for May*, 1992 (1995); *The Baby and Fly Pie*, 1993 (1996); *Loving April*, 1995; *Earth Giant*, 1995 (1997); *Junk*, 1996 (*Smack*, 1998); *Tiger, Tiger*, 1996; *Kite*, 1997 (2000); *The Copper Treasure*, 1998 (2000); *The Ghost Behind the Wall*, 2001 (2003); *Doing It*, 2003 (2004).

SUGGESTED READING: *Authors and Artists for Young Adults*, vol. 28, 2002; *Beacham's Guide to Literature for Young Adults*, vol. 12, 2001; *Contemporary Authors*, vol. 161, 2001; *Something About the Author*, vol. 146, 2004.

WEB SITE: *web.onetel.com/~melvinburgess/*

Betsy Byars
August 7, 1928–

"When I was a little girl, my father used to take me to the airport on Saturdays to eat popcorn and watch the planes take off and land. I began to develop a lifelong love of airplanes, and I also developed a lifelong love of popcorn.

"But my earliest love was books. My sister taught me to read at a very early age. I took books seriously and read every word, even a childhood dictionary I got for my seventh birthday.

"I didn't want to be a writer back then. I thought writers sat all day by themselves and typed, and that would be boring. I wanted action.

"In 1950 I married Ed Byars, a professor and pilot. We had courted in his 1931 Stintson airplane. It was five years later, when I was the mother of two, that I began to write. I started small, writing short pieces for magazines, but by the time we had four children, Laurie, Betsy Ann, Nan, and Guy—I was writing for them. Our family now includes nine wonderful grandkids.

"Ed and I now live on an airstrip in South Carolina. The bottom floor of our house is a hangar so we can just taxi out and take off when we want to. I got my pilot license as well and always enjoy our trips.

"So there was a sort of destiny in those long-ago lifelong loves of airplanes and books. And—I have to admit it—popcorn."

✿   ✿   ✿

Betsy Byars is best known for her realistic contemporary novels, though she has also written picture books, easy readers, fantasies, and historical fiction. Her writing sparkles with humor, warmth, emotional truth, and an unerring ear for dialogue. In a career that spans over 40 years and includes more than 50 books, she has delighted critics and young readers alike with her engaging characters and offbeat families. Whether those characters face unusually hard challenges or just the vagaries of everyday life, they live up to their author's faith in a child's resilience and ability to grow.

The younger daughter of a civil engineer, George Guy Cromer, and his wife, Nan, Betsy Cromer Byars was born and, except for a few years in a nearby town, raised in Charlotte, North Carolina. An intrepid child, curious and deeply interested in animals—one of her early ambitions was to work in a zoo when she grew up—Byars loved life outdoors with friends and was usually willing to try out a new experience like riding on a homemade skateboard or touching a mummy at the museum. School held less interest in those days, though she made sure she didn't fall too far below her family's expectations of acceptable grades.

Courtesy of PenguinPutnam Books for Young Readers

Betsy Byars

Byars attended Furman University for two years, majoring in mathematics like her sister before her, and then switched to the English Department at Queens College, North Carolina, where she earned her B.A. in 1950. While at Queens, she met her future husband, Edward Ford Byars, who was then teaching engineering at nearby Clemson University. They were married a few weeks after she graduated.

Though a lover of books since childhood, Betsy never considered writing until she went to Urbana, Illinois, where her husband attended graduate school. She was home alone with two children and another one soon to come. Living in student barracks where most of her neighbors worked or attended school, she says in her memoir, *The Moon and I*, "I really had two choices—write or lose my mind. I wrote." Starting with the magazine market, she wrote humorous articles for the *Saturday Evening Post* and *Look*, among other popular periodicals. As her family grew, she decided to write for children. Her first published work, a picture book called *Clementine*, came out in 1962 and was followed by *The Dancing Camel* in 1965. Early reviews of her work were disappointing, and Byars moved in and out of using personal material, trying to find what would please both editors and herself. It was in 1968 with *The Midnight Fox* that Betsy Byars demonstrated the highly individual writer she was becoming. Her sensitive portrayal of a shy city boy's fascination with a mother fox and her cub won critical notice, especially of her ability to speak so convincingly in the voice of a young boy.

That same year, she joined a volunteer program to work with children who had learning difficulties. That experience, plus three case studies found in a medical library and an article on how swans might leave a good pond for one that seems less supportive, became the basis of *The Summer of the Swans*. The story about 14-year-old Sara, who is caught up in the agonies of being a teenager, and her younger brother, Charlie, who is mentally impaired, treats the thoughts and emotions of both with sympathetic honesty and a complete lack of sentimentality. Discouraged by early responses to this novel, Byars had decided children's books were not her forte after all and had entered a master's program in special education at West Virginia University when she received a call to say that *The Summer of the Swans* had been awarded the Newbery Medal. That convinced Byars that she was indeed a children's book author. She began writing with greater confidence—and got a larger mailbox to contain her burgeoning fan mail.

Several more strong realistic novels followed, stories that involved children abused or abandoned by their parents. *The Pinballs* brings together a girl and two boys placed in a foster family who grow to the point of hoping they can have some influence over their own lives. What could have been a bitter, dark story of trauma and abuse becomes a frank, often humorous exploration of their new ability to make choices and value each other and themselves. Though not fostered out, the three siblings in *The Night Swimmers*, winner of a National Book Award, struggle to survive neglect by a selfish father, who thinks only of being a country-and-western music star until a near tragedy brings him to his senses. In *Cracker Jackson* we see an 11-year-old boy in a supportive family who discovers that a beloved former babysitter and her infant child are being threatened by her abusive husband. Here again, Byars addresses harsh truths—this time about battered women—with a deft hand, allowing the action to unfold through the feelings of her young protagonist. In one of the funniest scenes in all of Byars's books, we see underage Cracker and his friend trying to drive the woman to a shelter, demonstrating Byars's talent for mixing tragedy with comic relief to great effect.

From a boy facing a bully (*The 18th Emergency*), to a fourth-grader's first romance (*The Cybil War*), to the series of books about the life, loves, and humorous experiences of middle-schooler Bingo Brown, Byars has created lighter fare that still rings with eternal truth. Her Blossom Family series with its quirky family members and friends brims with laughter and yet manages to show how people living on the edge of society deserve as much respect and understanding as those whose lives

"I didn't want to be a writer back then. I thought writers sat all day by themselves and typed, and that would be boring. I wanted action."

The Not-Just-
Anybody Family

Betsy Byars

Illustrated by Jacqueline Rogers

Courtesy of Delacorte Press

seem more standard and normal. Byars's foray into mystery has produced the delightful character Herculeah Jones, daughter of a police chief and a private investigator, who first appeared in *The Dark Stairs*. *Keeper of the Doves* takes the reader back in time to view the lives of five sisters at the turn of the 20th century.

As delightful as her fiction, Byars's memoir is humorous and fast-paced. *The Moon and I*, filled with vignettes from her childhood, aspects of her writing life, and her persistent fascination with a blacksnake named Moon, shows readers how events in her own life have permeated her stories. Here, too, she describes her long struggle to write about her love of flying. "The problem," she says, "is that the only plot I could think of was something going wrong with the engine, the plane crashing, and the people having to survive. And I did not want to add to people's fear of flying. I wanted to make them love flying." She decided instead to write about a crotchety grandfather and his granddaughter flying across the country together. Byars and her husband flew from North Carolina to the West Coast to get a feel for such a trip. The result, after many drafts, is the novel *Coast to Coast*.

Betsy Byars has received the Regina Medal from the Catholic Library Association for the body of her work. A number of her books have been cited as ALA Notable Children's Books, and many have been adapted for TV, radio, and audiobooks. Her work has been translated into nine languages. Publishing seems to run in the Byars family. Her son, Guy, illustrated her humorous story *The Computer Nut*, which was published in 1984. Two of her recent titles have been co-authored with her two oldest daughters, Laurie Myers and Betsy Duffey. Betsy Duffey has become a well-known author in her own right and was profiled in the *Eighth Book of Junior Authors and Illustrators*.

SELECTED WORKS WRITTEN AND ILLUSTRATED: *The Groober*, 1967; *The Lace Snail*, 1975.

SELECTED WORKS: *Clementine*, illus. by Charles Wilton, 1962; *The Dancing Camel*, illus. by Harold Berson, 1965; *Rama, the Gypsy Cat*, illus. by Peggy Bacon, 1966; *The Midnight Fox*, illus. by Ann Grifalconi, 1968; *Trouble River*, illus. by Rocco Negri, 1969; *The Summer of the Swans*, illus. by Ted CoConis, 1970; *Go and Hush the Baby*, illus. by Emily A. McCully, 1971; *The House of Wings*, illus. by David Schwartz, 1972; *The 18th Emergency*, illus. by Robert Grossman, 1973;

The Winged Colt of Casa Mia, illus. by Richard Cuffari, 1973; *After the Goat Man*, illus. by Ronald Himler, 1974; *The TV Kid*, illus. by Richard Cuffari, 1976; *The Pinballs*, 1977; *The Cartoonist*, illus. by Richard Cuffari, 1978; *Goodbye, Chicken Little*, 1979; *The Night Swimmers*, illus. by Troy Howell, 1980; *The Cybil War*, illus. by Gail Owens, 1981; *The Animal, the Vegetable, and John D. Jones*, illus. by Ruth Sanderson, 1982; *The Two-Thousand-Pound Goldfish*, 1982; *The Glory Girl*, 1983; *The Computer Nut*, illus. by Guy Byars, 1984; *Cracker Jackson*, 1985; *The Not-Just-Anybody Family*, illus. by Jacqueline Rogers, 1986; *The Golly Sisters Go West*, illus. by Sue Truesdell, 1986; *The Blossoms Meet the Vulture Lady*, illus. by Jacqueline Rogers, 1987; *The Blossoms and the Green Phantom*, illus. by Jacqueline Rogers, 1987; *A Blossom Promise*, illus. by Jacqueline Rogers, 1987; *Beans on the Roof*, illus. by Melodye Rosales, 1988; *The Burning Questions of Bingo Brown*, illus. by Cathy Bobak, 1988; *Bingo Brown and the Language of Love*, illus. by Cathy Bobak, 1988; *Hooray for the Golly Sisters*, illus. by Sue Truesdell, 1990; *Bingo Brown, Gypsy Lover*, 1990; *The Moon and I*, 1991; *The Seven Treasure Hunts*, 1991; *Wanted . . . Mud Blossom*, illus. by Jacqueline Rogers, 1991; *Bingo Brown's Guide to Romance*, 1992; *Coast to Coast*, 1992; *McMummy*, 1993; *The Golly Sisters Ride Again*, illus. by Sue Truesdell, 1994; *The Dark Stairs: A Herculeah Jones Mystery*, 1994; *Growing Up Stories* (compiler), 1995; *Tarot Says Beware*, 1995; *My Brother, Ant*, illus. by Marc Simont, 1996; *The Joy Boys*, illus. by Frank Remkiewicz, 1996; *Tornado*, illus. by Doron BenAmi, 1996; *Dead Letter*, 1996; *Ant Plays Bear*, illus. by Marc Simont, 1997; *Death's Door*, 1997; *Disappearing Acts*, 1998; *My Dog, My Hero*, with Betsy Duffey and Laurie Myers, illus. by Loren Long, 2000; *Little Horse*, illus. by David McPhail, 2001; *Keeper of the Doves*, 2002; *Little Horse on His Own*, illus. by David McPhail, 2004; *The SOS File*, with Betsy Duffey and Laurie Myers, illus. by Arthur Howard, 2004.

Courtesy of Henry Holt & Co.

SUGGESTED READING: *American Writers for Children since 1960: Fiction*, 1986; *Authors and Artists for Young Adults*, vol. 19, 1996; Cammarano, Rita. *Betsy Byars*, 2002; *Children's Literature Review*, vol. 1, 1976; *Contemporary Authors*, vol. 183, 2000; *Dictionary of Literary Biography*, vol. 52, 1986;

Moran, Karen A. *A Visit with Betsy Byars*, 2001; Nakamura, Joyce. *Writers for Young Adults*, 1989; Pendergast, Tom and Sara, eds. *St. James Guide to Young Adult Writers*, 1998; Rees, David. "Little Bit of Ivory: Betsy Byars," in *Painted Desert, Green Shade: Essays on Contemporary Writers of Fiction for Children and Young Adults*, 1984; Silvey, Anita, ed. *Children's Books and Their Creators*, 1995; *Something About the Author*, vol. 108, 2000; *Something About the Author Autobiography Series*, vol. 1, 1986; Usry, Malcolm. *Betsy Byars*, 1995. Periodicals—Byars, Betsy, "Spinning Straw into Gold," *School Librarian*, March 1986; Cooper, Ilene, "The *Booklist* Interview: Betsy Byars," *Booklist*, January 15, 1993; Hansen, I. V., "Decade of Betsy Byars Boys," *Children's Literature in Education*, Spring 1984.

WEB SITE:*www.BetsyByars.com*

An earlier profile of Betsy Byars appeared in *Third Book of Junior Authors and Illustrators* (1972).

Courtesy of Ann Harwood

Meg Cabot

February 1, 1967–

"I was born in Bloomington, Indiana, on February 1, two years after Princess Stephanie of Monaco, who was also born on February 1. If you've ever visited southern Indiana, you'll understand why the majority of my childhood was spent in pursuit of air conditioning (for a long time, we didn't have AC in our circa 1920 house—cold in winter, hot in the summer). A primary—and free—source of AC proved to be the Monroe County Public Library, where I spent many hours, reading the complete works of Jane Austen, Judy Blume, and Barbara Cartland, among others.

"When the library was closed, I read in a rusty wheelbarrow in the front yard. Once a film company came to town to make the movie, and everyone was invited to come down to the stadium to see the bike race at the end (and earn a dollar for their efforts). I declined, preferring my wheelbarrow to a potential film career, because it was too hot.

"It occurred to me that the books I was always reading had been written by people who'd been paid money to write them. When I questioned my mother about the possibility of my being paid to write a book, she told me it was really hard to get published. So I quickly abandoned that plan and vowed to become a comic book illustrator, which seemed more doable.

"A lot of people ask me what I was like in high school. Was I, for instance, like any of the characters I write about? Well, I wasn't a princess, I didn't talk to ghosts, and I never got ESP or saved the president's life. I did, however, collect *Star Wars* comic books, babysit a lot, star in a few school plays and musicals, flunk freshman algebra twice, and sing in the school choir. In other words, I was a huge freak. Thank God for graduation, which couldn't seem to come soon enough.

"Four years at Indiana University and a fine arts degree later, I moved to New York City, intent upon pursuing a career in freelance illustration. But it turned out getting a job illustrating comic books was as hard as getting a book published . . . at least so far as I could tell. I decided I needed to go back to school to learn a skill a little more lucrative than drawing T-stroke jaw bones in superheroes, and got a job at New York University as the assistant manager of an undergraduate dormitory expressly because of the free tuition employee benefits.

"Shortly after this, my dad died suddenly. And it occurred to me that we don't have a lot of time on this planet, so we better make the most of what time we've got. I decided to send one of the many novels I'd written for fun to a publisher to see what would happen. What happened was that I got rejected. That rejection made me so angry that for a year I sent query letters to every agent in Manhattan until I finally got one to agree to represent me. She is still my agent today, and two years after she agreed to represent me, my first historical romance novel, *Where Roses Grow Wild* (written under the name Patricia Cabot), was published.

"It was while I was busy writing historical romances that a friend asked me why I didn't try writing a book for teen readers, since I worked with teens, watched so many teen TV shows, and had an unhealthy obsession with pop rock. I wasn't interested in writing for teens at first, but then one day, when I found out my mom was starting to date one of my teachers, I began writing the book that would become *The Princess Diaries*.

"Five years later, I'm working on many series of books for young adult readers, including The Princess Diaries, The Mediator, All-American Girl, and 1-800-Where-R-You. I now write full time and live in New York City with my husband and a one-eyed cat. I have loads of air conditioning."

"A lot of people ask me what I was like in high school. Was I, for instance, like any of the characters I write about?"

❄ ❄ ❄

Meggin Patricia Cabot's own story is as much of a fairy tale as her enormously popular Princess Diaries books. In 2000, before the first book, *The Princess Diaries*, was even published, the film version was already in production. Starring Julie Andrews as the regal grandmother to Anne Hathaway's reluctant princess, Mia, the movie rocketed Cabot to fame as the story's original author and created even more readers for the book, already enjoying word-of-mouth popularity on its own. Written with a finely

a novel

The
Princess Diaries

MEG CABOT

Courtesy of HarperCollins Children's Books

tuned ear for contemporary teen talk and a keen sense of popular teen culture, *The Princess Diaries* took on a life of its own. Sequels followed, and a second movie, based on an original story written by the Disney Studios, appeared in 2004. With film rights sold for her *All-American Girl* novel, and a television series based on her 1-800-Where-R-You series playing on the Lifetime channel (retitled *1-800-Missing*), Cabot has become a book/media phenomenon.

Ironically, the Princess series didn't start out to be about a princess at all. The original story was a way for Cabot to deal with the fact that her widowed mother was dating one of her former college professors. She wasn't sure why that bothered her so much; after all, Meg was in her thirties. So she wrote a story about a teenage girl who is embarrassed by the same situation, and then gave the story another twist by having Mia discover that her divorced father is the prince of the tiny country of Genovia and she is his heir. The movie version eliminated the father character, ostensibly to give a larger part to star Julie Andrews, and set the story in San Francisco rather than New York. But the characterizations of Mia and her friend Lilly are true to the way Meg wrote them and are immensely appealing on both the page and the screen. *The Princess Diaries* was named an ALA Best Book for Young Adults and an ALA Quick Pick for the Reluctant Reader.

Writing under the pseudonym Jenny Carroll, Meg has published other series books for teens. The Mediator series features a high school student who has an uncanny ability to communicate with ghosts, helping them resolve issues so they can move on to the next world. In her 1-800-Where-R-You series, another high school girl develops a psychic sense for finding missing children after being struck by lightning. Written under the name Patricia Cabot, Meg's historical romances are praised for their wit and wry humor along with fast-paced plots and interesting characters.

Today Meg Cabot lives with her husband, a financial market writer and a poet, and their one-eyed cat Henrietta on New York's Upper East Side. She enjoys writing, spending time with friends, and walking New York neighborhoods.

SELECTED WORKS: *The Princess Diaries*, 2000; *Princess in the Spotlight*, 2001; *Princess in Love*, 2002; *Nicola and the Viscount*, 2002; *All-American Girl*, 2002; *Victoria and the Rogue*, 2003; *Princess in Waiting*, 2003; *Princess Lessons: A*

Princess Diaries Guide, illus. by Chesley McLaren, 2003; *Project Princess*, 2003; *Princess in Pink*, 2004; *Perfect Princess: A Princess Diaries Book*, illus. by Chesley MacLaren, 2004; *Princess Mia Tells It Like It Is* (2-in-1 edition of the first two Princess Diaries books), 2004; *Teen Idol*, 2004; *The Highs and Lows of Being Mia* (2-in-1 edition of the third and fourth Princess Diaries books), 2004; *The Princess Present: A Princess Diaries Book*, 2004.

SELECTED WORKS: The Mediator series—as Jenny Carroll: *Shadowland*, 2000; *Ninth Key*, 2001; *Reunion*, 2001; *Darkest Hour*, 2001; as Meg Cabot: *Haunted: A Tale of the Mediator*, 2003. The 1-800-Where-R-You series—as Jenny Carroll: *When Lightning Strikes*, 2001; *Code Name, Cassandra*, 2001; *Safe House*, 2002; *Sanctuary*, 2002.

SELECTED WORKS FOR ADULTS: as Patricia Cabot—*Where Roses Grow Wild*, 1998; *Portrait of My Heart*, 1999; *An Improper Proposal*, 1999; *A Little Scandal*, 2000; "The Christmas Captive," in *A Season in the Highlands*, 2000; *Lady of Skye*, 2000; *Educating Caroline*, 2001; *Kiss the Bride*, 2002; as Meggin Cabot—*The Boy Next Door*, 2002; *She Went All the Way*, 2002; *Boy Meets Girl*, 2004.

SUGGESTED READING: *Children's Literature Review*, vol. 85, 2003; *Contemporary Authors*, vol. 197, 2002; *Something About the Author*, vol. 127, 2002. Periodicals—Kloberdanz, Kristin, "American Princess," *Book*, March/April 2003.

WEB SITE:*www.megcabot.com*

Michael Cadnum

May 3, 1949–

"I grew up near the beach in Southern California, and in the late afternoons and early evenings my mother and father and my three sisters would all pile into the family Ford and head down to the broad flat sands of Huntington Beach and enjoy the Pacific.

"The tides were always at their warmest in the weeks after school had started, the summer months over, and it was a treat to come home from school—with a new set of textbooks and a new, yet-to-be-tested teacher—and head down to the ocean. One evening as we swam near the pier in Newport Beach we could hear the sharp, distance-blurred reports of gunfire.

"We thought very little of it, enjoying the rise and fall of the warm water. There had been sharks all that summer—hammerheads, mostly—and they roamed the area near the pier where fisherman threw the entrails of perch and sand dabs back into the water. Sometimes people shot at them from the pier. We had never seen one of these menacing sea-hunters, however, and so we were surprised—amazed—when a shark approached along the line of the surf, making its progress toward us.

"We left the water, and stood watching as this shape knifed its leisurely way across the sunset-bright ocean. We were not hurt. But now when people ask me why I became a writer this incident comes to mind. Something about the quiet family interlude, the warm, safe, and sultry peace so completely disrupted. Something about the dignified pace of the carnivore. It all recalls to me the truth always hidden within the normal hours and quiet days of our lives: Things are not as they seem. Even the fact that the shark didn't hurt any of us that September evening reveals something. Maybe even sea monsters are not always what they are reputed to be.

"I have always read with great appetite. My favorite books were adventures, novels about knights and submarines, dinosaurs and the North Pole. I read books that were, in a way, really too hard for me at first—novels by Sir Walter Scott and Herman Melville. I was attracted to true stories, too, or tales that could have been true. Stories about Robin Hood particularly entranced me, so when I began to research and prepare my novels *In a Dark Wood*, about Robin Hood and the Sheriff of Nottingham, and *Forbidden Forest,* the story of Little John and Robin Hood, I drew on my years of love for this magical subject.

Courtesy of Sherina Cadnum

"I read and wrote poetry, too, starting with early attempts to write like such diverse poets as Edgar Allen Poe and Carl Sandburg, William Carlos Williams and Dylan Thomas. Sometimes I wrote not very well, I'm afraid, but I stayed with it. I wrote as often as I could, during lunch, before school or work, carrying my notebook wherever I went. I still write nearly every day. In all my own writing, and in the work of others, I am hoping for language that wakes us up and stirs us to greater life.

"Now I live beside San Francisco Bay with my wife, Sherina, and my Amazon parrot, Luke. My wife and I travel when we can, and these trips almost always lead to a book or a poem. My novel about the Crusades, *The Book of the Lion*, sprang from a visit to the ruined fortress of Acre in modern-day Israel, and my novels about the Vikings, *Raven of the Waves* and *Daughter of the Wind*, were rooted in a long walk my wife and I took beside a fjord in Norway.

"I think that the best sort of travel is the sort that requires neither wings nor freeway. We all enjoy it every time we open the pages of a book."

❉   ❉   ❉

Michael Cadnum's books for young adults are uncompromising, tightly plotted, and rich in emotional depth. All written in the first person, they are novels that take the reader into a character's mind, illuminating a painful dilemma or an entire historical period with psychological insight. His poetry and short stories have appeared in many periodicals, including *Commonweal*, *Virginia Quarterly Review*, *America*, and *Rolling Stone*.

Cadnum has worked at a variety of jobs—substitute teacher, data processor, shipping clerk—while writing constantly. A fellowship from the National Endowment for the Arts gave further impetus to his creative work. His contemporary novels for older teens deal with the pressures of modern life and the rage that many feel when their parents give them everything except attention. In *Breaking the Fall*, Stanley yields to an uncontrollable desire to risk everything while his home life is in shambles. The protagonist of *Taking It*, an ALA Quick Pick for Young Adults, plays a dangerous game of pretending to shoplift until she finds herself caught in a spiral of kleptomania. In *Heat* and *Edge*, Cadnum's characters take out their frustrations in the world of sport.

His historical novels are no less psychologically complex. *In a Dark Wood* tells of events in the Robin Hood legends, but from the point of view of the Sheriff of Nottingham, a disturbed and troubling personality. Turning to the Crusades in *The Book of the Lion* and *The Leopard Sword*, Cadnum depicts in vivid detail the weeks of tedium as well as the hours of terror that constitute a warring expedition.

Courtesy of Orchard Books

SELECTED WORKS: *Morning of the Massacre*, 1982; *Invisible Mirror*, illus. by Mary Hatch, 1987; *Foreign Springs*, 1988; *Nightlight*, 1990; *Sleepwalker*, 1991; *Calling Home*, 1991; *Saint Peter's Wolf*, 1992; *Breaking the Fall*, 1992; *Ghostwright*, 1993; *The Horses of the Night*, 1993; *Skyscape*, 1994; *Taking It*, 1995; *The Judas Glass*, 1996; *Zero at the Bone*, 1996; *Edge: A Novel*, 1997; *The Lost and Found House*, illus. by Steve Johnson and Lou Fancher, 1997; *Heat*, 1998; *In a Dark Wood*, 1998; *Rundown*, 1999; *The Book of the Lion*, 2000; *Redhanded*, 2000; *Raven of the Waves*, 2001; *Forbidden Forest: The Story of Little John and Robin Hood*, 2002; *The Leopard Sword*, 2002; *Daughter of the Wind*, 2003; *Ship of Fire*, 2003; *Blood Gold*, 2004.

SUGGESTED READING: *Authors and Artists for Young Adults*, vol. 23, 1998; *St. James Guide to Young Adult Writers*, 2nd ed., 1999; *Contemporary Authors*, New Revision Series, vol. 90, 2000; *Something About the Author*, vol. 121, 2001. Periodicals—Jones, Patrick, "People Are Talking About . . . Michael Cadnum," *The Horn Book*, March/April 1994; Campbell, Patty, "Sand in the Oyster," *The Horn Book*, May/June 1994; Cadnum, Michael, "The Eye Under Oath: Why Stories Are Alive," *ALAN Review*, Winter 1999.

Courtesy of Maureen Holla

Elisa Carbone

January 2, 1954–

"I wrote my first book before I learned how to write. When I was four and a half years old I announced to my father one day that I wanted to write a book and since I couldn't yet write, he would be taking dictation. We began a nightly ritual of me imagining my story and him patiently writing it down as I told it. I could hardly wait for him to get home from his veterinary clinic each evening so we could 'work on the book.' Our family left for vacation on Cape Cod, and there I could corner him any time of the day to say we had to get to work. I remember the two of us in front of the tiny prewar cottage, bits of grass on the lawn poking up through soil that was mostly sand, and Dad sitting in one of those wood and canvas folding beach chairs with a Cape Cod bay breeze threatening to blow the pages off his lap. I felt content that my story was not simply drifting away on the wind, but rather being preserved as a book. When, after several weeks, the 'book' was done, my mother typed it, I illustrated it, and I had my finished product. It gave me a wonderful feeling that I had created something solid from my imagination.

"Between age four and a half and my early thirties, which is when I decided to write my second book, I had a few adventures. After graduating from high school I went to school in Italy for a while, lived among my many cousins, and learned to speak Italian since none of my cousins speaks a word of English. I actually got to help with the wine making, including smashing the grapes with my feet! (Note: Stomping grapes is a lot more difficult and tiring and less romantic than one might think. Especially when you're covered with sticky grape juice up to your thighs and realize the town's running water has already been turned off for the day!) I got married when I was still a teenager and had two wonderful children. I was always interested in music and dance and spent time as a piano teacher, guitar teacher, dance teacher, and a professional dancer doing Appalachian clogging. When my kids were a little older I finally got around to finishing college, then got a master's degree and taught college classes. There was one hint that should have given me a clue as to my life's work: From first grade on, I read children's novels whenever I could find the time.

"These days I make my living as a writer. I use my imagination and then, by putting down on paper what I have imagined, I create a doorway that invites others to see what I have seen in my mind's eye. It leaves me with a sense of satisfaction that virtually nothing else in my life can give me. For all of my books, especially the historical ones, I add research to the imaginative process. Usually my research involves reading books, articles, and original records, doing interviews, and visiting the sites where my stories take place. But the research gets really interesting when I decide to re-enact some of the events in my characters' lives. Whether that's riding a train all night to Canada or trudging along the North Carolina beach during gale-force winds, re-enactment helps me truly understand what the people in my books must have experienced.

"When I'm not writing, I'm usually out having adventures. During the winter I spend a couple of months cross-country skiing before the climbing/paddling/windsurfing season starts again in the spring. Somehow, the intense physical exertion of the sports seems to balance out the mental exertion of writing. Also, the kind of mental focus that is necessary during these activities trains my mind to focus at other times, like when I'm imagining a scene and need to make it come alive on paper."

> *"When I'm not writing, I'm usually out having adventures."*

❈　❈　❈

Born in Washington, DC, and raised in Arlington, Virginia, adventurous Elisa Lynn Carbone received her B.A. from the University of Maryland in 1985 and later two master's degrees, one in speech communication and the other in education, from the same university. She married Jeff Nugent in 1973 and they had two children, Daniel Micah and Rachel Elisa. Divorced in 1987, she later married photographer Jim Casbarian. They now make their home part-time in the Washington, DC, area and part-time in the mountains of West Virginia. Nominated for an Excellence in Teaching Award at the University of Maryland, Elisa Carbone taught speech communication there and has also worked as an independent consultant and trainer of teaching and communication skills.

Carbone's first novel, originally published as *My Dad's Definitely Not a Drunk!* and then renamed *Corey's Story: Her Family's Secret*, involves a case of alcoholism and was intended to help young people who have alcoholics in their own families or know friends who are dealing with that situation. Two humorous contemporary novels, *Starting School with an Enemy* and *Sarah*

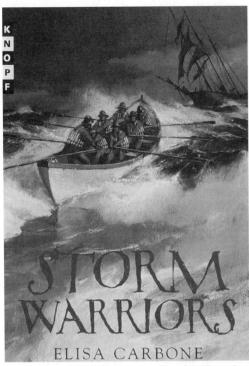

STORM WARRIORS

ELISA CARBONE

Courtesy of Alfred A. Knopf/Random House, Inc.

and the Naked Truth, which was an American Booksellers Association Pick of the Lists in 2000, follow the misadventures of a feisty 10-year-old named Sarah who attracts trouble—and friends to help her get out of it. *Stealing Freedom*, the tale of a 12-year-old slave in 1850s Maryland, is based on the true story of Ann Maria Weems, who risked her life to travel the Underground Railroad and find her family. *Stealing Freedom* was an ALA Best Book for Young Adults, nominated for many state book awards, and translated into Danish.

Carbone's next historical novel, *Storm Warriors*, portrayed a determined boy who wants to join the Pea Island Life-Saving Station on the Outer Banks of North Carolina. Though the boy is fictional, the rest of the story is true, including the dramatic rescue of the crew and passengers of the *E.S. Newman* during a hurricane. Much praised for its meticulous research and fast-paced plot, *Storm Warriors* was an ALA Notable Children's Book, a Bank Street College of Education Best Children's Book, a New York Public Library Book for the Teen Age, and the winner of the Virginia Library Association's Jefferson Cup Award.

SELECTED WORKS: *My Dad's Definitely Not a Drunk!*, 1992, reissued as *Corey's Story: Her Family's Secret*, illus. by Sally Davies, 1997; *Starting School with an Enemy*, 1998; *Teaching Large Classes: Tools and Strategies (Survival Skills for Scholars, 19)*, 1998; *Stealing Freedom*, 1998; *Sarah and the Naked Truth*, 2000; *Storm Warriors*, 2001.

SUGGESTED READING: *Contemporary Authors*, vol. 149, 1996; *Something About the Author*, vol. 81, 1995. Periodicals—Durango, Julia, "The Amazing Adventures of Elisa Carbone," *Daily Times* (Ottawa, Illinois), August 6, 2002.

WEB SITE: *www.elisacarbone.com*

Joe Cepeda

(seh-PEH-tah)

July 5, 1959–

"I grew up in East Los Angeles in the 1960s and '70s. From the beginning, I loved school. Even the stuff that wasn't very interesting, like math, was interesting enough. The joy of school started early in the day, beginning with the three blocks I covered to get to my classroom at Humphreys Avenue School. Sometimes I walked with friends, other times on my own. I never seemed to have problems with bullies or biting dogs lying in wait. In those few neighborhood blocks and the welcoming environs of school, I began to collect the rich visual memories that have become the library of images and sensibilities stored deep in my cranium.

"Our neighborhood was a working-class neighborhood. My brother and sister and I didn't have much, but we didn't want for much, either. Since we couldn't afford a new bike, I built one from parts of older abandoned bikes and parts I'd buy at swap meets. I had a strong appreciation for craftsmanship and the satisfaction of building something on my own from early on. My grandfather, who came to visit from Mexico, was a woodworker, and he crafted beautiful objects, including wonderful toys. He was an early mentor. He was also a Marxist.

"In school I was able to nurture that creative proclivity about half the time. When I was about ten, my mother, who saw that I liked to draw, was resourceful enough to enroll me in the Los Angeles Music and Art School, a small nonprofit school in East L.A. There I first smelled the strong aroma of oil paint and took afternoon classes once a week. In junior high school I relished my woodshop class. When I got to high school, though, there wasn't a shop class or an art class to be had. I stopped going to my afternoon classes for no real good reason that I can recall. I was always a good student, and after graduation I headed to Cornell University on a scholarship . . . to study engineering, of all things. What was I thinking?

"Eventually, after a 15-year scenic route through college (Cornell and I felt it best that I try something other than engineering), I ended up with a degree in illustration from Cal State Long Beach. I finally found something that allowed me to craft beautiful things and was a receptive depository for the memories that fell out of my head. Even though my memory banks are packed with 45 years of stuff (plenty of it worth looking at and some of it, not so much), I don't always have the easiest time

Courtesy of Juana Flores

accessing it. That's where illustrating comes in. It seems that with the reading and sharing of a good story, my brain gets tossed around enough for something particularly interesting to fall out onto the drawing board.

"I love the marriage between word and picture, and I do not take the visual commitment I bring to a story lightly. I feel an obligation to my craft and profession to go beyond just illustrating the text, to find the story within me. I look to express more than what I read, not because the manuscript is lacking, but because I'm inspired by it. If I surrender to it just right, the best little bits from my brain fall right out onto the page. I just try to make it look nice.

"As I watch my young son grow, running around the back yard with his dog, and hear my wife's sweet voice singing as she plays her guitar, I'm grateful for these new and beautiful images and how they replenish the heart of my inner library."

✿ ✿ ✿

Joe Cepeda received his B.F.A. in illustration from California State University at Long Beach in 1992. He has created illustrations for such corporate clients as Hilton Hotels and Land's End clothiers, and his art has appeared in many publications including the *Los Angeles Times*, *Latina*, *Hispanic Business*, and *Equal Opportunity Journal*. His work has appeared at Society of Illustrators shows in both New York and Los Angeles, and his vibrant illustrations have enlivened a wide variety of picture book stories. His strong sense of shape and form combines with richly saturated colors and an exuberant line to produce art that enhances every story in a special way.

One of his early books, *Gracias, the Thanksgiving Turkey*, written by Joy Cowley, was named a Notable Children's Trade Book in the Field of Social Studies. Cepeda's art was compared to that of Ezra Jack Keats in this story of a Puerto Rican boy in New York City who can't bear the thought of his pet turkey providing a meal for the family. *Big Bushy Mustache*, written by Gary Soto, received a commendation by the award jury for the Américas Award, and *Mice and Beans*, a story by Pam Muñoz Ryan, became an ALA Notable Children's Book and was cited by the Children's Literature Council of Southern California for excellence in total concept in both picture book text and illustration. In 2002, Cepeda was presented a Pura Belpré Honor Award for his illustrations in *Juan Bobo Goes to Work*, a Puerto Rican story retold by Marisa Montes about the classic Latino folklore character. He has also created jacket illustrations for well-loved novels with a Latino theme, including Pam Muñoz Ryan's *Esperanza Rising* and *Becoming Naomi León*.

Cepeda has illustrated stories of African and African American culture as well as Latino literature. He teamed with writer Julius Lester for an unconventional look at Heaven in *What a Truly Cool World*, which received a Blue Ribbon citation from the *Bulletin of the Center for Children's Books* and was named one of *Family Magazine*'s top 10 books of the year for children. Imagining a heaven where God is happy with his creation of the world until Shaniqua, "the angel in charge of everybody's business," points out a few deficiencies and suggests her own additions, Cepeda's rich colors and humorous characterizations perfectly match the tone of the text. A companion volume, *Why Heaven Is Far Away*, reintroduces the hip heavenly clan in Lester's retelling of an African American pourquoi story. A book Cepeda illustrated by author Carolivia Herron, *Nappy Hair*, is about the special qualities of Afro hair and a little girl who learns to love her looks. *Nappy Hair* became the center of

"I had a strong appreciation for craftsmanship and the satisfaction of building something on my own from early on."

controversy soon after it was published. Taken out of context, some of the images were thought to be derogatory, but that concern was largely discredited by Michelle Martin, a professor of children's and African-American literature writing in *The Horn Book* magazine.

Joe Cepeda met his wife, a musician and singer/songwriter, when he happened to hear her playing in a band. Their son was born in 1996, and they live today in Whittier, California.

Courtesy of Scholastic Press

SELECTED WORKS: *The Cat's Meow*, by Gary Soto, 1995; *Gracias, the Thanksgiving Turkey*, by Joy Cowley, 1996; *The Old Man and His Door*, by Gary Soto, 1996; *We Were Tired of Living in a House*, by Liesel Moak Skorpen, 1996; *Nappy Hair*, by Carolivia Herron, 1997; *Big Bushy Mustache*, by Gary Soto, 1998; *Pumpkin Fiesta*, by Caryn Yacowitz, 1998; *Koi and the Kola Nuts: A Tale from Liberia*, by Verna Aardema, 1999; *What a Truly Cool World*, by Julius Lester, 1999; *Rip's Secret Spot*, by Kristi T. Butler, 2000; *Vroomaloom Zoom*, by John Coy, 2000; *Juan Bobo Goes to Work: A Puerto Rican Folktale*, retold by Marisa Montes, 2000; *Captain Bob Sets Sail*, by Roni Schotter, 2000; *The Tapping Tale*, by Judy Giglio, 2000; *Mice and Beans*, by Pam Muñoz Ryan, 2001; *Why Heaven Is Far Away*, by Julius Lester, 2002; *Hey You! C'mere!: A Poetry Slam*, by Elizabeth Swados, 2002; *Who's That Girl?*, by Marisa Montes, 2003; *A Crazy Mixed-up Spanglish Day*, by Marisa Montes, 2003; *The Journey of Oliver K. Woodman*, by Darcy Pattison, 2003; *I, Freddy*, by Dietlof Reiche, trans. by John Brownjohn, 2003; *Captain Bob Takes Flight*, by Roni Schotter, 2003; *Try Your Best*, by Robert McKissack, 2004; *Freddy in Peril*, by Dietlof Reiche, trans. by John Brownjohn, 2004; *The Red Blanket*, by Eliza Thomas, 2004.

SUGGESTED READING: Bishop, Rudine Sims, "Heaven Is . . . Three African-American Literary Folktales," *The Horn Book*, March 1999; Martin, Michelle H., "Never Too Nappy," *The Horn Book*, May 1999.

WEB SITE: *www.joecepeda.com*

Yangsook Choi

March 1, 1967–

"At the age of 24 I came to America to finally pursue my dream of being an artist. Previously my mom had told me if I was talented I would have won some awards or recognitions early on. She also mentioned art would bring an ambiguous future. So I had kept my love for art abstract. Luckily I had two other dreams that seemed more hopeful to pursue. One was to be the first female Korean heavy metal singer. I felt my country deeply needed a strong female role model. The other was to be a biologist to feed my curiosity about life.

"But above all these, my determination was clear; no matter what I did I would use my profession as a channel to somehow connect with children. When I was little my heart was hardened by the injustices towards children caused by rules made by self-centered grown-ups. I felt I needed to do something about it when I grew up. I simply never expected myself to work this directly for children.

"Throughout my younger years I would draw whenever I found boredom and a piece of paper. On every submission of my art to teachers I would anticipate oohs and ahhs with freezing excitement, but instead no response was the response I got. So I kept art as a mindless and private habit. When I arrived in New York, I studied illustration at the School of Visual Arts. I reluctantly picked a children's folktale to illustrate for a thesis project. I chose this in response to the heaviness of conceptual illustration work that had burned me out previously. Through this I found that visual storytelling came natural to me. *The Sun Girl and the Moon Boy*, the folktale I illustrated, was published by Knopf.

"I met Peter Sís when he came to SVA to speak and he became my adviser for the thesis project. He proved to be a great inspiration. By showing me his selflessness and the importance of possessing a childlike heart, Peter helped me reach my full potential in children's book writing and illustrating. I got my first book contract before graduating from art school, and my publishing career took off without me quite realizing it. At about the same time it had taken me the whole year to memorize what the acronym for FSG, my publisher, stood for. Also, it took my parents in Korea two years and some overseas phone calls to finally stop asking me 'uh, what is it that you said you were doing over there in the States??'

"Despite that my only writing history consisted of a couple of C's from college writing classes, I had to move on to writing children's stories myself in order to create more illustration jobs. I simply could not wait around for a phone call to illustrate someone else's story. My storytelling started as a kid when my grandma was my only audience. She was a great audience, and she always slept well after hearing my stories. At the same time I did some acting at school and community events. Animating characters on stage made me feel alive. I think good writers are good actors on the page. Writing gives me the ability to bring the aliveness I felt on the stage to the paper. I have never imagined that I would enjoy the same creativity in writing! I don't always know what and how I want to write. All I know is that I want my voices and colors to be raw, and I will be happy as long as I have my art and heart in it."

✧ ✧ ✧

Yangsook Choi was born and raised in Seoul, Korea. After earning a B.A. degree from Sang-myoung University she worked as a flight attendant for Cathay Pacific for one year. Her first art class was in Kendall College of Art and Design in Michigan in 1991. Two years later she moved to New York City to pursue graduate study in illustration, and obtained a master's degree in fine arts from the School of Visual Arts. She was selected as one of the most promising new children's book artists of 1997 by *Publishers Weekly*. Her first picture book, *Nim and the War Effort*, written by Milly Lee, was an ALA Notable Book and a *New York Times* Outstanding Book of the Year; it won an IRA Children's Book Award in 1999 as well as a California Young Readers Medal.

Courtesy of Farrar, Straus and Giroux

New Cat, which she wrote and illustrated, was a Chicago Public Library Best Book and was selected for the Original Art exhibition at the Society of Illustrators. *The Name Jar* was an American Booksellers Association Pick of the Lists.

Rice Is Life was a Junior Library Guild Selection and a 2000 Parents' Choice Silver Honor. *This Next New Year* won a 2000 Oppenheim Toy Portfolio Gold Award. Choi's works have been exhibited in the Children's Museum of the Arts in New York City, the Society of Illustrators Museum of American Illustration, and New York Public Library. Her illustrations have been described as spare, elegant, lush, and vibrant. She worked on the Children's Program for the Asian Pacific American Heritage Festival for two years and taught a children's book writing workshop at the Asian American Writers' Workshop. Choi lives in New York City.

SELECTED WORKS WRITTEN AND ILLUSTRATED: *The Sun Girl and the Moon Boy*, 1997; *New Cat*, 1999; *The Name Jar*, 2001.

SELECTED WORKS ILLUSTRATED: *Nim and the War Effort*, by Milly Lee, 1997; *Basket Weaver and Catches Many Mice*, by Janet Gill, 1999; *Rice Is Life*, by Rita Golden Gelman, 2000; *This Next New Year*, by Janet S. Wong, 2000; *Earthquake*, by Milly Lee, 2001; *Goodbye, 382 Shin Dang Dong*, by Frances and Ginger Park, 2002.

SUGGESTED READING: "Children's Author Shows off Asian Culture," *Korea Herald*, June 27, 2002; Devereaux, Elizabeth, "Flying Starts," *Publishers Weekly*, June 30, 1997; Hong, Terry, "Being a Kid," *Asianweek*, July 19, 2002; Hong, Terry, "Drawn to Life," *Korean*, December 2002.

WEB SITE: *www.yangsookchoi.com*

Courtesy of R. Gregory Christie

R. Gregory Christie

July 26, 1971–

"I was recently told that the most adept observer of a society or a civilization is the one who views it from the outskirts—either from a highly spiritual standpoint or from the vantage point of a mendicant.

"These days I'm still trying to figure out my place in this rat race, but for a good part of my life, I've defined myself an outsider. I have been one who spends his time collecting information and connecting with people through their culture and attitudes only to isolate myself later in order to reflect upon my lessons. Generally speaking, I have come to the conclusion that all of us, linked by nature, are not all that much separated by culture. It takes tolerance and time, however, to comprehend another's desires and needs. And those who search long and hard enough—those who truly look and strive to see—will find an Asian or an African who needs the same things out of life as a European or a Middle Easterner. They will also find the expressions of beauty and creativity that all cultures offer.

"I grew up in a colonial suburban town in New Jersey. Near the main street was the Cannon Ball House; a block away stood the Stagecoach Inn. Both places had Revolutionary War historical roots; but in reality the town, the history, the people made me feel odd. As a quiet well-mannered youth, it took a great deal of time to accept myself. I had to get over the fact that I was a lot more different than the people around me. During this process of self understanding, I decided to find my place in this world. I moved from Scotch Plains, New Jersey, to the Upper West Side of New York in order to attend art school. I saw New York City as a place where cultures collide in order to make an organized sense of confusion. The paradoxes of the economy, culture, and attitudes were like a jungle for me to lose myself within. Eventually I grew accustomed to this jungle of ideas and became at ease surviving there. My time living there was an education in human nature and eventually defined my path as a painter.

"At this point in my life I've focused my energy upon creating children's books which deal with cultural or historical issues. I think that it's what is needed in the world. After being a bit of a nomad in and out of the United States, I've come to the conclusion that there's a greater need for understanding and acceptance between Americans. The generation of these books is therapeutic for me. It's my opportunity to share my talent and ideas with people in this society—a platform to tell each and every child that it's fine to be against the grain in a constructive way. At times one's inner treasures are buried. I feel that it's important to look inside oneself in order to find one's path. However, never be blind to the world around you. This philosophy has got me where I am today and I suspect will keep me here tomorrow as my art continues to be appreciated."

Courtesy of Lee & Low Books, Inc.

❈   ❈   ❈

Richard Gregory Christie has always been called by his middle name, a practice in his family that extends to both his brothers as well. Greg received a B.F.A. from the School of Visual Arts in New York City in 1993, but his interest in art extends back into his childhood. In an interview on one publisher's Web site he remembers being as young as five years old and copying characters from comic books. "Even then," he stated, "I always felt a sense of joy from painting and drawing." The support of a loving family and an artistic atmosphere at home were important to his growth—his brother and his father both enjoyed drawing, and his mother encouraged him to follow his dream of becoming an artist. While attending art school he spent time as an intern and spot illustrator for the *Newark Star Ledger*, where his first published work appeared; he also worked at art stores and in the Guggenheim Museum, where he was a bookstore clerk and later a security guard. His illustrations have appeared in many periodicals, including the *New York Times*, the *New Yorker*, the *Village Voice*, and *Atlantic Monthly*, as well as on promotional materials and CD covers.

In children's books, Gregory Christie made an auspicious beginning. In his very first book, *The Palm of My Heart*, he illustrated poems written by African American children and won a Coretta Scott King Honor Award for illustration, a significant achievement for a first-time book illustrator. The book also received a Reading Magic Award from *Parenting* magazine and was named to the Choices list of the Cooperative Children's Book Center (CCBC). His second book, *Richard Wright and the Library Card*, illustrated a story by William Miller that was based on a dramatic incident from Wright's autobiography. Christie's elongated figures and emotional intensity in this book were becoming the recognizable signature style that has characterized all his work. His art for a story by Anne Rockwell, *Only Passing Through*, dramatized with great feeling the life of Sojourner Truth and earned the artist a place in the prestigious Ten Best-Illustrated Children's Books list in the *New York Times Book Review* in 1997. *Only Passing Through* also won a Coretta Scott King Honor Award in illustration, received an ALA Notable Children's Book citation, and was named to the New York Public Library's 100 Titles for Reading and Sharing.

Continuing his depictions of strong African American role models and influences, Christie illustrated a poetic tribute to Langston Hughes, written by Tony Medina; *Love to Langston* was named a Best Book of the Year by *School Library Journal* and included on the New York Public Library's list. Children will relate easily to *Yesterday I Had the Blues*, in which Christie's art illuminates each color-enhanced mood of the characters and helped earn this title its Blue Ribbon designation from the *Bulletin of the Center for Children's Books*. With the inspiration of generations of African American experience and a palette influenced by the vibrancy of his New York neighborhoods, as well as his travels across Europe and around the world, Gregory Christie challenges his readers to look at the world through an artist's eye. Currently he lives in Brooklyn, New York.

SELECTED WORKS ILLUSTRATED: *The Palm of My Heart: Poetry by African American Children*, edited by Davida Adedjouma, 1996; *Richard Wright and the Library Card*, by William Miller, 1997; *Only Passing Through: The Story of Sojourner Truth*, by Anne Rockwell, 2000; *Rock of Ages: A Tribute to the Black Church*, by Tonya Bolden, 2001; *Deshawn Days*, by Tony Medina, 2001; *Stars in the Darkness*, by Barbara M. Joosse, 2002; *Love to Langston*, by Tony Medina, 2002; *Ruler of the Courtyard*, by Rukhsana Khan, 2003; *Yesterday I Had the Blues*, by Jeron Ashford Frame, 2003; *Hot City*, by Barbara M. Joosse, 2004.

SUGGESTED READING: *Something About the Author*, vol. 127, 2002. Periodicals—Donalds, Ariana, "Home and Away," *Print*, January 2001. Online—*www.leeandlow.com/booktalk/christie.html*.

"I grew up in Malden, Massachusetts, a suburb just outside of Boston, the daughter of two nurses and the youngest of three children. I consider myself very lucky to have grown up with a mother who loved to read. Each week my Mom would take me with her to our local library so that she could stock up on books. As I grew older I would venture off into the children's section and gather up my own collection to check out. Through my mother I realized that reading could become a wonderful escape, and writing even more so. When my mother gave me a diary as a gift, I first filled the pages with the 'very important' details of my life—adventures with my friends, secret crushes, and the many ways in which my family drove me crazy. Then I began creating my own stories.

"By the time I reached middle school, I had decided that I wanted to be a real writer, a journalist. I wanted to sniff out stories, conduct interviews, and write in-depth articles for a newspaper in New York City. After I attended a summer workshop for teens interested in journalism at Suffolk University in Boston, I realized that a career in journalism was the last thing I wanted. I was too shy to conduct interviews, hated working under tight deadlines, and did not enjoy factual writing. I wanted to create my own stories, or at least be able to put my own creative spin on the stories I wrote. By the time I finished high school, I had given up on the idea of any type of writing career.

"Though my mother started me on my writing journey, it was my teachers in school and throughout college who sustained it. With encouragement from my professors at Pratt Institute in Brooklyn, New York, I began writing for the college paper, and my passion for writing was renewed. After I graduated, I took my first job in the advertising department at Lord & Taylor, but soon realized that writing ad copy for catalogues would not be enough of a creative outlet.

"I became interested in children's books the year I married. My husband, James, was working on illustrating his first book, which allowed both of us to look at picture books in a new way. When we browsed in bookstores, he studied illustrations while I read the stories. I eventually completed a graduate degree in elementary education and through my coursework became truly immersed in children's literature.

Courtesy of Simon & Schuster

Lesa Cline-Ransome

July 12, 1965–

"When I was home after the birth of our first child, James would constantly suggest that I start writing for children. He had tons of ideas for books (none of which I liked), but then he showed me a collection of stories about champion athletes. When I read the section on Satchel Paige, the Negro League pitcher, I was hooked. In between my daughter's naps and another pregnancy, I read and researched and wrote for nearly a year before an editor at Simon & Schuster decided to take a chance on Satchel. Four years, four books (and four children) later, and I am still writing.

"Now as I make my weekly treks to the library with my own children to gather research and stock up on books, I am again reminded of just how lucky I am."

❂   ❂   ❂

"When I read the section on Satchel Paige, the Negro League pitcher, I was hooked."

Born in Malden, Massachusetts, Lesa Cline studied merchandising and fashion management at Pratt Institute in Brooklyn, New York. It was during her sophomore year there that she met her future husband, James E. Ransome. They met at a Purple Rain (all Prince music) party when he asked her to dance. Together they explored New York City's sights, restaurants, and museums. In their classes, he would help her with her art projects and she would help him with his writing assignments. They were married in 1989, and she combined his last name with her own.

After earning a bachelor of fine arts degree in 1987, Cline-Ransome worked as a fashion copywriter for Lord & Taylor and R. H. Macy, two of the largest department stores in New York City. Developing an interest in the field of education, she worked as a substitute teacher in the New York City school system. Later she became a teacher in the Living for the Young Family through Education (LYFE) program, which was designed to offer on-site infant and toddler child-care to teenage parents returning to high school to complete their education. While working for this program, she earned an M.A. from New York University in early childhood and elementary education.

Lesa Cline-Ransome resigned from her teaching position and began to think about writing for children when she was expecting her first child. Her first book, a carefully researched picture-book biography of Satchel Paige, illustrated with bold and vibrant oil paintings by her husband, was named an ALA Notable Children's Book and a Notable Social Studies Trade Book for Young People. Celebrating the combination of skill and showmanship that made Paige a legend in his own time, the book brings to life this baseball pioneer of the Negro Leagues, who was the first black ballplayer to pitch in a World Series. The Ransomes next collaborated on two concept books for young children, *Quilt Alphabet* and *Quilt Counting*, which presents letters and numbers in a fresh, original way, with rhyming verses and boldly colored illustrations. Their fourth collaboration, *Major*

Taylor, Champion Cyclist, chosen as a Junior Library Guild selection, highlights the life of a sports hero who is little known outside the annals of bicycle racing. Marshall Taylor, nicknamed "Major" when he was still young, won the world championship in bicycle racing in 1899 against tremendous odds, including the blatant racial prejudice directed toward black men of his time.

In addition to writing, Lesa Cline-Ransome visits schools to talk about her books and encourage children's creative responses. Recently she conducted a residency at the Claremont Neighborhood Center in the Bronx for 70 children during after-school hours to help them understand the importance of reading and writing. She lives in Rhinebeck, New York, with her husband and their four children: Jaime, Maya, Malcolm, and Leila.

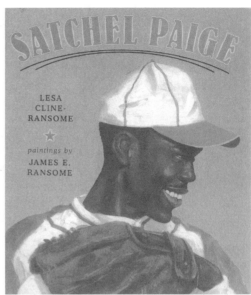

Courtesy of Simon & Schuster Books for Young Readers

SELECTED WORKS: *Satchel Paige*, illus. by James E. Ransome, 2000; *Quilt Alphabet*, illus. by James E. Ransome, 2001; *Quilt Counting*, illus. by James E. Ransome, 2002; *Major Taylor, Champion Cyclist*, illus. by James E. Ransome, 2004.

SUGGESTED READING: Sacks, Pamela H., "Major Taylor Finds Young Audience," *Worcester Telegram and Gazette* (Massachusetts), April 16, 2004.

WEB SITE: *www.jamesransome.com*

"My parents were very indulgent people. I believed as a child that I was from outer space . . . and they allowed me to think this was as normal as believing babies were dropped from the sky by a stork.

"I grew up on a street with all my relatives as my neighbors. My grandmother lived next door and cooked my breakfast every morning. In fact, my mother, my grandmother, my Aunt Nellie, or Aunt Mamie always cooked whatever I wanted to eat. I never needed to learn to cook. Thanks to these wonderful women I was permitted to daydream most of the day. I usually snuggled inside my grandmother's grape arbor creating stories to share with my family.

"My brother, Edward, loved my stories so much, he would pay me all his allowance and make my bed just to hear one of my stories. I made up tons of stories for him. I enjoyed the job so much that I began sharing my spoils with him in the end. His interest encouraged my creativity.

Evelyn Coleman

July 3, 1948–

"I was an extremely imaginative girl. I thought that was a good thing because my family encouraged and went along with all my fantasies. They all said I was different and they acted as though that was a marvelous thing. One winter I wore a blond horsetail in my hair. The next summer I refused to talk; I wrote everything down and my family read and read and read. Then there was the summer I believed that I had lived before in India. Even though I had never really seen an Indian from India I would only wear cloth wrapped around me like a sari. I am not sure to this day how I knew exactly how to wrap it, yet I did. No matter what I did my family treated me as though my behavior was normal, so I didn't know that this might be considered strange until I was older and went away to college at North Carolina Central University. By that time I had many messages from my family and community that I was normal, so it didn't bother me that people began to think I was weird or strange.

Courtesy of Shelia Turner

"My father died that year, and I was to struggle with the distress of his death for many years. I married, had two wonderful daughters, and went to work. Over the years I have held many jobs: a payroll clerk, a secretary, a telephone operator, an administrative assistant, a sales clerk, a library assistant (the hardest job I ever had), a math tutor, a journalist, a psychotherapist (for more than 13 years), and a business owner. I have owned a nursery school, a fish market, a garage, and a stress management company (using sensory deprivation tanks).

"After working for 13 years for mental health centers, I decided to retire in a typically drastic manner: I gave away or sold everything I owned except my car, a few books, and a set of dishes. My goal was to live a few years in a cave near the holy mountains of Tibet for my own pleasure and contemplation. However, the universe obviously had other plans for me, because the morning I was supposed to leave, a man fell asleep at the wheel on his way home from a night job and his car crashed into mine. It was while I convalesced that I began to write stories down. Not long after I was the first African American to win one of North Carolina's fiction fellowships. After this I began to educate myself as a writer.

"I wrote for the adult market for years to hone my skills in preparation for one day writing books for children. As you can read, I followed many paths back to the days of storytelling. I love writing for children. My stories have become my spoils that

I will share with everyone forever. There is nothing I'd rather do than to tell a story and indulge in the smiles of my readers."

☼　☼　☼

Evelyn Coleman was raised alongside her younger brother, Eddie Joe, and the many cousins of her extended family in Burlington, North Carolina. From these beginnings she developed a strong sense of connection with the earth and faith in the human spirit. In Coleman's freshman year at North Carolina Central University an English teacher, Linda Hodge, suggested that she was a wonderful writer. But it was many years, and many experiences later, before this suggestion would become a professional reality.

In each of Coleman's books for young readers, underlying themes deal with issues of slavery, racism, race relations, and the courage inherent in standing up for one's beliefs. *The Foot Warmer and the Crow* and *The Glass Bottle Tree* were both named Notable Children's Trade Books in the Field of Social Studies. *The Glass Bottle Tree*, in which a grandmother teaches her granddaughter a way to honor her ancestors, was also a Parents' Choice Honor Book. In *To Be a Drum*, the story is based on her father's teachings about listening for the heartbeat of the earth and discovering that strength within yourself. *The Riches of Oseola McCarty* relates the story of an African American washerwoman who donated her life savings to the University of Southern Mississippi to fund scholarships, so that deserving young people could have the education she herself missed. This inspiring biography was named a Smithsonian Notable Book, a Carter G. Woodson Honor Book, and a Society of School Librarians International Honor Book.

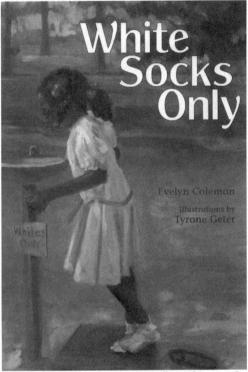

Courtesy of Albert Whitman & Co.

White Socks Only, a picture book in which a young girl confronts prejudice in the segregated South, was named an American Booksellers Association Pick of the Lists and a *Smithsonian* Notable Book. It also won a Bronze Award at the Worldfest Film Festival when it was made into an educational film by the Academy Award–winning producer Barbara Bryant of Phoenix Films.

In 1989 Coleman won a fiction fellowship from the North Carolina Arts Council for the articles and short stories she had published in adult journals, and in 1991 she attended workshops at Rice University and *Highlights* Writing School for Children on merit fellowships. In 2002 she received the Atlanta Mayor's

Fellowship for children's literature and was named Georgia Author of the Year for children's and young adult literature. A King Baudouin Exchange Fellowship allowed her to travel to Europe in 2003, where she spent most of her time in Belgium enhancing communications between American and Belgian authors.

Evelyn Coleman is married to Talib Din, a linguist and musician; she has two grown daughters and one granddaughter and lives in Atlanta, Georgia. In addition to her children's books she is currently writing adult thrillers and mysteries.

SELECTED WORKS: *The Foot Warmer and the Crow*, illus. by Daniel Minter, 1994; *Cymbals*, illus. by Sterling Brown, 1995; *The Glass Bottle Tree*, illus. by Gail Gorden Carter, 1995; *White Socks Only*, illus. by Tyrone Geter, 1996; *To Be a Drum*, illus. by Aminah Brenda Lynn Robinson, 1998; *The Riches of Oseola McCarty*, illus. by Daniel Minter, 1998; *Mystery of the Dark Tower* (American Girl History Mysteries, 6), illus. by Dahl Taylor and Greg Dearth, 2000; *Circle of Fire* (American Girl History Mysteries, 14), illus. by Jean-Paul Tibbles and Laszlo Kubinyi, 2001; *Born in Sin*, 2001.

SUGGESTED READING: Coleman, Evelyn, "Where's the Outcry? Maybe It Should Come from Within," *Obsidian III*, Spring/Summer 2001. Online—White, Claire E., "Interview with Evelyn Coleman," *Writers Write: The Internet Writing Journal: www.writerswrite.com/journal/apr98/coleman.htm.*

WEB SITE: *www.evelyncoleman.com/childhome1.htm*

Raúl Colón

December 17, 1952–

"Ever since I can remember, I've always loved to draw. I was always perfectly fine with pencil and paper in hand, even when I was ill. At a very young age, I suffered from chronic asthma. I spent days, even weeks at a time, locked up in my room trying to recover from a vicious attack. I could usually hear and see my New York neighborhood friends playing outside on beautiful sunny days. But what at first seemed to be a curse eventually became a blessing in disguise. Whenever I felt a little better and could sit up in bed, I'd collect all the composition notebooks I could find. I'd sharpen my pencil and fill every page with as many drawings as I could. The hours I spent at home allowed me to steadily sharpen my drawing skills. Of course, when I went back to school, my teachers were not impressed to find my homework surrounded by pictures of Spiderman, the Hulk, and Sgt. Rock.

"Obviously, comic book art was a major influence in my early development in the field of illustration. The heroic characters in these stories were my faithful companions during those long hours I spent alone in my room. Steve Ditko, Jack Kirby, and Joe Kubert were the draughtsmen who became my very first teachers. In trying to emulate their work, I was surely improving my own. I even tried to write my own comic book stories.

"When I was 11 or 12 years old, my family moved to a warmer climate. My health improved, as well as my line drawings. During my high school years, a federally funded program allowed me to study three years of commercial art. After graduation, I paid my dues by working at a printing company, spending endless hours doing what was then known as paste-up work. I did the same for a local periodical where, once in a while, I was allowed to draw the cover. I slowly worked my way into more art-oriented projects when I found full-time work in the art department for the audiovisual center of a local college. After three years, I decided to move to Fort Lauderdale, Florida, where I found a job in an instructional television center's graphic arts department. The television center produced educational programs for local schools. It was an exceptional learning experience for me and full of creative energy. I worked with four other magnificent artists who were as versatile as any I have ever met. We designed, produced, and built everything from puppets to animated films. We used hammer and nails to build television sets for different programs. We wrote and played music, performed in front of the cameras, and even worked the puppets. It seemed to be a poor man's *Sesame Street* type of production. For 10 years, I absorbed this creative experience as much as I could.

Courtesy of Raúl Colón

"But my big dream was to work as a freelance illustrator. Ever since I was a kid, I knew what an illustrator was. The large formats of magazines like *Life* and *Look* allowed me to appreciate the work of the first illustrator I came to know: Norman Rockwell. As I grew older, I came to love the artwork of others, like Brad Holland, Matt Mahurin, and Milton Glaser. I learned what I needed to do by reading magazines such as *Print* and *Communication Arts*. I spent a year putting a portfolio together. I had a number of postcards printed showing my best work. I made lists. I wrote to art directors. I did extensive mailings.

"Then I finally moved back to New York City in 1988. For the first six or seven months after the move, I made cold calls every morning, made appointments, and visited every art director willing to meet me. Slowly but surely I began getting pieces published in publications like *Business Week*, the *New York Times*, and the *Wall Street Journal*, and with RCA Records (now BMG). I also found myself an agent to help me in my efforts.

"Finally, children's books made their way into my oeuvre when one afternoon I received a call from an editor at Knopf, a division of Random House. She had seen my work in the *New York Times Book Review* and offered me a manuscript she thought I'd be interested in. It was called *Always My Dad*, by Sharon Dennis Wyeth, and became the first picture book I illustrated. Since then, I've illustrated dozens of picture books, including now the first book I've both written and illustrated, *Orson Blasts Off!*, published by Simon and Schuster.

"Today, most of my work consists of picture books. But I still like to diversify and do a lot of other types of artwork. I've done posters and even a mural for the New York Metro Transit Authority at the 191st Street station in Manhattan. I've worked on numerous book covers and still do some editorial work, like covers for the *New Yorker* and pieces for *Time* and *Business Week*. My wife and two sons (now grown up) have witnessed my ups and downs, but have also seen how rewarding it is to do what you love. I still spend a lot of time alone in my studio—not because I'm ill, but because what I'm doing is rewarding. So you see, my curse really did become a blessing, after all."

❈　❈　❈

"Obviously, comic book art was a major influence in my early development in the field of illustration. The heroic characters in these stories were my faithful companions during those long hours I spent alone in my room."

When he was 12 years old, Raúl Colón read about a place called the Famous Artists' School in one of his comic books. He wrote to the school to get a test from them to see how well he could draw. In response, the school sent a cartoonist to his home to tell him that, although he was too young yet to go to the school, he had artistic talent. From an early age, Raúl felt driven to be an artist and explored every avenue to achieve his goal. Today, Raúl Colón is an acclaimed illustrator whose work has appeared in magazines, journals, and newspapers and on theater posters, annual reports, advertisements, CD covers, and brochures for corporations and institutions such as American Express and Dean Witter. His awards include first place in the Florida Press Club contest for Excellence in Artist Illustration in 1987 and 1988; a 1988 Broadcast Designer's Award for his "Shaka Zulu" poster; and a fifth place in the 1990 AR Best Illustrated Annual Reports for the work he did for Johnson & Higgins.

Raúl Colón is especially renowned for his children's book illustrations. The first book he illustrated, *Always My Dad*, written by Sharon Wyeth, is the sensitive story of an absentee African American father and the daughter who cherishes his visits and savors the time he's around, even though she cannot ensure his return or control the world of adult comings and goings. Colón's art for this book won a Silver Medal at the Society of Illustrators' Original Art Exhibition. His second picture book, Libba Moore Gray's *My Mama Had a Dancing Heart*, won a Gold Medal from the Society of Illustrators, was selected for the *New York Times* Best Illustrated list, and was named an ALA Notable

Courtesy of Atheneum Books for Young Readers

Children's Book. *A Band of Angels*, with text by Deborah Hopkinson, was also designated an ALA Notable. In 1998, Colón received the Tomás Rivera Mexican American Children's Book Award from Southwest Texas State University for his illustrations for *Tomás and the Library Lady*, Pat Mora's story about an incident in the childhood of Rivera.

Jane Yolen's *Mightier Than the Sword: World Folktales for Strong Boys*, which won a 2003 Aesop Prize, is a collection of 14 stories—both well known and little known—from countries around the world, all united by the common theme of heroic effort. Colón's lively signature style of crosshatch with muted colors enhances each story. He has also illustrated picture book versions of myths in *Hercules* and *Pandora*, both written by Robert Burleigh. Many award-winning novels for young readers by such fine writers as Naomi Shihab Nye (*Habibi*) and Tony Johnston (*Any Small Goodness*) have been graced with Colón's distinctive jacket art.

In *Orson Blasts Off!*, his first book as both writer and illustrator, we catch a hint of the young asthmatic Colón stuck in his room with Orson's response to the jack-in-the-box's suggestion that he go outside: "Outside? I don't do outside." But when Orson does step out of his self-imposed boundaries, a journey of the imagination takes him by surprise. Wordplay and illustration combine for a delightful "lesson" when the boy uses his own imaginative resources rather than relying on his computer.

Raúl Colón lives in New City, New York.

SELECTED WORKS WRITTEN AND ILLUSTRATED: *Orson Blasts Off!*, 2004.

SELECTED WORKS ILLUSTRATED: *Always My Dad*, by Sharon Dennis Wyeth, 1995; *My Mama Had a Dancing Heart*, by Libba Moore Gray, 1995; *Grandmother's Garden*, by John Archambault, 1996; *Tomás and the Library Lady*, by Pat Mora, 1997; *Celebration!*, by Jane Resh Thomas, 1997; *Buoy, Home at Sea*, by Bruce Balan, 1998; *A Weave of Words: An Armenian Tale*, retold by Robert D. San Souci, 1998; *Hercules*, by Robert Burleigh, 1999; *A Band of Angels: A Story Inspired by the Jubilee Singers*, by Deborah Hopkinson, 1999; *The Snowman's Path*, by Helena Clare Pittman, 2000; *Secrets from the Dollhouse*, by Ann Turner, 2000; *A Shepherd's Gift*, by Mary Calhoun, 2001; *Pandora*, by Robert Burleigh, 2002; *Rise the Moon*, by Eileen Spinelli, 2002; *Mightier Than the Sword: World Folktales for Strong Boys*, by Jane Yolen, 2003; *What Is Goodbye?*, by Nikki Grimes, 2004.

SUGGESTED READING: Cummings, Pat. *Talking with Artists*, vol. 3, 1999.

WEB SITE: *www.raulcolon.com*

Barbara Cooney

August 6, 1917–
March 10, 2000

The following autobiographical sketch was written by Barbara Cooney in 1963 for *More Junior Authors*:

"My twin brother and I were born in Brooklyn, New York, where we lived for two weeks. Along with two younger brothers, we were brought up on Long Island during the school year and in Maine during the summer. The latter is still Mecca for all of us, and we return each year if we are able.

"My father was a stockbroker, but my mother was an artist. That I, too, am an artist is largely due to the tubes of paint, brushes, paper, and other art supplies that were always available to my mother's children. As far back as I can remember, I could always entertain myself by drawing pictures. I continued to do so during school and college years. Later I studied lithography and etching at the Art Students League in New York City.

"At about this time I began illustrating and haven't stopped since, with one exception: When my brother joined the army during World War II, I joined the WAC. During this period I married Guy Murchie, with whom I had two children, a girl named Gretel and a boy named Barnaby. I am now the wife of Dr. C. Talbot Porter, a general practitioner in Pepperell, Massachusetts. Two more children have been added to the family: Talbot Jr. and Phoebe. We live in a rambling old house surrounded by broad lawns, tall trees, and gardens. I couldn't ask for a pleasanter ivory tower. Possibly the term *ivory tower* is incorrect, for *ivory tower* doesn't generally connote hustle and bustle, which this house is full of.

"I am now working on my fiftieth book. My being an illustrator is a highly satisfactory arrangement for me. Wives of country doctors catch only fleeting glimpses of their husbands. But I can be busy and happy working, still see my children even though I'm a 'working mother,' and be right on hand when my husband returns at night.

"Although I am probably something of a romantic, I am quite realistic. I draw only the things I know about. Indeed, I am unable to draw any other way. I am always as truthful as I can possibly be. I draw from life whenever possible, and do not invent facts or 'suggest' with a vague line something I am not sure about. In spite of this, my pictures look realistic; they always look like me. However, they are the truth—as I see it—and my attempt to communicate about the things that matter to me."

❄   ❄   ❄

Barbara Cooney was one of the truly great creators of children's picture books in the 20th century. When she wrote her autobiographical sketch for this series, she was at the midpoint of her career; by the time of her death in 2000 she had produced 110 books, 12 of which she wrote as well as illustrated. Her career spanned 60 years—from *Ake and His World*, published in 1940, to *Basket Moon*, published in 1999—and garnered numerous prestigious awards and international fame. Her work was revered not just for the number of books she produced but for the beautiful, loving stories that she created.

She grew up on Long Island but spent her childhood summers with her family visiting her grandmother in Waldoboro, Maine, which would play a significant role in both her books and her life. Her mother, who was herself an artist, encouraged her artistic bent, and art became a lifelong passion. At Smith College Cooney took every course that was available in studio art and art history. When she graduated in 1938, her goal was crystal clear—to be an artist

Courtesy of Douglas Merriam

and illustrate children's books. One year after graduation her first illustrated book was published, and so was the first book she both wrote and illustrated, *King of Wreck Island*.

Cooney's love for her craft permeated her work, which received immense acclaim. Twice she won the Randolph Caldecott Medal for the most distinguished American picture book—first in 1958 for her own retelling of Chaucer's *Chanticleer and the Fox* with superb, full-color scratchboard illustrations, and second in 1980 for *Ox-Cart Man*, written by New England poet Donald Hall, with distinctive paintings in a primitive, folk-art style. Numerous times a book of hers was cited by the *New York*

Times as one of the Ten Best Illustrated Books of the Year. She was honored with the American Book Award for *Miss Rumphius* and received six major awards for her complete body of work, including the Silver Medallion of the University of Southern Mississippi in 1975 and the Kerlan Award in 1992. She was the United States nominee for the Hans Christian Andersen Medal, which is considered the children's book equivalent of being nominated for a Nobel Prize.

Cooney adopted the simple, folk-primitive look of *Ox-Cart Man* for her signature style. Throughout her career she meticulously researched a myriad of details—from the magpie (a bird of ill omen in medieval times) that perches on a pollarded tree in *Chanticleer* to Eleanor Roosevelt's embroidered baptismal gown in *Eleanor*. She once said: "My goal is to make the past come alive for children, to let them see it as it was, full of color and activity, and not as the static black-and-white photographs [with] which history books portray it." Whether she was illustrating a definite historical period, a classic children's story such as *Little Women* or *Bambi*, a fairy tale from the Brothers Grimm, a myth from Homer, or one of her many Christmas-themed books, her attention to detail and accuracy was always impeccable.

Cooney's later books exemplified the strong sense of place that she developed as her children grew older and she was able to travel to research such books as *The Little Juggler*, a legend from France, and *Mother Goose in French* and *Mother Goose in Spanish*. But eventually she settled in the place she loved the best, the coast of Maine. She built a house in Damariscotta and began the work for which she would be best remembered. Her first book in the Maine house was *Ox-Cart Man*. And then she created *Miss Rumphius*, based on a real woman who was known locally as Hilda the Lupine Lady. Cooney often called Miss Rumphius her favorite character and her alter ego; she herself became known as the Lupine Lady after the book was published. In 1989 the Maine Library Association created the Lupine Award with this book in mind, to honor outstanding children's books by Maine residents or authors of books about Maine. Cooney deemed the trio of *Miss Rumphius*, *Island Boy*, and *Hattie and the Wild Waves* "as near as I ever will come to an autobiography." In December of 1997 she made her love for Maine and for books tangible with the announcement that she was giving a Christmas present of nearly a million dollars to renovate the public library in her hometown of Damariscotta. In addition, she organized an auction of original art from children's picture books, donated by prominent illustrators, for the benefit of the town library.

In 1996 Barbara Cooney was designated an "official state treasure of Maine." She died in March of 2000, a few months before her 83rd birthday, and fans all over the world mourned the passing of this gracious woman who had enriched the field of chil-

> "My goal is to make the past come alive for children, to let them see it as it was, full of color and activity, and not as the static black-and-white photographs [with] which history books portray it."

Courtesy of Viking/PenguinPutnam Books

dren's literature for so many years. Cooney always adhered to the words of her favorite character, Miss Rumphius, who said: "You must do something to make the world more beautiful." Her great legacy is that her books for children will continue to do just that.

SELECTED WORKS WRITTEN AND ILLUSTRATED: *King of Wreck Island*, 1940; *The Kellyhorns*, 1942; *Chanticleer and the Fox*, adapt. from Chaucer, 1958; *The Little Juggler: Adapted from an Old French Legend*, 1961, reissued 1982; *A Little Prayer*, 1967; *Christmas*, 1968; *A Garland of Games and Other Diversions: An Alphabet Book*, 1969; *Little Brother and Little Sister*, 1982; *Miss Rumphius*, 1982; *Island Boy*, 1988; *Hattie and the Wild Waves: A Story of Brooklyn*, 1990; *Eleanor*, 1996.

SELECTED WORKS ILLUSTRATED: *Ake and His World*, by Bertil Malmberg, 1940; *Uncle Snowball*, by Frances M. Frost, 1940; *Shooting Star Farm*, by Anne Molloy, 1946; *The Rocky Summer*, by Lee Kingman, 1948; *American Folk Songs for Children in Home, School, and Nursery School*, by Ruth Crawford Seeger, 1948, 1993; *Kildee House*, by Rutherford Montgomery, 1949, 1994; *The Best Christmas*, by Lee Kingman, 1949, 1985; *The Man Who Didn't Wash His Dishes*, by Phyllis Krasilovsky, 1950, 1992; *Animal Folk Songs for Children*, by Ruth Crawford Seeger, 1950; *Hill Ranch*, by Rutherford Montgomery, 1951; *Quarry Adventure*, by Lee Kingman, 1951 (publ. in England as *Lauri's Surprising Summer*, 1957); *The Pony That Kept a Secret*, by Elisabeth Lansing, 1952; *Too Many Pets*, by Mary M. Aldrich, 1952;

Courtesy of Viking/PenguinPutnam Books

Where Have You Been?, by Margaret Wise Brown, 1952, 1966; *Christmas in the Barn*, by Margaret Wise Brown, 1952; *Let's Keep Christmas*, by Catherine Marshall, 1953; *American Folk Songs for Christmas*, by Ruth Crawford Seeger, 1953; *Peter's Long Walk*, by Lee Kingman, 1953; *A Pony Worth His Salt*, by Elisabeth C. Lansing, 1953; *The Little Fir Tree*, by Margaret Wise Brown, 1954; *The Five Little Peppers*, by Margaret Sidney, 1954; *Little Women*, by Louisa May Alcott, 1955; *Away We Go! One-Hundred Poems for the Very Young*, by Catherine S. McEwen, comp., 1956; *Friends with God: Stories and Prayers of the Marshall Family*, by Catherine Marshall, 1956; *City Springtime*, by Helen Kay, 1957; *Freckle Face*, by Neil Anderson, 1957; *Timmy's Search*, by Harry Behn, 1958; *Seasonal Verses Gathered by Elizabeth George Speare from the Connecticut Almanack for the Year of the Christian Era, 1773*, by Elizabeth George Speare, 1959; *The American Speller: An Adaptation of Noah Webster's Blue-Backed Speller*, 1961; *Peacock Pie: A Book of Rhymes*, by Walter de la Mare, 1961; *Le Hibou et la Poussiquette (The Owl and the Pussycat)*, by Edward Lear, trans. by Francis Steegmuller, 1962; *A White Heron: A Story of Maine*, by Sarah Orne Jewett, 1963; *Favorite Fairy Tales Told in Spain*, by Virginia Haviland, 1963; *Snow-White and Rose-Red*, by Jacob and Wilhelm Grimm, 1964; *Papillot, Clignot, et Dodo (Wynken, Blynken, and Nod)*, by Eugene Field, trans. by Francis Steegmuller and Norbert Guterman, 1964; *Mother Goose in French*, trans. by Hugh Latham, 1964; *Shaun and* the Boat: An Irish Story, by Anne Molloy, 1965; Katie's Magic Glasses, by Jane Goodsell, 1965; The Crows of Pearblossom, by Aldous Huxley, 1967; Mother Goose in Spanish, trans. by Alastair Reid and Anthony Kerrigan, 1968; The Owl and the Pussy-Cat, by Edward Lear, 1969; Christmas Folk, by Natalia Belting, 1969; Wynken, Blynken, and Nod, by Eugene Field, 1970; The Lazy Young Duke of Dundee, by William Wise, 1970; Dionysus and the Pirates, trans. by Penelope Proddow, 1970; Bambi: A Life in the Woods, by Felix Salten, 1970; Demeter and Persephone, trans. by Penelope Proddow, 1972; Seven Little Rabbits, by John Becker, 1973; Down to the Beach, by May Garelick, 1973; Squawk to the Moon, Little Goose, by Edna Preston, 1974; When the Sky Is Like Lace, by Elinor L. Horwitz, 1975; The Sad Story of the Little Bluebird and the Hungry Cat, by Edna Preston, 1975; Lexington and Concord, 1775: What Really Happened, by Jean Poindexter Colby, 1975; Burton and Dudley, by Marjorie Weinman Sharmat, 1975; The Donkey Prince, by the Brothers Grimm, adapt. by M. Jean Craig, 1977; Midsummer Magic: A Garland of Stories, Charms, and Recipes, comp. by Ellin Greene, 1977; Ox-Cart Man, by Donald Hall, 1979; "I Am Cherry Alive," the Little Girl Sang, by Delmore Schwartz, 1979; How the Hibernators Came to Bethlehem, by Norma Farber, 1980; Emma, by Wendy Ann Kesselman, 1980; Tortillitas para Mama and Other Nursery Rhymes: Spanish and English, sel. and trans. by Margot C. Griego, et. al., 1982; Spirit Child: A Story of the Nativity, trans. from the Aztec by John Bierhorst, 1984; Peter and the Wolf, by Sergei Prokofiev, 1985; The Story of Holly and Ivy, by Rumer Godden, 1985; Louhi, Witch of North Farm, by Toni de Gerez, 1986; The Year of the Perfect Christmas Tree, by Gloria Houston, 1988; Roxaboxen, by Alice McLerran, 1991; Snow-White and Rose-Red, by the Brothers Grimm, 1991; Emily, by Michael Bedard, 1992; Letting Swift River Go, by Jane Yolen, 1992; The Remarkable Christmas of the Cobbler's Sons, by Ruth Sawyer, 1994; Only Opal: The Diary of a Young Girl, by Opal Whiteley, sel. and adapt. by Jane Boulton, 1994; Basket Moon, by Mary Lyn Ray, 1999.

SUGGESTED READING: Children's Literature Review, vol. 23, 1991; Cummins, Julie, ed. Children's Book Illustration and Design, vol. 1, 1992; Silvey, Anita, ed. Children's Books and Their Creators, 1995; Something About the Author, vol. 96, 1998; vol. 123, 2001 (obituary). Periodicals—Cooney, Barbara, "Caldecott Medal Acceptance," The Horn Book, August 1959, August 1980; Hale, Robert D., "Interview with Barbara Cooney," The Horn Book, January/February 1994; Walton, Julie Yates, "Portrait of a First Lady to Be," Publishers Weekly, October 14, 1996. Online—www.lib.uconn.edu/about/exhibits/cooney/cnystment.htm.

Courtesy of WormWorks.com and WormWorks.co.uk
Photo © Neil Turner

Helen Cooper

May 19, 1963–

"I was born in London, and when I was two, we moved to a strange place where we collected the milk in a can from the farm, and bears lived inside cupboards under the stairs, and fairies lurked in the wildflowers outside. I liked Cumbria pretty well, although it rained a lot and there weren't enough kids to play with. There were compensations. Beautiful countryside, ponies, and lots of time to write stories, draw pictures, play the piano, and read. I've been writing stories, and illustrating them, almost as long as I can remember.

"One of my earliest efforts starred a sweet-shop owner, who married a teddy and had a koala bear instead of a human baby. We did write stories at school too, but my best memories there are of nature projects, and colouring in the outline of Jesus's kind hands, in pink and purple felt pen on graph paper. It was a time when kids were given only a sensible amount of schoolwork and homework, so there was plenty of spare time for hobbies. Just as well, because I've ended up making a living from drawing pictures and writing stories, playing the piano, and reading.

"I trained as a music teacher, then I played in a band, and got a day job painting posh china animals to make ends meet. In the evenings I taught myself to illustrate, using books I found in the wonderful local library. After I had been working hard at illustration for two years, *Kit and the Magic Kite* was published in 1987. Since then I've illustrated about another 16 picture books. I wrote most of them. I've also written a longer story called *Sandmare* for newly confident readers.

"My stories are often based on events that were desperately important to me when I was young. I try to design very sympathetic characters that young children can use as tools for expressing themselves, and a major part of the story takes place within the illustrations. However, picture books have such a mixed audience, from young children, their parents and grandparents (with older siblings listening in), to the teenage baby sitter and the adult collector. I'd love to think I've included something for everyone.

"Although I write my texts pretty quickly, my illustration process is fairly involved and painfully slow at times. I always end up working very long hours and it's a huge relief when I finish a book. I am sometimes sad to be saying goodbye to the characters, though. Actually there are a group of characters who wouldn't go away. I've had to write them another story, which is just about to be published, titled *A Pipkin of Pepper*.

"Now I live in Oxford with my husband, Ted Dewan. He also writes and illustrates picture books. Ted is American (we met at a party after he had moved to London), so we go to New England every fall to visit his family but also to visit the colours and the pumpkin piles, and the crazy golf, and the roadside graphics, which I put in many of my pictures. We have a small daughter called Pandora who was born in 1998; in fact, her date of birth can be found on the license plate of the bus in my book *Tatty-Ratty*. When she gives me time I still write stories, draw pictures, play the piano, and read. I hope I never have to stop."

☼ ☼ ☼

Unable to find a college that offered specialized courses in children's illustration, Helen Cooper learned her craft by studying books and talking to librarians about what they believed made good picture books. Her first book, *Kit and the Magic Kite*, featured an adventurous cat that was based on Tigger, a ginger and white cat she once owned. Another very independent cat is featured in *The House Cat*, which was selected for the Washington State Children's Choice Picture Book Award. *Little Monster Did It!*, an American Booksellers Association Pick of the Lists, tackles the issues of sibling rivalry. In *The Baby Who Wouldn't Go to Bed*, which won the Kate Greenaway Medal in 1996, a baby unwilling to go to bed is coaxed to sleep by a few friends, none of whom can play with him because they're on their way to bed and all of whom ultimately resemble the stuffed animals with which his mother finally tucks him to sleep. This book was published in the United States as *The Boy Who Wouldn't Go to Bed*.

The Bear under the Stairs, which won the Smarties Young Judges Prize, was based on an imaginary lion that Cooper herself believed lived in the cupboard under the stairs of her childhood home. He was so real to her that she fed him scraps of food and came to fear him as he grew. The spoiled food eventually was found by her mother, who helped Cooper clean away both the food and her fears. In the book, the lion becomes a bear and Cooper a little boy. "I wrote the book to persuade children that it's better not to keep fears bottled away," Cooper has said. "Fears usually stop being so real once you tell someone, and sooner or later they go away." In *Tatty-Ratty*, which was an IRA/CBC Children's Choice selection, a child's worry over the loss of her stuffed rabbit is softened by all the adventures she imagines he's having, including the adventure of how he'll find his way home to her.

In *Pumpkin Soup*, for which she won a second Kate Greenaway Medal, Cooper shows her animal characters weathering the changes and conflicts that friends must often face. In her acceptance speech for this award, the author/artist stated succinct-

"My stories are often based on events that were desperately important to me when I was young."

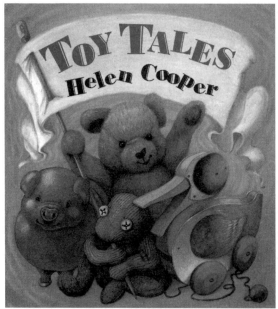

Courtesy of Farrar, Straus, Giroux

ly her beliefs about the importance of picture books: "Like a first-rate family film, picture books can be high-quality entertainment for all ages. And though they are educational, they're not just training wheels. They're visual poetry. An art form in their own right."

Helen Cooper's longer story, *Sandmare*, was illustrated by her husband, Ted Dewan. They live in Oxford, England, with their daughter, Pandora.

SELECTED WORKS WRITTEN AND ILLUSTRATED (Dates are for U.K. publication; U.S. publication dates, if different, are shown in parentheses): *Kit and the Magic Kite*, 1987; *Ella and the Rabbit*, 1990; *The House Cat*, 1993; *The Bear Under the Stairs*, 1993; *The Tale of a Bear*, 1995; *The Tale of a Duck*, 1995; *The Tale of a Frog*, 1995; *The Tale of a Pig*, 1995 (the previous four titles published in one volume as *Toy Tales*; 2000); *Little Monster Did It!*, 1996; *The Baby Who Wouldn't Go to Bed*, 1996 (*The Boy Who Wouldn't Go to Bed*, 1997); *Pumpkin Soup*, 1998 (1999); *Tatty Ratty* (*Tatty-Ratty*), 2002; *A Pipkin of Pepper*, 2004 (2005).

SELECTED WORKS ILLUSTRATED: *Solomon's Secret*, by Saviour Pirotta, 1989; *The Owl and the Pussycat*, by Edward Lear, 1991; *Christmas Stories for the Very Young*, ed. by Sally Grindley, 1998.

SELECTED WORKS WRITTEN: *Sandmare*, illus. by Ted Dewan, 2001 (2003).

SUGGESTED READING: *Something About the Author*, vol. 102, 1999. Periodicals—Bates, Sue, "Helen Cooper," *Carousel*, Winter 1997; Brennan, Geraldine, "Drawing on Memories of Vegas," *Times Educational Supplement*, January 31, 1997; Doonan, Jane, "Analysing a Picture Book," *Books for Keeps*, May 1994.

WEB SITE: *www.wormworks.com/*

Audrey Couloumbis

August 9, 1947–

"I remember learning to read *Run, Spot, Run* and *Dick and Jane*, and I remember wondering why this was important. Two or three years later, I read *Hans Brinker and the Silver Skates* when I had the measles and realized this was the answer to that question about *Dick and Jane*. I never made a decision to be a writer. Long before *Dick and Jane*, I told myself stories, and then told them to other people (this was generally called lying) and finally, when I was 12, it occurred to me to write these lies down. That's when I learned I was actually honest to a fault. I got into way more trouble telling the truth.

"I was a bit younger than Willa Jo (in *Getting Near to Baby*) when one of my aunts lost a child. A year later, my cousin and I woke to see our aunt striking out across a field. We wondered why she went off alone. We followed her to a ramshackle covered bridge. She climbed up, and we clambered up behind her. Whatever our aunt had in mind, she forgot about it in her concern that we would fall through because the roof was so thin in some places. We didn't get down, though—any of us. We sat and talked until our foreheads were sunburned—not about the baby who died, but about everything else. When we got home, none of us mentioned where we'd been. I don't think anyone even asked. A year or so later my cousin asked about that morning. My aunt looked bewildered. She either couldn't or wouldn't allow herself to remember anything about that day.

"At about the same time, a small child in a neighboring family died from drinking tainted water. The older women in the family knew this could happen, but the younger ones had no experience with such a danger. The younger women realized it could just as easily have happened to one of their children. These were the memories that sparked the incident around which *Getting Near to Baby* revolves.

"*Say Yes* grew out of something that happened to my husband's Aunt Adrienne a few years ago. Aunt Adrienne was once a beautiful young woman and is now a stunningly attractive old lady. No one who meets her thinks she's older than 70 although she's 92. Her hair is lovely, her nails are perfectly manicured. She still lives alone and takes the subway to shop for craft supplies, to do her banking, and to go to doctors' appointments. She's been hand-knitting a dress in very fine dark green yarn since the 1940s. She thinks she might need a new dress one of these days, and she doesn't find anything she likes in the stores anymore. The skirt could easily be used as a tablecloth. She makes ornate beaded Christmas stockings for everyone in the family, and she's working well into the next two generations now.

Courtesy of Neil Davidson

"Aunt Adrienne was robbed and she didn't tell anyone for several weeks. When she finally did tell about it, she told it to one person at a time, like it was a terrible secret. Her concerns were much like Martha Clark's in *Say Yes*. I began wondering what would make a child do this. But I didn't think about writing it until I accompanied Aunt Adrienne to the hospital for an X ray. While we sat in the cafeteria I noticed one of her fingernails had broken. I garden and nice-looking nails have never been my priority, but they've always been very important to her. She said she broke it scooting across the X-ray table and she said it in such an unconcerned way that it surprised me. I realized that Aunt Adrienne had changed in some vital way—and I began to write.

"People like to ask what I was doing when I found out that *Getting Near to Baby* was accepted for publication. After 15 years of writing and mailing out stories, of getting rejections, my reaction surprised me more than anyone else. I had just come in the door after being away all day and picked up the phone to hear the news from my agent. I was not thrilled. I felt like I was in terrible trouble, like when my mother found the stories I'd written and hidden under my mattress. It took me about three hours to get used to the idea that someone had found my story and I wasn't in trouble.

"Now it feels like I've come home."

Courtesy of PenguinPutnam Books

Born and raised in and around Springfield, Illinois, Audrey Couloumbis's early childhood was nearly idyllic, even though her parents divorced when she was two years old. Her mother remarried and her father left Illinois to work as an electrician for traveling shows such as Holiday on Ice. She made several trips to see him in such places as Paris, Brazil, Hawaii, Germany, Czechoslovakia, Italy, and Switzerland. Things changed for her when her stepfather became ill about the time she was entering junior high school. She lost interest in school, withdrew from her friends, and had a couple of long, hard years before she went to live with her father and his family in New York City when she was fourteen.

Audrey's love of reading began early, and she remembers how she enjoyed *The Five Little Peppers and How They Grew*. She didn't really see a picture book until a friend gave her Roger Duvoisin's *Petunia*. Unfortunately, the edition was in German and she couldn't read much of it, but she loved the pictures. The same friend gave her a copy of *Eloise*, written by Kay Thompson and illustrated by Hilary Knight. She could identify with Eloise and her life in the Plaza after all the time she had spent alone when she visited her father in exotic places. She, like Eloise, would wander the halls, making friends with the other hotel guests.

Audrey Couloumbis met her husband, Akila, when she flagged down a taxi in Brooklyn one day. The driver had his off-duty light on but agreed to take her to her address because it was only a few blocks from where his mother lived. Traffic was slow, which put the driver in a very bad mood; however, his mood lightened when the two began talking. Soon they had made a date to feed squirrels in the park, and they were married a year later. They've shared a long life together and have two grown children. Akila is an actor and director and has become the first reader of everything his wife writes. They share their home in upstate New York with a poodle named Phoebe. Phoebe and an ice cream soda were the two big treats Couloumbis indulged in when she received her first advance check for a manuscript.

Couloumbis's first published book, *Getting Near to Baby*, was named a Newbery Honor Book, an ALA Notable Children's Book, and a *School Library Journal* Best Book of the Year—a remarkable achievement for a first-time author. One of her main hobbies today is studying picture books.

SELECTED WORKS: *Getting Near to Baby*, 1999; *Say Yes*, 2002.

SUGGESTED READING: Sager, Jean, "South Fallsburg Resident: A Top Children's Author," *Sullivan County Democrat*, August 13, 2002. Online—*www.kidsreads.com/authors/au-couloumbis-audrey.asp*.

Joy Cowley
August 7, 1936–

"I was the eldest of five children, a slow learner who didn't read until she was nine. There were a number of reasons for this: family illness, poverty, changes in schools, and an archaic system of teaching that presented fragments of language without meaning. I must have absorbed some skills, but defeat was so entrenched that I was unwilling to try any challenge that could result in failure.

"Breakthrough came with the picture book *The Story of Ping*, by Margery Flack and Kurt Wiese. As I entered the story, I forgot that I was a 'bad reader.' I became a little duck lost on the Yangtze River, and when I came to the last page, I couldn't bear the adventure to finish. I turned the pages back and started again, and made an amazing discovery. The story was exactly the same with the second reading. Until then my experience had been of oral stories that tended to change with each telling. I had discovered the constancy of print.

"It seemed to me that I became, instantly, an avid reader. I know that wasn't so. No doubt I still struggled with letters, sounds, and word shapes. The change was in attitude. I had discovered that reading accessed story and that story empowered me. By the time I was 12, I was reading every book I could get, and those stories were overflowing, barely disguised, into my own writing.

"Twenty years later I was selling short stories, had published a couple of novels for adults, and was raising four children. Three of these youngsters took to reading like monkeys to a tree, but one son, Edward, was a slow beginner. His problems were different from mine. He was a left-brained learner who didn't relate to fiction, and he was sandwiched between sisters who had started to read before they were five. Edward was good at other things. He was not going to compete, and intervention was necessary. With his teacher's help, I wrote stories for him, for other children in his class, and then for neighbouring schools. Before long I was writing easy-to-read material for the publications of the New Zealand Education Department, and then, in 1978–1980, with editor June Melser, I wrote the Story Box Reading Programme, and writing for adults took a permanent back seat.

"The more I work with reluctant readers, the more I learn about their specific needs for affirmation, entertainment, and humour in their books. Adults don't read dull and meaningless material by choice, so why do we inflict that on children? Language skills are important, but they should be contained within the context of meaning, a story that gives a child pleasure.

"I have no doubt that the little girl who was told she was stupid is the source of my passion. I also write for children who are fluent readers—picture books, middle grade, and some Young Adult fiction—but my chief concern is the child with a frozen attitude to reading, the little one who is yet to discover that books are doorways to new worlds where he or she is the all-powerful ruler."

Courtesy of Terry Coles

❋　❋　❋

Born Cassia Joy Summers on a chicken farm in Levin, New Zealand, Joy Cowley nurtured her creativity in childhood after overcoming an early difficulty with reading. From the time she was 11, she had poems, stories, and drawings published on the children's page of the *Wellington Southern Cross* newspaper. Attending Girls' High School in Palmerston North, Wellington, she worked at an after-school job editing the children's page of the *Manawatu Daily Times*. When she left school she was offered a job as reporter for the same paper, but her parents felt the job was not the right environment for their daughter and found her employment as apprentice to a pharmacist. Though this job did not feed her creativity, she has said that it taught her a discipline that would help her writing later on.

BY JOY COWLEY · PHOTOGRAPHS BY NIC BISHOP

Courtesy of Scholastic Press

In 1956 Joy married Ted Cowley, a dairy farmer, and had four children in nearly as many years. Joining a writers' group helped her reclaim her love of writing, which had become dormant, and gave her the impetus to produce her own work. In the mid-1960s two of her short stories were published in *Short Story International*, a collection that came to the attention of Anne Hutchens, an editor in America. Hutchens encouraged her to write adult novels and published a number of those novels in the 1960s and 1970s. The Cowleys were divorced in 1968, but Joy's writing career was launched. In 1970 she married Malcolm Mason, a Wellington writer and accountant, who died in 1985. Since 1989, she has been married happily to Terry Coles; they live in Marlborough Sands in the northern end of the South Island of New Zealand.

A prolific writer of age-based developmental reading materials and programs for schools, Joy Cowley has enjoyed international fame for creating story-based reading programs, much more interesting than the sound-based reading materials that had discouraged her own early reading. The emphasis is on enjoyment and developing readers through interest in story. Joy also writes a variety of trade books that have had great success at home and abroad. She has twice won the New Zealand Children's Book of the Year award, for *The Silent One* and *Bow Down Shadrach*. Lifetime achievement awards in her native country include the Margaret Mahy Lecture Award and the New Zealand Commemoration Medal. In 1992 she was awarded the Order of the British Empire for services to children's literature, and in 1993 received an honorary degree from Massey University.

In the United States, Joy Cowley's books have also met with success. *Gracias: The Thanksgiving Turkey* was named a Notable Trade Book in the Field of Social Studies. *Agapanthus Hum and the Eyeglasses*, a story based on her own daughter Judith's mishaps wearing glasses while she "rushed at life with a song and a somersault," was named a *Publishers Weekly* Best Book. *Red-Eyed Tree Frog*, an evocative nonfiction picture book with stunning photographs by Nic Bishop, was named an Outstanding Science Trade Book, a *Horn Book* Fanfare title, an ALA Notable Children's Book, and the winner of the *Boston Globe–Horn Book* Award in the picture book category. A writer of prodigious energy, warmth, and humor, Joy Cowley has given great encouragement to younger authors and enjoys her life today surrounded by natural beauty, an assortment of animals, and visits from her 13 grandchildren.

SELECTED WORKS: *The Silent One*, illus. by Charles Robinson, 1980; *The Magician's Lunch*, illus. by Murray Grimsdale, 1989; *Bow Down Shadrach*, 1990; *The Mouse Bride*, illus. by David Christiana, 1995; *Singing Down the Rain*, illus. by Jan Spivey Gilchrist, 1997; *Big Moon Tortilla*, illus. by Dyanne Strongbow, 1998; *Agapanthus Hum and the Eyeglasses*, illus. by Jennifer Plecas, 1999; *The Rusty, Trusty Tractor*, illus. by Olivier Dunrea, 1999; *Red-Eyed Tree Frog*, photos by Nic Bishop, 1999; *Mrs. Wishy-Washy*, illus. by Elizabeth Fuller, 1999; *Nicketty-Nacketty Noo-Noo-Noo*, illus. by Tracey Moroney, 1999; *Gracias: The Thanksgiving Turkey*, illus. by Joe Cepeda, 1999; *The Video Shop Sparrow*, illus. by Gavin Bishop, 1999; *Starbright and the Dream Eater*, 2000; *Agapanthus Hum and Major Bark*, illus. by Jennifer Plecas, 2001; *Mrs. Goodstory*, illus. by Erica Dornbusch, 2001; *Weta: A Knight in Shining Armour*, photos by Rod Morris, 2002; *Mrs. Wishy-Washy Makes a Splash!*, illus. by Elizabeth Fuller, 2003; *Mrs. Wishy-Washy's Farm*, illus. by Elizabeth Fuller, 2003; *Agapanthus Hum and the Angel Hoot*, illus. by Jennifer Plecas, 2003; *Where Horses Run Free: A Dream for the American Mustang*, illus. by Layne Johnson, 2003; *The Wishing of Biddy Malone*, illus. by Christopher Denise, 2004; *Hunter*, 2004.

SELECTED WORKS FOR ADULTS: *Nest in a Falling Tree*, 1967; *Man of Straw*, 1970; *Of Men and Angels*, 1972; *Mandrake Root*, 1975; *The Growing Season*, 1978; *Classical Music*, 1999; *Holy Days*, 2001.

SUGGESTED READING: *Contemporary Authors*, New Revision Series, vol. 57, 1997; *Something About the Author*, vol. 90, 1997; *Something About the Author Autobiography Series*, vol. 26, 1998.

WEB SITE: *www.joycowley.com*

"I was born in Japan, a place where most Westerners still seem to think you are exposed to nothing but traditional Japanese or Chinese painting. On the contrary, I grew up almost exclusively exposed to Western art through my grandfather's collection of art books. They, of course, included Japanese art too, but I was very familiar with all of the Italian, French, and Flemish masters, as well as the illustrations of N. C. Wyeth, Maxfield Parrish, and others.

"Most of all I loved stories of any kind. I grew up with comic books (*manga*), which these days are known as graphic novels. My favorites were horror stories, which I still love, and I couldn't get enough of them even while still a small child. Sometimes I got so scared, I was even afraid to go to the bathroom, which in my home was in a separate part of the house. I also begged every adult who would listen to tell me stories. When I was a kid, whenever the electricity went out our father read stories to all of us by lamplight, including *Kwaidan*, a collection of Japanese ghost stories recorded by Lafcadio Hearn. However, more than any of the other stories, Homer's *Iliad* and *Odyssey* had the most profound influence on me. I was an insatiable reader as a child and read them over and over again. Those stories, all thanks to Homer, planted seeds in me that have led to almost everything else since.

Courtesy of Mahlon F. Craft

Kinuko Y. Craft

January 3, 1940–

"I have been drawing ever since my earliest memories. I am sure people encouraged me, including my grandfather, but I would have drawn whether anyone encouraged me or not. From the time I was a little child, light and color always fascinated me. I drew on any available surface, and when I was scolded for it, stole my sister's Cray-Pas when they took mine away. My parents gave me paint, paper, and canvas, and the opportunity to pursue what I loved, but beyond that they neither encouraged or discouraged me.

"From the top of the mountain behind my home, you could see the ocean, many miles away. One day when I was still a very little child, a friend of my grandfather's who lived with us took me up to the top and there we saw a water spout out on the sea. When I asked her what it was, she told me it was a dragon that had come down to drink the water. I only half believed her, but it was a beautiful way of describing what I saw. Looking back on that, and many other events of my childhood, it was like living in a fairy tale. In many ways as an adult I am still living in that fairy tale, and now, through my paintings, I am telling stories of my own."

❀ ❀ ❀

It will come as no surprise to admirers of Kinuko Craft's richly detailed, mystical illustrations that she was steeped in folklore and mythology as a child. Kinuko Craft has drawn on her memories of Japanese traditional tales and Greek mythology, as well as a deep knowledge of art history and her own imagination, to create the finely detailed and sumptuous illustrations in her versions of fairy tales and myths, such as *Cinderella* and *King Midas and the Golden Touch*.

Born Kinuko Yamabe, she received her bachelor of fine arts degree in 1962 from the Kanazawa Municipal College of Fine and Industrial Art (known in Japan as the Kanazawa Bidai). She then moved to the United States to study at the school of the Art Institute of Chicago, where she met her husband, Mahlon Craft. They were both students at the Institute's school in 1964. Mahlon was born and raised in Cincinnati, Ohio, and is a graduate of the Art Academy of Cincinnati. During their early years together, the Crafts lived in Chicago, where Mahlon served as art director for various companies and Kinuko worked in art studios. By the early 1970s, however, Kinuko had established a highly successful freelance career in commercial illustration and Mahlon was concentrating on the field of photography. Much of Kinuko's early work was done for the editorial and advertising markets and appeared in prestigious journals, newspapers, and corporate publications; other venues included greeting cards and posters. While still in Chicago, she began illustrating children's books for the Follett company.

In 1983 Kinuko had a one-woman show at the Society of Illustrators in New York. That same year the Crafts relocated to Norfolk, a small town in northwest Connecticut where they live and work today. They have one daughter, M. Charlotte Craft, who has written two of the folktale adaptations that Kinuko has illustrated. Recently Mahlon has become involved in the writing as well as the design of Kinuko's books. He created the text for her *Sleeping Beauty* and wrote an original story, *Christmas Moon*. Kinuko's special technique of painting in oils over a watercolor base imparts a luminous look to the many fairy tale retellings she has illustrated and adds richness and depth to the old stories, bringing them vividly to life.

In the course of her career, Kinuko Craft has won over 100 graphic arts awards, including five gold medals from the Society of Illustrators. In addition to picture books for children, she has designed book jackets for a wide variety of authors, from William Shakespeare to Stephen King, Isabel Allende, and Patricia McKillip. Her paintings have been featured in many museum exhibits and are in the permanent collections of the National Geographic Society, the Museum of American Illustration, and a number of corporations, among them Time Incorporated.

SELECTED WORKS WRITTEN AND ILLUSTRATED: *Cinderella*, retold by Kinuko Y. Craft, 2000.

"Looking back on that, and many other events of my childhood, it was like living in a fairy tale."

SELECTED WORKS ILLUSTRATED: *Gingerbread Children: Poems*, by Ilo Orleans, 1973; *Come Play with Me*, by Margaret Hillert, 1975; *Bear, Wolf, and Mouse*, by Jan Wahl, 1975; *Mother Goose ABC*, 1977; *The Cookie House*, by Margaret Hillert, 1978; *What Is It?*, by Margaret Hillert, 1978; *Treasure Island*, by Robert Louis Stevenson, adapted by June Edwards, 1980; *Bailey's Window*, by Anne Lindbergh, 1984; *Journey to Japan*, by Joan Knight, 1986; *The Twelve Dancing Princesses*, retold by Marianna Mayer, 1989; *Baba Yaga and Vasilisa the Brave*, retold by Marianna Mayer, 1994; *Cupid and Psyche*, retold by M. Charlotte Craft, 1996; *Pegasus*, retold by Marianna Mayer, 1998; *King Midas and the Golden Touch*, retold by Charlotte Craft, 1999; *The Adventures of Tom Thumb*, by Marianna Mayer, 2001; *Sleeping Beauty*, retold by Mahlon F. Craft, 2002.

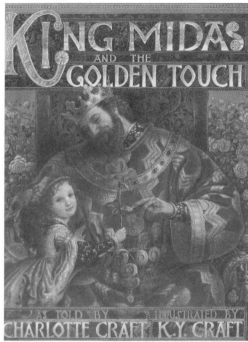

Courtesy of HarperCollins Children's Books

SUGGESTED READING: "Art and (Kinuko Y.) Craft," *Locus*, August 2002. Online— Darnel, Marisa, "Artist Interviews," *www.artistinterviews.com/art/kinukoycraft.html*, 2003; *www. duirwaighgallery.com*.

WEB SITE: *www.kycraft.com*

Nina Crews
May 19, 1963–

"Recently, a fourth grader asked me what my favorite subject had been in school. Without thinking I said art and English. Just as soon as I'd said it, I realized that I had managed to have a career that involved some of the very things that I loved most as a child.

"I was raised in a creative environment, by parents who were designers and authors/artists of picture books. I grew up in New York City and live there now. I love living in the city. As a child, our family would go exploring—regularly leaving our neighborhood streets and playgrounds to go uptown or downtown to take advantage of other parks, zoos, museums, restaurants, or to just look around somewhere new. I still explore the city. I have a younger sister and we are still very close. As kids, we shared a room, bunk beds, an AM radio, some toys, and a painting easel. Art materials were always accessible, because my parents' studio was in our house, and art projects were regular family activities. We had books of all kinds, and I don't recall ever being told that any were off-limits. My parents also had a large number of books about artists, which I would flip through for hours.

"I always felt that art would be a part of whatever career I chose, but I didn't originally consider children's books. Photography had become my favorite medium while I was in college, and I continued photographing in New York after moving back to the city, concentrating on personal projects. Even then I was interested in how photographs could tell stories and how a series of images might express that better. I worked animation production and found myself cutting, pasting, and collaging. Soon I was bringing collage techniques into my personal work and creating photo collages for editorial clients. Collage allowed me to use photography more playfully and became central to the look of my first picture books. By the time I had a portfolio meeting with Greenwillow Books just before writing *One Hot Summer Day*,

Courtesy of Amy Crews

I had a clear sense of how I might do a picture book and a strong desire to tell a story in images. Writing the story was a bit intimidating, as writing was a private pastime at that point. Creating a publishable story was thrilling.

"I chose to make photographic books because photography was and is my favorite medium to work in. As I've read my work to children, I have found that they respond enthusiastically to 'real' pictures. They love to hear about the children who pose for the books—their names, ages, and where they live. All of my photographic subjects are family and friends of friends. The books tell my stories but also record these children at certain ages—so they are stars. I write the story first, though most often a visual motivates me to start a book. Once the story is in place, I start to work with my models. The interaction between us always adds something to the project; their performances often generate new ideas. I try to keep the photography session as loose as possible, adding whatever I think might be interesting to the mix as I go along.

"I am always thrilled to learn that someone has copies of my books at home, or to see them on the shelves of libraries. I hope that my books play a small role in inspiring in children now the same love of a good story that I had as a child. Perhaps some may become book authors themselves."

❈ ❈ ❈

A talented creator of children's books in her own right, Nina Crews is the daughter of two well-known author/illustrators, Donald Crews and Ann Jonas. Born in Frankfurt, Germany, where her father was stationed for military service, Crews grew up in the West Village in lower Manhattan surrounded by art. After attending Music and Art High School, she went to Yale University, where she received her B.A. in 1985, majoring in art with an emphasis on photography. She worked as a freelance animation artist/coordinator while developing her photography and illustration portfolio and was a producer at Ink Tank, an animation studio in New York City, from 1995 to 1997.

Nina Crews's first picture book, *One Hot Summer Day*, appeared in 1995 with a combination of photographic collages and text celebrating a young girl's life in the city. Crews has stated that she wanted to express the joy of a child growing up in an urban environment after hearing so many people talk about the problems of city life. Praised for her creative use of photographs to bring out the mood and inner experiences of children, Crews went on to create *I'll Catch the Moon*, a fantasy picture book using a variety of photographs interspersed with pictures from the National Aeronautics and Space Administration (NASA). She has also used photography to illustrate biographical works by writers such as David Adler and Seymour Simon. *One Hot Summer Day*, *I'll Catch the Moon*, and *Snowball* were all named to the CCBC Choices list by the Cooperative Children's Books Center at the University of Wisconsin, Madison.

Courtesy of Greenwillow Books

Nina Crews lives and works in Brooklyn, New York, where she continues to create illustrations for her own stories and for those of other authors that reflect her interest in people, in the city where she grew up, and in the larger world.

SELECTED WORKS WRITTEN AND ILLUSTRATED: *One Hot Summer Day*, 1995; *I'll Catch the Moon*, 1996; *Snowball*, 1997; *You Are Here*, 1998; *A High, Low, Near, Far, Loud, Quiet Story*, 1999; *A Ghost Story*, 2001; *The Neighborhood Mother Goose*, 2004.

SELECTED WORKS ILLUSTRATED: *My Writing Day*, by David A. Adler, 1999; *When Will Sarah Come?*, by Elizabeth Fitzgerald Howard, 1999; *From Paper Airplanes to Outer Space*, by Seymour Simon, 2000; *We, the People*, by Bobbi Katz, 2000.

SUGGESTED READING: *Contemporary Authors*, vol. 163, 2001; *Something About the Author*, vol. 97, 1998.

A profile of Nina Crews's father, Donald Crews, appeared in *Fifth Book of Junior Authors and Illustrators* (1983); her mother, Ann Jonas, was profiled in *Seventh Book of Junior Authors and Illustrators* (1996).

Courtesy of Simon & Schuster Children's Books

Doreen Cronin

March 1966–

"I was born in Queens, New York, and grew up on Long Island with my parents, two brothers, and my younger sister. My father was a police officer in New York and would entertain us for hours with terrifying stories of a rough city (remember . . . we're talking about the 1970s) and hysterical stories about some of the characters he met in his line of work. One of his favorite assignments was working in the anti-crime unit where he would dress in street clothes, ride the subway, and pretend to be crazy. He would occasionally break into this routine at the dinner table and it always kept us in stitches.

"When my father died eight years ago, laughter became a rare commodity. My father passed away a few days before I was supposed to start law school at St. John's University in Jamaica, Queens. I put school off for a semester and continued to do some freelance writing. Late one night shortly after the funeral, I found myself wide awake and crying. I just missed my father so much. I walked over to the computer, sat down, and the story that became *Click, Clack, Moo* just flowed right out of me. The greatest kick of all was that when I finished it, I was laughing, and it felt like my Dad was right there with me. I had been sending out children's book manuscripts for quite a while, and had a box full of rejection letters to prove it. This one felt different; it was more than a story, it was a gift from my father. Today, any day spent reading *Click, Clack, Moo* with a roomful of laughing kids is like a day spent with my dad. An unbelievable gift given to me over and over again. Incidentally, the official publication date for *Click, Clack, Moo* was January 28th, which just happens to be my father's birthday. Enough said.

"The gap between acceptance of the manuscript and publication was a very long one. Long enough for me to graduate from law school, pass the bar, and begin to practice law. I worked at a Manhattan law firm where I practiced commercial and civil litigation. Brutal hours, but for the most part, I spent my time researching and writing, two of my favorite things to do. The attorney/children's book combo was definitely an interesting one and one that both my employer and I took some time getting used to. I remember having to take the morning off from the firm so I could meet up with Betsy Lewin and shoot an interview for Scholastic. Try explaining that to the managing partner. Not exactly billable time. After *Click, Clack, Moo* was featured on National Public Radio with Scott Simon and Daniel Pinkwater, one of the attorneys stopped me in the hallway to tell me what he had heard on *All Things Considered*. Seems he heard a very funny children's book read on the air, written by a Doreen Cronin, who, believe it or not, also happened to be an attorney. Although I hated to rain on his 'what a freaky coincidence' parade, I had to set him straight. 'That's not a coincidence, Jon. That's me.' The conversation ended rather abruptly, which is just as well, since casual conversation is not billable time!

"The firm was actually very supportive, and when Betsy Lewin took home a Caldecott Honor for her amazing illustrations, one of the partners came into my office with a copy of the *New York Times* article and kissed me on the head! See, lawyers aren't as heartless as you think they are! I juggled both careers for about six months, then realized it was time to make a choice. I wanted to accept invitations from school kids who wrote me asking me to come visit them. I wanted to spend more time writing. I wanted to visit bookstores. So I quit my law career and have been visiting, writing, and traveling ever since. By the by, I am still paying off my astronomical student loans, but I met my husband, Andrew, in law school so I think I came out ahead!

"When I am not reading or writing, I am probably out walking my dog or trying to learn how to cook. My husband and I love hiking, kayaking, and ordering pizza (because I am still trying to learn how to cook). We also have eight nieces and nephews who are the most lovable, interesting, and remarkable people I have ever known."

❈ ❈ ❈

"I juggled both careers for about six months, then realized it was time to make a choice."

Doreen Cronin was a journalism major at Penn State University, and much of that straightforward style of writing shows up in her picture book texts. Her understated, tongue-in-cheek humor can be enjoyed by children and adults together, over and over again. After graduating from college in 1988, she worked for Newbridge Communications, editing curriculum-based programs for elementary school teachers. Her boss, Vita Jimenez, also happened to run the Children's Choice book club, which offered parents inexpensive reprints of classic children's books. Given free access to that extensive library and reading through the shelves, Doreen Cronin found her love of children's books growing and developing into a desire to write her own stories.

Click, Clack, Moo took an unusually circuitous route from manuscript to published book, and during that time Doreen finished her law degree at St. John's University in 1998. Once published, though, it didn't take long for her first book, with Betsy Lewin's lively illustrations, to make history. Popularity as well as critical acclaim took *Click, Clack, Moo* from the *New York Times* bestseller list to *School Library Journal's* Best Books of the Year to being named a Caldecott Honor Book and an ALA Notable Children's Book. A second collaboration between Cronin and Lewin featured the same barnyard animals once again gaining

from the creators of CLICK, CLACK, MOO: Cows That Type
Courtesy of Simon & Schuster Books for Young Readers

the upper hand when Farmer Brown takes a vacation, leaving his clueless brother Farmer Bob to keep an eye on the farm. *Giggle, Giggle, Quack* also became a bestseller and a *School Library Journal* Best Book. *Duck for President*, third in the series about the stalwart barnyard crew, appeared in time for the 2004 election year.

Between writing the second and third books about the insurgent farm animals, Doreen published *Diary of a Worm*, with illustrations by cartoonist Harry Bliss. This picture book, a hilariously deadpan chronicle of the daily struggles of a young earthworm, quickly became a bestseller and was named a *School Library Journal* Best Book of 2003.

Doreen Cronin now faces classes of schoolchildren rather than judges and juries, and finds them a more demanding and much more rewarding audience. She lives with her husband, Andrew, in New York City.

SELECTED WORKS: *Click, Clack, Moo: Cows That Type*, illus. by Betsy Lewin, 2000; *Giggle, Giggle, Quack*, illus. by Betsy Lewin, 2002; *Diary of a Worm*, illus. by Harry Bliss, 2003; *Duck for President*, illus. by Betsy Lewin, 2004.

SUGGESTED READING: Odean, Kathleen, "Unanimous Verdict: For These Lawyers, the Decision's in: Kids Are a More Rewarding Audience Than Jurors," *Book*, July/August 2003.

Robert Crowther

May 25, 1948–

"I was born in Leeds in the north of England a long time ago—the same year as Prince Charles and the nationalisation of the British railways. I had few books as a child, but I loved looking at my pop-up *Story of Jesus* and *The Jolly Jump-ups*, a nursery rhyme pop-up. I've always liked drawing; my mother saved all my drawings from when I was three years old, and dad taught me how to trace *The Three Little Pigs* when I was five. My dad was a commercial traveller, so we moved around the north of England quite a bit when I was a boy, eventually settling in Knaresborough. When I was 18, Yorkshire Television Schools asked me to draw a storyboard for *The Three Little Pigs*—Dad's early training came in handy! I think this is where I developed the idea of drawing in black outline for simplicity and then colouring the illustrations afterwards.

"I started my foundations year at Leeds College of Art but was turned down there for the graphics course, so I went to Norwich School of Art in eastern England instead. At Norwich I was taught by John Farman and Graham Percy, and I think that is where my interest in pop-ups grew. I started to work with cardboard in 3-D and low relief and also used other media, including modeling clay and edible materials.

"At the Royal College of Art, I produced my *Most Amazing Hide-and-Seek Alphabet Book* as an art project. I taught myself pop-up mechanics by going into the local bookshop, Harrods, and peering between the pages to see how the mechanics were assembled. Then I'd hurry back to college to experiment with cardboard. My first alphabet book was printed at college in black and white and then hand-coloured, so it looked like a finished book—handy for showing publishers. Some interest was expressed in it at my degree show, but it was not published for another five years. In the meantime, I worked as a freelance designer for Madame Tussaud's, the London Planetarium, Chessington Zoo, and Warwick Castle. Whilst at Madame Tussaud's, I made cookie dough portraits of the Dutch royal family for their Amsterdam exhibition.

"Subsequently, I have designed almost 30 pop-up and lift-the-flap books since 1978. Sometimes I wish I could illustrate a straight book without cardboard additions . . . watch this space!

"These days I work only on books and travel up and down the country in England and in the U.S.A. doing pop-up workshops in schools and libraries. I have two daughters, Vicki and Kate, and three lovely granddaughters, Megan, Caris, and Freya. I live in a small village in Norfolk in eastern England with my American wife, Nancy, and our two cats and a dog. I work in a studio at the bottom of our lovely garden."

Courtesy of Robert Crowther

Robert Crowther

✻ ✻ ✻

Robert Crowther's creative, interactive picture books have proven enormously popular with children and adults alike. From alphabet, counting, and concept books for emerging readers to volumes on inventions, sports, and engineering feats for older children, his work has encompassed many ages beyond the young children who are traditionally considered the prime audience for books of pop-ups, pull tabs, and lift-the-flaps. Crowther has managed to appeal to many ages—including adults—with his intricate details and fine sense of humor and proportion.

Crowther received a diploma in art and design from the Norwich School of Art in 1970 and an M.A. from the Royal College of Art in London in 1973. In addition to his freelance design work, he has taught courses at various times at Oxford Polytechnic, Leicester Polytechnic, Exeter College of Art, and his own college, the Norwich School of Art. His work in children's books received early recognition when he was a runner-up for the Mother Goose Award to the "most exciting newcomer to British children's book illustration." In 2000 his *Deep Down Underground* received Honorable Mention at the Bologna-Ragazzi Awards in Italy. For the 100th anniversary of the modern Olympics, Crowther created his *Pop-Up Olympics: Amazing Facts and Record Breakers*, in which exciting bits of information from the 100-year history of the Games are integrated with movable parts to create a truly interactive learning experience for readers at all levels.

The paper engineering that is at the heart of Robert Crowther's book production often involves over 100 separate parts to a volume. There may be as many as 80 hidden pictures behind the flaps and pull tabs that extend the immediately visible text. The themes he chooses to illustrate are bright, exciting ones—fairs, sporting events, machinery, excavations—sometimes suggested by the children he meets on his visits to schools and libraries. He has said on occasion that his main motivation is to create books that will encourage children to read, and Crowther's bright, inventive books would be hard for anyone to resist.

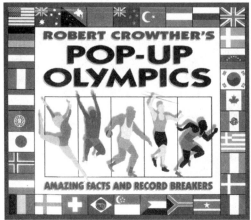

Courtesy of Candlewick Press

SELECTED WORKS WRITTEN AND ILLUSTRATED: *The Most Amazing Hide-and-Seek Alphabet Book*, 1977, 1999; *The Most Amazing Hide-and-Seek Counting Book*, 1981; *Jungle Jumble*, 1982; *The Most Amazing Hide-and-Seek Opposites Book*, 1985; *Pop Goes the Weasel!*, 1987; *Robert Crowther's Pop-Up Machines*, 1988; *How Many Babies on the Farm?*, 1990; *All the Fun of the Fair*, 1992; *Who Lives in the Country?*, 1992; *Who Lives in the Garden?*, 1992; *Animal Rap!: A Noisy Pop-Up Book*, 1993; *Animal Snap!*, 1993; *The Most Amazing Night Book*, 1995; *Robert Crowther's Pop-Up Olympics: Amazing Facts and Record Breakers*, 1996; *Dump Trucks and Diggers*, 1996; *Tractors and Trucks*, 1996; *My Pop-Up Surprise ABC*, 1996; *My Pop-Up Surprise 123*, 1997; *Deep Down Underground: Pop-Up Book of Amazing Facts and Feats*, 1998; *Robert Crowther's Most Amazing Hide-and-Seek Numbers Book*, 1999; *Amazing Pop-Up House of Inventions*, 2000; *Colors*, 2001; *Soccer: Facts & Stats, the World Cup, Superstars*, 2001; *Shapes*, 2002; *Let's Cook!*, 2004.

"Growing up in a small town of 4,000 people, my immediate world was small—until age five, when my mother took me to the public library to get a library card; then the world opened up for me. I made a life-enhancing discovery—books and reading. I loved books from that day on and that love became a passion, one that wound a course through high school, through college and graduate school, and eventually mapped out a career as a children's librarian and a profession as an advocate for library services for young people.

"There were several signs along the way. In high school I worked at the public library where I did almost everything from checking out books with the pencil stamp-dater to simple cataloging, typing 3 x 5 cards on a typewriter with a platen in the carriage to hold the cards in place. In college I devoured the one library science course and wrote witty columns (so I thought) for the college newspaper. After a slight detour via a graduate theater fellowship, I landed in library school. At the time I completed my degree, the field was wide open and I could have had any kind of job anywhere in the country, but my husband was located in Rochester, New York, so Rochester it would be. I was offered any job I wanted in the public library system, and since I had enjoyed making up stories for kids when I was a camp counselor, I chose the position of branch children's librarian. That was the true beginning. A stint on the bookmobile, head of the central children's room, and 11 years as children's services consultant gave me a full range of experience as a children's librarian.

"When I moved to New York City as the coordinator of children's service for the New York Public Library, it was culture shock in many ways—from the size alone, with 85 branch libraries. My 13 years in that position dramatically brought home to me the significance that books and reading play in children's lives. During the annual training of new children's librarians I always told them that what they did on a daily basis can and did make a difference in the lives of children.

"My first children's book was serendipitous. I was interviewing Roxie Munro for the reference book *Children's Books and Their Creators* and suggested that she needed to do a new Inside-Outside book—one on libraries. Her editor was there at the time and she said, 'Yes, let's do it!' And we did, in an unorthodox way for children's books. The three of us collaborated on determining the focus and what kind of libraries should be represent-

Courtesy of Blair Cummins

Julie Cummins

November 15, 1939–

ed; we storyboarded the sequence; and Roxie painted the illustrations first and I wrote the text for them afterward.

"A few years ago another discovery validated a prediction. Remember my small town? I was cleaning out papers and scrapbooks at my mother's house when I found my high school class prophecy. It was a mimeographed, stapled collection of pages (our class was too small to have a printed yearbook) and written as if a group of three classmates were taking a trip 10 years in the future. I kept reading it looking for my name—it didn't appear until the last page when the classmates traveled to New York City where Julia Fulmer was living and writing children's books. Every time I tell this story I get goose bumps, because now it's true."

❊   ❊   ❊

Courtesy of Dutton Children's Books

Born in Mansfield, Ohio, and growing up in nearby Loudonville, Julie Cummins developed a lifelong love of books and reading that carried her to the top of her profession in the field of children's librarianship. After receiving her B.A. degree from Mount Union College in Alliance, Ohio, in 1961, she spent a short time in a theater fellowship program at the University of Wisconsin. Deciding that she needed a more practical career than acting, she entered the Library Science School at Syracuse University, two weeks after marrying her college sweetheart, Blair Cummins. Julie received her M.S.L.S. from Syracuse in 1963, and after starting her career in Rochester, New York, convinced her husband to join her in the library profession; he has now been a library director for many years.

Julie Cummins's experience as a children's librarian and consultant has led her to many related ventures: teaching as an adjunct faculty member at Pratt School of Information and Library Science in New York City and several other colleges in New York State, television appearances to discuss children's books on the WCBS noon news in New York City, reviewing children's books for several journals, and a year as editor-in-chief of *School Library Journal*. She has held many important posts in both the New York Library Association and the American Library Association, served as chair of both the Newbery Award and Caldecott Award committees, and championed children's services as a member of the ALA Executive Board. She is the 2001 winner of the Grolier Award, the ALA's highest honor for lifetime contribution to children's reading, and the 2003 recipient of the Distinguished Service Award of the Association for Library Service to Children, a division of the American Library Association.

Cummins's first book for young readers, *The Inside-Outside Book of Libraries*, was named a *School Library Journal* Best Book of the Year. Her second book, a biography of early aviator Blanche Stuart Scott, grew out of her husband's interest in the history of flying. While accompanying him on a visit to the Glenn H. Curtiss Museum of Early Aviation in Hammondsport, New York, she noticed a reference to a woman aviator in the "Early Birds" display of pre-1916 pilots. She and her husband both put their librarian skills to work in ferreting out information about this interesting woman who was ahead of her time, resulting in Julie writing *Tomboy of the Air*, which was cited as a Notable Social Studies Trade Book for Young People. Julie Cummins's life today is a fine combination of writing, reviewing, consulting, lecturing, and travel. After many years of living in New York City, she and her husband, Blair, now reside in Canandaigua, New York.

SELECTED WORKS: *Children's Book Illustration and Design*, vol. 1, 1992; vol. 2, 1996; *The Inside-Outside Book of Libraries*, illus. by Roxie Munro, 1996; *Tomboy of the Air: Daredevil Pilot Blanche Stuart Scott*, 2001; *Country Kid, City Kid*, illus. by Ted Rand, 2002.

SUGGESTED READING: "A Country/City Hybrid," *American Libraries*, November 2002; Cummins, Julie, "Storyographies: A New Genre?" *School Library Journal*, August 1998; Cummins, Julie, "Taste Trends: A Cookie Lover's Assortment of Picture Book Art," *School Library Journal*, September 1996; Engberg, Gillian, "Julie Cummins' Country Kid, City Kid," *Booklist*, December 2002; Ward, Caroline, "A Passion for Her Profession," *School Library Journal*, September 2001.

Lynn Curlee

October 9, 1947–

"My children's book career began with a storybook. I was given the opportunity to illustrate *Horses With Wings* by Dennis Haseley for HarperCollins. With my second book I began writing myself, and started the series of nonfiction, informational picture books for older children which continues today.

"Book number two was *Ships of the Air*, the story of balloons and airships, for Houghton Mifflin. Number three was *Into the Ice: The Story of Arctic Explorations*.

"My fourth book was *Rushmore*, published by Scholastic. With it I found a solid niche—writing and illustrating books about great historical monuments and architectural icons. My wonderful editor, Brenda Bowen, subsequently moved to Simon & Schuster as publisher, and asked me to present new ideas there.

"This led to *Liberty, Brooklyn Bridge,* and *Seven Wonders of the Ancient World*. At this point, we wanted to find another American subject. We brainstormed, and came up with *Capital*—the story of the national mall in Washington, DC.

"The text was written, edited, and dummied. I began painting in June 2001, dutifully turning out painting after painting in a workman-like manner. Then the terrorist attacks of 9/11 happened. About one-third of the way into the painting, the importance of the subject was utterly transformed. What began as a pleasant job turned into a terribly serious and timely one. The very structures about which I was writing might have been destroyed even as I was doing the work.

"Paintings already planned and started took on a depth and richness for me that they might not have possessed before the tragedy. My feelings came to the forefront, and I think it shows in the finished book.

"I have had the rare privilege and honor of making books about some of the most important iconic monuments of our American heritage, and I thank my publishers and editors for this wonderful opportunity."

Courtesy of John D. Martin

Lynn Curlee was born and grew up in North Carolina. He attended the College of William and Mary, then graduated from the University of North Carolina in 1969. He received a master's degree in art history at the University of Pennsylvania two years later. Moving to New York in 1973, he began his career as a professional artist and exhibited in many galleries and shows. A client in one of his galleries suggested that his style of art would lend itself well to children's picture books. After visiting several publishers with his portfolio, he met an editor who matched his style with Dennis Haseley's manuscript for *Horses With Wings* and Curlee's career in children's books was launched.

Over the years he has garnered many awards and honors for books that portray extraordinary monuments and describe great feats of architecture and engineering, both ancient and modern. His book on Mount Rushmore was listed as a "recommended" title for the NCTE Orbis Pictus Award and was named a Notable Children's Trade Book in the Field of Social Studies. *Liberty*, which tells how the Statue of Liberty was built in France, shipped to the United States, and reassembled in New York harbor, was named an ALA Notable Children's Book and won an Honor Award in Social Studies from the Society of School Librarians International. *Brooklyn Bridge* captured a Robert F. Sibert Honor Book Award in 2002, was cited as an ALA Notable Children's Book, and was listed as both an Out-

Courtesy of Atheneum Books for Young Readers

standing Science Trade Book and a Notable Social Studies Trade Book for Young People. *Seven Wonders of the Ancient World*, Curlee's homage to the amazing engineering feats and creative vision behind these legendary monuments of history, was also named a Notable Social Studies Trade Book.

After living for 20 years in New York City, Lynn Curlee moved to the North Fork of Long Island. He creates his paintings on large canvases, usually 3 feet by 3 feet, and then has them photographed and reduced in size for the books. He has said that his background in art history helped him develop the research skills necessary to study in depth the various buildings and monuments that he writes about. Curlee continues to exhibit in galleries while pursuing new ideas for children's books.

SELECTED WORKS WRITTEN AND ILLUSTRATED: *Ships of the Air*, 1996; *Into the Ice: The Story of Arctic Exploration*, 1998; *Rushmore*, 1999; *Liberty*, 2000; *Brooklyn Bridge*, 2001; *Seven Wonders of the Ancient World*, 2002; *Capital*, 2003; *Parthenon*, 2004.

SUGGESTED READING: *Something About the Author*, vol. 98, 1998.

Courtesy of J.G. Dash

Joan Dash

July 18, 1925–

"When anyone asked my brother what he wanted to be when he grew up, he'd say, 'A pitcher. A lefty pitcher.' He usually had a mitt on one hand and a baseball in the other, and he spent his after-school time in an empty lot playing ball with other kids. When I was asked the same question, I'd say—slowly and thoughtfully, to show this was no passing fancy—'I'm going to be a writer.'

"Notice the difference. At the age of 10, Dick was already a pitcher—a left-handed one because he was born that way. I was five years older, which meant I had a head start, but I had never written a book. Nobody expected me to have written one. That was the beautiful part of wanting to be a writer, that you didn't have to hurry up and get started. You could put it off till you were 30, maybe even 50. Besides, I had been wearing glasses since fourth grade, so I looked like a writer. I was a bookworm, I devoured books the way Dick devoured baseball statistics, and learned a great many long words. It was another proof of my literary future.

"I went to Barnard College, at 116th Street in Manhattan, across the street from Columbia University, where I majored in English literature and became an editor of the *Barnard Bulletin*. I got good grades, which meant there was no time for writing my first book (although I had to admit that every now and then I wondered what it would be about). Dick went to college at Columbia and pitched for Columbia.

"In my junior year I got married. My husband was a physicist and his first job was in Los Alamos, New Mexico, the place where the atom bomb was born. Surrounded by high desert and the adobe villages of Pueblo Indians, we were sandwiched between tomorrow (nuclear power) and yesterday, the Tewa-speaking people who encouraged outsiders to watch their Eagle Dance and Buffalo Dance. We lived there for 10 years with our three children, and I continued to wonder what I'd find to write about when the time came to start writing.

"Our youngest child was 14 months old when we went to England for a year. In the lovely old university town of Cambridge we had a large house with gardens and a gardener, who tipped his cap whenever he saw me. There was also a nanny for the children, the two older ones who were already in school, and the baby. England felt foreign, or at any rate different. Daily life took a lot of getting used to.

"The house was supposed to be heated by eight gas grates, two coal-burning fireplaces, and something called a Neo-Classic Coke Boiler—that meant a heater in every room except the three bathrooms. They had no heat; English bathrooms never do. We had an old car, but the English drove on the left side of the road. I tried but couldn't. People stared at me on the street, then looked away in embarrassment; it took me a while to realize they had been staring at my blue jeans and sneakers, things they'd never seen before. Everyone was polite—even children were polite—but they kept to themselves. My friends were far away across the ocean, my husband seemed to move past me in a blur, and I felt lonely.

"Help was at hand, though; I found a battered typewriter, and before long I was discussing the differences between England and America with this elderly machine. The result was 10 short pieces that were published in one of the English newspapers—which didn't make me a writer, but it brought me closer.

"When we went home, we moved to Seattle, and an article I had written for an American magazine appeared on the newsstands. An editor at a publishing house asked if I could write a book on the same subject—the lives and marriages of distinguished women. That was my first book, and the second was a history-biography. After that I turned to history-biography for young readers, and each time I chose the subject because I wanted to find out more about a person, a place, or a period in time—not just what happened, but how I felt about it.

"As near as I can figure, writing is what I do to explain the world to myself."

"Did my brother become a pitcher for a big league team? No, he's a psychologist; whenever he passes a schoolyard where kids are playing baseball, he stops to watch, often for a long time. And did I come to realize that there were potential books everywhere—in Los Alamos, for example? Yes, I finally realized that. As near as I can figure, writing is what I do to explain the world to myself."

※　※　※

Joan Zeiger Dash was born and raised in Brooklyn, New York, when the Brooklyn Dodgers were still the Brooklyn Dodgers. She received her B.A. from Barnard College in 1946. While writing a book for adults, *A Life of One's Own: Three Gifted Women and the Men They Married*, she became interested in the particular challenges that faced Maria Goeppert-Mayer, a Nobel Prize winner for theoretical physics. This led her to write *The Triumph of Discovery*, a book for young readers about women scientists who have won the Nobel Prize. Her next book, *We Shall Not Be Moved*, explored women's activism in the labor movement in the early years of the 20th century and was named a Notable Children's Trade Book in the Field of Social Studies as well as an ALA Best Book for Young Adults.

THE
LONGITUDE PRIZE
Joan Dash

Pictures by Dušan Petričić

Courtesy of Farrar, Straus and Giroux

Dash's historical/biographical books are more than factual accounts of a life, a movement, or a cultural event. She re-creates the times she writes about with full descriptions of everyday life: the sights, the smells, the small details that bring a historical period to life for her readers. This was recognized especially upon the publication of *The Longitude Prize*, her vibrant account of the struggles of John Harrison in 18th century England to receive credit for inventing a way to measure longitude at sea. *The Longitude Prize* won the coveted *Boston Globe–Horn Book* Award for nonfiction as well as an Honor Book citation for the Robert F. Sibert Award for nonfiction in that award's inaugural year, 2001. *The Longitude Prize* was also named a Notable Social Studies Trade Book for Young People and an ALA Notable Children's Book. Dash's biography of Helen Keller, *The World at Her Fingertips*, became an ALA Notable Children's Book the following year.

SELECTED WORKS FOR ADULTS: *A Life of One's Own: Three Gifted Women and the Men They Married*, 1973; *Summoned to Jerusalem: The Life of Henrietta Szold*, 1979.

SELECTED WORKS FOR CHILDREN: *The Triumph of Discovery: Women Scientists Who Won the Nobel Prize*, 1991; *We Shall Not Be Moved: The Women's Factory Strike of 1909*, 1996; *The Longitude Prize*, illus. by Dušan Petričić, 2000; *The World at Her Fingertips: The Story of Helen Keller*, 2001.

SUGGESTED READING: *Contemporary Authors*, New Revision Series, vol. 57, 1997; *Beacham's Guide to Literature for Young Adults*, vol. 11, 2001. Periodicals—"2001 *Boston Globe–Horn Book* Awards: Nonfiction Award Winner," *The Horn Book*, January/February 2002.

Carmen Agra Deedy

September 11, 1960–

"When we are born, the first sentence of the book of our lives is written. But a story's beginning doesn't necessarily foreshadow its end.

"I was born into a Cuban family during the infant days of the Communist Revolution. Fidel Castro, a spirited young demagogue, had deposed Fulgencio Batista, a hated dictator. Those were heady days, full of turbulent political change, yet ripe with anticipation of the new democracy many hoped would follow. For my idealistic parents, who were strong human rights advocates, the new regime would become a crippling disappointment.

"I was three when we began the journey that would include our story among those of thousands of Cuban refugees who have found asylum in the United States. For my parents, who deeply loved their country, it was a soul-wrenching decision. My father was under mounting pressure to join the Communist Party. That, coupled with the chilling sounds of the *paredon*, the firing squads whose machine guns echoed from La Cabana, a notorious makeshift prison in Havana, was enough to cement their decision to emigrate. Both had been early supporters of the revolution, but joining the party that had so much fresh blood on its hands was something they could not, and would not, do. They would have to leave their homeland.

"We arrived in Decatur, Georgia, on a bitterly cold February day, in 1963. Years of food rationing and hardship had left us all undernourished and anemic. We were allowed to take only the clothes we had on. What a sight we must have made as we huddled on the tarmac, my mother's cotton dress whipping around us, my father trying desperately to hold on to his hat. How very vulnerable we all were, I think, as I look back now. How perilously young. Whenever I remember that encapsulated moment and the damp, bone-chilling wind, I can still feel my scalp prickle, and a shiver courses down my back. That was my first winter. I have now experienced nearly 41 of them in my adopted country.

"That frightened three-year-old? She's come to like winter—as long as it's accompanied by steaming cupfuls of *chocolate caliente*. She is now a middle-aged woman, a mother, a storyteller, and a writer.

Courtesy of Peachtree Publishers

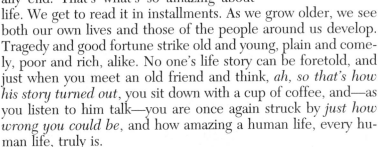

"That's how stories are. We are born. And the circumstances—whether we are born into splendid wealth, appalling poverty, or middle-class comfort—are not what decide how the story will unfold, or eventually end. That's what's so amazing about life. We get to read it in installments. As we grow older, we see both our own lives and those of the people around us develop. Tragedy and good fortune strike old and young, plain and comely, poor and rich, alike. No one's life story can be foretold, and just when you meet an old friend and think, *ah, so that's how his story turned out*, you sit down with a cup of coffee, and—as you listen to him talk—you are once again struck by *just how wrong you could be*, and how amazing a human life, every human life, truly is.

"And that, I suppose, is why I love stories."

❉   ❉   ❉

Carmen Agra Deedy's parents waited four years after the Castro Revolution before making the painful decision to take Carmen and her sister and leave their home in Havana. They found sanctuary in the United States under the JFK Cuban Refugee Act of 1963 and started their lives over in Decatur, Georgia, though not without a certain amount of culture shock. As an adult, Carmen has drawn on her dual heritage of Latin American and southern culture to become a renowned professional storyteller who has delighted audiences across the country in schools, museums, and festivals. She has performed at the National Storytelling Festival in Jonesborough, Tennessee; the Disney Institute in Orlando, Florida; the Kennedy Center in Washington, DC; and the New Victory Theater on New York's Broadway, to

Courtesy of Peachtree Publishers

name just a few. At the National Book Festival in 2002 she was one of three authors chosen to speak at a black-tie event at the Library of Congress. Her stories have also been heard on National Public Radio's weekend *All Things Considered.* Her audiotape collection, *Growing up Cuban in Decatur, Georgia*, won a Parents' Choice Gold Award and was named best storytelling audio by *Publishers Weekly.* While many of her stories reflect the themes of separation and deprivation of her early years, she is best known for her witty, entertaining style, emphasizing the importance of humor and perseverance in overcoming life's difficulties.

Carmen Deedy's books for children range in theme and setting from equatorial rain forests to the Arctic, from a Manhattan apartment to the streets of occupied Copenhagen during the Second World War. Each tale is unique and evokes many emotions, from a lighthearted fantasy about geese who want to reclaim their feathers in *Agatha's Feather Bed* to the gentle love story and lifelong friendship in *The Last Dance. The Library Dragon* received a Florida Reading Association Children's Book Award and was named to the Georgia Center for the Book's Top 25 Reading List. *The Secret of Old Zeb* brought the author an Award of Merit from the Southeast Library Association, and in 1993 Carmen Deedy was named Georgia Author of the Year for Juvenile Literature. Her most lauded book of all, *The Yellow Star*, recounts the legend that King Christian X of Denmark had a yellow star sewn on his clothes during the Nazi occupation of his country to protest the treatment of Denmark's Jewish citizens. The story alludes to the remarkable feat of those courageous Danes who managed to spirit most of their Jewish neighbors out of the country to neutral Sweden before Nazi soldiers could take them away to concentration camps. *The Yellow Star* won a Christopher Award, the Bologna Ragazzi Award, a Parents' Choice Gold Award, and an Honor Book Award from the Jane Addams Peace Association, among other recognitions.

Carmen Deedy lives in Tucker, Georgia. She has three grown daughters—Katherine, Erin, and Lauren.

SELECTED WORKS: *Agatha's Feather Bed: Not Just Another Wild Goose Story*, illus. by Laura L. Seeley, 1991; *The Library Dragon*, illus. by Michael P. White, 1994; *The Last Dance*, illus. by Debrah Santini, 1995; *The Secret of Old Zeb*, illus. by Douglas J. White, 1997; *The Yellow Star: The Legend of King Christian X of Denmark*, illus. by Henri Sørensen, 2000; *Treeman*, illus. by Douglas J. Ponte, 2000.

SUGGESTED READING: Coeyman, Marjorie, "Telling Tales of Bravery in Dark Times," *Christian Science Monitor*, October 30, 2001, p.16.

" **A** s a young boy, I was painfully shy and hated anything that might alter my life at home or with my friends. This is rather ironic since the word 'change' is what probably best describes my life and my work over the years. Somehow when I grew up the gypsy in me took over and gave me wings to travel, first to live outside of New England, and then to explore the unsafe world of making a living as an artist.

"When I was a kid, art was just another thing I liked to do, in addition to playing sports and being with family and friends. I would copy pictures of my heroes and do drawings of them that I would tape to my walls. When the Beatles were in their prime, my drawings were almost always of them. My parents were great role models. Although she didn't do it to make a living, my mother worked as a landscape artist. My father, a salesman, could also draw, and as a veteran pilot in WWII and an active pilot while I was growing up, he powered my imagination with books of planes and visits to air shows.

"I had a great imagination—nothing unusual for kids—but I always needed to have a costume to make the transition complete. My friends and I had Davy Crockett outfits, football outfits, soldier uniforms, and cowboy holsters with realistic-looking guns. My mother once asked me, 'Why is

Courtesy of Ethan Demarest

Chris L. Demarest

April 18, 1951–

it you need to have a costume for everything?' 'Because,' was my answer. Years later, after moving to a small town in Vermont and joining the volunteer fire department, on the drive home from the station looking over at my bunker gear I recalled her comment and laughed. Here I was, all these years later, still playing dress-up.

"After getting a B.F.A. in painting from the University of Massachusetts at Amherst, I bounced around for awhile. I worked as a house painter in Seattle, then in Boston; I tried my hand at becoming a freelance cartoonist. As a result, I did a lot of work for the *Atlantic Monthly* magazine. The art director at the *Atlantic Monthly* encouraged me to try children's book illustration and eventually introduced me to the late Emily MacLeod at Unicorn Books. It was from Emily that I learned there is no one right way to illustrate. There is room for many, many styles.

"I have let life give me the flexibility to move, and along with that, I've allowed my artistic thinking to branch out. My artistic style has changed to incorporate everything from simple pen-and-ink to watercolors done in quick strokes to opaque painting, from the woodcut style I studied in college to the cartoon style I was known for for over 25 years, to the realistic style I've just recently adopted.

"Recently all the elements of my past have come together to alter my career. The adventure and imagination from so long ago led me to explore books on firefighting, and my most recent book was inspired by the flights I've taken with the Coast Guard. Now not only do I draw the pictures of what I see, I get to experience it as well. With current projects again taking me airborne and beyond, I've begun to interpret realistic dramas with a realistic style, using pastels. Every book has now become a brand new adventure and a way to reach out to kids and show them life with all its possibilities. In many ways, I have come full circle, and in many ways, my life and work continue to evolve and change."

> "Now not only do I draw the pictures of what I see, I get to experience it as well. . . . Every book has now become a brand-new adventure and a way to reach out to kids and show them life with all its possibilities."

✻　✻　✻

Chris Demarest never thought he could be a famous artist. But art was in his blood, and after being inspired by a book of George Booth cartoons, he decided that what he wanted to paint were funny, playful situations that weren't about making artistic statements. He wanted to do something people could empathize with, so he built a portfolio of cartoon figures and scenarios, and for many, many years, this cartoon style dominated his work.

Demarest has won a number of awards, including a Ford Foundation Grant in 1975. His children's books have been popular favorites for many years. *Benedict Finds a Home* and *Clemens' Kingdom* were Junior Library Guild selections. *The Butterfly Jar: Poems* and *Bob and Jack: A Boy and His Yak* both received the Kentucky Bluegrass Award. These two titles were the result of a collaboration with Jeff Moss, a writer and composer for the *Sesame Street* television program and the creator of the Cookie Monster. *My Little Red Car*, which is about a boy who imagines driving to Paris and the North Pole in his toy car, received a Parents' Choice Picture Book Award in 1992. *Lindbergh*, a biography of the famous aviator in his youth, was named a *School Library Journal* Best Book in 1994. In the same year, *Smart Dog* was cited as an IRA/CBC Children's Choice selection and a Reading Rainbow book. *Casey in the Bath*, the tale of a fantastical bathtime aided by magic green goo and illustrated in Demarest's exuberant cartoon-style art, was also an IRA/CBC Children's Choice selection. *Bikes for Rent*, by Isaac Olaleye, featuring a young boy living in Nigeria, received a Children's Africana Honor Book Award.

While he continues to illustrate books in his cheerful cartoon style, most recently in the easy-reader Supertwins series by B. J. James, Chris Demarest has received great acclaim for the more realistic style of art found in recent titles that feature rescue workers. In *Firefighters A to Z*, his work was inspired by his own experience as a volunteer firefighter, and the book became one of the *New York Times*'s Notable Picture Books in 2000. *Smokejumpers One to Ten* was named a Notable Social Studies Trade Book, and *Hotshots!* received much praise for its depiction of brushfire fighters on the ground. When the U.S. Coast Guard invited Demarest to their base and gave him the chance to fly with them on several occasions, he was inspired to write and illustrate his most recent book, *Mayday! Mayday!*, which tells the story of a Coast Guard helicopter rescuing a yachtsman at sea during a fierce hurricane.

Born in Hartford, Connecticut, and raised in East Hartford, Demarest lives today in Claremont, New Hampshire. His son, Ethan, now in elementary school, is already showing his own artistic ability. He has expressed interest in visiting the bases his dad has dealt with, and they both look forward to sharing those experiences.

Courtesy of Margaret K. McElderry Books

SELECTED WORKS WRITTEN AND ILLUSTRATED: *Benedict Finds a Home*, 1982; *Clemens' Kingdom*, 1983; *Orville's Odyssey*, 1986; *Morton and Sidney*, 1987; *No Peas for Nellie*, 1988; *The Lunatic Adventure of Kitman and Willy*, 1988; *Kitman and Willy at Sea*, 1991; *My Little Red Car*, 1992; *Lindbergh*, 1993; *My Blue Boat*, 1995; *Plane*, 1995; *Ship*, 1995; *Bus*, 1996; *Train*, 1996; *Fall*, 1996; *Winter*, 1996; *Spring*, 1997; *Summer*, 1997; *All Aboard!* 1997; *Farmer Nat: A Lift-the-Flap Book*, 1998; *Honk!*, 1998; *The Cowboy ABC*, 1999; *Zookeeper*

Sue: A Lift-the-Flap Book, 1999; *Firefighters A to Z*, 2000; *Here Come Our Firefighters*, 2002; *Smokejumpers One to Ten*, 2002; *Heroes of the Sky: A Search-and-Rescue Pop-Up*, 2003; *Hotshots!*, 2003; *Little Lessons of Love*, 2003; *Mayday! Mayday!: A Coast Guard Rescue*, 2004.

SELECTED WORKS ILLUSTRATED: *Tree House Fun*, by Rose Greydanus, 1980; *Pooks*, by Elizabeth Isele, 1983; *Hedgehog Adventures*, by Betty Jo Stanovich, 1983; *Hedgehog Surprises*, by Betty Jo Stanovich, 1984; *World Famous Muriel*, by Sue Alexander, 1984; *World Famous Muriel and the Scary Dragon*, by Sue Alexander, 1985; *The Butterfly Jar*, by Jeffrey Moss, 1989; *Smedge*, by Andrew Sharmat, 1989; *Not Now! Said the Cow*, by Joanne F. Oppenheim, 1989; *I've Got Goose Pimples: And Other Great Expressions*, by Marvin Vanoni, 1990; *The Cows Are Going to Paris*, by David Kirby, 1991; *The Donkey's Tale*, by Joanne Oppenheim, 1991; *Missing Mother Goose: Original Stories from Favorite Rhymes*, by Stephen Krensky, 1991; *The Other Side of the Door: Poems*, by Jeff Moss, 1991; *Bob and Jack: A Boy and His Yak*, by Jeff Moss, 1992; *Two Badd Babies*, by Jeffie Ross Gordon, 1992; *What's on the Menu?* ed. by Bobbye S. Goldstein, 1992; *Whooo's There?*, by Lily Jones, 1992; *How Do You Wrap a Horse?*, by Diana Klemin, 1993; *Smart Dog*, by Ralph Leemis, 1993; *Today I'm Going Fishing with My Dad*, by N. L. Sharp, 1993; *Uh-Oh! Said the Crow*, by Joanne F. Oppenheim, 1993; *When Cows Come Home*, by David Lee Harrison, 1993; *Billy and the Magic String*, by Susan Karnovsky, 1994; *Hieronymus White: A Bird Who Believed That He Always Was Right*, by Jeff Moss, 1994; *Hooray for Grandma Jo!*, by Thomas McKean, 1994; *Time to Rhyme: A Rhyming Dictionary*, by Marvin Terban, 1994; *What Would Mama Do?*, by Judith Ross Enderle and Stephanie G. Tessler, 1995; *Casey in the Bath*, by Cynthia C. DeFelice, 1996; *Derek's Dog Days*, by Nancy Lee Charlton, 1996; *If Dogs Had Wings*, by Larry Dane Brimner, 1996; *A Dozen Dozens*, by Harriet Ziefert, 1997; *The Dad of the Dad of the Dad of Your Dad*, by Jeff Moss, 1997; *The Animals' Song*, by David L. Harrison, 1997; *I Need a Valentine!*, by Harriet Ziefert, 1998; *Mike Swan, Sink or Swim*, by Deborah Heiligman, 1998; *Who Walks on This Halloween Night?: A Lift-the-Flap Story*, by Harriet Ziefert, 1998; *Beep Beep, Vroom Vroom!*, by Stuart Murphy, 1999; *Who Loves Me Best?*, by Mary Packard and Kirsten Hall, 1999; *April Fool!*, by Harriet Ziefert, 2000; *I Can Jump Higher!*, by Paul Z. Mann, 2000; *Bikes for Rent!*, by Isaac Olaleye, 2001; *Brothers Are for Making Mud Pies*, by Harriet Ziefert, 2001; *DingDong, Trick or Treat!*, by Harriet Ziefert, 2001; *Sisters Are for Making Sand Castles*, by Harriet Ziefert, 2001; *My Best Friend*, by Kirsten Hall, 2001; *Someday We'll Have Very Good Manners*, by Harriet Ziefert, 2001; *BowWow Bake Sale*, by Judith Bauer Stamper, 2002;

The Princess and the Pea: A Pop-Up Book, by Sarah Aronson, 2002; *Snowy Winter Day*, by Estelle Feldman, 2002; *Supertwins Meet the Bad Dogs from Space*, by B. J. James, 2003; *Breakfast at Danny's Diner* (All Aboard Math Reader Series), by Judith Bauer Stamper, 2003; *Go Fractions* (All Aboard Math Reader Series), by Judith Bauer Stamper, 2003; *Supertwins and Tooth Trouble*, by B. J. James, 2003; *Supertwins Meet the Dangerous Dino-Robots*, by B. J. James, 2003; *Leaping Beauty: And Other Animal Fairy Tales*, by Gregory Maguire, 2004; *Supertwins and the Sneaky, Slimy Book Worms*, by B. J. James, 2004; *T. Rex at Swan Lake*, by Lisa Carrier and Lenore Hart, 2004.

SUGGESTED READING: *Something About the Author*, vol. 128, 2002.

"**M**y father died when I was three years old, so my older sister Beth and I were raised by our mother, Marie. I lived all my childhood in Redwood City, a suburb of San Francisco. I attended good schools with good teachers and made good grades, but I don't think it was school that first pointed me toward a writing career, nor do I think my first writing tool was either a pen or a pencil.

"I've rarely been lonely when I'm alone. As a child, I'd often take out my Tinker Toys and my plastic men and start building. I'd work my way out of my bedroom and down the hall toward the living room. As I laid out my toys, my mind would be going. Sometimes it was cowboys and Indians, sometimes cops and robbers. I frequently saved the nuns of St. Pius School from the Communists. Eventually I'd run out of raw materials. Then I'd look at my creation for a minute or two, pick up one of my plastic men, and for the next few minutes I was all-powerful, destroying everything I'd built. And there was great pleasure in that too.

"Of course I didn't spend all my time indoors. Many days I'd go in the backyard and hit clothespins with a stick, pretending I was Willie Mays. Off the wall was a single, above the window was a double, on the roof a home run. And there were long hikes (now I was Daniel Boone) in the woods behind our house. Always stories percolated inside my head. I would never have become a writer if I hadn't 'wasted' so many hours just kicking around, doing nothing.

Courtesy of Anne Mitchell

Carl Deuker

August 26, 1950–

"But you can't stay 10 years old forever. My mother and my sister never mocked my fantasy games, but my high school friends wouldn't have been so understanding. The Tinker Toys and the little plastic men went into the closet, and imaginary sports heroics gave way to organized sports. I was an okay athlete—good enough to make a few teams but not good enough to play much. As a result, I spent most of my time watching my more skilled teammates. That wasn't the worst thing for a future writer either, though I didn't like it at the time. Alone at the end of the bench I had time to dream.

"It takes more than dreaming to become a writer, though. One day a high school English teacher handed me a copy of James Joyce's *Portrait of the Artist as a Young Man*. 'Read this,' he said. *Portrait of the Artist* is a difficult book for an adult, impossible for a teenager, but I read it cover to cover. I understood almost nothing, but I did learn that words can be magical, powerful. I knew I was outside the candy store, and I wanted desperately to get in. A love of literature was born.

by Carl Deuker

Courtesy of Houghton Mifflin, Inc.

"That love of literature carried me through UC at Berkeley and the University of Washington, where I earned degrees in English literature, immersing myself in books. Like many English majors, I also wrote my own fiction, but I had no hope of ever being good enough to get any of my stories published.

"Later I married Anne Mitchell—the love of my life—and became a teacher. For many years I wrote movie and book reviews for a small Seattle alternative newspaper, all the while continuing to toy with fiction. My daughter Marian—the other love of my life—was born just about the time the newspaper went out of business. I thought to myself: 'Stop kidding yourself, if you want to write fiction, write fiction.' So I did, and with a lot of luck and a lot of help, have now published five young adult novels, all of which have had a sports theme. (Remember those hours I spent as a benchwarmer!) I used to make up stories as I played on the carpet. Now I sit at a computer and instead of using Tinker Toys, I use words. But it's still play, and it's still the little boy in me who's doing the writing."

❈   ❈   ❈

Combining a sports theme with stories about life issues for teens has become a hallmark of Carl Deuker's writing. After earning his B.A. in 1972 from the University of California at

Berkeley and his M.A. in 1974 from the University of Washington, he settled on teaching as a career and completed his teaching certificate at UCLA in 1976. Deuker's first position was at Saint Luke School in Seattle, Washington, where he has made his home since 1977. Currently he teaches fifth and sixth grades in the Northshore School District in Bothell, Washington.

Deuker achieved early success when his first book, *On the Devil's Court*, was named an ALA Best Book for Young Adults and won the South Carolina Young Adult Book Award. A combination of psychological thriller, superstition, and sports story, this book introduces high school student Joe Faust who, like his namesake in the medieval literature he studies in English class, may have agreed to sell his soul to the devil. *Heart of a Champion*, which *VOYA* called a "heartbreakingly beautiful book," was also cited as an ALA Best Book for Young Adults and received young readers' choice awards in Pennsylvania, Nebraska, and Tennessee. Introducing a main character whose father died when he was a child, *Heart of a Champion* contains one of the finest portrayals in young adult literature of a relationship between a teenage boy and his mother. *Painting the Black*, another ALA Best Book, was cited as a Blue Ribbon book by the *Bulletin of the Center for Children's Books*, as was *Night Hoops*. Ever aware of the tough moral choices facing teens, Deuker puts his characters into difficult situations where they must make hard decisions.

Though Carl Deuker writes about high school, he teaches in a middle school where he enjoys being able to change his focus from one subject to another during the day. In his spare time he plays golf, coaches softball, and enjoys attending the sports activities of his daughter Marian, who was born in 1989. The Deuker family live in Seattle with their very personable pet rats, and Carl is at work on a novel that will be his first departure from the theme of sports.

SELECTED WORKS: *On the Devil's Court*, 1989; *Heart of a Champion*, 1993; "If You Can't Be Lucky," in *Ultimate Sports: Short Stories by Outstanding Writers for Young Adults*, ed. by Donald R. Gallo, 1995; *Painting the Black*, 1997; *Night Hoops*, 2000; *High Heat*, 2003.

SUGGESTED READING: *Beacham's Guide to Literature for Young Adults*, vol. 7, 1994; *Something About the Author*, vol. 150, 2004. Online—Interview, *www.authors4teens.com*.

WEB SITE: *members2.authorsguild.net/carldeuker/*

Courtesy of Elspeth Hilbert

Jennifer Owings Dewey

October 2, 1941–

"When I was 10 I wrote my first book, an autobiography. That year was eventful for me. My grandmother died, a world leader died, and a war in Asia was ended. I felt the year deserved documentation, and so I went at it. I loved drawing back then, as I love drawing to this day, and so I illustrated my first book with various pieces of fruit, each representing a family member or a friend.

"I never seriously considered any profession other than to be a writer and illustrator since creating that child's version of my life story. I interviewed the wrangler on the ranch where I lived, interviewed his wife, and interviewed everyone I knew. Research, it turned out, was a wonderful thing. I had valid reasons to invade everyone's privacy.

"Many, *many* years later, I am basically still at it: writing stories and illustrating them. My favorite subject matter is nature, so I write nonfiction books about bats, spiders, snakes, and other wild creatures. In recent years I've written a few novels, and I've made the discovery that writing fiction is just as satisfying as writing nonfiction. My first fiction novel was *Navajo Summer*, and a few years later, I wrote *Borderlands* and *Minik's Story*.

"Writing at all is a blessing to me, a way to explore worlds well beyond the boundaries of the town where I live. Drawing is much the same in terms of satisfaction because I can explore with my pencils as one does with the written word. To research nonfiction often means to go to the region I will be writing about or drawing to experience first-hand observations, and so travel is part of what makes life interesting. My choice of what to do with my professional life has included traveling to strange, distant, and sometimes exotic places.

"My most extraordinary experience was a trip to Antarctica in the mid 1980s. I've always loved wild places, environments untroubled by the impact of humans, their roads and power lines and parking lots and malls. I applied for a grant from the National Science Foundation to travel to the Antarctic as a writer/illustrator doing research on birds. The base where I stayed is small, holding a maximum of 45 people, and while I was at the Palmer Station, I spent my time doing exactly what I'd always dreamed of doing: exploring, observing wildlife, writing, drawing, and day after day soaking up the visual beauty of the region. Two of the books that came out of this field work were *Birds of the Antarctic: The Adélie Penguin* and *Birds of the Antarctic: The*

Wandering Albatross. Antarctica defies description except to say it's a continent of extravagant brilliance and utter wildness.

"If I had to choose again what way of life I wanted I'd choose the same way of living. My early experience with writing an illustrated book was a good one, and so the rest, as they say, is history."

❀ ❀ ❀

Jennifer Owings Dewey was born in Chicago but moved to New Mexico when she was three years old. She was raised on a farm in the Southwest along with her twin sisters, a brother, and a great many pets. In high school Dewey became interested in writing and, with the help of her English teacher, had her first poems published. After attending the Rhode Island School of Design from 1959 to 1960, she returned home and entered the University of New Mexico, where she met her first husband, Keith Monroe. They had a daughter, Tamar, but her husband died in 1964.

After remarrying, Jennifer moved to California, where she exhibited her paintings in a show every year at Shorebirds Gallery in Tiburon. She also began illustrating children's books, and most of these were on subjects related to the outdoors, nature, and science. With her western upbringing, she would bravely venture into rugged and inhospitable places in order to capture accurately in her illustrations the amazing beauty she found in nature. In 1986, after illustrating a number of books for other writers, she published her first book as an author, which was *Clem: The Story of a Raven*, based on the raven that she kept in the early years of her first marriage. In the early 1990s, she began writing a number of books about the desert and its inhabitants, including several works for the Museum of New Mexico Press.

"Research, it turned out, was a wonderful thing. I had valid reasons to invade everyone's privacy."

Dewey has received a number of awards throughout her long career. In 1980, she was the recipient of the Bookbinders West Award for Illustration for *Idle Weeds*. In 1984, *The Secret Language of Snow* received both an Award for Illustration from the National Academy of Sciences, and a Children's Science Book Award from the New York Academy of Sciences. In 1986, *The Dinosaurs and the Dark Star* was selected as one of the Child Study Association of America's Children's Books of the Year. In 1995 she won an Orbis Pictus Honor Award from the National Council of Teachers of English for her compelling book on a wildlife veterinarian, *Wildlife Rescue: The Work of Dr. Kathleen Ramsay*. In 1998, *Mud Matters: Stories from a Mud Lover* was named a John Burroughs Young Reader winner and a Notable Children's Trade Book in the Field of Social Studies. *Stories on Stone*, about the rock art of the first peoples of the Southwest, was also chosen as a Notable Social Studies title. Several of her books have been named Outstanding Science Trade Books: *Living Fossils*; *Snowflakes*; *Clem: The Story of a Raven*; and *Pai-*

Courtesy of HarperCollins Publishers

sano, the Roadrunner. The National Science Teachers Association has presented her with its award for her body of work in the field of nonfiction for children.

SELECTED WORKS WRITTEN AND ILLUSTRATED: *Clem: The Story of a Raven*, 1986; *At the Edge of the Pond*, 1987; *Can You Find Me? A Book About Animal Camouflage*, 1989; *Birds of Antarctica: The Adélie Penguin*, 1989; *Birds of Antarctica: The Wandering Albatross*, 1989; *Prehistoric Swimmers and Flyers of the Southwest*, 1990 (with Lucy Lyon); *A Night and Day in the Desert*, 1991; *Animal Architecture*, 1991; *Prehistoric Mammals on the Rise: A Southwest Coloring Book*, 1992; *Spiders Near and Far*, 1992; *The Creatures Underneath*, 1994; *Cowgirl Dreams: A Western Childhood*, 1995; *Stories on Stone: Rock Art, Images from the Ancient Ones*, 1996 (reissued 2003); *Faces Only a Mother Could Love*, 1996; *Bedbugs in Our House: True Tales of Insect, Bug, and Spider Discovery*, 1997; *Rattlesnake Dance: True Tales, Mysteries, and Rattlesnake Ceremonies*, 1997; *Poison Dart Frogs*, 1998; *Family Ties: Raising Wild Babies*, 1996; *Mud Matters: Stories from a Mud Lover*, 1998 (photos by Stephen Trimble); *Antarctic Journal: Four Months at the Bottom of the World*, 2000; *Finding Your Way: The Art of Natural Navigation*, 2001.

SELECTED WORKS WRITTEN: *Wildlife Rescue: The Work of Dr. Kathleen Ramsay*, photos by Don MacCarter, 1994; *Navajo Summer*, 1998; *Borderlands*, 2002; *Once I Knew a Spider*, illus. by Jean Cassels, 2002; *Paisano, the Roadrunner*, photos by Wyman Meinzer, 2002; *Minik's Story*, 2003.

SELECTED WORKS ILLUSTRATED: *Frosty: A Raccoon to Remember*, by Harriet Weaver, 1974; *Idle Weeds*, by David Rains Wallace, 1980; *Living Fossils*, by Howard E. Smith Jr., 1982; *Song of the Sea Otter*, by Edith Thacher Hurd, 1983; *The Blue Planet*, by Louise B. Young, 1984; *Suburban Wildlife*, by Richard Headstrom, 1984; *The Secret Language of Snow*, by Terry Tempest Williams and Ted Major, 1984; *Walkers: Prehistoric Animals of the Southwest*, by David D. Gillette, 1984; *Birds of the Great Basin*, by Fred A. Ryser, 1985; *The Dinosaurs and the Dark Star*, by Robin Bates and Cheryl Simon, 1985; *Mammals and Their Milk*, by Lucia Anderson, 1985; *Snowflakes*, by Joan Sugarman, 1985; *Birds of the Great Basin: A Natural History*, by Fred A. Ryser Jr., 1985; *Wilderness Sojourn*, by David Douglas, 1987; *Strange Creatures That Really Lived*, by Millicent Selsam, 1987; *All about Arrowheads and Spear Points*, by Howard E. Smith Jr., 1989; *The Sagebrush Ocean: A Natural History of the Great Basin*, by Stephen Trimble, 1989 (10th anniversary edition, 1999); *The Village of Blue Stone*, by Stephen Trimble, illus. with Deborah Reade, 1990; *New Questions and Answers About Dinosaurs*, by Seymour Simon, 1993; *Creatures of Earth, Sea, and Sky: Poems*, by Georgia Heard, 1992; *Young Kangaroo*, by Margaret Wise Brown, 1993; *The Case of the Mummified Pigs: And Other Mysteries in Nature*, by Susan E. Quinlan, 1995; *Strange Nests*, by Ann Shepard Stevens, 1998; *Scott Gomez: Open on the Ice*, by Mark Stewart, 2001; *Reptiles: Explore the Fascinating Worlds of Alligators and Crocodiles, Lizards, Snakes, Turtles*, by Deborah Dennard, 2004.

SUGGESTED READING: *Something About the Author*, vol. 103, 1999.

"**I** was born in Philadelphia, Pennsylvania, in 1964. For the first five winters of my life, I got pneumonia. This was at the time when geographical cures were still prescribed. The doctor thought a warmer climate might help. And so, in 1969, my mother and brother and I moved to a small town in central Florida. And there I grew up outside—running around barefoot, swimming in the lakes and the ocean and the Gulf of Mexico, sitting high in the branches of a jacaranda tree and reading, reading, reading.

"In college, at the University of Florida, professors told me that I had a 'way with words.' I began to dream in earnest of becoming a writer, of telling stories for a living. And for nine years after college, I did exactly that.

"I dreamed.

"I wandered from job to job—selling tickets at Circus World, planting philodendrons in a greenhouse, calling bingo at a campground, running rides at an amusement park—and the whole time, I talked incessantly about being a writer and read books about writing and imagined, in great detail, my life as a writer.

"I did everything except write.

"And then, when I was 29 years old, I had an epiphany—it occurred to me that I could easily spend the rest of my life doing nothing but dreaming. So I sat down and thought very seriously

Courtesy of Lisa Beck

Kate DiCamillo

March 25, 1964–

about exactly what it took to be a writer. I came to the conclusion that one thing, absolutely, was required: writing.

"And so, scared, uncertain, terrified of failure, I began. I made myself write two pages a day. And in this way, I wrote a short story. It was a very bad short story. I rewrote it. It got marginally better. I rewrote it again. And again. And again. I sent it off to a magazine. They rejected it. And I was in business. Sort of.

"In 1994, I moved from Florida to Minnesota and got a job working as a 'picker' at a book wholesaler. I was assigned to the third floor—the floor where all the children's books were kept—and I spent my days filling orders for bookstores and libraries. Before long I started reading what I was picking. I read picture books and poetry books and board books, and one day I picked up a novel written for children called *The Watsons Go to Birmingham, 1963.* Christopher Paul Curtis's book changed my life. I read it and decided I wanted to try to write a novel for kids.

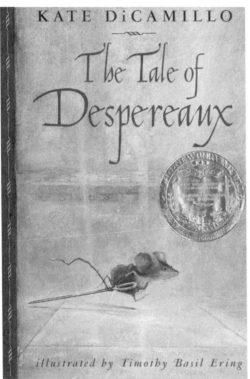

KATE DiCAMILLO

The Tale of Despereaux

illustrated by Timothy Basil Ering

Courtesy of Candlewick Press

"And so, during the worst winter on record in Minnesota, at a time when I was homesick for the warmth of Florida and suffering mightily from a disease I refer to as 'dog withdrawal' (I was living in an apartment where no dogs were allowed), I started to write a story about the South, about friendship, about a girl and her dog. The story eventually turned into a book called *Because of Winn-Dixie.* Amazingly, Candlewick Press offered to publish it. And 14 years after I started dreaming, the dream came true.

"Today I make my living as a writer, and the first thing I do every morning when I wake up is offer a small prayer of thanks. Then I sit down at my desk and get to work. I make myself write two pages. Even though I am (still) scared, uncertain, and terrified of failure, I do the work. I make myself tell the story that wants to be told."

✿　✿　✿

Kate DiCamillo grew up in Clermont, Florida, a small citrus town 30 miles west of Orlando where she moved with her mother and her older brother, Curt, when she was five years old, the year that her father deserted the family. She attended Rollins College and the University of Central Florida before she earned a B.A. in English from the University of Florida at Gainesville in 1987. A 1998 McKnight Artist Fellowship for Writers helped support her while she wrote her first book.

In her writing DiCamillo explores the recurring themes of loss, redemption, and the healing quality of friendship. In her first novel, *Because of Winn-Dixie*, she tells the story of India Opal Buloni, whose mother left the family when she was three. The companionship of a dog (a pet she names after the supermarket where she finds him) helps her break through her father's reserve and reach out to new friends as she comes to terms with her mother's desertion. This debut novel received immediate acclaim, appearing on all the year's best books lists, garnering the Josette Frank Award from Bank Street College as well as a Parents' Choice Gold Award, and culminating in winning a Newbery Honor Book in 2001. As popular with children as with critics, *Winn-Dixie* has also won a number of state-sponsored children's choice awards, including the Dorothy Canfield Fisher Award in Vermont, the Bluebonnet Award in Texas, and the Nutmeg Award in Connecticut. Her second novel, *The Tiger Rising*, was a finalist for the National Book Award in the youth category.

In 2004 Kate DiCamillo won the Newbery Medal for her animal fantasy/fairy tale novel, *The Tale of Desperaux: Being the Story of a Mouse, a Princess, Some Soup, and a Spool of Thread*. Written in a style that addresses the reader with asides throughout the story and uses many fairy tale conventions in a fresh and original manner, *The Tale of Desperaux* has become an instant favorite with children, parents and teachers, many of whom report it to be one of the best read-aloud experiences they have ever enjoyed. DiCamillo lives in Minneapolis where she takes part in a writing critique group that provides support and community while she is living her dream of being a writer.

SELECTED WORKS: *Because of Winn-Dixie*, 2000; *The Tiger Rising*, illus. by Chris Sheban, 2001; *The Tale of Despereaux*, illus. by Timothy Basil Ering, 2003.

SUGGESTED READING: *Contemporary Authors*, vol. 192, 2002; *Something About the Author*, vol. 121, 2001. Periodicals— *Orlando Sentinal*, September 28, 2001.

WEB SITE: *www.katedicamillo.com*

Brian Doyle

August 12, 1935–

"I began to write when I was in my ninth year. I wrote poems and stories and descriptions that I hid in a biscuit tin in our tumbling-down back shed in Lowertown, Ottawa, Canada. I was a secret writer. My mother was an unpublished poet whose poems my father used to make fun of. She'd hide her poems in a trunk beneath her bed. In my third year of high school, I submitted a poem to the yearbook and a short story to the school paper. Both were printed. I was out of the closet.

"Up to that point I had been disguised as a jock—gymnast, football player, track and field regular. I enrolled in journalism at Carleton College on First Avenue in Ottawa and was praised for my profiles of local Ottawa characters by Professor Wilfrid

Eggleston. Two other professors there, Gordon Wood and Michael Hornyansky, encouraged my aptitude for satire and narration. Another teacher, Professor M. Beattie, introduced me to James Joyce's wonderful novel *Ulysses*, from which I learned and still learn priceless lessons regarding the craft of writing.

"I mentioned my father earlier. He was not a writer, but he and all of his side of the family were professional-calibre raconteurs. My father could make you laugh and make you cry with his tales. In our log cabin on the Gatineau River, north of Ottawa and only an hour or so into Irish Quebec, I would lie on a top bunk and listen to my father and my aunts and uncles and sometimes my grandfather relate their stories into the night by the light of a coal oil lamp in the middle of the table. Often the narrations featured details of my *great-grandfather's* life in such a realistic way that I grew up feeling that I knew him and could hear and touch him, though he had died in 1921, 14 years before I was born. Even now, in this time of the early 21st century, I can easily reach back into the middle of the 19th! And I told myself then, in the dancing light and shadow–show of the coal oil lamp, that I would one day try to write down what I was hearing—the sounds of it, the rhythms of it, the timing, the musicality of it.

Courtesy of Megan Doyle

Brian Doyle

"After college, after work on an M.A. in English literature, after a number of different jobs, I went to teach in high schools. For many years, at Glebe Collegiate, Ottawa, while head of the English Department there, I wrote and staged, with my genius partner Stanley H. Clark, head of Music, 10 full-scale musicals with much local satirical content. We had an enormous fan base in the Ottawa Valley—they *had* to come and see—after all, the subject of these musical plays was themselves!

"My first published work, however, was right after graduation from university. A short story appeared in a small but prestigious literary quarterly called the *Fiddlehead*, Spring issue, 1960. The main branch of the Ottawa Public Library had one copy of the little magazine on their reading rack for three months. Whenever I went to the library, I would pick up the magazine and feel it to see if it had been handled very often, if at all. One day, as I entered the reading room, I saw a woman carrying the little magazine to a table. I watched her sit down, open the *Fiddlehead*, and begin browsing. She read some of the poems, flipped over some others, then stopped and began to read with interest. Was it my prose, my story, she was reading?

I strolled around behind her in the silent room until I could see the pages she was reading. It was my story: 'The Bird Watchers,' by Brian Doyle. I stood there in terror. What if she didn't finish it? I took a seat at the table in the far corner of the room. As I watched her read . . . a feeling, a strange and hypnotic wave of emotion in slow motion, gradually engulfed me . . . I saw her smile, then laugh; then grow sad as she finished, closed the covers, got up, left the table, placed the magazine carefully back in the rack.

"I walked home in a trance. I was a writer."

☼   ☼   ☼

One of Canada's most popular and best-loved authors of fiction for young people, Brian Doyle grew up in the Gatineau Hills north of Ottawa, an area steeped in the Irish culture of the people who had settled it 100 years earlier. His first book, *Hey Dad!*, was written to entice his daughter Megan to read, and the second he wrote for his son Ryan. Many of his books are set in the late 1940s, at a time when Doyle was the age of his readers. Each story is set in the environs of Ottawa, an area that he knows well. Writing stories that are rooted in a particular place is very important to Doyle. He also feels strongly that the voice in each book must be consistent in order to communicate and involve his readers; he refers to "straightforward talk" as the voice he works to achieve.

Doyle has won the Canadian Library Association's Book of the Year for Children Award four times: in 1983 for *Up to Low*, in 1988 for *Easy Avenue*, in 1997 for *Uncle Ronald*, and in 2004 for *Boy O'Boy*. Covered Bridge and *Uncle Ronald* both won Mr. Christie's Book Award, a prestigious award in Canada. Doyle's books cross borders easily; they have appeared in translation in France, Italy, Germany, Scandinavia, and South America. The German translation of *Angel Square* was nominated for the Jugendliteraturpreis, Germany's national award for children's literature, in 2001. In the United States, his titles have often appeared on New York Public Library's Books for the Teen Age list. *Spud Sweetgrass* and *Spud in Winter* both received Blue Ribbon citations from the *Bulletin of the Center for Children's Books. Mary Ann Alice* was named a *Horn Book* Fanfare title in 2002 and captured the Leishman Prize and a Mr. Christie's Book Award Silver Seal. Brian Doyle has been his country's nominee for the Hans Christian Andersen Award.

Mary Ann Alice

Courtesy of Groundwood Books

In July 2004 Doyle was selected as the 2005 laureate of the NSK Neustadt Prize for Children's Literature, awarded by the University of Oklahoma and its international quarterly, *World Literature Today*. The $25,000 NSK Prize was established in 2003 to honor an accomplished contemporary writer of children's literature every other year. In selecting Doyle, the jury made special mention of his 1984 novel *Angel Square*, in which, jurist Tim Wynne-Jones said, the author "charts for us one small corner of the world and, in doing so, reveals that it is no more out-of-the-way than anywhere else, really, once you give it a listen. He puts that one small place on the map and does so with humor and a great feeling of shared humanity."

Writing stories that show young people coping with conflicting emotions, everyday challenges, and the world around them, Brian Doyle has captivated readers with books that have the ring of truth and the insights to help them grow.

SELECTED WORKS: *Hey Dad!*, 1978; *You Can Pick Me Up at Peggy's Cove*, 1979; *Up to Low*, 1982; *Angel Square*, 1984; *Easy Avenue*, 1988; *Covered Bridge*, 1990; *Spud Sweetgrass*, 1992; *Spud in Winter*, 1995; *Uncle Ronald*, 1996; *The Low Life: Five Great Tales from Up and Down the River*, 1999; *Mary Ann Alice*, 2001; *Boy O'Boy*, 2003.

SUGGESTED READING: *Children's Literature Review*, vol. 22, 1991; *Something About the Author*, vol. 104, 1999; *Something About the Author Autobiography Series*, vol. 16, 1993. Periodicals—Budziszewski, Mary, "You Have to Think and Feel Like Your Readers," *CM Magazine*, March 1991. Online—*www.umanitoba.ca/outreach/cm/cmarchive/vol19no2/briandoyle.html*; *www.ou.edu/worldlit/NSK/NSK2005Laureate.htm*.

Tim Egan

September 24, 1957–

"Drawing pictures was always fun for me. I used to copy the Sunday comics and try to draw Norman Rockwell pictures, but mine never quite came out like his. In high school, I drew cartoons for the school newspaper, and by drawing week after week I started developing my own look. After high school, I attended the Art Center College of Design in Pasadena, California. It's an excellent school and they taught me far too much to include here, but what I learned most was that I enjoyed creating characters. Ridiculous characters with problems just like the rest of us.

"After graduating from Art Center, I worked in graphic design and advertising. I enjoyed it very much, but my wife, Ann, noticing that I was continually drawing pigs and ducks and strange people on just about everything, encouraged me to try doing children's books. It sounded like fun, so I did about 12 paintings based on Mother Goose rhymes and other children's literature. Filled with enthusiasm, I sent them off to the publishers in New York and Boston, ready to embark on my new career. They all thanked me for sending the pieces in politely worded, but very brief, rejection letters. I didn't like rejection letters, and for a short time I stopped sending. But Ann suggested I try writing a story of my own. By this time we had two sons, Chris and Brian, and it sounded like a fun idea. Strangely, my first stories were overly long and serious.

"They were rejected, too.

"But because I enjoyed it, I continued writing and, assuming the stories would be rejected anyway, I started to lighten up a little. I started writing more humorous stories. They were lighter and more fun to work on. I found that because I liked the stories more, I worked harder to make them right. I also found that if I liked the characters, even the rotten ones, other people would probably like them, too.

"I wrote a short little piece and sent it to Houghton Mifflin Company in Boston. Amazingly, the editor, Margaret Raymo, called me and asked me if I had any other stories. Naturally, I told her I had lots of stories, although, in truth, I didn't have *any* other stories at the time. When she suggested I send her some, I panicked and started writing like never before. After a few months, I sent her a story called *Friday Night at Hodges' Café*. When she called and told me they wanted to publish it, I danced around the studio. Since I'm not a very good dancer, I'm glad nobody saw me. But that phone call changed everything for me, and I've been writing and drawing ever since.

"I tend to draw first and write about the character or characters I've drawn. I give them problems and concerns and jobs and friends and enemies and then I write about them. For me, it's never as easy as it sounds.

"When asked where I get my ideas, I'm always at a loss for a decent answer. I wish I knew, and I wish I could just go there and find the ideas when I need them. But the truth is, I'm not sure where they come from. I only know that when they come, I work. When they don't, I just sit there and draw pigs and cows. It's a rather strange way to make a living, but I'm very fortunate.

"I get to do what I love."

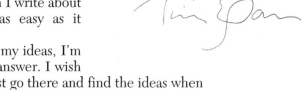

Courtesy of Tim Egan

❖ ❖ ❖

Tim Egan has established his own niche in the picture-book market with his distinctive ink and watercolor art and his droll, witty stories of offbeat animal characters. Each book imparts an

Courtesy of Houghton Mifflin, Inc.

important lesson, but with a large dose of tongue-in-cheek humor that appeals to adults as much as to the intended child audience. Indeed, these are stories that can tickle the funny bone as well as prick the conscience of readers of all ages.

After graduating with a B.F.A. in 1982 from the Art Center College of Design, Egan worked in graphic design and advertising. He received the Elan Award for best logo design in 1994 and for best billboard design in 1995. Happily, he heeded the urging of his wife, Ann, a floral designer whom he married in 1983, to submit his picture-book ideas to publishers. When *Friday Night at Hodges' Café* was published in 1994, Egan was featured in the "Flying Starts" column in *Publishers Weekly*, and his subsequent books have been well received by critics as well as children. Featuring nostalgic, often art deco–type settings in warm, muted tones, Egan's narratives and pictures thrive on dry wit and understated humor. In *Friday Night at Hodges' Café*, Hodges the elephant is assisted by a zany duck who precipitates a food fight when three tough-talking tigers invade the restaurant. With a theme of tolerance underlying the wacky action, the story delivers a message along with the mischief.

In *Metropolitan Cow* a lonely young calf challenges societal barriers in his city by making friends with a piglet, bringing together two families who discover they actually have a lot in common. The message of tolerance is reinforced by the sly humor of the illustrations, in which the slightest change in facial expression speaks volumes. *Metropolitan Cow* was a *School Library Journal* Best Book and won a Parents' Choice Gold Award as well as an Oppenheim Toy Portfolio Gold Award. *Burnt Toast on Davenport Street*, also named an *SLJ* Best Book, received an award that seems tailor-made for its author, the Southern California Book Council's "Truly Hilarious Words and Pictures" award. This story introduces an element of magic when a staid dog couple is offered three wishes by a frightened fly. In typical Egan fashion, the wishes become confused and mayhem ensues, but remarkably the dogs find their lives improved even though they don't get exactly what they wished for. *Serious Farm* is perhaps the most representative of Egan's books; the barnyard animals team up to convince Farmer Fred to take life a little more lightly, just as Tim Egan conveys the same message to his readers. He lives with his family in Southern California.

SELECTED WORKS WRITTEN AND ILLUSTRATED: *Friday Night at Hodges' Café*, 1994; *Chestnut Cove*, 1995; *Metropolitan Cow*, 1996; *Burnt Toast on Davenport Street*, 1997; *Distant Feathers*, 1998; *Blunder of the Rogues*, 1999; *A Mile from Ellington Station*, 2001; *The Experiments of Doctor Vermin*, 2002; *Serious Farm*, 2003; *The Trial of Cardigan Jones*, 2004.

SUGGESTED READING: *Something About the Author*, vol. 89, 1997. Periodicals—"Flying Starts," *Publishers Weekly*, December 19, 1994.

Ora Eitan

(AY-ten)

April 28, 1940–

"When I was little, I was very little—the smallest in my class. Therefore, I was always seated in the front row, just beneath the teacher's eyes. With a huge bow in my hair, two missing teeth, one lazy eye, and a pair of eyeglasses with a black patch on the right side, there was no chance to hide. While my left eye was lazy, my other eye was extremely useful. It worked very hard. In fact, it could see things normal eyes could never see.

"One day, when the teacher bent over me to check my work, a beam of sunshine broke on his gold-framed glasses. Beautiful, rainbow-colored shapes emerged in front of my eyes—both the lazy eye and the healthy one.

"'Fairies, fairies,' I called out loud, jumping to my feet.

"The class went crazy; the teacher went mad. I was expelled from class and ordered to write, 200 times, 'Fairies do not exist!' And so I wrote. But I added a 201st line: 'Fairies do not exist, or so my *teacher* says!'

"Years went by. I cut my hair, grew new teeth, and got rid of the black patch.

"But I still wear my glasses, and still spot fairies, elves, dwarves, and devils. These fantastic creatures, as I found out, were not born in my mind alone but in many minds before mine: They all live safe and happy in the pages of thousands of books. The world of words became my domain.

"Israel, where I was born and grew up, is a nation that cherished the written word, and books had exquisite literary quality, though poor visuals to match it. In the newborn country, still struggling to survive, color illustrations were rare. Such vibrant pictures could be found only in my parents' old European books, which I could not read.

"For my sixth birthday, my parents gave me a box of 24 imported crayons—a luxury at that time. It was, by far, the best gift I ever received. Years later, with a studio full of colors, I am still grateful for that gift, which allows me to this day to do what I love most: paint and write."

❀　❀　❀

Courtesy of Noah Tchernov

Ora Eitan's mother, Debora Urbach, immigrated to Israel from Lodz, Poland, with her parents and two siblings in 1924; her father was a Zionist. There she met Ora's father, Zeev Sandhause, a leader of a Zionist youth group called Hanoar Hezioni. Zeev had come to Israel in 1932. His parents, sister, and one brother who remained in Europe were killed in the Holocaust; but three other brothers escaped. Zeev was one of the builders of Tel Aviv.

Zeev and Debora's daughter Ora was born and raised in Tel Aviv and graduated from Bzalel Academy of Art and Design in Jerusalem, where she earned a B.F.A. in graphic design and fine art. She also received a teaching diploma. To support herself as a student, she worked in the botanic gardens of the Hebrew University, where she met a young biologist, Eitan Tchernov. They shared an interest in nature, music, literature, art—and each other. Eventually they married and settled in Jerusalem. When Ora began publishing, she created a pen name for herself from her first name and her husband's first name.

Ora started her career as an illustrator and writer for a children's magazine, *Haareth Shelanu*. Shortly before giving birth to her son Dan, in 1967, she received her first assignments in book illustration, as well as a job at a daily newspaper where she worked as an illustrator, caricaturist, and reporter. After daughter Noa was born in 1971, the family went to Africa. They spent a sabbatical in Nairobi, traveling, camping, and going on safaris. The book *Donkey's Tale*, which Ora wrote, illustrated, and designed, came out of these trips and won the Israeli Book Contest award for Distinguished Book Design.

Since 1977, Ora has taught illustration at her alma mater, Bzalel Academy. At the same time, she became a member of the editorial board of *Pilon* children's magazine. In addition, Ora has designed and illustrated book and magazine covers, posters, and postcards. But her main interest has always been books. Ora's illustrated books have earned her 37 awards, including Israel's nomination and a certificate of honor for IBBY's Hans Christian Andersen Award (1978); the Nachum Gutman Award (1988); and the Ben Izhak Medal for Distinguished Illustration (1978, 1988, and 1996). Though she was well-known in Israel, it wasn't until the 1990s that Ora's work began to appear in the United States. Her whimsical, light-hearted illustrations for writers such as Tony Johnston, Christine Loomis, and Jennifer Ericsson have been highly praised.

Ora enjoys using different artistic techniques, tailoring her approach to suit a book's content and spirit. Although she uses the computer, she has never neglected her painting. She also participates in art shows and exhibitions. Venues at which her artwork has been exhibited include the Albatros Gallery, Prague; the Israel Museum, Jerusalem; Every Picture Tells a Story, Los Angeles; the Art Institute of Chicago; the Widener Library, Harvard University; and the Society of Illustrators, New York.

Courtesy of HarperCollins Publishers

SELECTED WORKS WRITTEN: *Sometimes Big, Sometimes Small*, illus. by Elchanan, 1992.

SELECTED WORKS ILLUSTRATED: *Sun Is Falling, Night Is Calling*, by Laura Leuck, 1994; *Inch by Inch: The Garden Song*, by David Mallett, 1995; *Little Wild Parrot*, by Tony Johnston, 1995; *Hanna's Sabbath Dress*, by Itzhak Schweiger-Dmi'el, 1996; *Cowboy Bunnies*, by Christine Loomis, 1997; *No Milk!*, by Jennifer Ericsson, 1999; *Dance, Sing, Remember: A Celebration of Jewish Holidays*, by Leslie Kimmelman, 2000; *Astro Bunnies*, by Christine Loomis, 2001; *A Tisket, a Tasket*, by Ella Fitzgerald, 2003; *Scuba Bunnies*, by Christine Loomis, 2004.

"I was born in Boston and grew up in a 300-year-old Colonial house on a river in Ipswich, Massachusetts. It is a mostly suburban area, but with woods and vast salt marshes that lead to the beaches and the ocean beyond. We were close enough that even as a child I could row a small boat to the sea from our house. My father, illustrator Ed Emberley, was in love with boats

Michael Emberley

June 2, 1960–

of all kinds, but especially sailboats. As a family we sailed most summers around the area from Maine to Nantucket. And though I was to adopt the habit of drawing from my father, I never developed his passion for the sea. It was the bicycle, and racing the winding roads of New England, that grabbed me with a similar intensity. And to this day I spend at least as much time riding as drawing, probably more. I pursue it with passion . . . but I also pursue other things with passion. I am curious, above all. Curious about how and why things are the way they are. What makes a lightbulb work? Curious about how people behave and what drives them. Why do we eat with a fork, and when did it start? Silly things. In school I was told I asked too many questions, but I was a classic underachiever. I have only a little formal art instruction at the college level. A few months here and there. The Rhode Island School of Design is the best known of the lot. I think I was there three months.

Courtesy of Shireen Agherdiem

"So I became an author/illustrator for two reasons: It was around the house—my mother and father, my sister Rebecca, and I were always dabbling in arts and crafts, including helping my father with his work. Then I woke up one day as a late teenager and realized I needed to get a job. My second revelation was that I was not qualified for much and, with my work ethic at school, I would have trouble getting into a university. I could draw a little, so I tried illustrating. My prospects were limited. I had little choice.

"This is how it started. Not with a higher calling, or the pursuit of a lifelong dream. I needed a profession, I needed money. Even though this sounds a little crass or unromantic, this is the reason many great artists and writers have been motivated to produce. I even had my first book published before I got into art school, but I did not tell anyone because it seemed kind of pretentious.

"After doing three books, two of which were drawing books almost identical to my father's more famous work, I stopped illustrating and took a job creating computer graphics for an oil industry educational publisher. I had to bluff my way into the job since I had only spent about an hour on a computer in my life. But I was a fast learner.

"Then I took a year to travel to Australia and New Zealand, and to decide what to do for the rest of my life. With prospects still limited, I chose children's books, but this time I really chose it, and decided to teach myself to write too (with the help of some understanding friends who read and commented on early drafts). This took about another year of living very close to the poverty line as I wrote and illustrated five dummy books to take to publishers.

"*Ruby* was the first of this second batch of books, followed by *The Present* and *Welcome Back Sun*. After I met author Robie Harris at an autographing event, we embarked on a series of nonfiction books about growing up and sexuality. A stretch, you might think—but remember I am curious about everything, and Robie sold me on her vision and on her ability. We are good friends as well as partners, and the long hours we spend trying to make complicated topics into readable, useful books have been incredibly rewarding.

"I do what pleases me, even when it means doing far more work than I could ever be compensated for. I like to do things the best way I know how. I like to be challenged . . . and then hope for the best. If I am happy and interested, I do my best work. If I get bored with what I am doing, it shows. I began illustrating because I needed money, but now I truly appreciate what I do. I like doing a variety of book projects and using different techniques. This is more difficult than mastering one style but it is the only way for me.

"I can also pretty much make my own schedule, which makes it easier to train and race the bicycle. And it allows time to stare into space, which is something I have learned is important for me. If I don't have a good deal of 'nothing time,' my creativity and motivation dry up. All of this limits how much work I can produce, but I have accepted the trade-off of money (and possible fame!) for a slower, more varied quality of life. I simply could not work at my desk all day every day like some artists or writers do. I still think I'm getting away with something, and one day I'll be told I have to get a real job. It frightens me. Being an author and illustrator allows me to learn and discover about people and the world. I weave all my curiosity into each paragraph and drawing. And going through my mind the whole time is the question: 'Is this good enough?' and the answer: 'No, but the next one is going to be really good!' "

> *"I am curious, above all. Curious about how and why things are the way they are."*

❋　❋　❋

That Michael Emberley turned to illustrating children's books as a career is no surprise, given his family background. Growing up with his parents, Ed and Barbara Emberley, who had collaborated on the 1968 Caldecott Award–winning *Drummer Hoff*, Michael was surrounded by art. His mother had majored in fashion design, and his father's series of books on how to draw have been staple items in library collections since the 1970s. Michael and his older sister, Rebecca, both assisted their father with his books when they were teenagers, but as they began to create their own books both developed distinctive individual styles. The contrasting styles of the Emberley family may be seen in the one

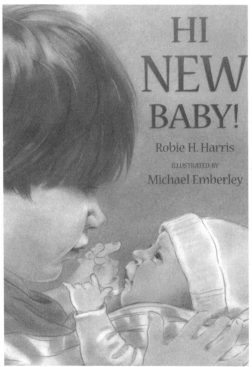

HI NEW BABY!

Robie H. Harris

ILLUSTRATED BY

Michael Emberley

Courtesy of Candlewick Press

volume they created together: *Three: An Emberley Family Scrapbook*. Each artist contributed a section to the book, based on the concept of "three"—Ed's section features his computer-generated graphics, Rebecca's her signature collage illustrations, and Michael's his exuberant watercolor, ink, and crayon pictures—to produce a unique family album of artistic styles.

Michael's own picture books have received recognition from the beginning. *Ruby* is a clever spoof on the fairy tale of "Little Red Riding Hood" with a mouse as the main character and a cat playing the part of the wolf. *Welcome Back Sun*, the charming story of a Norwegian girl who wants to hasten a long-awaited spring in her far-northern environment, received a Blue Ribbon citation from the *Bulletin of the Center for Children's Books*. Working with other authors, Michael created evocative illustrations for Robie Harris's *Happy Birth Day!*, enhancing a story about a new baby that was named a *School Library Journal* Best Book for 1996, and his complementary art to Mary Ann Hoberman's poetry in *You Read to Me, I'll Read to You* resulted in a book that became an ALA Notable Children's Book in 2002.

It was his illustrations for Robie Harris's groundbreaking book on sexuality, *It's Perfectly Normal: A Book About Changing Bodies, Growing Up, Sex, and Sexual Health*, that brought Michael Emberley his most widespread recognition. The book won a *Boston Globe–Horn Book* Honor Award for nonfiction and was an ALA Notable Children's Book and a *New York Times* Notable Book of the Year; it appeared on nearly every Best of the Year list in 1994. Major media attention was drawn to this title in newspapers around the country, often because of concerns voiced by conservative groups that the information was too frank and the illustrations too graphic; but Harris's approach to the subject and Emberley's tastefully accurate illustrations have been commended by educational organizations, reviewers, and library professionals for their honesty, openness, and respect for young people. The team of Harris and Emberley also produced *It's So Amazing!: A Book About Eggs, Sperm, Birth, Babies, and Families*, on the same topic for younger children, and this title was named an ALA Notable Children's Book, a *Horn Book* Fanfare title, a *School Library Journal* Best of the Year, and a Parents' Guide to Children's Media Award winner. It has also attracted national print, television, and radio coverage, including a feature article in the *Boston Globe* and a recommendation in *Child* magazine.

Michael Emberley lives and works in San Diego, California.

SELECTED WORKS WRITTEN AND ILLUSTRATED: *Dinosaurs: A Drawing Book*, 1980; *The Sports Equipment Book*, 1982; *More Dinosaurs! and Other Prehistoric Beasts: A Drawing Book*, 1983; *Ruby*, 1990; *The Present*, 1991; *Welcome Back Sun*, 1993; *Three: An Emberley Family Scrapbook* (with Ed Emberley and Rebecca Emberley), 1998; *Ruby and the Sniffs*, 2004.

SELECTED WORKS ILLUSTRATED: *Rudolph's Second Christmas*, by Robert Lewis May, 1992; *Rudolph the Red-Nosed Reindeer*, by Robert Lewis May, 1994; *It's Perfectly Normal: A Book About Changing Bodies, Growing Up, Sex, and Sexual Health*, by Robie H. Harris, 1994; *Happy Birth Day!* by Robie H. Harris, 1996; *It's So Amazing!: A Book About Eggs, Sperm, Birth, Babies, and Families*, by Robie H. Harris, 1999; *You Read to Me, I'll Read to You: Very Short Stories to Read Together*, by Mary Ann Hoberman, 2001; *Growing Up Stories Up to 1: When Benny Was a Baby*, by Robie H. Harris, 2002; *Go! Go! Maria!: What It's Like to Be One*, by Robie H. Harris, 2003; *You Read to Me, I'll Read to You: Very Short Fairy Tales to Read Together*, by Mary Ann Hoberman, 2004; *Sweet Jasmine, Nice Jackson: What It's Like to Be Two*, by Robie H. Harris, 2004.

SUGGESTED READING: *Something About the Author*, vol. 119, 2001.

WEB SITE: *www.michaelemberley.com*

A profile of Michael Emberley's parents, Ed and Barbara Emberley, appeared in *Third Book of Junior Authors* (1972). His sister, Rebecca, was profiled in *Eighth Book of Junior Authors and Illustrators* (2000).

Karen English
June 12, 1947–

"I was born in Vallejo, California, but grew up in Los Angeles. I was the middle child in a family of five. Some of my most vivid childhood memories are of the books I read. In the fourth grade, I wanted to be Beverly Cleary's character, Ellen Tebbits, in her book, *Ellen Tebbits*. In the fifth grade, I wanted to be the title character in Carol Ryrie Brink's book, *Caddie Woodlawn*.

"At that time, in children's literature, there were no young female African American characters—mainstream or historical. I was aware of this, but it was like being aware of the sun. It was just something that was. In some ways, I wasn't bothered by this because emotions have no color, and it was easy to relate to Ellen Tebbits's horror mixed with satisfaction when she accidentally-on-purpose slapped her best friend, Austine, over a pulled sash.

"Like most writers, I began as a reader. I remember the sound of cracking open one of those little Golden Books you could buy in the supermarket. I remember the candy-like scent of the binding. And I remember the excitement in my stomach when a book was compelling from the start.

"I began writing early. My mother called my stories the 'Miss Flouncy Stories.' I wrote them on a thick pad of lined newsprint with a fat pencil when I was seven. I don't remember what I wrote, but I remember the process and how wonderful it felt. There was one story I wrote as a child that I do remember vividly. When I was in the fifth grade, I attempted to write a novel about a little girl who had to move from the city to the country (I knew nothing about the country). This was after the Miss Flouncy days. We had a housekeeper then. If I did a few chores, she would listen to each new excerpt and would allow me to read from the beginning just so she could hear the new part in the right context. (That was my idea. She probably daydreamed through it.) The sad thing was, although I knew I was writing about a little black girl, I could not make her description black. I gave her long blonde hair and blue eyes, but rationalized that she was still kind of secretly 'colored' (a word we used then).

Courtesy of Yervard/Royal Photography

"Midyear a girl named Linda Shannon entered 42nd Street School, which was the school I attended. She was not in my class because she was a grade behind. But, voilà, she was colored with long blonde braids (straight) and green eyes. I felt vindicated. I'd never seen a black character in a book outside of *Little Black Sambo*. There were almost no black characters on television or in the movies. Hence, my imagination just did not stretch that far. Thank God things have changed.

"As an adult, I began writing for children seriously when my own children reached a level of independence where they weren't so emotionally consuming for me. I had to be in a place where there wasn't an interruption threatening me every 15 minutes. I love writing. I consider it a blessing from God. It makes life much more interesting to see a fragment of a plot or character in almost everything and everyone. The journey of an idea or a notion or a thought to a whole complete novel seems almost miraculous.

"Today I teach second grade at Martin Luther King Elementary School in Oakland, California. I am also the mother of four grown children (Ain, 33 years old; Kenneth, 31; Erin, 25; and Isaac, 22) and the grandmother of one (Gavin Young, 15 months old)."

✹ ✹ ✹

Karen English received her bachelor of arts degree in psychology from California State University at Los Angeles, where she also completed her course work in elementary education. A book-aholic by nature, English loves to visit bookstores and browse the shelves. If she knows she doesn't have time to read a particular book right away, she still has a need to have it on her shelves. Two of her current favorite authors are Kevin Henkes and Cynthia Rylant. She loves their humor.

Though she had written stories as a child, English did not consider writing for publication until 1993, when *Newsweek* magazine accepted an essay from her for a column called "My Turn." She wrote about media coverage of the violence that ensued after the first Rodney King verdict, coverage which she felt had unfairly characterized the African American population in South-Central Los Angeles as approving of lawlessness and crime. When *Newsweek* printed her piece, the elementary teacher began to think she could attempt writing, and children's books seemed the right market for her. She published several picture books, but her greatest success began with a rejection letter.

Courtesy of Farrar, Straus and Giroux

An editor returned a picture book manuscript saying it seemed more like the beginning of a novel, so she began to expand the story into the book that became *Francie*. English grew up hearing her mother talk about the prejudice that existed during her own childhood. Based on the time and place in which her mother lived (the pre–civil rights era in North Carolina), *Francie* is, nevertheless, largely fictional. The story centers on 12-year-old Francie, who befriends a 16-year-old boy she is tutoring in reading; trouble erupts when he is accused of the attempted murder of a white man and Francie comes to his aid. "Most of what I write is based on research mixed with what I've experienced emotionally," says English. "The details are fiction. I've never used, specifically, someone I know or have known in a story. Characters can be a composite. I'm acutely aware that everyone has a story and every situation could be part of a novel. Just that awareness colors how I see and experience everything. It's kind of like sensory overload. The challenge is sifting through all the data to come up with a story." *Francie* was named a Coretta Scott King Honor Book, an ALA Notable Children's Book, an IRA Notable Book for a Global Society, and a *School Library Journal* Best Book. It also received the Northern California Book Award and was designated a Distinguished Work of Fiction by the Children's Literature Council of Southern California.

English's very first book was the picture book *Neeny Coming, Neeny Going*, a bittersweet story about growing up, letting go, the loss of old loves, and the importance of remembering one's roots. Illustrated by Synthia Saint James, *Neeny Coming, Neeny Going* received a Coretta Scott King Honor Award for Illustration. According to English, the difference between writing a picture book and writing a novel is that a novel requires a lot more sustained energy and you live with the novel's characters for a much longer period of time. Characters in novels become old friends, while characters in picture books forever remain new ones.

SELECTED WORKS: *Neeny Coming, Neeny Going*, illus. by Synthia Saint James, 1996; *Big Wind Coming!*, illus. by Cedric Lucas, 1996; *Just Right Stew*, illus. by Anna Rich, 1998; *Francie*, 1999; *Nadia's Hands*, illus. by Jonathan Weiner, 1999; *Speak English for Us, Marisol!*, illus. by Enrique O. Sánchez, 2000; *Strawberry Moon*, 2001; *Hot Day on Abbott Avenue*, illus. by Javaka Steptoe, 2004; *Speak to Me (And I Will Listen Between the Lines)*, illus. by Amy June Bates, 2004.

SUGGESTED READING: English, Karen, "South-Central Exposure" (My Turn column), *Newsweek*, May 24, 1993; Roper, Ingrid, "A Testament to Perseverance," *Publishers Weekly*, December 20, 1999.

Shane Evans

December 26, 1971–

"I can remember, as far back as five years old, being interested in art and always being encouraged to pursue that interest. I had an aunt and an uncle who were artists and they both insisted that whatever project I was working on, I do it myself. My mom was a teacher and my dad worked for the government in customs at the Canadian border. They were both a huge influence on me and were very supportive of all my efforts. They recognized early that art was important to me and sent me to the Buffalo Academy of Visual and Performing Arts from 5th to 9th grade. There I was surrounded by other students who were interested in the arts, and we had extra time in our school day to pursue whatever branch of the arts we wanted to: drawing, painting, sculpture, photography, music, dance.

"When my mom got a job in Rochester, I moved there to attend another school of the arts through my high school years. There I became interested in the performing arts, which expanded my horizons. Many of my friends went on to become actors and musicians; in that school my peers were as encouraging as my teachers. One art teacher in particular, Ms. Medler, taught me how to stay focused on my work by keeping a sketchbook and being aware of all the influences around me. She was a former English teacher, so she made sure we paid attention to our spelling and grammar too, which would be a big help to me when I got into working on books.

"I majored in illustration at Syracuse University. The school of the arts was very prominent on the campus, and I studied photography and painting as well as computer work and design. I followed creative pursuits in my free time, too, and performed as a vocalist in a band. My friend Taye Diggs got me involved in working on plays and musicals; we grew up together and went to college together, and now he's gone on to a career in professional acting.

"After graduation, I was approached by both Hallmark Cards and *Rolling Stone* magazine to do internships. I decided to spend the summer of 1993 in the internship at *Rolling Stone,* and it was a great experience. They brought in four individuals to be interns and we worked on 3 or 4 issues. I was the design intern and spent that summer around a lot of influential people in various branches of the media. It was a tremendous learning experience. At the end of the summer, I moved to Kansas City to take the job with Hallmark, where I learned so much. Some people say working at Hallmark is like going to paid graduate school, and in many ways that is true. We had workshops and seminars available to us for developing our creativity in many ways. We had ceramics facilities available to us. I learned to design and to build furniture. I was inspired by working beside many creative people. I also kept up my computer skills, which are so relevant to my work today. Through that time I was working on children's book projects at night. Finally in 2000 I had to make a choice, and I decided to pursue my illustration work full time.

Courtesy of Topher Cox

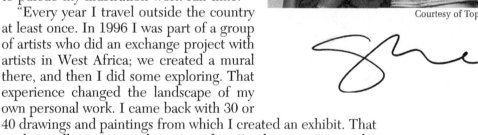

"Every year I travel outside the country at least once. In 1996 I was part of a group of artists who did an exchange project with artists in West Africa; we created a mural there, and then I did some exploring. That experience changed the landscape of my own personal work. I came back with 30 or 40 drawings and paintings from which I created an exhibit. That work is still instrumental to me today. I've been to Japan, the Dominican Republic, Venezuela, Australia, and other places. Each day on a journey I sketch or write or take photographs, something to open my mind and heart to what is around me. I have been blessed in my life to be surrounded by supportive, creative people, but it is most important to believe in yourself and stay open to the world around you."

✼   ✼   ✼

Born in Oakland, California, Shane Evans moved to upstate New York when he was just a few years old and was raised in Buffalo and Rochester, New York. He received his B.A. degree in 1993 from the Syracuse University School of Visual and Performing Arts. His career at Hallmark Cards, from 1993 to 2000, included many opportunities for further study in a variety of media, including ceramics, computer graphics, welding, and furniture design. Since 2000 Evans has concentrated on his freelance career, which includes theater posters, advertising, CD designs, and studio art, as well as an impressive number of books for young readers.

In his first children's book, Shane Evans teamed with basketball star Shaquille O'Neal to create a unique and vibrant retelling of several traditional folk tales with actual photos of O'Neal inserted into Evans's broad, cartoon-style art. *Shaq and the Beanstalk* is a rollicking rendition of nursery favorites updated for modern children and reluctant readers. Evans also found critical acclaim in illustrating the recollections of a sharecropper's daughter, Osceola Mays, as retold by Alan Govenar, with stylized oil paintings of a hard life lived with dignity. *Osceola* was named a *Boston Globe–Horn Book* Honor Book for nonfiction, an Orbis Pictus Honor Book, an ALA Notable Children's Book, and a Notable Social Studies Trade Book for Young People.

Courtesy of Candlewick Press

The influence of a month of work and travel in West Africa is evident in Evans's illustrations for *Bintou Braids*, the story of a young girl living in West Africa and a book that appeared in the annual Choices list of the Cooperative Children's Book Center. *The Way a Door Closes*, a heartfelt collection of poems about situations faced by today's children, illustrated with great sensitivity by Evans, was named a *School Library Journal* Best Book; and *No More!: Stories and Songs of Slave Resistance*, powerful writings selected by Doreen Rappaport and illustrated by Evans with equally powerful paintings, received a Parents' Choice Gold Award and was included on the New York Public Library's annual list of 100 Titles for Reading and Sharing.

Each new book illustrated by Shane Evans reveals another aspect of this artist's remarkable talent—from the astounding perspectives of *Take It to the Hoop, Magic Johnson* to the warm family relationships in *Down the Winding Road*; from the poignant endurance and determination seen in the faces in *No*

More! to the hope of overcoming prejudice seen in the eyes of the young girl in Andrea Davis Pinkney's *Fishing Day.* Shane Evans lives in Kansas City, Missouri.

SELECTED WORKS ILLUSTRATED: *Shaq and the Beanstalk and Other Very Tall Tales,* by Shaquille O'Neal, 1999; *Osceola: Memories of a Sharecropper's Daughter,* collected and edited by Alan Govenar, 2000; *Take It to the Hoop, Magic Johnson,* by Quincy Troupe, 2000; *Down the Winding Road,* by Angela Johnson, 2000; *Bintou Braids,* by Sylviane A. Diouf, 2001; *Shanna's Doctor Show,* by Jean Marzollo, 2001; *Shanna's Princess Show,* by Jean Marzollo, 2001; *Shanna's Teacher Show,* by Jean Marzollo, 2002; *Shanna's Ballerina Show,* by Jean Marzollo, 2002; *Here We Go Round,* by Alice McGill, 2002; *Homemade Love,* by bell hooks, 2002; *No More!: Stories and Songs of Slave Resistance,* by Doreen Rappaport, 2002; *The Way a Door Closes,* by Hope Anita Smith, 2003; *Fishing Day,* by Andrea Davis Pinkney, 2003; *Free at Last!: Stories and Songs of Emancipation,* by Doreen Rappaport, 2004.

WEB SITE: *www.shaneevans.com*

"I was born in Connecticut in 1959. As a boy, I attended the Long Ridge School in Stamford. At the age of fourteen, I was sent away to the Cambridge School of Weston in Massachusetts. Both schools were liberal, experimental, and progressive and allowed me to spend serious time concentrating on my artistic interests. For this I cannot thank my parents enough.

"After experiencing such a lovely, tolerant, and nurturing environment, however, I was caught completely off guard by the cold realities of collegiate academia. New York University gently asked me to leave after my sophomore year. I then spent two years at Parsons School of Design in New York before transferring to Otis Art Institute in Los Angeles.

"In Los Angeles, I began my career as an artist. I also started working with the painter David Hockney. I first assisted him on revivals of some of his earlier opera productions . . . later I began collaborating with him, designing sets and costumes for new productions of *Tristan and Isolde* for the Los Angeles Opera, *Die Frau Ohne Schatten* for Covent Garden and *Turandot* for the Chicago Lyric and San Francisco Operas. It was here that I learned the ancient and delicate art of transforming a large, difficult, aggressive, middle-aged dramatic soprano into an 18-year-old virgin princess.

Courtesy of Roddy McDowell

Ian Falconer

August 25, 1959–

"In 1995 I moved back to New York, where I have continued painting and stage design for theater, mostly ballet, notably Stravinsky's *Scènes de Ballet* for the New York City Ballet and his *Firebird* for the Boston Ballet. Also, I started working for the *New Yorker* magazine, my first time doing illustration. I am now working on my fourteenth cover for them.

"At the same time, I began fooling around with an idea for *Olivia*. I intended it originally as a little Christmas present for my niece of the same name. The real Olivia is an extremely headstrong, imaginative child who, even at the age of three (she is older now, of course), could argue (or stonewall, or bulldoze, or filibuster) through any 'inconvenience' to achieve her goal. (Always in the nicest way, I might add; she's very charming.)

"At any rate, the drawings and the character became better and better, so I began to really develop it in earnest. Eventually, I brought it to a large Manhattan agency, where I was told that although they loved the drawings, they felt that I should be paired with a professional writer. Well, having so carefully created this character, I am afraid my vanity wouldn't allow me to relegate myself to 'illustrated by.' I also thought my instincts about the story were, if unpolished, right on target, and had happened organically with the pictures.

Courtesy of Atheneum Books for Young Readers

"So, I sat on it. Then a couple of years later, Anne Schwartz at Simon and Schuster called me. She liked my *New Yorker* work and asked if I would be interested in doing a children's book. I brought her *Olivia*."

Ian Falconer has had a varied career spanning the worlds of publishing, opera, ballet, and fine arts. Born in Ridgefield, Connecticut, Falconer studied art history at New York University and painting at Parsons School of Design and Otis Art Institute. His career in set design and costume design for stage, opera, and ballet was well established and his cover art for the *New Yorker* magazine well recognized when he ventured into the field of children's books.

An illustrated story that began as a 1997 Christmas present for Olivia Crane, the daughter of Falconer's sister, Victoria, *Olivia* was published in the year 2000 to immediate critical acclaim and wide popularity with children and adults alike. A day in the life of curious, active, and self-confident Olivia is depicted in shadowed vignettes that make it clear she is always center-stage in her own world. Falconer's minimalist approach employs tones of gray, black, and white with accents of red gouache and generous use of white backgrounds, which set off the character of the precocious piglet.

Olivia captured a Caldecott Honor Award as well as being named an ALA Notable Children's Book and appearing on virtually all the "best books of the year" lists. The following year, *Olivia Saves the Circus* was also named an ALA Notable Children's Book, a *School Library Journal* Best Book and a *New York Times* Best Illustrated Book. Falconer has created board books about the same character that illustrate concepts for the very young. Selling over one million copies to date in the United States, the Olivia books have been translated into 17 languages. In 2001, Falconer teamed with humor writer David Sedaris to create a comic story, "Pretty Ugly," for the collection *Strange Stories for Strange Kids (Little Lit 2)*. Ian Falconer lives and works in Manhattan.

SELECTED WORKS WRITTEN AND ILLUSTRATED: *Olivia*, 2000; *Olivia Saves the Circus*, 2001; *Olivia Counts*, 2002; *Olivia's Opposites*, 2002; *Olivia . . . and the Missing Toy*, 2003.

SELECTED WORKS ILLUSTRATED: "Pretty Ugly," by David Sedaris, included in *Strange Stories for Strange Kids (Little Lit Book 2)*, ed. by Art Spiegelman, 2001.

SUGGESTED READING: *Something About the Author*, vol. 125, 2002. Periodicals—Brown, Jennifer, "Ian Falconer," *Publishers Weekly*, December 18, 2000; "No stone or story left unturned (the home of artist Ian Falconer in New York)," *New York Times*, December 6, 2001; "Pig Tales," *People Weekly*, February 4, 2002.

Cathryn Falwell

March 17, 1952–

"I was born in Kansas in 1952 and moved several times—to Missouri, Wisconsin, Minnesota, and Connecticut—before entering high school. Each time I started at a new school, kids would ask me if I had a dog named Toto, since they only knew about Kansas from *The Wizard of Oz*.

"Being the 'new kid' had its challenges. One way I made friends was by drawing. I loved to draw and always carried a sketchbook around with me. It was a good way to start a conversation with someone. Other kids would peer over my shoulder to see what I was drawing. Sometimes I was shy about my artwork. A teacher might hold up my work to show the class and say, 'Look at this lovely picture, boys and girls.' I would whisper to those nearby: 'Yours is really better,' or 'She didn't see yours. You draw really well.' Having friends was more important to me than having my work praised. My memories of drawing and making friends later inspired the story for my book *David's Drawings*.

"I have always loved to draw and paint and make things, and also to write stories and poems. When I was in the second grade, I told my mother that I wanted to make books for children when I grew up. I did many other things before finally making picture books. After graduating from college, I was a printmaker, a waitress, a teacher, a graphic designer, and then a mother with two children before my first book was published. That book was *Where's Nicky?*, and it's a simple little picture book for babies and toddlers. It was the first of a series of six books about Nicky. To make the illustrations for those books, I used cut paper collage. I enjoyed the technique because it allowed me to change my mind easily. If I didn't like the color of a T-shirt, for example, I could just tear it gently off the paper and glue on a new one It was much easier than trying to erase crayon, pastel, or paint.

"Since the *Nicky* books, I've had many more books published. For all of them, I have used cut paper collage. Sometimes I also add scraps of cloth, leaf prints, rubber-stamped patterns, or torn tissue collage. I enjoy exploring a variety of materials and techniques, so right now I'm using paint for the illustrations of a new book. After more than 20 books, I wanted to try something completely different.

"My husband and I have two sons—Alex and Nick. Both were born in Hartford, Connecticut. The elementary school they attended there was a wonderfully diverse, multi-ethnic community that helped them to grow into kind, talented, creative young men. Now we live in Maine, on Frog Song Pond. Every day I look to see if there are any 'new kids' at the pond. Sometimes I see a mother mallard with her ducklings, a new butterfly testing its wings, or the footprints of a deer in the snow. We have a dog, too— but his name is Bailey, not Toto."

Courtesy of Kate Greenman

✻ ✻ ✻

Cathryn Falwell earned her B.F.A. in art from the University of Connecticut School of Fine Arts. In addition to writing and illustrating books, she is involved in many volunteer projects in her community. She recently painted large murals in the new children's area of her town's library, the Baxter Memorial Library in Goreham, Maine. As a child, Falwell enjoyed picture books that had hidden things to look for in the illustrations, and so in these murals, she has included many things for children to find—little faces peek from behind stones, a faint castle appears in the clouds, insects and small animals are tucked under the leaves. She loves watching the library's young visitors make discoveries in the murals.

Falwell also visits schools and libraries in many states, where she presents interactive programs for children about books and creativity. She encourages children to use their imaginations to make books of their own. With scraps from old magazines, wrapping paper, and colored envelopes, she shows them how to cut and paste collages to make the illustrations. Cutting and pasting paper has been a lifelong activity for Falwell. As a young child, she received a box of special papers from her aunt, who was an artist. The beautiful papers—foils, prints, textured and flocked sheets—seemed too precious to use. It was many years before she found the courage to take her scissors to them. Her book *Butterflies for Kiri*, which was a Parents' Guide to Children's Media Award winner and named one of Bank Street College of Education's Best Children's Books of the Year, is reminiscent of this experience. A young girl receives a package of beautiful origami papers and is hesitant to play with them until her creative energy finally motivates her to use them in an imaginative way.

Turtle Splash was named an ALA Notable Children's Book and received an Oppenheim Toy Portfolio Gold Award. A combination counting book and nature tale, this story in verse also received an outstanding merit citation on Bank Street College of Education's Best of the Year list, and became an Honor Book for Maine's Lupine Award and a PBS *Science Friday* recommended book. Another counting book, *Feast for Ten*, features a rhyming text about a family buying groceries and preparing a meal. In a different type of concept book, *The Letter Jesters*, which was chosen as a *Reading Rainbow* Review Book, Falwell introduces children to the world of typography and the influence that fonts and typefaces have on a reader's emotions.

In *David's Drawings*, named a Parent's Guide to Children's Media Award winner and one of Bank Street College of Education's Best Children's Books of the Year, Falwell re-creates a dilemma from her own childhood. A shy boy blossoms and makes

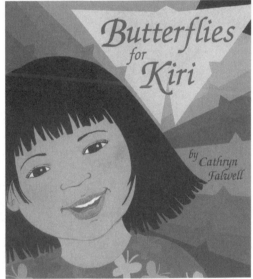

Courtesy of Lee & Low Books, Inc.

friends by letting his classmates help him draw a class picture, even while he continues to explore his own creative nature in private. *Word Wizard*, named a Notable Children's Book in the Language Arts and featured as a Junior Library Guild selection, is about a girl who can create anagrams out of alphabet cereal letters with a magic spoon. Another wordplay adventure, *Clowning Around*, was named a *Parenting* magazine Best Book of the Year and features a clown juggling eye-catching letters and manipulating them into words. Falwell's skill with mixed media illustrations in bold and lively colors enhances each story with a special sense of joy and purpose.

SELECTED WORKS WRITTEN AND ILLUSTRATED: *Where's Nicky?*, 1991; *Nicky, 123*, 1991; *Nicky and Grandpa*, 1991; *Nicky's Walk*, 1991; *Clowning Around*, 1991; *Nicky Loves Daddy*, 1992; *Nicky and Alex*, 1992; *Shape Space*, 1992; *Feast for Ten*, 1993; *We Have a Baby*, 1993; *The Letter Jesters*, 1994; *Dragon Tooth*, 1996; *P.J. & Puppy*, 1997; *Christmas for Ten*, 1998; *Word Wizard*, 1998; *David's Drawings*, 2001; *Turtle Splash!: Countdown at the Pond*, 2001; *Butterflies for Kiri*, 2003.

SELECTED WORKS ILLUSTRATED: *New Moon*, by Pegi Deitz Shea, 1996; *Hands!* by Virginia Kroll, 1997; *It's About Time*, by Florence Perry Heide, Roxanne Heide Pierce, and Judith Heide Gilliland, 1999.

Courtesy of Hyperion Books

Jules Feiffer

January 26, 1929–

"So far, I've been a political and social cartoonist, a playwright, a novelist, a screenwriter, a satirist, a college professor, and a children's book author. Writing children's books is fairly new to my résumé. In 2000, in my mid-sixties, I decided to start off the millennium by reinventing myself as a children's book author. My inspiration came from my three daughters. This new perspective—looking at the world through a child's eyes—was really an old perspective and gave me the chance to see things in a way I had almost forgotten. What I love about entering the children's book field at this age is being stupid. The problem with doing a weekly cartoon for as many years as I had was that I'd grown too sophisticated. I wish that I could start from scratch and know how to be dumb about it, but I can't. Being dumb about children's books makes me child-like in the best way because it returns me to my innocence.

"I was born in the Bronx in 1929 and started drawing at an early age. When I was five, I won a gold medal in an art contest. That's when I decided what I wanted to be when I grew up. I studied unimpressively at James Monroe High School and, after graduation, from 1947 to 1951, I attended drawing classes at Pratt Institute in Brooklyn. Around the same time, I started working for Will Eisner, the soon-to-be-legendary cartoonist. Eisner allowed me to write scripts for his classic comic, 'The Spirit.'

"In 1949, Eisner gave me the back page of his 'Spirit' section to start my own strip, and 'Clifford' was born. He became a Sunday cartoon-page regular, my first feature in print, which ran in six newspapers from 1949 to 1951. Serving two years in the Signals Corps, I spent my free hours experimenting with what was to be my first satirical cartoon narrative, a picture book for adults called *Munro* about a four-year-old boy who's drafted by mistake into the army. It took six years to find its way into print. Returning to civilian life, I then went from one job to another, managing not to get fired until I worked the six months necessary to earn unemployment insurance, until finally the *Village Voice* began to print my weekly political cartoon in 1956. It ran for 42 years. Eventually, these strips were pulled together and, in 1958, were published as a book called *Sick, Sick, Sick: A Guide to Non-Confident Living*. In April of 1959, *Munro* was finally published, bought for animation, and in 1961, it was awarded an Oscar by the Academy of Motion Picture Arts and Sciences as the best short-subject cartoon of the year. My cartoons have been collected into about 19 or 20 books, and have appeared in such publications as the *New Yorker, Esquire, Playboy,* and the *Nation*. At one point, I was commissioned by the *New York Times* to create its first op-ed page comic strip, which ran monthly until 2000, when I decided to give up political cartoons for children's books.

"I'd written books before, but *The Man in the Ceiling* was my first book for children. Although many people claim it's a study of the byways of the creative process (a theme I only saw in there after I was told), I thought the book was about failure. It was important to me as a father and as a former boy to get this out. Having been a smart, sensitive kid who often didn't live up to his own expectations of himself, and having had two children very much the same way, I wanted to deal with the rather un-American idea of failure as a process. In a country where we talk about winners and losers and being number one, we don't give any attention to failure as being one of the more necessary learning tools of life. One of the things that I've learned over the years, having taken a lot of lumps along with a lot of success, is that it's not failure that counts; it's how you treat failure and what your attitude towards it turns out to be. Because if you do anything that is of value, it has to involve risk and the chance of screwing up.

"I've written plays that were raved about that were inferior to the plays that got slammed. I decided early on that I am not going to let the critics determine my own judgment about my work. I am not going to let strangers make judgments on me that prevail in my own mind. But kids do that all the time. And sometimes they—themselves—are the critics. When something they do doesn't work out, they can drive themselves nuts. 'I stink. I'm no good. I'm lousy.' Until you see them through this tantrum, they won't give themselves a break. Sometimes they never give themselves a break.

"The secret of my success comes from the creative use of failure and ineptitude in my life."

"In a country where we talk about winners and losers and being number one, we don't give any attention to failure as being one of the more necessary learning tools of life."

❄ ❄ ❄

Jules Feiffer was born and raised in the Bronx, and has spent a good part of his life in New York City. A Pulitzer Prize–winning cartoonist, as well as a novelist, playwright, and screenwriter, Feiffer has also taught as an adjunct professor at Southampton College, the Yale School of Drama, and Northwestern University. He has been a Senior Fellow at Columbia University's National Arts Journalism Program, is a member of the Dramatists Guild Council, and was elected to the American Academy of Arts and Letters in 1994. He is the only cartoonist to have had a comic strip published as a regular feature by the *New York Times*.

Jules Feiffer recently donated some of his papers and several hundred cartoons and manuscripts to the Library of Congress. In 2003, the New York Historical Society presented a retrospective exhibit of his work spanning his entire professional career, including early cartoons for the *Village Voice* and manuscripts for his plays *Little Murders* and *Carnal Knowledge*. His awards include a Pulitzer Prize for editorial cartooning in 1986, an Academy Award for his animated short cartoon *Munro* in 1961, Obie Awards for his plays *Little Murders* and *The White House Murder Case*, a Tony award nomination for his play *Knock, Knock*, and a Venice Film Festival Best Screenplay award for *I Want to Go Home*. *Little Murders* also received the London Theatre Critics and Outer Circle Critics awards. It was filmed in 1971, as was *Carnal Knowledge*, with Feiffer writing both screenplays.

> "The secret of my success comes from the creative use of failure and ineptitude in my life."

Early in his career, Feiffer created the illustrations for the now classic children's story *The Phantom Tollbooth*, written by Norton Juster. Feiffer and Juster became friends when they lived in the same apartment building in Brooklyn. They shared an apartment for a while, and as an escape from a more mundane project, Feiffer started making drawings as Juster was writing chapters. In fact, some of the characters Juster wrote into *The Phantom Tollbooth* were actually conceived as a challenge to his illustrator-friend, such as the Triple Demons of Compromise, "one tall and thin, one short and fat, and the third exactly like the other two." Enjoying the wordplay and offbeat humor, the two friends created a book in which the text and art are perfectly complementary. First published in 1961, *The Phantom Tollbooth* was an immediate bestseller and has remained a standard favorite ever since.

Jules Feiffer returned to the children's book market nearly 30 years later after establishing his reputation as a political and social cartoonist and playwright. His cartoons had always provided a fresh and witty look at life, touching on social and political issues in his signature style of successive scenes without borders between them, the "panel-less panel cartoon," as *Print Magazine* called it. Looking for a new direction to his work in the early 1990s, and inspired by his own young children as well as a grandchild born to his oldest daughter, Feiffer reinvented himself as a children's book creator.

His first book written and illustrated for children, *The Man in the Ceiling*, was selected by *Publishers Weekly*, *Booklist*, and the Library of Congress as one of the best children's books of 1993. The New York Public Library placed it on both their lists for children and for young adults as a best book of the year. Feiffer explores the theme of failure in this story of a boy who is no good at sports, doesn't do well in school, and only wants to draw cartoons. His optimism, comic though it seems, carries him through his father's disapproval and the ups and downs of friendship. Illustrated with Feiffer's energetic black-and-white cartoons that capture the trials of the main character, the book was a hit with critics and readers alike.

I Lost My Bear was inspired by his daughter, who had misplaced a treasured toy in their New York apartment. Told completely from the angst-ridden child's point of view, this familiar family melodrama comes to a satisfying conclusion after escalating to the verge of crisis through Feiffer's energetic art and dialogue. Named an ALA Notable Children's Book, a *Bulletin of the Center for Children's Books* Blue Ribbon title, and a *Horn Book* Fanfare, among other honors, it became an instant success. *Bark, George*, a hilarious cumulative story that is a kind of reversal on the old story of the lady who swallowed a fly, was also named an ALA Notable Children's Book as well as a *School Library Journal* Best Book of the Year.

Bark, George was made into an animated video by the Weston Woods Studios with actor John Lithgow providing the narration and premiered at the New Haven Film Festival in September of 2003 in both the adult and children's part of the program. It was named an ALA Notable Video and won the Best Short Animation Classic in the International Family Film Festival. A film version of *I Lost My Bear*, also produced by Weston Woods and released in the fall of 2004, is narrated by Feiffer's daughter Halley, who is currently a student at Wesleyan University.

Jules Feiffer and his wife, Jenny Allan, a writer and stand-up comic, live in New York City with their two daughters. His oldest daughter (from a former marriage) and grandchild live on Martha's Vineyard.

SELECTED WORKS ILLUSTRATED FOR YOUNG READERS: *The Phantom Tollbooth*, Norton Juster, 1961, reissued 1989, 1996 (with an appreciation by Maurice Sendak); *Some Things Are Scary*, by Florence Parry Heide, 2000.

SELECTED WORKS WRITTEN AND ILLUSTRATED FOR YOUNG READERS: *The Man in the Ceiling*, 1993; *A Barrel of Laughs, a Vale of Tears*, 1995; *Meanwhile . . .* , 1997; *I Lost My Bear*, 1998; *Bark, George*, 1999; *I'm Not Bobby!*, 2000; *By the Side of the Road*, 2001; *The House Across the Street*, 2002; *The Daddy Mountain*, 2004.

SELECTED WORKS FOR ADULTS: *Sick, Sick, Sick*, 1958; *Passionella*, 1959; *The Explainers*, 1960; *Harry: The Rat with Women*, 1963; *The Unexpurgated Memoirs of Bernard Mergendeiler*, 1965; *Feiffer on Civil Rights*, 1966; *Feiffer's Marriage Manual*, 1967; *Pictures at a Prosecution, Drawings and Text from the Chicago Conspiracy Trial*, 1971; *Feiffer on Nixon*, 1974; *Ackroyd*, 1977; *Tantrum*, 1979; *Jules Feiffer's America from Eisenhower to Reagan*, 1982. Plays and films—*Munro* (animated short subject), 1961; *Little Murders*, 1968; *The White House Murder Case*, 1970; *Carnal Knowledge*, 1971; *Knock, Knock*, 1976; *Popeye*, 1980; *Grownups*, 1982; *Elliot Loves*, 1988; *Anthony Rose*, 1989; *I Want to Go Home*, 1989; *A Bad Friend*, 2003.

SUGGESTED READING: *Contemporary Authors*, New Revision Series, vol. 59, 1998; Hochman, Stanley. *McGraw-Hill Encyclopedia of World Drama*, vol. 2, 1984; Horn, Maurice, ed. *100 Years of American Newspaper Comics*, 1996; Wakeman, John, ed. *World Authors 1970–1975*, 1980. Periodicals—Gussow, Mel, "Jules Feiffer Finds New Visibility," *New York Times*, March 6, 2003; Heller, Steven, "Jules Feiffer: Cartoonist, Author, and Playwright," Interview, *Print*, May/June 1998; Stevens, Carol, "Baby Teeth: Five Prominent Artists . . . Turn Their Eye to Children's Books," *Print*, May/June 1999.

WEB SITE: *www.julesfeiffer.com*

"I am not actually a born illustrator. After a great deal of effort by my mother, I was actually born a baby in Irvington, New Jersey. And then, after a lot of crying, crawling, and carrying on, I became a toddler. It was at this point that I picked up a white crayon and created what my mother thinks was an astronaut floating in space. I then spent a number of years as a child. I remember drawing many battle scenes involving cavalry soldiers and their mounts and a particularly enjoyable day drawing the fallow deer at the Turtle Back Zoo. For fourth grade back-to-school night at Beechwood School in Mountainside, New Jersey, I drew a picture of a Siberian husky that hung on Mrs. Podmeir's classroom wall. I was particularly proud of my effort.

"When puberty started to take hold of me, my attention turned from Legos and drawing to basketball, and the center of my universe became the backboard in our driveway. Unfortunately, my basketball career barely escaped ninth grade. A couple of years later, I rediscovered my artistic ability and love of drawing. This was reinforced by a lovely young lady who sat next to me in an art class my last year in high school.

"Upon successfully graduating from my youth and high school, I attended Bucknell University. It was in my second year of college that I created a drawing that made me think that maybe I had a future with my talent. Believe it or not, it was a drawing of my jeans, and it had the perfect texture and just looked really, really good. That was about the time I discovered illustration as a career. Although I was pursuing a degree in animal behavior, my animal behavior adviser, as well as my roommate, encouraged me to continue drawing. My plans of medical or dental school became sidetracked as I went off to the Philadelphia College of Art after graduating from college.

"I had been doing magazine illustration and advertising storyboards for seven years after college when Margie Palatini's rough manuscript for *Piggie Pie* landed on my drawing table. Harry Devlin, an illustrator I knew, had always encouraged me to do children's books, and the text was so clever and funny, I did a mock-up of the book. Margie's agent had shopped it to a couple of publishers, but I thought I had better access to art directors as an illustrator, since it was common for illustrators to show their portfolios in person. I brought it to Clarion Books, where I was showing my portfolio, and an editor who saw the dummy bought it on the spot. *Piggie Pie* was very well received and led to a career in children's picture books.

Courtesy of Howard Fine

Howard Fine
February 6, 1961–

"Drawing and painting all day, although enjoyable, is also lonely, so around the time I started in picture books, I also went to dental school. I now divide my days between illustrating animal misbehavior and the oddly more social activity of performing root canals and other dental procedures on the fair folk here in Westchester County, New York, where I also live with my wife, Rona, and my three children."

❖   ❖   ❖

Howard Fine's career as an artist has taken a lot of turns. Before becoming a children's book artist, he did magazine illustrations for such trade journals as *ATT*, *Medical Economics*, and *Forbes*. He also worked in advertising, doing storyboards for Margie Palatini's husband, Rich, who was then an art director for Gianettino and Meredith, an advertising agency in Short Hills, New Jersey. So Fine actually knew Margie Palatini's husband before he ever met the writer who became the author of his first book.

"I now divide my days between illustrating animal misbehavior and the oddly more social activity of performing root canals and other dental procedures."

When illustrating a manuscript, Fine usually tries to imagine the scenes running through his mind as if they were in a movie. This helps him develop the characters' movements, mannerisms, and other visual character traits. As much as possible, he tries to illustrate around the text. That is, he tries to include information, and maybe even characters and visual jokes, not mentioned by the author. When it comes to visual point of view, Fine says he learned not to view everything from his own eye level from an illustrator who taught at Philadelphia College of Art. This instructor used to work as a courtroom artist, and during lengthy trials, he became so familiar with the courtroom characters that he would sometimes draw the scenes from vantage points other than where he was physically sitting. This left a lasting impression on Fine, who says, "The viewer's point of view (and I mean that literally), forcing perspectives, dramatic and altered lighting, value and colors all go into creating interest and content in a scene."

Piggie Pie won several state awards, including the Vermont Red Clover Children's Choice Picture Book Award, the Colorado Children's Book Award in the Picture Book category, the Kentucky Bluegrass Award for grades 4–8, and the Maryland Black-Eyed Susan Picture Book Award. *Piggie Pie* was also named an ALA Notable Children's Book and received the 1998 Kansas Reading Association's Bill Martin Jr. Picture Book Award. *Zak's Lunch*, also written by Margie Palatini, about a boy who is bored with his ham and cheese sandwich and conjures up a waitress to serve him all kinds of tasty delights, received the Bank Street College of Education's Irma S. and James H. Black Award for Excellence in Children's Literature.

A 1998 graduate of the University of Medicine and Dentistry of New Jersey, Fine is a practicing dentist even while he continues to illustrate children's books. When asked if he would ever

Courtesy of Clarion Books

consider combining his two careers—perhaps writing and illustrating a picture book about going to the dentist—Fine's response was: "I'm still waiting for that movie to make its première in my head." Until then, he continues to draw inspiration from his children: Ben, who is going into third grade; Elana, who is just entering kindergarten; and Emma, who is just starting preschool. He lives with his family in White Plains, New York.

SELECTED WORKS WRITTEN AND ILLUSTRATED: *A Piggie Christmas*, 2000.

SELECTED WORKS ILLUSTRATED: *Piggie Pie*, by Margie Palatini, 1995; *The Upstairs Cat*, by Karla Kuskin, 1997; *Zak's Lunch*, by Margie Palatini, 1998; *Zoom Broom*, by Margie Palatini, 1998; *Ding Dong, Ding Dong*, by Margie Palatini, 1999; *Steamboat Annie and the Thousand-Pound Catfish*, by Catherine Wright, 2001; *Broom Mates*, by Margie Palatini, 2002; *Dinosailors*, by Deb Lund, 2003; *Raccoon Tune*, by Nancy Shaw, 2003; *Seven Scary Monsters*, by Mary Beth Lundgren, 2003; *Bed Hogs*, by Kelly S. Dipucchio, 2004.

"When I was young, my family says, I hid among the kitchen cabinet pots when people came to visit. Once, they say, grandfather, James Rosseau, came to our house and began to hand out money to me, my two sisters, and three brothers. I was a toddler. He was a big man with a big, booming voice. 'What a foolish child,' I'm told he said, as I ignored the money and ran for the pots. I was too young to know then that fear

Sharon Flake

December 24, 1955–

would be a character trait that would stick with me most of my life.

"In elementary school, I slept in bed with my two older sisters. I'd be in the middle. Once the lights went off, clothing hanging across doors or lying on dressers turned into monsters in my mind. I remember saying more than once, that if the monster came he'd get my sister Daphne first, because she'd sleep on the edge of the bed. Then he'd get my sister Veronica, because she was the oldest. And he'd say I was too little to be bothered with, I think.

"Looking back at it now, I think my fears were driven by my insecurity—an insecurity many young people have. But I also think my fear was driven by something else that was untamed—creativity. It sounds funny, but I think it's true. There were tons of emotions running through me. Tons of scenes I played out in my mind. I made monsters out of sweaters. I turned boys on the corner simply conversing with one another into glaring flirts who made me so uncomfortable I went blocks out of my way to avoid them.

Courtesy of Sharon Flake

"In middle school, my insecurities made it so I didn't go outside with friends very often. I stayed inside and watched television and read a lot. I wasn't sad or lonely, though. My house was always filled with laughter and light debates on everything from current affairs to classroom antics. My parents were natural-born storytellers (though I didn't realize it at the time) and always told stories about what it was like for them growing up.

"My parents always made us believe we could do anything. I guess that's why, in spite of my fears, I have always had an adventurous spirit. In high school I played on the tennis team and went out for the chess team, even though I was too afraid to go to the prom. Later on, though I was still afraid of boys, I became the first person in my family to go to college in another city. I attended the University of Pittsburgh, six hours from my home in Philadelphia. Still afraid of the dark, I slept with the lights on. But I had a big mouth, a curious spirit, and made friends easily so people didn't really know what I felt deep, down inside.

"While at Pitt, I took several English classes and discovered that I was good at writing. I'd write poetry, fiction, newspaper articles, and stories from a teenage girl's perspective. But there was a problem. My papers would come back with loads of red marks—circled spelling and grammatical mistakes. I thought the

A or B I received on my papers was simply my professors' way of being nice to me. Once, I was offered an internship at a major local newspaper. I accepted the position, but I never showed up for the job. I thought that I didn't really have any talent. 'They're just being nice to me,' I said.

"After college, I worked with young people in foster homes for eight years. Following that, I worked at the University of Pittsburgh in public relations. In my spare time I wrote for national magazines, and wrote short stories at home. By the time my first book, *The Skin I'm In*, came out in 1998, I was 42 years old. I love being an author. I love knowing that my fears and insecurities have helped other people open up about their own fears. I love that I can stand in front of a group of hundreds of people unafraid—not even once wanting to run and hide among the pots. Being an author is a great way to get all of those feelings and thoughts I have out of my head—and into the world! As a writer, I get to take all the feelings and fears I have and turn them into people, places, and things. Now I know why I felt so many things when I was young. My heart and head were being prepared to give birth to stories—to characters with strong opinions, various personalities, and world views like many of my readers'. "

✿   ✿   ✿

Sharon G. Flake grew up in Philadelphia, Pennsylvania. She received her B.A. degree from the University of Pittsburgh in English writing in 1978. While working in the Public Relations office at the University of Pittsburgh, she took a writing course at a children's bookstore. Making contact with editor Andrea Davis Pinkney through an article in *Essence* magazine, she sent her an outline of the book she had started. Pinkney worked with her to get the manuscript ready for publication. *The Skin I'm In* is about a dark-

Courtesy of Hyperion Books for Children/Jump at the Sun

skinned girl who gets picked on by her peers and has to find a way to stand up for herself and appreciate her own talents. This book earned her the Coretta Scott King–John Steptoe New Talent Award and was selected as an ALA Best Book for Young Adults, a Quick Pick for Reluctant Readers, and a Book for the Teen Age by the New York Public Library. *Publishers Weekly* called her an author to watch.

Interested more in issues within the African American community than confrontations between races, Flake focuses on problems such as self-image and stereotypes of personal appearance, problems that all teenagers find troubling. In her second novel, *Money Hungry*, she introduces 13-year-old Raspberry Hill, who has a strong need to ensure that she and her mom will never be homeless again. In the book's sequel, *Begging for Change*, named a Blue Ribbon title by the *Bulletin of the Center for Children's Books*, Raspberry is one year older, a lot tougher, and once again confronting issues of greed, anger, and the true meaning of friendship.

As an African American author, Flake believes her mission is to show the world that inner city people also work, love, and laugh the same as others. The short stories in *Who Am I Without Him?* all focus on girls and boys in various stages of relationships. These thought-provoking vignettes, with their unique twists and turns, introduce readers to characters that make them laugh, cringe, and cheer—teenagers they can immediately relate to and feel compelled to talk about with family and friends. Sharon Flake lives in Pittsburgh, Pennsylvania, with her teenage daughter, Brittney.

SELECTED WORKS: *The Skin I'm In*, 1998; *Money Hungry*, 2001; *Begging for Change*, 2003; *Who Am I Without Him?: Short Stories about Girls and the Boys in Their Lives*, 2004.

SUGGESTED READING: "Flying Starts," *Publishers Weekly*, December 21, 1998.

WEB SITE: *www.sharonflake.com*

Sid Fleischman

March 16, 1920–

"I sometimes think I was born to set a bad example. My writing habits are eccentric; an aspiring author will follow them at great risk. I don't write a rough first draft. And, defying common sense, I don't plot my novels in advance. I find an opening scene, jump in, and wonder what's going to happen next. Improvising daily, I hope that I will find a plot before I finish. I don't know how my stories will end until I reach the last pages.

"Improvising daily—isn't that just like life?

"I embraced my creative bad habits when as a teenager I had my life plotted out—I was going to be a magician. But I failed to follow my carefully devised plan. I discarded that plot and improvised myself into a writer. During those early years when I was teaching myself sleight of hand from library books, I was on my way to becoming a writer. I just didn't know it. While still in high school, I sat down at the family's noisy old typewriter to explain some original magic tricks. I accumulated a growing stack of pages without quite realizing that I had written a short book. When it was issued by a publisher of texts for magicians and I saw my name glowing on the cover, my aspirations took a shift.

"Become an author? Instead of pulling rabbits out of hats, could I pull stories out of my head? In due time I sat down to write a mystery novel—they were a kind of magic trick, weren't they? All one needed was a dead body, a detective, and the ability to hocus-pocus a clue or two. I could do that. That's when I found another folly to embrace. I discovered that rewriting the hasty and clumsily-written first draft pages of a long novel filled me with dread. Instead, I began to rewrite and polish each page as it emerged from the typewriter. Only when I felt that the sentences were ready for the printer did I venture on to the next page.

"I still work that way. These methods can chew up time and energy, but it's a price I'm happy to pay. Readers don't and shouldn't care how long it took the author to pluck the novel out of thin air. Each writer discovers for himself or herself the best methods of working. There is no right or wrong way. There is only one's own way.

"I often think back to my misspent youth when I wrote for adults. In those days, I rarely received a letter from any of my readers—if I had any readers. When I came to my senses and began writing books for young people, kids' letters began dropping into my mailbox. That mail, sometimes in hard-to-read scrawls, is one of the special rewards that come to us who write for children.

"Books matter to kids. They may hate them, they may adore them, but young people can't ignore books. Kids are born honest and often give me earnest advice ('Why don't you write a story about the blob that ate New York?') ('When are you going to STOP writing?') or encourage me with their whimsey ('Dear Mr. Big Shot Writer—'). I always find time for answers, brief as my replies may necessarily be.

"After having written more than 60 books, for adults, for children, and for magicians, one would think I'd have the grace to quit. But as I write this I have just finished a new novel (*The Giant Rat of Sumatra*, to be published in winter 2005). And I have no doubt that before long I'll stumble over an idea for an opening scene and jump into a new story just to find out what happens next."

Courtesy of Rhonda Williams

Sid Fleischman

❋   ❋   ❋

To say that Sid Fleischman works magic with words is no exaggeration. His experience as a magician and his keen sense of humor make him one of the most accomplished and humorous voices in American literature for children. In an interview with Michael Cart, he said, "Language is a wondrous toy and I have great literary fun with it." Both critical and popular acclaim of his books testify to that. He is regarded as a master of the tall tale and noted for writing action-filled adventures that weave together exciting plots, well-researched historical facts, rollicking wit, and clever wordplay.

But his pathway to writing humorous books for children was far from a straight and narrow one. Although he was born in Brooklyn, New York, his family relocated when he was two to San Diego, California, where he grew up. His father laid the groundwork for Sid's future career with his zest for storytelling and his mother with the books she read to him, *Robin Hood* being his favorite. As a small boy, Fleischman developed a strong interest in magic, voraciously reading every book on the subject that he could find in the public library. In his Newbery acceptance speech for *The Whipping Boy*, he took the opportunity to express his gratitude to the public library for his career: "As a writer, I am almost entirely a product of the free public library system." At age 17 he decided to write a book on his original magic tricks, and when *Between Cocktails* was published when he was 19, he was hooked on writing books.

Books for adults would come first. After high school Fleischman toured with a magic show during the last days of vaudeville. His encounters with folk speech and folk tales began to germinate, but they wouldn't begin to bud until later. He married Betty Taylor in 1942, and during World War II he served in the U.S. Naval Reserve on a destroyer escort in the Pacific and Asia. After the war, he attended San Diego State College and wrote pulp fiction for adults, mostly detective and suspense stories. Stints as a reporter for the San Diego *Daily Journal* and as an associate editor of *Point* magazine ensued, but in 1951 he turned to writing full-time. In 1955 he adapted his own novel *Blood Alley* for the film version, starring John Wayne.

He wrote his first children's book for his own children. *Mr. Mysterious & Company*, published in 1962, is a story about a family who travels to California via a covered wagon that the father dubbed, "a traveling temple of mystification, education, and jollification." These are words that describe Fleischman's work as well. The book was so successful, capturing a *Boston Globe–Horn Book* Honor Award among other honors, that he began writing children's books exclusively. His first novel was quickly followed by *By the Great Horn Spoon!* in 1963, *The Ghost in the Noonday Sun* in 1965, and *Chancy and the Grand Rascal* in 1966. Fleischman had found his niche with colorful characters, mysterious identities, rough-and-tumble scenarios, and tall-tale tempos. The stories were ripe for the screen, too. In 1974 *The Ghost in the Noonday Sun* was made into a movie starring Peter Sellers, and in 1967 *By the Great Horn Spoon* was filmed by Disney as *Bullwhip Griffin*.

Also published in 1966 was the first in a series of tall tales, *McBroom Tells the Truth*, about a father rearing a family of 11 children on a marvelous Iowa farm where super-fertile soil produced magnificent crops and remarkable stories. The robust humor was so popular that Fleischman wrote a dozen or more tales

> *"I find an opening scene, jump in, and wonder what's going to happen next. Improvising daily, I hope that I will find a plot before I finish."*

about the McBrooms. *McBroom the Rainmaker* was a Golden Kite honor book in 1974. Another series of books began to appear in 1981 featuring The Bloodhound Gang, a trio of junior detectives. The books were originally written as scripts for the Children's Television Workshop program *3-2-1 Contact*.

Sid Fleischman has a unique ability to introduce historical accuracies seamlessly into his narratives. He keeps a research notebook for each novel. Drawn from American folklore and pioneer history, his larger-than-life characters are as flamboyant as their names: Pitch-Pine Billy Pierce, Mississippi MacFinn, Cut-Eye Higgins, Shagnasty John, and Praiseworthy, to mention but a few. The names of his towns (Bed Bug, Hangtown, Rough and Ready) have a similar character and add to the rich, pungent imagery. That folkloric finesse won him the *Boston Globe–Horn Book* Award in 1979 for *Humbug Mountain,* as well as a National Book Award nomination. Over the years, many of his works have been cited as ALA Notable Children's Books and *School Library Journal* Best Books and gathered numerous other accolades as well. He has won many state-sponsored awards in which children themselves are the judges, a test of his popular appeal with his intended audience in addition to the critical approval he has won from adults.

Courtesy of Greenwillow Books

The story that garnered the Newbery Medal in 1986 was a departure from his others, many of which were rooted in 19th-century America. The idea for *The Whipping Boy* sprang from his discovery of that term's medieval origin while researching another book—"A boy educated with a prince and punished in his stead." It was an idea that wouldn't let go, but it took Fleischman 10 years to write because he first envisioned it as a picture book story. He shelved the story numerous times until he realized it needed to be longer, and then the rollicking melodrama of a spoiled prince and a streetwise, resourceful orphan finally took shape. Under the pseudonym Max Brindle, he later wrote the screenplay for the 1994 movie adaptation starring George C. Scott. The story was also produced as a musical by the Seattle Children's Theatre with play and lyrics written by Sid Fleischman.

Having written over 60 books, Fleischman used examples from his personal writing experiences to tell his own story in *The Abracadabra Kid: A Writer's Life.* Published in 1996 and told in his typical lively, engaging style, this autobiography also offers entertaining advice to young aspiring authors. His own son Paul has become an author and a Newbery Award medallist as well (for *Joyful Noise* in 1989); they are the first and to date the only father-son duo to capture that prestigious award. Paul calls his father a prestidigitator of words, and Fleischman himself has described his writing as sleight-of-mind. In 2003 he received a fine accolade from his peers when the Society of Children's Book Writers and Illustrators established the Sid Fleischman Humor Award, with Fleischman himself as the first recipient for his body of work. The award, which will be given to authors whose work exemplifies excellence of writing in the genre of humor, was established because humorous writing is so often overlooked by other award committees. In presenting the first award, SCB-WI president Stephen Mooser said of Sid Fleischman, "It's one thing to make someone laugh. But his ability to do that in so many stories with such poignancy is nothing short of magic."

Courtesy of Greenwillow Books

SELECTED WORKS: *Mr. Mysterious & Company*, illus. by Eric von Schmidt, 1962; *By the Great Horn Spoon!*, 1963; *The Ghost in the Noonday Sun*, illus. by Warren Chappell, 1965, illus. by Peter Sís, 1989; *Chancy and the Grand Rascal*, illus. by Eric von Schmidt, 1966; *McBroom Tells the Truth*, illus. by Kurt Werth, 1966, illus. by Walter Lorraine, 1981, illus. by Amy Wummer, 1998; *McBroom and the Big Wind*, illus. by Kurt Werth, 1967, illus. by Walter Lorraine, 1982; *McBroom's Ear*, illus. by Kurt Werth, 1969, illus. by Walter Lorraine, 1982; *Longbeard the Wizard*, illus. by Charles Bragg, 1970; *McBroom's Ghost*, illus. by Robert Frankenberg, 1971, illus. by Walter Lorraine, 1981, illus. by Amy Wummer, 1998; *Jingo Django*, illus. by Eric von Schmidt, 1971; *McBroom's Zoo*, illus. by Kurt Werth, 1972, illus. by Walter Lorraine, 1982; *The Wooden Cat Man*, illus. by Jay Yang, 1972; *The Ghost on Saturday Night*, illus. by Eric Von Schmidt, 1974, illus. by Laura Cornell, 1997; *Mr. Mysterious's Secrets of Magic*, illus. by Eric von Schmidt, 1975; *McBroom Tells a Lie*, illus. by Walter Lorraine, 1976, illus. by Amy Wummer, 1999; *Kate's Secret Riddle Book*, illus. by Barbara Bottner, 1977; *Me and the Man on the Moon-Eyed Horse*, illus. by Eric von Schmidt, 1977; *Humbug Mountain*, illus. by Eric Von Schmidt, 1978; *Jim Bridger's Alarm Clock and Other Tall Tales*, illus. by Eric von Schmidt, 1978; *McBroom and the Beanstalk*, illus. by Walter Lorraine,

1978; *The Hey Hey Man*, illus. Nadine Bernard Westcott, 1979; *McBroom and the Great Race*, illus. by Walter Lorraine, 1980; *The Bloodhound Gang in the Case of Princess Tomorrow*, illus. by Bill Morrison, 1981; *The Bloodhound Gang in the Case of the Cackling Ghost*, illus. by Anthony Rao, 1981; *The Bloodhound Gang in the Case of the Flying Clock*, illus. by William Harmuth, 1981; *The Bloodhound Gang in the Case of the Secret Message*, illus. by William Harmuth, 1981; *The Bloodhound Gang in the Case of the 264-pound Burglar*, illus. by Bill Morrison, 1982; *McBroom the Rainmaker*, illus. by Walter Lorraine, 1982, illus. by Amy Wummer, 1999; *The Bloodhound Gang's Secret Code Book*, illus. by Bill Morrison, 1983; *McBroom's Almanac*, illus. by Walter Lorraine, 1984; *The Whipping Boy*, illus. by Peter Sís, 1986; *The Scarebird*, illus. by Peter Sís, 1988; *McBroom's Wonderful One-Acre Farm: Three Tall Tales*, illus. by Quentin Blake, 1992; *Here Comes McBroom: Three More Tall Tales*, illus. by Quentin Blake, 1992; *Jim Ugly*, illus. by Jos. A. Smith, 1992; *The 13th Floor: A Ghost Story*, illus. by Peter Sís, 1995; *Abracadabra Kid: A Writer's Life*, 1996; *Bandit's Moon*, illus. by Jos. A. Smith, 1998; *A Carnival of Animals*, illus. by Marylin Hafner, 2000; *Bo & Mzzz Mad*, 2001; *Disappearing Act*, 2003.

SUGGESTED READING: Cameron, Eleanor. *The Green and Burning Tree*, 1969; Cart, Michael. *What's So Funny: Wit and Humor in American Children's Literature*, 1995; Cullinan, Bernice and Diane Person, eds. *The Continuum Encyclopedia of Children's Literature*, 2001; *Fantasy Literature for Children and Young Adults*, 4th ed., 1995; Sadker, Myra Pollack and David Miller Sadker. *Now Upon a Time: A Contemporary View of Children's Literature*, 1977; *Something About the Author*, vol. 148, 2004; *Twentieth-Century Children's Writers*, 4th ed., 1995; Townsend, John Rowe. *Written for Children: An Outline of English Language Children's Literature*, rev. ed., 1974. Periodicals—Fleischman, Sid, "Newbery Medal Acceptance," *The Horn Book*, July/August 1987; Johnson, Emily Rhoads, "Profile: Sid Fleischman," *Language Arts*, October 1982; Steinberg, Sybil, "What Makes a Funny Children's Book?: Five Writers Talk about Their Method," *Publishers Weekly*, February 27, 1978.

WEB SITE: *www.sidfleischman.com*

An earlier profile of Sid Fleischman appeared in *Third Book of Junior Authors* (1972). A profile of his son Paul can be found in *Fifth Book of Junior Authors and Illustrators* (1983).

Courtesy of Liz Demott

Susan Fletcher

Susan Fletcher

May 28, 1951–

"My early years were full of stories. Stories heard on my mother's lap: of a goose who lost her galoshes, of a stray kitten looking for a home. Old family stories: antics of my eccentric great-uncle Charlie, escapades of my father and his dog, Betsy. Stories that I read to myself: *Ellen Tebbits, A Wrinkle in Time, Wuthering Heights*. Stories we made of our lives, now grown so familiar with the telling that a single phrase can evoke a particular time, a particular place: *Remember when . . . .* When my pet cockatiel flew away over the trees at our grandparents' house, but returned to my whistle the following day. When my mother caught a baby rattlesnake, slapped it into a peanut butter jar, and named it Skippy. When, in a rowboat, we washed ashore on Santa Barbara Island . . . into the middle of a pod of basking sea elephants. When, in another small boat, we unexpectedly found ourselves in the midst of a school of sharks.

"No one believes this last story, but it, like the others, is true.

"My family moved four times before I finished elementary school—from where I was born, in Pasadena, California, to Houston, Texas; San Gabriel, California; Brecksville, Ohio; and Palos Verdes, California.

"I spent lots of time alone—partly because I was shy and it took me a while to make friends after each move. Partly as well because I grew to like being alone. I loved to read—to dive deep down into another world, another life, to surface hours or even days later. I loved to wander through Ohio woods or California meadows. I wrote stories about my wanderings, illustrated them with crayons, and stapled them together into 'books.'

"Before I married, my name was Susan Clemens. One day when I was in third grade, our teacher told us about a famous author named Mark Twain, whose real name was Samuel Clemens, and he had a daughter named Susan. *Susan Clemens.* That was my name. So I thought, 'I'll become an author!' Not very logical—picking your career because of a name. But my love of stories—already well established—made it stick. Eventually I did make friends, and with them and my three younger siblings, I ice-skated on Jacobys' pond, tobogganed down Suicide Hill, and swung on vines across the ravine behind the Hoffman place.

"In college, upon discovering that I could actually earn credit for *reading stories*, I decided to major in English. Afterward, I wrote advertising copy; I met my husband, Jerry, in an advertising agency in Denver. Later, I freelanced writing magazine articles at home as I cared for our daughter, Kelly. Perusing the library in search of stories to close the circle—to read to Kelly as she sat in *my* lap—I rediscovered children's literature. Magic, multiplied: pleasure for myself, pleasure for Kelly, my pleasure in her pleasure. I decided that *this*—writing children's books—was what I wanted to do.

"Although I have written contemporary novels, I am also attracted for reasons beyond my understanding to the long ago and faraway. To compensate for the fact that I don't live in medieval Wales or ancient Persia or even 19th-century California, I do extensive research. I prowl around in libraries; I buy books and videos; I talk to experts; I fill binder after binder with notes. To come to know the worlds of my stories, I have spent a night in a lighthouse and received a custom-tailored showing in a planetarium. I have explored three different kinds of caves and flown in a glider. I have cut up baby chickens and mice for a hawk's dinner and watched a falcon hunt.

"My favorite days are the ones in which I get to submerge myself inside my characters and explore the world through their eyes. To tell you the truth, writing is not easy. But to me, there's nothing more satisfying. The best life I can imagine is one that is full of stories."

❋ ❋ ❋

From the time she received her B.A. in English from the University of California at Santa Barbara in 1973 and her M.A. in English from the University of Michigan in 1974, Susan Clemens Fletcher has involved herself, one way or another, in a life of writing. She worked in Minneapolis as an advertising copywriter and as a freelance magazine writer, seeing her articles published in *Ms.*, *Woman's Day*, *Family Circle*, and the *New Advocate*, among others. Married to Jerry Fletcher in 1977, she lives in Wilsonville, Oregon, with her husband and their daughter, Kelly. She has been on the faculty of the Vermont College M.F.A. in Writing for Children and Young Adults program since 2000.

Courtesy of Atheneum Books for Young Readers

A versatile writer, Susan Fletcher creates believable worlds with strong, multifaceted heroines in works of fantasy and historical fiction as well as contemporary novels. The first of her fantasies, *Dragon's Milk*, drew immediate attention from reviewers and readers alike for its inventive plotting and strong characterization. *Dragon's Milk* received the 1990 Oregon Book Award and was a 1991 IRA Young Adults' Choice. *Flight of the Dragon*

Kyn, a prequel that introduces more background to the land and politics of this series, was named an ALA Best Book for Young Adults and an IRA Young Adult's Choice in 1995. *Sign of the Dove*, a sequel to *Dragon's Milk*, continues the story.

Fletcher wrote *The Stuttgart Nanny Mafia* in a lighter vein, showing the trials and tribulations of having to cope with new family members. It was an International Youth Library Selection in 1992. *Shadow Spinner* brings the world and legend of Scheherezade (of *Arabian Nights* fame) to life through the eyes of Fletcher's young heroine, Marjan, a handmaid to the beleaguered storyteller. Marjan's frank, lively commentary and the tales she gathers in the city form the basis for this involving adventure that was named a *School Library Journal* Best Book, an ALA Notable Children's Book, an ALA Best Book for Young Adults, and a Notable Children's Trade Book in the Field of Social Studies. In *Walk Across the Sea*, a historical novel, 13-year-old Eliza Jane McCully lives in a lighthouse on an island off the Pacific coast in 1886 and meets a Chinese boy who changes her life. That theme—of people or dragons or events that change one's life and perspective—pervades all of Susan Fletcher's writing.

SELECTED WORKS: *Dragon's Milk*, 1989; *The Stuttgart Nanny Mafia*, 1991; *Flight of the Dragon Kyn*, 1993; *Sign of the Dove*, 1996; *Shadow Spinner*, 1998; *Walk Across the Sea*, 2001.

SUGGESTED READING: *Authors and Artists for Young Adults*, vol. 37, 2001; *Contemporary Authors*, New Revision Series, vol. 71, 1999; *Something About the Author*, vol. 110, 2000.

Alex Flinn

October 23, 1966–

"The three biggest influences on my writing were law school, junior high, and my mother. Law school strikes people first, because my characters are usually embroiled in the legal system. But law school was last. My mother was first. When I was five, my mom asked me what I wanted to be when I grew up. 'How about . . . an author?,' she suggested. 'An author is a lady who writes books.' Well, that sounded fine to me, so I agreed. From that day, we both assumed I'd be a writer. Mom did her part by sending poems I wrote in school to *Highlights* magazine. I was collecting rejection letters at age eight!

"I loved to read. As a child, I often dressed up as literary characters for Halloween—I have photographs of myself as both Pippi Longstocking (with pipe cleaners in my braids to make them stick out) and Laura Ingalls Wilder. An early school memory involves a classmate telling me I wasn't allowed to read such thick books because they were for the sixth graders. Favorites included fantasy authors like P. L. Travers and Roald Dahl. I read *A Little Princess* at least 10 times! But as I got older, I switched to more realistic fiction, and that is where I stayed.

"Although my other ambition was to be a musical theater star (and I would attend college on a voice scholarship), writing was never far from my mind. I wrote poetry, journals, and, especially, plays for the neighborhood kids to perform. I had an ordinary, happy childhood. Nothing much was going on, but I had fun.

"It wasn't until I was 12 that something interesting happened. My family moved from Long Island to Miami, Florida, just as I was starting junior high. I was painfully shy, and I had tremendous difficulty making friends. So, lacking friends, I watched other people. Watching is something all writers must do, and it was in junior high that I learned to do it.

"Perhaps because of all the watching I did in junior high, I eventually decided to write for teenagers. When I close my eyes and visualize myself, I am 12 or 13, running around the school track, wearing an extremely unflattering baggy white gymsuit. So I try to write books that gymsuit girl would enjoy—exciting books where something *happens* because nothing was happening in my real life at the time. I was very impatient—I was always *waiting* for something to happen.

Courtesy of J.A. Cobrera

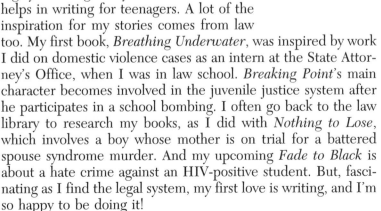

"It was middle school that taught me empathy too. I have a great deal of empathy for anyone who's having a hard time. I believe this ability to see another's viewpoint has served me well as a writer. I love when teens write, asking if my stories are true or saying they feel that I'm writing about them. I feel like I am writing about them, too.

"Oh, and the lawyer thing: Well, I learned to write in law school. Legal writing requires a great economy with words, the ability to get one's points across quickly. If you can get a tired judge to read your writing, you can get anyone to read it! That helps in writing for teenagers. A lot of the inspiration for my stories comes from law too. My first book, *Breathing Underwater*, was inspired by work I did on domestic violence cases as an intern at the State Attorney's Office, when I was in law school. *Breaking Point*'s main character becomes involved in the juvenile justice system after he participates in a school bombing. I often go back to the law library to research my books, as I did with *Nothing to Lose*, which involves a boy whose mother is on trial for a battered spouse syndrome murder. And my upcoming *Fade to Black* is about a hate crime against an HIV-positive student. But, fascinating as I find the legal system, my first love is writing, and I'm so happy to be doing it!

"I no longer practice law, but I still read, write, and sing. I live in Miami, Florida, with my husband, Gene; two daughters, Katie and Meredith; cat, Ravel; and dog, Ginger."

✳ ✳ ✳

Alexandra Flinn was born in Syosset, New York, a town on Long Island where her family lived until moving to Miami when she was twelve. She spent her high school years taking part in various performing arts programs in Miami and studied opera in college. In 1988 she received her bachelor of music in vocal performance from the University of Miami. Her law degree came four years later from Nova Southeastern University Law School.

Courtesy of HarperCollins Children's Books

She met her husband in college. It was after their first daughter was born in 1995 that Alex returned to writing and literature and began to rework a novel she had started in college. She read a variety of young adult books, especially those of Richard Peck, and then met him in person at a workshop of the Key West Literary Seminar, an event that she has called "an inspiring experience." She also credits a friend and fellow author, Joyce Sweeney, with helping her along the way.

Alex Flinn made an auspicious debut as a writer of young adult fiction when her first novel, *Breathing Underwater*, was named one of the Top Ten Best Books for Young Adults by the American Library Association in 2003. It was also named a Quick Pick for Reluctant Young Adult Readers, a Booksense 76 Title, and an American Booksellers Pick of the Lists. Told from the point of view of Nick, a high school student who doesn't understand his own quick-tempered behavior toward his girlfriend, the story explores the contemporary problems of dating violence and abusive behavior at home. Telling the story from Nick's point of view, the author creates an immediacy and suspense in the book that make for compelling reading. In her second book, Flinn tackled the difficult themes of school violence and peer pressure. *Breaking Point* was named an ALA Quick Pick for Reluctant Young Adult Readers and a New York Public Library Book for the Teen Age. Both these books are receiving rave reviews from teens around the country as they appear on state award reading lists.

SELECTED WORKS: *Breathing Underwater*, 2001; *Breaking Point*, 2002; *Nothing to Lose*, 2004.

FLOCA

SUGGESTED READING: Odean, Kathleen, "Unanimous Verdict: For These Lawyers, the Decision's in: Kids Are a More Rewarding Audience Than Jurors," *Book*, July/August 2003; "Flying Starts," *Publishers Weekly*, June 25, 2001.
WEB SITE: *www.alexflinn.com*

"**I**'ve been drawing since before I can remember, and for me drawing has always been tied up with stories. Keep that Abstract Expressionism; the pictures I've always liked and always drawn have narratives. Something is happening to someone; someone is doing something. How that childhood love of drawing stories became how I spend my adult days can perhaps be suggested by sharing seven (7) telling moments:

"(1) Early on, I would draw on typing paper that my father brought home from work. I still remember the excitement I would feel on seeing him come through the door with a packet of clean, white paper.

"(2) In the second grade, my teacher Mrs. Martin kept an old bathtub filled with pillows in the middle of her classroom. If you finished work early, you gained the much coveted privilege of lounging in the tub with a book. I hardly ever made it in—I spent all my time making my own books, comic books, about a succession of invented superheroes. One was a cape-wearing, anthropomorphized automobile tire, Terrific Tire. His antagonist was an ersatz version of Godzilla, whose film work had made a big impression on me. (As a kid I loved books, but B-movies, too.)

"(3) In the fourth grade Mrs. Persons used my drawings as illustrations on the lesson plans she handed out, even though my drawings were often concerned with, say, the Death Star, and the lesson plans were not. I still remember the cool chemical aroma of those mimeographs and seeing my drawings printed in that bluish ink. A taste for publication was whetted.

"(4) At Temple High School I cartooned for the school newspaper. I went from drawing Darth Vader to drawing the principal. The school was lucky to have a clutch of wonderful teachers, including my art teacher, Sally Bales, who inspired all manner of creative work from students. Those teachers were the saving grace of a place that often seemed to invest itself more in football championships than academics and art.

Courtesy of Brian Floca

Brian Floca
January 11, 1969–

"(5) At Brown University I majored in studio art and, just as important to me as my major, I cartooned for the *Brown Daily Herald*. The *BDH* was available at no charge at the cafeteria entrance, and the combination of free printed matter and long lines for turkey tetrazzini guaranteed the paper a readership. My strip ran four days a week, and though sometimes my term papers were late, I always got that strip in on time. It was great fun, but I had little sense of how to convert my love of drawing and cartooning into something I could do after college. Then, in the nick of time, I took the right class, and caught a break.

"(6) Brown was just up College Hill from the Rhode Island School of Design, and students at one school could take classes at the other. I was slow to sign up for a RISD class; the schools had different academic calendars, and that made cross-registering a bit of a hassle. Finally, I learned that David Macaulay taught at RISD, and the idea of class with the author and illustrator of *Cathedral* and *Castle* got me down the hill. Macaulay's class was shot through with the intelligence and wry humor that characterized his books. It would have been a highlight of college even if Macaulay hadn't, midway through the semester, introduced me to Avi.

"(7) That introduction led to my working with Avi and his editor, Richard Jackson, on a book idea that eventually became the comic-book novel *City of Light, City of Dark*. I knew right away that I'd had a break, but I knew so little about children's publishing that I couldn't appreciate how extraordinary that break was. After years of work and friendship with both Avi and with Dick, I am ever more amazed at my good fortune.

"In conclusion: It seems pretty straightforward, laid out like that, but of course the above list of incidents is selective, it omits various ups and downs, books and projects and other things, plenty of other things, that didn't work out. But I don't doubt that I'm lucky. Most days I get up and go to my studio and roam around in stories, someone else's or my own, and think about the ways in which pictures can help bring those stories to life. It's work that feels deep and true and honest to me, and that's a great gift."

> *"At Temple High School I cartooned for the school newspaper. I went from drawing Darth Vader to drawing the principal."*

❉ ❉ ❉

Brian Floca was born and raised in Temple, Texas, where his mother, Kathy, had been an elementary school teacher, and his father, Ted, ran his own business in bottling soda. Brian and his younger sister, Elizabeth, were always told that they could do anything they wanted when they grew up. Elizabeth now works for the family business and is married; her daughter Lauren was born in time to have her uncle Brian dedicate *The Racecar Alphabet* to her, a book that became an American Library Association Notable Children's Book and was included on the New York Public Library's 100 Books for Reading and Sharing list.

As a child, Brian loved dinosaurs, movies, and books, and was particularly enthralled by the original *Star Wars* movies and the *Lord of the Rings* books, which he says he found as involving as any movie. His ability to stay in touch with many of the passions of childhood is reflected in his work, whether it is dinosaurs, trucks, racecars, fantasy worlds, or animal tales. His first book was a collaboration with Avi, a graphic novel for middle-grade readers, *City of Light, City of Dark*, which was named a *Publishers Weekly* Best Book of the Year. This was the first of many novels on which he would collaborate with Avi, who said in an acceptance speech for the *Boston Globe–Horn Book* Award that Brian Floca's art is full of "vision, meaning, and wit." Floca uses a variety of artistic styles and techniques. At times he works in delicate and intricate pencil drawings, as in his illustrations for Avi's *Poppy*, an ALA Notable Children's Book and winner of the *Boston Globe–Horn Book* Award. At other times, he employs a broad flat style, as in his illustrations for *Dinosaurs at the Ends of the Earth*, which was named a *Horn Book* Fanfare title and a Notable Social Studies Trade Book for Young People. *The Racecar Alphabet* features large, colorful pages that burst with the energy and motion of the track.

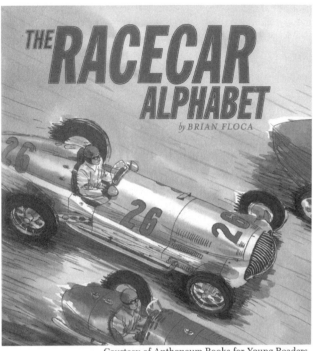

Courtesy of Antheneum Books for Young Readers

Brian Floca attended Brown University, where he did cartooning for the *Brown Daily Herald* and graduated with an A.B. in 1991. He received an M.F.A. from the School of Visual Arts in 2001. He has lived in various places after leaving college and has traveled to Prague and to Rome. Currently he lives in New York City.

SELECTED WORKS WRITTEN AND ILLUSTRATED: *The Frightful Story of Harry Walfish*, 1997; *Five Trucks*, 1999; *Dinosaurs at the Ends of the Earth*, 2000; *The Racecar Alphabet*, 2003.

SELECTED WORKS ILLUSTRATED: *City of Light, City of Dark*, by Avi, 1993; *Poppy*, by Avi, 1995; *Luck with Potatoes*, by Helen Ketteman, 1995; *The Voyager's Stone: The Adventures of a Message-Carrying Bottle Adrift on the Ocean Sea*, by Robert Kraske, 1995; *Jenius: The Amazing Guinea Pig*, by Dick King-Smith, 1996; *Where Are You, Little Zack?*, by Judith Ross Enderle and Stephanie Gordon Tessler, 1997; *Mixed-up Max*, by Dick King-Smith, 1997; *Poppy and Rye*, by Avi, 1998;

Lightning Liz, by Larry Dane Brimner, 1998; *King Max*, by Dick King-Smith, 1998; *Sports! Sports! Sports!: A Poetry Collection*, ed. by Lee Bennett Hopkins, 1999; *Ragweed*, by Avi 1999; *Ereth's Birthday*, by Avi, 2000; *Ethan Out and About*, by Johanna Hurwitz, 2002; *The Mayor of Central Park*, by Avi, 2003; *Ethan at Home*, by Johanna Hurwitz, 2003; *Uncles and Antlers*, by Lisa Wheeler, 2004.

SUGGESTED READING: Avi, "*Boston Globe–Horn Book* Acceptance Speech," *The Horn Book*, January/February 1997; Downes, Lawrence, "Indiana Bones," *New York Times Book Review*, May 14, 2000.

WEB SITE: *www.brianfloca.com*

Courtesy of David Frampton

David Frampton

November 4, 1942–

"I come from a family of artists, and so I can say with some authority that artists' families are different from normal families. For one thing, in an artist's home everyone plays with clay or crayons or anything else at hand, soap for instance. I will never forget the little row of animals marching across the back of the bathroom sink. My father had carved them from bars of Ivory soap and put them on the sink to surprise my brother and me one morning.

"In the artist's home where I grew up there was no living room, that room having been converted into a studio where all the fun stuff happened. Like getting to sit at my father's drawing board and make pictures. Or like the time my brother and I entered the studio and saw toys, toys everywhere, on tables, on shelves, and covering the floor! It looked like Santa's Workshop. We ran from toy to toy looking and touching. I remember we even, shyly, opened the little doors to the toy stove and refrigerator that were clearly (back then) 'toys for girls.' To my brother and me, the moment seemed magical, but really it was just an art job. The toys were sent to my father to illustrate for a spread in a newspaper. This was back in the 1940s and 1950s, when an illustrator could make a toaster, a top hat, or a toy look more beautiful than a photograph.

"Now I really can't tell of that magic moment without telling you about a similar but somewhat less delightful one. It was another art assignment. My father was sent a big box filled with gloves and mittens of all different sizes, styles, and materials to illustrate. Unlike the toy job, the gloves did not have to go back to the client. 'Just throw them away,' they told him. Never! Not my parents, not with four boys. We would wear them. One problem: The client, in order to save on shipping costs, had sent only one of each glove or mitten, since you only need one to do the art. My parents said, 'No big deal, just pick out a left and then find a right from a different style. It will be fun. You might even start a fad. All the kids will want to do the same.' So there we were with a large leather glove on one hand and small wool mitten on the other. (It varied from brother to brother.) The kids at school thought we were weird. It was awful, but it could have been worse. It could have been shoes.

"Still, I loved the studio and I loved making pictures when I was a kid. I am somewhat grown up now and have been an illustrator for about 30 years. I have my own studio, where my kids and I play with clay. I have had lots of fun assignments for newspapers, magazines, and books. I would have to say that books are the most fun, especially children's books. It's nice to illustrate classic literature, but there are always too many words between pictures. Not so with children's books. Making a children's book is like making a movie; the only difference is that in a movie they turn the pages faster. I should mention here that all my pictures in all my books are cut from wood. Woodcuts, where each color or picture is cut on a separate block of wood and then, one by one, inked and printed on a piece of handmade rice paper. Yes, it takes a lot of time to make a woodcut, but there is something so nice about a print. Also, woodcuts were meant for books. There was a time when nearly all the pictures in books were woodcut. The history of the book is, in a sense, the history of woodcuts. I love to look at the old books from the 15th, 16th, and 17th century. I study the work of the great masters of the book woodcut. I learn so much from them. I can only hope that these masters won't mind that I have taken what I have learned and used it to create some very silly pictures for kids. Perhaps they too sat in their studios and said to their children, 'Hey kids, you wanna play with clay?'"

"In the artist's home where I grew up there was no living room, that room having been converted into a studio where all the fun stuff happened."

✻   ✻   ✻

David Frampton, who was born in Brooklyn, New York, and spent his teen years in suburban Katonah, now makes his home in the New Hampshire woods. He and his wife, Margaret, have raised a son and daughter without benefit of a television set but with plenty of creative time and exposure to art. David graduated from Rhode Island School of Design with a B.S.A. in 1965. After his military service, he earned his M.F.A. at Pennsylvania State University, where he studied printmaking. He then began a successful commercial art career creating illustrations for magazines, newspapers, and periodicals, some of which were published as far away as India and South Africa.

David has always worked with woodcuts, an ancient art that he practices with a modern flair, using bright colors and geometric designs and borders, as well as motifs from traditional cul-

Courtesy of Clarion Books

tures. Unlike classic woodcuts, where the images are often dark, the woodcuts David creates for children's books are designed to be inviting. He enjoys suiting his art to his subject. He mixed colors to create a sense of whimsy in *My Son John*, and in a book for older children, Eve Bunting's *Riding the Tiger*, he mixed the real and fantastic to show the beauty and brutality of the tiger and highlight a moral dilemma. *Clouds of Glory*, for which he was awarded a Silver Medal from the Society of Illustrators, uses pictures that recall stained glass windows to illuminate familiar Bible stories. *Clouds of Glory* was also a *Horn Book* Fanfare book.

For a more somber subject, as in *When Plague Strikes*, David's woodcuts reflect the seriousness of the writing with dark tones and heavy lines. *When Plague Strikes* was chosen as a *School Library Journal* Best Book and a Notable Children's Trade Book in the Field of Social Studies. *Whaling Days* and *When Plague Strikes* were both named ALA Notable Children's Books. *Whaling Days* was also included on the *Bulletin of the Center for Children's Books* Blue Ribbon list. *Bull Run* and *Of Swords and Sorcerers* were cited as Notable Children's Trade Books in the Field of Social Studies.

SELECTED WORKS WRITTEN AND ILLUSTRATED: *The Whole Night Through: A Lullaby*, 2001; *My Beastie Book of ABC*, 2002.

SELECTED WORKS ILLUSTRATED: *Waterway West: The Story of the Erie Canal*, by Mary Kay Phelan, 1977; *The Seventh Day: The Story of the Jewish Sabbath*, by Miriam Chaikin, 1980; *Joshua in the Promised Land*, by Miriam Chaikin, 1982; *The Old Man and the Sea*, by Ernest Hemingway, 1985; *Fresh Paint: New Poems*, by Eve Merriam, 1986; *Jerusalem, Shining Still*, by Karla Kuskin, 1987; *Just So Stories*, by Rudyard Kipling, 1991; *The Scarlet Letter*, by Nathaniel Hawthorne, 1992; *Of Swords and Sorcerers: The Adventures of King Arthur and His Knights*, by Margaret Hodges and Margery Evernden, 1993; *Whaling Days*, by Carol Carrick, 1993; *Bull Run*, by Paul Fleischman, 1993; *My Son John*, by Jim Aylesworth, 1994; *When Plague Strikes: The Black Death, Smallpox, AIDS*, by James Cross Giblin, 1995; *Miro in the Kingdom of the Sun*, by Jane Kurtz, 1996; *Clouds of Glory: Legends and Stories about Bible Times*, by Miriam Chaikin, 1997; *Riding the Tiger*, by Eve Bunting, 2001; *Rhyolite: The True Story of a Ghost Town*, by Diane Siebert, 2003.

"Children read pictures. They really do. That is why it is such a pleasure to draw pictures for them. They notice every detail, every sequential action, every parallel, secondary, or counterpoint story line. This makes the illustrator of children's books a writer of sorts—a visual storyteller. One of my most treasured compliments came from a second grader who wrote, 'Dear Marla Frazee, I like the stories that you draw.'

"Often the story I'm telling in the illustrations is different from the story that is being told in the words. Of course the word-story and the picture-story should work together to create a seamless whole. That is the unique challenge of picture books, and the reason it gives me such pleasure to illustrate them.

"Drawing picture-stories is something that I've always done. As soon as I could read and write, I was crayoning my way through a story, writing words to go along with the pictures, and clumsily stapling it all together to make a tiny book. When I was in the third grade, my best friend wrote a story and I illustrated it. This was my first collaborative effort. Our book was made out of construction paper and held together with brass fasteners—a pretty simple affair—but it won an award and was prominently displayed in our elementary school library for years. I remember sneaking peeks at the shelf it sat on as our class filed in for library time, and seeing it keeping company with real books.

"In fifth grade, my teacher, Mrs. Holcomb, made some predictions about what her students would be when they grew up. She said I would illustrate children's books, painting outdoors in a sunlit meadow. So far, I've never painted in a meadow. I used to work in one of the three bedrooms of our home. The walls were painted a deep turquoise, and I found this restful—like diving into the deep end of a swimming pool—which, by the way, is a lot like beginning work on a new story. Now I work in a small cabin studio in our backyard, nestled in the shade of an avocado tree, within shouting distance to the house, in case anyone needs me.

"Creating pictures for my books generally takes me a year. I submerge myself in the project. I usually start by getting to know the characters, because once I know who they are, I can then imagine where they live and how they act. As I'm thinking about the characters and setting, I begin to visualize the book as a physical object. What size should it be? Is it horizontal, vertical, or

Courtesy of Tim Bradley

Marla Frazee

January 16, 1958–

square? At what point in the text will the page turn? Where is the type and where is the image? Finding the answers to these questions can take months. And then after I've sketched the book, I begin to paint the finished art. This takes even longer.

"As the mother of three boys, I fit my work time in between carpool schedules, loads of laundry, after-school activities, homework, and sibling squabbles. Certainly, the exuberance and disarray of our household have found their way into my illustrations. Child-friendly chaos, the quirks and endearments of children trying to find their way in our complex adult world, their subversive nature and unbounding energy—these are the themes that I am drawn to. My children sing in the choir. The kids arrive running, screaming, stomping, pushing, and shoving. Somehow this energy is harnessed into a purity of sound. But as soon as it is over, they fall back into their natural state of wild

Courtesy of Harcourt, Inc.

abandon. I love this duality. In the struggle to control these impulses, and often the failure to do so, there are amazing stories to tell.

"It is wonderful to work for an audience of children. They are the most appreciative, most observant, and most open-hearted group of people I've ever encountered!"

Marla Frazee is a passionate Southern Californian. She was born in Los Angeles and graduated with distinction in 1981 from the Art Center College of Design in Pasadena. It was there that she met her husband, Tim Bradley, who later became the chair of the Art Center's Photography Department. This meant that the family would put roots down in Pasadena, and they have been there ever since, enjoying their proximity to the beach and the mountains.

Frazee begins each day hiking the mountain trails near her home with her dog, Rocket. Then she settles down to a day of work in her small cabin studio, which has a tiny porch with a rocking chair and a birdhouse. She often listens to music while she works—choral, folk, or bluegrass. She also teaches children's book illustration at the Art Center College of Design.

Frazee wasn't always so comfortable in front of a group. Because she was very shy, she spoke to no one but her mother and one neighbor until she was three years old. Nursery school wasn't a possibility for her because of her shyness, and when she went to kindergarten, she spent the first weeks in tears. Frazee remembers, "My teacher always stood up so straight and rigid that from my vantage point as a short five-year-old child, I could not see her face. Ever. I remember looking at the class picture with consuming interest because it was the first time I had seen what my teacher really looked like straight on." However, soon after she started school, she became known as the class artist. From that point on she drew and painted her way though each assignment and each grade level. After seeing *Where the Wild Things Are* and *Blueberries for Sal* she knew that she wanted to be a children's book illustrator.

Marla Frazee's books, acclaimed for their colorful and comical illustrations, have earned numerous awards. *Everywhere Babies*, written by Susan Meyers, was honored as a *Horn Book* Fanfare book, named a *School Library Journal* Best Book, and received a *Parenting* magazine Reading Magic Award. *That Kookoory!*, *Hush, Little Baby: A Folk Song with Pictures*, and *Roller Coaster* were all named ALA Notable Children's Books. *Hush, Little Baby* also was named a *School Library Journal* Best Book and a *Horn Book* Fanfare title. *The Seven Silly Eaters, On the Morn of Mayfest*, and *Harriet, You'll Drive Me Wild!* were chosen as American Booksellers Pick of the Lists. In 2002 Marla Frazee won the Golden Kite Award in the picture book illustration category for *Mrs. Biddlebox*.

SELECTED WORKS ILLUSTRATED: *World Famous Muriel and the Magic Mystery*, by Sue Alexander, 1990; *That Kookoory!*, by Margaret Walden Froehlich, 1995; *The Seven Silly Eaters*, by Mary Ann Hoberman, 1997; *On the Morn of Mayfest*, by Erica Silverman, 1998; *Hush, Little Baby: A Folk Song with Pictures*, 1999; *Harriet, You'll Drive Me Wild!*, by Mem Fox, 2000; *Everywhere Babies*, by Susan Meyers, 2001; *Mrs. Biddlebox*, by Linda Smith, 2002.

SUGGESTED READING: *Something About the Author*, vol. 151, 2004.

WEB SITE: *www.marlafrazee.com/*

Kristine O'Connell George

May 6, 1954–

"As I write this, I am sitting on my back patio with my feet propped up on a chair. The rooster next door is crowing hoarsely—and has been since 4 A.M.! Amber, our golden retriever, is lying next to me keeping a drowsy eye on the birdbath in case the robins try anything funny. A squadron of hummingbirds is zinging around the feeder, and Mighty, the donkey up the road, is braying loudly. (Just what does that donkey sound like? A rusty hinge?)

"When I was a student, the idea of becoming a writer who works from her back patio never entered my imagination. Instead, I dreamed of becoming a microbiologist, a marine biologist, a physical therapist, or perhaps a drummer in a rock and roll band. After graduating with a bachelor of science degree, I did what I thought a grown-up was supposed to do: get a job in 'Corporate America.'

"My first corporate job was as a sales representative with a territory that included Colorado, Nebraska, and Wyoming. Later, as a manager for a Fortune 500 telecommunications company, I marketed voice and data network services to aerospace firms. Even then, however, I was notorious for finessing writing into my job description. My sales reports were more likely to feature an account of the tornado that chased me down a highway in Nebraska than a dry recap of sales statistics. I began to write essays in my spare time, and when my daughter was born, I rediscovered children's literature. Eventually, I enrolled in a course in children's poetry taught by the legendary poet and anthologist, Myra Cohn Livingston. During that first class, Myra read aloud David McCord's poem, 'This Is My Rock.' How did David McCord compress so much emotion into so few words? Why did that handful of words sound so wonderful?

Courtesy of Mike George

"The challenge of writing poetry motivated me to study with Myra for the next eight years, during which I filled a large plastic laundry basket with stacks of poems. My years with Myra were rich with discoveries. We studied the forms, tools, and structure of poetry. She introduced us to poets from around the world, and I marveled at the range and depth of poetry written for children. My personal experiences emerged as the catalyst for my own poems—riding a 'rent-a-horse,' losing a favorite tree in a storm, or skipping rocks on a river. Observations and experiences from my 15 different homes in Colorado, Texas, Oregon, Ohio, Idaho, and California crept into my poetry. In fact, many of the feelings I had as the 'new kid' in seven different schools surfaced years later in *Swimming Upstream: Middle School Poems*.

"Even though I did not become a rock and roll drummer, writing allows me to experiment with rhythm and the sounds of language. Poetry feels like music to me. Writing poetry also satisfies my scientific side because I can indulge my curiosity and love of observation. Best of all, I have a challenging and fascinating career that allows me to work outside on my patio. Amber is now sound asleep and snoring softly. She's missing the lizard doing push-ups on the flagstones and the robins splashing two feet away in the birdbath. Perhaps there is a poem in this—right here, on my back patio!"

✣   ✣   ✣

In an introduction to Kristine O'Connell George's first book of poetry, her mentor Myra Cohn Livingston wrote: "it is not only refreshing but urgent that our children hear poetry resonating with music, keen observation, fresh metaphor, personification, and meaningful flights of imagination." That Kristine George is able to create that resonance has been proved by the delight of her audience and the resounding praise of critics. *The Great Frog Race*—her first book of poetry—received both the Lee Bennett Hopkins Poetry Prize from the Pennsylvania Center for the Book and the International Reading Association's Lee Bennett Hopkins Promising Poet Award. Since then many of her titles have been recognized on such prestigious lists as *School Library Journal*'s Best of the Year, *Horn Book* Fanfare, "Capitol Choices," *Riverbank Review*'s Books of Distinction, New York Public Library's 100 Titles for Reading and Sharing, and the Los Angeles Public Library's 100 Best Books.

Little Dog Poems, inspired by George's own dog Spri, was named an ALA Notable Children's Book, and *Old Elm Speaks* received a Golden Kite Award from the Society of Children's Book Writers and Illustrators. George has twice won the Myra Cohn Livingston Poetry Award from the Children's Literature Council of Southern California, for *Old Elm Speaks* and *Toasting Marshmallows*. Writing for a wide range of ages, she is equally adept at addressing the concerns of middle school students in *Swimming Upstream: Middle School Poems*, which was an IRA/CBC Children's Choice book, and exploring the world of the toddler in *Book!*, an Oppenheim Toy Portfolio Award winner.

Courtesy of Clarion Books

Born in Denver, Colorado, Kristine George lived in many different states and homes as a child. She received her B.S. degree from Colorado State University in 1976 and now lives with her husband, Mike, and daughter, Courtney, in Southern California. She taught in the UCLA Writer's Program, where she first encountered the courses of Myra Cohn Livingston and developed her own love of writing children's poetry. She has served as a poetry consultant for PBS's *Storytime* and in her spare time enjoys crafts, hiking, photography, golf, and tennis.

SELECTED WORKS: *The Great Frog Race and Other Poems*, illus. by Kate Kiesler, 1997; *Old Elm Speaks: Tree Poems*, illus. by Kate Kiesler, 1998; *Little Dog Poems*, illus. by June Otani, 1999; *Book!*, illus. by Maggie Smith, 2001; *Toasting Marshmallows: Camping Poems*, illus. by Kate Kiesler, 2001; *Little Dog and Duncan*, illus. by June Otani, 2002; *Swimming Upstream: Middle School Poems*, illus. by Debbie Tilley, 2002;

Hummingbird Nest: A Journal of Poems, 2004; *One Mitten*, illus. by Maggie Smith, 2004.

SUGGESTED READING: Fletcher, Ralph, "Interview with Kristine O'Connell George," in *Poetry Matters*, 2002; Janeczko, Paul, comp. *Seeing the Blue Between: Advice and Inspirations for Young Poets*, 2002; *Something About the Author*, vol. 110, 2000. Periodicals—George, Kristine O'Connell, "Where Do Poems Come From?" *Book Links*, April/May 2002.

WEB SITE: *www.kristinegeorge.com*

Courtesy of Dion Ogust

Laura Godwin

September 2, 1956–

"My mother says that I have always enjoyed causing trouble. When I was a child and my brothers and sister were peacefully reading in the back of our car, a Travelall, or on the chesterfield in the rumpus room, I, apparently, would feel compelled to poke one of my siblings and cause a ruckus. It's not that I don't enjoy tranquility, I only like it to a point. After that point, restlessness sets in along with the desire to act. And the delight in a reaction—even a negative one—is irresistible. I suppose that I felt that my existence was then confirmed, my place in the family ensured.

"I grew up in rural Alberta, Canada, as the oldest of four children. We were very close in age, and by the time I was six, with three younger siblings, I was the grownup. I had lots of chores and responsibilities (mostly having to do with looking after my younger siblings), and mostly I was happy to do them. We lived about a mile from school and every day, even in the midst of the Canadian winter when it was very cold, we walked. When I was in the first grade, I occasionally walked to school on my own. Even though at home I was the big kid, in the wider world I was really just a little kid. I was pretty gullible, and sometimes older kids would walk me home from school and tell me that they knew a short cut. But for some reason, those short cuts always took far longer than the regular route. I can remember coming home late and my mother asking what took me so long. I'd always say that the big kids were showing me a short cut, and I believed it was true.

"My entrée into the world of writing was at the age of seven when my beloved guinea pig, George the First (also known as Georgie), died. I remember writing a commemorative poem for him that was set to the tune of a melody made popular by Herb Alpert and the Tijuana Brass. Words and music merged, and in my mind, I not only wrote the poem but also became the composer of the melody, a fact that, to my chagrin, my mother firmly but gently disputed.

For Georgie

Georgie, I loved you,
More than my heart can ever say.
Georgie, I loved you,
Please come back to me someday.

I hope you're happy
In the place that you have found.
In your snug burrow
Far beneath the solid ground.

[Repeat first verse.]

"The sadness over losing my pet was partly offset by the pride in writing what I considered to be a beautiful poem in his memory. I buried one carefully folded copy of that poem with Georgie, and kept another for myself. I still have it. The joy of writing in response to a feeling was born in me that day, and I became a rather sporadic but passionate composer of Poems For Occasions. Another poem was written about being late (often) for school: 'Time is a never-ending thing / It makes the clocks chime and the school bells ring / O! Time is a never-ending thing.' Finally, I had found something more satisfying than poking my brothers and sisters. I was hooked on writing.

"Now that I'm a grownup I still like to write poems in response to feelings or events. I wrote *Central Park Serenade* in response to an afternoon in the park taking pictures, and as a way to tell my two-year-old nephew about one of the most special places in New York City. And I wrote *Barnyard Prayers* on the plane coming home from my parents' farm in Alberta on my way back to my apartment in New York City. I've found that thinking up stories and poems and writing them is even more fun than causing a ruckus. When I write, I can create any kind of trouble that I want and any kind of reaction to the trouble. If I poke someone in real life, he will probably poke me back. But if I write a story or poem about him, he might even thank me! That's why, these days, I save most of my trouble-making skills for my characters. They never poke me back, and if I tell them we're taking a short cut, they believe me."

> "The joy of writing in response to a feeling was born in me that day, and I became a rather sporadic but passionate composer of Poems For Occasions."

✿　✿　✿

BY LAURA GODWIN · PICTURES BY BARRY ROOT

CENTRAL PARK
SERENADE

Courtesy of HarperCollins Publishers

Laura Godwin was born in Fairview, Alberta, Canada, and grew up in the small Alberta towns of Vermillion and Olds. Her family spent their summers at the Pelly River Ranch, the northernmost farm in North America, and she enjoyed a childhood close to the natural world. She spent time during her college years traveling in Europe and in the Yukon Territory, where she worked as a waitress at the Burwash Landing Lodge at Mile 1098 on the Alaska Highway. Graduating from the University of Calgary in 1982 with a major in General Studies and a minor in English Literature, Godwin eventually found her way to New York City to visit a friend she had met in Switzerland. She worked a succession of jobs during this time and finally applied to read unsolicited manuscripts at a major publishing house. That led to becoming an assistant to editor Robert Warren at Harper & Row (now HarperCollins) and working also with the well-known editor Charlotte Zolotow.

In 1987, Godwin moved to Henry Holt and Company as an assistant editor, gradually working up to her current position with Holt as vice president and publisher of children's books. Her own writing began as an idea for a packaging project to create a small packet of books that could be given out at Halloween as an alternative to candy. Asked by an editor what would be in the books, Laura Godwin wrote the text, which was eventually published under the pseudonym of Nola Buck. Under that name Godwin also published her first chapter books, *Oh, Cats!* and *Sid and Sam*, as well as *Christmas in the Manger*, which was illustrated by Felicia Bond. The first book she wrote under her own name was an easy-to-read story that refers back to Godwin's childhood in Canada. *Forest* tells of a young girl who finds a fawn in the woods, and of her mother, who convinces her that a wild creature cannot become a pet. With great facility of language and a sure sense for what interests young children, Godwin has created a number of stories for newly independent readers, including the popular series about a dog named Happy and a cat named Honey. Her picture book *Central Park Serenade*, illustrated with evocative and colorful paintings by Barry Root, is an homage to the great chunk of the natural world that is found within her adopted city.

Teaming with her good friend Ann M. Martin, the award-winning author and creator of the Babysitters Club, Godwin co-authored *The Doll People* and *The Meanest Doll in the World*. The two collaborators started out with the idea of creating a picture book together, but as they developed the story, they began to see that it was much longer than a picture-book text. It took five years for the two friends to work out all the story's details and divide up the writing of the novel, but in the year 2000 *The Doll People* was published to great acclaim. It was named an ALA Notable Children's Book and a *School Library Journal* Best Book of the Year. Illustrated by Brian Selznick, the story follows the adventures of an antique doll, Annabelle, who makes friends with Tiffany Funcraft, the daughter of a modern, plastic doll family. Together they set out to solve the mysterious disappearance of Annabelle's aunt many years before. Dramatic tension and the totally believable details of these miniature lives made this book an instant success with both readers and critics.

Laura Godwin divides her time between a home in New York City and one in upstate New York, which she shares with an ever-changing menagerie. In addition to reading and writing she is passionate about animals and enjoys playing the violin, a love she inherited from her grandfather, who was an avid fiddler.

SELECTED WORKS: *Forest*, illus. by Stacey Schuett, 1998; *Little White Dog*, illus. by Dan Yaccarino, 1998; *Barnyard Prayers*, illus. by Brian Selznick, 2000; *The Flower Girl*, illus. by John Wallace, 2000; *Happy and Honey*, illus. by Jane Chapman, 2000; *Honey Helps*, illus. by Jane Chapman, 2000; *The Doll People*, with Ann M. Martin, illus. by Brian Selznick, 2000; *The Best Fall of All*, illus. by Jane Chapman, 2002; *Central Park Serenade*, illus. by Barry Root, 2002; *Happy Christmas, Honey!*, illus. by Jane Chapman, 2002; *What the Baby Hears*, illus. by Mary Morgan, 2002; *The Meanest Doll in the World*, with Ann M. Martin, illus. by Brian Selznick, 2003.

SELECTED WORKS (as Nola Buck): *The Basement Stairs: A Spooky Pop-Up Book*, illus. by Jonathan Lambert, 1993; *Christmas in the Manger*, illus. by Felicia Bond, 1994; *The Littlest Witch: A Spooky Pop-Up Book*, illus. by Jonathan Lambert, 1994; *Gotcha!: A Spooky Pop-Up Book*, illus. by Jonathan Lambert, 1994; *Halloween Parade: A Spooky Pop-*

Up Book, illus. by Jonathan Lambert, 1994; *Creepy Crawly Critters and Other Halloween Tongue Twisters*, illus. by Sue Truesdell, 1995; *Sid and Sam*, illus. by G. Brian Karas, 1996; *Morning in the Meadow*, illus. by Holly Keller, 1997; *Santa's Short Suit Shrunk and Other Christmas Tongue Twisters*, illus. by Sue Truesdell, 1997; *Oh, Cats!*, illus. by Nadine Bernard Westcott, 1998; *Hey, Little Baby!*, illus. by R. W. Alley, 1999.

Courtesy of Candlewick Press

Bob Graham

October 20, 1942–

"My growing up in the early 1950s in Beverly Hills, a suburb of Sydney, Australia, leaves a whole confusion of images in my mind; not least was the Saturday afternoon matinee at the local cinema. First the newsreel, still showing images of a recent war-torn Europe, then a B-grade support movie along with much whistling and stamping if any tender love scene were to be played out between hero and heroine. Balled-up silver chocolate wrappers looped up through the light of the cinema projector. I can still see the angry flash of the usher's torch as it raked back and forth across the crowd, which was always on the edge of anarchy. But after an interval, Hopalong Cassidy could always be relied upon to avoid all the love stuff in his relentless quest to rid the West of its baddies. (Why did they always wear black and be none too keen on shaving?)

"The highlight of the afternoon was always for me the cartoon—Donald Duck, Tom and Jerry, or Mickey Mouse—and is it any wonder that along with the traditional children's books coming out of Europe that I was also an avid reader of comic books from America? I learnt to draw Mickey when I was very young and when he had very thin legs and two buttons on his shorts. My mother, father, sister, and live-in grandmother gave me praise and encouragement enough, and I guess that my future was set. I could never have believed way back then that someday I might be lucky enough to sit at home all day and draw pictures and write stories.

"So that is how it started and has more or less continued ever since. Between then and now I have managed to go to art school and learn painting and drawing, marry Carolyn (whom I met at art school), have two children, Naomi and Pete, and numerous dogs of all shapes and sizes over the years.

"I never planned to be an author and illustrator of children's books. I never planned very much at all; it just happened. A small blue parakeet flew into our back garden one morning, stayed with us for a while, and one day flew out again. It was a simple story, but nevertheless worth telling, so one day I stayed home from work and started to make small drawings . . . and to write a few words . . . and it became my first book, *Pete and Roland*. I have continued to make books ever since—about a profusion of dogs we have lived with, people we have known (or heard about), and also my imagination let off the leash.

"I would like my books to be a little like opening someone's family photo album and looking inside, then recognising that the people inside might be someone you know, or you, even. I have also managed to read heaps of books over the years since those first Walt Disney comics. I have read them to myself, and I have read them to my children. Now I read them to my granddaughter Rosie. My, oh my! Life flies along."

❄ ❄ ❄

Bob Graham's books have been characterized as having an overall theme of empathy and tolerance for those who are different, but these messages are always presented with a light touch of humor and exuberant, cartoon-style illustrations. Graham grew up in a suburb of Sydney, Australia, with his mother, father, grandmother, sister, and a dog called Tigger. While his sister always enjoyed the words in the books they had around the house, Bob would mostly pore over the pictures. "I still remember the strange creepy feeling of Arthur Rackham drawings, always at arms' length, and the comfortable and friendly atmosphere that infused E. H. Shepard's pictures, that certain hunch of Pooh Bear's shoulders," he told an interviewer when he won the Greenaway Medal in 2002 for *Jethro Byrde, Fairy Child*. His own ink-and-watercolor style is influenced by these early experiences with line and color, and delightfully enhanced by his lifelong love of cartoon art.

After high school, Graham worked for Qantas Airlines for four years before attending the Julian Ashton School of Art in Sydney from 1964 to 1967. He met his English wife, Carolyn, in art school, and they have lived in both Australia and England. It was while they were living in Manchester, England, that their daughter, Naomi, was born. Back in Australia, Graham spent two years with New South Wales Government Printers, designing safety posters and brochures and drawing Father Christmas on lottery tickets. Later, while working for the Department of Technical and Further Education of the Australian National University, he put together a children's picture book, using his young son, Pete, as a character, and it became his first published book. Since 1982 he has been a freelance author and illustrator. He and his wife currently live in Hawthorn, Australia. His daughter, Naomi, now lives in London, and his son, Pete, is a contemporary artist in Melbourne, Australia.

"The highlight of the afternoon was always for me the cartoon— Donald Duck, Tom and Jerry, or Mickey Mouse."

Courtesy of Candlewick Press

Well known in his native country, Bob Graham has won the picture book award of the Children's Book Council of Australia four times, for *Crusher Is Coming!*, *Greetings from Sandy Beach*, *Rose Meets Mister Wintergarten*, and *Let's Get a Pup!* Other books of his have been commended, shortlisted, and cited as Honour Books for that award. *Buffy* has won two state awards, in Tasmania and Victoria, and *Max* won the state award in Victoria. Equally appreciated in Great Britain, Graham has won both the Smarties Prize, for *Max*, and the Kate Greenaway Medal, for *Jethro Byrde, Fairy Child*. In the United States, *Max*—a picture book about a gentle young superhero—appeared on many lists of best books and was also named an ALA Notable Children's Book and an Oppenheim Toy Portfolio Platinum winner. *Let's Get a Pup!*, which had been shortlisted for the Greenaway Medal in Britain, was published in America as *Let's Get a Pup! Said Kate* and captured the *Boston Globe–Horn Book* Award in the picture book category, in addition to the KIND Children's Book Award from the Humane Society of the United States.

The universality of Graham's humorous cartoon style has been recognized with international prizes as well. In 1994 he was named the UNICEF Bologna Illustrator of the Year, and in 1998 he was given a Certificate of Honour for Illustration by the International Board on Books for Young People for *First There Was Frances*. His appealing stories and art have graced school texts as well as award-winning picture books.

SELECTED WORKS WRITTEN AND ILLUSTRATED (U.S. publication dates, if different, are shown in parentheses): *Pete and Roland*, 1981 (1984); *Pearl's Place*, 1983 (1985); *Here Comes Theo*, 1983 (1988); *Here Comes John*, 1983 (1988); *Libby, Oscar & Me*, 1984 (1985); *Where Is Sarah?*, 1985 (1988); *Bath Time for John*, 1985; *First There Was Frances*, 1984 (1986); *The Wild*, 1986 (1987); *The Adventures of Charlotte and Henry*, 1987; *Crusher Is Coming!*, 1987 (1988); *The Red Woollen Blanket*, 1987 (1988); *Has Anyone Here Seen William?*, 1988; *Grandad's Magic*, 1989; *Greetings from Sandy Beach*, 1990 (1992); *Rose Meets Mr. Wintergarten*, 1992; *Spirit of Hope*, 1993 (1996); *Queenie the Bantam* (U.S. title: *Queenie, One of the Family*), 1997; *Buffy: An Adventure Story* (U.S. title: *Benny: An Adventure Story*), 1999; *Max*, 2000; *Let's Get a Pup!* (U.S. title: *Let's Get a Pup! Said Kate*), 2001; *Jethro Byrde: Fairy Child* (U.S. title: *Jethro Byrd: Fairy Child*), 2002; *Tales from the Waterhole*, 2004.

SELECTED WORKS ILLUSTRATED: *A Boggle of Bunyips*, comp. by Edel Wignell, 1981; *Poems for the Very Young*, ed. by Michael Rosen, 1990; *Babies: Unsentimental Anthology*, ed. by Iona Opie, 1990; *This Is Our House*, by Michael Rosen, 1996; *Full House*, by Nigel Gray, 1998; *In Every Tiny Grain of Sand*, ed. by Reeve Lindbergh, 2000.

SUGGESTED READING: *Something About the Author*, vol. 151, 2004.

"I grew up in St. Louis in the 1950s. Since both my parents worked full time, I spent my days as a little girl playing alone under the not-so-watchful eyes of babysitters. I pored over picture books, learning the words by heart. I also loved to draw. At age two and a half, I was sent off to nursery school. Even there, surrounded by children and teachers, I was always something of a loner. There is a class picture of me then, tall with curly dark hair, frowning in the back row. My world changed in second grade when my mother became ill and could no longer continue her career in the advertising business. Her recuperation took a long time. During those months when my brother and I crept around the house and talked in low voices, books and reading became even more important to me. I lost myself in stories. My favorite books were about girls who were abandoned and then rescued, as in Frances Hodgson Burnett's classic story, *A Little Princess*, which I read over and over again.

Courtesy of Maureen Greenberg

Jan Greenberg

December 29, 1942–

"One Christmas I was given a small white diary with a gold key, and every night, under the covers with a flashlight, I recorded my daily life. One of my favorite entries was a description of my first girl/boy party in sixth grade. I rewrote it in *A Season in Between*, my autobiographical novel about the year my father died of cancer. I always tell young writers to save everything they write because you never know when you can use it again. In high school, I was more of an observer than a participant in the love life and dating scene of my friends. Even then, I viewed the world with some skepticism and always had a fine sense of the ridiculous. Hopefully this comes out in my novels for young readers.

"In college, I came into my own. I majored in English literature, had poetry published in the university literary journal, and fell in and out of love. I met my husband when I was a junior, and we were married eight months later. I remember being the only pregnant woman in my graduating procession at Washington University. This was the 1960s, the height of the Women's Movement, and although I was busy having babies (three daughters), I wanted a career as well. I went back for a graduate degree and began teaching at Webster University in an innovative arts education program. When my daughters entered middle school, I was flooded with so many memories of my own childhood that I started writing an autobiography to share some of my family history with them. Somewhere along the way my imagination took over, and I found myself embellishing and exaggerating the facts of my life. To my surprise and delight, my first attempt at writing fiction was actually published. During the next 10 years, I wrote six more novels, including *The Iceberg and Its Shadow*, about a girl who is bullied at school, and *No Dragons to Slay*, based on my best friend's son, who survived a serious illness.

"In 1972 my husband opened an art gallery, committed to showing works by contemporary American artists. We filled our rambling old house with these brash new artworks. The large, abstract paintings bewildered and disturbed many people, especially the teenagers who visited our daughters. What was it they were reacting against? I discovered that there were no books, especially for young people, that helped develop a dialogue with new art. Eventually in 1990 I got together with my first editor, Sandra Jordan, to write *The Painter's Eye: Learning to Look at Contemporary American Art*. Our collaboration has continued for over 10 years and includes biographies of a number of artists, such as Louise Bourgeois, Chuck Close, and the architect Frank Gehry. We spend hours in museums and galleries looking and talking about art. Visiting the artists in their studios and interviewing them has formed the basis for our books. We discovered that there is a strong correlation between what an artist experiences as a child and the art he or she creates as an adult. I also discovered that the loner in me is the loner in many creative people. In writing a biography or inventing a fictional character, it is wonderful to peel back the layers and get inside the mind of someone else. It puts my own life in perspective and helps me to tolerate my own weaknesses, as well as to cherish my strengths."

> *"We discovered that there is a strong correlation between what an artist experiences as a child and the art he or she creates as an adult."*

❋   ❋   ❋

Jan Greenberg has lived all her life in St. Louis, Missouri, but has traveled far in pursuit of the interests that inform her award-winning books for youth. She received her B.A. in English from Washington University in St. Louis and a M.A.T. in communication arts from Webster University in 1972. She has taught creative writing and art appreciation in the St. Louis public schools and at several colleges. Webster University has honored her with a Distinguished Alumni Award in 1992 and a School of Education Outstanding Alumnus Award in 2001. She and her husband, Ronald Greenberg, currently live in St. Louis; their three daughters—Lynne, Jeanne, and Jackie—have grown up and are all living in New York City.

Jan Greenberg's novels for teens, inspired by her daughters' growing years and her own memories, were well received, and she has also published numerous short stories, articles, and book reviews for the *Saint Louis Post Dispatch* and the *New York Times*; but her writing has had its greatest impact in the area of nonfiction. Stimulated by her interest in contemporary art and by contact with the artists who showed their work in her husband's gallery, she teamed with Sandra Jordan to explore a variety of ways to introduce modern artists and art concepts to today's children and young adults. Their first joint project, *The Painter's Eye*, was cited on many lists of the best books of the year and named an ALA Notable Children's Book. An upbeat writing

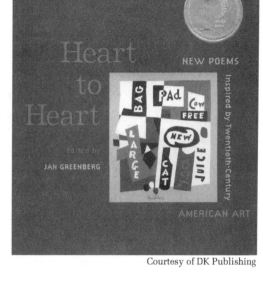

Courtesy of DK Publishing

style, strong book design, and intense personal interest in the subject made a winning combination for readers and critics alike, and this success was followed by *The Sculptor's Eye*, also an ALA Notable Children's Book, and *The American Eye*, cited as a Notable Children's Trade Book in the Field of Social Studies.

The dynamic writing duo then turned to individual artists in books that were as startling in their originality as the artists they introduced. *Chuck Close Up Close*, with its graphic representation of Close's style, besides being an ALA Notable Children's Book, was awarded a *Boston Globe–Horn Book* Honor Award for nonfiction and received the Norman Sugarman Award for Biography. *Frank O. Gehry: Outside In* introduced young readers to the controversial architect with splashy design, crisp photography, and a personal approach derived from direct interviews with Gehry and his staff. Named an ALA Notable Children's Book, it was also cited by the *New York Times* as "one of the best introductions to architecture that we have."

Vincent Van Gogh garnered a Robert F. Sibert Honor Award as well as being cited by the ALA as a Notable Children's Book and a Best Book for Young Adults. In 2001, Jan Greenberg received a Michael Printz Honor Award for a groundbreaking book that she edited on her own. For this book, *Heart to Heart*, she contacted a number of poets, asking them to respond by writing a poem inspired by a work of 20th-century art. The book that grew out of this project represents a dance between visual art and word pictures, with the poems grouped according to the form of the poet's response to the visual art: as stories, voices, impressions, and expressions. Jan Greenberg exhibited great editorial creativity in bringing this disparate group of artists and poets together. Teamed once again with Sandra Jordan and with illustrator Robert Andrew Parker for a dynamic picture book about Jackson Pollack, *Action Jackson*, she received a second Sibert Honor Award, another Notable Book citation and inclusion on many of the best-of-the-year lists. In 2004 *Runaway Girl: The Artist Louise Bourgeois* was named an ALA Best Book for Young Adults, cited as a *School Library Journal* Best Book, and received a Blue Ribbon citation from the *Bulletin of the Center for Children's Books*. *Romare Bearden* was also a *Bulletin* Blue Ribbon book. Greenberg continues to explore modern art, helping her readers to see with a new eye and experience the visual world with new understanding.

SELECTED WORKS: *A Season in Between*, 1979; *The Iceberg and Its Shadow*, 1981; *The Pig-out Blues*, 1983; *No Dragons to Slay*, 1984; *Bye Bye Miss American Pie*, 1985; *Exercises of the Heart*, 1987; *Just the Two of Us*, 1989; *The Painter's Eye: Learning to Look at Contemporary Art* (with Sandra Jordan), 1991; *The Sculptor's Eye: Looking at Contemporary American Sculpture* (with Sandra Jordan), 1993; *The American Eye: Eleven Artists in the Twentieth Century* (with Sandra Jordan), 1996; *Chuck Close Up Close* (with Sandra Jordan), 1998; *Frank O. Gehry: Outside In* (with Sandra Jordan), 2000; *Vincent Van Gogh: Portrait of an Artist* (with Sandra Jordan), 2001; *Heart to Heart: New Poems Inspired by Twentieth-Century American Art* (as editor), 2001; *Action Jackson* (with Sandra Jordan), illus. by Robert Andrew Parker, 2002; *Runaway Girl: The Artist Louise Bourgeois* (with Sandra Jordan), 2003; *Romare Bearden: Collage of Memories*, 2003; *Andy Warhol: Prince of Pop* (with Sandra Jordan), 2004.

SUGGESTED READING: *Something About the Author*, vol. 125, 2002.

An earlier profile of Jan Greenberg appeared in the *Sixth Book of Junior Authors and Illustrators* (1989).

Stephanie Greene

September 12, 1950–

"I grew up with four siblings in a drafty old New England house with a great sledding hill in the side yard, acres of wood, and a river running through the property. We accidentally fell into the river every spring when we wanted to swim and our mother said it was too early. We also had a tall, skinny pine tree next to the garage in which we built sheet forts and sang songs from the top as it swayed in the wind. I swam in the Long Island Sound in the summer and practiced figure skating on the river in the winter. It wasn't a perfect childhood, but it was pretty darned good.

"I was a reader long before I thought about being a writer. When I did think about writing as a career, I wanted to be a newspaper reporter, because my grandfather was the managing editor of a newspaper in New York City and he was the most glamorous man I knew. Not glamorous because he made lots of money, but because he had interesting friends and knew powerful people and seemed incredibly serene and content. I think that's what writing does for a person; it gives them a healthy outlet for the thoughts and fears and dreams that other people keep pent up inside them. When you finally write something that pleases you, you get the most incredible feeling of accomplishment and deep-seated harmony. Sometimes, after I've just sold a book, I'll be in the middle of a checkout line in the grocery store, when I'll suddenly think: 'I did it. I really did it.' Nothing else I do gives me that feeling.

"I tried newspaper writing for a few years and liked it very much. But I've always been a restless person who likes to try new things, so I moved to New York City and became an advertising copywriter. I married George Radwan, an art director, and we worked in South Africa and Hong Kong for a few years. Then we settled down on the Hudson River where our son, Oliver, was born, and I stopped working. As soon as he was old enough, Oliver and I would go to the library and come back with a huge stack of picture books and lie on the couch side by side and read through them all, then go back for another stack. It was while reading to him and watching the way he loved books and learned from them that the age-old thought popped into my head: *I can do that.*

"So, of course, I began with picture books, which I soon discovered (as all writers do) are the hardest books to write. After that, I never tried to write to a certain length again; I simply wrote what was waiting in the wings and let it end up whatever length it wanted to. When I finally started my first Owen Foote book, it flowed out of the tips of my fingers and I thought: 'Yes. Now you have it.' And I did have it. It took several revisions, 10 unsolicited submissions, and taking my place in line in a pub-

Courtesy of Oliver Radwan

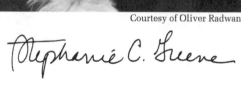

lisher's slush pile, but I made it. Now, every time I get a letter from a little boy who says, 'Owen is me,' I feel the most enormous happiness, because I know that the books that got me through life as a child were those that made me realize there were other kids out there like me, that I wasn't alone.

"All I want to do is to write one good book every year for the rest of my life and have each one be better than the one before. And have children turn to my books when they're happy or sad. And make them laugh and feel brave and capable and comforted. That may be asking too much, but asking too much is the story of my life."

✿ ✿ ✿

Stephanie Greene was born in New York City and grew up on the Silvermine River in Norwalk, Connecticut. Her mother, Constance Greene, wrote books for young readers. Stephanie saw her mother writing at their round dining-room table every day, and every night they had to push the papers and typewriter aside to set the table for dinner. Living in the midst of all those piles of books, notes, and wadded-up, crumpled sheets of paper made her think that the lifestyle of a writer was simply the norm. (Stephanie was the model for Isabelle in her mother's book *Isabelle the Itch*.)

Attending the University of Connecticut, Stephanie Greene spent her junior year in Rouen, France, and graduated with a B.A. in French in 1972. She worked as a reporter for the *Norwalk Hour* in Connecticut for several years before becoming an advertising copywriter in New York. She married George Radwan in 1976. Today she lives with her husband and her son in Chapel Hill, North Carolina, where they moved to escape the harsh northern winters. Currently she reads once a week to her "Lunch Bunch," a group of third graders at the local elementary school, and tutors an adult through the local Literacy Council. She also works part time as the editorial director of the Chapel Hill Press, which helps writers to self-publish.

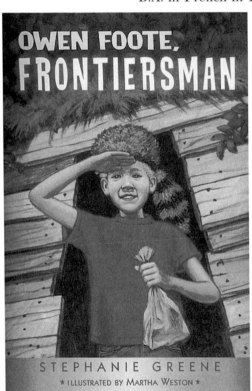

Courtesy of Clarion Books

Greene's stories about Owen, the smallest boy in his class at school, have been very popular with young readers, who respond to the humor of these books, which are told entirely from a child's perspective. *Owen Foote, Frontiersman* was a *School Library Journal* Best Book of the Year for 1999. *Owen Foote, Money Man* was named an American Booksellers Pick of the Lists in 2000.

SELECTED WORKS: *Owen Foote, Second Grade Strong Man*, illus. by Dee De Rosa, 1996; *Owen Foote, Soccer Star*, illus. by Martha Weston, 1998; *Show and Tell*, illus. by Elaine Clayton, 1998; *Owen Foote, Frontiersman*, illus. by Martha Weston, 1999; *Owen Foote, Money Man*, illus. by Martha Weston, 2000; *Not Just Another Moose*, illus. by Andrea Wallace, 2000; *Owen Foote, Super Spy*, illus. by Martha Weston, 2001; *Falling into Place*, 2002; *Betsy Ross and the Silver Thimble*, illus. by Diana Magnuson, 2002; *Owen Foote, Mighty Scientist*, illus. by Cat Bowman Smith, 2004.

SUGGESTED READING: *Something About the Author*, vol. 127, 2002.

A profile of Stephanie Greene's mother, Constance Greene, appeared in *Fourth Book of Junior Authors and Illustrators* (1978).

"I became a writer of rhyming children's stories because I love making up stories and working with rhyme. The ability to make up stories is something that I learned from my parents, who were always making up stories for me and my five younger brothers and sisters. My mom had a good technique for making up stories. First she would think of a hero for her story, then she would think of a predicament for the hero to get into, then she would think of all of the crazy things that could happen to that hero in that predicament, and suddenly she would have a story. She often did not know how her stories were going to come out; she would just make them up as she went along. That is how I make up stories today. I just start with a main character who is in some sort of predicament and then let my imagination wander, thinking of all the bizarre things that could happen to that character in that predicament until ultimately a story unfolds. And like my mom, I often do not know how my stories are going to turn out until I am done, which is one of the things that makes making up stories so much fun.

Courtesy of Bill Grossman

Bill Grossman

Bill Grossman

April 21, 1948–

"Another reason I became a writer of rhyming children's stories is that I love rhyme. All my life I have written silly limericks and other rhyming poems. I also acquired an appreciation for rhyme during the many Saturdays that I had to spend memorizing poetry in high school. At my high school, if you were late for school or were overly playful in class you would receive a demerit. After so many demerits you would have to come in on a Saturday and would not be allowed to leave until you had memorized a fairly lengthy poem. Being a highly playful person who is always late (my book *The Guy Who Was Five Minutes Late* is about me), I spent many Saturdays memorizing poetry.

"While those Saturday sessions never cured my playfulness or lateness, they did give me an appreciation for rhyme and a sense of what makes good rhyme. It was fun to read certain rhyming poems, such as Coleridge's *The Rime of the Ancient Mariner* (of which I had to memorize the first 84 lines one Saturday) or Poe's *The Raven* (which I had to memorize in its entirety on another Saturday). I noticed that what distinguished these good rhyming poems from rhyming poems of lesser quality was that the good rhyming poems always had a superb rhythm, or beat, to them. This led me to develop a very definite philosophy about rhyming poems, which is this: A good rhyming poem has a flawless rhythm to it, whereas even minor flaws in the rhythm can make an otherwise good rhyming poem sound bad.

"So now when I write a rhyming story the thing that I work the hardest on is making sure that the lines have perfect rhythm. Whenever I create a new draft of a rhyming story I have as many people as possible read the story aloud to me, and I always rewrite any lines that are not read with the proper beat. Hopefully somebody memorizing one of my rhyming stories on a Saturday will find it fun to read.

"All in all, being a writer of rhyming children's stories is a good job for a playful person who enjoys making up stories and working with rhyme. And since writers generally do not have to be anywhere at any particular time, it is also a good job for someone who is always late."

❋   ❋   ❋

"Whenever I create a new draft of a rhyming story I have as many people as possible read the story aloud to me, and I always rewrite any lines that are not read with the proper beat."

With a Catholic grammar and high school education, an M.S. and M.B.A. from Rensselaer Polytechnic Institute, and a master's degree in education from the University of Hartford, Bill Grossman has a wide-ranging background as well as being a master of rhymed storytelling. Over the years, he has held a number of different jobs, from fast-food griller to art school model to grave digger to fork lift operator to U.S. Marine. From 1977 to 1983 he was a computer software engineer and systems analyst, and from 1983 to 1988 he was an insurance actuary in Hartford, Connecticut. For several years he taught third grade and middle-school math at the Hebrew Academy of Greater Hartford in Bloomfield, Connecticut. He has taught mathematics at the University of Hartford in West Hartford and is currently on the faculty of Housatonic Community College in Bridgeport, Connecticut. His favorite jobs have been teaching and writing; he also enjoys visiting schools to talk about his books.

Before becoming a children's book writer, Grossman wrote short stories for adult periodicals such as *Northwest*. His first picture book, *Donna O'Neeshuck Was Chased by Some Cows*—a rhyming story featuring a character named for his former wife (Donna Anischik) who attracted not only cows but a host of other animals and humans with her irresistible head pats—was named a 1989 IRA/CBC Children's Choice selection. *Tommy at the Grocery Store* was Grossman's second book. Tommy's story is one of continual mistaken identity as he is identified only for individual body parts. One shopper thinks he's a potato because he has eyes; another is sure he's a banana because he has skin; a third is certain he's a bottle because he has a neck. Tommy is mistaken for a salami, a ruler, a corncob, a table, and a chair before his mother finds him and recognizes him as Tommy, the child she loves. Reminiscent of a folksong, *Tommy at the Gro-*

cery Store appeared on the Library of Congress list of Best Books for Children and was a *Publishers Weekly* Editors' Choice. In *The Guy Who Was Five Minutes Late*, Grossman tells the story of a baby who was born five minutes late and remains five minutes late all his life. Finally he meets a princess who is also always a few minutes late, and together they decide that the rest of the world is really just five minutes early. This rollicking read-aloud was an IRA/CBC Children's Choice selection.

In *My Little Sister Ate One Hare*, the narrator's sister will eat anything—ants, snakes, bats, shrews, mice, polliwogs, worms, lizards—and can keep them all down until she finally eats 10 nutritious but unpalatable peas, whereupon everything comes back up with the peas, alive and well. A counting book that uses humor to educate, *My Little Sister Ate One Hare* was named a *School Library Journal* Best Book of the Year and received the Indiana Young Hoosier Book Award and the South Dakota Prairie Bud Award, both in the grade K–3 category.

Courtesy of Random House, Inc.

Born in Cleveland, Ohio, Bill Grossman currently lives in Windsor, Connecticut. He is the father of three children, named Joshua, Adam, and Sally.

SELECTED WORKS: *Donna O'Neeshuck Was Chased by Some Cows*, illus. by Susan G. Truesdell, 1988; *Tommy at the Grocery Store*, illus. by Victoria Chess, 1989; *The Guy Who Was Five Minutes Late*, illus. by Judith Glasser, 1990; *Cowboy Ed*, illus. by Florence Wint, 1993; *The Banging Book*, illus. by Robert Zimmerman, 1995; *My Little Sister Ate One Hare*, illus. by Kevin Hawkes, 1996; *The Bear Whose Bones Were Jezebel Jones*, illus. by Jonathan Allen, 1997; *Timothy Tunny Swallowed a Bunny*, illus. by Kevin Hawkes, 2001; *My Little Sister Hugged an Ape*, illus. by Kevin Hawkes, 2004.

SUGGESTED READING: *Something About the Author*, vol. 126, 2002.

Vicki Grove

December 24, 1948–

"Sometimes I'm asked, 'When did you become a writer?' That's an easy one—it was in third grade. That year I discovered two wonderful things—how to write in cursive, and the hayloft that formed the second story of our old oak barn. The hayloft had always been there, of course. The barn had loomed for probably 100 years behind the tiny one-room schoolhouse we'd lived in all my life. My grandparents and great-grandparents lived within a mile of us there on the Illinois prairie. They had all attended the school we now used for a home when they were children, and you could see both of their big white farmhouses from up in our hayloft.

"But you weren't allowed to climb up there alone until you were grown up enough to be in third grade. When I turned eight, I was given permission to go up to the hayloft all by myself, without my father standing watching below, ready to catch me if my foot slipped from the wide-spaced rungs of the high and rickety ladder. It was good timing. I needed such a place just then, because of cursive. 'Children, now that you're learning cursive, there'll be no stopping your hand,' Mrs. Peters was telling us in class each day. 'Try it! Why, you can write whole stories now! Find a quiet place to be by yourself, think of what's interesting to you, and then let your mind range free as the wind.'

Courtesy of Michael Grove

"And so I crept up to the hayloft each afternoon and wrote about my pet rabbit, my grandfather with just one thumb, my grandmother using her hoe to kill a coon that was in her garden, Beth Apple winning a ribbon at the county fair that I deserved to win since my embroidery might not have been as perfect as hers but was way more original, my sister getting red boots, my baby brother getting all the attention, a storm that was like a cloud dance. The more I poured my life onto wide-lined notebook paper, the more I wanted to. I couldn't climb the gym rope at school, and I was shy and self-conscious. But up there in the hayloft, with the pictures in my mind turning into word paintings, I was powerful. Sometimes I punched the air and bounced my heels against the old wood floor in excitement when I got a paragraph just right.

"Would I be a writer today if I hadn't had that hayloft through my last important years of elementary school? Oh, I imagine I'd have found some other private, quiet, wonderful place to pour myself onto wide-lined notebook paper. Still, I recently met a girl who had read all my books and she pointed out to me that four of my narrators sit in haylofts to write in their journals each day! Yes, writers do draw from the truth of their own lives. (And before I forget—thanks, Mrs. Peters.)

"A tornado pretty much destroyed our little schoolhouse when I was ready to start junior high. My dad left farming, got a job in Oklahoma, and through junior high and high school I added a wild and wooly frontier layer of experience to the peaceful farm experiences of my early life. I turned 13 in 1961, so I was very much a teen during the turbulent 1960s. The actions and reactions of people facing the Vietnam War and the Civil Rights era are sometimes reflected in my books, particularly in *The Starplace*.

"We moved to Kansas City when I was 18, and I met my husband in graduate school in Missouri. He's a music teacher and a church choir director, and we've raised two amazing children, Michael and Jennifer, in an old white farmhouse we have on a few acres of land here outside Ionia, Missouri (population 118, counting 4 horses). We have a goldfish pond where I love to sit early in the morning and brainstorm my stories. About 10 years ago, my father and husband built me a little playhouse out in our hayfield. It's just about big enough to hold my computer and rocking chair, and it's where I spend most of my time working on my books and short stories. For company out here in the playhouse, I have a little tree toad who lives in a small birdhouse I hammered beside the window. His name is Joop.

"Oh, and yes—nearly every afternoon, just before twilight, I take my looseleaf notebook up to my hayloft and let my life come pouring out on the page. When I get a paragraph exactly right, so it tells the truth of something deep inside me, I punch the air and bounce my heels against the old wood floor in excitement."

✿　✿　✿

"Sometimes I'm asked, 'When did you become a writer?' That's an easy one—it was in third grade."

Vicki Grove is steeped in the life of rural America. The converted schoolhouse she grew up in was a few miles from the tiny town of Keyesport, and she was surrounded by a loving family filled with storytellers. Her younger sister and much younger brother were partners in her imaginative play, and her elementary teachers still hold a warm place in her heart. Grove earned a B.A. in 1972 and an M.A. in 1974, both from Central Missouri State University, where she met her husband. Their children are now grown, but the Groves still share their lives with an assortment of animals and continue to live in the American Midwest, the setting for many of Vicki's novels.

Vicki Grove began writing professionally when she was in her early thirties. It happened by accident. She sent some articles to magazines and was surprised when they were accepted. So she continued, and about eight years later wrote a book about the world she knows best. A story about a farm foreclosure told from the viewpoint of a 12-year-old girl, *Goodbye, My Wishing Star* won Putnam's Fiction Prize for a First Novel for Children and was an American Booksellers Pick of the Lists. Grove's career as a writer for young adults was launched.

While she never expected young adults to be her audience, she now says, "I absolutely love to write in the voice of a 13- or 14- or 16-year-old." Many of her books are about middle graders or young adults who face enormous personal challenges and rise above them. She was shocked when she realized that many youngsters live a life very different from the one she knew, and she wanted to offer them courage to persevere and conquer their

THE STARPLACE

VICKI GROVE

Courtesy of Penguin Putnam Books for Young Readers

difficulties. She explores such issues as moving from a beloved home, suffering peer rejection, battling a weight problem, homelessness, the death of a parent, and the cruelty of racism, addressing all of these issues with grace and compassion.

The Fastest Friend in the West, the story of two lonely girls who quickly become best friends, was an IRA/CBC Children's Choice in 1990. *Reaching Dustin* and *The Starplace* were on *School Library Journal's* Best Books list of 1998 and 1999, respectively, and *Destiny* was the winner of the 2001 Midland Author's Award for Children's Fiction.

SELECTED WORKS: *Goodbye, My Wishing Star*, 1988; *Junglerama*, 1989; *Fastest Friend in the West*, 1990; *Rimwalkers*, 1993; *Crystal Garden*, 1995; *Reaching Dustin*, 1998; *The Starplace*; 1999; *Destiny*, 2000.

SUGGESTED READING: *Authors & Artists for Young Adults*, vol. 38, 2001; *Contemporary Authors*, vol. 195, 2002; *Something About the Author*, vol. 151, 2004.

WEB SITE: *mowrites4kids.drury.edu/authors/grove*

Brenda Guiberson

(GUY-ber-son)

December 10, 1946–

"As a child, I never thought about being an author or illustrator, but wondered how I might become a jungle explorer. I rarely read books and attended an elementary school without a library. I grew up with five sisters, two brothers, and, for a while, three foster children from Cuba. Much of my childhood was spent swimming in the Columbia River, watching geese and salmon (and younger siblings), searching for arrowheads and other artifacts, and building things or taking them apart. I was curious about everything and had a lot of patience for observation. If a bird flew into the yard, I'd look for it again and again, trying to discover where it lived and what it ate.

"In high school and college, I loved science classes. But as I put myself through the University of Washington in Seattle, it was easier to schedule evening English classes than afternoon science labs, so I graduated with B.A. degrees in English and fine art.

"I married William R. Guiberson in 1973, and we continue to live near Seattle. I was introduced to children's literature while reading numerous books to our son, Jason. When he went off to elementary school, I volunteered in the school library and classroom and really enjoyed the enthusiasm and delight of the kids as they discovered new things about the world around them.

"After taking exciting trips that involved a 50-foot cactus, a hungry alligator, and spoonbills, I got interested in trying to create a book for children that would be like a field trip. As a writing voice developed in *Cactus Hotel*, *Turtle People*, and *Spoonbill Swamp*, I found that I liked a book to speak for itself with lots of dramatic, visual detail that came from doing extensive research.

"Research, to me, is a great adventure. I love it, do a lot of it, and then leave out about 90 percent of what I have learned. Nothing is wasted, though, because parts of it shift my thinking, lead to new interests, and emerge in other books. Having a deep pool of information to draw on also helps in the writing and rewriting process. I want a book to be intriguing and poetic as well as accurate.

"I include direct observation, talking to experts, searching through archival collections, and reading about a subject from many different angles. I am always looking for objects or facts that awaken my kid-like sense of wonder, astonishment, and fresh association. Fieldwork is a favorite method and has involved such events as a night in a haunted lighthouse, counting sea turtle eggs in Costa Rica, and watching flamingos on a salty island in the Bahamas. It is not possible to learn all that needs to be known through field research. For instance, how can we observe a cactus or sea turtle living out its entire life cycle? However, a journey to the source is a good place to get the emotion, the big picture, and a sense of awe. If a field trip is not possible, then I try to get an emotional connection through music, videos, photos, or artwork. This is what I try to put into a book.

Courtesy of Doug Zangar

Brenda Z Guiberson

"After collecting a tremendous amount of research for each book, I focus on the most exciting and meaningful items. These I weave into a story, listening for flow, poetry, and lots of visual images. When I first wrote *Cactus Hotel* and *Spoonbill Swamp*, I thought I was writing fiction and was surprised when my editor said it was nonfiction. I hope that readers will experience not only the facts but the emotions that I pull into a dramatic narrative. Whether I am writing about emperor penguins, kudzu, or mummies, I try to convey a strong sense of wonder, adventure, and survival. I feel that an awareness of the connections between plants and animals, between past and present, between environment, weather, and opportunity, will help us all take better care of the planet."

❋   ❋   ❋

Courtesy of Henry Holt & Co.

Brenda Zangar Guiberson was born in Denver, Colorado, but when she was five her family moved to Richland, Washington, where her father worked as an engineer at the Hanford Nuclear Reservation. After graduating from the University of Washington, Guiberson worked at a variety of jobs: copy editor, manager, woodworker, and stained glass artist. When her son was born, she found herself drawn to children's books—through reading to him, volunteering in his school library, and finally writing and (often) illustrating her own books.

Guiberson has written fiction, but she has found her strongest narrative voice in nonfiction, writing books that are a blend of storytelling and research. She can combine primary source material, action scenes, and poetic prose to create books that are fun to read, yet filled with factual information. Her first book, *Turtle People*, a novel that is laced with facts about Native American history, was named a Junior Library Guild selection. *Cactus Hotel*, *Spoonbill Swamp*, *Lobster Boat*, and *Spotted Owl* have all been named Outstanding Science Trade Books. *Spoonbill Swamp*, *Into the Sea*, and *The Emperor Lays an Egg* have been cited as *School Library Journal* Best Books of the Year. *Cactus Hotel* also received a Parents' Choice Award, was chosen as a Teachers' Choice by the IRA, and named a Notable Trade Book in Language Arts by the NCTE.

In addition to writing and illustrating children's books, Guiberson is an instructor at the University of Washington in the Advanced Writing for Children program. She and her husband live in Seattle.

SELECTED WORKS WRITTEN AND ILLUSTRATED: *Salmon Story*, 1993; *Spotted Owl: Bird of the Ancient Forest*, 1994; *Lighthouses: Watchers at Sea*, 1995; *Mummy Mysteries: Tales from North America*, 1998; *Tales of the Haunted Deep*, 2000; *Mud City: A Flamingo Story*, 2004.

SELECTED WORKS WRITTEN: *Turtle People*, 1990; *Cactus Hotel*, illus. by Megan Lloyd, 1991; *Instant Soup*, 1992; *Spoonbill Swamp*, illus. by Megan Lloyd, 1992; *Lobster Boat*, illus. by Megan Lloyd, 1993; *Winter Wheat*, illus. by Megan Lloyd, 1995; *Into the Sea*, illus. by Alix Berenzy, 1996; *Teddy Roosevelt's Elk*, illus. by Patrick O'Brien, 1997; *Exotic Species: Invaders in Paradise*, 1999; *The Emperor Lays an Egg*, illus. by Joan Paley, 2001; *Ocean Life*, 2001; *Sharks*, 2002; *Rain, Rain, Rain Forest*, illus. by Steve Jenkins, 2004.

SUGGESTED READING: *Something About the Author*, vol. 124, 2002. Periodicals—Bowlan, Cheryl, "Author Profile: Brenda Guiberson," *Northwest Reading Journal*, Fall 2000.

WEB SITE: *www.brendazguiberson.com*

"**I** am the youngest of five children, and for a long time, my life story seemed boring, and hardly worth telling. But then at some point, I realized that like all of us, little people or VIPs, I had been born in a tide of history. And the tide was rushing along in a torrent. Once you wake up and decide to swim, especially against the current, life becomes very interesting indeed.

"Like the character Emi in my book *Be-Bop-A-Do-Walk!*, I was born into the culturally diverse slums of the Lower East Side of post–World War II New York City. The year was 1949. Before we moved up to West Harlem, six of us lived in a three room flat with a toilet in the hall. But I didn't know we were poor because we didn't have a television set to tell me so.

"My dad was an actor, a bohemian, and I grew up with be-bop: Bird and Diz and Prez [Charlie "Bird" Parker, Dizzy Gillespie, and Lester Young]. At night, I listened to my father recite Shakespeare and Neruda and Lorca. By day, I read *Dick and Jane*. Everything I know about art I attribute to this early exposure to brilliant musicians and writers. Thankfully, my father was smart enough not to think: hmm, what grade level is *The Heights of Machu Picchu?*

Courtesy of Julia Casteliero

Sheila Hamanaka

August 1, 1949–

"My parents had made their way to New York after their release from Jerome, one of 10 concentration camps that held over 110,000 Japanese Americans during the war. The government destroyed the Japanese American community, using a tactic they had practiced with Native Americans: removal. My father had become a rebel after he read, at age 18, *War and Peace* by Tolstoy. The book turned him into a pacifist at a time when it was not popular to be one (after all, the United States was fighting Hitler and the Nazis). Had he not been a pacifist, he might have joined the 442nd, which, because of the Army's policy of segregation, was all Japanese American. The 442nd and the 100th, Japanese Americans from Hawaii, were the most decorated units of their size in all of U.S. military history. They were wounded and killed at a rate five times higher than average.

"We never talked about this in my family. Many things, especially how to deal with racism, are learned nonverbally. They simmer beneath the surface until the tide swells up and swimmers stick their heads above water, see the mountain top, and yell 'FREEDOM!' That tide was the Civil Rights Movement, which gave my community the guts to demand an apology, and reparations. In 1990, I wrote *The Journey: Japanese Americans, Racism, and Renewal*. I had been part of the anti-war movement of the late 1960s, which led me to write *Peace Crane*, and to compile artwork, prose, and poetry from 60 different authors and illustrators in the beautiful book *On the Wings of Peace*. It commemorated the 50th anniversary of the bombings of Hiroshima and Nagasaki, and though it is now, sadly, out of print, you may find it in your library.

"I am inspired to write about peace, or multiculturalism, or the strength of girl power. I hope there will be a tide of these kinds of books and that the imagery in *All the Colors of the Earth* will become the norm, because that's what our country looks like now. I hope that one day someone will say to me, 'I decided to work for peace after reading your book.' Every bit of mass culture that glorifies violence helps take someone else's life away. Literature can give life. Like my father before me, I owe my life to Tolstoy. I hope to return the favor."

> *"Once you wake up and decide to swim, especially against the current, life becomes very interesting indeed."*

❉ ❉ ❉

Sheila Hamanaka attended public schools in New York City, including the High School of Music and Art (now called LaGuardia), where she majored in art. When it was tuition-free, she studied at City College of New York and later took art courses at Indiana University. Asked how she became interested in illustrating children's books, Hamanaka says she "fell into it." She was in an exercise class with an editor who introduced her to an art director at Morrow Junior Books.

For some years, Hamanaka illustrated humorous middle grade novels, mystery stories, and books of humorous poetry that were very popular with children and received a number of children's choice state book awards. Among these were stories written by Johanna Hurwitz (*Class Clown* and *School's Out*) and *The Twenty-Four-Hour Lipstick Mystery*, by Bonnie Pryor. She is currently working with author/illustrator Pat Cummings on a series of mystery/fantasy novels for middle grade readers to be called *Snapshots*. But it is her own illustrated books that have brought her the greatest recognition, books that explore in text and in art ideas and emotions that spring from her own experience and family background.

The Journey: Japanese Americans, Racism, and Renewal, which became a Jane Addams Peace Award Honor Book winner and a *School Library Journal* Best Book, was originally a painting in Hamanaka's studio that one of her editors, Dick Jackson, saw and liked. He convinced her to expand the painting into a book about the Japanese American experience during World War II with particular emphasis on internment camps. Continuing her exploration of Japanese culture, Japanese American experience, and the theme of peace, she has had

Courtesy of Morrow Junior Books

six titles named Notable Children's Trade Books in the Field of Social Studies: *All the Colors of the Earth*, *Be-Bop-a-Do-Walk!*, *Peace Crane*, *I Look Like a Girl*, *In Search of the Spirit*, and *On the Wings of Peace*. *In Search of the Spirit: The Living National Treasures of Japan*, which was also named an ALA Notable Children's Book, offers an intriguing look at Japanese culture by describing six extraordinary artists and their arts (Yuzen dyeing, bamboo basket weaving, Bunraku puppetmaking, swordmaking, Noh theater, and neriage ceramics). *All the Colors of the Earth*, which celebrates in verse the richness and diversity of the world's children, was included on Reading Is Fundamental's 100 of the Decade's Best Multicultural Read-Alouds for the 1990s.

Sheila Hamanaka lives in Tappan, New York, with her Alaskan Malamute whose name, Kalluck, means thunder. She has two grown children: a daughter, Suzuko, and a son, Kiyoshi, as well a six-year-old granddaughter, Sachiko.

SELECTED WORKS WRITTEN AND ILLUSTRATED: *The Journey: Japanese Americans, Racism, and Renewal*, 1990; *Screen of Frogs: An Old Tale*, 1993; *All the Colors of the Earth*, 1994; *Be-Bop-a-Do-Walk!*, 1995; *Peace Crane*, 1995; *I Look Like a Girl*, 1999; *In Search of the Spirit: The Living National Treasures of Japan*, with Ayano Ohmi, 1999; *Grandparents Song*, 2003.

SELECTED WORKS ILLUSTRATED: *Class Clown*, by Johanna Hurwitz, 1987; *Teacher's Pet*, by Johanna Hurwitz, 1988; *Juliette Gordon Low: America's First Girl Scout*, by Kathleen V. Kudlinski, 1988; *The Twenty-Four-Hour Lipstick Mystery*, by Bonnie Pryor, 1989; *A Poem for a Pickle: Funnybone Verses*, by Eve Merriam, 1989; *Beverly Sills: America's Own Opera Star*, by Mona Kerby, 1989; *Chortles: New and Selected Wordplay Poems*, by Eve Merriam, 1989; *Class President*, by Johanna Hurwitz, 1990; *Molly the Brave and Me*, by Jane O'Connor, 1990, 2003; *School's Out*, by Johanna Hurwitz, 1991; *The Terrible EEK: A Japanese Tale*, retold by Patricia A. Compton, 1991; *The Heart of the Wood*, by Marguerite W. Davol, 1992; *Sofie's Role*, by Amy Heath, 1992; *A Visit to Amy-Claire*, by Claudia Mills, 1992; *Quiet, Please*, by Eve Merriam, 1993; *The Hokey Pokey*, words by Larry La Prise, Charles P. Macak, and Tafft Baker, 1996.

SELECTED WORKS EDITED: *On the Wings of Peace: Writers and Illustrators Speak Out for Peace, in Memory of Hiroshima and Nagasaki*, comp. with an introduction by Sheila Hamanaka, 1995.

SUGGESTED READING: Cummings, Pat, *Talking with Artists*, vol. 2, 1995.

Virginia Hamilton

March 12, 1936–
February 19, 2002

The following autobiographical sketch was written by Virginia Hamilton for the *Fourth Book of Junior Authors and Illustrators* (1978):

"I was born the fifth child of Etta Belle and Kenneth James Hamilton in the village of Yellow Springs, Ohio. At six months of age I fell from my cradle on the porch to the ground and landed on my back. Ever since, I have been particularly fond of Ohio skies. My childhood and youth I remember as being mostly pleasant, my family having considered me 'the baby' until the time I went off to college. My four brothers and sisters flattered me and my parents spoiled me, thus instilling me with an abundant sense of my own importance.

"By age six I sang solos in the local African Methodist Episcopal church. This coincided neatly with my discovery of, and extreme fascination with, public school. I fairly ran the mile to school each morning and quickly cracked the mysteries of math and reading. Where my family left off in paying me attention, the schools now took on the burden. For the next 12 years my career as one of many teacher's pets was marked by overachievement. I had old-fashioned teachers who seemed to indulge every child with liberal doses of warmth and discipline. I graduated from high school with honors and had no thought of attending university when Antioch College offered me a full scholarship.

"Somewhere along the line, and at any early age, I started to write. It soon became a pleasant habit, but I don't remember ever making much of a fuss about it. When I entered college it seemed natural to drift to the departments of literature and creative writing, where at once my prose was given respect. Such attention now induced feelings of claustrophobia; and after three years I dutifully left Antioch for Ohio State University. Many writing courses and literature classes later, I struck out for New York City, where, I was told, a great gold kettle of publishers was waiting just for me. No rockets exploded in air on my arrival. More writing courses, more study, and after 10 years my first book was published. In that time I learned about city life and self-survival. I also learned how to write the best way—by living.

"I am extremely fond of children and of singing. But for the most part, I write and sing for myself. My greatest pleasure is sitting down and weaving a tale out of the mystery of my past and present."

❆ ❆ ❆

Virginia Hamilton, over the course of a long, illustrious career, earned recognition as one of the most distinguished writers for young people of our time. From her first two books, *Zeely* in 1967 and *The House of Dies Drear* in 1968, she made the children's book world sit up and take notice. Though very different, the stories about a young black girl's admiration of a tall, regal black woman and an African American family's eerie experiences in a house that had once been on the Underground Railroad, were indicative of Hamilton's innovative writing, which incorporated unique characters, compelling narratives, and African American culture. Time, place, and family were at the heart of the fiction she created.

Hamilton wrote nearly 40 books, handling with finesse a great variety of genres that included mysteries, biography, science fiction, folk tales, love stories, and picture books—each one original, engaging, and always in Hamilton's inimitable voice. Writ-

Courtesy of Scholastic, Inc.

ing was a part of her life from a young age. A native of Yellow Springs, Ohio, Hamilton had strong roots that would nourish her stories. She was the youngest of five children on a small truck farm in Ohio, with parents who were gifted storytellers and grandparents who had once been slaves. She attended Antioch College on a scholarship and majored in writing but left after three years for Ohio State University, where three significant things occurred that would shape her life: she met Arnold Adoff, a poet and author, whom she would marry three years later; she won her first writing award for a short story, a story that later became her first book, *Zeely*; and an OSU instructor encouraged her to leave college and test her writing skills in New York City. And she did. She and Arnold were married in New York in 1960. Then, while working as a bookkeeper, she studied writing at the New School for Social Research.

Hamilton and Adoff's two children have inherited their parents' passion for music and writing. Their son, Jaime Levi (named for Hamilton's grandfather), has performed in a band and published a book of poems about music, *The Song Shoots Out of My Mouth*, as well as a novel for young adults. Daughter Leigh is pursuing a career as an opera singer. Family was always of primary importance to Hamilton, and the theme of family solidarity and history is a thread that runs through all of her novels, which often include parents, grandparents, aunts, uncles, and cousins of her main characters. A groundbreaking picture book about her own interracial family was written by her husband in 1973, *Black Is Brown Is Tan*, celebrating the everyday life of a biracial couple and their two children. Reissued in 2002 in a larger format and with updated illustrations by the original artist, Emily Arnold McCully, the book continues to be a joyous depiction of multicultural diversity and the power of family love.

Early notice of Hamilton's writing skill came when she received an Edgar Allen Poe Award at the beginning of her career for the mystery story *The House of Dies Drear*. National recognition of her distinctive talent continued in 1972 with a Newbery Honor Award for *The Planet of Junior Brown*, one of the first books about homeless children. The Newbery Medal followed in 1974 for *M. C. Higgins, the Great*, in which the main character sits atop a 40-foot pole watching as a strip mine encroaches on his family's mountain home. Hamilton was the first African American author to receive a Newbery Award, and in the same year she also won the National Book Award. She received Newbery Honor Awards twice more for *Sweet Whispers, Brother Rush*, and *In the Beginning*. Three of her books were chosen for the Coretta Scott King Award: *The People Could Fly*; *Sweet Whispers, Brother Rush*; and *A Little Love*; and three times she received Coretta Scott King Honor citations. Sixteen of her books were cited as ALA Notable Children's Books over the years, and a number of those titles were also named Best Books for Young Adults. Her audience indeed crossed over age boundaries in response to her excellence of style, provocative themes, and joyous spirit.

Virginia Hamilton loved folklore, and she retold many old myths and tales from her own ancestry to restore pride in a rich ethnic heritage. Titles like *The People Could Fly*, *In the Beginning*, *A Ring of Tricksters*, and *When Birds Could Talk and Bats Could Sing* reflect her gentle sense of humor, her delight in the stories she grew up hearing, and a deep sense of cultural pride. In an article for the Children's Book Council Web site, she once said, ". . . the fact that my grandfather Levi was a fugitive from the Civil War South gave me the impetus to research centuries

"I learned about city life and self-survival. I also learned how to write the best way—by living."

of plantation-era history and folklore. I then recast certain historical and folk narratives into contemporary collections of stories and tales for the young." The biographies she wrote also grew out of her family history, and were recognized for their fine style and substance. *Anthony Burns: The Defeat and Triumph of a Fugitive Slave* won a *Boston Globe–Horn Book* Award for nonfiction as well as the Jane Addams Peace Prize. In her biographies of W. E. B. DuBois and Paul Robeson and in *Many Thousand Gone: African Americans from Slavery to Freedom*, she chronicled historic African American struggles in this country through distinctive individual voices.

In 1992 Hamilton became one of the few Americans to win the Hans Christian Andersen Medal, the top international prize for children's literature, for her body of work. In her acceptance speech, she spoke of her desire to mark the history and traditions of African Americans. She had achieved that goal with integrity and distinction, making those traditions a universal celebration of humanity. In 1995 she received the American Library Association's Laura Ingalls Wilder Award for lifetime achievement; in that same year, she became the first children's book author to receive a coveted fellowship from the MacArthur Foundation. In 2000 she was honored by her home state with the Ohio Governer's Award in the Arts and in 2001 she was presented the University of Southern Mississippi's Medallion for her significant contribution to children's literature. The Regina Medal from the Catholic Library Association in 1991, the May Hill Arbuthnot lectureship in 1993, and honorary degrees from several universities are among the other significant achievements of Hamilton's distinguished career.

Courtesy of Blue Sky Press/Scholastic, Inc.

Virginia Hamilton completed her last novel shortly before her death, and it seems fitting that the story is semi-autobiographical. *Time Pieces* relates how an Ohio girl discovers the powerful family history of her grandfather's escape from slavery in Virginia to the free state of Ohio. In all of her work as novelist, biographer, and reteller of folktales, Hamilton strove to portray what she liked to call a "parallel culture community" in American society, all the while pointing out the universality of human experience. Her books are a treasured legacy to future generations.

SELECTED WORKS: *Zeely*, illus. by Symeon Shimin, 1967; *The House of Dies Drear*, illus. by Eros Keith, 1968; *The Time-Ago Tales of Jahdu*, illus. by Nonny Hogrogian, 1969; *The*

Planet of Junior Brown, 1971; *W. E. B. DuBois*, 1972; *Time-Ago Lost: More Tales of Jahdu*, illus. by Ray Prather, 1973; *M. C. Higgins, the Great*, 1974; *Paul Robeson: The Life and Times of a Free Black Man*, 1974; *Arilla Sun Down*, 1976; *Justice and Her Brothers*, 1978; *Dustland*, 1980; *Jahdu*, illus. by Jerry Pinkney, 1980; *The Gathering*, 1981; *Sweet Whispers, Brother Rush*, 1982; *The Magical Adventures of Pretty Pearl*, 1983; *Willie Bea and the Time the Martians Landed*, 1983; *A Little Love*, 1984; *Junius Over Far*, 1985; *The People Could Fly: American Black Folktales*, illus. by Leo and Diane Dillon, 1985; *A White Romance*, 1987; *The Mystery of Drear House*, 1987; *In the Beginning: Creation Stories from Around the World*, illus. by Barry Moser, 1988; *The Bells of Christmas*, illus. by Lambert Davis, 1989; *Cousins*, 1990; *The Dark Way: Stories from the Spirit World*, illus. by Lambert Davis, 1990; *The All Jahdu Storybook*, illus. by Barry Moser, 1991; *Drylongso*, illus. by Jerry Pinkney, 1992; *Many Thousand Gone: African Americans from Slavery to Freedom*, illus. by Leo and Diane Dillon, 1993; *Plain City*, 1993; *Her Stories: African American Folktales, Fairy Tales, and True Tales*, illus. by Leo and Diane Dillon, 1995; *Jaguarundi*, illus. by Floyd Cooper, 1995; *When Birds Could Talk and Bats Could Sing*, illus. by Barry Moser, 1996; *A Ring of Tricksters: Animal Tales from America, the West Indies, and Africa*, illus. by Barry Moser, 1997; *Second Cousins*, 1998; *Anthony Burns: The Defeat and Triumph of a Fugitive Slave*, 1998; *Bluish*, 1999; *The Girl Who Spun Gold*, illus. by Leo and Diane Dillon, 2000; *Time Pieces: The Book of Times*, 2002; *Bruh Rabbit and the Tar Baby Girl*, illus. by James E. Ransome, 2003; *Wee Winnie Witch's Skinny: An Original African American Scare Tale*, illus. by Barry Moser, 2004.

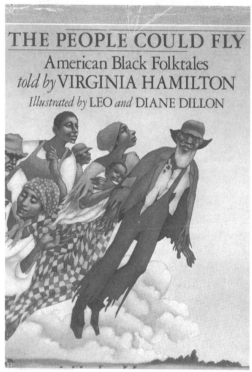

THE PEOPLE COULD FLY
American Black Folktales
told by VIRGINIA HAMILTON
Illustrated by LEO *and* DIANE DILLON

Courtesy of Alfred A. Knopf

SUGGESTED READING: *Black Writers*, 2nd ed., 1994; Cullinan, Bernice, and Diane Person, eds. *The Continuum Encyclopedia of Children's Literature*, 2001; Hopkins, Lee Bennett. *More Books by More People*, 1974; Hopkins, Lee Bennett. *Pauses: Autobiographical Reflections of 101 Creators of Children's Books*, 1995; McElmeel, S. L. *100 Most Popular Children's Authors*, 1999; Mikkelsen, Nina. *Virginia Hamilton*, 1994; Silvey, Anita. *Children's Books and Their Creators*, 1995; *Something About the Author*, vol. 123, 2002; Townsend, John Rowe. *A Sounding of Storytellers: New and*

Revised Essays on Contemporary Writers for Children, 1979; Wheeler, Jill. *Virginia Hamilton*, 1997. Periodicals—Hamilton, Virginia, "The King and I," *School Library Journal*, May 1999; Hamilton, Virginia, "Newbery Acceptance Speech," *The Horn Book*, August 1975; Langton, Jane, "Virginia Hamilton the Great," *The Horn Book*, December 1974.

WEB SITE: *www.virginiahamilton.com*

A profile of Virginia Hamilton's husband, Arnold Adoff, appeared in the *Fourth Book of Junior Authors and Illustrators* (1978).

"**K**ids and adults always ask me, 'When did you publish your first book?' 'In kindergarten,' I answer. And they all look quite surprised. In my kindergarten class, the first thing we did every morning was to draw a picture and tell our teacher a story about our drawing. Each day, our teacher would write down our story. At the end of the year, each student's stories and drawings were compiled into a book. I named that book—my first book—'Robie's Stories.' It was 'published' in June 1946.

"From second grade on, the first thing we did every morning was to write—anything—for 15 minutes. Our teacher told us not to worry about spelling. We could fix that later. Once a week, we would read aloud what we had written, and our classmates would tell us what did and didn't work. The next day we would revise our writing—until we got it 'right.' I still write numerous drafts—maybe more than 30 for each book! I still read what I wrote out loud to myself at the end of each day, so I can hear the parts that work and the parts that don't work. The next afternoon, I work on the parts that didn't work. To this day, almost every day, I still write first thing in the morning—a habit I learned in second grade.

"My closest friend and first cousin, children's book author Elizabeth Levy, and I attended the same elementary school. Liz and I are each other's first readers and toughest critics—a practice we both learned from our remarkable elementary school teachers. I never planned to be a children's book author. It just happened. But I always liked making books. I was editor of my high school newspaper and college yearbook. After graduate school, I became a teacher at the Bank Street School for Children in New York City and taught children how to write.

Courtesy of Harry Robie

Robie H. Harris

April 3, 1940–

"A few years later, I worked with two veteran and talented children's book authors, Irma Black and Bill Hooks, at the Bank Street Writer's Laboratory. Five mornings a week, sitting together with pencil, paper, and a toy piano, we wrote a song and the five-minute opening segment for ABC's *Captain Kangaroo* show. Here I learned to spend the morning writing and the rest of the day rewriting, and to work with others to create something better than anything I could create by myself. Collaboration became a habit, and today I work closely with extraordinarily talented illustrators—Michael Emberley, Nicole Hollander, Jan Ormerod, and Harry Bliss—so that, hopefully, my text and their art become seamless.

"I grew up in a home where all the neighborhood children played and hung out. The home my children grew up in was that way as well. My mother adored and respected children as I do— from babies to adolescents. I find them refreshingly honest and always fascinating. Perhaps that's why children, not animals, are the characters in my books. The 'Bird' and 'Bee' characters I created (for *It's Perfectly Normal*) are really the voices of children.

"What I love to write about are the real and powerful feelings children have and the ways in which they express those strong and perfectly normal feelings."

"What I love to write about are the real and powerful feelings children have and the ways in which they express those strong and perfectly normal feelings. Hence, it's no surprise that my picture books explore the inner life of children and deal with topics such as love, attachment, independence, loss, sibling rivalry, and even anger and hate. My father was a radiologist, my mother worked in a biology laboratory, and my brother is a neurosurgeon. I am quite sure their love of science influenced me greatly and is probably why my nonfiction books explore such topics as infancy, early childhood development, puberty, reproduction, cells, genetics, viruses, and sexual health. My own experience as a wife and mom, and now a grandmother, also influences my writing. My husband's work and the work of my two grown children and their spouses all center on children. I learn from each one in my family all of the time. And I can't wait to see the ways in which my wonderful new grandchildren will weave themselves into my future books!"

✿ ✿ ✿

Robie H. Harris was born Robie Heilbrun and grew up in Buffalo, New York. She received her A.B. degree from Wheaton College in Massachusetts in 1962 and has also earned an M.A.T. from the Bank Street College of Education in New York City. Married to William Harris since 1968, she has two grown children, Ben and David, and is now a grandmother. Her education experience includes: master teacher for second grade at the Bank Street School for Children; director of the After-school Program for Bank Street College Early Childhood Center, Head Start Model Program; and teacher at the Smallwood Drive School in Williamsville, New York. In 2000 she was awarded an honorary degree, doctor of humane letters, from Lesley College in Boston for her work in the field of children's books, and in 2002 she received a Distinguished Alumnae Award for her contributions to education from the Bank Street College of Education.

Harris's books for young children met with early success. *Before You Were Three*, written with her cousin Elizabeth Levy, was named an Outstanding Science Trade Book for Children, and *Rosie's Double Dare* was named to the Children's Choices list. Her series of picture books, illustrated by Michael Emberley, about the life of the very young—*Happy Birth Day, Hello Benny!*, and *Hi, New Baby!*—have been mentioned on many lists of the best books of the years in which they were published and have won numerous prizes, from the Oppenheim Toy Portfolio Gold Seal Award to the *Parenting* Reading Magic Award. The same is true for her picture book about death, *Goodbye Mousie*, sensitively illustrated by Jan Ormerod.

Courtsey of Candlewick Press

While Harris has written picture books, nonfiction books, and chapter books, she is best known for her text for the groundbreaking *It's Perfectly Normal: A Book About Changing Bodies, Growing Up, Sex, and Sexual Health*. This honest and witty discussion of sexual maturation won a *Boston Globe–Horn Book* Honor Book Award for nonfiction and was named an ALA Notable Children's Book, cited as a *New York Times* Notable Book of the Year, and listed in nearly every Best of the Year list in 1994, as well as being designated a Wil Solimene Award Winner for Excellence in Medical Communication. Major media attention was paid to this title around the country, often because of concerns voiced by conservative groups that the information was too frank and the illustrations too graphic. Harris's approach to the subject has been lauded by educational organizations, reviewers, and library professionals, however. Her research for the book included meetings with parents, librarians, teachers, psychologists, and health care professionals to ensure accurate, up-to-date information that would also be understandable and psychologically appropriate for the intended audience. Nevertheless, *It's Perfectly Normal* was cited by the American Library Association's Office of Intellectual Freedom as the most challenged nonfiction book of 1998.

It's So Amazing!: A Book About Eggs, Sperm, Birth, Babies, and Families, on the same topic but for younger children, was also an ALA Notable Children's Book, a *Horn Book* Fanfare title, a *School Library Journal* Best of the Year, and a Parent's Guide to Children's Media Award winner. It has attracted national print, television, and radio coverage, including a feature article in the *Boston Globe* and a recommendation in *Child* magazine. In an interview on *TeachingBooks.net*, Harris said, "Our kids already know or have heard about 99.9 percent of this stuff. What concerns me is that they have a lot of misinformation, no matter how much they tell us they know, and I wanted them to get accurate information. So, I think the litmus test for me was: What's in the best interest of the child, what's going to help a child stay healthy."

SELECTED WORKS: *Before You Were Three: How You Began to Walk, Talk, Explore, and Have Feelings*, with Elizabeth Levy, photos by Henry E. F. Gordillo, 1977; *Rosie's Double Dare*, 1980; *I Hate Kisses*, illus. by Diane Paterson, 1981; *Rosie's Razzle Dazzle Deal*, 1982; *Messy Jessie*, illus. by Nicole Hollander, 1987; *Hot Henry*, illus. by Nicole Hollander, 1987; *It's Perfectly Normal: A Book About Changing Bodies, Growing Up, Sex, and Sexual Health*, illus. by Michael Emberley, 1994; *Happy Birth Day*, illus. by Michael Emberley, 1996; *Hi, New Baby!*, illus. by Michael Emberley, 2000; *Goodbye, Mousie*, illus. by Jan Ormerod, 2001; *I Am Not Going to School Today*, illus. by Jan Ormerod, 2001; *Hello Benny! What It's Like to Be a Baby*, illus. by Michael Emberley, 2002; *Go! Go! Maria! What It's Like To Be 1*, illus. by Michael Emberley, 2003; *Don't Forget To Come Back!*, illus. by Harry Bliss, 2004; *Sweet Jasmine, Nice Jackson: What It's Like To Be 2—And To Be Twins!*, illus. by Michael Emberley, 2004.

SUGGESTED READING: *Something About the Author*, vol. 147, 2004. Periodicals—McCullough, Bob, "Toward a Younger Audience: Author, Illustrator Gear Sex Ed Book for Readers 10 and Up," *Boston Globe*, October 23, 1994; Stevenson, Deborah, "The Big Picture," *Bulletin of the Center for Children's Books*, October 1994; Zvirin, Stephanie, "The *Booklist* Interview: Robie Harris," *Booklist*, May 1, 1996. Online—Elias, Tana, "The Perfectly Amazing Robie Harris: An Interview," *www.soemadison.wisc.edu/ccbc/friends/harris.htm*.

Marc Harshman

October 1, 1950–

"I was a lucky boy. The once-a-week trip to town from the farm for groceries always included, as well, a trip to the Carnegie Library. My clearest, early memory of home was of mother in one chair, father in another, and a stack of books at both their elbows. I recall, too, the similar good fortune of hearing my father's voice wrapped around the poems of James Whitcomb Riley—this was Randolph County, Indiana, near the small town of Union City—'Little Orphant Annie's come to our house to stay, / An' wash the cups an' saucers, an' brush the crumbs away, . . .' To this day I am enchanted by dialect, by real voices informed by local culture. I believe that had I not had such a 'language-rich' extended household as I did, I would never have gone on to write a single published word. This early start, I earnestly believe, was far more important to my development as a writer than all the university education I would later receive.

"Lucky. In many ways. I was sick a lot as a kid and, though I doubt that I thought of it as lucky at the time, I wonder now if, in fact, it wasn't. There were endless days spent under the counterpane deep inside the wonders of countless books. Those sure look like lucky days now. John McGahern, the Irish novelist and short story author, has written: 'There are no days more full in childhood than those that are not lived at all, those days lost in a favourite book.' I believe a good part of my childhood was so lost.

"I remember my grandparents, the supper table there, how when the dishes were 'red up' we would continue to sit for what seemed to me hours at a time. We would stay put, sitting and talking and, I realize now, storytelling—the rich reminiscences of the old ones mixing with the day's gossip and news: whose cows were down sick, how great grandad had shot a wildcat in the woods behind the very house where we're now sitting, giant blacksnakes, the talk from the Wednesday night prayer meeting. It was all there, creating what I think of now as a story table. It is a table I fear is lost from most of our families, a table I feel we must re-create as authors, teachers, librarians wherever we encounter children today, a table at which not only do we bring our stories, but at which we, too, sit and listen.

Courtesy of Carthrine Feryok

My favorite remark from the large wisdom of Thomas Merton is this: 'The peculiar grace of a Shaker chair is due to the fact that it was made by someone capable of believing that an angel might come and sit upon it.' I like to have that chair in mind when I think of our children, their chairs, and the tables around which they gather. Which of us knows how precious each of those lives may be?

"My wife and daughter and I live in a simple house in the foothills along the Ohio River. Here and there goes on the kind of independence, self-reliance, neighboring, and husbandry that I value and which reminds me of the energetic attentiveness necessary to pursuing any craft and so nurtures, in part, my own writing. To paraphrase Wendell Berry I find that region, in the sense that it matters to me, is a place where 'local life is aware of itself.' I have nearly always lived in such places. I know the man next door and he knows me. And he, too, knows these names. And with these and much else we can still speak with a shared language and shared knowledge of our community. This is what matters most to me about the place where I live.

"I have always lived in neighborhoods, places where people have known each other. Whether next door or out the ridge, there were names and faces known and trusted. Living in the foothills of West Virginia along the Ohio River these past 30 years has given a singular blessing to my work as both a poet and children's writer."

✿ ✿ ✿

Raised in Randolph County, Indiana, Marc Harshman has lived most of his adult life in West Virginia, and it is clear from his writing that rural America has had a great influence on his life and work. He received his B.A. from Bethany College in West Virginia in 1973 and a master's degree from Yale University Divinity School in 1975; he also holds an M.A. from the University of Pittsburgh. For many years he taught fifth and sixth grades at the Sand Hill School, one of the last of the three-room country schools. Marc is married to Cheryl Ryan, a librarian and author, and they live near Wheeling, West Virginia, with their daughter, Sarah.

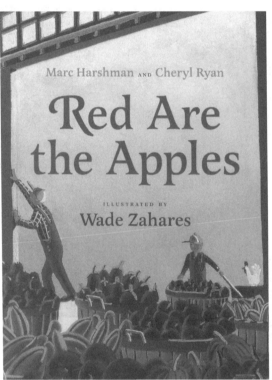

Courtesy of Harcourt, Inc.

The author of nine picture books for children, Marc is also a poet and storyteller; a chapbook of his poems, *Rose of Sharon*, was published by Mad River Press, and he received a West Virginia Arts Commission Fellowship in Poetry for the year 2000. His excellence in teaching was recognized when he was named the West Virginia English Teacher of the Year by the West Virginia English Language Arts Council in 1995. In 1994 he received the Ezra Jack Keats/Kerlan Collection Fellowship from the University of Minnesota for research in Scandinavian myth and folklore; his retelling of an Icelandic tale has recently been published in *Cricket Magazine*.

Marc Harshman's picture book texts reflect his roots in rural America and celebrate the values and experiences of children living in the country, ranging from everyday happenings to disruptions in children's lives, as in *Moving Days*, to traumatic events such as fires and tornadoes. *Only One*, an exploration of math concepts found in the setting of a county fair, was selected as a *Reading Rainbow* review book by PBS. *All the Way to Morn-*

ing was an American Booksellers Pick of the Lists. In *The Storm*, Harshman captures the fear and determination in a boy's reaction to an approaching tornado, showing the small acts of heroism that occur so often in country living. *The Storm* was a Parents' Choice Gold Seal Winner, a *Smithsonian* Notable Children's Book, a Notable Children's Trade Book in the Field of Social Studies, and a Junior Library Guild Selection. Marc Harshman enjoys world travel, and his children's books have been translated into Spanish, Danish, and Swedish.

SELECTED WORKS: *A Little Excitement*, illus. by Ted Rand, 1989; *Snow Company*, illus. by Leslie W. Bowman, 1990; *Rocks in My Pockets* (with Bonnie Collins), illus. by Toni Goffe, 1991, 2002; *Only One*, illus. by Barbara Garrison, 1993; *Uncle James*, illus. by Michael Dooling, 1993; *Moving Days*, illus. by Wendy Popp, 1994; *The Storm*, illus. by Mark Mohr, 1995; *All the Way to Morning*, illus. by Felipe Davalos, 1999; *Red Are the Apples* (with Cheryl Ryan), illus. by Wade Zahares, 2001; *Roads*, illus. by Mary Newell DePalma, 2002.

SUGGESTED READING: *Contemporary Authors*, vol. 180, 2000; *Something About the Author*, vol. 109, 2000.

WEB SITE: *www.marcharshman.com*

Yumi Heo

November 26, 1964–

"This is a tale mostly of beginnings—my beginnings—a child of Korea, an artist, a New Yorker.

"The first published book I ever illustrated was *The Rabbit's Judgment*, a retelling of a Korean folktale by Suzanne Crowder Han. This was a story I had known since I was a child in Korea, and I felt a real connection with it. And from the start, I was very comfortable with the artistic process I used for the illustrations. I would say that this art came from inside of me. Fortunately, the critics agreed with me. One reviewer called my style 'a pleasing blend of sophisticated design, ethnic reference, and visual storytelling,' which was very reassuring.

"The first book I both wrote and illustrated was *One Afternoon*. I came to America from a small town in Korea, and when I was at the School of Visual Arts in New York City, I did a book about the racial disharmony there. An editor told me it would be difficult to publish, but he encouraged me to write a Korean immigrant story. So I wrote and illustrated *One Afternoon*. It's just the story of a little boy who spends his day running around doing errands with his mother, but the child's experiences of the big buildings, noises, and excitement of New York City were like my own. The second book I wrote and illustrated was *Father's Rubber Shoes*, about a boy whose family has just moved to America from Korea. The boy is lonely, but his father tells him a story about how he was so poor in Korea as a child that he carried his shoes around rather than wearing them so they wouldn't wear out. This is actually a story that my mother told me when I was little. The basis for the story is that when Koreans come to this country, they don't come with a lot of money. They start from the bottom and try to work their way up. They try to do better for their children.

"Another first for me was the 30-piece colored-glass art installation of 'Q Is for Queens.' I illustrated a book called *A Is for Asia* by Cynthia Chin-Lee, and that book was what gave me the idea for 'Q Is for Queens.' There is a brightly colored glass panel for each letter of the alphabet, from 'A Is for Aqueduct Raceway' to 'Z is for Zoo,' as well as four additional panels denoting special landmarks and events. The New York Metropolitan Transit Authority sponsored the project, and the panels were installed in subway stops at 33rd Street, 40th Street, and 46th Street in Queens. I am now a bona fide New Yorker."

❊ ❊ ❊

Courtesy of Steven Dana

Yumi Heo was born and raised in Wonju, a small town in South Korea's countryside. Before coming to the United States in 1989, she studied graphic design in Korea. In 1991, she received an M.F.A. in illustration from the School of Visual Arts in New York City. While she was attending the School of Visual Arts, she met Steven Dana, whom she married in 1992. An artist himself, Dana currently teaches graphic design at the School of Visual Arts.

Known for her quirky, lively characters, detailed backgrounds, textured collage, and unique perspectives, Heo is stylistically both traditional and tradition-breaking, her art both primitive and sophisticated. Her distinctive artwork has been lauded for its visual storytelling, unusual arrangement of details, and the whimsical approach which represents the world as a child might see it. Many of these unique characteristics can be seen in her award-winning books. *The Rabbit's Judgment*, her first picture book, was cited by the *Bulletin of the Center for Children's Books* as a Blue Ribbon Title, and *The Rabbit's Escape* was named an ALA Notable Children's Book. Both stories were written by Suzanne Crowder Han. In *The Lonely Lioness and the Ostrich Chicks*, a Masai tale retold by Verna Aardema, Heo combined several art forms, including pencil, paper collage, and oil paints, in a style that tosses details across the background like wallpaper. For this distinctive title she earned a citation as one of the *New York Times* Best Illustrated Books of the Year. *So Say the Little Monkeys*, Nancy Van Laan's version of a Brazilian story, gave Heo yet another cultural venue for artistic interpretation and was named a *School Library Journal* Best Book of the Year, as well as a *Bulletin* Blue Ribbon title.

Courtesy of Atheneum Books for Young Readers

In Heo's own retelling of a Korean folktale, *The Green Frogs*, two naughty frog brothers love to disobey their mother until her death makes them regret all the mischief they caused. *The Green Frogs* was named a *Bulletin* Blue Ribbon book and a *Horn Book* Fanfare title. *Henry's First-Moon Birthday*, in which Heo's whimsical and energetic pencil-oil-collage compositions enhance Lenore Look's story of a young girl helping her grandmother prepare for a traditional Chinese celebration of her baby brother's first moon (one month) birthday, was named an ALA Notable Children's Book, a *Smithsonian* magazine Notable Book for Children, and a Notable Social Studies Trade Book for Young People.

Yumi Heo currently lives in White Plains, New York, with her husband and their two children—Auden, who was born on September 3, 1997, and Sara Jane, who was born on April 25, 2000.

SELECTED WORKS WRITTEN AND ILLUSTRATED: *One Afternoon*, 1994; *Father's Rubber Shoes*, 1995; *The Green Frogs*, 1996; *One Sunday Morning*, 1999.

SELECTED WORKS ILLUSTRATED: *The Rabbit's Judgment*, by Suzanne Crowder Han, 1994; *The Rabbit's Escape*, by Suzanne Crowder Han, 1995; *The Lonely Lioness and the Ostrich Chicks: A Masai Tale*, by Verna Aardema, 1996; *A is for Asia*, by Cynthia Chin-Lee, 1997; *Pets!* by Melrose Cooper, 1998; *So Say the Little Monkeys*, by Nancy Van Laan and Verna Aardema, 1998; *The Not So Itsy-Bitsy Spider*, by

Dawn Bentley, 1999; *Dandelion: Celebrating the Magical Blossom*, by Amy S. Wilensky, 2000; *Sometimes I'm Bombaloo*, by Rachel Vail, 2000; *Yoshi's Feast*, by Kimiko Kajikawa, 2000; *Henry's First-Moon Birthday*, by Lenore Look, 2001; *Snake's Tales*, by Marguerite W. Davol, 2002; *Pirican Pic and Pirican Mor*, by Hugh Lupton, 2003; *Uncle Peter's Amazing Chinese Wedding*, by Lenore Look, 2003; *Moondog*, by Alice Hoffman, 2004; *Smile, Lily!* by Candace Fleming, 2004.

SUGGESTED READING: *Something About the Author*, vol. 146, 2004. Periodicals—*Bulletin of the Center for Children's Books*, November 1997.

Courtesy of Reven Wurman

Jennifer Holm

1968

"When I was a kid, I liked to read. A lot. One of our neighbors said recently that his clearest memory of me as a child was watching me rake the lawn one-handed while I read a book with the other. In fact, the highlight of a particular summer vacation was not, for me, going on the water slide at an amusement park but rather stopping at a bookstore with a great kid's section and discovering—gasp!—that my favorite author, Lloyd Alexander, had written *four* more books.

"I was born in California across from a zoo and then we lived on Whidbey Island in the Puget Sound and then moved again to Audubon, Pennsylvania, where I spent most of my childhood. My dad was a pediatrician, and my mom a pediatric nurse. We had a dog named Ruffy who had a bad habit of chasing skunks and a hamster named Sneaker who liked to curl up in my hair and fall asleep (he was a very mellow hamster).

"But my childhood was marked by something else—boys. Specifically, brothers. I had a pack of them. Four to be exact, and I liked to do everything they did—softball, kickball, climbing trees, spitting contests, swimming in the creek, you name it. I guess it left a lasting impression. Even my husband admits that it takes me less time to get ready in the bathroom than him!

"My childhood has always been my main source of inspiration for my writing. You can see glimpses of it in my book *The Creek*, and also in *Our Only May Amelia*. Another big influence during those years were comic books and cartoon strips. My brothers and I would fight over the big color funnies section of the Sunday newspaper. I still love comic books and graphic novels and I think reading them has helped make me a better writer.

"I attended Audubon Elementary School, where I had a wonderful librarian named Mrs. Ellenburg. After surviving middle school (barely), I attended Methacton High School. In high school I did lots of different things—I was in the marching band, I was on the debate team, and I played lacrosse. So I guess you could say I was hard to pigeonhole. I graduated and went to Dickinson College in Carlisle, Pennsylvania, and that's where I really started writing.

"After I graduated from college, I moved to New York City, where I became a broadcast producer of television commercials and music videos for clients like Nickelodeon and MTV and American Express and Hershey's and even Huggies (yes—baby wipes). I enjoyed working in television, but I had always wanted to be a writer. My father's stories of the family farm in Naselle, Washington, intrigued me, and so when a family member sent me a photocopy of a diary kept by my great aunt, Alice Amelia Holm, when she was a young girl, I got the spark. May Amelia and the Jackson family were born. I was incredibly fortunate to receive a Newbery Honor for my first novel, *Our Only May Amelia*, and that allowed me to eventually become a full-time writer. My books have been translated into several languages and the Seattle Children's Theatre staged *Our Only May Amelia* in 2002.

"I'm trying to stay out of trouble these days. I still prefer reading to amusement parks, and on occasion, I rake the lawn while reading a book (although I confess I don't seem to get many leaves up that way). I now split my time between writing and taking care of my son, Will Aaron. My husband, Jonathan Hamel, and I recently collaborated on a series called The Stink Files about a British international cat of mystery. We all live in Maryland with one slightly stinky cat named Princess Leia Organa the Cat."

Courtesy of HarperCollins Publishers

❀ ❀ ❀

As a child Jennifer Holm played with her brothers and the neighborhood children in the deep woods behind their houses, generally getting into trouble that their parents never found out about. It felt like a totally separate world in the woods, one created out of imagination, play, and problem-solving—the kind of world few adults ever inhabit. She loved to read, and her favorite books were the Boxcar Children mysteries by Gertrude Chandler Warner and anything by her idol, Lloyd Alexander, especially his Chronicles of Prydain series. She often fantasized about becoming a writer, but as time went on, the idea seemed intimidating.

During her college years, Jennifer worked in the Dickinson College Archives, where she came to appreciate and enjoy long hours of research and discovery and began to see the wonderful stories that could be found. She graduated in 1990 with a B.A., majoring in international studies, and immediately headed for New York City to produce television commercials and music videos. When her father became ill, Holm began visiting him more frequently, and the stories he told her about his youth and his family in the state of Washington made her consider the idea of writing again.

Ten years later, her first book, *Our Only May Amelia*, won a Newbery Honor Award. It featured a character not unlike herself—a tomboy with lots of brothers. May Amelia resents being expected to act "like a lady" even while she hopes the baby her mother is having will be a girl so she'll have some company in the family. This book, inspired in part by her father's stories and the diary of her own Great Aunt Alice Amelia Holm, a Finnish-American girl born in the 19th century on the Nasal River in Washington state, was also named an ALA Notable Children's Book, a Notable Social Studies Trade Book for Young People, and a *Publishers Weekly* Best Book and won a Parents' Choice Silver Award. Her second novel, the first book in the Boston Jane series, called *Boston Jane: An Adventure*, was named an ALA Best Book for Young Adults and won the Women Writing the West Silver Award. Set in 1854, it also features a tomboy, but this time a reluctant one. When prim and proper Jane Peck leaves Boston for the Northwest to meet her fiancé, she must abandon her upbringing and schooling in order to survive in the rough-and-tumble world of the Washington Territory.

Recently Jennifer has begun collaborating with her husband, Jonathan Hamel, on a nine-book series called The Stink Files, in which the nine books represent the nine lives of cats. The idea came from the time when they were first married and their two cats, who had a hard time getting along, bickered and argued and even slapped each other. "It was so human," Holm said, "that we began to think that cats really do have a whole world order of their own." Since her husband had always been her first editor, even before she sent her manuscripts to the publisher, it seemed natural for them to become writing partners. The first book in the series is called *The Stink Files, Dossier 001: The Postman Always Brings Mice*.

After living in Brooklyn, New York, for a time, Holm has moved to Hunt Valley, Maryland, with her husband and their son.

SELECTED WORKS: *Our Only May Amelia*, 1999; *Boston Jane: An Adventure*, 2001; *Boston Jane: Wilderness Days*, 2002; *The Creek*, 2003; *Boston Jane: The Claim*, 2004; *The Stink Files,*

Dossier 001: The Postman Always Brings Mice, with Jonathan Hamel, illus. by Brad Weinman, 2004.

SUGGESTED READING: *Something About the Author*, vol. 120, 2001. Online—"Growing up Weird," author profile on *Book Sense: www.booksense.com/people/archive/holmjennifer.jsp*; Newman, Patricia, "An Author Profile: Jennifer Holm," *Acorn: Newsletter for the North/Central California Region of the SCBWI*, September 2003 (*scbwinorca.org/news/acorn/ acornfall2003.pdf*).

WEB SITE: *www.jenniferholm.com*

"When people ask me how long it takes me to write a book I say, 'Do you want the short answer or the long one?' The short answer is 'about one and half years,' but the most honest answer is 'all my life.' Often I can pinpoint the inspiration for the story, and usually that inspiration can be traced back to a moment in my childhood. Therefore, a lifetime of experiences must be factored into the amount of time that forms the story.

"I was born in Pensacola, Florida, during Hurricane Donna while my father was stationed there in the U.S. Navy. The next 18 years included travels to destinations all over the world, including Paris, France. Although I don't speak French now, as a young child I spoke it fluently, and it became the first language I learned to read. I also lived in Virginia, Guam, Washington, and various cities in Louisiana.

"I wanted desperately to grow up in one place, but my father's Navy career kept us moving. Between transfers, my family visited my grandparents in Forest Hill, Louisiana. That small piney-woods town became my emotional home.

Courtesy of Fugua Photography, Inc.

Kimberly Willis Holt

September 9, 1960–

"Years later the author Richard Peck told me he thought I wrote to find home. I believe Peck is right. My characters always seem to be redefining or searching for home. I can identify with the plight of my main characters because I was often the 'new girl.' Although each move meant making new friends, I grew up with two younger sisters, Alicia and Angela. Sometimes I borrow from their experiences or aspects of their personalities and use them in my stories, but it is never to the extent that they claim. I think it's cheating to plop a real person in a story. Almost anyone can do that. I'd like to think my characters are lifelike, but also original.

"I've wanted to be a writer ever since I was 12 and read *The Heart Is a Lonely Hunter* by Carson McCullers. That was the first time I'd read a book where the characters seemed like real people to me. I wanted to write like that. I didn't pursue my dream until many years later. On June 15, 1994, I picked up a pen and decided to write. I called myself a writer and wrote six days a week. I acted like writing was my job, even though I didn't get a paycheck. Soon the voice of Tiger Ann Parker came to me, and I wrote my first book, *My Louisiana Sky*, on yellow legal pads. I treasure those pads because they represent the beginning. Almost two years to the day after I began to write, *My Louisiana Sky* sold to the publisher Henry Holt and Company.

"Today I live in the Texas Panhandle with my husband, Jerry, my daughter, Shannon, and our poodle, Bronte. With Bronte at my feet, I write my first drafts by hand, usually sitting in a bedroom chair and covered with a heating blanket. I've learned I can write anywhere—in airplanes, coffee shops, and hotel rooms. As long as I have paper, pen, and a block of time, I can write. On school visits, I tell students to believe in themselves, work hard and their dreams can come true. Whenever I'm grumpy, I remind myself that I have the privilege of living my dream. What other job lets you stay home and work in your pajamas?"

Courtesy of Henry Holt & Co.

✾ ✾ ✾

After moving constantly during her growing-up years, Kimberly Willis Holt stayed in the Louisiana of her family's roots at age 18 to attend the University of New Orleans and Louisiana State University, where she studied broadcast journalism. She worked as a radio news director, sold advertising time for the same radio station, and spent about seven years doing interior decorating before she decided to fulfill her childhood dream of becoming a writer. She married her husband, Jerry Holt, in 1985, and their daughter, Shannon, was born in Arlington, Texas.

Holt's first book, *My Louisiana Sky*, was inspired by a memory from her childhood; while she was visiting her Louisiana grandparents, she noticed a woman walking along the side of the road. Her mother told her that both the woman and her husband were mentally retarded and had many children. The voice of a girl growing up in that situation came to Kimberly as she started writing many years later; *My Louisiana Sky* received a *Boston*

Globe–Horn Book Honor Book citation for fiction and was named one of the ALA Top Ten Best Books for Young Adults, as well as an ALA Notable Children's Book, a remarkable achievement for a first novel. Successes continued when her second book, *Mister and Me*, became a Junior Library Guild selection and was included on New York Public Library's list of 100 Titles for Reading and Sharing.

When Zachary Beaver Came to Town was also inspired by a childhood memory, a trip to the Louisiana State Fair when Kimberly was 13. She paid two dollars to see the "fattest teenage boy in the world." Exploring the emotions of that situation years later, she created the novel that earned her a National Book Award. The poignant story of Zachary Beaver was also in the Top Ten of ALA's Best Books for Young Adults and was named an ALA Notable Children's Book, a *Horn Book* Fanfare title, and a *School Library Journal* Best Book. *Dancing in the Cadillac Light*, her next book, was designated a *School Library Journal* Best Book, and *Keeper of the Night*, which draws on Holt's memories of living in Guam during her 5th and 6th grade years, became an ALA Notable Children's Book, a Best Book for Young Adults, and a *Kirkus* Editors' Choice.

Writing about the emotions and situations that feel most true and important to her, Kimberly Willis Holt has carved a special niche for herself in contemporary literature for young people.

SELECTED WORKS: *My Louisiana Sky*, 1998; *Mister and Me*, illus. by Leonard Jenkins, 1998; *When Zachary Beaver Came to Town*, 1999; *Dancing in the Cadillac Light*, 2001; *Keeper of the Night*, 2003.

SUGGESTED READING: *Something About the Author*, vol. 122, 2001. Periodicals—Horning, Kathleen T., "Small Town Girl," *School Library Journal*, February 2000.

WEB SITE: *www.kimberlywillisholt.com*

Deborah Hopkinson
February 4, 1952–

"My sister says what she remembers most about me as a child is that I was always reading. I expect she's right. It wasn't unusual for me to read until two, three, or even four in the morning on summer nights, my head buried in a book.

"I grew up in Lowell, Massachusetts, and attended the University of Massachusetts at Amherst. I majored in English, in part because I didn't know what else to do. In my sophomore year I participated in a domestic exchange program at the University of Hawaii at Manoa. I fell in love with Hawaii and returned in 1975 to pursue a master's degree in Asian studies. While there I met my husband, Andy Thomas, an artist, and we moved to a small house in the back of Manoa Valley, which we shared with centipedes, cockroaches, and geckos!

"After graduate school I still didn't have much of a career plan. Back in sixth grade I'd won the spelling bee for my school, and a little blurb about me had appeared in the newspaper. At that time I wrote that I wanted to be a writer or a doctor. Here it was years later, and I wasn't doing either one.

"As it turned out, though, the first job I landed after graduate school was as the staff writer for the American Red Cross in Honolulu. That started me on a career in fund-raising for nonprofit organizations, something I've pursued ever since. I began working for the University of Hawaii in 1985. In 1994 we moved back to the mainland so I could accept a position at Whitman College in Walla Walla, Washington. I've been there ever since and work full-time as director of Grants and Advancement Services.

"I've enjoyed my career in higher education, but after our daughter, Rebekah, was born in 1984, my early desire to be a writer returned. I didn't see how I'd have time to write a long

novel, but as Rebekah and I began to read picture books together, I thought this might be something I could try. And so I began to write and submit short pieces. It took two years of rejections before I sold my first story to *Cricket* magazine. I'll never forget the excitement of holding that acceptance letter in my hand. I continued to sell magazine stories, as well as a nonfiction book about Pearl Harbor. Then, in 1989, while listening to National Public Radio one morning, I heard an interview with an African American quilter that inspired me to write *Sweet Clara and the Freedom Quilt.*

Courtesy of Rebekah Hopkinson

"It wasn't easy to get this story published either. After a year of submitting it I was about to give up. Finally, one October morning in 1990, I sent the story off to about 10 publishers simultaneously. Three weeks later I received a phone call from an editor named Anne Schwartz who said, 'I like your story.' Anne has continued to be my editor, and we are now working on our ninth book together.

"Selling this book enabled Andy and me to adopt our son, Dimitri, who at the time was almost six years old and was living in an orphanage in Russia. Both my children are extremely active and creative. Rebekah, now attending college, is an extraordinary actor. Dimitri breeds chickens, doves, and pigeons, is a budding antiques dealer, and has his own yard business. I love being able to take my kids on trips to conferences and even school visits. Sometimes Dimitri gets more requests for autographs than I do, from kids who want to know all about his pets!

"Thinking back to my early years, it's clear that my love of reading has stayed with me, although most of my reading now is research-related. In many ways, I feel writing historical fiction has been like going to school all over again, and I love studying and learning about the past. But every once in a while I take time off from research to read a good novel. And I still love to stay awake until all hours of the night to finish it!"

❉   ❉   ❉

Deborah Hopkinson's work is largely about opening windows to the past. Her first picture book, *Sweet Clara and the Freedom Quilt*, was inspired by a story on National Public Radio about a Williams College quilt exhibition marking the centennial of their first African American graduate. It won a 1994 International Reading Association Award and was a *Reading Rainbow* Selection, as well as a Notable Children's Trade Book in the Field of Social Studies. *Birdie's Lighthouse*, set in 19th-century Maine, received a Parents' Choice Silver Honor, was a Junior Library Guild Selection, and was named a Blue Ribbon book in the *Bulletin of the Center for Children's Books*. *A Band of Angels* was named an ALA Notable Children's Book and received a Golden Kite Award for picture book text. *Fannie in the Kitchen* was a *Smithsonian* Notable book and a *Publishers Weekly* Best Book of 2001, while *Bluebird Summer* received a Golden Kite Honor Award for picture book text. *Under the Quilt of Night*, a companion book to *Sweet Clara*, was named one of the 100 Best Children's Books of 2002 by the New York Public Library and included on the Capitol Choices List.

Hopkinson earned her B.A. in English from the University of Massachusetts, Amherst, in 1973, and she completed a master's degree in Asian studies at the University of Hawaii in 1978. She wrote her first book, *Pearl Harbor*, during the years she lived in Honolulu. For many years she has contributed stories to children's periodicals such as *Cricket, Ladybug*, and Scholastic's *Storyworks Magazine*. Her interest in history leads her to search for subjects in many places, and her wide-ranging topics have led to many awards as well as delight and attention from young readers. A popular title with students is *Girl Wonder: A Baseball Story in Nine Innings*, which won the Great Lakes Book Award chosen by children, as well as being a Jane Addams Award Honor book and an Oppenheim Toy Portfolio Gold Award winner.

Fannie in the Kitchen was initially inspired by a chapter in a book on women inventors, augmented by memories of her own childhood—eating in a Fannie Farmer coffee shop and enjoying Fannie Farmer candies, both without ever knowing that Fannie Farmer was a real person. *Fannie in the Kitchen* is more highly fictionalized than some of Hopkinson's other books, because she wasn't able to locate the kind of source materials that had informed those works. By contrast, her book about the tenement life of immigrants to New York City, *Shutting Out the Sky*, was the result of extensive research into the wealth of material available about that era. This much-honored title won an Orbis Pictus Honor Book award, was named a *Booklist* Editors' Choice and

"Thinking back to my early years, it's clear that my love of reading has stayed with me, although most of my reading now is research-related. . . . I love studying and learning about the past."

Courtesy of Alfred A. Knopf

was cited as a Notable Social Studies Trade Book for Young People. Regardless of the degree of fictionalization individual characters and their stories may require, Hopkinson strives to provide an accurate picture of the events about which she writes, and to awaken in her readers an excitement about history and the many absorbing stories it holds.

SELECTED WORKS: *Pearl Harbor*, 1991; *Sweet Clara and the Freedom Quilt*, illus. by James Ransome, 1993; *Birdie's Lighthouse*, illus. by Kimberly Bulcken Root, 1997; *A Band of Angels*, illus. by Raúl Colón, 1999; *Maria's Comet*, illus. by Deborah Lanino, 1999; *Bluebird Summer*, illus. by Bethanne Andersen, 2001; *Fannie in the Kitchen: The Whole Story from Soup to Nuts of How Fannie Farmer Invented Recipes with Precise Measurements*, illus. by Nancy Carpenter, 2001; *Under the Quilt of Night*, illus. by James Ransome, 2002; *Pioneer Summer*, illus. by Patrick Faricy, 2002; *Cabin in the Snow*, illus. by Patrick Faricy, 2002; *Girl Wonder: A Baseball Story in Nine Innings*, illus. by Terry Widener, 2003; *Shutting Out the Sky: Life in the Tenements of New York, 1880–1924*, 2003; *Our Kansas Home*, 2003; *The Klondike Kid: The Long Trail*, illus. by Bill Farnsworth, 2004; *A Packet of Seeds*, illus. by Bethanne Andersen, 2004; *Apples to Oregon*, illus. by Nancy Carpenter, 2004.

SUGGESTED READING: *Contemporary Authors*, New Revision Series, vol. 72, 1999; McElmeel, Sharron. *100 Most Popular Picture Book Authors and Illustrators*, 2000; *Something About the Author*, vol. 108, 2000. Periodicals—"The Missing Parts," *The Horn Book*, November/December 2002; "History Must Be Seen," *Library Talk*, November/December 2001; "Reach for the Stars," *Book Links*, March 2000; McElmeel, Sharron, "Author Profile: Deborah Hopkinson," *Library Talk*, November/December 1998; "Shining Light on History," *Book Links*, November 1997.

WEB SITE: *www.deborahhopkinson.com*

"I grew up in Kalamazoo, Michigan, and in Lake Nebagamon, Wisconsin, in the summer. I much preferred the summers in Wisconsin and vowed when I grew up that I would live some place with lots of pine trees and not many people. Currently I am living in Metchosin, British Columbia, with lots of pine trees, not many people, and the ocean—an added bonus. I wanted to live on the rocky cliffs of Maine, in a lighthouse. I'm not living in a lighthouse but otherwise have succeeded admirably in my housing pursuits.

"From the time I was eight, I have wanted to be a writer. Probably I wanted to be a writer even earlier but it wasn't until I learned cursive and could get the stories down quickly enough, that I began to pursue this as a career. I spent many years in Kalamazoo either sitting in trees writing, sitting on gravestones writing (those accounted for the grave tones of my early poetry), or sitting on the roof of my house writing. I don't actually remember writing poetry on the roof of my house, but the neighbors like to remind me of this every time I visit my mother, so it must be true. Very early on it occurred to me that I would need a day job and that it had better be something interesting. I decided I would either be a ballerina or a nun by day. Since it turned out there were no diurnal nuns, I opted for ballerina. Then, when it turned out I wasn't as tippy-toed as I thought, I settled for being a dance teacher.

"I went to the Canadian College of Dance and then to New York City for a while and finally ended up teaching in Montreal, marrying Arnie Keller, and having two little girls, Emily and Rebecca. When Rebecca was born, we moved to Victoria, British Columbia, where I decided to give up my day job and concentrate on babies and writing books. Five years later, after endless househunting, our family finally moved to the bear-infested woods of Metchosin, where we remain very happily with our dog, Keena, and our horse, Zayda, both of whom we acquired in a random manner along the way. A few koi came and went. Don't ask where they went.

"Currently I am writing full time: young adult novels, middle reader novels, adult novels, stories for magazines, and various other things. When I'm not writing, I take walks in the woods and think about writing. I no longer sit on the roof and write poetry, but I will rule nothing out in my declining years."

Courtesy of Arnie Keller

Polly Horvath

January 30, 1957–

✵ ✵ ✵

Courtesy of Farrar, Straus and Giroux

It is particularly fortunate for today's readers that Polly Horvath turned from a career in dance to her first love—writing. Perhaps it could be argued that her training at the Canadian College of Dance in Toronto and the Martha Graham School of Contemporary Dance in New York has, indeed, influenced her witty novels, with their resilient characters, twists and turns of plot, and insightful humor that lightens difficult situations. Her first novel, *An Occasional Cow*, put a city girl in a country setting, visiting relatives in Iowa and finding more than she expected. *Booklist* called it a story that "heralds a promising new writer" and Horvath's career was launched.

Since that beginning, her writing has grown to capture some of the most prestigious awards available. *The Trolls*, which introduced eccentric Aunt Sally and her talent for conveying family history, was named an Honor Book for the *Boston Globe–Horn Book* Award, a finalist for the National Book Award, and an ALA Notable Children's Book. *Everything on a Waffle*, the story of Primrose Squarp, a supposed orphan, captured another *Boston Globe–Horn Book* Honor Award and a Newbery Honor Award, as well as a Parents' Choice Gold award. In Canada, the book received Mr. Christie's Award in the 8–11 age category.

In 2003 *The Canning Season* captured the National Book Award for Young People's Literature and was named an ALA Best Book for Young Adults. It appeared on many lists of the best books of the year, including the *Kirkus Review*'s Editors' Choice, the *Horn Book* Fanfare, and New York Public Library's 100 Titles for Reading and Sharing. Once again, Horvath placed a young protagonist in a situation with elderly relatives—this time it is twin great-aunts of 91—who teach their 13-year-old charge that the best person to rely on in life is yourself. Wry, sometimes dark, humor permeates the lively writing in this novel, which appeals to readers of all ages.

Polly Horvath lives on Vancouver Island in British Columbia, Canada, with her husband and two daughters.

SELECTED WORKS: *An Occasional Cow*, illus. by Gioia Fiammenghi, 1989; *No More Cornflakes*, 1990; *The Happy Yellow Car*, 1994; *When the Circus Came to Town*, 1996; *The Trolls*, 1999; *Everything on a Waffle*, 2001; *The Canning Season*, 2003; *The Pepins and Their Problems*, illus. by Marylin Hafner, 2004.

SUGGESTED READING: *Children's Literature Review*, vol. 90, 2003; *Something About the Author*, vol. 140, 2003. Periodicals—Horvath, Polly, "The Cloud of Unknowing," *School Library Journal*, February 2004; Parravano, Martha, "Who Is This For?" *The Horn Book*, May/June 2003 (editorial). Online—Interview with Polly Horvath, *www.nancymatson.com/authorinterviews/horvat.htm*.

WEB SITE: *www.pollyhorvath.com*

"I was born in Vienna, Austria, before the war. My mother was a playwright, my father a scientist. They were both gifted people, but the marriage was unhappy and they soon went their separate ways, so that my childhood was spent shuttling back and forth in trains across Europe, from one to the other. The theme of a child incessantly commuting on a train is one I've used for Minette in *Island of the Aunts* and comes into many of my stories.

"The advent of Hitler sent my father to Great Britain, and my mother, after remarriage to a Russian philosopher, soon followed him. I changed languages and spent the rest of my childhood in a progressive boarding school striving to become British. I fell in love with the English language quite quickly, but found it harder to adapt to being allowed to do what I liked!

"I took a degree in physiology at London University and was there for part of the Blitz. (This wasn't nearly as frightening as the persecution and prejudice in Austria, since the bombs were directed at everybody equally whereas Hitler had it in just for me and my family back home.) I went on to do research at the University of Cambridge, but I found the experiments I had to perform on living animals extremely distressing and was much alarmed by the enormous rabbits who understandably scratched me horribly whenever I tried to take their rectal temperatures. Moreover, the results of my experiments were so peculiar that when a fellow student, Alan Ibbotson, suggested I would do less harm to science by leaving it and marrying him, I accepted thankfully.

"We went to live in Bristol, then in Newcastle in the north of England, where my husband took a university post teaching agricultural biology. Four children followed—a girl and three boys—and it was at this time I started writing short stories, which could be fitted in between my domestic chores.

Courtesy of Simon Veit-Wilson

Eva Ibbotson

Eva Ibbotson

January 21, 1925–

"When my youngest son started school, I wrote my first full-length novel for children—*The Great Ghost Rescue*—and subsequently wrote books for children and adults alternately. Although I personally had not suffered directly from the Nazis, the turmoil of those times and the horrors of the war made me want to comfort and cheer my readers, and I'm afraid I have never been able to write a book with an unhappy ending! It is only now that I realise my work often has the theme of children finding a place where they can stay and put down roots, as I had never been able to do.

"Another theme—a concern for animals (even the most unusual ones!)—was strengthened by my long marriage to a naturalist, who kept an ant nest under his bed when I first met him and tried to breed edible snails in our garages.

Courtesy of Dutton Children's Books

"Since my husband's death three years ago I have gone on living in our old house, finding in the writing of stories a consolation and a reason for going on. Fortunately, my children and my grandchildren keep my nose to the grindstone! This is the time of my life when I realise how fortunate I am to have a profession in which I do not have to retire."

❁   ❁   ❁

Eva Ibbotson's stories combine humor, imagination, and the psychological truths of childhood in a way that has proven popular with her many readers. Born Eva Wiesner, she was forced to leave her Austrian homeland in the years before World War II. Her father, whose heritage was partly Jewish, took a position at the University of Edinburgh; her mother and stepfather eventually moved to England as well. She received her B.S. from the University of London in 1945. Though she did take a diploma in education from the University of Durham in 1965, and has worked as a research worker, university teacher, and schoolteacher, she discovered her true calling in the writing of books for both children and adults.

For many years, her writing alternated between books for children and books for an adult audience. Her children's books—highly imaginative, and often peopled with ghosts and hags, wizards and witches, mermaids and mistmakers—all are rich in humor. Frightened by ghost stories as a child, Ibbotson felt that telling these tales with laughter would help children to be less afraid. Her supernatural characters are actually underdogs, people who live outside of society and need the reader's concern and sympathy. Her plots are full of old-fashioned adventure, with villains who are driven by greed and a lust for power, two traits that she finds especially unpleasant in human beings.

Three of Ibbotson's novels, when published in the United States, were named *School Library Journal* Best Books of the Year—*Secret of Platform 13, Island of the Aunts*, and *Journey to the River Sea*. In Britain she received a Carnegie Medal commendation in 1979 for *Which Witch?* In 2003, *Journey to the River Sea* was the Gold Winner for the Smarties Prize in the 9–11 age category, was runner-up to Philip Pullman for the Whitbread Prize, and was cited as an ALA Notable Children's Book in the United States. Ibbotson's themes of kindness to animals, respect for those who are different from oneself, and solid reverence for the natural world are present in all of her stories, but especially strong in this remarkable adventure story about an orphan girl who goes to live on the edge of the Amazon jungle in Brazil.

Eva Ibbotson lives in Newcastle-on-Tyne in the north of England.

SELECTED WORKS (Dates are for British editions, U.S. publication dates, if different, shown in parentheses): *Which Witch?*, illus. by Annabel Large, 1979 (1999); *The Worm and the Toffee-nosed Princess, and Other Stories of Monsters*, 1983; *The Haunting of Hiram C. Hopgood*, 1987; *Not Just a Witch*, 1991 (illus. by Kevin Hawkes, 2003); *The Secret of Platform 13*, illus. by Sue Porter, 1994 (1998); *Dial-A-Ghost*, illus. by Kerstin Meyer, 1996, (illus. by Kevin Hawkes, 2001); *Island of the Aunts*, illus. by Kevin Hawkes, 2000; *Journey to the River Sea*, illus. by Kevin Hawkes, 2002; *The Great Ghost Rescue*, illus. by Kevin Hawkes, 2002.

SUGGESTED READING: *Something About the Author*, vol. 103, 1999. Online—Grant, Gavin J., Interview with Eva Ibbotson, *www.booksense.com/people/archive/ibbotsoneva.jsp*.

"Growing up in Michigan, except for Saturday morning cartoons, my two older brothers and I were never allowed to watch television during the daytime. Daytime meant going outside to play. Other kids in the neighborhood had little wooden sandboxes. We had a sand yard, filled by a dump truck; and when we scattered that, we had another dump-truck load of sand. With my father's patient and kind instruction, we built wooden ships that sailed the grassy seas on our acre of yard. We melted lead to make soldiers and mixed root beer in the basement laundry tub, bottled it, and drank the ones that didn't explode.

"One brother was always playing with fire. He had a tiny cannon about four inches high that would fire the lead balls that we molded, and he would aim at the backyard sailing ships from my parents' second-story bedroom windowsill. We had toy pirates,

Kathy Jakobsen

October 8, 1952–

kings, knights, queens, robbers, soldiers, Indians, cowboys, and animals with magical powers. Their adventures and the news of our world was recorded in our tiny newspapers, which also included ads and the latest 'wanted criminal' posters.

"On rainy days spent indoors, I read books, especially horse books. My next door neighbor's horse Cuddy was the inspiration and model for my early artwork. We spent many happy years together and I still include horses in my oil paintings, if at all possible. Speedy, our orange-and-white cat, appears in many paintings. In tribute to his eccentric personality, Speedy is hidden in every painting of both of the *My New York* books. My mother painted landscapes and portraits, so I grew up with the smell of oil paint. She kept my first oil painting (of my doll, at age five).

Courtesy of Keith Hallquist

I am thankful for her encouragement, creativity, her wacky sense of humor, and that she was a stay-at-home mom. My brothers and I had a lot of freedom and a lot of fun. Not too surprisingly, we all ended up in creative careers.

"In my paintings, I almost never focus attention on the negative side of life. I want my paintings to invite the viewer into a world that creates a positive and uplifting effect. I know the dark side is out there, it's just that I would rather keep my attention focused in a positive direction, on the way I would like things to be. When I am creating, time is suspended, I have (almost!) infinite patience, and I feel a spiritual light-heartedness. Even though I have done over 600 oil paintings since I started working full time in 1978, I feel as though I have barely begun, there are so many subjects that I would like to explore. I love detail, and delight in putting friends and family members and their pets in my paintings. That was one inspiration for doing children's books. My husband and I thought it would be fun for our kids to see themselves in a real book. Since then, children's books have opened up a whole new world and created many exciting opportunities. Instead of my paintings hanging in someone's living room and being enjoyed by one family, now they can be viewed by a much larger audience. I am amazed and thrilled by the response. I love going to schools and book signings and meeting the kids. I don't read my books aloud, I just do 'guided tours' of all the special details! It takes several years and thousands of hours to do each book, so I try to choose subjects that are timeless and inspiring."

❖   ❖   ❖

Kathy Jakobsen grew up in Dearborn Township, now the city of Dearborn Heights, in Michigan. Nurtured by her creative family, she is basically a self-taught artist and has called her mother her greatest teacher. She was fortunate to have been discovered and encouraged by the late Dr. Robert Bishop. She met him in 1976, when he worked at the Henry Ford Museum in Greenfield Village, near her home. Kathy wanted to create *frakturs* of Benjamin Franklin quotes to sell in the museum gift shop for the U.S. Bicentennial. A *fraktur* is an ornate document featuring a unique form of Gothic-style lettering and colorful decorations in the manner of Pennsylvania Dutch folk art. Bishop also had a gallery in his living room and asked her to create more folk art to sell there. The following year he was named director of the Museum of American Folk Art (now called the American Folk Art Museum) in New York City.

Bishop's partner, Jay Johnson, took over their gallery business and invited Kathy to have a one-woman show. At the time she was selling Good Humor ice cream, which left little free time for art. She took a new job working in a bumper sticker factory to allow more time for painting, and when she had enough pieces for an entire show, she went to New York. The show was to last 10 days, but when the entire show sold out, Kathy Jakobsen became a confirmed lover of New York and stayed for nearly 10 years. She lived in a studio apartment on 30th Street formerly occupied by Georgia folk-artist Mattie Lou O'Kelley, about half a block from Madison Square Garden.

Kathy Jakobsen left the Big Apple and moved to Mini-Apple-us (Minneapolis, Minnesota) in 1985 and married Keith Hallquist, who had proposed after seeing her three times. The pair moved around the country while Kathy continued to produce her folk paintings and mail them to the gallery in New York. Their three children were all born in different parts of the United States: Elizabeth Starlight ("Becky") in 1986 in Los Angeles, Martin in 1988 in Clearwater, Florida, and Alana in 1991 in Weston, Connecticut, where the family now resides. When her first child was born, Jakobsen jokingly commented to Robert Bishop that now she should publish a children's book. He put her in touch with Melanie Kroupa, an editor at Little, Brown & Co., and soon she found herself illustrating Reeve Lindbergh's poem, *Johnny Appleseed*. Her folk art beautifully captured the character of John Chapman's remarkable life, and in 1992 she traveled to Japan for eight days to celebrate the Japanese edition of *Johnny Appleseed*, with an exhibition of the original art sponsored by Tokyo Gas.

Jakobsen's love affair with New York City culminated with the publication in 1993 of a book of her New York City paintings, called *My New York*. Written as a letter from a young girl to a friend in the Midwest, the book features the cheesecake bakery around the corner from her original 30th Street apartment, along with many more widely recognized landmarks. With lively

"In my paintings, I almost never focus attention on the negative side of life. I want my paintings to invite the viewer into a world that creates a positive and uplifting effect."

Courtesy of Little, Brown, and Company

text and brightly colored, intricately detailed oil paintings in Jakobsen's folk-primitive style, *My New York* captures all the excitement, rhythm, and variety of that great city and was named to the New York Public Library's list of 100 Titles for Reading and Sharing. It received an Oppenheim Toy Portfolio Platinum award, was designated Best Jacket at the 1994 New York Book Show, and received a glowing first-page review by Frank Rich in the *New York Times Book Review*. In 2003, a 10th anniversary sequel was published. Expanded to 48 pages and a larger 9x12 format, it features 23 new paintings, including the Macy's Thanksgiving Day Parade, the Rockefeller Center Christmas Tree, the Apollo Theater in Harlem, New Year's Eve at Times Square, and the New York Public Library. The book also contains seven fold-out images, a new story, and a tribute to the World Trade Center.

Working with Woody Guthrie's daughter Nora, Kathy Jakobsen created glowing and detailed illustrations for the folksinger's most beloved song in a book by the same title, *This Land Is Your Land*. Chosen as an ALA Notable Children's Book, it was included on the Best of the Year lists of *Publishers Weekly*, *School Library Journal*, *Parenting* magazine, the New York Public Library, and *The Horn Book*. In 2000 it was released in a version that includes a CD featuring Woody's recorded voice with Nora and her brother Arlo Guthrie singing along. A Weston Woods video version of the book was narrated by Nora.

Kathy Jakobsen was named "one of the best landscape folk painters of the century" by the editors of the *Encyclopedia of Twentieth-Century Folk Art and Artists*. She has exhibited in many venues in the United States, Europe, and the Far East. Her work appears in such permanent collections as the Smithsonian Institute, the American Museum of Folk Art, and the New York City Transit Museum. In 2001 the Housatonic Museum of Art mounted a 25-year retrospective of Jakobsen's career that included pieces by her mother, grandmother, and daughter Becky—a four-generation show. In 2004 the Metropolitan Transit Authority of New York commissioned her to create an original oil painting to celebrate the 100th anniversary of the New York subway system.

SELECTED WORKS WRITTEN AND ILLUSTRATED: *My New York*, 1993; *Meet Me in the Magic Kingdom*, 1995; *My New York New Anniversary Edition*, 2003.

SELECTED WORKS ILLUSTRATED: *Johnny Appleseed: A Poem*, by Reeve Lindbergh, 1990; *This Land Is Your Land*, by Woody Guthrie, 1998, issued with CD, 2000.

SUGGESTED READING: *All-American Folk Arts and Crafts*, 1986; *American Folk Art of the Twentieth Century*, 1983; Lewis, Richard W. *Absolut Book*, 1996; Rosenak, Chuck, and Jan Rosenak. *Museum of American Folk Art Encyclopedia of Twentieth-Century American Folk Art and Artists*, 1991; Secord, William. *A Breed Apart*, 2001. Periodicals—*Country Home Magazine*, December 1993 and December 1987.

WEB SITE: *www.hcc.commnet.edu/artmuseum/exhibits/ 2001/jakobsen/artistof.html*

Courtesy of Laura Jimenez

Francisco Jiménez

(hee-MEN-ez)

June 29, 1943–

"I was born in a small village in Mexico, and when I was four years old, my family and I entered the United States without documentation, hoping to leave our poverty behind. We began our new life as migrant farmworkers, moving from place to place, following seasonal crops throughout the Central Valley of California. We lived in farm labor camps, often in tents or old garages. My older brother and I worked in the fields alongside our parents from the time I was six years old.

"I started school not knowing a word of English. In fact, I had to repeat the first grade because I did not know English well enough. When I was fourteen, my family and I were caught by the Border Patrol and deported to Mexico. We returned months later with proper papers and settled permanently in Santa Maria, California, where my brother and I worked part-time as janitors while attending school to support our family of eight (my father could not continue working in the fields because of severe back problems).

"My motivation for writing and my love for literature are due to Ms. Bell, my sophomore high school English teacher. She regularly assigned our class to write narrative accounts of personal experiences. Even though I had difficulty expressing myself, I enjoyed writing about my migrant childhood. In one of my classes, she commented that the experiences I wrote about were moving and that my writing showed promise. She then had me read *The Grapes of Wrath*. It was a difficult novel to read, but I could not put it down. I was able to relate my family's life to the life of the Joad family. For the first time I realized the value and power of language to move hearts and minds.

"After graduating from high school, I entered Santa Clara University with three scholarships and a federal loan. There I discovered that my migrant experiences were both an obstacle and a blessing. They were an obstacle to the extent that I did not enjoy the same social, economic, and educational experiences most of my classmates enjoyed. However, they were a blessing because they served as a constant reminder of how fortunate I was to be in college. Those experiences convinced me that I should do everything within my power to forge ahead in my studies and not give up. I compare my situation then to a man who is drowning. A man who is drowning uses the water, the very substance that threatens his life, to save himself. So I used poverty and those experiences that initially pulled me down to boost myself up. Whenever I felt discouraged, I would reflect on and write about my childhood experiences. These recollections later became the subject matter for my books, which are largely autobiographical.

"Upon graduating from Santa Clara University, I was awarded a Woodrow Wilson fellowship to attend graduate school at Columbia University, where I received my Ph.D. in Latin American literature and where I began my teaching career. My mission as a teacher and writer is to fill the need for cultural and human understanding. Through my writing, which is inspired by the community of my childhood, I hope to give readers an insight into the lives of migrant farmworkers and their children of yesterday and today whose backbreaking labor puts food on our tables. Their courage and struggles, hopes and dreams for a better life for their children and their children's children give meaning to the term 'American dream.' Their story is the American story."

Francisco Jiménez

Courtesy of Houghton Mifflin, Inc.

❋ ❋ ❋

Francisco Jiménez writes books that arouse a sense of compassion and respect for all humanity, often evoking the extraordinary trajectory of his own life. He was born in San Pedro, Tlaquepaque, Mexico, the second son of Francisco, a farm laborer, and Maria, a cannery worker; he became a United States citizen while studying for his B.A. at Santa Clara University. A highly successful academic, with a Ph.D. from Columbia University in 1972, he has never forgotten his roots in the farm labor camps and writes eloquently of his childhood experiences as a migrant worker. Much of his writing is for adults, but the few books that he has written for young people have been widely honored. Critics praise them for their moving depictions of the problems and hardships a migrant worker faces—poverty, prejudice, and transience—and for their faith in the power of the human spirit. They also deal with issues that all children face on one level or another: the puzzling behavior of adults, the struggle to grow up in a confusing and challenging society, and how imagination can provide a way to cope with life's frustrations.

Jiménez's first book for children, *The Circuit: Stories from the Life of a Migrant Child*, received the *Boston Globe–Horn Book* Award for Fiction, the Américas Award, and a Jane Addams Peace Prize Honor Book Award. In *Breaking Through* he continued the story into his adolescence, adding the problems of a teenager to the family's struggles and treating family members— particularly the embittered, authoritarian father—in greater depth. *Breaking Through* also received the Américas Award, as well as the Tomás Rivera Mexican American Book Award and a Pura Belpré Honor Book Award. Both of these titles were named ALA Best Books for Young Adults and cited by New York Public Library on its Books for the Teen Age list. Both volumes have been translated into Spanish by the author; *The Circuit* is also available in Chinese and Japanese translations.

The Christmas Gift / El regalo de Navidad, a poignant bilingual tale of a young boy realizing how hard it is for his parents to have so little to give at Christmastime, received the Cuffie Award from *Publishers Weekly* for "Best Treatment of a Social Issue" and was named an ALA Notable Children's Book as well as a Notable Social Studies Trade Book for Young People. In *La Mariposa* Jiménez tells the story of a boy who uses his imagination to rise above the difficulties he faces upon entering first grade without knowing English. Named to the Américas Award Commended List, it was also recommended by Parents' Choice and named a *Smithsonian* magazine Notable Book for children.

Today Francisco Jiménez is a professor of modern languages and Latin American literature at Santa Clara University. His wife works with the University's Eastside Project, an academic support program that allows students to integrate community-based learning with the academic curriculum. The couple have three grown sons.

SELECTED WORKS: *The Circuit: Stories from the Life of a Migrant Child*, 1997; *La Mariposa*, illus. by Simón Silva, 1998; *The Christmas Gift/El regalo de Navidad*, illus. by Claire Cotts, 2000; *Breaking Through*, 2001.

SUGGESTED READING: *Contemporary Authors*, vol. 131, 1991; *Something About the Author*, vol. 108, 2000. Periodicals— Bold, Kathryn, "The Grapes of Wrath," *Santa Clara Magazine*, Spring 1996; Carlile, Susan, "Challenges Give Meaning to Our Lives," *ALAN Review*, Fall 2004.

WEB SITE: *www.scu.edu/SCU/Programs/Diversity/frjim.html*

Courtesy of Medora Hebert

D. B. Johnson

November 30, 1944–

"Sometimes the things that are best for your whole life happen when you're very young. I was three years old. My father moved our family into a house he had built on a country road in New Hampshire. The house was unfinished inside, so we were able to see through the open framework from the living room all the way to the far bedroom. That first winter we kids, all five of us, scrunched up around the fireplace at night before racing through the walls to our cold bedrooms. There inside the covers at the foot of our beds, my mother had placed warm bricks wrapped in newspaper. In the morning we could see our breath and touch the ice inside our windows. It was a great polar adventure.

"Summers meant family picnics and relatives from the city. With them we flew kites and balsa airplanes in the field across the road. Every year Uncle Herb, the printer, brought a box of paper left over from a year's printing jobs. Uncle Bud, the architect, drew wild characters he dreamed up on the spot. Once he gave us a Walter Foster drawing book. That year I used hundreds of sheets of paper copying his crazy faces and adding others from the drawing book. Every summer after that, I dived into that big box of paper and drew some more.

"All that drawing got me a lot of friends. In school I became the 'class artist,' but I didn't take art very seriously. Mostly I roamed the woods and fields up and down our road. I loved the mile walk to the two-room schoolhouse. Each afternoon my mother, from the kitchen window, would glimpse me two hills away. To her, that meant I'd be home in 15 minutes. But one day after 30 minutes I still hadn't arrived. When I finally walked in the door an hour late, she was very angry. 'What took you so long?' she demanded. I didn't understand why she was so upset. 'Mom!' I said, 'I took the shortcut.' There it was. I lived in my own world of stonewalls, woodchuck holes, and swamps.

"In high school when I read Henry David Thoreau's book *Walden,* I was surprised to hear the words of someone who loved the earth as much as I did. Later when I studied history and government in college, I read Thoreau's words again. This time I understood, not just his ideas about nature but also his ideas about how to live. If people weren't working so hard to buy stuff, he said, they could spend more time doing what they love. That was an important idea. I decided to spend my life doing art.

Courtesy of Houghton Mifflin, Inc.

"And so I have. More than 30 years ago, after I got married, my wife and I moved back to my small New Hampshire town. Here I worked for the local newspaper drawing cartoons for the 'letters page.' Those cartoons were both funny and serious. Over the years my art became more illustration than cartoon, and it was printed in newspapers and magazines all over the United States.

"From the beginning my wife and I made decisions about our family's way of life that had nothing to do with money. Artists don't get paid a lot, so we had to think about what kind of life we wanted and not what kinds of things we would buy. Except for the very earliest of our children's growing-up years, I worked at home all day drawing pictures. My children could come into the studio any time to talk or to draw. In our home there was no television to watch, but there were library books, and we read aloud to our kids until they were almost teenagers.

"So I've done the work I love, closest to the people I care about—something I learned from *Walden*. That's why I wrote the Henry books. Now children don't have to wait until high school to find out about Thoreau's ideas."

※ ※ ※

The contented artist and lover of the simple life D. B. (Don) Johnson was born in Derry, New Hampshire. After earning a B.A. in government from Boston University in 1966, he became a staff artist with the Valley News in Lebanon, New Hampshire, before working entirely out of his own studio as a technical illustrator, comic strip artist, editorial cartoonist, nationally syndicated op-ed artist, and author/illustrator of children's books. He and his wife, Linda, make their home in Lebanon, where they've raised their three children, who are now grown.

D. B. Johnson's first picture book, *Henry Hikes to Fitchburg*, features two bear friends living in the 19th century who decide to go to Fitchburg and enjoy the country. Henry, an ursine young Henry David Thoreau, claims that the fastest way to Fitchburg is to walk; his friend thinks the train will get him there faster and says he will work to earn the fare and still arrive before Henry. So the two friends start out. Henry relishes every minute of his walk, finds ferns and flowers, climbs a tree, rafts across a river, and, within a mile of Fitchburg, stops to pick and feast on blackberries. His friend works hard, cleaning, hoeing, sweeping, and painting to earn his train fare and does indeed arrive first—though without having enjoyed his day. Johnson based his story on a paragraph from Thoreau's *Walden*. The artist said in his *Boston Globe–Horn Book* acceptance speech he chose to make Henry a bear because, "To me, Thoreau was a bear: large, free roaming, independent . . . When it came down to it, Henry knew how to have fun. I wanted this book to reflect that fun, and to draw kids to other gentle ideas: It's okay to be different; you can get where you want to go without money; we're all part of nature; keep life simple." In fresh, bright, angular paintings, beautifully composed, the artist succeeds admirably, with appealing views of nature to match Henry's viewpoint, never losing sight of the fun of a race.

As well as receiving the 2000 *Boston Globe–Horn Book* Award for Picture Books, *Henry Hikes to Fitchburg* was a *New York Times* Editors' Choice and Best Illustrated Book, a *School Library Journal* Best Book of the Year, a *Booklist* Editors' Choice, a *Publishers Weekly* Best Book of the Year, and a Society of Illustrators Silver Medal winner. D. B. Johnson also won the 2001 Ezra Jack Keats New Writer Award for this work. His next picture book, *Henry Builds a Cabin*, shows Thoreau (as a bear once again) constructing a cabin on the shore of Walden Pond and, as always, doing it his own way. *Henry Builds a Cabin* was included on the New York Public Library's list of 100 Titles for Reading and Sharing for 2002. Johnson's colored pencil and paint illustrations are as inviting as his character's determination to live life on his own terms.

SELECTED WORKS WRITTEN AND ILLUSTRATED: *Henry Hikes to Fitchburg*, 2000; *Henry Builds a Cabin*, 2002; *Henry Works*, 2004.

SUGGESTED READING: "Flying Starts," *Publishers Weekly*, June 26, 2000; "2000 *Boston Globe–Horn Book* Awards," *The Horn Book*, January/February 2001.

WEB SITE: *www.HenryHikes.com*

"**P**rovincial America boasts many small towns with strange and amusing names. Mousie, Kentucky, my hometown, is one of them. It lies in the heart of the Appalachian mountain chain. Here I grew up alongside coal trains, annual hog killings, Sunday dinners on the ground, and a whole lot of whittling and spitting. I often spent long summer days with my grandfather, helping him tend to his honeybees and listening to his doubtful tales.

"I began to draw and paint early on. With sketchbook in hand, I spent many an afternoon sprawled on a grassy bank, drawing and dreaming. My parents were very supportive of my special interest and saw to it that I received private art lessons from the instructors at nearby Alice Lloyd College.

"After high school at Hindman, Kentucky, I attended the University of Kentucky in Lexington, where I continued my art studies. I often found myself at odds with my professors, most of whom embraced the prevailing abstract-expressionist mode. Mine was a more romantic bent— and remains so.

Courtesy of Diane Lawless

Paul Brett Johnson

May 19, 1947–

"In college conventional wisdom held that one could not likely make a living as an artist, so I earned a teaching degree. But I soon discovered that teaching, while a valiant profession, was not my calling. Then in 1974, after a string of short-lived jobs, including graphic artist for a theater group, designer and artist for a display company, and illustrator of educational booklets for a state agency, I decided it was time to devote my full energy to producing my own work. Since then I have maintained a studio in Lexington.

"My interest in writing and illustrating picture books first surfaced when I was still at the university. Just for fun, I had taken a class in children's literature. I was enthralled, and I wrote and illustrated a story of my own. Looking back, I see that it was not very good—trite and condescending. Nonetheless, a seed had been planted. Periodically during the next two decades, I found myself entertaining the thought of writing and illustrating children's stories as something I would really like to do. Occasionally I went as far as working up a manuscript and submitting it. But I found the rejection slips too discouraging and so, each time, I shelved the idea.

"Eventually, however, the desire to make my dream reality took over. I read every how-to article and book I could find. I wrote to publishing houses for their catalogs. I spent endless hours at the library. Then I sat down to write my first published book, *The Cow Who Wouldn't Come Down*, and I realized that it had all the elements of a good story—inventiveness, action, and believable characters—along with the tall-tale humor of a folk heritage that was my own.

"Today when I work, I often go back to those grassy creek banks of my youth—if not physically, then in my mind. There I draw upon a reservoir of memories, emotions, and lessons learned. In that sense, a little bit of Mousie, Kentucky, finds its way into each new book."

❋ ❋ ❋

Paul Brett Johnson's picture books, noted for their down-home humor and storytelling qualities, draw heavily on his Appalachian roots and the stories he heard as a child. Many of the books he has written as well as illustrated are, in fact, interpretations of age-old folktales with generous doses of slapstick humor. Johnson graduated from the University of Kentucky with an M.A. in education in 1970 but taught elementary school for only one year. He had been earning his living as a commercial artist for more than 20 years before he published his first book, *The Cow Who Wouldn't Come Down*. Called by *School Library Journal* "a virtuoso debut," this book was named an American Booksellers Pick of the Lists, a *Bulletin of the Center for Children's Books* Blue Ribbon winner, and one of *School Library Journal's* Best Books of 1993. Johnson's career in children's books was launched.

illustrated and adapted by Paul Brett Johnson

Fearless Jack

Courtesy of Margaret K. McElderry

Farmers' Market was designated a notable book of the year by *Smithsonian* magazine. Three of Johnson's Appalachian folk tale adaptations—*Old Dry Frye, Fearless Jack*, and *Jack Outwits the Giants*—have been chosen by the New York Public Library for its annual list, 100 Titles for Reading and Sharing. Not all of Johnson's work is limited to his Kentucky roots, however. *Lost*, co-authored with Celeste Lewis and illustrated by Johnson, tells a poignant story of a lost beagle struggling to survive in a barren desert landscape and was named to *School Library Journal's* Best Books list in 1996. *A Perfect Pork Stew*, based on the Russian legend of Baba Yaga, was the winner of a Kentucky Bluegrass Award.

In addition to his own stories, Johnson has illustrated books written by other authors, bringing his clever, warm, engaging style to those texts as well. His illustrations often use wit and humor combined with bright colors to create the energy that delights his readers. Johnson lives in an old house in downtown Lexington, Kentucky, with three porches and a cat named Carly who, he says, "thinks she's the most important family member of all."

SELECTED WORKS WRITTEN AND ILLUSTRATED: *The Cow Who Wouldn't Come Down*, 1993; *Lost* (with Celeste Lewis), 1996; *Farmers' Market*, 1997; *A Perfect Pork Stew*, 1998; *The Pig Who Ran a Red Light*, 1999; *Bearhide and Crow*, 2000; *Mr. Persnickety and Cat Lady*, 2000; *Fearless Jack*, 2001; *Old Dry Frye*, 1999; *The Goose Who Went Off in a Huff*, 2001; *Jack Outwits the Giants*, 2002.

SELECTED WORKS ILLUSTRATED: *Saint Patrick and the Peddler*, by Margaret Hodges, 1993; *Insects Are My Life*, by Megan McDonald, 1995; *Too Quiet for These Old Bones*, by Tres Seymour, 1997; *An Appalachian Mother Goose*, by James Still, 1998; *A Traveling Cat*, by George Ella Lyon, 1998; *Bedbugs*, by Megan McDonald, 1999; *Reptiles Are My Life*, by Megan McDonald, 2001; *The Best Kind of Gift*, by Kathi Appelt, 2003.

SUGGESTED READING: *Something About the Author*, vol. 83, 1996.

WEB SITE: *www.paulbrettjohnson.com*

"I hated being a kid. If I tell you about my mother-the-artist who drew paper dolls of the heroines of all my favorite books, my father who played badminton and croquet with us after dinner, my grandmother who wrote musical comedies about world peace and taught us songs around the piano, and my five semi-adorable younger brothers and sisters, and the orchard where we had picnics under the trees, and the stream behind our house where we caught salamanders—you probably will say, it sounds like a good deal to me. What are you whining about? And you'd be right in a way. For someone stuck being a kid, I was happy enough. I had my share of heartaches and broken dreams, but I also had lots of books and art supplies, and after a while we moved near Lake Erie on the West Side of Cleveland so I could go to the beach every day if I wanted to. Still, it was clear to me that adults made all the rules and had all the real fun. What can I say? I was cranky and lazy, and I couldn't wait to grow up.

"I was born on April Fool's Day in Pittsburgh, Pennsylvania. As long as I can remember I knew that someday I would be a writer. At age seven, on a rainy Saturday afternoon, I wrote and illustrated my first sixteen-page book, carefully folding and stapling it, then printing my name on the cover before presenting it to my parents. They praised my efforts and gently pointed out several debts to the authors of *Tootle the Train* and *Winnie the Pooh*, but assured me that I would get better with practice. Then

Sandra Jordan

April 1, 1947–

they gave me my own box of the good kind of soft colored pencils which were much better for illustrating than crayons, and I kept at it.

"When I was in the third grade we moved to Cleveland, Ohio, living first in the suburb of Seven Hills and later in Bay Village. By the time I reluctantly entered high school I wasn't sure why I had to be there except that 14-year-olds are not allowed to rent their own apartments. I had friends (even, to my amazement, a popular boyfriend), but I never felt comfortable in the high school scene. All the girls in my school yearned to be like 'Tracy,' the captain of the cheerleaders, homecoming queen, and all-around school star. While I hoped by some miracle I would wake up one morning looking like 'Tracy' and marveled at her seemingly effortless ability to be nice to everyone, I wanted to be like Françoise Sagan, the French teenager whose novel, *Bonjour Tristesse*, I had found on my parents' bookshelves. Françoise Sagan, my parents told me, was only 18 when her book became an international best-seller. In magazine stories I looked up in the library, I found out the things my parents hadn't bothered to mention—young Françoise dressed in black clothes, hung out in Parisian cafes with other angst-filled intellectuals, smoked unfiltered French cigarettes, drove expensive sports cars at high speeds down poplar-lined French roads, and didn't have a curfew. My complete heroine.

Courtesy of Roaring Brook Press

Sandra Jordan

"After graduating from high school I attended Simmons College, which I enjoyed not least because it was in Boston. Simmons was next door to the Isabella Stewart Gardiner Museum and around the corner from the Boston Museum of Fine Arts, so I took many art history classes and looked at great paintings almost every day. I also took all the English, writing, and journalism classes I could cram into my schedule, and one day, almost on a whim, I signed up for a class in children's literature. It was amazing! Until then, I had not thought of editing children's books as a career, but now I had a new life goal—receiving a salary for reading all day! Once I graduated, and spent several years writing two unfinished novels that even I thought were boring, I moved to New York City to look for an entry-level job that would lead to becoming a children's book editor. I was lucky enough to find one at the Thomas Y. Crowell Company (now part of HarperCollins), working for the legendary editor Ann Beneduce. I loved everything about editing children's books, in spite of the discovery that the reading of manuscripts and books would take place on what previously had been my nights and weekends. Days were spent meeting with authors, illustrators, designers, copy editors, production people, advertising directors, and all the other people involved in the fascinating business of publishing.

"By 1989, editing was still fun, but I began to feel restless. Maybe it was time to try writing again. There are people who manage to be editors and also write their own books, but the knack of it eluded me, so I resigned. A few weeks later, during an art-filled discussion with my friend Jan Greenberg (whose first novel I had edited), she asked me to join with her in writing what would be the first of our many books together, *The Painter's Eye*. My next book came about over dinner. About 10 years earlier, I had become obsessed with photography and set up a darkroom at home. One evening while sharing pasta and gossip with my friend Neal Porter, an editor, I told him about a perfect afternoon I had spent at a Christmas tree farm in Rhode Island. He said, 'Sounds good. What about writing me a book?' His determined nagging led to the first of my photo essays, *The Christmas Tree Farm*.

"Even though I never wrote an international best-seller, or led the racy life in France I imagined as a teenager back in Ohio, I have found the perfect job for a former cranky, lazy kid. Because I'm doing exactly what I want to do—writing, talking to artists about their work, researching, looking at art, writing, taking and making photographs—in exactly the way I want to do it, I can't be bothered to be lazy. And since I'm lucky enough to have found a writing partner who shares my passion for work, and talented editors who are committed to making the finished books match my (and our) vision, I don't have much to be cranky about. While that might not be the final secret of a happy life, it's working for me so far."

"By 1989, editing was still fun, but I began to feel restless. Maybe it was time to try writing again. There are people who manage to be editors and also write their own books, but the knack of it eluded me, so I resigned."

※　※　※

Concentrating at different times on her various talents as editor, writer, and photographer, Sandra Jordan has made an important impact on the field of children's book publishing. After her first jobs at Thomas Y. Crowell as an assistant and then an editor, Sandra moved on to become editor-in-chief of children's books at Farrar, Straus & Giroux in 1977, where she worked with Paula Fox, Madeleine L'Engle, Uri Shulevitz, Isaac Bashevis Singer, and Betsy and Jamie Wyeth, among others. In 1981 she married Bob Verrone, who was a children's book publisher at Bradbury Press in partnership with Dick Jackson. Changing her focus to adult books, Sandra worked at the New American Library, but after Bob's untimely death in 1984 she eventually returned to the children's book field as editor-in-chief for the New York office of Orchard Books until 1989.

ACTION JACKSON

Jan Greenberg and Sandra Jordan Illustrated by Robert Andrew Parker

Courtesy of Roaring Brook Press

Sandra's interest in photography was sparked by courses she took in New York, including classes in darkroom technique at the International Center for Photography. In her photo-essays about natural settings, she keeps a narrative flow in mind as she takes the pictures, then uses the pictures to guide her in writing the text. Through this process, she creates a child's-eye view of each subject—a barnyard, a pond, a Christmas tree farm. Teamed with Jan Greenberg, Sandra has found many ways to introduce modern artists and art concepts to today's children and young adults. Their first joint project, *The Painter's Eye*, was cited on many lists of the best books of the year and named an ALA Notable Children's Book. An upbeat writing style, vibrant book design, and personal interest in the subject have characterized each of the books produced by this writing duo. Their first success was followed by *The Sculptor's Eye*, also an ALA Notable Children's Book, and *The American Eye*, cited as an ALA Best Book for Young Adults and as a Notable Children's Trade Book in the Field of Social Studies.

Turning to individual artists in books that were as startling in their originality as the artists they introduced, Jordan and Greenberg continued to have great success. *Chuck Close Up Close*, with its graphic representation of Close's style, was named an ALA Notable Children's Book and received a *Boston Globe–Horn Book* Honor Award for nonfiction as well as the Norman Sugarman Award for biography. *Frank O. Gehry: Outside In* introduced young readers to the controversial architect with splashy design, crisp photography, and a personal approach derived from direct interviews with Gehry and his staff. Named an ALA Notable Children's Book, it was also cited by the *New York Times* as ". . . one of the best introductions to architecture that we have." *Vincent Van Gogh* garnered a Robert F. Sibert Honor Award and was cited as an ALA Notable Children's Book and an ALA Best Book for Young Adults. *Action Jackson*, which teamed the writing pair with veteran illustrator Robert Andrew Parker to capture the spirit of Jackson Pollock in a picture book, was also named a Sibert Honor Book and a *Booklist* Editors' Choice. The aim in each of these books is to help young people look beyond first impressions and personal reactions to art, and learn to develop a sense of the artist's intent.

Sandra Jordan lives in New York City.

SELECTED WORKS: *The Painter's Eye: Learning to Look at Contemporary Art* (with Jan Greenberg), 1991; *Christmas Tree Farm*, 1993; *The Sculptor's Eye: Looking at Contemporary American Sculpture* (with Jan Greenberg),

1993; *The American Eye: Eleven Artists in the Twentieth Century* (with Jan Greenberg), 1996; *Down on Casey's Farm*, 1996; *Chuck Close Up Close* (with Jan Greenberg), 1998; *The Pond Book*, 1999; *Frank O. Gehry: Outside In* (with Jan Greenberg), 2000; *Vincent Van Gogh: Portrait of an Artist* (with Jan Greenberg), 2001; *Action Jackson* (with Jan Greenberg), illus. by Robert Andrew Parker, 2002; *Frog Hunt*, 2002; *Runaway Girl: The Artist Louise Bourgeois* (with Jan Greenberg), 2003; *Andy Warhol: Prince of Pop* (with Jan Greenberg), 2004.

"**I** always chuckle a little bit when people ask me how I got started writing and illustrating children's books, because the truth is a bit surprising; it was almost a complete accident. *Serendipity* is a lovely word, and over time I have come to have great respect for its role in shaping a life.

"I always loved to paint and draw as a child, but by the time I got to high school I was increasingly pulled in other directions. I went to the High School of Music and Art and left after a year because I was more engaged by some of the academic subjects. When it was time to apply to college I thought again about studying art and went to Sarah Lawrence College. But somehow I ended up with a concentration in American history and a master's degree from Columbia in the department of political science. I was really stuck in an internal tug of war.

"At Hunter High School in New York City, where I went after leaving Music and Art, Latin was a required subject, though definitely not my favorite. By the end of my senior year I wanted to do something to bring up my grade, and my very nice teacher, Mr. Kizner, offered the possibility of doing an extra translation. 'Anything you like,' he said. The text I chose was 'Little Red Riding Hood.' I translated it into Latin, illustrated it, and put it all in dummy form, though of course at the time I didn't know what that was. The old wolf didn't look half bad in a toga, and it was a wonderfully satisfying project. But I was so happy with my 'A' that I failed to notice that writing and illustrating books could be a fine resolution of my seemingly divergent interests.

"A husband and two children later I started printmaking in a studio at Manhattanville College. I was working on a series of etchings, and the instructor observed that my work looked very

Courtesy of Holly Keller

Holly Keller

February 11, 1942–

suitable for children's book illustration. Slowly the idea began to take root in my brain, and I started to make sketches of what eventually became my portfolio. But writing was still nowhere in my mind.

"At that time I was living near Danbury, Connecticut, and the public library there sponsored a series of 'meet the author/illustrator' presentations. I became a regular attendee. One week Janina Domanska was speaking, and I was very anxious to hear her. Unable to get a babysitter for my son, Jesse, who was then about four years old, I decided to take him along and hope for the best. Jesse wasn't a patient listener, and he took out his frustration by kicking the back of the chair in front of him. At the end of her talk, Ms. Domanska turned to the poor woman sitting in that chair and introduced her as her editor, Susan Hirschman. 'Ah hah,' I said to myself, 'Greenwillow Books is definitely one place I'll never go to look for work!' But life is strange, and when I was finally ready to show my portfolio I looked over the long list of publishers and art directors graciously sent by the Children's Book Council and there was only one name I recognized. I wrote to Susan and confessed to being the mother of the annoying child who kicked her chair. Susan wrote back a characteristically warm letter. 'Since we're already friends,' she said, 'come and see me.'

"When I arrived at Susan's office feeling more nervous than I think I had ever felt in my life, she explained that there were more illustrators in the world than there were manuscripts and it would make much more sense for me to write my own stories. Nothing could have been more unexpected. I'm sure that I must have gasped out loud because Susan laughed, but she was not deterred. She selected a drawing from my portfolio and said that I should go home and write the story that went with it. She was going to Bologna and would be back in two weeks to read it. I can tell you that during those two weeks my family ate a lot of pizza, if they ate at all, and I have no idea how the children got off to school or if they ever took a bath. I was lost in the world of rabbits. When I surfaced exactly two weeks later and Susan read the story, she said that it was good. I knew that something remarkable had happened.

"That story was called *Cromwell's Glasses*, and it contains several of the themes that have remained important to me over the years—themes like difference and the love of family. It was the first of many books that I have written (though I have managed to illustrate some books by other authors along the way) and the start of a perfect career.

"When we read fiction it often gives us a chance to try on a different reality or to be someone other than we are. It is pure bliss. I think that the same thing can be true of writing fiction. I have inhabited many worlds over the years and tried out many personae. The same mental magic that is at work for the reader works for the writer too. Dreams can be realized, wrongs set

" I always chuckle a little bit when people ask me how I got started writing and illustrating children's books, because the truth is a bit surprising; it was almost a complete accident."

Courtesy of Greenwillow Books/HarperCollins Publishers

right, and patience and courage can be within your grasp. Each new book has brought me to a new place and it is always a wonderful place to be. *Serendipity* is indeed a lovely word!"

❋　❋　❋

For Holly Keller, drawing was an early form of self-entertainment. Among other things, she copied all the bird illustrations from a book by John James Audubon. But it wasn't until the age of 40 that her career as a children's book author and illustrator actually began. She has illustrated many titles of nonfiction for young children in the fields of nature study and animal behavior. Her own picture book stories often feature animal protagonists drawn in a minimalist, cartoon style, though *Ten Sleepy Sheep* focuses on a human child who can't fall asleep, even with the help of a rambunctious crowd of sheep who end up having a party in his room. This title was named the 1983 Children's Book of the Year by the Library of Congress.

Keller has created a menagerie of engaging characters who appear in more than one of her books. One hallmark character is an endearing piglet named Geraldine. Geraldine and her baby brother Willie resolve a bout of sibling rivalry with a heart-to-heart talk and a bedtime story in the middle of the night in *Geraldine's Baby Brother*, an American Booksellers Association Pick of the Lists. *Geraldine's Blanket*, in which the piglet turns her favorite blanket into the more socially acceptable doll clothes,

Ninth Book of Junior Authors and Illustrators 273

was a *School Library Journal* Best Book of the Year. Another memorable Keller character is a spotted leopard named Horace. Adopted by tiger parents, Horace feels out of place among cousins who all have stripes. Inspired when the author met a child troubled by the knowledge that she was adopted, *Horace* was named to *Horn Book*'s Fanfare and became a *Reading Rainbow* Review Book.

Holly Keller's stories handle many sensitive subjects for preschoolers. In *Goodbye, Max*, which was a Child Study Association Book of the Year and an IRA/CBC Children's Choice, Keller explores a child's grieving process over the loss of his dog. Two of her books were named Notable Children's Trade Books in the Field of Social Studies: In *The Best Present* a worried Rosie tries to look older so she can visit her grandmother in the hospital to give her some flowers, and in *Grandfather's Dream* a Vietnamese grandfather wants to lure cranes back to the wetlands while his daughter wants to farm the land. This conservation theme was based on Keller's experience with an Earthwatch project. A subtle lesson in human nature occurs in *The New Boy*, an American Booksellers Association Pick of the Lists, when a new boy in class is victimized but eventually becomes one of the crowd when a newer boy arrives in class. Another ABA Pick of the Lists title was *Island Baby*, a beautifully oblique tale of passages, in which a young boy nurses a baby bird before releasing him back into the wild, just as the adults in the boy's life are preparing him to go off to school.

Equally adept at writing and illustrating picture books, Holly Keller won the 2003 Charlotte Zolotow Award for picture book text for *Farfallina & Marcel*. In this story, Keller considers whether drastic changes might alter a friendship as one friend, a caterpillar, becomes a butterfly, and the other friend, a gosling, becomes an adult goose. All her picture books are known for evoking a variety of universal emotions with ease and style through her beautifully understated texts and vibrant pictures.

SELECTED WORKS WRITTEN AND ILLUSTRATED: *Cromwell's Glasses*, 1982; *Ten Sleepy Sheep*, 1983; *Too Big*, 1983; *Geraldine's Blanket*, 1984; *Will It Rain?*, 1984; *Henry's Fourth of July*, 1985; *When Francie Was Sick*, 1985; *A Bear for Christmas*, 1986; *Goodbye, Max*, 1987; *Lizzie's Invitation*, 1987; *Geraldine's Big Snow*, 1988; *The Best Present*, 1989; *Maxine in the Middle*, 1989; *Henry's Happy Birthday*, 1990; *What Alvin Wanted*, 1990; *Horace*, 1991; *The New Boy*, 1991; *Furry*, 1992; *Island Baby*, 1992; *Harry and Tuck*, 1993; *Geraldine's Baby Brother*, 1994; *Grandfather's Dream*, 1994; *Pearl's New Skates*, 1995; *Geraldine First*, 1996; *I Am Angela*, 1997; *Merry Christmas, Geraldine*, 1997; *Angela's Top-Secret Computer Club*, 1998; *Brave Horace*, 1998; *A Bed Full of Cats*, 1999; *Jacob's Tree*, 1999; *What I See*, 1999; *That's Mine, Horace*, 2000; *Geraldine and Mrs. Duffy*, 2002; *Cecil's Garden*, 2002; *Farfallina & Marcel*, 2002; *What a Hat!*, 2003.

SELECTED WORKS ILLUSTRATED: *Clever Raccoon*, by Jane Thayer, 1981; *Why I Cough, Sneeze, Shiver, Hiccup, & Yawn*, by Melvin Berger, 1983; *Air Is All Around You*, by Franklyn M. Branley, 1986; *Snow Is Falling*, by Franklyn M. Branley, 1986; *Snakes Are Hunters*, by Patricia Lauber, 1988; *Shooting Stars*, by Franklyn M. Branley, 1989; *An Octopus Is Amazing*, by Patricia Lauber, 1990; *Ears Are for Hearing*, by Paul Showers, 1990; *Sponges Are Skeletons*, by Barbara Juster Esbensen, 1993; *Be a Friend to Trees*, by Patricia Lauber, 1994; *From Tadpole to Frog*, by Wendy Pfeffer, 1994; *Who Eats What?: Food Chains and Food Webs*, by Patricia Lauber, 1995; *You're Aboard Spaceship Earth*, by Patricia Lauber, 1996; *The Best Bug Parade*, by Stuart J. Murphy, 1996; *What's It Like To Be a Fish?*, by Wendy Pfeffer, 1996; *Morning in the Meadow*, by Nola Buck, 1997; *Let's Go Rock Collecting*, by Roma Gans, 1997; *Sounds All Around*, by Wendy Pfeffer, 1999; *Growing Like Me*, by Anne Rockwell, 2001; *Hear Your Heart*, by Paul Showers, 2001.

SUGGESTED READING: *Children's Literature Review*, vol. 45, 1998; Silvey, Anita, ed. *Children's Books and Their Creators*, 1995; *Something About the Author*, vol. 108, 2000; Ward, Martha E. *Authors of Books for Young People*, 3rd ed., 1990.

Steven Kellogg

October 6, 1941–

"I was born in October, my favorite month of the year, in the suburban town of Norwalk, Connecticut. When I was six years old my family moved to nearby Noroton Heights, where we lived until I was halfway through high school. Among my most vivid memories were the hours I spent in the few acres of woodland (among the last in the town) that were located at the end of my road. The woods were being systematically eradicated by the epidemic growth of the houses and streets all around, but when I left the asphalt pavement and the suburban clamor and disappeared into the leafy shadows I felt like I had slipped into a forest primeval. When neighborhood friends and I made our way along the sun-dappled paths our imaginations transformed us into tribesmen in the Amazon jungle, or explorers probing the frontiers of an undiscovered continent, or the resident wolf pack of a Nordic wilderness.

"Every day after school I looked forward to losing myself in the serenity of that magical woodland. I loved the soaring trees, the dense thickets, the tiny stream, and the fascinating variety of birds and small animals that had also found a refuge there. Back in my room I made drawings of the wildlife that I had observed in the woods, and then I thumbtacked the pictures from floor to ceiling, completely covering the wallpaper. In favorite books and magazines about animals I studied the illustrations and photographs of larger species, and I began giving myself drawing assignments in which I would attempt to depict all the North American owls, or the great cats of the world, or the varieties of antelope in Africa. To my parents' dismay the compulsive cycle of replacing old pictures with more recent ones soon left my walls terminally damaged by thousands of thumbtack holes!

"Initially the materials I used were pencils and crayons and small pieces of paper, but it wasn't long before I was eager for more variety and a larger format. I hired myself out to do odd jobs around my neighborhood so I could afford to purchase watercolors, tempera paints, and large sheets of art paper. My dream was to become an illustrator for a magazine like *National Geographic*. I could imagine nothing more exciting and satisfying than to be sent on assignments around the world to paint wild animals in remote and exotic locations.

"In addition to assuring the availability of art supplies, the money I earned fueled another passion: collecting books, especially books about animals and nature. *Black Beauty* was a particular favorite, and I reread it often. The author Anna Sewell's exposure of the insensitive and cruel treatment to which the horses were subjected resonated deeply with me. I was particularly moved (and still am) by the chapter that revealed the death of my favorite horse, the proud and high-spirited Ginger. Another book that I constantly reread was Eric Knight's classic, *Lassie Come Home*. The dignity, courage, and loyalty of the heroic collie who traveled hundreds of miles to find the boy from whom she had been forcibly separated never failed to inspire me.

Courtesy of Penguin Putnam Books for Young Readers

Steven Kellogg

"My fascination with books motivated me to create stories of my own. I particularly enjoyed making up tales to entertain my two younger sisters. A format evolved that began with me taking a seat between them with a stack of paper in my lap. I had a very imprecise idea of what direction the plot would follow, but I would spontaneously push a succession of events forward while I briskly scribbled sketches to accompany my narration. The chatter and the flow of pictures would continue at a frantic pace until both my imagination and audience were exhausted. We called this process 'telling stories on paper,' and I'm sure it was an early symptom of what was to become a happy lifetime obsession with words, images, and the world of the picture book.

"During my high school years I continued to draw and paint constantly. I spent after-school hours and the weeks of summer vacation working in dog kennels that were within biking distance of my house. I loved taking care of the dogs, and I enjoyed doing portraits of them, which I gave to their owners. During my senior year I received a Pitney Bowes scholarship, which allowed me to enroll at the Rhode Island School of Design, where I majored in illustration and took some wonderful classes in art history, literature, world history, and psychology. But the best part of my college experience came when a European Honors Fellowship sent me to Italy for my senior year. I was fascinated by the beauty of the Tuscan countryside and the artistic wealth and magnificence of Florence, where I spent the majority of my time. I was amazed to find myself in a country where art was so highly valued, and I was deeply grateful for the warmth, enthusiasm, and hospitality of all the Italian people who befriended me. In that supportive and exhilarating environment I could feel myself opening up and growing as an artist and as a person. Many years have passed since I returned from Italy, but most of the details of my experiences and impressions remain vivid; I remember that entire period with deep appreciation and wonder.

"Upon my return I did some graduate work at American University, where I taught etching. I exhibited my etchings and paintings in the Washington, DC, area. At the same time I began developing ideas for children's books, and I started submitting illustrated manuscripts and showing portfolios of my artwork to New York publishers. During 1966 I was asked to illustrate George Mendoza's trio of stories, *Gwot! Horribly Funny Hairticklers*. Newly married and having acquired six stepchildren, I moved back to Connecticut to devote myself full time to writing and illustrating children's books. Throughout the 1970s, 1980s, and 1990s I published about three books a year, and that pace continues. I vary the writing of my own stories with illustrating books written by others. For me each book is an intriguing new challenge and a fresh adventure. I enjoy exploring all the ways that words and pictures can be orchestrated within the format of the turning pages of a picture book so that the visual and the verbal voices blend and intertwine in a duet that totally immerses the reader-observer in the world that the story creates.

"My childhood fascination with stories, animals, and nature expresses itself in the books that I write and illustrate. I enjoy pointing this out to audiences of children during my frequent visits to schools and libraries around the country. I hope that my books will heighten their awareness of the complexity and beauty of the natural world and encourage them to put their thoughts, feelings, and experiences into stories of their own. One of the questions that I am asked most often when I am doing programs for children is how I feel about my job. My response is that I love it, and my greatest hope is that the time my readers share with me and my work will prove to be an enjoyable experience for them—one that will encourage a lifetime association with pictures, words, and books."

"Every day after school I looked forward to losing myself in the serenity of that magical woodland. I loved the soaring trees, the dense thickets, the tiny stream, and the fascinating variety of birds and small animals that had also found a refuge there."

❋   ❋   ❋

Steven Kellogg is one of the most beloved and revered children's book illustrators of the present day. His childhood interest in drawing, and especially in drawing pictures of animals and birds, grew into a prolific career in book illustration and an impressive body of work in picture-book art and writing. Since his first published book appeared in 1967 he has garnered many awards from critics as well as great appreciation from children. In 1970 his witty pen-and-ink illustrations for a new edition of Hilaire Belloc's satirical takeoff on Victorian cautionary tales, *Matilda, Who Told Lies and Was Burned to Death*, earned him a place on the *New York Times* Best Illustrated list. This honor coming very early in his career was followed by a second citation as a *New York Times* Best Illustrated Book in 1974 for *There Was an Old Woman*. In 1977, he received the Irma S. and James H. Black Award celebrating excellence in picture book art from the Bank Street College of Education for *The Mysterious Tadpole*.

Throughout the last 35 years many of his books have appeared on the ALA Notable Children's Books List. In 1989 he was presented with the Regina Medal from the Catholic Library Association, and in 1996 he received a Lifetime Achievement Award from the New England Booksellers Association. He has also been a recipient of the David McCord Children's Literature Citation from Framingham State College for "significant contribution to excellence in the field of children's books." Kellogg uses a variety of techniques for his children's books, including pen-and-ink, colored inks, watercolors, and acrylics. An energetic line and profusion of detail inviting his readers to linger over every page have been hallmarks of his work from the beginning. His books abound with an explosive humor that earned him the 1998 Jo Osborne Award for Humor given by the Children's Literature Conference of Ohio State University. This award honors humor that "provides perspective on human pomposity and foibles," and Steven Kellogg has certainly spent his entire career creating that sort of perspective.

One of Kellogg's most popular original characters is Pinkerton, a huge, gangly Great Dane whose adventures are based on his own family's rambunctious pup, the real-life Pinkerton who grew to weigh 180 pounds. *Pinkerton, Behave!* introduced the endearing dog in 1979 and chronicled the family's exasperation with his perpetual puppyhood. Many more Pinkerton stories followed. An assertive cat born wild in the Catskill Mountains and adopted by the Kelloggs became Pinkerton's foil in *A Rose for Pinkerton*. The stories recount hysterical situations that end up with complete confusion, chaos, and delight for all concerned. Reflecting the joy that Pinkerton and many other Kellogg characters have brought to countless young fans, a retrospective compilation of 11 of Kellogg's best-loved stories over the years was published in 2004, entitled *Pinkerton and Friends*. Another favorite Kellogg original story is *The Island of the Skog*, an imagi-

"I was amazed to find myself in a country where art was so highly valued, and I was deeply grateful for the warmth, enthusiasm, and hospitality of all the Italian people who befriended me."

native ecology story that countless school-children have watched Steven energetically re-create for them on a huge drawing pad while he performs the story at school assemblies.

STEVEN KELLOGG

Clorinda

by Robert Kinerk

Many of the stories Kellogg has illustrated over the years have been written by the finest picture book authors writing today— Margaret Mahy, Peggy Parish, Trinka Hakes Noble, Amy Ehrlich, and Bill Martin Jr., among others. His newest personable animal character is Clorinda, created for Robert Kinerk's whimsical story about a determined cow who wants to be a ballet dancer. While most of his work has been fictional and fanciful, Kellogg's art has also occasionally enhanced nonfiction titles, such as David Schwartz's books on numerical concepts. Their first collaboration, *How Much Is a Million?*, won a *Boston Globe–Horn Book* Honor Award in 1985 and was followed by *If You Made a Million* in 1989 and *Millions to Measure* in 2003. Kellogg met the challenge of illustrating mathematical concepts with the same imaginative verve and humor found in his fictional stories. His picture-book version of the song "Yankee Doodle," originally published for the American Bicentennial year of 1976, was reissued in a larger format in 1996 and contains historical notes on the song and language of the era along with exuberant illustrations for each verse of this Revolutionary War favorite.

Kellogg's own retellings of folk tales and tall tales have brought these age-old stories to a new audience with fresh humor and rollicking good fun. Paul Bunyan, Pecos Bill, Mike Fink, Sally Ann Thunder Ann Whirlwind Crockett, and other stars of the uniquely American brand of tall tale humor have gained new life through Kellogg's words and art. Characters from his other books, such as Pinkerton, sometimes make a cameo appearance in the folk stories. His version of *Pecos Bill* won the SouthWest Book Award for outstanding literature for any age about the American Southwest. These larger-than-life characters are a perfect match for Kellogg's witty texts and energetic, vibrant art that often includes cartoon-style dialogue balloons. His delightful retellings of nursery tales such as *Chicken Little*, *Jack and the Beanstalk*, and *The Three Little Pigs* are written and illustrated to entice children's attention and expand their horizons. There is always a subtext beyond the words in his drawings, in true picture-book tradition going back to 19th-century illustrators like Randolph Caldecott. In Kellogg's rendition of *The Three Sillies*, for example, a cat appears in the illustrations who is obviously more sensible than any of the human characters and shows great disgust at their ridiculous antics, though she is never mentioned in the text.

Steven Kellogg takes his work very seriously, for all the humor that it exudes. He believes that the picture book serves as a child's first introduction to art and literature and, as such, should provide as dramatic and stimulating an experience as possible. In one of his most challenging projects, he stepped outside the picture-book genre and created 18 paintings for a Books of Wonder edition of Mark Twain's *Adventures of Huckleberry Finn*. "It was a privilege," he said in an interview, "to be immersed for many months in the power, the beauty, and the humor of Twain's magnificent writing." After living for many years in southern Connecticut, Steven and his wife, Helen, bought a historic house on Lake Champlain in Essex, New York, with a breathtaking view of mountains and water. There, with his studio in a converted barn, he continues to create unique and distinctive picture books for new generations of children.

Courtesy of HarperCollins Children's Books

SELECTED WORKS WRITTEN AND ILLUSTRATED: *The Wicked Kings of Bloon*, 1970; *Can I Keep Him?*, 1971; *The Mystery Beast of Ostergeest*, 1971; *The Orchard Cat*, 1972; *Won't Somebody Play With Me?*, 1972; *The Island of the Skog*, 1973; *There Was an Old Woman*, 1974; *The Mystery of the Missing Red Mitten*, 1974; *Much Bigger than Martin*, 1976; *The Mysterious Tadpole*, 1977 (reissued with new illustrations and text, 2002); *The Mystery of the Magic Green Ball*, 1978; *Pinkerton, Behave!*, 1979; *The Mystery of the Flying Orange Pumpkin*, 1980; *A Rose for Pinkerton*, 1981; *Tallyho, Pinkerton!*, 1982; *The Mystery of the Stolen Blue Paint*, 1982; *Paul Bunyan: A Tall Tale*, 1984; *Chicken Little*, 1985; *Pecos Bill: A Tall Tale*, 1986; *Best Friends*, 1986; *Prehistoric Pinkerton*, 1987; *Aster Aardvark's Alphabet Adventures*, 1987; *Johnny Appleseed: A Tall Tale*, 1988; *Jack and the Beanstalk*, 1991; *The Christmas Witch*, 1992; *Mike Fink: A Tall Tale*, 1992; *Sally Ann Thunder Ann Whirlwind Crockett: A Tall Tale*, 1995; *I Was Born about 10,000 Years Ago: A Tall Tale*, 1996; *The Three Little Pigs*, 1997; *A-Hunting We Will Go!*, 1998; *The Three Sillies*, 1999; *Give the Dog a Bone*, 2000; *The Missing Mitten Mystery*, 2000; *A Penguin Pup for Pinkerton*, 2001; *Pinkerton and Friends: A Treasury of 11 Stories*, 2004.

SELECTED WORKS ILLUSTRATED: *Gwot! Horribly Funny Hairticklers*, by George Mendoza, 1967; *The Rotten Book*, by Mary Rodgers, 1969; *Matilda, Who Told Lies and Was Burned to Death*, by Hilaire Belloc, 1970, reissued 1992;

Mister Rogers' Songbook, by Fred Rogers, 1970; *Mrs. Purdy's Children*, by Ruth Loomis, 1970; *Can't You Pretend?*, by Miriam Young, 1970; *Granny and the Desperadoes*, by Peggy Parish, 1970; *Abby*, by Jeannette Caines, 1973; *Come Here, Cat*, by Joan L. Nødset, 1973; *You Ought to See Herbert's House*, by Doris Lund, 1973; *Kisses and Fishes*, by Liesel Moak Skørpen, 1974; *How the Witch Got Alf*, by Cora Annett, 1975; *The Great Christmas Kidnapping Caper*, by Jean Van Leeuwen, 1975; *The Boy Who Was Followed Home*, by Margaret Mahy, 1975; *The Most Delicious Camping Trip Ever*, by Alice Bach, 1976; *Steven Kellogg's Yankee Doodle*, by Edward Bangs, 1976; *Grouchy Uncle Otto*, by Alice Bach, 1977; *Barney Bipple's Magic Dandelions*, by Carol Chapman, 1977; *Appelard and Liverwurst*, by Mercer Mayer, 1978; *The Pickle Plan*, by Marilyn Singer, 1978; *Uproar on Hollercat Hill*, by Jean Marzollo, 1980; *The Day Jimmy's Boa Ate the Wash*, by Trinka Hakes Noble, 1980; *Liverwurst Is Missing*, by Mercer Mayer, 1981; *Leo, Zack, and Emmie*, by Amy Ehrlich, 1981; *Jimmy's Boa Bounces Back*, by Trinka Hakes Noble, 1984; *Iva Dunnit and the Big Wind*, by Carol Purdy, 1985; *How Much Is a Million?*, by David M. Schwartz, 1985; *Leo, Zack, and Emmie Together Again*, by Amy Ehrlich, 1987; *Jimmy's Boa and the Big Splash Birthday Bash*, by Trinka Hakes Noble, 1989; *Is Your Mama a Llama?*, by Deborah Guarino, 1989; *If You Made a Million*, by David M. Schwartz, 1989; *Engelbert the Elephant*, by Tom Paxton, 1990; *The Day the Goose Got Loose*, by Reeve Lindbergh, 1990; *The Wizard Next Door*, by Peter Glassman, 1993; *Parents in the Pigpen, Pigs in the Tub*, by Amy Ehrlich, 1993; *The Great Quillow*, by James Thurber, 1994; *The Adventures of Huckleberry Finn*, by Mark Twain, 1994; *The Rattlebang Picnic*, by Margaret Mahy, 1994; *Frogs Jump: A Counting Book*, by Alan Brooks, 1996; *Library Lil*, by Suzanne Williams, 1997; *A Beasty Story*, by Bill Martin Jr., 1999; *The Baby Beebee Bird*, by Diane Redfield Massie, 2000; *Big Bear Ball*, by Joanne Ryder, 2002; *Millions to Measure*, by David M. Schwartz, 2003; *Clorinda*, by Robert Kinerk, 2003; *Jimmy's Boa and the Bungee Jump Slam Dunk*, by Trinka Hakes Noble, 2003; *Santa Claus Is Comin' to Town*, by J. Fred Coots and Haven Gillespie, 2004.

SUGGESTED READING: *Children's Literature Review*, vol. 6, 1984; Cummings, Pat. *Talking with Artists*, 1992; Pendergast, Tom. *Saint James Guide to Children's Writers*, 5th ed., 1999; Silvey, Anita, ed. *Children's Books and Their Creators*, 1995; *Something About the Author*, vol. 130, 2002. Periodicals—Elleman, Barbara, "Born to Draw: A Profile of Steven Kellogg," *Language Arts*, September 2001; Nagler, Eve, "Tales of Whimsy, Boas, and Great Danes," *New York Times*, May 22, 1994; Thomas, Barbara, "Drawing Kids In," *Hartford Courant* (Connecticut), December 18, 1997.

WEB SITE: *www.stevenkellogg.com*

An earlier profile of Steven Kellogg appeared in *Fourth Book of Junior Authors* (1978).

Courtesy of Penny Millar

Elizabeth Cody Kimmel

Elizabeth Cody Kimmel

October 23, 1964–

"One of my favorite photographs of myself was taken in Cape Cod when I was about five years old. I am lying on my stomach in the living room near the fireplace, chin propped up by one hand, an open book spread in front of me. I am smiling, because I always loved having my picture taken, but there is also a hint of impatience in my expression. Clearly I want to get back to the book, which I'm fairly certain is *Alice in Wonderland,* as soon as possible. As I write this, the bulletin board over my desk is covered with snapshots, including a recent photograph, taken at my mother-in-law's house in Kentucky last Christmas. I am stretched out in front of a roaring fire, head propped up on a pillow, reading (for the tenth time) Susan Cooper's *The Dark Is Rising* (which I have just given my niece for Christmas, then just as quickly borrowed back).

"All the years that passed by in between the taking of those two photographs could contain thousands of similar snapshots. Wherever I have lived, wherever life has taken me, reading has been my great constant. Whether I am visiting a friend's house or traveling to a foreign country for the first time, I am always evaluating my surroundings for their readability. Is that a good couch for some reading time? Can I sneak away to that hammock and get to the end of this novel? Is there a bookstore down that inviting little lane? Reading has been my sanctuary, my escape, my gift to myself, and in the last eight years reading has also been part of my job. Sometimes I have to pinch myself to make sure this last part is true. Whether I am reading new young adult novels to see what is selling, or plowing through a biography as research for a nonfiction project, keeping up with my reading is at the heart of my writing.

"I have always loved to write as well as to read. Several of my childhood stories, most of them involving secret passageways and curious children, have survived in attic boxes. But though I always knew I was a writer, it never seriously occurred to me to try to make a living as one. That just seemed too good to be true. It would have been like deciding to be a movie star—I just assumed everyone in the world wanted to do the same thing, and there was very little point in trying. But life nudged me ever closer in that direction. One year I was working with published writers. The next year, I was signing my first book contract.

"It gives me great pleasure to see how similar my 39-year-old self is to my five-year-old self. The two of us know what we want, know what makes us happy, know what makes us feel at home. If that five-year-old Beth Cody had known that the grown-up version of herself would make a life and living from books, I'm sure she would have rejoiced in a dream come true—at least for a minute. Then she would have to get back to what really consumed her—the open book waiting on the rug."

✳   ✳   ✳

Elizabeth Cody Kimmel was born in New York City and grew up in Westchester County, just north of the city. When she was nine years old, her family moved to Brussels, Belgium, for two years in connection with her father's job. While living in Brussels she discovered the books of British author Enid Blyton—and was astonished to discover when the family returned home that Blyton was virtually unknown in America. Elizabeth attended Emma Willard School and Kenyon College, where she majored in English and drama (playwriting). After graduation, she worked for a literary agent, where she read countless manuscripts for children and young adults. After eight years, she decided to write her own young adult novel. This resulted in her forming a collection of the publishing industry's kindest rejection letters. Taking the advice of her boss (now also her agent), she immediately began work on a second novel, which was accepted for publication and launched her writing career.

That first published book, *In the Stone Circle*, a skillful blending of a young adult coming-of-age story and a ghost story, was

Courtesy of Clarion Books

a Junior Library Guild selection and remains one of the author's bestselling books. Equally adept at writing nonfiction, Kimmel focuses on adventurous history books. Her narrative skill can bring vividly to life the accounts of an Antarctic explorer (*Ice Story: Shackleton's Lost Expedition*) or a Viking adventurer (*Before Columbus: The Leif Eriksson Expedition*) or the amazing accomplishments of Lewis and Clark in early 19th-century America (*As Far As the Eye Can Reach*). Kimmel's heroes are not exclusively human. One of her most popular titles, *Balto and the Great Race*, recounts the extraordinary journey of a sled dog to Nome, Alaska, in 1925, a trip that delivered life-saving medicine to that remote settlement.

Kimmel's research skills led her to writing historical fiction as well as fact. Using the few facts known about the early years of her own distant relative, Buffalo Bill Cody, she has created a series of fictional adventure tales for middle grade readers, beginning in the year 1854, when young Bill is eight years old and moves to the Kansas Territory with his family. The second book in the series, *One Sky Above Us*, tells how the security of Bill's family (with its strong abolitionist stand) is affected by the slavery issue raging in the Territory. *One Sky Above Us* was named a Notable Social Studies Trade Book for Young People in 2002; *Ice Story* had received the same distinction, then phrased as Notable Children's Trade Book in the Field of Social Studies, in 1999. In her latest book, *Lily B. on the Brink of Cool*, Kimmel has returned to the young adult novel with new humor, for a story that is as poignant as it is funny.

Beth Kimmel lives in New York's Hudson Valley with her husband, an actor, and her daughter, a future artist/veterinarian /actress/rock climber (but not necessarily in that order). Her books have been published in England, Germany, and Japan, as well as the United States.

SELECTED WORKS: *In the Stone Circle*, 1998; *Balto and the Great Race*, illus. by Nora Koerber, 1999; *Ice Story: Shackleton's Lost Expedition*, 1999; *Visiting Miss Caples*, 2000; *To the Frontier* (The Adventures of Young Buffalo Bill, 1), 2002; *One Sky Above Us* (The Adventures of Young Buffalo Bill, 2), illus. by Scott Snow, 2002; *As Far As the Eye Can Reach: Lewis and Clark's Westward Quest*, 2003; *Before Columbus: The Leif Eriksson Expedition*, 2003; *What Do You Dream?*, illus. by Joung Un Kim, 2003; *In the Eye of the Storm* (The Adventures of Young Buffalo Bill, 3), illus. by Scott Snow, 2003; *Lily B. on the Brink of Cool*, 2003; *The Look-It-Up Book of Explorers*, 2004.

Jackie French Koller

March 8, 1948–

"**I** am not one of those authors who knew from the day she was born that she was destined to write. As a matter of fact, I didn't think that was something an ordinary person could do. I thought you had to be rich or famous to be able to get a cool job like writing books. I did love to read though, and I had a vivid imagination. We didn't have a TV when I was very young, and even after we got one, we didn't spend much time in front of it. My mother was a great advocate of us kids getting outside for 'a little fresh air' no matter what the weather. We didn't have a million activities lined up to entertain us, either. My mother didn't even have a car. If we wanted to play baseball, we dug a bat and a ball out of a cardboard box in the basement and tore up some other hunks of cardboard to make bases. If we wanted to dance, we set up an old record player in the garage. If we wanted to be in a play we hung a sheet over the clothesline to make our stage. 'Swimming lessons' consisted of flopping around in a plastic blow-up pool or jumping in and out of the sprinkler. Instead of video games we played board games. Instead of sticking a movie into the VCR when we were bored, we read books or drew pictures or did crafts. There was no end to the things we could make with colored paper, paste, empty thread spools, food cartons, buttons, Popsicle sticks, and the endless other odds and ends we'd find around the house. And quiet time was okay, too—just hanging upside down from the monkey bars and watching the clouds go by, or lying in the grass on a hot summer day, listening to the cicadas buzz, or climbing a tree and just being alone with your thoughts. I did a lot of that as a kid—a lot of thinking, imagining, dreaming . . . and I know that's why it's so easy for me to dredge up those memories now, as a writer, and use those memories to create characters who think and feel like real kids.

"So when did I start writing? I fooled around with it a little bit in the sixth grade. I actually wrote a short novel, bringing it into school chapter by chapter and reading it to my friends on the playground. Either they were very tolerant or they actually liked it because when it was finished, they encouraged me to start another one, which I did, but then lost interest and went on to other things. I found both stories later, when I was in high school and had the self-esteem of a slug, and I hastily threw them away for fear that someone else might discover that I'd written them and think I was some kind of weirdo. How I wish I hadn't done that, but so ended my short-lived attempt at early authorship.

"I didn't try writing again until I had children of my own. Even before they were old enough to hold their heads up, I was reading to them the way my mother had read to me as a child. Story time became my favorite time of day, and before long all those wonderful books were triggering my imagi-

Courtesy of George Koller

Jackie French Koller

nation, and I began getting ideas for stories of my own. At first I wrote them just for my children, but eventually I got up the courage to show them to other people. People seemed to like them and soon I was hooked. I finally knew what I wanted to do with my life and I set out to make my dream a reality. It would be a long haul—ten years of rejection before my first book, *Impy for Always*, was published in 1989. But then things started happening fast, and since then so many dreams have come true— picture books, chapter books, novels—even a movie! Every day is a new adventure when you're a writer, and I can hardly wait to see what tomorrow will bring."

✿　✿　✿

Jackie French Koller was born in Derby, Connecticut, to parents who had both overcome difficult backgrounds. Her mother, Margaret, was one of nine children of an abusive, alcoholic father. Raised in poverty in New York City during the Depression, she was forced to drop out of high school to help the family make ends meet. Koller's father, Ernest, was only a teenager when his own father, also an alcoholic, was imprisoned for manslaughter for his role in a hit-and-run accident. Nevertheless, Ernest was able to graduate from high school and engineering school, working four jobs to pay his way through college. When he and Margaret had children of their own, they had a lot to teach about persistence and determination, lessons that served their daughter Jackie well on the long road to becoming a published author. More than that, her parents' family backgrounds gave her a true empathy for characters faced with hard lives and difficult choices.

Koller remembers her own childhood as happy and creative. Her artistic talent was encouraged by teachers. She planned to attend art school until her father convinced her of the tenuous nature of an artistic career. Instead, she studied interior design at the University of Connecticut, from which she graduated with a B.A. in 1970. While in college she worked summers on a factory assembly line and, to relieve the boredom of the job, made a game of making up stories based on characters or situations suggested by co-workers.

> "Every day is a new adventure when you're a writer, and I can hardly wait to see what tomorrow will bring."

At the university she met George Koller and the two married in 1970. They have three grown children: Kerri teaches middle school math in eastern Massachusetts; Ryan is an engineer and designer of aircraft engines; Devin, the youngest, is an engineer as well.

Today Koller, her husband, and their Labrador Cassie live on 10 acres on a mountaintop in western Massachusetts. Koller enjoys reading, painting, gardening, hiking, and making gingerbread houses.

Koller's writing ranges from easy readers and early chapter books to young adult novels; from fantasy to reality to history. *The Falcon* and *The Primrose Way* were both named ALA Best Books for Young Adults. *A Place to Call Home* was designated an ALA Notable Children's Book, and *No Such Thing* was cited as a Blue Ribbon Book by the *Bulletin of the Center for Children's Books*. *Last Voyage of the Misty Day* became a selection of the Junior Library Guild, as did *No Such Thing* and *One Monkey Too Many*. Many of Koller's titles have appeared on New York Public Library's Books for the Teen Age list, and her early chapter books about Mole and Shrew, as well as her Dragonling series, have proven very popular with emerging readers. *If I Had One Wish . . .* was adapted as a Disney Channel TV movie. Renamed *You Wish*, it was telecast early in 2003.

SELECTED WORKS: *Impy for Always*, illus. by Carol Newsom, 1989; *The Dragonling*, illus. by Judith Mitchell, 1990; *Nothing to Fear*, 1991; *If I Had One Wish . . .*, 1991; *Mole and Shrew*, illus. by Stella Ormai, 1991; *The Primrose Way*, 1992; *Mole & Shrew Step Out*, illus. by Stella Ormai, 1992; *Last Voyage of the* Misty Day, 1992; *A Dragon in the Family*, illus. by Judith Mitchell, 1993; *A Place to Call Home*, 1995; *Mole and Shrew All Year Through*, illus. by John Beder, 1997; *No Such Thing*, illus. by Betsy Lewin, 1997; *Dragon Quest*, illus. by Judith Mitchell, 1997; *The Falcon*, 1998; *The Promise*, illus. by Jacqueline Rogers, 1999; *Bouncing on the Bed*, illus. by Anna Grossnickle Hines, 1999; *Nickommoh!: A Thanksgiving Celebration*, illus. by Marcia Sewall, 1999; *One Monkey Too Many*; illus. by Lynn Munsinger, 1999; *Mole and Shrew are Two*, illus. by Anne Reas, 2000; *Mole and Shrew Have Jobs to Do*, illus. by Anne Reas, 2001; *Mole and Shrew Find a Clue*, illus. by Anne Reas, 2001; *Someday*, 2002; *Baby for Sale!*, illus. by Janet Pedersen, 2002; *The Keepers—Book One: A Wizard Named Nell*, 2003; *The Keepers—Book Two: The Wizard's Apprentice*, 2004.

SUGGESTED READING: *Authors and Artists for Young Adults*, vol. 28, 1999; *Children's Literature Review*, vol. 68, 2001; *Contemporary Authors*, vol. 170, 1999; *Something About the Author*, vol. 109, 2000.

WEB SITE: *www.jackiefrenchkoller.com*

Courtesy of Simon & Schuster Books for Young Readers

Mary Kay Kroeger

February 27, 1950–

"When I have time to fill, I plan to search used bookstores for my first favorite book, *365 Bedtime Stories*. The cover was glossy, the bindings cracked when I last remember holding that book. My book, my dad, and me. What cozy memories those short, single-page tales hold.

"I was born in 1950, on February 27, in Cincinnati, Ohio, and after the turn of a new century you can still find me there. I live two miles from where I grew up. Even though I was an only child, I had a family of six cousins living right across the street. My family ate dinner at 5:15 P.M. every evening. After spending the ritual 15 minutes 'letting my food digest,' my mother let me go across the street just in time to sit at my cousins' dinner table. Lucky for me there was always room for me to squeeze in between Linda and Marcia, the two cousins closest in age to me.

Aunt Alice was always so gentle and welcoming to me and to the rest of the neighborhood children. She was probably my inspiration to become a teacher.

"Of course that dream surfaced long after I hung up my Annie Oakley holster and climbed down from the back of the wingback chair that I 'rode' through the dusty western streets of my imagination. Later that chair became my favorite reading spot for series like the Bobbsey Twins, Cherry Ames, and, of course, Nancy Drew. Even *Jane Eyre* read best in that chair in our front window.

"Reading to my two children, Carrie and Joe, was treasured time in our home. Since then, I have added many new books to my shelves. I guess that's why grandchildren were invented!

Courtesy of Lifetouch

Mary Kay Kroeger

Eighteen years ago I began teaching language arts. At the same time, a dear friend started to share new children's books with me. Soon my own two children, as well as my students, became intrigued with the language and stories of children's literature. How natural it became to coach children in writing, using rich literature as models for their stories.

"The Ohio Writing Project is another experience in my life that brings me to this page. The Project guided me to put my heart on paper and share meaningful events in my life. When I listened with pride to my father tell me the story of his life as a paperboy, I knew I wanted it to be recorded for my family to read for years and years. Soon Louise Borden helped me see how to add poetry to a story . . . and *Paperboy* was eventually published. Writing with a friend can be like playing make-believe. Together we can be anyone and anywhere we wish!

"Of course, when we are writing biographies like *Fly High!* we must be very accurate. Writers need to spend a lot of time following their research to the Library of Congress in Washington, to Chicago, and even to New York! Now that our children are married, my husband, Dan, and I intend to find more time to do the things we love to do: read books, watch movies, and spend time with our friends and families. I'll be enjoying that and continuing to watch for stories to tell."

✵ ✵ ✵

Mary Kay Kroeger, born Mary Kay Weich, received her B.S. degree in education in 1972 and a master of education degree in reading in 1996, both from the College of Mount St. Joseph-on-the-Ohio. For 20 years she taught in Catholic schools, most of that time teaching fourth- through eighth-grade math and science in multi-level classrooms. An understanding principal adjusted her schedule to part-time when her children were born, though Kroeger did take a year off when her son's kindergarten schedule didn't fit well with her teaching day. When both children were in school full time, she moved to a third-grade teaching post in another Catholic school for eight years.

While Kroeger was teaching for the Archdiocese of Cincinnati, she received a fellowship to attend the Ohio Writing Project offered by Miami University of Ohio. An intensive six-week course, the Project strives to help participants learn how to teach writing by first becoming writers themselves. The experience of being immersed in a writing community spurred Kroeger to want to tell her own stories as well as encourage her students. For the last 10 years she has been teaching fourth-grade language arts and social studies with the Mariemont City Schools.

Kroeger first heard the story that became *Paperboy* on her 40th birthday, as the family ate ice cream and cake. She had just finished the Writing Project and was looking for stories to tell when her father shared his memories of selling newspapers as a boy. The names were changed, but all the details came straight from her father's memory in her picture-book story of a boy who showed up to sell papers with the fight results that no one in his neighborhood wanted to hear—the defeat of Jack Dempsey by Gene Tunney in 1927. As a reward for his diligence, Willie Brinkman gets a chance to move up to a big corner, just as Kroeger's father, William Weich, did when he was a boy. Kroeger's friend, the writer Louise Borden, urged her to write the story, and eventually the two friends worked on it together, meeting at a hamburger restaurant halfway between their homes to play with words and phrasing. *Paperboy* received a starred review in *Publishers Weekly*.

Courtesy of Clarion Books

Another collaboration between the two came about when they discovered they had both torn out the same article from the Cincinnati *Enquirer*—a short piece about Bessie Coleman that appeared during Black History Month, when a different hero was highlighted each day in the paper. The courage and determination of this woman made both of them want to tell her story, so they agreed to collaborate again on *Fly High!: The Story of Bessie Coleman*, which received a starred review in *School Library Journal*. Kroeger's students are always interested in hearing about her writing process, although occasionally a new student who has missed out on the fact she is a published writer will bring one of the books to class to point out the coincidence that the author has the same name as hers.

SELECTED WORKS: *Paperboy*, with Louise Borden, illus. by Ted Lewin, 1996; *Fly High!: The Story of Bessie Coleman*, with Louse Borden, illus. by Teresa Flavin, 2001.

Courtesy of Hank Kudlinski

Kathleen V. Kudlinski

October 5, 1950–

"My family was always on the move when I was growing up. In each new town I searched anew for people to talk to. Books—and their authors—were the only friends who traveled across the country with me. Unlike anyone else in my family, I loved nature and art, and I had a secret longing to be great someday. I spent my days climbing trees to look into nests or digging in streambeds to find salamanders. Books by Robert McClung and, later, Sally Carrigher and Rachel Carson, honored my interest. I could ask any nature question, however odd or embarrassing, and find the answers for myself, in books.

"When I wasn't nature-watching, I was drawing birds, horses, castles, or monsters. How-to books showed me ways to sketch and paint. I read dozens of biographies looking to see how people became great. I never thought about becoming a great author. I thought writers were tidy people with good grades and perfect spelling. My bedroom was always full of shed snakeskins and feathers, piles of books, art projects, and camping gear. My report card was a mess and my spelling was worse.

"During high school in Westport, Connecticut, I volunteered at a local museum—sketching, caring for wild animals, and teaching about nature. It seemed a perfect match for my talents and hobbies. I studied science in college at the University of Maine, where I met my future husband, Hank. After we graduated in 1972, I decided to teach in schools instead of in museums. For three years I taught science at an elementary school in North Carolina in a classroom crowded with cages of gerbils and snakes, parakeets and tarantulas. For three years after that, my animals and I taught fifth grade in New Hampshire. I had found a way to be important in the lives of many kids, doing what I love.

"Then my husband took a new job in Massachusetts where there was no need for schoolteachers—even those with dozens of classroom animals. I spent months trying to find something good to do with my life. When I saw an ad for a conference of the Society of Children's Book Writers and Illustrators in nearby Northampton, I decided to drop in. One of the speakers, Jane Yolen, was as excited and happy with writing as I had been with teaching. I bought her book, *Writing for Children*, and stood in a long line waiting for her to sign it. As we inched along I thought about perhaps trying to write, someday. But Jane didn't write 'good luck' in the book. In black ink, she wrote 'from one writer to another.'

"I stumbled away from the table, my life changed. The great Jane Yolen had given me permission to think of myself as an actual writer. I went home and began work on my first book.

"Over the next four years, Jane and I became friends. I had two children and dozens of rejections. I wrote for magazines and newspapers, doing stories about nature. Every month I met with a writers' group, led by Jane and including Robert McClung and Patty MacLachlan. We talked about getting books published and then critiqued each other's books-in-progress. The encouragement and support of these famous people kept me from being discouraged by rejections. I finally signed a book contract for *Rachel Carson, Pioneer of Ecology* six years after Jane told me I was a writer.

"In 1985 our family moved to Connecticut, where we still live. I've written more than two dozen books here, sitting at my desk overlooking a deep, wild pond. Sometimes now I take my computer up to our log cabin in the woods of Vermont. I write about the things that fascinate me: nature and art and greatness. Every week I write and illustrate a newspaper article about nature too. In writers' groups, I pass on the same encouragement I got when I was just beginning. I often visit classrooms, where I talk about writing well and the joy of finding a life full of the things you love."

❋   ❋   ❋

> *"I never thought about becoming a great author. I thought writers were tidy people with good grades and perfect spelling."*

Kathleen (Kay) Kudlinski was born Kathleen Veenis in Philadelphia, Pennsylvania; she remembers that children would tease her because her name was like the planet Venus, but spelled differently. She spent her childhood traveling with her family from Philadelphia to Pittsburgh, to Chicago, and then to Connecticut. Her father worked as an executive in his own business, selling copper to the gravure industry, where it is used to print dollar bills and magazines. After she grew up she continued to travel: to Maine for college, then on to North Carolina, New Hampshire, and Massachusetts. Kathleen's husband now works for the family business, and he continues to travel, but she prefers to stay at their home in Guilford, Connecticut, where she has finally taken root.

A prolific writer, with over 25 books and many newspaper columns and articles to her credit, she is often working on two or three books at once. She writes about the natural world, plants and animals, always with painstaking research and facts clearly

ART ENCOUNTERS

The *Spirit* *An Encounter with Georgia O'Keeffe* Catchers

KATHLEEN KUDLINSKI

Courtesy of Watson-Guptill Publications

presented. She also writes about courage, both in biographies of famous people and in fictional stories of young people in historical settings. Where appropriate, her style can be described as breezy and entertaining, often friendly and conversational. Yet she deals with issues of prejudice carefully and is a defender of rights for all those treated badly, whether slaves or immigrants, animals or nature itself. Her very first book, *Rachel Carson: Pioneer of Ecology*, has been translated into Japanese and excerpted in a literature textbook by Mc-Graw-Hill. Her 1989 biography of Helen Keller was cited as a Notable Trade Book in the Field of Social Studies, and her informative *Dandelions* was named an Outstanding Science Trade Book in 1999. *Juliette Gordon Low: America's First Girl Scout* and *Earthquake!: A Story of Old San Francisco* were both *Weekly Reader* Book Club selections, and several more titles have become Scholastic Book Club selections.

Kay Kudlinski is generous with her support of other writers. She has been designated a Master Teaching Artist by the Connecticut Commission on the Arts and is an active member of the Society of Children's Book Writers and Illustrators, acting as a regional critique group leader for many years. She is also an active member of the Outdoor Writers Association of America. From 1997 to the present she has written "The Naturalist," a weekly illustrated column in the *New Haven Register* Sunday edition, receiving Outdoor Writers awards in both Outdoor Ethics and Natural History. While she continues to be fascinated by animals of all kinds, her personal menagerie has shrunk in recent years to consist of a tomcat and two poodles, all the same size, with the tomcat firmly in charge. She also enjoys viewing native birds at her windowledge bird feeder. The birds, enjoying the wild sanctuary she and her husband have created with apple and cherry trees, look in on her as she works, offering encouragement and inspiration to a writer who admires nature, courage, and all wild things.

SELECTED WORKS: *Rachel Carson: Pioneer of Ecology*, illus. by Ted Lewin, 1988; *Juliette Gordon Low: America's First Girl Scout*, illus. by Sheila Hamanaka, 1988; *Helen Keller: A Light for the Blind*, illus. by Donna Diamond, 1989; *Pearl Harbor Is Burning: A Story of World War II*, illus. by Ronald Himler, 1990; *Hero Over Here: A Story of World War I*, illus. by Bert Dodson, 1990; *Animal Tracks and Traces*, illus. by Mary Morgan, 1991; *Night Bird: A Story of the Seminole Indians*, illus. by James Watling, 1993; *Earthquake!: A Story of Old San Francisco*, illus. by Ronald Himler, 1993; *Facing West: A Story of the Oregon Trail*, illus. by James Watling, 1994; *Lone Star: A Story of the Texas Rangers*, illus. by Ronald Himler, 1994; *Shannon: A Chinatown Adventure*, illus. by Bill Farnsworth, 1996; *Marie: An Invitation to Dance: Paris 1775*, illus. by Lyn Durham, 1996; *Shannon: The Schoolmarm Mysteries*, illus. by Bill Farnsworth, 1997; *Shannon: Lost and Found*, illus. by Bill Farnsworth, 1997; *Venus Flytraps*, photos. by Jerome Wexler, 1998; *Popcorn Plants*, photos. by Jerome Wexler, 1998; *Dandelions*, photos. by Jerome Wexler, 1999; *Rosa Parks: Young Rebel*, illus. by Meryl Henderson, 2001; *Harriet Tubman: Freedom's Trailblazer*, illus. by Robert Brown, 2002; *Franklin Delano Roosevelt: Champion of Freedom*, illus. by Meryl Henderson, 2003; *Sojourner Truth: Voice of Freedom*, illus. by Lenny Wooden, 2003; *Boy, Were We Wrong About Dinosaurs!*, illus. by S. D. Schindler, 2004; *The Spirit Catchers: An Encounter with Georgia O'Keefe*, 2004.

SUGGESTED READING: *Something About the Author*, vol. 150, 2004. Periodicals—"Local Author's New Book Honors Women's History Month," *Guilford Courier* (Connecticut), March 20, 2003; "FDR for Kids, Candid New Book by Guilford Author," *Guilford Courier*, September 11, 2003.

Laura McGee Kvasnosky

January 27, 1951–

"**M**y little brother and sister were the audience for my first stories. I used a squeaky voice to channel 'The Adventures of Kitty' through a gray stuffed cat. Kitty vanished when I was eight. I suspect my mom was behind his mysterious disappearance. She'd had enough of that squeaky voice.

"My dad was my first writing teacher. Every Wednesday after dinner we would go over the column I wrote for his newspaper in Sonora, California. It was called Campus Letter, about the goings-on at my high school. We worked at the kitchen counter, next to the just-washed dinner dishes. Weekly, I offered up my small sheaf of freshly-typed pages. Weekly, he dove in with his big black copy pencil. And the lessons began: lead sentence, writing tight, word choice, punctuation, checking facts. Usually these lessons were offered with humor and affection, but sometimes his impatience made me cry. For most of four years, we worked together Wednesday nights in the kitchen. I came to know myself as a writer and as his daughter—two qualities that define me to this day. Despite the tears, I learned the satisfaction of getting it right.

"Occidental College in Los Angeles was my next stop after high school. I changed my major so often that I ran out of spaces on the registration card. Eventually I defaulted to journalism, which necessitated a term at the University of Missouri Journalism School. A lucky twist of fate, as it would turn out. There I crossed paths with a tall, New Jersey–born broadcast student, John. We married in December 1972 and moved to Seattle a year or so after.

"Although I have always loved writing, I was waylaid for awhile by graphic design, which I did from our home while our children, Tim and Noelle, grew. During those years, some of our best times were spent piled in a big chair, lost in a book together. I first admitted I dreamed of being a children's book creator when I turned 40. I only told my closest family. My sister Nancy gave me Uri Shulevitz's *Writing with Pictures*, inscribed 'to help you with your dream.' Seven years later when I received two Golden Kite Awards for *Zelda and Ivy* from the Society of Children's Book Writers and Illustrators, Mr. Shulevitz was a fellow recipient.

Courtesy of John Kvasnosky

"My stories mostly come from my childhood. As the middle of five kids, I'm sitting on a mother lode of material. For instance, my insider's view of sibling rivalry has come in handy when inventing stories for the fox sisters, Zelda and Ivy. The first Zelda and Ivy book is dedicated: 'To my sisters Susan, Nancy, and Kate and my brother Tim, with love from the favorite.'

"Albert Camus once said that the whole of a person's artistic expression is the attempt to recapture through art those two or three images in whose presence your soul first opened. For me, one of those times was sleeping out under the summer stars with my siblings. We kids, small and snug in our sleeping bags, the vast universe sparkling above us. You can see this scene in *Zelda and Ivy and the Boy Next Door*, where Zelda spots a shooting star. My Seattle house is in that painting, too. It turns out I live across the street from the fox sisters.

"In 2002, Dutton published my first novel, *One Lucky Summer*. After the concise discipline of picture books, it was exhilarating to get to use all those words. This story is based on the love/hate relationship I had growing up with my cousin Jerry. Like the characters in the book, Jerry and I nearly drowned in a Siamese Twins swim race in Twain Harte Lake.

"Last week at a school visit a second grader asked me how long I plan to keep making books. I told him I plan to keep making books as long as I can. Why would I stop? I get to do what I love. It's the world's best job."

✵　✵　✵

Born in Sacramento, Laura McGee Kvasnosky stayed in California for most of her college years, graduating with a B.A. in journalism from Occidental College in Los Angeles in 1973. She has continued to study in areas that she enjoys: design at the University of Washington, writing with Jane Yolen at Centrum in Port Townsend, Washington, and illustration with Keith Baker at Seattle's School of Visual Concepts.

Since entering the field of children's books, Kvasnosky has written and illustrated her own picture books as well as illustrating those of others. *A Red Wagon Year*, written by Kathi Appelt, was an American Booksellers Association Pick of the Lists in 1996. She draws on her own sibling experiences with a popular series of stories about the red fox sisters, Zelda and Ivy, in which she captures the gentle squabbling as well as the love and warmth that sisters share. The first in the series, *Zelda and Ivy*, was named a *Booklist* Editors' Choice and a Blue Ribbon Book of the *Bulletin of the Center for Children's Books* as well as an ALA Notable Children's Book and a *School Library Journal* Best Book. It was also named a Golden Kite Honor Book for both picture book writing and illustration by the Society of Children's Book Writers and Illustrators. In addition to their publication in the United States and Britain, Zelda and Ivy stories are also available in Denmark, where the sisters are called "Nina og Marie." Kvasnosky and her husband live in Seattle. She works in her studio, formerly the garage, and enjoys gardening and singing in her spare time. She often travels to visit schools and especially enjoys the stories she hears from kids and their parents when she is facilitating her workshop, entitled "Drawing on Family Stories."

Courtesy of Candlewick Press

SELECTED WORKS WRITTEN AND ILLUSTRATED: *Pink, Red, Blue, What Are You?* 1994; *One, Two, Three, Play with Me*, 1994; *See You Later, Alligator*, 1995; *Mr. Chips!*, 1996; *Zelda and Ivy*, 1998; *Zelda and Ivy and the Boy Next Door*, 1999; *Zelda and Ivy One Christmas*, 2000; *One Lucky Summer*, 2002; *Frank and Izzy Set Sail*, 2004.

SELECTED WORKS WRITTEN: *What Shall I Dream?*, illus. by Judith Byron Schachner, 1996.

SELECTED WORKS ILLUSTRATED: *There Once Was a Puffin*, by Florence Page Jacques, 1995; *A Red Wagon Year*, by Kathi Appelt, 1996; *If Somebody Lived Next Door*, by Libby Hough, 1997.

SUGGESTED READING: *Something About the Author*, vol. 93, 1997.

Courtesy of Judith Petrovich

Madeleine L'Engle

Madeleine L'Engle

November 29, 1918–

"I was born in New York City on the snowy night of November 29, 1918, and lived in New York for the next 12 years, with a jaunt or two to Europe. My father, Charles Wadsworth Camp, was a writer, and my mother, Madeleine Hall Barnett Camp, a pianist. The house was always full of artists of one kind or another. When I was 12 we moved to Europe, where we lived mostly in France and Switzerland, and I went to a Swiss boarding school. Then followed school in South Carolina and Smith College.

"After graduating from Smith in 1941, I took an apartment in Greenwich Village with three other girls, two of whom were aspiring actresses. Because I wanted to be a writer, I was the lucky one to get jobs in the theater. (I thought it an excellent school for writers, and it is.) When I was in Chekhov's *The Cherry Orchard* I met the actor Hugh Franklin, and I married him a year later when we were both in *The Joyous Season*. Our first child was born in 1947, and in 1952 he retired from the theater 'forever.'

"We had an old white farmhouse in northwestern Connecticut, and Hugh wanted to settle down, put down roots, and get away from the tensions of the city and the theater. In order to earn a living, we acquired a defunct general store. I must honestly admit that helping to build up a dead general store, participate in the life of a small but very active community, run a large old farmhouse, and raise three small children is the perfect way not to write a book. However, I did manage to write at night. I have written since I could hold a pencil, much less a pen, and writing is for me an essential function, like sleeping and breathing.

"The store was a smashing success, and then suddenly the fun and the challenge were gone. So we decided to move back to the quiet life of New York and the theater. There, too, we were drawn into civic and church affairs, but we found the life of the theater and New York infinitely more peaceful than that of a tiny village. There is nothing more exciting than seeing a magnolia burst into bloom in the middle of Broadway!

"We spent the next decades pursuing our crafts. Hugh was on *All My Children* for 14 years, and I continued to write and teach. I traveled a great deal, leading writers' workshops and retreats, speaking to school and church groups. I always loved coming home to New York where I could walk my dog to my office at the Library of the Cathedral of St. John the Divine. Summers are still spent in Connecticut.

"My husband died in 1983, and I miss him every day. My granddaughters lived with me while they were going to college, and they did a good job of bringing me up. Though I am no longer able to travel, my family is close by; all four of my great-grandchildren live in walking distance from me."

❋ ❋ ❋

Since the publication of *A Wrinkle in Time* and the Newbery Medal it received in 1963, Madeleine L'Engle has been a much-revered author of children's books. But the path to that lofty position was not easy. Her first published works were for the adult market, and after the initial success of *A Small Rain* in 1945, her second novel was not well received. She wrote two books for teen readers, *And Both Were Young* in 1949 and *Camilla Dickinson* in 1951, but for several years after that she found her stories and novels being rejected and decided to cover her typewriter for good. When she realized that she was working out a novel about failure in her head, she knew she had to write, even if she never published again.

L'Engle was born Madeleine L'Engle Camp, but dropped the last name when she published her first book. Until the age of 12 she lived on the Upper East Side in New York City and had a lonely childhood. An only child, whose parents were considerably older than her classmates', she attended a school where she felt bullied and unhappy, much as Meg does in *A Wrinkle in Time*. When her parents traveled to Europe they enrolled her in a Swiss boarding school. Returning to the United States when Madeleine was fifteen, the family moved to Jacksonville, Florida, the home of Mrs. Camp's family. Madeleine completed her high school years at a boarding school in Charleston, South Carolina, called Ashley Hall, where the teachers recognized her intelligence. She responded with delight to the literature and drama program and was elected class president. During her senior year, her father, whose health may have been compromised by service in World War I, died of pneumonia.

Graduating from Smith College in 1941, L'Engle returned to New York. She took some courses at the New School for Social Research during 1941–1942, performed in several plays, and published her first book. In January 1946 she married Hugh Franklin, an actor, and the following summer they bought an old farmhouse in the northwestern corner of Connecticut. Their daughter Josephine was born in 1947, and in 1950 the Franklins moved to Connecticut to live year-round. Soon after, their son Bion was born, and in 1956 they adopted a third child, Maria, whose parents, friends of the Franklins, had both died suddenly. After 10 years of country living, the family returned to New York City, where L'Engle has lived ever since.

In 1960, soon after her move back to New York, L'Engle published *Meet the Austins*, which was named an ALA Notable Children's Book. In this story of a family living in an old house in the

"I have written since I could hold a pencil, much less a pen, and writing is for me an essential function, like sleeping and breathing."

country, narrated by 12-year-old Vicky Austin, the family takes in a girl whose parents have died suddenly. Many children's books today deal with the subject of death, but in 1960 it was a taboo theme, which caused many publishers to shy away from the manuscript. According to May Hill Arbuthnot and Zena Sutherland, writing in *Children and Books*, this was the first time an author had explored the subject of death and handled it so well since Louisa May Alcott in *Little Women*, nearly 100 years earlier. L'Engle wrote many more stories about the Austin family during the next 40 years; the most widely known are *The Moon by Night*, *The Young Unicorns* (a *School Library Journal* Best Book), and *Ring of Endless Light* (an ALA Notable Book and a Newbery Honor Book.)

L'Engle's own children were her first audience for the book that continues to be her best-known and best-loved work, *A Wrinkle in Time*. Though it was rejected by publishers over 25 times as being too complicated for children, L'Engle knew the book had worth, and it was at last published by Farrar, Straus & Giroux in 1962, beginning L'Engle's long association with that publishing firm. In the story, Meg Murry, her younger brother Charles Wallace, and her friend Calvin O'Keefe embark on a harrowing interplanetary journey in search of Meg's physicist father. They are aided by three supernatural women—Mrs. Whatsit, Mrs. Who, and Mrs. Which—who take them traveling through time "wrinkles" called tesseracts to the planet Camazotz. An evil disembodied brain called It and a society that has relinquished all individual freedoms for security are the forces the children must fight against to rescue Dr. Murry and save themselves. Meg accomplishes the task by relying on her stubborn determination and the power of her love for her family. Combining elements of Einstein's relativity theory, quantum physics, mathematics, cosmology, adolescent psychology, and theology, the story is a challenging one. And it is a challenge that young readers for over 40 years have been eager to accept. Many have written to the author to tell her that the book changed their lives, and adults often continue to read it throughout their lives. In 2004 a made-for-TV movie adaptation aired on the ABC network, reflecting the enduring qualities of the characters, plot, and themes of the book.

In the sequel, *A Wind in the Door*, which appeared 10 years later, L'Engle intrigues her readers with the relativity of size when Meg and Calvin journey into the microcosm of the human body rather than the larger universe. *A Swiftly Tilting Planet*, which received a National Book Award, once again finds Charles Wallace traveling through time with the help of a unicorn named Gauditor. *Many Waters*, a story that features the youngest of the Murry children, twin brothers Sandy and Dennys, completes what has come to be called L'Engle's Time Fantasy Quartet. A second quartet involves the next generation, as Meg Murry and Calvin O'Keefe marry and have children, and the combination

> *"We found the life of the theater and New York infinitely more peaceful than that of a tiny village."*

of suspense, romance, science, and exotic locales in these titles—*The Arm of the Starfish*, *Dragons in the Waters*, *A House Like a Lotus*, and *An Acceptable Time*—have kept many readers engaged throughout their teens and beyond. A unique blend of science, religion, suspense, and fantasy, Madeleine L'Engle's books also allow fans to encounter familiar characters at various stages of their lives the way they might in a large extended family.

Over the years, Madeleine L'Engle has received many awards and much recognition for her writing. In 1978 she was awarded the University of Southern Mississippi Medallion and in 1984 the Catholic Library Association presented her with its Regina Medal. The Kerlan Award followed in 1990, and the Empire State Award from the New York Library Association came in 1991. For significant contributions to literature for young adults, she was presented the ALAN Award by the National Council of Teachers of English in 1986 and the American Library Association's Margaret A. Edwards Award in 1998. She has taught as a writer-in-residence at various colleges, including Wheaton College in Illinois, which holds a collection of her papers. In 1984 she was honored with the Sophia Smith Award for distinction in her chosen field by her alma mater, Smith College. In 1966 she took the position of librarian at the Cathedral of St. John the Divine near her home on the Upper West Side of Manhattan and still maintains an office in the Cathedral Library.

Courtesy of Farrar, Straus and Giroux

In addition to her children's books, L'Engle has also published novels, poetry, and nonfiction books that explore religious subjects and family relationships for adults. In 1997 a collection of her writings on a familial relationship, *Mothers and Daughters*, was published with vibrant photographs by her adopted daughter, Maria Rooney. *Mothers and Sons*, another collaborative book with Rooney, appeared in 1999. In 2001 readers saw a new dimension of her talent when she published her first picture book, *The Other Dog*, with illustrations by Christine Davenier. With a wry humor, the story explores the feelings of a poodle who is distressed by a new addition to the family—a "dog" that has yet to be housebroken (which is, in actuality, a new baby). A fresh approach to discussing sibling acceptance of a new child in the family, the story shows yet another aspect of L'Engle's perennial theme of family issues, including the animal characters that have often played minor roles in her novels.

Madeleine L'Engle's books have achieved popular acclaim as well as critical recognition. Both *Publishers Weekly* and *American Bookseller* have ranked her among the most popular children's authors in the country, and *A Wrinkle in Time* continues to be one of the best-selling children's books of all time. L'Engle's ability to connect with a reader's deepest longings and darkest fears, and to leave the reader with a sense of hope and optimism are perhaps her ongoing legacy to literature for young people.

SELECTED WORKS: *The Small Rain*, 1945, 1984; *And Both Were Young*, 1949; *Meet the Austins*, 1960; *A Wrinkle in Time*, 1962; *The Moon by Night*, 1963; *The Twenty-four Days Before Christmas: An Austin Family Story*, illus. by Inga, 1964; *The Arm of the Starfish*, 1965; *Camilla*, 1965; *Journey with Jonah* (a play), illus. by Leonard Everett Fisher, 1967; *The Young Unicorns*, 1968; *Lines Scribbled on an Envelope, and Other Poems*, 1969; *Dance in the Desert*, illus. by Symeon Shimin, 1969; *A Wind in the Door*, 1973; *The Risk of Birth*, 1974; *Everyday Prayers*, illus. by Lucile Butel, 1974; *Prayers for Sunday*, 1974; *Dragons in the Waters*, 1976; *A Swiftly Tilting Planet*, 1978; *The Weather of the Heart: Poems*, 1978; *Ladder of Angels: Scenes from the Bible*, illus. by Children of the World, 1979; *A Ring of Endless Light*, 1980; *The Anti-Muffins*, 1980; *The Sphinx at Dawn*, 1982; *A House Like a Lotus*, 1984; *Many Waters*, 1986; *A Cry Like a Bell*, 1987; *An Acceptable Time*, 1989; *The Glorious Impossible*, 1990; *Anytime Prayers*, 1994; *Troubling a Star*, 1994; *Wintersong: Christmas Readings*, with Luci Shaw, 1996; *Mothers and Daughters*, with Maria Rooney, 1997; *Miracle on 10th Street, and Other Christmas Writings*, 1998; *Mothers and Sons*, with Maria Rooney, 1999; *A Full House: An Austin Family Christmas*, 1999; *The Other Dog*, illus. by Christine Davenier, 2001.

Courtesy of Farrar, Straus and Giroux

SUGGESTED READING: Chase, Carole F., comp. *Madeleine L'Engle Herself: Refections on a Writing Life*, 2001; *Current Biography*, 1997; Colby, Vineta, ed. *World Authors, 1985–1990*, 1995; *Contemporary Literary Criticism*, vol. 12, 1980; *Dictionary of Literary Biography*, vol. 52, 1986; Gonzales, Doreen. *Madeleine L'Engle*, 1991; L'Engle, Madeleine. *A Circle of Quiet*, 1972; L'Engle, Madeleine. *Trailing Clouds of Glory: Spiritual Aspects in Children's Literature*, with Avery

Brooke, 1985; Shaw, Luci, ed. *The Swiftly Tilting Worlds of Madeleine L'Engle*, 1998; Townsend, John Rowe, *A Sense of Story: Essays on Contemporary Writing for Children*, 1971. Periodicals—L'Engle, Madeleine, "Newbery Acceptance Speech," *The Horn Book*, August 1963; Zarin, Cynthia, "The Storyteller: Fact, Fiction, and the Books of Madeleine L'Engle," *New Yorker*, April 12, 2004. Videos—*The World of Madeleine L'Engle*, 1998.

WEB SITE: *www.madeleinelengle.com*

An earlier profile of Madeleine L'Engle appeared in *More Junior Authors* (1963).

"The grandmother in my story *The Raft* is a merging of my mother and paternal grandmother. My mom is a kind, intelligent, practical, 'no whining, please' kind of woman. She has a strong optimistic nature, and she teaches more with example than lecture. When I was 10 or so, on a dare, I jumped off a neighbor's roof. As I hit the ground war-whooping, my knee slammed into my chin, and with my two buckteeth I bit a neat hole into my tongue. I ran home wailing, tongue hanging like a dog, blood running down my neck and chest. My mom calmly looked me over and said, 'We'll put some ice on it, and for crying out loud, stop jumping off garages.'

"My grandmother had been a Depression-era mother. She knew hard work and what has been referred to as comfort foods: pot roasts, homemade soups, breads, pies, and, of course, pan-fried fish. She taught herself pastel drawing and seemed to be a natural impressionist. My grandpa framed her art in the basement woodshop. I have one of her drawings hanging on my dining room wall. It's a soft, warm scene of a pine-lined dirt road on a summer evening. It looks as fresh and alive as if it had been drawn yesterday.

"My grandparents had a cottage on an isolated lake in northern Wisconsin. Like the boy in *The Raft*, I spent a part of each summer 'up north' at the cabin. There was no plumbing, television, or neighbors except for the occasional bear. We spent our days fishing, swimming, picking berries, and playing a game my older brother invented. I'd row out on the lake just a couple of feet further than my brother could throw a stone from shore. As I rowed back and forth John would hurl golf ball–sized rocks at me. He improved his baseball talents and I learned how to quickly maneuver a rowboat.

Courtesy of Jim LaMarche

Jim LaMarche

November 25, 1952–

"In spite of the Cuban missile crisis and a cold war it was a simpler and freer time to be a child. I lived in a small town, went to a small Catholic school, and skated and swam on the river that ran through town. We pretty much had the run of the place. We could go anywhere our legs, bikes, or skates could take us. Disputes were quickly settled with wrestling matches or the occasional punch in the nose, and then forgotten. It was too small a town to have much of a class system.

"My dad taught biology at the high school. He was more of an ecologist than a frog-splitter. The time we spent fishing or hiking with my dad was always a lesson in plant identification or our local glacial history. By nature or nurture I've always been in love with the flora and fauna of the natural world, which I'm sure is evident in the stories I choose to create. I like small quiet stories with quiet magical moments.

"When my sons were young I bought them two battery-operated metal detectors for Christmas. A couple of days later at breakfast I read to them, out of the morning paper, a story about a lost Spanish treasure presumed to be scattered in the hills just outside of town. Of course they insisted we immediately go out with the metal detectors and hunt for the treasure. Sure enough, in a short while each boy had found a bag of rare Spanish coins, which coincidentally looked an awful lot like the coins my mother-in-law had brought back from Europe. Many years had passed since then and the metal detectors sat in the back of the boys' closet, forgotten. I found them one day recently and asked my college boys if they remembered the time I had hidden the Spanish treasure for them. 'That was you?' My jaded and slightly cynical sons were shocked. Up until that moment their memory of the hunt had been real. They had never questioned how they had been able to find a lost treasure so quickly. Of course I'm sorry now that I told them about the set-up; I should have let the memory stay that way, touched by magic.

"That is the gift of creating children's books, both words and illustration. We share stories of goodness and kindness and magic. And we hope that the core of those stories and ideals stays with our readers. I'm lucky to be a part of that."

> "That is the gift of creating children's books, both words and illustration. We share stories of goodness and kindness and magic. And we hope that the core of those stories and ideals stays with our readers. I'm lucky to be a part of that."

✤ ✤ ✤

Jim LaMarche grew up in Kewaskum, Wisconsin, a place that he has described as a "Norman Rockwell kind of town." The landscape of his childhood—rivers, lakes, and birch trees—is present in many of his books and takes center stage in the semi-autobiographical picture book he both wrote and illustrated, *The Raft*. Jim attended the University of Wisconsin, where he was a fine arts major, graduating in 1974. He met his wife when they were both VISTA volunteers at an American Indian school in Bismarck, North Dakota. He began his art career by doing illustration work for advertisements but was soon creating portraits and then book illustrations. In 1992 his illustrations for *The*

Rainbabies, written by Laura Krauss Melmed, won the international Bologna Book Fair Picture Book Award. This gentle story of a couple who long for a child was brought to life by LaMarche's illustrations, which are suffused with light and perfectly capture the tone of the writing.

Parental love is also the theme of a second collaboration between LaMarche and Melmed. *Little Oh* tells the story of an origami doll who belongs to a lonely Japanese woman. LaMarche's evocative paintings create strong characterizations set in a richly realized Japanese culture. This gentle fantasy tale was named an ALA Notable Children's Book and a Notable Trade Book in the Field of Social Studies. For *Carousel*, Liz Rosenberg's story of a magical merry-go-round, LaMarche made lustrous nighttime illustrations that enhance the mystical atmosphere of the story. Based on an actual restored carousel in upstate New York, this book was an American Booksellers Association Pick of the Lists, a *New Yorker* Notable Book, a *Parents Magazine* Best Book, and a *Reading Rainbow* Review Book. For *The Raft*, the first book in which he created the text as well as the illustrations, Jim LaMarche turned to his own memories of boyhood adventures in the natural world while paying tribute to the adults in his life, who encouraged him to pursue artistic expression. *The Raft* was a *School Library Journal* Best Book of the Year and won the Irma Simonton Black and James H. Black Award from the Bank Street College of Education.

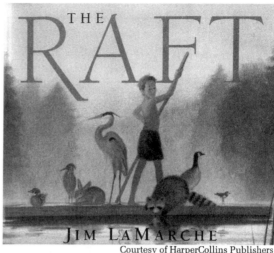

Courtesy of HarperCollins Publishers

Jim LaMarche's style is a unique blend of watercolor, acrylics, and colored pencil that lends a luminous quality to each of his books. Known for his deeply felt natural scenes and evocative characterizations, he has chosen stories to illustrate that often have a touch of mystery or fantasy. His own adaptation of the Grimm Brothers tale *The Elves and the Shoemaker*, named an IRA/CBC Children's Choice, is a fine example of how he excels at placing fantasy tales within a realistic, yet classical setting. For *Albert*, Donna Jo Napoli's quirky story of a city apartment dweller who sticks his hand out the window and unintentionally supplies the support for a cardinal's nest, Jim's colored pencil drawings bring a bit of magic into everyday life, and brought *Albert* recognition as one of the *New York Times* Best Illustrated Books of the Year in 2001. Jim and his wife have three boys: Mario and Jean-Paul are college age, and Dominic is in high school. They make their home in Santa Cruz, California.

SELECTED WORKS WRITTEN AND ILLUSTRATED: *The Raft*, 2000; *The Elves and the Shoemaker*, retold from the Brothers Grimm, 2003.

SELECTED WORKS ILLUSTRATED: *My Daddy Won't Go to Work*, by Madeena Spray Nolan, 1978; *Two Places to Sleep*, by Joan Schuchman, 1979; *My Minnie Is a Jewel*, by Tricia Springstubb, 1980; *A Matter of Pride*, by Emily Crofford, 1981; *Mandy*, by Barbara D. Booth, 1991; *The Rainbabies*, by Laura Krauss Melmed, 1992; *The Walloping Window-Blind*, by Charles E. Carryl, 1994; *The Carousel*, by Liz Rosenberg, 1995; *Grandmother's Pigeon*, by Louise Erdrich, 1996; *Little Oh*, by Laura Krauss Melmed, 1997; *Albert*, by Donna Jo Napoli, 2001; *A Story for Bear*, by Dennis Haseley, 2002; *Old Town in the Green Groves*, by Cynthia Rylant, 2002.

SUGGESTED READING: Lodge, Sally, "All the Pretty Horses: Old-Fashioned Carousels in Upstate New York Inspire a New Picture Book," *Publishers Weekly*, October 23, 1995.

Courtesy of Yun Soon Jeon

Laurie Lawlor

April 4, 1953–

"In early grade school I realized that the only way I'd ever get some peace and quiet was to tell terrifying stories to my five noisy younger brothers and sisters. In this way I achieved a miracle. If my tales worked, there would be places in our house that my brothers and sisters dared not go. One particularly horrible creature, named Evil Peter Pan, secretly lurked in the vent of our attic ceiling fan. I told so many stories about Evil Pan that no one dared go up into the dim, dusty third floor. Voilà! This out-of-the-way spot became my refuge— the place I could read Trixie Belden and Dana Girl mysteries and nobody would bother me.

"Telling stories that are so convincing that people think they are true provided me with a real sense of power. I began practicing these skills on not only my brothers and sisters but also other unsuspecting neighborhood children. One of the most gullible kids on the block was Greggy. Poor Greggy! Whenever he got scared, his mouth made a perfect O-shape and he howled like a dog. One day I dragged a big stick into our back yard. I managed to tip it upright and lower it into a hole, which I stamped around with my foot. There it was. A perfect tree.

"Greggy watched me from the back porch. He walked a little closer and asked me what I was doing. And I didn't say anything. I just kept stamping the dirt around the tree with my foot and looking up at the sky. 'Whatcha doin'?' he yelled. And still I didn't answer. So finally, he climbed over our chain link fence and got his pants caught only three times. 'Whatcha doin'?' he asked, his voice nervous and warbly now.

"I couldn't help myself. 'You know the story about Jack and the Beanstalk?' I asked. Of course he knew that story. 'Well,' I said, 'there's a giant up there in the sky and he's going to come down this tree and eat the first little boy he sees.' That was enough for Greggy. His mouth made a perfect O-shape and he howled like a dog. His howling gave me a very satisfying feeling. This was the second indication that I would one day become a writer.

"I wrote poetry all through grade school and my best friend drew the pictures. We stapled pieces of paper together and shared these books with our friends. We made plays in our garage using stories we invented or stole. I continued writing poetry throughout high school and college, worked on the newspaper in high school and majored in journalism in college. In 1977 I started writing for children while still doing freelance writing and editing for Chicago magazines and newspapers. I sold my first book, *Addie Across the Prairie*, in 1984. My son and daughter, who are grown now, provided me with many ideas and insights when they were young. In fact, they used to warn their friends when they came to our house, 'Don't talk too much in front of Mom. She might put you in her book.'

"I think that all of us have some special gift. Some of us know how to howl like a dog. Some of us tell scary stories. Some of us have the ability to create spellbinding jokes or blinding true pieces of art. Others can understand the feelings and bring out the best in other human beings in spite of incredible odds. Stubbornness—the stamina and ability not to give up, the energy to keep going no matter what—is what all writers need. It is the one absolutely necessary resource to keep a talent alive and well and to keep growing throughout life. Creating convincing characters and exciting adventures for children remains for me the ultimate challenge of imagination and craft. Young readers are the most demanding, vigilant, astonishing, and rewarding readers of all."

"Stubbornness— the stamina and ability not to give up, the energy to keep going no matter what—is what all writers need."

✿ ✿ ✿

Born in Oak Park, Illinois, Laurie Lawlor was raised in La-Grange, where she lived until she went to Northwestern University. The family spent their summers in a small mountain town in Colorado where Laurie's father directed a summer stock repertory theater company that was run by her mother. She worked on her high school newspaper before attending the Medill School of journalism at Northwestern and earned her B.S. degree in journalism in 1975. Lawlor worked for many years as a freelance writer and editor, but today she spends her time writing fiction and nonfiction for children and young adults and as an artist-in-residence teaching writing workshops to elementary and junior high students throughout the country. For the past several years she has taught writing workshops at National-Louis University, where she earned an M.A. in teaching in 1992. She also teaches at Columbia College, where she won the 2000–2001 Excellence in Teaching Award.

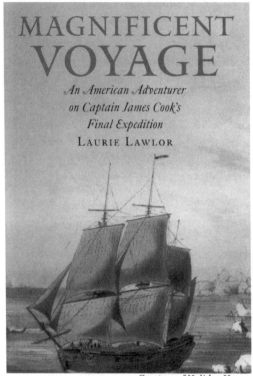

MAGNIFICENT
VOYAGE
*An American Adventurer
on Captain James Cook's
Final Expedition*
LAURIE LAWLOR

Courtesy of Holiday House

Lawlor's grandmother was a compelling storyteller and told about her grandparents who traveled by covered wagon from Iowa to the wilds of the Dakota Territory in the 1880s. The story was so interesting that Laurie researched tape-recorded interviews from the 1960s with people who had pioneered as children in South Dakota. *Addie Across the Prairie*, her first published book, was the result. It was the first of a popular series that also includes *Addie's Dakota Winter*, *Addie's Long Summer*, and *George on His Own*.

Lawlor's love of research led her to the investigation of other people's stories, the stories of extraordinary individuals such as frontiersmen Daniel Boone and John Chapman (Johnny Appleseed) and writer/activist Helen Keller. *Shadow Catcher: The Life and Work of Edward S. Curtis* earned a Golden Kite Honor Book award for nonfiction and was on ALA's list of Best Books for Young Adults. *Helen Keller: Rebellious Spirit* was a *School Library Journal* Best Book, and *Daniel Boone* was a *Booklist* Editors' Choice. *Shadow Catcher: The Life and Work of Edward S. Curtis* and *Where Will This Shoe Take You?: A Walk Through the History of Footwear* were both named Notable Children's Trade Books in the Field of Social Studies; *Helen Keller: Rebellious Spirit* achieved the same distinction as a Notable Social Studies Trade Book for Young People.

Laurie Lawlor lives with her husband, her two large Labrador retrievers, and a parakeet in Evanston, Illinois. Her son is finishing college and her daughter is now a teacher. Lawlor enjoys reading, swimming, and traveling to do research for her books, as well as writing fiction and nonfiction for young readers.

SELECTED WORKS: *Addie Across the Prairie*, illus. by Gail Owens, 1986; *How to Survive Third Grade*, illus. by Joyce Audy Zarins, 1988; *Daniel Boone*, illus. by Bert Dodson, 1989; *Addie's Dakota Winter*, illus. by Toby Gowing, 1989; *Second-Grade Dog*, illus. by Gioia Flammenghi, 1990; *Addie's Long Summer*, illus. by Toby Gowing, 1992; *George on His Own*, illus. by Toby Gowing, 1993; *Shadow Catcher: The Life and Work of Edward S. Curtis*, 1994; *Gold in the Hills*, 1995; *The Real Johnny Appleseed*, illus. by Mary Thompson, 1995; *Where Will This Shoe Take You?: A Walk Through the History of Footwear*, 1996; *Addie's Forever Friend*, illus. by Helen Cogancherry, 1997; *Biggest Pest on Eighth Avenue*, 1997; *The Worst Kid Who Ever Lived on Eighth Avenue*, illus. by Cynthia Fisher, 1998; *West Along the Wagon Road: 1852*, 1998; *Titanic Journey Across the Sea: 1912*, 1998; *Window on the West: The Frontier Photography of William Henry Jackson*, 1999; *Voyage to a Free Land: 1630*, 1999; *Wind on the River*, 2000; *Helen Keller: Rebellious Spirit*, 2001; *Old Crump: The True Story of a Trip West*, illus. by John Winch, 2002; *Magnificent Voyage: An American Adventurer on Captain James Cook's Final Expedition*, 2002; *The School at Crooked Creek*, illus. by Ron Himler, 2004.

SUGGESTED READING: *Something About the Author*, vol. 80, 1995. Periodicals—Kurtz, Jane, "Author's Stories Draw on Her Family's History," *Grand Forks Herald* (North Dakota), May 3, 1992.

"I grew up surrounded by books. My father had hundreds of them, and read them all. There were encyclopedias, an ancient Koran, the journals of Scott, and the poems of Omar Khayyám. Every night he read us a story. We were always encouraged to take them from the shelves, and long before we started school, my older brother and I spent our days among books. We learned that there was nothing like a set of encyclopedias for building little forts and castles.

"Every few months we packed them up and moved along to somewhere else. My father, always looking for a better job, took us back and forth across Canada. We moved so often that by the time I finished Grade 7 I'd been to eight different schools. I had never had a friendship that had lasted more than a year. For much of the time, I hadn't had a friend at all. But our family was very close. We played board games in the evenings and went for long, rambling trips on the weekends, in old cars that seemed to be forever breaking down. From a home in Calgary we traveled through Montana, through Saskatchewan, or westward to the coast. We hiked the Rockies, hunted dinosaur bones in the Badlands, and explored a wartime bomber abandoned in a field. From Toronto we went north to the forests, east to Maine, out to the edge of the continent at the tip of Nova Scotia.

"There was always a big canvas tent in the back of the car and some sort of boat on the roof. At first it was just a plastic one, like a little floating wading pool, that almost drowned me in a river on the prairies. Later it was a sailing dinghy that I bought

Courtesy of Donald Lawrence

Iain Lawrence

February 25, 1955–

at 16, with money from my first summer job. We sailed that boat in two oceans and two of the Great Lakes, before Muffin the cat scratched a hole right through its hull of pressed foam.

"My Grade 3 teacher predicted that I would be a writer. But the idea didn't occur to me until my last years of high school, when journalism began to appeal to me. My father introduced me to Richard Needham, a columnist with the *Toronto Star*, and I went to see him in an office that shuddered with teletype machines. He told me that to be a writer I should drive taxis or dig ditches, but not write for newspapers. I took his advice for a while, working at odd and sporadic jobs while churning out short stories that met with no success. Then I studied journalism in Vancouver and spent the next 10 years as a reporter and editor on small newspapers in northern British Columbia. In the port city of Prince Rupert, at the *Daily News*, I began sailing again and bought another boat. For the first time in a decade, I took up fiction writing, and joined a writers' group. There I met Kristin Miller, who was working on a book about quilting. A fish-farmer, she lived in a little seaside cabin with no electricity or running water. I loved her outdoor lifestyle and her community of boating friends and soon moved into her cabin. I quit my newspaper job to work at the fish farm. When it went bankrupt two years later, we were living on 'the hill,' caretaking a remote radio-transmitter site on a nearby island.

Courtesy of Delacorte Press

"With no rent and few bills to pay, we lived very cheaply for 10 months of the year and went sailing in the summers, up and down the northern coast in my little wooden boat. I wrote two books about our voyages and started writing novels. Kristin finished her book and sold it through an agent, Jane Jordan Browne of Multimedia Product Development. At Kristin's encouragement, I sent my novels to Jane, who took an immediate interest. But it was a dozen novels later before I went back to one of my first ones, a tale for boys about storms and ship-wreckers. Jane sold the new version quickly, and since then I've written nothing but novels for children and have no interest in doing anything else.

"I write every day, with the habit learned from journalism. From morning to afternoon I feel as though I become a child again, telling myself the same sorts of stories that my father read to me at bedtime. I have the same eagerness now to see how they all turn out. And in my writing I see constant echoes of my childhood. I write about lonely boys who try very hard to please their parents, and especially their fathers."

✻ ✻ ✻

Iain Lawrence's exciting adventure stories in the High Seas Trilogy—*The Wreckers*, *The Smugglers*, and *The Buccaneers*—made an immediate impact on readers and critics alike. Characterized by fast-paced action and enigmatic characters that keep the reader guessing which ones are the villains and which the heroes, these volumes follow the fortunes of young John Spencer on sea and land. *The Wreckers* and *The Smugglers* were both named ALA Best Books for Young Adults, Quick Picks for Young Adults, and Blue Ribbon titles by the *Bulletin of the Center for Children's Books*. They were also included on New York Public Library's Books for the Teen Age. In Lawrence's native Canada, *The Wreckers* won the Geoffrey Bilson Award for historical fiction. As much a mystery as a high adventure tale, it was nominated for an Edgar Allen Poe award. This atmospheric story of Cornish villagers luring sailing ships onto the rocks so as to pillage their contents is based on solid historical research and written to create the same thrill of adventure that Lawrence felt as a boy when reading *Treasure Island* and similar books.

In *Ghost Boy*, the author explores the feelings of an outsider, a small-town Midwestern boy who is teased beyond endurance for his albino coloring. Joining a traveling circus, he learns much about acceptance and understanding while the show journeys to Oregon. Strong character development, theme, and setting characterize this novel, which was named a Notable Children's Book and a Best Book for Young Adults by the American Library Association, and a Best Book by *School Library Journal*. *Lord of the Nutcracker Men*, included on the New York Public Library's list, 100 Titles for Reading and Sharing, as well as *Publishers Weekly*'s Best Books of the Year list, expands the theme of intolerance to a global scale when a British toymaker goes off to World War I leaving his son with a set of carved wooden soldiers. Sent away from London for safety, the lonely boy plays with the soldiers and each new one his father sends with his letters. But the letters change in tone as the father encounters the true horrors of war, and the boy wonders what powers he unleashes with his toy soldiers' mock battles.

Returning to the theme of the sea, *The Lightkeeper's Daughter* is a haunting contemporary story set on a fictional island but based on one that Lawrence knows well from his sailing off the coast of British Columbia. Family secrets, love, and blame all intertwine in this taut psychological drama about the loneliness and loveliness in the lives of a lighthouse keeper and his family. *The Lightkeeper's Daughter* had the distinction of being named one of the Top Ten on ALA's Best Books for Young Adults list in 2003.

Iain Lawrence lives today on Gabriola Island, near Vancouver Island, British Columbia, with his partner Kristin, a dog and a cat, and a sailboat in the dock.

SELECTED WORKS FOR YOUNG READERS: *The Wreckers*, 1998; *The Smugglers*, 1999; *Ghost Boy*, 2000; *The Buccaneers*, 2001; *Lord of the Nutcracker Men*, 2001; *The Lightkeeper's Daughter*, 2002; *B Is for Buster*, 2004.

SELECTED WORKS FOR ADULTS: *Sea Stories of the Inside Passage: In the Wake of the* Nid, 1997.

SUGGESTED READING: *Something About the Author*, vol. 135, 2002. Periodicals—Hulick, Jeannette, "Rising Star: Iain Lawrence," *Bulletin of the Center for Children's Books*, December 1, 2001.

Courtesy of Marian Wood Kolisch

Ursula K. Le Guin

Ursula K. Le Guin

(luh GWIN)

October 21, 1929–

"I had a good childhood. My parents were loving, kind, intelligent, lively people. I had a great-aunt who was an extra mother to me, and three beautiful older brothers. And everybody in the family was glad I was a girl, which makes it a lot easier to be glad to be a woman when you get there.

"My father was a university professor, so we didn't have as hard times as many people did during the Depression of the 1930s. We lived in Berkeley, California, in a redwood house on a hill, and spent summers on an old ranch in the hills of the Napa Valley. I went to public schools, where I got an excellent education. I was too shy to speak to anybody in school until fourth grade, and though I did finally make a few dear friends, school was social torture, and I was always glad to be home.

"If home was a refuge it was a lively one, with us four kids and lots of visitors, talk and argument and discussion about everything, endless books, music, games. My brothers and I were brought up to read and think and work and enjoy. My father wrote every day, and I grew up knowing writing as both an important thing and an ordinary thing—a life's work.

"During the Second World War my brothers went into the navy and air corps, and the summers in the Valley became lonely ones, with just me and my parents in the old house. There was no TV then; we turned on the radio once a day to get the war news. Those summers of solitude and silence, a teenager wandering the wild hills on my own, with no company, 'nothing to do,' were very important to me. I think I started making my soul then.

"And I read and wrote, and read and wrote.

"Unexpectedly (because my father taught for a year at Harvard and I could go for free), I went to Radcliffe College, where I got more excellent education and made new friends. I majored in French language and literature, so that I could teach; as my father had pointed out, very few writers make a living from their writing, and I'd better have a salable skill. Anyhow, I loved learning languages. And didn't want to be told what to read or write in my language. English was the instrument of my art, and I knew I had to find my own way of using it, in my own time, on my own terms. Although shy and unadventurous, I was stubborn as rock about some things, as I think any artist has to be.

"I fell in love several times in college; the last time was a real disaster. I went on to Columbia University for my graduate degree, and after two years there got a Fulbright scholarship to France. On board the *Queen Mary* I met a student from Georgia named Charles Le Guin. We got married in Paris, just before Christmas. All our friends went off to Spain that night and so we stayed put in Paris for our honeymoon. I recommend it highly.

"We lived first in Georgia while my husband got his doctorate, then in Idaho where our daughter Elisabeth was born. Then we moved to Portland, Oregon, where Charles taught at Portland State College, and Caroline and Theodore were born, and we bought the house where we have now lived for over 40 years.

"I wrote poetry and stories all the way through college, and began to find my own voice as a writer, particularly after I began setting stories in the imaginary country of Orsinia. I passionately love California where I grew up and Oregon where I have lived so long, and I have written about them; but mostly, in order to tell a story, I have to invent (find) the place, just as I invent (find) the characters. So I came to Orsinia, and later to Earthsea, and Gethen, and other worlds of my mind.

"I began my first novel the summer after college and wrote four more novels that were refused by publishers (one, *Malafrena*, was revised and published much later; the others will not be). I did have a fair number of poems printed in magazines, but though I also submitted my fiction regularly, it was about 10 years before I had a short story accepted—an Orsinian tale named for a Schubert song, 'And Die Musik.' That was the crack in the ice. From then on I was able to sell most of what I wrote.

"Most of my fiction has been published as science fiction and fantasy because that field of literature was far more open to invention and innovation than 'literary' (realistic) fiction was. Later on I got the courage to write for children (it can be scary—children are tough readers). And I continue to write poetry.

"When the children were little I wrote at night, but morning is the best time. I usually start with a notebook and a pen, and then begin revising or composing directly on a keyboard—a 1957 Underwood typewriter for years, now a bright orange iBook.

"Writing is what I do best. Fortunately it's also what I like best to do. What luck!"

"I passionately love California where I grew up and Oregon where I have lived so long, and I have written about them; but mostly, in order to tell a story, I have to invent (find) the place, just as I invent (find) the characters."

✿　✿　✿

Considered one of America's finest writers of fantasy and science fiction, Ursula K. Le Guin continues to astonish her readers with the beauty of her prose, the strength of her imaginative creations, and her willingness to break new ground. Praised by other well-known authors and literary critics for her work in many forms, Ursula Le Guin has written novels, short stories, poetry, screenplays, essays, young children's books, books for young adults, verbal texts for musicians, and voicetexts for performance or recording. Her celebrated Earthsea books have been translated into 16 languages, and the three earlier titles—*A Wizard of Earthsea*, *The Tombs of Atuan*, and *The Farthest Shore*—have now been continuously in print for over 30 years.

Born in Berkeley, California, Le Guin is the daughter of the anthropologist Alfred Kroeber and the writer Theodora Kroeber, author of *Ishi in Two Worlds*. In a home filled with visiting scientists, writers, students, and California Indians, she grew up with talk about different cultures and issues all around her. And stories. Her father translated stories he'd heard from Indians in their native languages. Her mother shared the many collections of myths and legends she'd gathered. Le Guin read widely in Celtic and Teutonic lore, explored Sir James Frazer's *The Golden Bough*, and discovered the writer Lord Dunsany and his original fantasies. Dunsany's books showed Le Guin that adult authors actually wrote fantasies for adults and had a profound influence, as did stories by Hans Christian Andersen, Padraic Colum, and, later, J. R. R. Tolkien. She began writing poetry at the age of five and her first story at the age of nine. She and her next-in-age brother bought copies of the magazine *Astounding Stories* to feed their taste for science fiction. After high school, Le Guin attended Radcliffe College, where she majored in French. She received her A.B., magna cum laude, and joined Phi Beta Kappa in 1951. She went on to study Romance languages at Columbia University, earning a master's degree in 1953. Just after starting work on a Ph.D. in French and Italian renaissance literature at Columbia University, Le Guin received a Fulbright fellowship to France. Returning to the United States with her new husband, she worked on her writing while raising her family, and had published several adult novels before she tried writing for young people.

In 1968 she published her first book intended for young readers, *A Wizard of Earthsea*. A fantasy as well as a coming-of-age story, the plot follows the adventures of Ged, a bright, talented boy with a gift for wizardry, who must learn how to make responsible use of the magic powers he possesses. Though he meets an evil sorceress and a dragon, the greatest darkness he faces at last is the shadow he himself brought into the world. The theme of responsibility, of actions and consequences and gathering self-knowledge, is at the heart of many of Le Guin's novels but never, perhaps, as clearly delineated as in *A Wizard of Earthsea*. Winner of the 1968 *Boston Globe–Horn Book* Award and designated

> *"Writing is what I do best. Fortunately it's also what I like best to do. What luck!"*

an ALA Notable Children's Book, as well being named to numerous "best" lists, it is included in Anita Silvey's *100 Best Books for Children* and has won its place as a modern classic in children's and young adult literature.

Le Guin's second book in the Earthsea series, *The Tombs of Atuan*, continues the adventures of Ged and introduces the girl priestess Arha, who has lost her real name and serves an insatiable god. Ged discovers her name, Tenar, since the secret of true naming is the basis of a wizard's power, and together they bring out of the Tombs a treasure that may allow the return of a great king. *The Tombs of Atuan* celebrates the capacity of a young woman, no matter how indoctrinated by the beliefs of a strange cult, to grow into an individual, able to make her own decisions and gain the courage to choose a new way of life. It won a 1972 Newbery Honor Book Award, was named an ALA Notable Children's Book, and was a finalist for the American Book Award for Children's Literature. In the third book of the series, *The Farthest Shore*, Ged is Arch-

Ursula K. Le Guin

CATWINGS

Illustrations by
S. D. SCHINDLER

Courtesy of Scholastic Press

mage, powerful and wise, and challenged to find out what is threatening the very roots of wizardry. He journeys with young Arren, a prince, to find the source of the evil spreading through the islands and, in a final test of power and sacrifice, gives up his own magic for the sake of the future of Earthsea. It is a high price but with it comes the return of wholeness to his world and the long-awaited king. Winner of the National Book Award for Children's Literature, *The Farthest Shore* completed the Earthsea story at that time. The hero Ged grew into manhood and personal responsibility with an understanding of the requirements of relationships; he was able, finally, to face his own mortality and death. Filled with satisfying adventure and permeated by themes of balance, the power of language, the need for a continual re-examination of the nature of human beings and how they use power, the trilogy combines concepts from Jung and the Tao, from European hero tales and Native American legends. Le Guin's capacity to build a fully realized fantasy world, rich with a sense of languages, nature, myths, and history, is often compared to that of J. R. R. Tolkien or C. S. Lewis.

But that wasn't the end of the Earthsea books. Le Guin continued to grow in her own understanding of herself, especially in the light of the nascent feminism of the 1960s and '70s. Though it took some years for her to develop and then integrate her changing viewpoint, she began to reconsider the nature of gender and of power. She began to "re-vision" Earthsea, considering what would bring true equilibrium and how women's wisdom might be essential to the future of that world. In *Tehanu*, published 18 years after *The Farthest Shore*, events are seen through the eyes of Tenar, heroine of *The Tombs of Atuan*. A widow now, living on a small farm, Tenar rescues a badly abused child, Therru, and tries to nurture her. Soon after, Ged comes to Tenar as well, exhausted and without his magical powers. Together they help to heal Therru, who assumes her true name, Tehanu, and in turn rescues them with her capacity to call dragons. *The Other Wind* extends the story further into a new tale of Tenar and Tehanu and their attempt to both save Earthsea and free the spirits of the dead from the Dry Land. Here, Le Guin re-visions the world of the dead seen in *The Farthest Shore* and shows the destiny of dragons. In *Tales from Earthsea* Le Guin collected short stories from various eras of her fully realized world, filling in gaps in chronology between the novels and supplementing the historical background.

Courtesy of Atheneum Books for Young Readers

Ursula Le Guin was one of the first women to successfully enter the world of adult science fiction. Her groundbreaking *The Left Hand of Darkness* won the Nebula Award and the Hugo Award for science fiction writing in 1969. Since this recognition came during the time her *A Wizard of Earthsea* was receiving accolades and garnering many enthusiastic readers, Le Guin was highly praised for her capacity to write both extraordinary fantasy and award-winning science fiction. Her novels *The Dispossessed* and *Always Coming Home* followed soon after, illuminating her highly original exploration of the nature of utopias. Among the many awards she has won are finalist for the Pulitzer Prize, five Hugo Awards, five Nebula Awards, the PEN/Malamud Award for Short Fiction, and lifetime achievement awards from the *Los Angeles Times* and the Pacific Northwest Booksellers Association. She has been designated a Grand Master by the Science Fiction and Fantasy Writers of America. In 2004 she delivered the May Hill Arbuthnot Honor Lecture for the American Library Association, in a program held at Arizona State University, and she was the recipient of the Margaret A. Edwards Award administered by *School Library Journal* and the Young Adult Library Services Association, a division of the American Library Association. In awarding this honor for lifetime service to literature for young adults, the committee said of Le Guin: "A fantasy writer and social activist since her youth, she has inspired four generations of young adults to read beautifully constructed language, visit fantasy worlds that inform them about their own lives, and think about ideas that are neither easy nor inconsequential."

Though best known for her other-worldly works, LeGuin has also published a realistic young adult novel, *Very Far Away from Anywhere Else*, a sensitive study of a boy and a girl who are confused by the impact of sexuality and peer pressure on their friendship and must find their own ways of understanding how to be individuals and true to themselves. At the earlier end of the age spectrum, Le Guin has published several picture book stories and turned to animal fantasy in a series of short novels for young children. *Catwings* is a gentle tale about a litter of kittens born with wings who must venture from their original environment on a search for safety and love. The adventures continue in *Catwings Return*, and more characters appear in *Wonderful Alexander and the Catwings* and *Jane on Her Own*. Evocatively illustrated by S. D. Schindler, these stories are a fine introduction for young readers to the power of Le Guin's prose and her ability to create memorable characters and settings.

Ursula Le Guin lives today in Portland, Oregon, with her husband. She leads a private life, but is occasionally involved in political activities and maintains an ongoing connection to other writers, the public library, Oregon Literary Arts, and the Soapstone Foundation.

SELECTED WORKS FOR CHILDREN AND YOUNG ADULTS: *A Wizard of Earthsea*, 1968; *The Tombs of Atuan*, 1970; *The Farthest Shore*, 1972; *Very Far Away from Anywhere Else*, 1976; *Leese Webster*, illus. by James Brunsman, 1979; *Cobbler's Rune*, illus. by Alicia Austin, 1983; *Catwings*, illus. by S. D. Schindler, 1988; *Solomon Leviathan*, illus. by Alicia Austin, 1988; *A Visit from Dr. Katz*, illus. by A. Barrow, 1988; *Catwings Return*, illus. by S. D. Schindler, 1989; *Fire and Stone*, illus. by Laura Marshall, 1989; *Tehanu*, 1990; *Fish Soup*, illus. by P. Wynne, 1992; *A Ride on the Red Mare's Back*, illus. by Julie Downing, 1992; *Wonderful Alexander and the Catwings*, illus. by S. D. Schindler, 1994; *Jane on Her Own: A Catwings Tale*, illus. by S. D. Schindler, 1999; *Tales from Earthsea*, 2001; *The Other Wind*, 2001; *Tom Mouse*, illus. by Julie Downing, 2002.

SELECTED WORKS FOR ADULTS: *Rocannon's World*, 1966; *Planet of Exile*, 1966; *City of Illusion*, 1967; *The Left Hand of Darkness*, 1969; *The Lathe of Heaven*, 1972; *The Dispossessed: An Ambiguous Utopia*, 1974; *The Ones Who Walk Away from Omelas*, 1976; *The Wind's Twelve Quarters*, 1976; *The Word for World Is Forest*, 1976; *Orsinian Tales*, 1977; *Malafrena*, 1979; *The Beginning Place*, 1980; *The Compass Rose*, 1982; *The Eye of the Heron*, 1983; *Always Coming Home*, 1985; *Buffalo Gals*, 1988; *Searoad*, 1991; *A*

Fisherman of the Inland Sea, 1994; *The Telling*, 2000; *Gifts*, 2004; *The Wave in the Mind: Talks and Essays on the Writer, the Reader, and the Imagination*, 2004.

SUGGESTED READING: *American Writers for Children Since 1960: Fiction*, 1986; *Authors and Artists for Young Adults*, vol. 9, 1992; Bittner, James. *Approaches to the Fiction of Ursula K. Le Guin*, 1984; Bucknall, Barbara J. *Ursula K. Le Guin*, 1981; Cogell, Elizabeth Cummins. *Understanding Ursula K. Le Guin*, 1990; Cogell, Elizabeth Cummins. *Ursula K. Le Guin: A Primary and Secondary Bibliography*, 1983; *Contemporary Authors*, New Revision Series, vol. 52, 1996; *Contemporary Novelists*, 7th ed., 1994; Jones, Libby Falk, and Sarah Webster Goodwin. *Feminism, Utopia, and Narrative*, 1990; Keulen, Margarete. *Radical Imagination: Feminist Conceptions of the Future in Ursula Le Guin, Marge Piercy, and Sally Miller Gearhart*, 1991; Reginald, Robert, and George Edgar Slusser, eds. *Zephyr and Boreas: Winds of Change in the Fiction of Ursula K. Le Guin*, 1996; Reid, Suzanne Elizabeth. *Ursula K. Le Guin*, 1997; Rochelle, Warren G. *Communities of the Heart: The Rhetoric of Myth in the Fiction of Ursula K. Le Guin*, 2001; *St. James Guide to Science Fiction Writers*, 4th ed., 1996; Silvey, Anita, ed. *Children's Books and Their Creators*, 1995; Slusser, George Edgar. *Between Two Worlds: The Literary Dilemma of Ursula K. Le Guin*, 2nd ed., 1995; *Something About the Author*, vol. 149, 2004; *Twentieth-Century Children's Writers*, 1989; *Twentieth-Century Young Adult Writers*, 1994; Wakeman, John, ed. *World Authors 1970–1975*, 1980; White, Donna R. *Dancing with Dragons: Ursula K. Le Guin and the Critics*, 1998; *Writers for Young Adults*, 1995.

WEB SITE: *www.UrsulaKLeGuin.com*

An earlier profile of Ursula K. Le Guin appeared in *Fourth Book of Junior Authors* (1978).

Arnold Lobel

May 22, 1933–
December 4, 1987

The following autobiographical sketch was written by Arnold Lobel for the *Third Book of Junior Authors* (1972):

"Shortly after the wedding ceremony, my father and mother got on a train heading west to California. They had both grown up in Schenectady, New York, but my father had decided that his particular 'pot of gold' lay somewhere on the sunny shores of that far state. Of course, in the early 1930s, there were very few 'pots of gold' anywhere. Several years later, they arrived back in Schenectady and, along with their disappointment, they carried with them a screaming, red-faced, ill-tempered infant of six months. That was me!

"The house in which I grew up in Schenectady was large and ramshackle. The wide front lawn sloped down to a pleasant tree-lined street and, for the most part, my very early childhood was quite happy. Later, however, a series of illnesses kept me hospitalized for long periods of time. I can remember sitting on the sundeck of the hospital looking out at the school playground across the street and feeling isolated and separate from the children I saw playing there.

"With adolescence came improved health, as well as the knowledge that I wanted to be an artist. After high school, with this end in mind, I applied for admission and was accepted at Pratt Institute in Brooklyn. The sense of independence and the excitement of the Big City was a heady combination for a young man fresh from a quiet town in upstate New York. In settling down to my studies at Pratt, I discovered that book illustration was the special branch of art that intrigued me the most . . . .

"Most of the ideas for my books, I find, have not really come from observing my own children as much as from my own childhood. I find that the majority of my books have as their central characters 'child substitutes' rather than real children. My first book was *A Zoo for Mister Muster*, and the gentleman of the title would most certainly fit into that description. A portly and friendly little man with a passion for zoo animals and a general distrust of adult institutions, he has all the attributes of a child but moves through the story with the independence of an adult.

Courtesy of HarperCollins Publishers

"In *Giant John* we meet an enormous young man of unspecified age who, while being devoted to his mother in a manner with which children may identify, goes forth to achieve fame and some fortune through his own efforts and cleverness. Small Pig is a 'child' in every way but physical form. His momentary burst of independence brings him adventure and some misery, but in the end, he is a richer pig for it.

"I never like to use the same illustrative technique over and over, but rather to use a repertory of styles as they suit the mood of the manuscript. I cannot think of any work that could be more agreeable and fun than making books for children."

❈ ❈ ❈

During his distinguished career Arnold Lobel wrote and/or illustrated over 70 books for children, but he is best remembered for four simple, endearing stories about a frog and a toad who become friends. These gentle stories of friendship reflect Lobel's own persona and most certainly stem from his own childhood. *Frog and Toad Are Friends*, *Frog and Toad Together*, *Frog and Toad All Year*, and *Days with Frog and Toad* are considered classics because they exemplify acceptance and steadfastness within a child's familiar world.

Arnold Lobel's parents divorced when he was a baby, leaving him to be raised by his grandparents in Schenectady, New York. Ill health caused him to miss a year of school, and when he returned to third grade he felt excluded. But as a natural-born storyteller, he told and illustrated stories for his classmates, which helped him to recover physically and emotionally. His fascination with stories and illustration continued through high school and into college. He graduated from Pratt Institute in Brooklyn with a B.F.A. in 1955, and that same year he married Anita Kempler, a fellow student and textile designer.

Lobel began his art career in advertising, but the storyteller in him was beckoning. As he made the rounds of publishing houses, Susan Hirschman, an editor at Harper & Row, spotted a drawing of a cricket in his portfolio and asked if he could "do" salmon. His over-confident answer assured her he could (though he had never done so), and *Red Tag Comes Back* by Fred Phleger became his first published book, in 1961. It was the beginning of a long-standing relationship with the publishing house that is known today as HarperCollins. The first book he wrote as well as illustrated was *A Zoo for Mr. Muster*, published in 1962 and illustrated in just two colors because he didn't think the publisher would do full color for an unknown illustrator. *A Holiday for Mr. Muster* followed in 1963 along with *Prince Bertram the Bad* and *Giant John*, which he described as "cartoony" because he was influenced by watching his two young children as they watched television in the apartment when he was working.

> "Most of the ideas for my books, I find, have not really come from observing my own children as much as from my own childhood."

During this time he was accepting any manuscripts that came his way because the family needed income; when an editor called, he often didn't ask what the book was about. His breakaway title from the cartoonish stiffness of his early work was *Red Fox and His Canoe* by Nathaniel Benchley, and it was a step forward in finding his own style. It was also among the first of many "I Can Read" books for beginning readers, a series for which many of Lobel's best-loved titles were created.

Lobel considered 1970 as a watershed year for him because that is when he began to enjoy illustrating books and his style and feelings began to gel. From early on he was inspired by Beatrix Potter and Edward Lear, whom he referred to as his artistic mother and father, and the legacy of those revered writer/illustrators can be seen in *Frog and Toad Are Friends*, which was published that year. The stories had grown out of the summers that the family spent in Vermont, and it was the first time that Lobel was able to write about himself and childhood. The book won a Caldecott Honor Award, which was the first of many honors for his work.

The next year he received another Caldecott Honor Award for his evocative black-and-white illustrations for *Hildilid's Night*, by Cheli Durán Ryan. And the following year, *Frog and Toad To-*

gether received a Newbery Honor for distinguished writing, a rarity for an easy-reader picture book for young children. Lobel had clearly found his stride as both an author and illustrator, though he always felt less comfortable about his writing than his artwork. He wrote and polished his stories before illustrating them. Then he would often establish the mood by setting his cartoon animals in pastoral and Victorian settings through his artwork; dressing his animals in formal Victorian attire enabled him to portray human foibles humorously. The wonderful combination of warmth, humor, and sensitivity in his writing and drawing communicated the intrinsic values of friendship, compassion, and community. And those qualities are most evident in Lobel's Caldecott Award–winning book, *Fables*. This collection of moral tales depicts in a wonderfully witty way the proverbial sayings that are born out of human idiosyncrasies. Two morals from his tales in *Fables* perhaps best provide insight into the creative genius of Lobel: "Satisfaction will come to those who please themselves" (from "The Camel Dances"), and "Knowledge will not always take the place of simple observation" (from "The Elephant and His Son").

It seemed inevitable that at some point Lobel would team up with his wife, Anita, who was also creating children's books. The four titles on which they collaborated, with Arnold writing the text and Anita illustrating, were all very successful. *How the Rooster Saved the Day* was a *School Library Journal* Best Book; *Treeful of Pigs* was an ALA Notable Children's Book; *On Market Street* earned Anita a Caldecott Honor Award, and *The Rose in My Garden* received a *Boston Globe–Horn Book* Honor designation. Eventually, however, Arnold and Anita's careers and their lives took different paths, and the pair separated.

Over the years many accolades came to Arnold Lobel. Eleven of his titles were named to the *New York Times* Best Illustrated Books of the Year. *Frog and Toad Are Friends* was a National Book Award finalist. He received a Christopher Award twice, for *On the Day Peter Stuyvesant Sailed into Town* and for *Frog and Toad All Year*. In 1985 he was presented the University of Southern Mississippi's Silver Medallion for distinguished service to children's literature. It was a sad day for the world of children's books when Arnold Lobel died on December 4, 1987, at the age of 54. But the friends he created on paper will continue to touch the lives of children and adults alike. From the gentle Frog and Toad stories to the spooky, scary images in Jack Prelutsky's *Nightmares*, Lobel's puckish nature, sly sense of humor, and love for story imbued his charming characters with life, as they learn to observe and to please themselves, twin discoveries that are universal attributes of childhood.

SELECTED WORKS WRITTEN AND ILLUSTRATED: *A Zoo for Mr. Muster*, 1962; *A Holiday for Mr. Muster*, 1963; *Prince Bertram the Bad*, 1963; *Giant John*, 1964; *Martha the Movie Mouse*, 1966; *Lucille*, 1964; *The Great Blueness and Other Predicaments*,

"I never like to use the same illustrative technique over and over, but rather to use a repertory of styles as they suit the mood of the manuscript. I cannot think of any work that could be more agreeable and fun than making books for children."

Courtesy of HarperCollins Children's Books

1968; *Small Pig*, 1969; *Frog and Toad Are Friends*, 1970; *The Ice-Cream Cone Coot and Other Rare Birds*, 1971; *On the Day Peter Stuyvesant Sailed into Town*, 1971; *Frog and Toad Together*, 1972; *Mouse Tales*, 1972; *The Man Who Took the Indoors Out*, 1974; *Frog and Toad All Year*, 1976; *Mouse Soup*, 1977; *Grasshopper on the Road*, 1978; *Days with Frog and Toad*, 1979; *Fables*, 1980; *Ming Lo Moves the Mountain*, 1982; *The Book of Pigericks: Pig Limericks*, 1983; *Whiskers and Rhymes*, 1985; *Owl at Home*, 1987; *Uncle Elephant*, 1987; *The Turnaround Wind*, 1988.

SELECTED WORKS ILLUSTRATED: *Red Tag Comes Back*, by Fred Phleger, 1961; *Terry and the Caterpillars*, by Millicent Selsam, 1962; *The Little Runner of the Longhouse*, by Betty Baker, 1962; *Greg's Microscope*, by Millicent Selsam, 1963; *The Secret Three*, by Mildred Myrick, 1963; *Red Fox and His Canoe*, by Nathaniel Benchley, 1964; *Let's Get Turtles*, by Millicent Selsam, 1965; *Someday*, by Charlotte Zolotow, 1964; *Oscar Otter*, by Nathaniel Benchley, 1966; *Benny's Animals and How He Put Them in Order*, by Millicent Selsam, 1966; *Let's Be Early Settlers with Daniel Boone*, by Peggy Parish, 1967; *The Microscope*, by Maxine Kumin, 1968; *Ants Are Fun*, by Mildred Myrick, 1968; *The Four Little Children Who Went Around the World*, by Edward Lear, 1968; *Sam the Minuteman*, by Nathaniel Benchley, 1969; *I'll Fix Anthony*, by Judith Viorst, 1969; *The New Vestments*, by Edward Lear, 1970; *Hildilid's Night*, by Cheli Durán Ryan, 1971; *The Master of Miracle: A New Novel of the Golem*, by Shulamith Ish-Kishor, 1971; *Miss Suzy's Easter Surprise*, by Miriam Young, 1972; *Seahorse*, by Robert A. Morris, 1972; *As I Was Crossing Boston Common*, by Norma Farber, 1973; *The Clay Pot Boy*, adapt. from the Russian by Cynthia Jameson, 1973; *Good Ethan*, by Paula Fox, 1973; *Circus*, by Jack Prelutsky, 1974; *Dinosaur Time*, by Peggy Parish, 1974; *Miss Suzy's Birthday*, by Miriam Young, 1974; *As Right As Right Can Be*, by Anne K. Rose, 1976; *Nightmares: Poems to Trouble Your Sleep*, by Jack Prelutsky, 1976; *Merry, Merry Fibruary*, by Doris Orgel, 1977; *Gregory Griggs and Other Nursery Rhyme People*, sel. by Arnold Lobel, 1978; *The Mean Old Mean Hyena*, by Jack Prelutsky, 1978; *Tales of Oliver Pig*, by Jean Van Leeuwen, 1979; *The Headless Horseman Rides Tonight: More Poems to Trouble Your Sleep*, by Jack Prelutsky, 1980;

The Tale of Meshka the Kvetch, by Carol Chapman, 1980; *More Tales of Oliver Pig*, by Jean Van Leeuwen, 1981; *The Random House Book of Poetry for Children*, comp. by Jack Prelutsky, 1983; *A Three Hat Day*, by Laura Geringer, 1985; *The Random House Book of Mother Goose*, sel. by Arnold Lobel, 1986 (reissued as *The Arnold Lobel Book of Mother Goose*, 1997); *Tyrannosaurus Was a Beast: Dinosaur Poems*, by Jack Prelutsky, 1988; *Arnold Lobel's Mother Goose for Babies*, 2004.

SELECTED WORKS WRITTEN (all illus. by Anita Lobel): *How Rooster Saved the Day*, 1977; *A Treeful of Pigs*, 1979; *On Market Street*, 1981; *The Rose in My Garden*, 1984.

Courtesy of Alfred A. Knopf, Inc.

SUGGESTED READING: Butler, Francelia, et al. *Triumphs of the Spirit in Children's Literature*, 1986; Cullinan, Bernice, and Diane Person. *The Continuum Encyclopedia of Children's Literature*, 2001; Cummins, Julie. *Children's Book Illustration and Design*, vol. 1, 1992; Hopkins, Lee Bennett. *Pauses: Autobiographical Reflections of 101 Creators of Children's Books*, 1995; Kingman, Lee, comp. *Illustrators of Children's Books, 1957–1966*, 1968; Shannon, George. *Arnold Lobel*, 1989; Silvey, Anita, ed. *Children's Books and Their Creators*, 1995; *Something About the Author*, vol. 54, 1989; *Twentieth-Century Children's Writers*, 2nd ed., 1983. Periodicals— Lobel, Arnold, "Caldecott Medal Acceptance," *The Horn Book*, August 1981; *New York Times*, December 6, 1987 (obituary).

A profile of Anita Lobel appeared in *Third Book of Junior Authors* (1972).

"I was born in Ithaca, New York, where my father was finishing his doctorate in soil science at Cornell University. The second-born of five children, I was quiet and shy. I have fond memories of my mother reading *Winnie the Pooh*, *The House at Pooh Corner*, *When We Were Very Young*, *The Pokey Little Puppy*, and *The Little Engine that Could*. My mother, now in her 80s, memorized many of A. A. Milne's poems and has repeated them on appropriate occasions throughout our lives. Sometimes, after stories, my father would sit in the hallway, where all five of us could hear from our bedrooms, and play soft tunes on his recorder (sort of a wooden flute with mellow tones) to help us go to sleep.

Sylvia Long

September 29, 1948–

"I loved to draw—clowns, flowers, then horses, etc. I remember copying some of the drawings in *The Tale of Peter Rabbit*. My favorite Christmas present was new 'colors,' whether a new box of Crayolas, a set of paints, or pencils. I was quite young when my family identified me as the 'family artist,' in charge of making cards for every occasion, in which my parents, sister, and brothers would then write their GET WELL SOON or HAPPY BIRTHDAY messages.

"Even though I loved to draw and paint, I didn't consider it as a profession until I was a senior in high school. Most of my family ended up with advanced degrees in the sciences. Enjoying nature and animals, I had a vague idea that I might be a veterinarian. My art teacher encouraged me to apply to a private college, Maryland Institute of Art, in Baltimore. I also applied for—and received—a four-year full tuition scholarship, so was able to attend and graduate with a B.F.A. in 1970, with a painting/drawing major and ceramics minor.

Courtesy of Thomas Long

"I don't recall a time in my life when I wasn't working in some sort of art medium. When my boys, Matthew and John, were small, I'd work while they were napping, or they would draw along with me in my studio. Being a mother is the most important thing in my life, and I was very fortunate to have a profession that didn't take me out of the house. For nearly 25 years, I showed my work in galleries and museums and entered competitive shows around the country.

"My method of working was to have an idea for a series of pictures and then visually investigate the idea until it held no more interest for me, changing mediums to suit the exploration of the idea. Some of these series would consist of a dozen or so pieces; others, more than 100. It was while I was working on a series called Native American Rabbits that my first children's book was born. A friend, Virginia Grossman, came to visit while my family was living on the Wind River Indian Reservation in Fort Washakie, Wyoming. She thought the images would be a good vehicle for a children's book. We collaborated on *Ten Little Rabbits* long-distance (between Washington and Wyoming). It was published in 1991 by Chronicle Books in San Francisco and received the honor of Best Picture Book of the Year from the International Reading Association. That was a huge encouragement for me to continue on that path.

"There is nothing I'd rather do than illustrate children's books. It has been extremely rewarding for me in many ways. I was very fortunate to have an editor who saw potential in my work and taught me about the fine points of illustrating. She encouraged me to use different perspectives and new formats, to vary my style to suit the manuscript, etc. With each new project, I learn something new about my craft.

"I currently live in Scottsdale, Arizona, and enjoy working in my bright studio with my golden retriever, Amigo, at my feet."

❋ ❋ ❋

Sylvia Long's distinctive ink and watercolor paintings have graced a variety of children's books and are a natural extension of the nature-based paintings she has shown in galleries for many years. From her first book, a collaboration with Virginia Grossman that grew out of her series of rabbit paintings depicting Native American costumes and customs, she has wedded her art with deeply felt stories about living comfortably within an environment. *Ten Little Rabbits* received a California Book Award as well as a Best Book citation from the International Reading Association. This early recognition of Long's work was an omen of praises to come. Her illustrations for *Alejandro's Gift* by Richard E. Albert are perfectly suited to the story of an old man living alone in the desert in harmony with his surroundings and helped earn that book a CLASP award as a Commended Book of the Year for Latin American Studies. It was also chosen as a *Reading Rainbow* title.

Hawk Hill, a story in which a lonely boy is befriended by an elderly woman who shares his passion for birds of prey, was named a *Smithsonian* magazine Notable Book. Long's art was praised as much for its portrait of the gruff, kindly Mary as for its accurate portrayal of the birds. Similarly, in *Bugs for Lunch*, a *Parenting* magazine Reading Magic Award book, the pictures of tarantulas, bats, and toads had dramatic impact as well as scientific precision. In *Any Bear Can Wear Glasses*, Long teamed up with her son and her physician husband for a humorous look at endangered species, to gently induce an awareness of threats to the animal kingdom in children.

Venturing into creating her own texts, Sylvia Long has reworked some classic literature to produce her own unique versions of old favorites. Disturbed by the grasping overtones of the traditional lullaby "Hush Little Baby," she rewrote the text to have the mother sharing wonders of the natural world with her baby rather than offering to buy a succession of gifts. Illustrated with Long's signature-style bunnies, the book was named one of *Child* magazine's best books of the year in 1997. Two years later *Sylvia Long's Mother Goose* appeared, with many of the illustrations and some text changes creating more positive images for the old favorite rhymes, yet without compromising the basic integrity of the originals. When the cradle falls in the "Rock-a-bye

"I was very fortunate to have an editor who saw potential in my work and taught me about the fine points of illustrating."

Courtesy of Chronicle Books

Baby" verse, for example, the illustration shows a baby bird flying out on its first solo flight, encouraged to leave the nest.

Besides creating children's books, Sylvia Long continues to exhibit her art in a gallery in Arizona and on the Internet. Some of her books have been translated into French, German, Japanese, and Korean.

SELECTED WORKS WRITTEN AND ILLUSTRATED: *Hush Little Baby*, 1997; *Sylvia Long's Mother Goose*, 1999; *Deck the Hall: A Traditional Carol*, 2000.

SELECTED WORKS ILLUSTRATED: *Ten Little Rabbits*, by Virginia Grossman, 1991; *The Most Timid in the Land: A Bunny Romance*, by Oliver Herford, 1992; *Fire Race: A Karuk Coyote Tale about How Fire Came to the People*, retold by Jonathan London with Lanny Pinola, 1993; *Liplap's Wish*, by Jonathan London, 1994; *Alejandro's Gift*, by Richard E. Albert, 1994; *Any Bear Can Wear Glasses*, by Matthew Long and Thomas Long, 1995; *Hawk Hill*, by Suzie Gilbert, 1996; *Bugs for Lunch*, by Margery Facklam, 1999; *Twinkle, Twinkle, Little Star: A Traditional Lullaby*, by Jane Taylor, 2001; *Snug As a Bug*, by Michael Elsohn Ross, 2004.

SUGGESTED READING: *Something About the Author*, vol. 120, 2001.

Lenore Look

March 12, 1962–

"I first began making picture books in kindergarten because my parents couldn't afford to buy them. My other career option at the time was to steal the books from my teacher when she wasn't looking. But a life of crime required practice and patience, neither of which I had, so I settled into honest industry, working as fast as my fat crayons could go, so that I would have something to read.

"Publishing was no problem in those days, not like it is now. By first grade, I could put words in my books, and because copying the same story was easier than writing it the first time, I also became a publisher. My parents were delighted. My dad nailed some pieces of wood together and made me a bookcase. I was the featured author on every shelf, and there was no brighter literary star in my universe. I held readings and instructed my two younger brothers and the neighborhood kids in the useful skill of queuing for autographed copies. I don't know where I ever got that idea. We lived on Seattle's Beacon Hill, now the setting for my books, but then the Gobi Desert of author events until my debut. I charged 25 cents a book (an enviable paperback royalty today), but also accepted candy.

"By third grade, I had abandoned the literary scene. My parents bought an old piano. I practiced for weeks, and then after we saluted the flag one day, I marched to the front of the class and belted 'America the Beautiful' in my best vibrato. My prodigious talent left no jaw undropped. Some time after that, I came across a book about Maria Tallchief, and became a ballerina. I weighed only 40 pounds and could leap and pirouette all day without stopping. Then I read *All Creatures Great and Small* and opened a veterinary clinic. Then I read *The Making of a Surgeon*, and my brothers fled for their lives.

"My friend Vivian, with whom I shared all secrets, suddenly and without any warning wrote a fairy tale about a king with ten golden balls. It changed my life. She submitted it to a contest I'd never heard of, and before I could submit my story about a king with several hundred golden balls, she'd won. And her story got published, with illustrations. Suddenly, Vivian was a star, and I was not. Vivian declared that she would become an author when she grew up. And I declared that I would become an architect. Where I got that idea, I'll never know. It was the sixth grade, and I had a talent for alliteration.

"I have no memory of junior high, but in high school I had begun writing for our school newspaper. Everyone liked my ditties and encouraged me to write more. So I did. I wrote so much that I couldn't stop writing. In college, I was an art historian, philosopher, Chinese scholar, and Secretary of State, all in a single morning. I became *moong cha-cha*, which in Cantonese means *very confused, fuzzy in the head*, but every afternoon I was at the campus newspaper doing what I really loved—writing. After graduation, I moved to Los Angeles to work as a newspaper reporter. Beat reporting was not easy. It required practice and patience, which I still did not have. I

Courtesy of James J. Kriegsmann, Jr.

fell asleep at school board meetings. I got to press conferences just in time to see them cart off the microphones. The police station that I visited for stories was at the best of all possible places to work (on a suntan, that is)—the beach. But worst of all, I kept writing stories that had nothing to do with my beat.

"It wasn't until I became a mother and began reading children's books again that I felt what the Chinese call *yun feen*, which means a continuing of work begun in past lives. I had long forgotten my early foray into picture books, the thread I'd dropped in kindergarten, a thin rig, like the one a spider would use in rising. I had journeyed nearly 30 years down through space by then, unaware of my silken strand. Then one afternoon, with my two preschoolers clamoring for something to do, I showed them how to fold paper into a book . . . picked up some crayons and a pen, and then . . . felt myself rising . . . returning to that place where I began, that brief age in which I had so many talents, and leapt and pirouetted into the sun, and could not stop."

✿ ✿ ✿

Raised in Seattle, Washington, Lenore Look earned her B.A. from Princeton University in 1984. She began her writing career as a reporter, first for the *Los Angeles Times*, 1984–1985, and then for the *Trenton* (NJ) *Times*, 1985–1987. She also wrote political speeches for a short time. The mother of two daughters, she and her family live in Randolph, New Jersey.

Courtesy of Atheneum Books for Young Readers

Published in 1999, Look's first picture book, *Love As Strong As Ginger*, was based on the life of Lenore's own grandmother and immediately won attention for its poignancy and strong sense of family love. Illustrated by Stephen T. Johnson, it is the tale of Katie who visits the cannery where her Chinese immigrant grandmother GninGnin works. The crab cannery is a place of terrible smells and noise, and after a long, grueling day, GninGnin barely makes enough money to pay for bus fare home and food for their dinner. Katie returns from that experience understanding how hard her grandmother has worked to make a better future for her family, including Katie. *Love As Strong As Ginger* was named a *Booklist* Editors' Choice, a *New York Times* Bookshelf selection, an IRA Notable Book for a Global Society, and a Notable Trade Book in the Field of Social Studies. Her next picture book, *Henry's First-Moon Birthday*, illustrated by Yumi Heo, introduces readers to a joyous Chinese American family's celebration of a baby's one-month birthday through the eyes of Jen, Older Sister. As in Look's first book, the special relationship between a grandmother and her granddaughter is highlighted. *Henry's First-Moon Birthday* was an ALA Notable Children's Book, a *Smithsonian* Notable Book of the Year, and a *Booklist* Editors' Choice. It was also on the Highly Commended list for the Charlotte Zolotow Award for excellence in picture book writing.

SELECTED WORKS: *Love As Strong As Ginger*, illus. by Stephen T. Johnson, 1999; *Henry's First-Moon Birthday*, illus. by Yumi Heo, 2001; *Ruby Lu, Brave and True*, illus. by Anne Wilsdorf, 2004.

"**I** was born on the lucky day of April First in Iowa City, Iowa. Before I was two my family moved to Cambridge, Massachusetts, but not for long. My father was getting established as a college professor and new opportunities kept coming up for him. We went on to Urbana and then Chicago in Illinois, then Palo Alto, California; West Boylston, Massachusetts; and Lawrence, Kansas. Finally, when I was twelve, we settled down in Oskaloosa, Kansas. All of this moving around turned me into a watcher and a listener. In each new town and school I had so much to learn. Did the girls tuck their skirts into their snow pants or let them stick out like tutus? Could it be true that we were allowed to play only on the asphalt and never on the grass of the schoolyard? Did that boy's teasing mean that he liked me or that he thought I was a weird outsider? I had to pay attention, watch, and listen.

"I also became a great reader. I discovered that everywhere we lived there was a public library and every library felt like home. I always found books that were already friends of mine and new books to become acquainted with. One day when I was eight I noticed that every book on the shelves of the Palo Alto Children's Library had a person's name on it. That person, I learned, was the author, the man or woman who had created the people and the story in the book. An author! I dreamed of walking into a library and seeing a book on the shelf with my name on it.

"However, being an author truly seemed to be my impossible dream. I was a very slow writer and I had terrible handwriting. I only wrote what I was required to and made that as short as possible. But there were stories bubbling inside me that had to come out somehow. My parents told stories to my brother and sister and me, mostly about things that happened to them when they were growing up. I decided that I could tell stories, too. And I had a wonderful listener, my younger sister, Lucy. My parents didn't tell fairy tales, so I read as many as I could and told them to Lucy. Sometimes I made up stories about an imaginary girl named Oklahoma Wingate, or Bixby, a magical dog.

"In high school I learned to type, not very well but well enough that I was able to write essays and stories for the school paper. But I was busy, and my dream of being an author retreated to the back of my mind. In university my typing got better and I even took a writing course on the side while I studied history. When I graduated I decided to go back to my favorite place, the library. I became a children's librarian.

Courtesy of Trevor Black

Celia Barker Lottridge

Celia Barker Lottridge

April 1, 1936–

"As a children's librarian I could do things I loved: read books, talk about books, arrange books properly on shelves, and most of all, tell stories. I worked in public libraries and then in elementary school libraries. Of course, I kept up my family tradition of moving around and lived in New York City; San Diego, California; Providence, Rhode Island; Somerville and Brookline in Massachusetts before I settled down in Toronto, Ontario, Canada. In Toronto I found work in the Children's Book Store, a magical place dedicated to selling the best of children's books. And at the Children's Book Store it at last occurred to me that some of those stories I had been telling might make books and that I should write them.

"So I finally did become an author. All of my watching, listening, traveling, reading, and storytelling goes into my books. Some are my versions of old stories which I like to tell; others are based on stories my father told me about growing up on a farm in Alberta, and still others come from places where I grew up and people and animals I have known. I divide my work between writing books and telling stories in schools and at festivals. And in my spare time I travel and listen and watch, always looking for new ideas for stories."

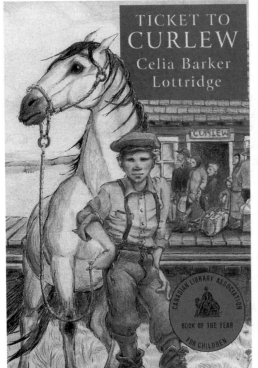

Courtesy of Groundwood Books

❋ ❋ ❋

Celia Lottridge received her B.A. from Stanford University in 1957 and a master's degree in library science from Columbia University in 1959. Her marriage to a Navy man that same year took her to San Diego, where she worked as a children's librarian. Returning to New York when her husband began graduate work in Russian at Columbia, Celia became a librarian at the Dalton School, and it was there she developed her skills as a storyteller for all grade levels. In 1964–1965 she accompanied her husband on a 10-month exchange program in Moscow, returning to live in Rhode Island where he taught at Brown University and she set up an inner-city library. Her son Andrew was born in Providence in 1967. When the marriage ended seven years later, Celia and Andrew moved to Toronto, where she had relatives, and found the city a congenial place to live and raise a child. Working at the Children's Book Store put her in a perfect spot to be at the center of children's literature and storytelling activities.

Pursuing her love of folktales and storytelling, Celia became one of the founders of the Storytellers School of Toronto, an active group that promotes storytelling activities in schools and the community. She has performed, conducted workshops for children, and offered classes for teachers, librarians, and the general public in the art of telling stories. She is also one of the founders and developers of the Parent-Child Mother Goose Program, a social service program in which nursery rhymes, games, and stories are used as a means of improving parent-child relationships. She served as director of the program for 10 years, until 2001.

Books that Celia Lottridge has written have often grown out of her storytelling experience and have received many accolades in her adopted country, Canada. *The Name of the Tree*, her picture-book retelling of a Bantu tale, received the Mr. Christie Award, as did another folktale adaptation, *The Little Rooster and the Diamond Button*. *Music for the Tsar of the Sea* garnered the Ruth Schwartz Award, and *Ten Small Tales*, relatively unfamiliar stories for the very young collected from many cultures around the world, earned the Toronto area IODE (International Order of Daughters of the Empire) Award.

Celia Lottridge's storytelling abilities are equally apparent in her novels. *Ticket to Curlew* came into being while she was writer-in-residence at the Regina Public Library in Saskatchewan in 1991. Based on stories her father had told about his family leaving Iowa to farm in Alberta, Canada, in the early years of the 20th century, the book was a popular and critical success, winning the Canadian Library Association's Book of the Year Award as well as the Bilson Award for historical fiction. In the sequel, *Wings to Fly*, Celia told of the same time period from a female point of view, using many of the stories related to her by her aunts. The book is a tribute to the courage and hard work of women who settled the prairies of both Canada and the United States, and won the national IODE prize, the Violet Downey Award. Celia Lottridge lives in Toronto and continues to tell and write stories that are close to her heart.

SELECTED WORKS: *One Watermelon Seed*, illus. by Karen Patkau, 1986, 1997; *The Name of the Tree: A Bantu Tale*, illus. by Ian Wallace, 1989; *Ticket to Curlew*, illus. by Wendy Wolsak-Frith, 1992 (publ. in the United States as *Ticket to Canada*, 1995); *Ten Small Tales: Stories from Around the World*, illus. by Joanne Fitzgerald, 1993; *The Wind Wagon*, illus. by Daniel Clifford, 1995; *Mother Goose: A Sampler*, illus. by Barbara Reid, Marie-Louise Gay, et. al., 1996; *Wings to Fly*, illus. by Mary Jane Gerber, 1997; *Music for the Tsar of the Sea: A Russian Wonder Tale*, illus. by Harvey Chan, 1998; *The Little Rooster and the Diamond Button: A Hungarian Folktale*, illus. by Joanne Fitzgerald, 2001; *Berta: A Remarkable Dog*, illus. by Elsa Myotte, 2002; *Stories from the Life of Jesus*, illus. by Linda Wolfsgruber, 2004; *Stories from Adam and Eve to Ezekiel*, illus. by Gary Clement, 2004.

SUGGESTED READING: *Something About the Author*, vol. 112, 2000. Periodicals—Ellis, Sarah, book review of *Ten Small Tales*, *The Horn Book*, January/February, 1994.

Courtesy of Katie Ambrose

Sue Macy

May 13, 1954–

"When I was about eight years old, I hit a line drive that broke a pane of glass in a lamppost across the street from my house. It was one of the proudest moments of my childhood. My brother and the other boys in our neighborhood always seemed to be causing property damage with balls they threw, kicked, or hit. By doing so myself, I felt like I had crashed some boys-only club and shown them that I, too, should be taken seriously.

"In the 1950s and '60s, the sports world was dominated by boys and men. It wasn't until I was in college that I learned women had played just about every sport for decades. But most of their exploits were either ignored, overlooked, or forgotten. That fact, along with my background as an athlete and a sports fan, gave me a natural focus when I set out to write about things that mattered to me.

"My introduction to early female athletes was memorable. When I was a summer intern at my local newspaper in 1973, I was assigned to interview Althea Gibson, the first African American to win a major tennis tournament. (She won the French nationals in 1956 and both Wimbledon and the U.S. nationals in 1957 and 1958.) I had heard of Gibson, but nothing had prepared me for the experience of meeting her. She was awe-inspiring; tall, with huge hands and an office full of trophies, including her two massive winner's plates from Wimbledon. If it wasn't for the photographer who accompanied me, I might never have gotten up the nerve to ask my first question.

"After speaking to Gibson and other sports pioneers, I started to realize the unique place early women athletes occupied in American history. More often than not, their participation in sports allowed them to lead more liberated lives than other women, who were still treated as second-class citizens at work and at home. For female athletes, the very act of competing was a liberating experience. By pursuing their love of sports, they personally rebelled against the constraints of society.

"All of that came into focus when I took classes in history and women's studies at Princeton University. But I wasn't only interested in women's sports from an academic standpoint. Watching Martina Navratilova smash a tennis ball or Nancy Lopez sink a 10-foot putt reawakened the competitor in me. And even though my tennis shots tended to sail over fences and my average score on a golf hole was a quadruple bogey, I could relate to Navratilova and Lopez because they were women. Their accomplishments inspired me to set my own goals.

"One of my aims in writing about women and sports is to find new role models for myself and my readers. But I've been lucky to have strong role models in my life all along. My grandmothers were both amazing. My mom's mother grew up in Poland and was the only girl in her town to study the Talmud, a complex collection of Jewish commentaries interpreting the Bible. My dad's mother spent six days a week running her women's clothing store—until she was 92 years old. She also baked incredible cakes and pastries for us on Sundays, her only day off.

"I grew up in Clifton, New Jersey, with a father who is a certified public accountant (and a huge sports fan!) and a mother who was a business teacher before she became a full-time mom. I have a younger brother who was a great Little League pitcher and tennis player and was always willing to play catch with me. As a kid, I read two newspapers a day and learned a lot about writing from the *New York Times*. I was the editor of my junior high and high school newspapers and worked for my local paper for three summers during high school and college.

"I chose a career as a writer (and editor) because writing empowers me. It allows me to express myself and shine the spotlight on the exploits and achievements of people who were ignored, overlooked, or forgotten. By learning about them, we can all learn something about ourselves."

✳ ✳ ✳

Born in New York City and raised in New Jersey, where she now makes her home, Sue Macy brings an elegant, spare style and enthusiastic flare to writing about women in sports. A reader of the *New York Times* since she was a child, she became interested in journalism because of a scholarship she won to Northwestern University's summer high school journalism institute.

Courtesy of Henry Holt & Co.

After receiving a B.A. from Princeton University in 1976, Macy became a research coordinator for Scholastic, Inc., then an editor for *Scholastic Newstime*. She left Scholastic to become a freelance writer but returned later to be the editorial director of Scholastic's science and math magazines and a project editor for Scholastic Reference, where she served as editor-in-chief for the *Scholastic Children's Dictionary*.

A lover of sports, history, and social issues, Macy interviewed several players in the historic All-American Girls Professional Baseball League, which began in 1943 and continued until 1954. Fascinated by their experiences, she decided to write her first book about the league's women athletes and the times in which they played. The result, *A Whole New Ball Game*, won her both critical acclaim and praise from the league players. It was named a *School Library Journal* Best Book, an ALA Best Book for Young Adults, a Notable Children's Trade Book in the Field of Social Studies, and a New York Public Library Book for the Teen Age.

Winning Ways: A Photohistory of American Women in Sports became a *School Library Journal* Best Book, an ALA Best Book for Young Adults, an ALA Notable Children's Book, and a New York Public Library Book for the Teen Age. *Play Like a Girl: A Celebration of Women in Sports* is an accessible, inspiring collection of photos and quotations that was an ALA Quick Pick for Reluctant Young Adult Readers, a Cooperative Children's Book Center Choice, and a New York Public Library Book for the Teen Age. *Girls Got Game: Sports Stories and Poems* was cited as a Top 10 Sports Book for Youth by *Booklist*, as well as being a Cooperative Children's Book Center Choice.

Turning to another remarkable woman in history, Macy wrote *Bull's-Eye: A Photobiography of Annie Oakley*, telling the tale of Phoebe Ann Moses, the legendary sharpshooter. As in all her biographical studies, Macy worked to provide a rounded view of her subject, the times in which she lived, and social norms for women of those times. *Bull's-Eye* was a *School Library Journal* Best Book, a Notable Social Studies Trade Book for Young People, an ALA Notable Children's Book, and the winner of a 2001 Gold Medal for Non-Fiction from the National Parenting Publications Association.

SELECTED WORKS WRITTEN: *A Whole New Ball Game: The Story of the All-American Girls Professional Baseball League*, 1993; *Winning Ways: A Photohistory of American Women in Sports*, 1996; *Barbie: Shooting Hoops*, 1999; *Bull's-Eye: A Photobiography of Annie Oakley*, 2001; *Swifter, Higher, Stronger: A Photographic History of the Summer Olympics*, 2004.

SELECTED WORKS EDITED: *Play Like a Girl: A Celebration of Women in Sports*, 1999; *Girls Got Game: Sports Stories and Poems*, 2001.

SUGGESTED READING: *Contemporary Authors*, vol. 152, 1997; *Something About the Author*, vol. 134, 2003.

Margaret Mahy

(MAH-hee)

March 21, 1936–

"'Once upon a time there was a big black-maned Abyssinian Lion . . .' This was the beginning of a story, invented and told to me by my father when I was very young. It is probably the first story I can remember hearing, and in a curious way links up with my own first published story, *A Lion in the Meadow*. At any rate it seems to me that the lion in my father's story had secretly haunted me for more than 30 years, only to emerge, transformed, illustrated, and somehow authenticated by its library binding.

"I was the oldest of five children, all of whom had stories read to them incessantly. My sister and I both wrote stories ourselves when we were young, but I was obsessed not only with writing the stories down, but with trying to get them glorified by print. I will never forget the astonishment that flooded me when, at age eight, I opened a local newspaper to the children's column and saw a story of mine in print for the first time. Publication transformed it. It was both mine and not mine. It still belonged to me (as writer) but now it belonged equally to everyone who was able to read it.

"Getting stories published by the New Zealand School Publications (now called Learning Media) was a wonderful advance for me, and it was through School Publications and the New Zealand *School Journal* that my stories came to the attention of Helen Hoke Watts of Franklins Watts, Inc. in the United States. In due course Franklin Watts published, simultaneously, five of these stories as picture books, the first being *A Lion in the Meadow.*

"I have been a persistent and prolific writer over many years now, and a full-time writer since 1979, writing television scripts and short stories for educational publishers, as well as a large number of trade books at many different levels: texts for picture books, collections of short stories, books for both the middle and senior school, along with several young adult novels. The shortest story I ever had published was nine words long. The longest book I have ever written consisted, when finished, of 800 crowded pages. However, that one has never been published.

"As I am not one of those reclusive writers, I have willingly talked about books over and over again—both my own and other people's—at many conferences in New Zealand, Australia, Britain, and the U.S.A. I am now 68 years old—galloping towards 70, I feel—and, during my writing life, the book world has changed around me in many ways. When I was a child, like most European New Zealanders I was told stories with English settings—tales by Beatrix Potter, A. A. Milne, and Kenneth Grahame, for example—and experienced an odd imaginative displacement. It was as if the true world of the imagination existed in some place other than my own. However, over the years I have been able to return to, and re-explore with growing confidence, my essential identity as a

Courtesy of Vanessa Hamilton

New Zealander, at the same time as New Zealand and Australia have been learning to celebrate strong and varied children's literature of their own. This has happened at a time when children's reading time is being eaten into, predictably enough, by the combined impact of television programmes, play stations, and organized sport. But for all that, stories are still vital threads in the human psyche, and the pleasure of telling and listening to stories or reading them in silence is a necessary part of human communication—both communication with those around us and a mysterious inner communication—part of the process by which we define and form ourselves.

"I live in the same house I have lived in for over 30 years, sharing it, over time, with a series of cats, dogs, and children, and currently with grandchildren. I have five grandchildren living on a harbour peninsula five minutes away from me—two older girls who play tennis, ride horses, and sail yachts, a Down-syndrome boy who spends time with me every week, and younger identical twin girls who think the world was created entirely for their pleasures. I have another grandson in Auckland, but we visit one another regularly, exchanging books and reading stories to one another. I still work hard as a writer but I do a lot of baby-sitting as well, so I think I am leading a life that resounds with entertainment and unexpectedness. No grandmother can afford to take anything for granted, and life with children constantly involves one with jokes, with apprehension, and with the sort of creative surprise that connects one with stories of the past along with events that might—just might—evolve into future tales of wonder."

✻ ✻ ✻

A remarkable storyteller, who has published for young people of all ages, Margaret Mahy has created award-winning picture books, middle grade fiction, and young adult novels for over 35 years. Known for her rollicking, rambunctious picture books and supernatural tales that often mix humor with horror, as well as her poignantly emotional teen stories and solid middle-grade fiction, this New Zealand writer has enthralled audiences all over the world.

Born in the town of Whakatane, Margaret Mahy graduated from Auckland University College in 1955. Later she earned her librarian's diploma from the New Zealand Library School in Wellington and worked for a number of years as a children's librarian, both in the School Library Service in Christchurch and in public libraries. She has been a major force in creating a strong base for children's literature set in New Zealand and written by New Zealanders; indeed, she has been a great encouragement to many New Zealand authors in pursuing their careers. Mahy has won the Esther Glen Award, the highest children's book award in her country, six times: for *A Lion in the Meadow*, *The First Margaret Mahy Storybook*, *The Haunting*, *The*

> "Stories are still vital threads in the human psyche, and the pleasure of telling and listening to stories or reading them in silence is a necessary part of human communication—both communication with those around us and a mysterious inner communication—part of the process by which we define and form ourselves."

Changeover, Underrunners, and *24 Hours.* *The Haunting* and *The Changeover* both won the coveted Carnegie Medal in Britain. These two titles are examples of the fine way in which Mahy weaves the supernatural into everyday life, with such clearly drawn characters that their reactions to mysterious events are totally believable. This quality is pervasive in *The Tricksters,* an intricate story that blends many of Mahy's recurring themes: a girl on the brink of growing up, a story rooted in a particular landscape, the complexity of family relationships, the importance of written expression, and the development of a sense of ethical purpose in the lives of young people. In her latest novel, *Alchemy*—winner of the New Zealand Post Award for young adult fiction—Mahy once again mixes magic and terror with the everyday world for a powerful story of the struggle between good and evil and the importance of remaining true to ideals.

Courtesy of Margaret K. McElderry Books

Not all of Mahy's stories include supernatural and fantastic elements. *Memory* is a poignant novel of the tentative friendship that develops between an angry teenage boy, haunted by the memory of his sister's death, and a gentle old woman whose memory is lost to Alzheimer's disease. Highly praised for its sensitive handling of an intergenerational relationship and complex issues, *Memory* was named an Honor Book for the *Boston Globe–Horn Book* Award. *Underrunners,* set in the landscape near the author's home, is a multilayered story of two children who seek comfort from each other when the world around them doesn't provide it. In a harrowing climax, they both learn more about themselves and the frightening aspects of their earlier lives. *The Catalogue of the Universe* features two young protagonists—attractive Angela, longing to find the father she has never known, and Tycho, her brainy friend who loves her and isn't sure how to show it. When Angela does confront her father, with disappointing results, Tycho's comforting presence awakens her romantic feelings for him. Another character, Hero in *The Other Side of Silence,* chooses self-imposed mutism to deal with her personal demons and family issues. Suspenseful encounters with a family that is stranger than her own bring Hero out of her lonely silence. In each of these beautifully crafted novels full of rich language, symbolism, and imagery, Mahy provides a compelling story while urging her readers to look beneath the surface for deeper meanings that may illuminate their own lives.

Mahy's talents are equally apparent in her more humorous writings and her light verse. Her felicitous use of words, rhyme, and rhythm has delighted readers of such books as *17 Kings and 42 Elephants* and *Bubble Trouble & Other Poems and Stories.* An irrepressible delight in the absurd informs hilarious stories that live up to the promise of their titles: *The Blood-and-Thunder Adventure on Hurricane Peak, Raging Robots and Unruly Uncles,* and *The Great Piratical Rumbustification & The Librarian and the Robbers.* The latter title, combining two stories in one volume and ebulliently illustrated by Quentin Blake, is indicative of Mahy's wit. Pirates hired by unwitting parents as baby-sitters enliven an otherwise dull neighborhood, while in the second story a kidnapped librarian reforms a group of dastardly villains by reading aloud to them when they come down with the measles. Wordplay, alliteration, and outrageous humor abound in these and other quintessential Mahy treats. Contagious humor permeates her many picture book stories, illustrated by such stellar artists as Steven Kellogg, Patricia MacCarthy, and Jonathan Allen. In *The Great White Man-Eating Shark: A Cautionary Tale* a misanthropic young man pretends to be a shark to frighten people off the beach, leaving him free to swim alone . . . until he attracts the attention of an amorous female shark.

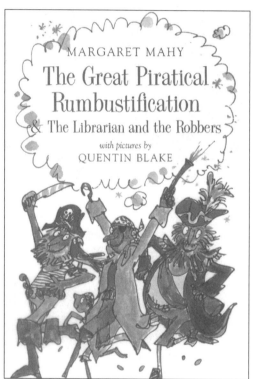

Courtesy of David R. Godine, Publishers, Inc.

Margaret Mahy's books have been published in the United States to great acclaim. Many titles have been named ALA Notable Children's Books and Best Books for Young Adults. In 1989 she delivered the May Hill Arbuthnot Honor Lecture for the American Library Association in Pittsburgh, Pennsylvania. Few authors have ever matched Mahy's remarkable versatility, writing for so wide an age range and in so many different genres. The mother of two grown daughters, she lives today outside Christchurch in the South Island of New Zealand in a house with a large library, an assortment of pets, and most of her grandchildren nearby. In 1993 Margaret Mahy received the Order of New Zealand, the highest honor her country can bestow.

SELECTED WORKS: *A Lion in the Meadow*, illus. by Jenny Williams, 1969; *The Dragon of an Ordinary Family*, illus. by Helen Oxenbury, 1969; *Mrs. Discombobulous*, illus. by Jan Brychta, 1969; *The Procession*, illus. by Charles Mozley, 1969; *Pillycock's Shop*, illus. by Carol Barker, 1969; *The Little Witch*, illus. by Charles Mozley, 1970; *Sailor Jack and the 20*

Orphans, illus. by Robert Bartelt, 1970; *The Boy with Two Shadows*, illus. by Jenny Williams, 1971; *The Princess and the Clown*, illus. by Carol Barker, 1971; *The Man Whose Mother Was a Pirate*, illus. by Brian Froud, 1972; *Rooms for Rent*, illus. by Jenny Williams, 1974; *The Witch in the Cherry Tree*, illus. by Jenny Williams, 1974; *The Boy Who Was Followed Home*, illus. by Steven Kellogg, 1975; *UltraViolet Catastrophe! or, The Unexpected Walk with Great-Uncle Magnus Pringle*, illus. by Brian Froud, 1975; *Leaf Magic*, illus. by Jenny Williams, 1976; *Nonstop Nonsense*, illus. by Quentin Blake, 1977; *The Haunting*, 1982; *The Changeover: A Supernatural Romance*, 1984; *Aliens in the Family*, 1985; *Jam: A True Story*, illus. by Helen Craig, 1985; *The Catalogue of the Universe*, 1985; *The Tricksters*, 1986; *17 Kings and 42 Elephants*, illus. by Patricia MacCarthy, 1987; *Memory*, 1987; *The Adventures of a Kite*, illus. by David Cowe, 1988; *The Birthday Burglar & A Very Wicked Headmistress*, illus. by Margaret Chamberlain, 1988; *My Wonderful Aunt*, illus. by Deirdre Gardiner, 1988; *Clever Hamburger*, illus. by Rodney McRae, 1989; *The Blood-and-Thunder Adventure on Hurricane Peak*, illus. by Wendy Smith, 1989; *A Very Happy Bathday*, illus. by Elizabeth Fuller, 1989; *The Great White Man-Eating Shark: A Cautionary Tale*, illus. by Jonathan Allen, 1990; *Making Friends*, illus. by Wendy Smith, 1990; *The Seven Chinese Brothers*, illus. by Jean and Mou-Sien Tseng, 1990; *The Chewing-Gum Rescue*, illus. by Jan Ormerod, 1991; *The Queen's Goat*, illus. by Emma Chichester Clark, 1991; *Keeping House*, illus. by Wendy Smith, 1991; *Dangerous Spaces*, 1991; *The Girl with the Green Ear: Stories about Magic in Nature*, illus. by Shirley Hughes, 1992; *The Horrendous Hullabaloo*, illus. by Patricia MacCarthy, 1992; *Underrunners*, 1992; *A Tall Story and Other Tales*, illus. by Jan Nesbitt, 1992; *Bubble Trouble & Other Poems and Stories*, 1992; *A Busy Day for a Good Grandmother*, illus. by Margaret Chamberlain, 1993; *Raging Robots and Unruly Uncles*, illus. by Peter Stevenson, 1993; *The Good Fortunes Gang*, illus. by Marian Young, 1993; *A Fortunate Name*, illus. by Marian Young, 1993; *The Pirates' Mixed-Up Voyage: Dark Doings in the Thousand Islands*, illus. by Margaret Chamberlain, 1993; *The Three-Legged Cat*, illus. by Jonathan Allen, 1993; *The Great Piratical Rumbustification & The Librarian and the Robbers*, illus. by Quentin Blake, 1993; *The Christmas Tree Tangle*, illus. by Anthony Kerins, 1994; *The Greatest Show Off Earth*, illus. by Wendy Smith, 1994; *A Fortune Branches Out*, illus. by Marian Young, 1994; *Tick Tock Tales: Stories to Read Around the Clock*, illus. by Wendy Smith, 1994; *Tangled Fortunes*, illus. by Marian Young, 1994; *The Pirate Uncle*, illus. by Barbara Steadman, 1994; *The Rattlebang Picnic*, illus. by Steven Kellogg, 1994; *Clancy's Cabin*, illus. by Barbara Steadman, 1995; *Tingleberries,*

Tuckertubs, and Telephones: A Tale of Love and Ice-Cream, illus. by Robert Staermose, 1995; *The Other Side of Silence*, 1995; *The Five Sisters*, illus. by Patricia MacCarthy, 1996; *Boom, Baby, Boom, Boom!*, illus. by Patricia MacCarthy, 1997; *A Summery Saturday Morning*, illus. by Selina Young, 1998; *The Horribly Haunted School*, 1998; *Beaten by a Balloon*, illus. by Jonathan Allen, 1998; *Simply Delicious!*, illus. by Jonathan Allen, 1999; *Down the Dragon's Tongue*, illus. by Patricia MacCarthy, 2000; *24 Hours*, 2000; *Dashing Dog!*, illus. by Sarah Garland, 2002; *Alchemy*, 2003.

SUGGESTED READING: *Children's Literature Review*, vol. 78, 2002; *Contemporary Authors*, New Revision Series, vol. 38, 1993; Gilderdale, Betty. *Introducing Margaret Mahy*, 1987; Hipple, Ted. *Writers for Young Adults*, vol. 2, 1997; Mahy, Margaret. *My Mysterious World*, photos by David Alexander, 1995; *St. James Guide to Children's Writers*, 5th ed., 1999; Silvey, Anita. *Children's Books and Their Creators*, 1995; *Something About the Author*, vol. 119, 2001. Periodicals—Mahy, Margaret, "A Dissolving Ghost: Arbuthnot Honor Lecture," *Journal of Youth Services in Libraries*, Summer 1989; Mahy, Margaret, "Future Classics: Flint Heart," *The Horn Book*, November/December 2000; Mahy, Margaret, "Looking Inward, Exploring Outward," *The Horn Book*, March/April 2004; Mahy, Margaret, "The Mysteries of Book Ownership," *The Horn Book*, November/December 1994.

WEB SITE: *library.christchurch.org.nz/Childrens/MargaretMahy/*

An earlier profile and first-person statement of Margaret Mahy appeared in *Fourth Book of Junior Authors and Illustrators* (1978).

Sandra Markle

November 10, 1946–

"Writing nonfiction science has given me an excuse to get to know many fascinating people and has taken me to amazing places—even to the end of the earth. For example, while working on *Growing Up Wild: Penguins*, I went to Antarctica and spent a summer living with 60,000 Adélie penguins while they were raising their chicks. *Pioneering Space* had me test-driving the MMU (Manned Maneuvering Unit) trainer, putting on a space suit, and standing with the press, watching Sally Ride's Space Shuttle launch. *Growing Up Wild: Bears* took me to Denali National Park in Alaska to see bears up close. I got so close to my subject for *Outside and Inside Snakes* that I was bitten on the forehead by a large boa constrictor. Luckily, they're non-poisonous, so my adventures are still continuing.

"The journey that led to my writing science books for children started when I was in the fifth grade. That was about the time *Sputnik* made everyone decide kids should learn about science but before anyone had yet published an official science textbook. So my first experience with science was when the one and only science teacher arrived twice a month in my hometown of Fostoria, Ohio, to guide my class through hands-on experiments or take us outdoors to explore the world for ourselves. As far as I was concerned, science was magical, amazing, and fun. I was hooked!

"For me, every book I write is a journey of discovery, but my journeys to Antarctica have truly changed my life. I was fortunate to be selected twice to receive grants from the highly competitive U.S. Antarctic Program's Artists and Writers program. That took me to the South Pole, to McMurdo Station, aboard a research vessel in the Ross Sea where even the maps were wrong, and to amazing remote sites. I will never forget being on my knees photographing penguins just an arm's length from the open sea when a killer whale stuck its head up and looked me in the eye. I will also never forget huddling in my sleeping bag while my only shelter—a tent—was ripped apart by hurricane-force winds. From these experiences came four books: *Growing Up Wild: Penguins*; *Pioneering Frozen Worlds*; *Super Cool Science: The South Pole Station Past, Present, and Future*; and *A Mother's Journey*. My trips to Antarctica also led to my producing one of the first-ever interactive Web sites about my experiences. And that led to my development of the Kit & Kaboodle Program, which was funded by grants from the National Science Foundation and NASA. It produced interactive, online science materials used by thousands of schools throughout the United States and in 11 other countries. In recognition of this work, I was named one of 1999's Women of the Year by Women in Technology International.

Courtesy of Sandra Markle

Sandra Markle

"I taught for 11 years in Ohio, North Carolina, and Georgia. I quit teaching in order to write full time—except that I never really quit teaching. Even now, I continue to present science and writing workshops for children and teachers. I'm also still remembered as 'Ms. Whiz' from a local television program that aired in Atlanta, Georgia, and today I continue to be 'Ms. Whiz,' performing science magic for school assembly programs and for conventions of librarians and teachers.

"I co-authored a couple of books with William Markle, my exhusband. After my divorce, I met my husband Skip Jeffery while working in Antarctica. Skip has helped me with my books by supplying photographs for some of my recent titles, including *Can You Believe: Volcanoes* and *Outside and Inside Big Cats*. Skip and I were from opposite sides of the United States and while trying to decide where to live, we realized that we both really loved New Zealand—a country we came to know because it is the place you come to in order to fly to Antarctica. It is a very beautiful country and still largely untouched. I now live outside Christchurch, New Zealand, just two minutes from the beach and within an hour of the Southern Alps. Having lived here for five years now, I feel New Zealand has become my adopted, very special home.

"Today, I am as intrigued by science and the whole world of exploration as I was in the fifth grade. I'm continuing to write, producing books that range from guides to hands-on science activities to real-life stories about wildlife and science discoveries. Some of my newest titles include the Animal Predator series, *Outside and Inside Mummies*, *Rescues*, the Biggest! Littlest! series, and *A Mother's Journey*. With each book, my goal is to make readers feel they're sharing my journey of discovery too from cover to cover."

❄ ❄ ❄

"The journey that led to my writing science books for children started when I was in the fifth grade."

Sandra Markle graduated magna cum laude from Bowling Green State University in 1968. She did graduate work at Ohio University and the University of North Carolina. A former elementary school teacher and radio presenter on science topics, she has written over 70 nonfiction books for young readers. She has also developed science specials on CNN and PBS and produced numerous magazine and newspaper articles on science and mathematics for adults. Widely recognized as a science education consultant, Markle has helped produce an elementary science textbook series, was on the planning committee for *Peanut* (a magazine for IBM-PCJunior users), wrote the "Hands-On Science" column for *Instructor* magazine for 11 years, and frequently contributes articles to *Family Fun* and *Parenting* magazines. She is noted for developing "On-Line Expedition: Antarctica," one of the first online educational programs, and its sequel "On-Line Expedition: New Zealand." In 1997, she founded the nonprofit organization CompuQuest, Inc., to continue developing quality Internet-based educational materials. This project, funded with a two-year $500,000 grant from the National Science Foundation and $55,000 from NASA, as well as additional corporate support, developed Markle's Kit & Kaboodle curriculum program. An independent evaluation conducted by Georgia State University has shown that students using this program score as much as 10 percent higher on science achievement tests.

Markle's books have received a number of awards. *Outside and Inside Bats* won a *Boston Globe–Horn Book* Honor Award for Nonfiction and *Outside and Inside Birds* was named an ALA Notable Children's Book. The Outside and Inside books provide children with a scientific understanding of a wide variety of interesting plants and animals. She received the Best of Children's

Courtesy of Simon & Schuster Books for Young Readers

Nonfiction Georgia Author of the Year Award in several different years for *Discovering Graph Secrets, Outside and Inside Bats, Outside and Inside Alligators,* and *Outside and Inside Kangaroos.* Many of her books have been cited as Outstanding Science Trade Books, including *Exploring Winter, Outside and Inside Birds, Outside and Inside Spiders, Science to the Rescue, Outside and Inside Kangaroos,* and *Growing Up Wild: Penguins.* Two of her titles were named to the Bank Street College of Education's list of Best Children's Books of the Year: *Outside and Inside Trees* and *Growing Up Wild: Wolves.*

The Fledglings, which was about a runaway orphan's attempts to discover her own heritage and the care she gives to a fledgling eagle, was named an IRA Young Adult Choice in 1994 and received a Society of School Librarians International Honor Book Award in Language Arts. *Down, Down, Down in the Ocean* received the Parents' Choice Award, and *Growing Up Wild: Bears* received a Parent's Guide to Children's Media Nonfiction Award. *After the Spill,* which explores the effects of the *Exxon Valdez* oil disaster, won the Utah Children's Book Award.

Many of Markle's books are illustrated with her own drawings or with photographs she has taken on her many journeys and adventures of discovery. She currently resides with her husband in the South Island of New Zealand, where she enjoys being close to nature, fishing along wild streams and lakes, and capturing the beauty of the landscape in her watercolors. She has two children, Scott and Holly.

SELECTED WORKS WRITTEN AND ILLUSTRATED: *Primary Science Sampler*, 1980; *Science Sampler*, 1980; *Kids' Computer Capers: Investigations for Beginners*, 1983; *The Programmer's Guide to the Galaxy*, 1984; *In Search of Graphics: Adventures in Computer Art*, with William Markle, 1985; *Digging Deeper: Investigations into Rocks, Shocks, Quakes, and Other Earthy Matter*, 1987; *Exploring Summer*, 1988; *Exploring Winter*, 1988; *Hands-On Science*, 1988; *Power Up: Experiments, Puzzles, and Games Exploring Electricity*, 1989; *Exploring Spring*, 1990; *The Kids' Earth Handbook*, 1991; *Earth Alive!* 1991; *Exploring Autumn*, 1991; *Science Mini-Mysteries*, 1991; *The Fledglings*, 1992; *Pioneering Space*, 1992; *Math Mini-Mysteries*, 1993; *Outside and Inside Trees*, 1993; *Outside and Inside Birds*, 1994; *Outside and Inside Spiders*, 1994; *Science to the Rescue*, 1994; *Measuring Up*, 1995; *Outside and Inside Snakes*, 1995; *Pioneering Ocean Depths*, 1995; *What Happens Next?*, 1995; *Creepy, Crawly Baby Bugs*, 1996; *Outside and Inside Sharks*, 1996; *Pioneering Frozen Worlds*, 1996; *What Happens Next?* vol. 2, 1996; *Outside and Inside Bats*, 1997; *Discovering Graph Secrets*, 1997; *Super Science Secrets*, 1997; *Outside and Inside Alligators*, 1998; *Super Cool Science: South Pole Stations Past, Present, and Future*, 1998; *After the Spill: The* Exxon Valdez *Disaster, Then and Now*, 1999; *Outside and Inside Kangaroos*, 1999; *Growing Up Wild: Bears*, 2000; *Outside and Inside Dinosaurs*, 2000; *Growing Up Wild: Penguins*, 2001; *Growing Up Wild: Wolves*, 2001; *Outside and Inside Rats and Mice*, 2001; *Sea Babies*, 2002; *Outside and Inside Big Cats*, 2003; *Outside and Inside Giant Squid*, 2003; *Predators*, 2003; *Animal Predators: Wolves*, 2003; *Animal Predators: Crocodiles*, 2004; *Animal Predators: Great White Sharks*, 2004; *Animal Predators: Killer Whales*, 2004; *Animal Predators: Lions*, 2004; *Animal Predators: Owls*, 2004; *Animal Predators: Polar Bears*, 2004; *Chocolate: A Sweet History*, 2004; *Outside and Inside Killer Bees*, 2004.

SELECTED WORKS WRITTEN: *Computer Tutor*, illus. by Beverly Armstrong, 1981; *Computer Tutor Junior*, illus. by Beverly Armstrong, 1982; *Weather / Electricity / Environmental Investigations*, illus. by Beverly Armstrong, 1982; *A Young Scientist's Guide to Successful Science Projects*, illus. by Bob Byrd, 1989; *Discovering Science Secrets*, illus. by June Otani, 1991; *Outside and Inside You*, illus. by Susan Kuklin, 1991; *Discovering More Science Secrets*, illus. by June Otani, 1992; *A Rainy Day*, illus. by Cathy Johnson, 1993; *Science: Just Add Salt*, illus. by June Otani, 1994; *Science in a Bottle*, illus. by June Otani, 1995; *Creepy, Spooky Science*, illus. by Cecile Schoberle, 1996; *Icky, Squishy Science*, illus. by Cecile Schoberle 1996; *Science Surprises*, illus. by June Otani, 1996; *Gone Forever: An Alphabet of Extinct Animals*, with William Markle, illus. by Felipe Dávalos, 1998; *Weird, Wacky Science*, illus. by Cecile Schoberle, 1998; *Down, Down, Down in the*

Ocean, illus. by Bob Marstall, 1999; *Magic*, illus. by Jamie Smith, 2001; *Can You Believe: Hurricanes*, illus. by Jo-Ellen C. Bosson, 2002; *Can You Believe: Insects*, illus. by Jo-Ellen C. Bosson, 2002; *Can You Believe: Volcanoes*, illus. by Jo-Ellen C. Bosson, 2002; *That's Amazing!: Earthquakes*, illus. by Jo-Ellen C. Bosson, 2002; *Amazing Human Body*, illus. by Jo-Ellen C. Bosson, 2002; *Science Dares You: Build a Room Alarm and 16 More Electrifying Projects!*, illus. by Eric Brace, 2003; *Science Dares You: Grow a Giant Beanstalk and 15 More Amazing Plant Projects!*, illus. by Eric Brace, 2003; *Spiders: Biggest! Littlest!*, illus. by Simon Pollard, 2004.

SUGGESTED READING: *Something About the Author*, vol. 148, 2004.

"I have always hated being bored, so school was not a very pleasant experience for me. Most of the teachers were boring, or bullies, or both. I had two good years, in Grade 4 and Grade 6, when I had creative, warm, generous, and good-natured teachers, which made quite a difference. All the way through high school I sat in the back of the class thinking 'There must be a better way to teach than this. Why do they have to be so cold and unfriendly?' I was at a military school, where they believed that a teacher who was friendly with the students was weak, and this would lead to a complete collapse of the educational system.

"The ways I eased my boredom in school were to read and to write. I read, I don't know how many, several thousand books during my childhood and adolescence, and often tried writing things, always fiction, and usually imitative and clichéd. After leaving school I tried law but didn't like it. I had an idea that I would enjoy teaching, but there was an attitude of contempt in my family towards teachers, and as a result I was reluctant to go down that path. However, when I was about 28, I decided that teaching had to be better than selling pizzas, or working in a mortuary, or being a motor-bike courier, or operating a hospital switchboard, or any of the other jobs I'd tried, so I enrolled in a course in primary (elementary) teaching.

"I loved it! It enabled me to be creative, to be subversive, to engage with people on a daily basis—and to make a difference. As part of the course we had to read some children's fiction, and so for the first time in 15 or 16 years I found myself going to the

Courtesy of Katie Morgan

John Marsden

*September 27,
1950–*

children's section of the library. I was overwhelmed by the quality of the books I found there: titles like *Smith* by Leon Garfield, *The Nargun and the Stars* by Patricia Wrightson, and *Elidor* by Alan Garner. As it turned out I taught high school rather than primary school, but I loved that too. It was disappointing, however, to find that the range of fiction available to adolescents was inferior to the quality of the books for younger readers. Apart from Paul Zindel and Judy Blume, no one else seemed to be breaking new ground or writing material that teenagers might find accessible and attractive.

"I spent a short vacation writing a novel that I thought my Grade 9 students might enjoy, and eventually, on the seventh attempt, found a publisher who was willing to take it on. This book, *So Much to Tell You*, became one of Australia's biggest selling novels and won the Christopher Medal in the U.S.A. Needless to say, I decided this was good fun, so I continued to write for teenagers and have done so pretty much to this day, except for a small group of books for younger readers.

"I've now published 31 titles (not all of them are available in the U.S.A.). I still enjoy what I do, although the work generated by writing has meant that I have had to quit full-time teaching, which I regard as something of a loss. What I have done instead is to set up my own writing centre, on 1,100 acres of beautiful forest just outside Melbourne in Australia, where I run residential courses and camps for young people and adults who want to improve their writing skills. At the same time I'm able to preserve an important piece of Australian bush, with lots of kangaroos and wallabies and koalas!

"I suppose my most satisfying experience in writing has been the success of the Tomorrow, When the War Began series, which has sold over 3 million books in Australia alone—a country which has a population of only 19 million. And I continue to love reading and writing as much as I did back in primary school."

"I have always hated being bored, so school was not a very pleasant experience for me. Most of the teachers were boring, or bullies, or both."

✿   ✿   ✿

John Marsden was born in Melbourne, Australia, but his early childhood was spent in quiet country towns, first in Kyneton, where his family moved when he was two. He lived in Devonport, on the north coast of Tasmania, between the ages of 6 and 10. When he was 10 his family moved to Sydney, where he was sent to the King's School, a spartan conservative boarding school run along military lines, and he remained there throughout his secondary education. In 1969, Marsden pursued a law degree at the University of Sydney for a time, but abandoned it for a series of interesting jobs, which included guarding a mortuary at night and working in a sideshow. At age 28, he decided to become a teacher, receiving his degree from Mitchell College Bathurst and starting his career as an English teacher at All Saint's College Bathurst. Perhaps reacting against the tedium of his own school years, Marsden became a passionate teacher. He then taught at Geelong Grammar School from 1982 until 1990, becoming head of the English Department.

During a school vacation, Marsden wrote the book that became his first published title in 1987, *So Much to Tell You.* Winner of Australia's Children's Book of the Year Award and the Victorian Premier's Literary Award, the book went on to success abroad and captured the Christopher Medal in the United States. The story was inspired by two real people: a woman whose face had been damaged by a gunshot wound and a 14-year-old girl Marsden had once met who would not speak. That girl's spirit haunted Marsden as he told the story of a mute and physically scarred girl who had been hurt when her father attempted to pour acid on her mother, missed, and injured her instead. *So Much to Tell You* became one of Australia's best-selling novels and has been published in 16 countries. Marsden returned to the mental hospital setting in *Checkers*, a political novel about a girl who has a nervous breakdown after a family crisis resulting from her father's unethical business practices.

Courtesy of Houghton Mifflin, Inc.

Marsden's books sometimes evoke controversy for his unsentimental portrayal of sex and violence, but he is also applauded for not talking down to his teen readers and providing adventure stories in which the heroes and heroines must face moral and ethical issues. In one of his most compelling stories, *Letters from the Inside*, a chilling psychological drama plays out in the correspondence between two teenage pen pals, one of whom is incarcerated in a maximum security prison. Based on a newspaper account of a murder, a television interview with a murderer's girlfriend, and a conversation the author had with a young girl about her violent brother, *Letters from the Inside* also draws on the author's own experiences in a Tasmanian prison after he was arrested during a conservation demonstration. Named an ALA Best Book for Young Adults, *Letters* was also a runner-up for the Dutch Children's Book of the Year and won the Grand Jury Prize in Austria.

The first title in Marsden's landmark young adult series bears the same name as the series—*Tomorrow, When the War Began.* A group of Australian teens return from a camping trip to find their homes destroyed, their families incarcerated, and an invading force taking over their country. A fast-paced survival story with elements of romance and moral dilemma, the book was an instant hit with readers. Winner of the older section of every state award in Australia judged by teen readers themselves, it was named an ALA Best Book for Young Adults in the United States. Subsequent titles in the series have continued to earn awards and break sales records in Australia, as well as being successfully published around the world. The seventh and final book in the series, *The Other Side of Dawn*, appeared in the United States in 2002. Many of Marsden's books have been cited as New York Public Library Books for the Teen Age, including *A Killing Frost, Checkers*, and *The Dead of Night*.

John Marsden has also written for younger children, including such picture books as the thought-provoking *A Prayer for the Twenty-First Century*, which poetically combines modern anxieties with basic fears, all in the form of a prayer, and *The Rabbits*, an allegorical picture book about devastating ecological and cultural destruction with evocative illustrations by Shaun Tan, which won the Children's Book Council of Australia Picture Book of the Year Award. His books continue to win awards around the world. *The Third Day, the Frost* received the most coveted award in Germany for young people's books, and *Tomorrow, When the War Began* was chosen in Sweden as the book most likely to inspire teenagers to read. Marsden now teaches writing workshops for adults and young people on the Tye Estate in Melbourne.

SELECTED WORKS (dates are for Australian editions; U.S. dates are in parentheses): *So Much to Tell You*, 1987 (1989); *The Journey*, 1988; *Staying Alive in Year Five*, 1989; *Out of Time*, 1990; *Letters from the Inside*, 1992 (1994); *Take My Word for It*, 1992 (1993); *Tomorrow, When the War Began*, 1993 (1995); *Everything I Know about Writing*, 1993; *Looking for Trouble*, 1993; *The Dead of the Night*, 1994 (1997); *Cool School*, 1995; *This I Believe: Over 100 Eminent Australians Explore Life's Big Question*, as editor, 1995 (1996); *Checkers*, 1996 (1998); *The Third Day, the Frost*, 1996 (U.S. title: *A Killing Frost*, 1998); *Darkness, Be My Friend*, 1997 (1999); *Burning for Revenge*, 1997 (2000); *A Prayer for the Twenty-First Century*, 1997 (1998); *The Night Is for Hunting*, 1998 (2001); *Secret Men's Business*, 1998; *The Rabbits*, illus. by Shaun Tan, 1999 (2003); *The Other Side of Dawn*, 1999 (2002); *Marsden on Marsden: The Stories Behind John Marsden's Bestselling Books*, 2000; *Winter*, 2000 (2002); *I Believe This: 100 Eminent Australians Face Life's Biggest Question*, as editor, 2004.

SUGGESTED READING: *Authors and Artists for Young Adults*, vol. 20, 1997; *Something About the Author*, vol. 146, 2004.

WEB SITE: *www.johnmarsden.com*

"I have always loved the sound of words. When I was a child growing up on our dairy farm in Maine I would say the names of our cows, just to hear them—Riceland Marathon Indigo, Bonheur Chieftan Neva. Words such as 'Marathon' or 'Bonheur' had no meaning for me, yet I enjoyed those sounds as much as I enjoyed running barefoot in wet grass or eating fresh raspberries.

"I did not think then that I would grow up to be a writer. It wasn't that I didn't know stories. My mother read us Thornton Burgess stories from the newspaper; but I had no sense of Thornton Burgess as a person who got up every morning, ate breakfast, and went to his desk to write. We had a series of books containing poems, tales, fables, and my favorite—the tale of Paul Bunyan; but all the stories in those books had been set down a long time ago. A hired man from Denmark had given us a book of the works of Hans Christian Andersen. I read and re-read those fairy tales and can still recall the wonder of the stories, the just-right-for-my-hand size of the book, and the feel of the paper; but I knew Hans Christian Andersen was dead.

"So I did what children do: played with my brothers and sisters and my cousins, played with my imaginary friend, Seekie. We tipped lawn chairs over and played our own invented game called 'fox and rabbits.' We spent hours at kick-the-can and hide-and-seek. We made little 'apartments' in the line of cedar trees that grew next to a stone wall. And I collected memories. I remember the cow who fell in the well and broke her hip bones. I remember the hurricane that blew down trees and stretched them out along the ground so we could walk the entire length of the trunk. I remember eating spaghetti served out of an old tin kettle at the edge of the field. That was our own kind of picnic. My father could jump off the tractor during a busy day and join us—if we brought the picnic to him.

"I wrote book reports and school reports. I wrote one essay in third grade—why farmers should keep registered Holsteins—and sent it in to a state contest. It won third prize! But I still did not think of myself as a writer. When I got to high school one of my teachers suggested I think of a career involving writing. But I was too busy with high school to think of careers. I went to college and met many others who seemed to have greater claim to the title of 'writer' than I did.

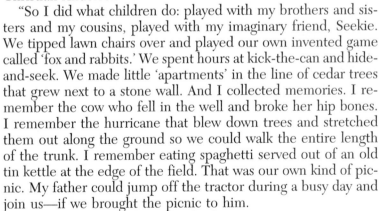

Courtesy of Sharron McElmeel

Jacqueline Briggs Martin

April 15, 1945–

"Eventually I married and moved to a rented house on a pig farm in Iowa with my husband and two young children. My husband went to work every morning and Sarah and Justin and I had the day to fill with our own activities. We played. And we read books—stacks of children's books. *Curious George, Babar the Elephant, Bartholomew Cubbins*, and *Chicken Soup with Rice* were some of our favorites. It was then that I began to want to be a writer. I wanted to write stories which children and parents could enjoy as much as we had enjoyed the stories we read and re-read.

"I recalled the words of my high school teacher. Armed with those words, a new tablet of paper, and a new pen, I began to write. I got up very early in the morning and wrote before the sun came up. In the corner of the dining room, by the light of one lamp, I invented people and places. Many of those people and places never got further than a box in our basement. But eventually I found my way to write stories which others have wanted to read.

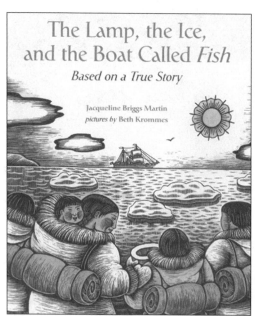

The Lamp, the Ice, and the Boat Called *Fish*

Based on a True Story

Jacqueline Briggs Martin
pictures *by* Beth Krommes

Courtesy of Houghton Mifflin, Inc.

"I am grateful every day that I get to work with words, to watch the world and pick out the parts which make me want to sing or laugh or cry, and tell about them. And I am grateful that in this busy, bustling time there are children and parents, children and friends, teachers, aunts, uncles, grandparents who sit in chairs, on beach blankets, under trees and read books."

Growing up in Maine gave Jacqueline Briggs Martin a fine appreciation for nature and history, two themes that are woven throughout her most successful books for children. After graduating from Wellesley College in 1966, she married Richard Martin, a college professor, the following year. Her husband teaches at Cornell College in Iowa, where they raised their two children, who are now grown. Their daughter, Sarah, lives in California with her husband and young son, and their son, Justin, lives in Honduras. Jackie attended the University of Minnesota Institute for Child Development in 1971 and for many years taught preschool, getting up early in the morning to write before going to teach. But her real love was writing, and today she spends her time creating picture book texts and visiting schools to talk about her books.

Jackie Martin writes picture books for a wide age range; her early books were directed toward the preschool audience, but many of her later titles appeal to older children and adults with their historical settings and scientific themes. *Snowflake Bentley*, which was included in nearly all the lists of best books for 1998 and won a Caldecott Medal for Mary Azarian's striking illustrations, is a picturebook biography of the 19th-century Vermont farmer who was fascinated by photography and snowflakes. Martin first heard of him when she and her children read an article in *Cricket* magazine in 1979, and she remembered for years her fascination with Bentley's life. *Snowflake Bentley* was also named an Outstanding Science Trade Book of the year.

Several of Martin's books have appeared on lists of Notable Social Studies Trade Books for Young People: *Washing the Willow Tree Loon*, *Green Truck Garden Giveaway*, and her fascinating account of survival in the Arctic, *The Lamp, the Ice, and the Boat Called Fish*. Based on a true story of a 1913 expedition, this sensitive tale of disparate cultures learning from each other was also an ALA Notable Children's Book and a *Smithsonian* magazine Notable Children's Book. *Grandmother Bryant's Pocket* was named an ALA Notable Children's Book, won the Lupine Award of the state of Maine, and appeared on many of the year's Best Books lists. Set in Maine in 1787, the story relates how wise grandparents help a young girl recover from the death of her beloved dog. *On Sand Island*, about a fishing community in Lake Superior in the early 20th century, was a *Publishers Weekly* Best Book in 2003.

SELECTED WORKS: *Bizzy Bones and Uncle Ezra*, illus. by Stella Omai, 1984; *Bizzy Bones and Moosemouse*, illus. by Stella Omai, 1986; *Bizzy Bones and the Lost Quilt*, illus. by Stella Omai, 1988; *The Finest Horse in Town*, illus. by Susan Gaber, 1992; *Good Times on Grandfather Mountain*, illus. by Susan Gaber, 1992; *Washing the Willow Tree Loon*, illus. by Nancy Carpenter, 1995; *Green Truck Garden Giveaway: A Neighborhood Story and Almanac*, illus. by Alec Gillman, 1997; *Grandmother Bryant's Pocket*, illus. by Petra Mathers, 1996; *Higgins Bend Song and Dance*, illus. by Brad Sneed, 1997; *Button, Bucket, Sky*, illus. by Vicki Jo Redenbaugh, 1998; *Snowflake Bentley*, illus. by Mary Azarian, 1998; *The Lamp, the Ice, and the Boat Called Fish*, illus. by Beth Krommes, 2001; *The Water Gift and the Pig of the Pig*, illus. by Linda Wingerter, 2003; *On Sand Island*, illus. by David A. Johnson, 2003.

SUGGESTED READING: *Something About the Author*, vol. 98, 1998. Online—"Picture Book Potpourri," with Jacqueline Briggs Martin, Institute of Children's Literature, *www.institutechildrenslit.com/rx/tr01/ jacqueline_briggs_martin.shtml*.

Courtesy of Elaine S. Martens

Robert McCloskey

September 15, 1914–June 30, 2003

The following autobiographical sketch was written by Robert McCloskey for *The Junior Book of Authors* (1951):

"I was born in Hamilton, Ohio. I attended public school, and from the time my fingers were long enough to play the scale I took piano lessons. I started next to play the harmonica, the drums, and then the oboe. The musician's life was the life for me; that is, until I became interested in things electrical and things mechanical. I collected old electric motors and bits of wire, old clocks and Meccano sets. I built trains and cranes with remote control; my family's Christmas trees revolved, lights flashed and buzzers buzzed, fuses blew and sparks flew! The inventor's life was the life for me; that is, until I started making drawings for the high school paper and the high school annual. I was presented with a scholarship to an art school in Boston, and from Boston I went to New York to attend the National Academy of Design. I painted during the summers on Cape Cod and received a scholarship to study in Rome. The artist's life became the life for me.

"It is just sort of an accident that I write books. I really think up stories in pictures and just fill in between the pictures with a sentence or a paragraph or a few pages of words.

"Besides being an artist, I am the husband of my wife, Margaret, and the father of my daughter, Sarah. During the war [World War II] we lived in Alabama. I was a sergeant and drew training pictures for the army. Now at last we have a home on an island off the coast of Maine.

"When I was young I surrounded myself with musical instruments and tried the musician's life. Then I worked for hours with motors and wires and tried the inventor's life. With paints and brushes and such I have lived the artist's life. But you know, living on the sea I have been spending a lot of time with sea gulls and fish lately. Just this morning while I was shaving, I noticed a very slight difference in my whiskers. I examined them carefully, but it is too early to tell whether they are changing into scales or feathers."

❈ ❈ ❈

If asked to name their favorite childhood picture book, throngs of people would respond, *Make Way for Ducklings*. Robert McCloskey created children's books that were quickly recognized as classics and have attained the enduring life of beloved family memories. McCloskey's own boyhood passions for music and invention would become the taproots for his children's books. His musical talent and inventive mechanics gained him an after-school job at the YMCA teaching hobbies to boys, including playing the harmonica, making model airplanes, and carving figures from soap—all experiences that would later appear in his children's books.

In his senior year in high school he won a nationwide Scholastic Award for his woodcut engraving, earning him a scholarship to the Vesper George School of Art in Boston. After three winters of study there and three summers of counseling in a boys' camp in Ohio, he moved to New York City and in 1935 called on May Massee, editor of Junior Books at Viking. She told him to shelve his paintings of dragons, Pegasus, and limpid pools and go back and learn to draw. And he did. For two years he studied at the National Academy of Design in New York and then returned to Massee in 1939 with a humorous story and drawings about a boy who learns to play the harmonica. *Lentil* was born, and McCloskey's first children's book was published by Viking in 1940 with double-spread sepia artwork that captured the flavor of an American hometown, circa 1914. It was the precursor of all his books stemming from keen observation and first-hand experience.

That same year he married Margaret Durand, a children's librarian and the daughter of Ruth Sawyer, a Newbery Award–winning writer and a well-known storyteller. Children's books had become a family affair. In 1942 two events occurred, one that would be a milestone for McCloskey: he joined the army and *Make Way for Ducklings* won the Caldecott Medal. This, his most beloved book, had begun years earlier, when McCloskey was working on a mural commission in Boston. He came across the story of the ducks in the Public Gardens and was taken with the novelty of an animal family charming a big city. A book idea took shape. As he drew the final sketches, he realized he knew very little about mallards. Being meticulous about details, he visited the Museum of Natural History in New York, an ornithologist, and the Washington Market in Manhattan, where he bought four ducks from a poultry dealer.

In his Caldecott acceptance speech, McCloskey described what happened: "With pride I took my purchases home to the studio and displayed them to Marc Simont, my roommate at that time. He didn't even bat an eye when he found that all six of us were going to live together. The ducks had plenty to say— especially in the early morning. I spent the next weeks on my hands and knees, armed with a box of Kleenex and a sketch book, following ducks around the studio and observing them in the bathtub." Years later the enormously popular story inspired sculptor Nancy Schon, who created the bronze statues of the ducks that were installed in Boston's Public Gardens in 1989 and continue to attract visitors today. *Make Way for Ducklings* was named the official state book of Massachusetts in 2003.

"When I was young I surrounded myself with musical instruments and tried the musician's life. Then I worked for hours with motors and wires and tried the inventor's life. With paints and brushes and such I have lived the artist's life."

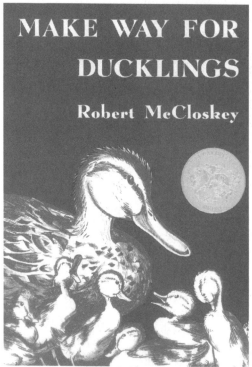

Courtesy of Viking/PenguinPutnam Books

World War II was under way when Mc-Closkey joined the army, but he wanted to finish another book before he went. His three years in military service (1942–1945) were spent making visual aids for the infantry at Fort McClellan, Alabama. He laughingly reported in an article, "My greatest contribution to the war effort was inventing a machine to enable short second lieutenants to flip over large training charts in a high breeze." Of considerably more merit was the book he completed. *Homer Price*, published in 1943, was a chapter book written for older children that related six blithe tales about the title character, illustrated with McCloskey's sprightly line drawings, similar in style to those in *Lentil*. Homer's invention of a continuous doughnut machine that wouldn't stop became a favorite story, and the illustration of the contraption was clearly and cleverly the product of McCloskey's inventive mind. *Centerburg Tales*, a follow-up book continuing Homer's adventures, was published in 1951, set again in the same small town as *Lentil*.

After being discharged from the army, the McCloskeys, now a family of three with young daughter Sally born in 1945, headed for Maine. His last four books were all inspired by his family life there. *Blueberries for Sal*, 1948, is a perfectly designed book: oversized, with blueberry-colored lithograph drawings that flawlessly frame the scenario of the mix-up between Sal and her mother and a mother bear and her cub on a berry-picking outing. The satisfying balance and simplicity of the story, the spare text, and the lively illustrations, modeled upon McCloskey's own wife and daughter and the family kitchen, created another favorite that became a classic.

One Morning in Maine (1952) captures the charm of everyday family life near the water and the excitement of a childhood moment when the younger of two sisters loses a tooth. Navy blue lithographs highlight the momentous occasion; the family scenes were based on sketches of McCloskey's two daughters, Sally and her younger sister, Jane. *Time of Wonder* (1957) was a departure from McCloskey's previous books. Three years in the making, it was his first book created in full color, using watercolors. The text was joyfully poetic, with rich imagery that conveyed his love for his Maine island home. The book won the 1958 Caldecott Medal, and McCloskey became the first artist to win the award twice.

In a personal commentary following McCloskey's second Caldecott speech, Marc Simont described his friend: "Bob McCloskey's talent for devising mechanical contraptions is topped only by his ability to turn out books that carry off the Caldecott Medal." Over 12 years, McCloskey not only won the medal twice but also received three Caldecott Honors: for *Blueberries for Sal, One Morning in Maine*, and *Journey Cake, Ho!*. An old folktale about a runaway johnny-cake, this last story was retold by his mother-in-law, Ruth Sawyer; McCloskey's rollicking drawings matched the humor of the story and depicted the down-home charm of its Appalachian setting. Six years later, in 1963, he produced his second full-color book splashed with lavish caricature paintings. *Burt Dow: Deep-Water Man* is a playful tall tale of an old Maine fisherman who puts to sea in a leaky dory and almost winds up in the belly of a whale.

Robert McCloskey's artistic ability was recognized early when he received the President's Award from the National Academy of Design in 1936 and the Tiffany Foundation prize, Prix de Rome, in 1939. In addition to these artistic awards, McCloskey was presented the Regina Medal in 1974 for his distinguished contribution to children's literature. In his Caldecott acceptance speech for *Make Way for Ducklings*, he said: "I'm not a children's illustrator. I'm just an artist who among other things does children's books. Like a musician who likes to have his music listened to, the architect who likes to build houses that are homes, I like to have my pictures looked at and enjoyed."

Though his output was not prodigious— he wrote and illustrated eight books of his own and illustrated 10 for other authors— the impact of McCloskey's work far outweighs that of many more prolific writers and illustrators. His use of line, composition, and page design was masterful. On April 24, 2000, Robert McCloskey was designated a "Living Legend" by the Library of Congress. He was one of six children's book authors among the 78 honorees cited. This mark of distinction is bestowed upon people who have advanced and embodied the American ideals of individual creativity, conviction, and exuberance, qualities that have enriched the nation.

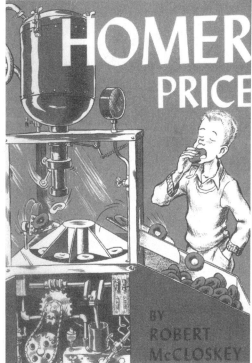

Courtesy of Viking/Penguin Putnam Books

It is the credibility of his pictures and words that appeals to children and adults, while the gentle humor, kindness, compassion, and integrity of his work provide a protective frame for the exuberance of childhood. As Norman Rockwell was to magazine illustration, Robert McCloskey was to children's literature: Both artists portrayed slices of Americana spiced with wit, grace, and keen observation. Their art has endeared them to generations, and without a doubt they enjoyed every moment of it.

SELECTED WORKS WRITTEN AND ILLUSTRATED: *Lentil*, 1940; *Make Way for Ducklings*, 1941; *Homer Price*, 1943; *Blueberries for Sal*, 1948; *Centerburg Tales*, 1951; *One Morning in Maine*, 1952; *Time of Wonder*, 1957; *Burt Dow, Deep-Water Man: A Tale of the Sea in the Classic Tradition*, 1963.

SELECTED WORKS ILLUSTRATED: *Yankee Doodle's Cousins*, by Anne Malcolmson, 1941; *Tree Toad*, by Robert Hobart Davis, 1942; *The Man Who Lost His Head*, by Claire Hutchet Bishop, 1942; *Trigger John's Son*, by Tom Robinson, 1949; *Journey Cake, Ho!*, by Ruth Sawyer, 1953; *Junket*, by Anne H. White, 1955; *Henry Reed, Inc.*, by Keith Robertson, 1958; *Henry Reed's Journey*, by Keith Robertson, 1963; *Henry Reed's Baby Sitting Service*, by Keith Robertson, 1966; *Henry Reed's Big Show*, by Keith Robertson, 1970.

SUGGESTED READING: Cullinan, Bernice, and Diane Person. *The Continuum Encyclopedia of Children's Literature*, 2001; Hopkins, Lee Bennett. *Books Are by People*, 1969; Hopkins, Lee Bennett. *Pauses: Autobiographical Reflections of 101 Creators of Children's Books*, 1995; Marcus, Leonard. *A Caldecott Celebration*, 1998; Marcus, Leonard. *Ways of Telling: Conversations on the Art of the Picture Book*, 2002; Silvey, Anita, ed. *Children's Books and Their Creators*, 1995; *Something About the Author*, vol. 100, 1999. Periodicals— McCloskey, Robert, "Caldecott Medal Acceptance," *The Horn Book*, July 1942; McCloskey, Robert, "Caldecott Award Acceptance," *The Horn Book*, August 1958; *New York Times*, July 1, 2003 (obituary).

Tom McGowen

May 6, 1927–

"Some of my earliest recollections, from the age of four or five, are of my mother reading to me at bedtime from the marvelous *Oz* books of L. Frank Baum. I think those readings gave me the love of fantasy that has been a major factor in my life, and in my writing. The period of my childhood, the 1930s, was when science fiction was just coming into its own, and there was a profusion of science fantasy magazines available. These fed my appetite for fantasy and also probably helped instill an interest in aspects of science that has always been a major part of my character. The books of British author H. G. Wells, known as the 'father of science fiction,' were also instrumental in teaching me how science fiction can be useful in examining social and technological problems and extrapolating them to determine how they might affect the future.

"Farther up the line, when I was in my thirties, I found the writer who affected my work most of all—J. R. R. Tolkien, whose gems *The Hobbit* and *The Lord of the Rings* trilogy I regard as the major fantasy achievement of the 20th century. His effect on my own writing may be seen most readily in my 1970 fantasy novel, *Sir MacHinery*, which to this day elicits letters and comments from people who relished it when they were children as well as people whose children were affected by it. It may well be my major contribution to the field of children's literature.

"Like many writers, I began making up stories and writing them down at a very early age; in my case about seven or eight. Throughout childhood and adolescence I continued to write stories because it was fun to do, and during my time of service in the U.S. Navy during World War II, I often whiled away periods of boredom by writing. At the age of 38, after some years as an advertising artist and writer, I made the decision that what I real-

Courtesy of Nicholas Litrento

ly wanted to do was write for children, possibly because by that time I had four children of my own who seemed entertained by the stories I made up for them. After suffering no more than two years of rejections, I had the amazing good fortune of having two books accepted by two different publishers within about three weeks of each other.

"At the age of 42 I began what was to be a long period of utter satisfaction, when I joined the firm then known as Field Enterprises Educational Corporation, publisher of World Book Encyclopedia and also of the Childcraft books for children. I spent the next 19 years happily working at writing books for children five days a week for Childcraft, and then spending a good part of my evenings and weekends writing my own books for children at home. I published 17 'in house' books with Childcraft, and 60 more titles were published by various publishers in the 36 or so years since I began writing for children. Of the latter, seven were 'storybooks' for younger kids, 11 were fantasy novels, 40 were nonfiction, chiefly in areas of natural and physical science, history, and military history. One was a Dungeons and Dragons 'Endless Quest' book, with which the reader could actually construct a number of different stories by making a particular choice at certain points in the narrative.

"At the end of 1987 I retired from the firm (now called World Book, Inc.) and concentrated on my own books, most recently nonfiction dealing with events of World War II. As a veteran of that war, I feel it is important that I try to pass along an understanding of that time when the world was actually saved from conquest by the horrible system of fascism in a truly epic struggle. At the present moment, I have several interesting nonfiction projects lined up. People sometimes ask me when I'm really going to retire, and the answer is, I'm not; I love writing too much to ever want to quit!"

✿　✿　✿

Tom McGowen was born in Evanston, Illinois. He attended Roosevelt College of Chicago (now known as Roosevelt University) and the American Academy of Art. His experience of serving in the United States Navy during World War II has informed his most recent nonfiction books for young readers, but over a 40-year career in children's books, he has covered many subjects in science and social history as well. His series of Album books was especially well received in the 1970s and 1980s. Many of the titles have been published in German, Danish, Swedish, and British editions. *Album of Prehistoric Man* was named a Notable Children's Trade Book in the Field of Social Studies, and *Album of Whales* was cited as an Outstanding Science Trade Book in 1981, as was *Radioactivity* in 1987. *The Great Monkey Trial* appeared on the New York Public Library's list of Books for the Teen Age in 1991.

McGowen's fantasy novels have been favorites of many young readers over the years. *The Magician's Apprentice* was named a *Booklist* Editors' Choice and has appeared on several state award nominations lists. *Trial of Magic* was cited by the Child Study Committee of Bank Street College as a Book of the Year in 1992. McGowen's earlier picture books also enjoyed great success. *Dragon Stew*, illustrated by Trina Schart Hyman, was translated into German, Danish, and Swedish and produced as an animated cartoon. His first book, the self-illustrated humorous story *The Only Glupmaker in the U.S. Navy*, was a Junior Literary Guild selection in 1966. He has also published short stories in several anthologies for children.

Tom McGowen lives in Norridge, Illinois, and continues to write challenging nonfiction for the middle school reader, primarily in the field of history.

SELECTED WORKS WRITTEN AND ILLUSTRATED: *The Only Glupmaker in the U.S. Navy*, 1966.

SELECTED WORKS WRITTEN: *Apple Strudel Soldier*, illus. by John E. Johnson, 1968; *Dragon Stew*, illus. by Trina Schart Hyman, 1969; *Sir MacHinery*, 1970; *Album of Dinosaurs*, illus. by Rod Ruth, 1972, 1987; *Album of Prehistoric Animals*, illus. by Rod Ruth, 1974, 1989; *Album of Prehistoric Man*, illus. by Rod Ruth, 1975, 1987; *Odyssey from River Bend*, 1975; *The Spirit of the Wild*, 1976; *Album of Sharks*, illus. by Rod Ruth, 1977, 1987; *Album of Astronomy*, 1979, 1987; *Album of Whales*, illus. by Rod Ruth, 1980, 1987; *Album of Rocks and Minerals*, 1981, 1987; *Encyclopedia of Legendary Creatures*, illus. by Victor G. Ambrus, 1981; *Album of Spaceflight*, illus. by Lee Brubaker, 1983, 1987; *Midway and Guadalcanal*, 1983; *War*

> *"People sometimes ask me when I'm really going to retire, and the answer is, I'm not; I love writing too much to ever want to quit!"*

Gaming, 1985; *Radioactivity: From the Curies to the Atomic Age,* 1986; *The Magician's Apprentice,* 1987; *The Circulatory System,* 1987; *The Time of the Forest,* 1988; *The Magician's Company,* 1988; *The Magician's Challenge,* 1989; *Chemistry: The Birth of a Science,* 1989; *The Great Monkey Trial: Science Versus Fundamentalism in America,* foreword by Stephen Jay Gould, 1990; *The Shadow of Fomor,* 1990; *The Magical Fellowship,* 1991; *A Trial of Magic,* 1992; *A Question of Magic,* 1993; *Lonely Eagles and Buffalo Soldiers,* 1995; *"Go for Broke": Japanese-Americans in World War II,* 1995; *Adventures in Archeology,* 1997; *African-Americans in the Old West,* 1998; *The Battle for Iwo Jima,* 1999; *Sink the Bismarck,* 1999; *Robespierre and the French Revolution in World History,* 2000; *Giant Stones and Earth Mounds,* 2000; *The Battle of Midway,* 2001; *Carrier War: Aircraft Carriers in World War II,* 2001; *Air Raid!: Bombing Campaigns of World War II,* 2001; *Assault from the Sky: Airborne Infantry of World War II,* 2002; *Assault from the Sea: Amphibious Invasions in the Twentieth Century,* 2002; *The Attack on Pearl Harbor,* 2002; *Frederick the Great, Bismarck, and the Building of the German Empire,* 2002; *D-Day,* 2004; *The Revolutionary War and George Washington's Army in American History,* 2004; *The Surrender at Appomattox,* 2004.

SUGGESTED READING: *Contemporary Authors,* New Revision Series, vol. 101, 2002; *Something About the Author,* vol. 109, 2000.

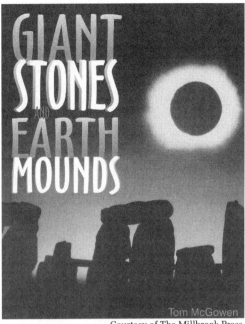

Courtesy of The Millbrook Press

The following autobiographical sketch was written by Eloise McGraw for *More Junior Authors* (1963):

"I was born in Houston, Texas, but after five years my parents moved to Oklahoma City, and it was there I grew up. I began to write early—I believe my first story occurred when I was eight years old and was written in school, when I should have been doing arithmetic. It was called 'The Cedar Pencil Boys' and I remember nothing about it except that its heroes were two animated cedarwood pencils. I had just acquired such a pencil, the first I had ever seen, and it struck me as fascinatingly exotic—so different from the ordinary yellow affairs with red erasers. I have always loved pencils, notebooks, paper, pens—all the tools of

Eloise Jarvis McGraw

December 9, 1915–November 30, 2000

writing—and hang over that counter in the dime store to this day, wanting to buy everything.

"I wrote other stories, once I'd begun, all highly fanciful, all mercifully perished long ago. I was entranced by the Oz books and had no higher ambition than to write such things someday. I have wondered since if my intense interest in imaginative stories as against realistic ones could have been a first indication of my strong tendency now to write about colorful eras of the past rather than modern-day fiction. At any rate, even then I was determined to be a writer if I possibly could, though I held such an exaggerated and reverent view of writers that I never really believed I might someday join their rarefied company.

"During high school in Oklahoma City I wrote much poetry,

Courtesy of Vern Uyetaka

crammed with adjectives and descriptions. I was madly in love with words, and my poems were scarcely more than excuses to string together words like *purple* and *scintillating* and *dusk*—or, in the case of the better ones, to describe a mood or scene which had affected me deeply. Since almost everything affected me deeply at that time, I wrote a great deal of terrible poetry, and have adjectivitis to this day unless I watch myself closely.

"The strongest influence on me during this time and, indeed, during my whole life, was the summers we spent on my uncle's Oregon farm. The Oregon country is beautiful and its forests and streams a real foretaste of heaven; moreover, the farm and country living were a constant delight to me. Later, I made use of my stored-up memories in my first three books, all of which were laid in Oregon. Shortly after completing the third of these, I actually enticed my own family up here to live, and I think they love it as much as I.

"In college I went on for a while with writing, then suddenly turned to oil painting instead, and changed my ambition. I became proficient enough to earn several commissions for portraits and murals, and had no idea I would ever return to writing. But after a bit of postgraduate work at the Universities of Oklahoma and Colorado—in sculpture and painting—and after teaching oil painting a couple of years at Oklahoma City University, I married a newspaperman from Des Moines, Iowa, William Corbin McGraw. His work took us to Athens and Cleveland, Ohio; to Oklahoma City again; and finally to La Jolla, California. By this time we had two children, a boy, Peter, and a girl, Laurie. I had dropped painting for theater work, puppet work, a little radio, and a great deal of modern dance, and was becoming interested in ceramics. However, I was possessed of a conviction that my husband should write books, not newspaper stories. Since he was slow about doing this, I wrote one myself, to nudge him a little. To my astonishment, it was accepted by Coward-McCann and published. I was a writer after all. My husband looked at the book thoughtfully and sat down at his typewriter. The following year he had his first young people's novel published and I had my second.

"At length we moved to Oregon, bought a filbert orchard and an old farmhouse to remodel, acquired two or three saddle horses, two dogs, and innumerable cats, and are now both settled firmly into our chosen trade. I work with copper and enamel now instead of ceramics and would go back to painting as a hobby if only I had time. But my decision at the age of eight was obviously the right one—I am not really a painter, a dancer, or any of those other things. I first saw that cedar pencil. And though it is not so glamorous as I thought it would be, it is even more satisfying."

✿ ✿ ✿

As a writer of historical fiction, mysteries, and fantasy, Eloise Jarvis McGraw sweeps her readers into adventure in richly imagined, fascinating locales. Her third book, *Moccasin Trail*, won a Newbery Honor Medal in 1953, as did *The Golden Goblet* in 1962. Both stories attest to her ability to re-create a historical era, frontier America in the first instance, ancient Egypt in the second. Her last book, *The Moorchild*, published when the author was 81 years old, explored the realms of fantasy that so fascinated her in her own childhood and won her a third Newbery Honor Award. *The Moorchild* also garnered a *Boston Globe–Horn Book* Honor and a Golden Kite Award. A popular workshop leader and teacher known for her generosity and willingness to share her knowledge with new authors, McGraw also published articles about writing and compiled a successful textbook called *Techniques of Fiction Writing*.

Born in Houston, Texas, where she spent her first five years, Eloise McGraw was the daughter of a successful merchant, Loy Hamilton Jarvis, and a feisty woman from Oklahoma Territory, Genevieve Scoffern Jarvis. An imaginative only child with a multitude of relatives, she grew up listening to family tales from East Texas and Oklahoma and never lost her taste for a good story wherever she found it. Many of those tales turn up, transformed, in her own novels. Always involved in one kind of class or another from early childhood—piano, dancing, theater, art—she wanted to explore every aspect of creativity that she could. While she was attending Principia College, where she received a B.A. degree in 1937, a much-loved professor of English told her to choose one discipline and stick to it or she'd "scatter her fire." So for the remainder of her college career she majored in art and even taught art classes at Oklahoma City University when she was in her twenties.

"I believe my first story occurred when I was eight years old and was written in school, when I should have been doing arithmetic."

While in college she met her husband-to-be, William Corbin McGraw, in a creative writing class, and married him in 1940. They grew to know each other before their marriage more through correspondence than actual time spent together, which Eloise McGraw always thought fitting for two writers. They lived first in Athens, Ohio, where Bill had a job as a small newspaper's only reporter, then in Cleveland, Ohio, where he worked at the telegraph desk of the Cleveland *Plain Dealer*. Their first child, Peter Anthony, was born in Cleveland. But their time there was cut short because of the attack on Pearl Harbor and America's involvement in World War II. Knowing Bill would be entering one of the armed services, the McGraws moved their small family back to Oklahoma City. Eloise's first article was published about this time, a piece on raising a two-year-old that appeared in *Parents* magazine. When their daughter, Lauren Lynn, was born, Eloise decided she couldn't combine child-rearing with serious art. She threw out her paints. Bill went into the navy and trained in San Diego. In 1945, the war over, the family moved to La Jolla, California, where Bill had a job at the *San Diego Union-Tribune*.

At this point, Eloise McGraw settled down to learning the craft of writing. She later told other would-be writers that in spite of all the workshops and creative writing classes, each writer must do his own apprenticeship and find his own way. The lessons she herself learned about how she could best develop a full novel are mentioned in a series of articles she contributed to the journal the *Writer*. Eventually those articles were collected and became the basis of her textbook, *Techniques of Fiction Writing*. For the setting of her first novels—always an important element to McGraw—she chose Oregon. *Sawdust in His Shoes*, her first novel for young people, was about a trick rider in a circus who tries to adapt to an Oregon farm. Talking about this book, she stressed how naive she was in those days. She knew Oregon, but she knew nothing about circuses and discovered through her editor that knowing what you're talking about is essential in fiction. Her second book, *Crown Fire*, was an honor book in the *New York Herald Tribune* Children's Book Festival. The German translation was awarded the Deutschen Jugenbuch–Sonder Preis. The Newbery Honor–winning historical adventure *Moccasin Trail* came next, with her hero, Jim Keath, desperately trying to sort out his obligations to the family that bore him and the Indian tribe that raised him and to achieve his own freedom.

Always fascinated by history, McGraw delved into ancient Egypt for *Mara, Daughter of the Nile*, a fast-paced adventure about a young slave girl who is drawn into the intrigue and danger of the royal court of the pharoahs. Later, using a similar setting in *The Golden Goblet*, she created a harrowing story about a young artist who discovers the half-brother to which he is apprenticed is a thief and barely escapes with his life. For *Master*

> "The strongest influence on me during this time and, indeed, during my whole life, was the summers we spent on my uncle's Oregon farm."

Cornhill she moved to late-17th-century England to follow the trials and tribulations of an orphaned 11-year-old survivor of the Great London Fire and the plague who must find a new place for himself. *The Striped Ships* brings to life the time of the Norman invasion of England in 1066. Juliana, the daughter of a well-to-do Saxon thane, delivers her little brother safely to Canterbury and escapes slavery to find work on the Bayeux Tapestry. A lively, practical heroine, Juliana matures into a self-reliant young woman of medieval times.

Combining fantasy and mystery with a historical setting, McGraw's *A Really Weird Summer* received the Edgar Award for best juvenile mystery of the year from the Mystery Writers of America. It involves a 12-year-old finding a secret passageway in an old inn and meeting an unknown boy whose family is trapped in a pocket of time. In her final novel and third Newbery Honor Book, *The Moorchild*, she also blended genres. McGraw believed that a fantasy novel, even more than a realistic one, must

Courtesy of Margaret K. McElderry Books

have a myriad of details to anchor the material and establish a convincing setting. Drawing on historical research as well as the lore of the supernatural, she interwove realistic details of medieval life with a fanciful tale about the legendary fairy folk, or "moorfolk," who live underground on the windswept moors. Her protagonist, the changeling Saaski, is caught between worlds, not fully part of either and therefore shunned by both. Saaski, once she understands who and what she is, rescues the human child who was stolen from the village when she was left in its place, and in so doing goes through the painful process of learning to accept her own true nature, in spite of those around her. A thoughtful, powerful tale, *The Moorchild*, is both an original fantasy and a deeply felt coming-of-age novel.

McGraw wrote in an article for the *Writer* that a good mystery for young readers requires three things: a secret, a child investigator, and a believable opponent. Her own mysteries have all those ingredients. In *The Money Room*, a boy named Scotty is trying to find his great-grandfather's "money room" before his rival does. The *Tangled Webb* introduces Juniper Webb as the investigator who confides to her diary that her new stepmother has a secret that Juniper is determined to discover.

Fascinated by the Oz books of L. Frank Baum when she was a child, Eloise co-authored two new Oz books with her daughter, Lauren Lynn McGraw: *Merry Go Round in Oz* in 1963 (which was reissued in 1989) and *The Forbidden Fountain of Oz* in 1980. Their joint work received the L. Frank Baum Memorial Award in 1983. In a lecture to the Winkie Convention of the International Wizard of Oz Club, mother and daughter explained how they collaborated on these books and discussed the enjoyment as well as the limitations of two authors working in tandem. Eloise's last published work was another, Oz book, *The Rundelstone of Oz*, which she finished in the year that she died. It was published the following spring.

Though she never regretted choosing to be a writer, McGraw continued to take art courses and create artworks in various mediums throughout her life. She found that in the fallow period immediately after finishing a novel, before the next was to begin, she needed such activity. Near the end of her career, she even painted the jacket pictures for two of her novels. Eloise Jarvis McGraw received a lifetime achievement award from the Willamette Writers' Organization in Oregon in 1998. She died in 2000, a year after her husband. They had been married for 59 years.

SELECTED WORKS: *Sawdust in His Shoes*, 1950; *Crown Fire*, 1951; *Moccasin Trail*, 1952; *Mara, Daughter of the Nile*, 1953; *The Golden Goblet*, 1961; *Steady, Stephanie* (one-act play), 1962; *Merry Go Round in Oz*, with Lauren McGraw, 1963; *Greensleeves*, 1968; *Master Cornhill*, 1973; *A Really Weird Summer*, 1977; *Joel and the Great Merlini*, 1979; *The Forbidden Fountain of Oz*, with Lauren McGraw, 1980; *The Money Room*, 1981; *Hideaway*, 1983; *The Seventeenth Swap*, 1986; *The Trouble with Jacob*, 1988; *The Striped Ships*, 1991; *Tangled Webb*, 1993; *The Moorchild*, 1996.

SUGGESTED READING: *Authors and Artists for Young Adults*, vol. 41, 1988; *Contemporary Authors*, New Revision Series, vol. 82, 1999; *Major Authors and Illustrators for Children and Young Adults*, 1993; McGraw, Eloise. *Techniques of Fiction Writing*, 1959; Pendergast, Tom and Sara. *St. James Guide to Young Adult Writers*, 1998; *Something About the Author*, vol. 67, 1992, and vol. 123, 2001 (obituary); *Something About the Author Autobiography Series*, vol. 6, 1988. Periodicals— "Author, Correspondent, Friend: Tributes to Eloise Jarvis McGraw," *Baum Bugle*, Autumn 2001; "Eloise Jarvis McGraw 1915–2000," *Publishers Weekly*, December 18, 2000; "Hands-on Research," *Writer*, October 1997; McGraw, Eloise, "Some Clues to the Juvenile Mystery," *Writer*, July 1996; McGraw, Eloise, "A View from the Deck," *Writer*, March 1994; McGraw, Lauren Lynn, "Eloise Jarvis McGraw, 1915–2000," *Baum Bugle*, Autumn 2001.

"Growing up, everyone in my extended family—we had those in those days—liked to sit around and tell funny stories. My grandmother was famous for her jokes and sense of the incongruous. My dad told stories that involved animals and funny phrases and sound effects. My brother was fixated on Joan of Arc and medieval heroism. And I wrote stories about rabbits. I thought all families did this and didn't realize till sixth grade that most people had been watching TV that whole time. Then they told each other the plots of various shows or movies that I'd never seen: *The Twilight Zone*, the *Psycho* shower scene, *The Fugitive*.

"Early on, I identified with Laura Ingalls. I read all the Little House books over and over again. We lived with my grandfather, who lived to be 102, in a large farmhouse 15 miles from New York City. The suburbs sprung up all around us, while in the backyard we made cider and jam, picked apples, raised chickens, and brewed our own root beer. When I was seven, we sailed on a steamship to England for a year. Again I seemed to enter another time period. Northern England in 1960 was still recovering from World War II. There were bomb shelters, bombed-out buildings, and coal fires for heating. On weekends, we toured ruined castles and peered at sheep on foggy moors.

"At that time, school in England was very different from school in the U.S.A. Boys and girls didn't play together on the playground. Children were caned for minor infractions. Watching children having their hands beaten by teachers outraged me. It was an injustice I have never forgotten.

"With an out-of-sync childhood like this, it seemed natural for me to become an avid reader. I read in the car, while I was walking, instead of playing sports, instead of lunch period, instead of watching TV. I guess I was a geek. And I continued in my geekdom by going to Bryn Mawr College, where I majored in English literature with the thought of becoming an English teacher. Later I studied art education and became an art teacher.

"I moved to Maine 28 years ago, married, and had two sons, who are now grown up. And then I developed a chronic illness. I left teaching and began to write for kids.

"My first book was called *Little Wind Takes Off*, inspired by a line of laundry. It was never published. It took me over two years (I'm stubborn) to realize that people were supposed to be the main characters in books and not chunks of canned pineap-

Courtesy of Pierce Studio

Alice Mead (signature)

Alice Mead

January 11, 1952–

ple or recently laundered underpants! I wrote my first realistic novel in 1993. I gave my first human character, Rayanne, in *Crossing the Starlight Bridge*, a box of crayons just like the one I had when I was young. It turned out that suddenly I was known for writing realism. I wrote about outsiders—people on the edge, refugees, displaced people, kids in projects, on islands, in Kosovo, in the former Yugoslavia, and in Sudan.

"But there are books/things I haven't written about yet—my big blue bear, a shepherd kid in Scotland in 1603, a kid whose dad gambles away their house and then dies, an illiterate witch. For some reason, these stories remain fragments, as yet undeveloped. Waiting . . . or maybe I will never write those books. Subjects seem to emerge from some kind of wordless place in me. I haven't quite figured it out. But that's okay. I like mysteries."

❊   ❊   ❊

Alice Weber Mead was born and grew up in Portchester, New York. The year her family spent living in Yorkshire made a lasting impression on her—the postwar devastation of an industrial city as well as the legends surrounding ancient castles and landscapes. While attending Bryn Mawr College, she worked as an art counselor at a Fresh Air camp for inner-city children one summer. This experience convinced Mead to pursue a career that would encourage creativity in children. She received her B.A. from Bryn Mawr in 1973 and a master's degree in education from Southern Connecticut State University two years later. After moving to Maine and marrying Larry Mead in 1983, she earned a degree in art education from the University of Southern Maine.

Teaching art in junior high schools and preschools over the years 1974–1992, Alice Mead often worked with children living in poverty, children living on the edges of society. Her interest in children living under difficult circumstances extended to other parts of the world, and she has traveled to Eastern Europe to document the conditions of children's lives there. She has visited Kosovo several times and has worked to make the world aware of the plight of the Kosovars, producing a videotape titled *Kosovo and the Death of Yugoslavia* and writing many letters and articles. Her novel *Adem's Cross*, cited as an ALA Best Book for Young Adults, tells the story of one Albanian boy caught in the horrors of ethnic wars, the strong family ties of his people, and

Junebug in Trouble

ALICE MEAD

Courtesy of Farrar, Straus and Giroux

his attempt to escape to a better life. In her series of stories about Junebug, Mead introduces readers to a likable, kindhearted boy whose life in the projects of an American inner city is often difficult and confusing. When his mother finds a better home for the family, Junebug learns that even in his new surroundings, he will be faced with problems that at times seem overwhelming. *Junebug and the Reverend* was named a Notable Trade Book in the Field of Social Studies in 1999.

Alice Mead and her husband have two grown sons and live in Cape Elizabeth, Maine, in a small house near a cliff overlooking Casco Bay.

SELECTED WORKS: *Crossing the Starlight Bridge*, 1994; *Junebug*, 1995; *Walking the Edge*, 1995; *Adem's Cross*, 1996; *Junebug and the Reverend*, 1998; *Soldier Mom*, 1999; *Billy and Emma*, illus. by Christy Hale, 2000; *Girl of Kosovo*, 2001; *Junebug in Trouble*, 2002; *Year of No Rain*, 2003; *Madame Squidley and Beanie*, 2004.

SUGGESTED READING: *Contemporary Authors*, vol. 159, 1998; *Something About the Author*, vol. 146, 2004.

"My friends put up with a lot from me when I was a kid. For one thing, I was always pestering them to perform plays I adapted from fairy tales like *Snow White* and *Rapunzel*. Naturally, I served as producer, director, and star rolled into one. During recess I organized elaborate games of 'family'— ongoing soap operas that took place in whatever culture I was reading about and was enthralled with at the moment, be it Chinese, Eskimo, or British (the last involving much tea-drinking with crooked pinky while periodically exclaiming 'my word!'). After coming across a volume of Edgar Allen Poe's stories, I told gory tales of terror during sleepovers.

"I grew up in New York City in a leafy section of Queens. In those simpler times the neighborhood was our kingdom as long as we made it back home in time for dinner. We climbed and swung in the spacious playground next door or bounced pink 'spaldeen' balls off the walls of our apartment building's back courtyard. We dared each other to run through the murky basement with its groaning monster furnace and cobwebs that clung to your skin. In summertime we lounged on the roof, playing cards, painting our toenails, and staging our fairy tale productions. Hot nights caused neighbors to haul beach chairs up there from stifling apartments to kibitz under starry skies.

"My mother read to me from early on—Golden Books and picture books from the library. I loved the language in *A Child's Garden of Verses* and poured over the art by the Provensens. A cherished collection of poems and stories about elves and fairies had dazzling illustrations by Garth Williams. Once I entered school I came down with bronchitis every winter, staying home from school for days on end. Keeping up with language arts was

Laura Krauss Melmed

October 13, 1947–

easy—I went through every adult book brought home by my father, an avid and wide-ranging reader. (To verify that learning math was a different story, refer to my checkbook register.) When at school I eagerly awaited trips up a tower stair to the P.S. 101 library. There I wandered through the rainbow shades of the Andrew Lang Fairy Books and, as a wistful only child, reveled in the adventures of the large Pepper, March, and Melendy clans.

"I also loved drawing and painting. My mother bought me art supplies, took me to museums, and even let me paint flowers on her kitchen walls. In junior high I entered an accelerated program, completing three grades in two years. When I moved on to my huge urban high school I felt younger than everyone else.

Courtesy of Thomas W. Radcliffe

Laura Krauss Melmed

I still had strong opinions but worried about sharing them. I got high grades on papers and exams (except in those pesky subjects, Geometry and Algebra) and took honors classes but never raised my hand. I dreamed of one day writing for a living and signed up for journalism, then was too shy to conduct an interview. But I felt honored when in senior year my poem on the recent assassination of President Kennedy was featured in the school literary magazine.

"Happily, I emerged from my shell in college. I learned to live with a group, majored in sociology, and met my future husband, Allan. After marrying we moved to New Orleans for several years, where I got a graduate degree in early childhood education and taught kindergarten. After settling in our permanent home, Washington, DC, I went to work for the U.S. government, writing pamphlets and brochures. Soon along came our daughter, Stephanie, and sons, Jonathan and Michael. Being a mother has been the greatest reward of my life, followed by writing for children. I wrote the poem that became my first book, *The First Song Ever Sung*, to answer a bedtime question posed by my son Jonathan. Since then I've written other lullaby books, such as *I Love You as Much*; original folktales like *The Rainbabies* and *Moishe's Miracle*; and nonfiction books like *Capital!* I love the discipline and challenge of writing a rhythmic picture book text. It's a strange phenomenon, but while I'm at my computer the hands of the clock spin faster than normal. Hours spent in this way speed by like mere minutes. I guess that's a sign of doing something you love. I feel very fortunate to have discovered this joy in my life and in being able to share it with my readers."

❄ ❄ ❄

Laura Krauss Melmed fell in love with books early in life, thanks to parents who taught by example that reading is valuable. She remembers staggering home with armloads of books from the Forest Hills Branch of the New York Public Library week after week as a child. She earned a bachelor's degree in sociology at the State University of New York at Buffalo and a graduate degree at Tulane University. After she moved with her husband to Washington, DC, where he served his medical internship and residency, she worked for the General Services Administration of the U.S. government. They decided to make Washington their permanent home, and it was there that Melmed wrote her first book, *The First Song Ever Sung*. Ironically, since it took four years from contract to publication, her second book, *The Rainbabies*, was actually published first.

The Rainbabies, illustrated by Jim LaMarche, won the Bologna Book Fair Graphics Prize. In the judges' decision, they described the book as "a timeless tale turning on a classic archetype in which illustration and text combine to create a truly memorable book . . . an outright modern classic." *The Rainbabies* began with a very personal experience. For the first 10 years of their marriage, Laura and her husband had no children; then they had three in quick succession. According to Laura, "It often seemed to be raining babies at the Melmed house!" Babies do literally rain down from the sky on an elderly childless couple in the story, fulfilling their wish for children.

Her next original fairytale, *Little Oh*, is about an origami doll who longs to visit the world and springs to life, bringing wonderful changes into the lives of the people she touches. *Little Oh* won a 1997 National Parenting Publications Award and was named an ALA Notable Children's Book, a Notable Children's Trade Book in the Field of Social Studies, and an American Booksellers Association Pick of the List. *A Hug Goes Around*, recipient of a Parents' Choice Award, has an opening phrase that was a gift from Melmed's editor, Susan Pearson, who was looking for a sequel to *I Love You As Much* and came up with: "A mountain goes up/A valley goes down/Where does a hug go?/A hug goes around." Melmed also won an Oppenheim Toy Portfolio Gold Award for *This First Thanksgiving Day: A Counting Story*, and her *The Marvelous Market on Mermaid* was selected for the IRA/CBC Children's Choices list.

Melmed is always impressed by the depth of children's interests and their willingness to share thoughts and advice on her books. Once, reading *Moishe's Miracle* to children at the Hebrew Day School, she recalls how the children were eager to improve her pronunciation of "Hanukkah." For *Moishe's Miracle* she received a National Jewish Book Award for her "remarkable contribution to the world of Jewish letters and learning."

Laura Krauss Melmed lives with her physician husband in Washington, DC. Their three children are now grown, and she has left her government job to write full time.

"In those simpler times the neighborhood was our kingdom as long as we made it back home in time for dinner."

Courtesy of HarperCollins Publishers

SELECTED WORKS: *The Rainbabies*, illus. by Jim LaMarche, 1992; *The First Song Ever Sung*, illus. by Ed Young, 1993; *I Love You As Much*, illus. by Henri Sørensen, 1993; *Prince Nautilus*, illus. by Henri Sørensen, 1994; *The Marvelous Market on Mermaid*, illus. by Maryann Kovalski, 1995; *Little Oh*, illus. by Jim LaMarche, 1997; *Jumbo's Lullaby*, illus. by Henri Sørensen, 1999; *Moishe's Miracle: A Hanukkah Story*, illus. by David Slonim, 2000; *This First Thanksgiving Day: A Counting Story*, illus. by Mark Buehner, 2001; *Fright Night Flight*, illus. by Henry Cole, 2002; *A Hug Goes Around*, illus. by Betsy Lewin, 2002; *Capital!: Washington from A to Z*, illus. by Frané Lessac, 2003.

SUGGESTED READING: Leggett, Karen, "Authors in Your Neighborhood: Meet Laura Krauss Melmed," *Washington Parent*, July 2002 (*washingtonparent.com/articles/0207/author.html*).

WEB SITES: *www.childrensbookguild.org/melmed.html*

Ben Mikaelsen

November 24, 1952–

"Growing up in South America, Spanish was my strongest language. I had terrible problems with English, spelling and grammar. My handwriting looked like worms had mud-wrestled on the page. I thought this meant I was a bad writer. Yet I loved to hide under the covers at night with a flashlight in my mouth, scribbling ideas and stories on a piece of paper.

"Not until college did the idea of actually being an author creep into my head. An English professor called me in after class to comment on an assignment I had written. He told me my grammar skills were those of a fifth grader. Fearful, I asked if I should drop the class. 'Oh, no, no, no!' he replied. 'I just finished reading 300 stories, and only one made me laugh and cry. That was yours. You're a storyteller. That's writing!'

"What a great discovery. Now when I visit schools, I find other young writers having trouble with the mechanics of English. I encourage them to work on the mechanics, but more importantly, I want them to understand that writing is storytelling! The story is what holds the magic and power. The story is why we created language.

"What is it that brings a tear or scares the tapioca pudding out of you? What makes you choke laughing? Much of my research finds me searching for those feelings—the heart of my story. In libraries I find wonderful facts and information, but only on the streets can I discover the haunted stares of homeless children digging through garbage cans. Only in forests can I find frightened bear cubs that have lost their mother to a hunter.

"When students ask me how to become a better writer, I answer, 'Go out and live! You can't pour water from an empty bucket. Experience life. Then never quit writing about it!'

"As a child growing up in South America, I knew early the sting of racist comments. I can remember being held down by bullies and having mud smeared in my face so I wouldn't be a white 'gringo.' My parents sent me away to a boarding school where strict English matrons ruled with an iron fist. We wore uniforms—saddle shoes with bobby socks, and leather knickers with a blouse type shirt and bow tie. Not knowing any better, I wore these clothes here in the United States on my first day of seventh grade. The ridicule was immediate and severe.

"Luckily I never learned to conform. In high school I started skydiving and flying. Later, I rode a horse cross-country from Minnesota to Oregon. Being a bit of a loner, I enjoyed training animals. During college I raced sled dogs in northern Minnesota. After moving to Montana, I played horse polo and adopted a black-bear cub named Buffy. Buffy is now a 750-pound member of our family.

"As a child I had been ashamed of who I was, but slowly I discovered that my differences were what made me special: they were my strengths. Now I grin when I see children proud of their differences. How wonderful!

"One of the greatest discoveries anyone can make in life is that he or she is an author. Not only of words on paper, but also of reality. You can mold and affect your own life as surely as you can create with words on a blank white page.

Courtesy of Denver Bryan

"I've been asked if it's realistic to have my characters doing all the wild things they do in my stories. I laugh when I answer, 'You bet it is!' I know a child can fly an airplane, parachute, survive storms alone, love the night, and much, much more. I know because as a child I did those things. With time, each experience and discovery became a stepping stone to larger and greater things. Now when someone asks me, 'Is it realistic for a bad student to grow up to become an author?' I say, 'You bet it is!'"

❊ ❊ ❊

Ben Mikaelsen began his life adventure in La Paz, Bolivia, the son of John Mikaelsen, a radio engineer, and his wife, Luverne. Unhappy in school, he rarely felt that he fit in with others in Bolivia or, later, in middle school in the United States. To prove to others and to himself that he was special, Ben chose daring hobbies such as high-cliff diving and skydiving. Along with these activities he continued his habit of writing, though he kept that to himself until he attended college. His college years were divided between Concordia College in Moorhead, Minnesotta, during 1971–1972 and Bemidji State University during 1975–1979, with a two-year stint in the U.S. Army in between. After college, Mikaelsen and his wife, Melanie, chose the mountains of Bozeman, Montana, as their home, moving there in 1980. For a few years he owned an awards and engraving business, then a woodworking business. In 1984, he and Melanie adopted Buffy, a declawed black-bear research cub, who changed their lives. Afraid of humans when he came to the Mikaelsens, Buffy needed a great deal of time, love, and understanding, as well as a large

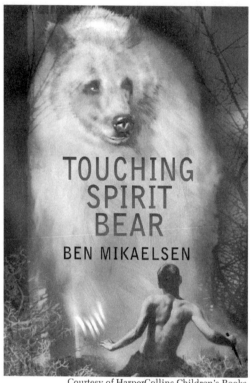

TOUCHING
SPIRIT
BEAR

BEN MIKAELSEN

Courtesy of HarperCollins Children's Books

living space with pond, playground, eating place, and den. Mikaelsen devoted himself to the cub. Later, as a writer, he began scheduling his book tours and other business in winter when Buffy was hibernating. In an interview, he said, "The question people always ask me is, do you really trust Buffy? But the proper question is, does he really trust me? In his mind, he owns me. And in my mind, I am his."

The lessons Buffy taught Ben, and the methods Ben learned to use to help their relationship, stood him in good stead as the Fish and Game Department in Bozeman began bringing him cubs who needed temporary homes until a place could be found for them. Spring bear hunting orphaned most of these visitors to the Mikaelsen home. Shooting a mother bear is against the law in Montana, but it is impossible to enforce that law. Because of these cubs, and the fact that some needed to be destroyed when no permanent home could be found for them, Mikaelsen researched and wrote his first book.

Rescue Josh McGuire, a story that follows young Josh's desperate struggle to save a cub after its mother is killed by Josh's alcoholic father, won the Golden Spur Award from the Western Writers of America, Inc., and a Children's Book Award from the International Reading Association in 1991. For his next novel, *Sparrow Hawk Red*, the author lived among the homeless in Mexico to understand how it looked and felt. The result, a taut adventure about a boy determined to track down his mother's murderers, teems with realistic scenes of Mexican street life and was a California Young Reader Medal winner. *Stranded*, which focuses on a girl who had lost her foot a few years earlier yet manages to rescue a mother dolphin and its calf, emerged from Mikaelsen's own experiences working at a dolphin research facility. *Petey*, an ALA Notable Children's Book and winner of a Golden Spur Award, follows the life of a boy with cerebral palsy who spends his entire life in institutions because the disease is so badly misunderstood in his day, the early 20th century. *Touching Spirit Bear*, a story of physical and emotional survival, was an ALA Best Book for Young Adults, and *Red Midnight* was named to the Young Adult Choices list of the International Reading Association. Both *Red Midnight* and *Tree Girl*, Mikaelsen's 2004 novel, deal with children in flight from the savage civil wars of Central America.

SELECTED WORKS: *Rescue Josh McGuire*, 1991; *Sparrow Hawk Red*, 1993; *Stranded*, 1995; *Countdown*, 1996; *Petey*, 1998; *Touching Spirit Bear*, 2001; *Red Midnight*, 2002; *Tree Girl*, 2004.

SUGGESTED READING: *Authors and Artists for Young Adults*, vol. 37, 2001; *Children's Literature Review*, vol. 38, 1996; *Contemporary Authors*, vol. 139, 2002; *Something About the Author*, vol. 107, 1999. Periodicals—Marvel, Mark, "Imagine a World where People and Animals Live Together Like One Big Happy Family," *Interview*, February 1994.

WEB SITE: *www.benmikaelsen.com*

William Miller

February 8, 1959–

"I have always loved to read. Reading has always been my inspiration to write. Today, as a published author, I stress to my students that I'm a reader first and a writer second. When I read something I enjoy, I still feel the old inspiration to write something myself. . . . My favorite form of reading has always been biographies. I love to learn about the lives of other people, and this reading led to my first poems. As a children's book author, I have been inspired by and written about the lives of famous African Americans, including Zora Hurston and Richard Wright.

"When I was twelve, I suffered from a bone disease, osteomylitis, and had to stay out of school for a year. I spent that year reading and writing. I knew then that I wanted to be a writer. I also knew that I would need to study creative writing with teachers who could help me find my voice. At the age of sixteen, I was accepted by the Alabama School of Fine Arts. I wrote poetry and received a lot of personal attention to my writing. Charles Ghigna, the poet and children's author, encouraged me and made me feel that my poetry was good enough for publication.

"I went on to study creative writing at Eckerd College, Hollins College, and Binghamton University. I considered myself a poet first and a fiction author second. At this point in time I had no desire to write for children and began to publish my first poems and stories. I had published my second collection of poetry when I ran into my high school creative writing teacher, Charles Ghigna, at a book-signing I was giving. He was now a successful children's author and challenged me to write a book for children. I had no idea what to write about, but writing a book for children intrigued me. I finally decided to write a book based on a poem I had written about the death of Zora Hurston's mother. I had been teaching African American Literature at York College and loved Hurston's work. I decided to expand the poem into what I thought was a children's picture book. I added material from Hurston's early life and kept the poetic language from the poem. I sent my finished manuscript to Lee and Low books, and to my surprise they showed a great deal of interest. After some more editing, the book was accepted and titled *Zora Hurston and the Chinaberry Tree*. The book received many awards and was chosen as a *Reading Rainbow* selection.

Courtesy of Lee. M. Friedman

"Since *Zora*, I have published 11 other books for children, all on African American subjects. The question I am most frequently asked at conferences and book signings is, Why does a white author choose to write about African Americans? The answer to this question is a complex one. I love African American literature and have been teaching it for 15 years. Before I wrote picture books, I wrote poetry about the lives of famous African American authors. In my children's books, I do not appropriate an African American voice. I write from a third person, neutral, authorial perspective. If there is any use of dialect, it is in the dialogue between characters in the story. The illustrators for my books have primarily been African Americans. They interpret my words visually, which makes each book a truly multicultural project."

❈   ❈   ❈

Born and raised in Anniston, Alabama, William Miller attended high school at the Alabama School of Fine Arts in Birmingham. He received his B.A. from Eckerd College in 1982, an M.A. from Hollins College in 1983, and a Ph.D. in English and American literature from the State University of New York at Binghamton in 1988. Currently he teaches creative writing and African American literature at York College in York, Pennsylvania. A published poet, Dr. Miller has received great acclaim for children's books that combine his love of language and poetic expression with his deep respect for African American lives and literature. In an interview on his publisher's Web site, Miller states that he is "drawn to the themes of struggle, renewal, and celebration" in the writings of African Americans and finds inspiration in the works of Zora Neale Hurston and Richard Wright, among others.

Zora Hurston and the Chinaberry Tree, his first children's book, movingly portrayed this remarkable writer as a child, suffering the grief of her mother's death but determined to reach for the sky as her mother taught her. Designated a *Reading Rainbow* selection, it was also named an American Booksellers Association Pick of the Lists and a Notable Children's Trade Book in the Field of Social Studies. Miller portrayed another heroic African American in *Frederick Douglass: The Last Day of Slavery*, which received a Paterson Prize from Passaic County Community College and was designated a Notable Children's Book by *Smithsonian* magazine. Always celebrating the resilience of African Americans in the face of adversity, Miller tells the story of a little-known custom in the 1930s when parties would be organized to help those in need in *Rent Party Jazz*, which was acclaimed as a Notable Social Studies Trade Book for Young People. *Richard Wright and the Library Card*, a story that dramatizes an incident from Wright's autobiography, earned Miller another Notable Children's Book citation from *Smithsonian*.

Courtesy of Lee & Low Books, Inc.

Perseverance and determination are exemplified by the young man in *Night Golf*, Miller's story of a boy encountering prejudice while trying to learn golf in the 1950s. A timely book that gave contemporary young readers some perspective on the achievements of Tiger Woods, the story is accompanied by a timeline of notable African American golfers and was awarded a Parents' Choice Gold Award and named a Notable Book for a Global Society by the International Reading Association. William Miller brings a distinctive voice to each of his picture book texts, a poetic intensity of feeling conveyed by characters who are determined to succeed.

SELECTED WORKS: *Zora Hurston and the Chinaberry Tree*, illus. by Cornelius Van Wright and Ying-Hwa Hu, 1994; *Frederick Douglass: The Last Day of Slavery*, illus. by Cedric Lucas, 1995; *The Conjure Woman*, illus. by Terea D. Shaffer, 1996; *The Knee-High Man*, illus. by Roberta Glidden, 1996; *A House by the River*, illus. by Cornelius Van Wright and Ying-Hwa Hu, 1997; *Richard Wright and the Library Card*, illus. by Gregory Christie, 1997; *Bus Ride*, illus. by John Ward, 1998; *Night Golf*, illus. by Cedric Lucas, 1999; *Tituba*, illus. by Leonard Jenkins, 2000; *The Piano*, illus. by Susan Keeter, 2000; *Rent Party Jazz*, illus. by Charlotte Riley-Webb, 2001; *Joe Louis, My Champion*, illus. by Rodney S. Pate, 2004.

SUGGESTED READING: *Something About the Author*, vol. 116, 2000.

Courtesy of Nelson Mitchell

Margaree King Mitchell (signature)

Margaree King Mitchell

July 23, 1953–

"From as early as I can remember I could express myself better through writing than through speaking. While a student in school, if I had something really important to say I wrote it down because I knew every point I wanted to make would be clearly stated. I also loved making up stories to tell my younger sisters. Stories like there being a store in a ditch near our house that sold all sorts of candy. And I was the only one who could get there. The interesting thing is, they believed me. So at an early age I realized that I had the power to captivate audiences with stories.

"Nevertheless, while growing up, I never had any idea I would become a writer. Being a writer was not a career choice I was presented with. My grandparents wanted me to become a teacher. I grew up on my grandparents' farm in Holly Springs, Mississippi. I basically had a carefree life. I remember going on long walks down the dirt road across from our house and just daydreaming about the future. I always wondered what other parts of the world were like. I had visions of seeing the world.

"It wasn't until I got to college—Brandeis University, in Waltham, Massachusetts—that I met a professor who recognized my ability to create stories and craft words onto paper in an interesting way. This professor encouraged me to pursue writing as a career. I tried all forms of writing to see which I loved best. I decided to focus on short stories, plays, and screenplays. However, it wasn't until my son was in kindergarten that I decided to write books for children. One day his school had Grandparents' Day, in which the students could invite their grandparents to spend the whole day with them. We were living in Memphis, Tennessee, at the time. My son's grandmothers lived far away. One lived in Atlanta, Georgia, and the other lived in Kansas City, Kansas. So he had no one to bring to school that day.

"Some students brought grandmothers to school and some brought their grandfathers. When my son returned home that day he was very sad. 'I don't have any grandfathers,' he said. I explained to him that both of his grandfathers had died before he was born. But he didn't understand. I thought if I had pictures to show what kind of lives they had led, he would better understand my stories about them.

"So I went to libraries and bookstores looking for picture books that were set in the past. But I could not find what I was looking for. That's when I decided to write the books myself. I wanted each book to be set in the South. Each book would focus on a different aspect of history. And each book would have something in it that my grandfather had taught me.

"When my son was in first grade we had moved to Little Rock, Arkansas. As I volunteered in his classroom I realized that the book I was writing for my son would be beneficial to other boys and girls. I wanted students all over the world to know that they could be anything they wanted to be if they didn't give up their dreams."

❉ ❉ ❉

Daughter of Joe King, a farmer, and Susie Mae Bowen, Margaree King Mitchell grew up in Mississippi, leaving that state to get her B.S. at Brandeis University in 1975 and marrying Kevin Lee Mitchell, an account executive, in 1982. They have one son, named Nelson. Mitchell served as the Drama Department director for the Monumental Baptist Church in Memphis, Tennessee, 1987–1990, and was later active with the Little Rock School District Biracial Committee as well as both of the elementary schools her son attended. The family now lives in Houston, Texas.

Courtesy of Simon & Schuster Books for Young Readers

Initially, Mitchell wrote for adults, creating a script, "Corporate Lies," which was a finalist for the Writers Guild of America, East Foundation Fellowship Program, in 1991. That same year, her play, *The Hi-Rise*, was chosen as a finalist in the 1991 Theatre Memphis New Play Competition. In 1992, "Once Upon a Drama," was presented in an Arkansas Screen Writers Association workshop. A television script, "School's Out," followed in 1994.

Uncle Jed's Barbershop, Margaree King Mitchell's first picture book for children, takes place in the 1920s in the segregated South. Sarah Jean's favorite relative, Uncle Jedediah, is an itinerant barber with the dream of having his own barber shop. Twice Uncle Jed sees his savings disappear, once to get his niece medical care and again when banks fail during the Depression. He doesn't give up but keeps saving and at the age of 79, he opens the barbershop he has hoped and worked for all those years. Sarah Jean says at the end of the story, "Uncle Jed died not long after that, and I think he died a happy man. You see, he made his dream come true even when nobody else believed in it. He taught me to dream too." A Coretta Scott King Honor Award winner for illustration, *Uncle Jed's Barbershop* was also named a Notable Children's Trade Book in the Field of Social Studies, an ALA Notable Children's Book, and an American Booksellers Association Pick of the Lists. The book also won a

Charlie May Simon Honor Book Award and was featured on *Reading Rainbow*.

Granddaddy's Gift, Mitchell's second book, was an IRA/CBC Teachers' Choice and received a 1998 *Skipping Stones* Award (an international award for promoting respect for cultural diversity). Set in segregated Mississippi, *Granddaddy's Gift* is the story of a black man insisting that his granddaughter go to school, even if it is only a poor, segregated school, so that she will have choices he didn't when she grows up. He is the first in the community to volunteer to register to vote and takes his granddaughter with him. She sees him humiliated by an angry white crowd but not giving up, not even when their church is set on fire in the night. It's a story of bravery and one that continues Margaree Mitchell's theme that one must never give up a dream.

SELECTED WORKS: *Uncle Jed's Barbershop*, illus. by James Ransome, 1993; *Granddaddy's Gift*, illus. by Larry Johnson, 1997; *Susie Mae*, illus. by Melodye Benson Rosales, 2003.

SUGGESTED READING: *Contemporary Authors*, vol. 150, 1996; *Something About the Author*, vol. 84, 1996.

Susie Morgenstern

March 18, 1945–

"I used to read my homework to my mother—compositions, poems, book reports—and she'd look at me as if I were Jane Austen, Shakespeare, the sun, the moon, and the stars. This is what comes to mind when I try to pinpoint the drive it takes to write one word after another, sentence to sentence and page by page. How she rejoiced when I got an A and how she consoled when I got a tragic A-. And then when I married a Frenchman and moved to Nice, she sat and read my books looking up every word in a French-English dictionary. I wonder if people who don't have mothers who gave them confidence and permanent wonder can eventually become . . . .

"Confidence and doubt have been my partners in this crime. The world could crumble around me and I sit steadfast and write. Things used to pile up: dishes, ironing, laundry, but it was only when my children didn't have one pair of panties left that I'd take the drastic measure of filling the machine and pushing the button. Even now, my children grown with their own children, I sit here overlooking the sea in Nice, and ask myself: Why aren't you on the beach? Is writing an act of participating in life or of fleeing life?

"I don't know if growing up in Belleville, New Jersey, made a writer of me, but life in my boisterous family pushed me in the right direction. I could never get a word in edgewise in family discussions, so the only way for me to talk was to write. I guess it became a habit. Becoming a French writer is one of the funny accidents life prepares for us. First I read and read and read until I thought my brain would burst for my doctoral thesis in comparative literature, and then I thought: Enough literary criticism; let me take my own stab at literature. I tried it out on my children, who have always been the inspiration for it all. After the first day of starting to write my first book, quite naturally in English, I re-read those few pages and was surprised to see that I had written them in French. I sent this first manuscript anonymously to a competition sponsored by the French Youth Ministry, who were trying to encourage FRENCH writers to write for children and to stop the tidal wave of translations of American books. I won, and when I showed up at the prize ceremony to receive the generous check, they were horrified by my thick American accent and flustered that they had to give the award to a miserable Yankee.

"There have been about 50 books since. Sometimes I would translate a book that had been successful in France and send it round and round to American publishers, who always told me it was too European or too this or too that. I have a brilliant collection of these rejection letters. It took a good fairy in the form of an American exchange student to do the trick. This young college girl happened into my home for two weeks and enjoyed her stay here. Years later she wrote me a postcard that she had become an editor and would I send her some of my recent books. French-speaking Jill Davis has become my editor at Viking. Always be nice to people, lest they be angels!

"And now by another quirk of life, I've written my first novel in English . . . for adults. I don't know how that happened either. Isn't it wonderful how mysterious life is?"

Courtesy of Beatrice Heyligers

Susie Morgenstern [signature]

❋   ❋   ❋

Susie Hoch Morgenstern was born in Newark, New Jersey. She attended Hebrew University and Rutgers University, where she received her B.A. in 1967. Continuing with her studies in comparative literature at the University of Nice, France, she received her M.A. in 1969 and a Ph.D. in 1972. In France she met her husband, the mathematician Jacques Morgenstern, and they had two daughters, Aliya and Mayah. Susie Morgenstern has been a professor of English at the University of Nice since 1971, and a literary critic and writer. Although she is an American, she has written most of her books in French, with much help from her husband, who is now deceased, and their daughters, who would often correct her French grammar and spelling mistakes. Gill Rosner, another American living in Nice, has provided the English translations for many of Morgenstern's novels.

Her first book, *Alphabet Hébreu*, was published in 1977. Subsequent titles have been enormously popular in Europe, many translated into such diverse languages as Greek, Hebrew, Dutch, Danish, Spanish, Italian, Japanese, and Korean. Over the years she has received several major awards in France, including the Grand Prix du Livre pour la Jeunesse in 1982 for *C'est pas juste!* (*It's Not Fair!*). Her characters are often quirky, usually humorous, sometimes wistful. From an elderly teacher who inspires his students to read, to a boy who leaves school in order to find out why he might want to return, to princesses who need more than palaces, she brings her unexpected characters vibrantly to life.

When she was nominated for the Hans Christian Andersen Award by the French section of the International Board on Books for Young People, it was noted in the nomination statement that "it doesn't matter in which language you read her. Her voice goes straight to the heart. She was the first writer in France to adopt the point of view of children and adolescents and to evoke day-to-day life in children's literature." When at last her children's books were translated into English, *Secret Letters from 0 to 10* and *A Book of Coupons* were both named ALA Notable Children's Books and were awarded a Mildred L. Batchelder Honor Book citation for best books in translation.

Courtesy of Viking Children's Books

SELECTED WORKS FOR CHILDREN IN ENGLISH TRANSLATION (French titles and original publication date in parentheses): *It's Not Fair!* illus. by Kathie Abrams, 1983 (*C'est pas juste*, 1982); *Secret Letters from 0 to 10*, trans. by Gill Rosner, 1998 (*Lettres d'amour de 0 à 10*, 1996); *A Book of Coupons*, illus. by Serge Bloch, trans. by Gill Rosner, 2001 (*Joker*, 1999); *Three Days Off*, trans. by Gill Rosner, 2001 (*Trois jours sans*, 1998); *Princesses Are People Too: Two Modern Fairy Tales*, illus. by Serge Bloch, trans. by Bill May, 2002 (*Même les princesses doivent aller à l'école*, 1991); *Sixth Grade*, trans. by Gill Rosner, 2004 (*La sixième*, 1985).

SUGGESTED READING: *Contemporary Authors*, vol. 202, 2003; *Something About the Author*, vol. 133, 2002.

"I was born in Calgary in the province of Alberta, Canada, spent a few years in Winnipeg (Manitoba) and grew up in a small town outside of Montreal (Quebec) called Two Mountains. When I was in high school I knew I wanted to make pictures. I had always loved doing art, geography, and science projects and hoped to someday work for an advertising agency. During those years I spent lots of time outdoors: camping, hiking in summer, and skiing in winter. I began art school at Grant MacEwan College (Alberta) then went on to a three-year illustration course at Sheridan College (Ontario) followed by a year at the Ontario College of Art. While in school I produced a number of animation and video works and also worked in the photography lab. I began freelancing doing magazine, editorial, and some advertising illustration.

Courtesy of Steve Wolf

Paul Morin

January 14, 1959–

"My parents were living in Guinea, West Africa, and each year I would travel there and experience the 'heartbeat' of that continent. Soon I was collecting drums and assorted instruments. In my constant quest for adventure I began to travel to remote areas of North, Central, and South America. My reputation as an artist grew, and I was getting more challenging work when I was approached to illustrate *The Orphan Boy*, my first children's book. I knew instantly that I would need to travel back to Africa and research the Maasai people, who are the subject of the story. I thought that it would be nice to work on a series of paintings, and the trip would satisfy my interest in travel, music, and anthropology. Late one night by a campfire I met Salutan ole Debe, a Maasai warrior, and we became friends. I visited his village at night and we made recordings of Maasai songs with his friends. The experiences I had gave me a tremendous amount of inspiration, and I realized that I wanted to illustrate more stories of traditional cultures. Since then I have illustrated 15 books and traveled around the world.

"I usually begin a project by doing extensive research. I travel with lots of film, two cameras, video and recording equipment, and a sketchbook so that I can observe, absorb, and capture experiences to influence the images I create. During each trip I make recordings of nature, and when I return home my friends and I improvise musical compositions to these recordings. I listen to these recordings while I'm painting to further influence the mood or atmosphere of each project. Many of the paintings have their own musical score. I have produced several documentaries and released CDs, including location recordings and music for each book.

Courtesy of Candlewick Press

"While preparing the illustrations for *The Vision Seeker*, I was exposed to Native American sweat lodge ceremonies, and we continue to attend sweats. During my travels I have met traditional healers, and we host elders from many countries who come to share their ceremonies. Over the past decade, I have lectured at conferences, schools, and libraries across North America on art, music, and traditional cultures. I live with my wife, Janine, and sons, Palmer and Kadin, in a cedar house, and my studio is located at the edge of a forest by a wetland near Rockwood, Ontario, Canada. For years I have been drawn to nature and man's connection with it. In order to express this, I prepare exhibitions which feature my fine art in installations that combine paintings, sculpture, music, sound, and video designed to transport the viewer to a time and place where one can hear the 'Voices of the First Day.' In life I attempt to walk in harmony with the Earth, to allow some of the teachings of nature to influence my daily existence. If you touch the Earth, it is easy to learn to respect it."

❋　❋　❋

In a freelance career that has spanned the past 25 years, Paul Morin has worked for major advertising agencies and publishers across North America. His artwork has been exhibited in museums throughout Canada, including the Museum of Civilization. His illustrations have appeared in *Newsweek*, *Macleans*, and the yearbooks of the Society of Illustrators. Morin's career in children's books had an auspicious beginning with his illustrations for Tololwa Mollel's story, *The Orphan Boy*, in 1990. In his native Canada, the book won the Governor General's Literary Award for Illustration, the Amelia Frances Howard-Gibbon Illustrator's Award, and the Elizabeth Mrazik-Cleaver Canadian Picture Book Award. It also earned him a place on Canada's IBBY Honour List and was shortlisted for the Kate Greenaway Medal in Britain. In the United States, *The Orphan Boy* was named a Notable Children's Book by the American Library Association.

It is traditional cultures that interest Paul, because they are grounded in nature, spirit, harmony, and wisdom. He has traveled to Africa, Australia, and China as well as throughout North, Central, and South America to research the background for each story he has illustrated. Whether it is a realistic story from an unfamiliar culture, a folktale from the past, a collection of poetry, or an interpretation of animal behavior, each of Paul Morin's books stands out for the integrity of his artistic vision. Three of his books have been named Notable Children's Trade Books in the Field of Social Studies: *Ghost Dance*, *Animal Dreaming*, and *Flags*. He won a second Amelia Frances Howard-Gibbon Illustrator's Award for *The Dragon's Pearl* in 1993 and a Society of Illustrators Award in 1993 and 1998.

A multimedia artist, Paul Morin has combined his talent for producing video and musical recordings with his fine art and illustration work in solo exhibitions that enlighten viewers and listeners about natural settings and Native cultures as much as they delight the eye and ear.

SELECTED WORKS WRITTEN AND ILLUSTRATED: *Animal Dreaming: An Aboriginal Dreamtime Story*, 1998.

SELECTED WORKS ILLUSTRATED: *The Orphan Boy*, by Tololwa Mollel, 1990; *The Dragon's Pearl*, by Julie Lawson, 1992; *Fox Song*, by Joseph Bruchac, 1993; *The Mud Family*, by Betsy James, 1994; *The Ghost Dance*, by Alice McLerran, 1995; *The Vision Seeker*, by James Whetung, 1996; *Lasting Echoes*, by Joseph Bruchac, 1997; *Flags*, by Maxine Trottier, 1999; *At Break of Day*, by Nikki Grimes, 1999; *Panther: Shadow of the Swamp*, by Jonathan London, 2000; *Crocodile: Disappearing Dragon*, by Jonathan London, 2001; *What the Animals Were Waiting For*, by Jonathan London, 2001.

SUGGESTED READING: *Canadian Who's Who*, 2003; Cummins, Julie. *Children's Book Illustration and Design*, vol. 2, 1996. Periodicals—Cundiff, Brad, "Paul Morin," *Studio Magazine*, July/August 1992.

"I was born in 1943 and went to school first of all at St. Matthias Church of England Primary School. After that there followed two boarding schools: the Abbey in Sussex and, when I was 13, the King's School in Canterbury. I was an undistinguished student, rather better on the rugby field than in the classroom. A brief period in the army at Sandhurst was followed by marriage to my wife, Clare, in 1963 and then three years as an undergraduate at King's College, London. The best that can

Michael Morpurgo

October 5, 1943–

be said for my degree was that it was unexceptional. I went from university straight into teaching. We had three children during my teaching time.

"Then came a crossroads. Clare's father, Sir Allen Lane, was founder of Penguin Books in England and a son of what is known as the West Country, the counties of Devon and Cornwall. Clare and I decided to embark on an innovative educational project while going back to those roots. Conscious of the fact that many children, particularly in the inner cities, were missing out at school for various reasons—the limitations of school, family circumstances, etc.—we decided to see if there was something we could do to enrich the lives of these children. After much research, we thought a farm would be a way to do this, a farm for children, where children would actually learn to become the farmers. Perhaps a chance to live for a week in the country, to be around animals and the natural world, and to experience a landscape that was not man-made would help these children. So in 1975 we set up a charity called Farms for City Children. We purchased a farm and a house near Iddesleigh in Devon, formed a partnership with the Ward family, our farming neighbours, and invited schools to come.

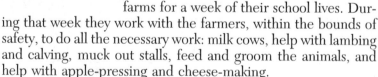

Courtesy of Elaine S. Martens

"The first year nine schools came, but two years later we were full and, with the exception of seven months during the Foot and Mouth scare, the farm has been full ever since. The late poet and author Ted Hughes was our founding president and Princess Anne is our patron. There are now three Farms for City Children: Nethercott, the Devon one; Treginnis, near St. David's in Pembrokeshire (Wales), and one near the city of Bristol called Wick Court. Some 3,000 primary and secondary children a year now come with their teachers to the farms for a week of their school lives. During that week they work with the farmers, within the bounds of safety, to do all the necessary work: milk cows, help with lambing and calving, muck out stalls, feed and groom the animals, and help with apple-pressing and cheese-making.

"During this time I began writing my stories, short stories at first, then novels, picture books, screenplays, and libretti for opera. In my 30 years of writing I have published 100 titles. The books have been translated into 26 languages and have won prizes in England and abroad, more in France than anywhere. In 1999 Clare and I were both awarded the MBE (Member of the Order of the British Empire) for our work for children, and in 2003 I was made children's laureate. I am a fellow of King's College, London, and hold an honorary doctor of education from the University of Plymouth."

✵ ✵ ✵

Michael Morpurgo was born in St. Albans, outside of London, and became interested in writing for young people during his 10 years of teaching in both state and private schools in Kent. He read a book called *Poetry in the Making* by the poet Ted Hughes, a book he has called a "persuasive invitation to write." Discovering that his students enjoyed and paid attention to the stories he told them, he began to write those stories down. Since 1976, when he and his wife established their Farms for City Children program, Michael's books have been written alongside his work on Nethercott Farm in Devon, interacting with the children whose week-long residence at the farm can often be a life-changing experience. During their residence week, many children develop new self-confidence as they learn to be responsible and take pride in their work. In the evenings on the farm, Michael shares his stories, and the children in turn provide inspiration for the storyteller.

One summer's evening, while walking in the water meadows on the farm, Michael encountered Ted Hughes walking along the river, the very poet whose work had so inspired him. The two became great friends. Hughes was appointed England's poet laureate, and one night after dinner, the two friends brainstormed an idea for a children's laureate position. When they enlisted the help of Lois Beeson, a children's literature advocate, their idea became a reality. In 2003 Michael Morpurgo was named the third children's laureate (Quentin Blake and Ann Fine had been the first two). A two-year position, it entails traveling to visit schools and fairs, libraries and bookstores, and advocating children's reading.

> *"I was an undistinguished student, rather better on the rugby field than in the classroom."*

Throughout the years, Michael's books have garnered many awards. His passionate love of the countryside and of animals is evident in his stories, and he takes his inspiration from the life and history he finds everywhere he goes. His novel *War Horse*, which has been compared to *Black Beauty* for its empathic power, was based on a true story of a farm horse from Devon pressed into military service during World War I. Several of his books are set in the Isles of Scilly, where Michael and his family have vacationed. *Why the Whales Came*, about children befriending an outcast old man and joining forces with him to save a beached whale, has been made into a feature film. *The Wreck of the Zanzibar*, another tale that evokes the magic of the Isles, won the Whitbread Award in 1996.

The Butterfly Lion, which draws on some of Michael's least happy memories of boarding school, was presented the Smarties Gold prize. This gentle story of a man's lifelong love for a wild animal, and the healing qualities that imparts to another child

MICHAEL MORPURGO

Kensuke's Kingdom

Courtesy of Scholastic Press

much later, is a quiet blend of realism and fantasy. Morpurgo honors the riches of folklore and heroic literature in his collaborative work with illustrator Michael Foreman in such books as *Arthur, High King of Britain*; *Robin of Sherwood*; and *Joan of Arc*. Some of his books have been adapted for the theater, and five have been made into films. Several have been shortlisted for the Carnegie Medal, and *Kensuke's Kingdom* won the Children's Book Award. As Morpurgo says above, his books have received notice outside of Britain as well. In the United States, *The War of Jenkins' Ear* was cited as an ALA Best Book for Young Adults; *Waiting for Anya*, a tense story of rescue in the Pyrenees during World War II, became a *School Library Journal* Best Book, and *Twist of Gold* was included on the list of Notable Trade Books in the Field of Social Studies. In 2004 *Kensuke's Kingdom* was named a Notable Children's Book by the American Library Association.

Michael Morpurgo lives with his wife in Devon when he is not on the road. They have three grown children and six grandchildren.

SELECTED WORKS (Dates are for British publication; U.S. publication dates, if different, appear in parentheses): *It Never Rained: Five Stories*, illus. by Isabelle Hutchins, 1974; *Thatcher Jones*, illus. by Trevor Ridley, 1975; *Long Way Home*, 1975; *Do All You Dare*, photos by Bob Cathmoir, 1978; *The Day I Took the Bull by the Horn*, 1979; *The Ghost Fish*, 1979; *Love at First Sight*, 1979; *The Nine Lives of Montezuma*, illus. by Margery Gill, 1980; *The White Horse of Zennor: And Other Stories from Below the Eagle's Nest*, 1982; *The War Horse*, 1982 (1983); *Twist of Gold*, 1983 (1993); *Little Foxes*, 1984; *Why the Whales Came*, 1985; *Jo-Jo, the Melon Donkey*, illus. by Chris Molan, 1987, illus. by Tony Kerins, 1995; *King of the Cloud Forests*, 1988; *Waiting for Anya*, 1990 (1991); *The Sandman and the Turtles*, 1991 (1994); *The War of Jenkins' Ear*, 1993 (1995); *Snakes and Ladders*, 1994; *Arthur, High King of Britain*, illus. by Michael Foreman, 1994 (1995); *The Dancing Bear*, illus. by Christian Birmingham, 1994 (1996); *Muck and Magic: Tales from the Countryside*, 1995; *The Wreck of the Zanzibar*, illus. by Christian Birmingham, 1994 (1995); *Blodin the Beast*, illus. by Christina Balit, 1995; *Beyond the* Rainbow Warrior: *A Collection of Stories to Celebrate 25 Years of Greenpeace*, (as editor), 1995; *Sam's Duck*, illus. by Keith Bowen, 1996; *The*

Ghost of Grania O'Malley, 1996; *Robin of Sherwood*, illus. by Michael Foreman, 1996; *Farm Boy*, illus. by Michael Foreman, 1997; *Escape from Shangri-La*, 1998; *Joan of Arc*, illus. by Michael Foreman, 1998 (1999); *The Rainbow Bear*, illus. by Michael Foreman, 1999; *Kensuke's Kingdom*, 1999 (2003); *The Kingfisher Book of Great Boy Stories: A Treasury of Classics from Children's Literature*, (as compiler) 2000; *Billy the Kid*, illus. by Michael Foreman, 2000; *Wombat Goes Walkabout*, illus. by Christian Birmingham, 1999 (2000); *The Silver Swan*, illus. by Christian Birmingham, 2000; *Toro! Toro!*, illus. by Michael Foreman, 2002; *Out of the Ashes*, illus. by Michael Foreman, 2002; *Private Peaceful*, 2003 (2004); *The Gentle Giant*, illus. by Michael Foreman, 2004.

SUGGESTED READING: *Authors and Artists for Young Adults*, vol. 37, 2001; Carey, Joanna. *An Interview with Michael Morpurgo* (Telling Tales series), 1999; *Children's Literature Review*, vol. 51, 1999; *Contemporary Authors*, vol. 158, 1998; McCarthy, Shaun. *All About . . . Michael Morpurgo*, 2004; Pendergast, Tom and Sara. *St. James Guide to Young Adult Writers*, 1999; *Something About the Author*, vol. 143, 2003. Periodicals—Cooper, Ilene, "The *Booklist* Interview," *Booklist*, January 1 & 15, 1996; "Interview," *Young Writer*, April 1999; Kellaway, Kate, "Sword's Lore," *Observer*, March 24, 2002; "The Making of *Anya*, or a Tale of Two Villages," *Children's Literature in Education*, December 1993.

WEB SITES: *www.childrenslaureate.org*; *www.farmsforcitychildren.org*.

Gerald Morris
October 29, 1963–

"I grew up between worlds. Most of my childhood I lived in Singapore, where my parents were missionaries in the Chinese churches there and where I was a curiosity—an undersized boy with a white-blond crewcut and pink cheeks that seemed to be just right for pinching and cooing over. When I was small, I reacted against the Chinese and Malay and Indian cultures that surrounded me by proudly declaring myself American and turning up my nose at everything Singaporean. Thus I rejected all sorts of mouth-watering foods in favor of such true American specialties as Velveeta cheese and Wonder bread. I would have eaten library paste if I'd thought it would make me more American. The paste would have tasted better.

"Then, on visits back to the United States, I discovered that I was just as much an outsider in my own country as I was in Singapore. It wasn't just that the other kids I met in the States didn't know anything about other cultures or people, but they didn't seem to want to know. I began to appreciate Singapore as I never had. For the rest of my childhood and teen years, I tried to work out how to love both the country of my birth and the country that was my home for all they were worth. One thing was sure, though: I would never be just an American or just a Singaporean.

I was like a pollywog, stuck somewhere between tadpole and frog.

"I was the same way concerning my plans for the future. I was going to be a minister, a teacher, or a writer, depending on which day you asked me. Even as I went to college, my career picture never really became clear. I had officially decided to become a minister, but I majored in English and began writing poetry and short stories. I went to ministerial school and, while there, began writing novels. I became pastor of a small church in Muncie, Indiana, and while I drove around making pastoral visits, I composed light verse about church history in my head. I decided to become a religion professor and got a Ph.D. in Hebrew and Greek, but I kept on writing fiction. None of my books are 'religious' novels. I began teaching in the religion department of a Baptist university, where I mostly hung out with English professors.

"I was 33 years old and still a pollywog.

"I don't mean to say that I'm unstable. (I might be, but I certainly don't intend to say so.) Certain things do stay the same throughout my life: my faith, my love for my wife (Rebecca) and children (William, Ethan, and Grace), my enjoyment of words, my tendency to forget appointments, my habit of trailing off in mid-sentence and losing my train of thought . . . .

"But in many ways I'm still between worlds. Now I am the part-time pastor of a small Baptist church in Wisconsin, an occasional substitute teacher, an occasional instructor in a university extension program, and a children's novelist. Often the people I meet in one of my worlds don't understand my other lives. Literary people who find out I'm a minister are frequently astonished. ('How interesting!' they say doubtfully, as if they had just discovered that I lived entirely on a diet of worms.) On the other hand, many people in my own church would be shocked if they ever read my novels, which are full of sorcery and beheadings and fairies and elves and other things that you hardly ever find in Sunday School books. I'm not what anyone in any of my worlds expects me to be.

"The poet Walt Whitman once wrote 'Do I contradict myself? Very well then, I contradict myself. (I am large. I contain multitudes.)' I don't think I'm as large as Whitman—I'm only a pollywog, after all—but I guess it's all right for me to be bigger than other people's notions of what I'm supposed to be."

Courtesy of Greg Behrendt

❊ ❊ ❊

Born in Riverside, Wisconsin, Gerald Morris received his B.A. from Oklahoma Baptist University in 1985. He married Rebecca Hughes in 1986, and they are the parents of William, Ethan, and Grace. Earning a M.Div. from Southern Baptist Theological in 1989 and a Ph.D. in 1994, Morris put together a varied working career. He's taught Hebrew and biblical studies and English as a second language, and tutored students in Greek. He's also been a substitute teacher and was a landscaper before becoming the pastor of the First Baptist Church in Wausau, Wisconsin. His first published work was for the academic world, entitled *Prophesy, Poetry, and Hosea* (1996).

Morris began writing novels for young people while he was in graduate school, and not long after he'd finished his doctorate, *The Squire's Tale* was accepted for publication. Inspired by Arthurian legends, *The Squire's Tale* introduces 14-year-old Terence, who leaves the hermit who has raised him to adventure forth with Gawain on his quest to be a Knight of the Round Table. Humorous, filled with lively characters and engaging dialogue, it won immediate acclaim by reviewers. His next book, *The Squire, His Knight, and His Lady*, named an ALA Best Book for Young Adults in 2000, provides a fresh look at the tale of Sir Gawain's meeting with the Green Knight and introduces both Terence's true identity and his unexpected love, the Lady Eileen. *The Savage Damsel and the Dwarf*, an ALA Best Book for Young Adults in 2001, brings another Arthurian legend to life with a delightful twist and a tart exploration of bravery and intelligence. Each of these titles as well as the recent *Parsifal's Page* have in common an insistence that it's important to look beyond bold deeds to the intentions behind them. Each also celebrates the world of Faerie, of enchantment, and how it interfaces with the world of humankind.

Courtesy of Houghton Mifflin, Inc.

SELECTED WORKS: *The Squire's Tale*, 1998; *The Squire, His Knight, and His Lady*, 1999; *The Savage Damsel and the Dwarf*, 2000; *Parsifal's Page*, 2001; *The Ballad of Sir Dinadan*, 2003; *The Princess, the Crone, and the Dung-Cart Knight*, 2004.

SUGGESTED READING: *Contemporary Authors*, vol. 196, 2002; *Something About the Author*, vol. 150, 2004.

Courtesy of Harcourt, Inc.

Marissa Moss (signature)

Marissa Moss

Sepember 29, 1959–

"When I was a kid, I constantly told myself stories and drew pictures to go along with them. I even sent my first book to publishers when I was nine. (Even though that story was never published, I wasn't deterred from writing more.) I loved the way stories allowed me to make things happen the way I wanted them to. I was a very small, skinny, asthmatic kid, so making up stories made me feel powerful. It still does.

"I remember vividly the satisfaction I felt creating something outside of myself worthy of other people's notice, and when I wrote in my private journal, I felt a similar satisfaction as events and emotions were sifted through and made meaningful by writing them down. It always amazed me that just by naming something, I understood it better.

"Although I started my career making picture books with *Amelia's Notebook*, I stumbled upon a format that let me write and draw the way I had as a kid. More than conventional picture books, the notebook format allows me to leap from words to images, and this free-flowing back-and-forth inspires my best work. It reflects the way I think—sometimes visually, sometimes verbally—with the pictures not there just to illustrate the text but to replace it, to tell their own story. Often the art allows me a kind of graphic shorthand, a way of conveying a thought that is much more immediate than words. Kids often ask me which comes first, the words or the pictures. With Amelia, it can be either—and I love that fluidity.

"But there are places Amelia, as a contemporary child, can't go, and so I started a new notebook series, with books in the format of historical journals. Like Amelia's notebooks, the pages resemble real notebook pages, with drawings and objects detailed on every page, but in the new series the main character is from the past. The first book, *Rachel's Journal: The Story of a Pioneer Girl*, is the diary of a 10-year-old who takes the Oregon Trail from Illinois to California in 1850. I spent months doing the necessary research, first reading general histories, then digging into the archives of the Bancroft Library at the University of California, Berkeley, where I found actual manuscripts written by men, women, and children who had traveled by covered wagon across this immense continent.

"The accounts were, for the most part, riveting reading, and I was impressed with what an enormous undertaking—what a leap of faith—it was for pioneers to travel west. It was a dangerous trip. Indian attacks, river crossings, storms, and especially sickness were feared. But I was struck by the difference between how men and women viewed the long journey and how children saw it. To kids it was a great adventure—troublesome at times, tedious and terrifying at others, but ultimately exciting. These children showed tremendous courage and strength of character, and I tried to capture some of that, as well as the exhilaration of traveling into the unknown, in *Rachel's Journal*. The book provided an opportunity for me to try yet another kind of writing as I searched for a convincing voice and character. And I hope it inspires a different kind of reading from kids—a hunger for historical sources and the way they can make a strange, vague period of the past vivid and familiar.

"My second historical notebook is the diary of a 10-year-old girl trapped in British-occupied Boston during the Revolutionary War. Again I was fascinated by the richness of the period, the personal and national dramas that played out, and the psychological journey the colonists made from seeing themselves as proud British subjects to seeing themselves as independent Americans. While researching *Emma's Journal: The Story of a Colonial Girl*, I unearthed gems of stories about falling hairpieces, clever spy systems, churches turned into riding rings with pews used as pigsties. Once again a period that had seemed bland to me, a set of clichés, came alive with the many details of daily life. As I step forward with Amelia's notebooks, I step backward with my historical journals in the Young American Voices series. I can't wait to see where the books will take me next."

❋   ❋   ❋

Marissa Moss has been able to convey the feelings and thoughts of a young person in each of her books, whether in a historical work or in the more contemporary Amelia notebooks. She does this through a journal format, combining words and pictures in a unique blend that has become her signature style. This ability to connect with her audience has made her books enormously popular with young readers and has established her place in the children's book field today.

Though she was born in Pennsylvania, Marissa's family moved to California when she was two years old, and she considers herself a West Coast person. She grew up in a variety of places around the Los Angeles area and also in the Bay area of San Francisco, but wherever the family lived, her life was filled with books, stories, and pictures. Going to the library was a weekly event for her. She remembers most vividly the years that she was 9 and 10, so it's not surprising that her heroines are usually that age. Her quirky, unsentimental style is refreshing and appealing, but there is plenty of substance in her many "notebooks" about Amelia and also in her growing list of historical journals. For these she does extensive and meticulous research to create a pic-

"I was a very small, skinny, asthmatic kid, so making up stories made me feel powerful. It still does."

Courtesy of Harcourt, Inc.

ture of what life was like for a child at that particular time in history and in that particular place. In *Hannah's Journal: The Story of an Immigrant Girl*, for example, Hannah travels bravely from her home in a Lithuanian village to make a new life in America at the beginning of the 20th century. Each detail of the journey has been carefully studied and incorporated into an exciting plot to keep the reader involved; Moss gives readers just enough information to come away feeling they know the heroine and want to know her better.

Marissa Moss's work has been recognized by critics as well. *Amelia's Notebook* was named an American Booksellers Association Pick of the Lists book. *My Notebook (with Help from Amelia)* won a 2000 Parent Council Outstanding Award for informational content. *Oh Boy, Amelia!* received a Parent's Guide to Children's Media Award and an IRA Children's Choice Award. Seven of her historical books have been designated as Notable Children's Trade Books in the Field of Social Studies (since 2000, called Notable Social Studies Trade Books for Young People). The titles so honored were *Rachel's Journal, Hannah's Journal, Rose's Journal, Galen: My Life in Imperial Rome, True Heart, Brave Harriet*, and *In America*.

Marissa Moss received her B.A. in art history from the University of California and has attended California College of Arts and Crafts. She and her husband, Harvey Stahl, a professor, and their three children—Simon, Elias, and Asa—live in Berkeley, California.

SELECTED WORKS WRITTEN AND ILLUSTRATED: *Regina's Big Mistake*, 1990; *After-School Monster*, 1991; *Knick Knack Paddywack*, 1992; *Amelia's Notebook*, 1995; *The Ugly Menorah*, 1996; *Amelia Writes Again*, 1996; *Amelia Hits the Road*, 1997; *Amelia Takes Command*, 1998; *Rachel's Journal: The Story of a Pioneer Girl*, 1998; *Luv, Amelia, Luv, Nadia*, 1999; *Emma's Journal: The Story of a Colonial Girl*, 1999; *Amelia's Family Ties*, 2000; *Hannah's Journal: The Story of an Immigrant Girl*, 2000; *Rose's Journal: The Story of a Girl in the Great Depression*, 2001; *Galen: My Life in Imperial Rome*, 2002; *Max's Logbook*, 2003.

SELECTED WORKS WRITTEN: *True Heart*, illustrated by C. F. Payne, 1998; *Brave Harriet: The First Woman to Fly the English Channel*, illus. by C. F. Payne, 2001; *Mighty Jackie: The Strike-Out Queen*, illus. by C. F. Payne, 2004.

SUGGESTED READING: *Something About the Author*, vol. 104, 1999

"There are several incidents in my childhood which I remember that seem 'improbable' at least, but they're vivid in my mind and they have stayed with me. We had a cherry tree in the back yard, and I remember that if I rode my tricycle just fast enough, I could fly higher and higher in circles around its top. The image of looking back down at my great-grandmother, Gramma Muth, as she hung out the bed sheets on the clothesline stays with me as if it were yesterday.

"I was raised until the age of seven by Gramma Muth. My parents would both leave for work early in the morning and often get home very late at night. There were no children my age for me to play with, so I remember my early life as being with her. I would see the treetops waving and the wind was always blowing then, so I was sure that the trees made the wind blow. I remember my bed silently floating out of my room, down the hall and down the stairs, and I would wake up the next morning in my great-grandmother's bed. Gramma Muth was a very gentle and strong spirit. When I started going to school, she would walk me the mile to school and then walk home, only to do it again a few hours later to meet me when school was over. Often, we would then go another three miles to the market with her pushing me in a grocery cart. She was 78 then. I remember the first time she wasn't able to come and pick me up from school. A leaf followed me all the way home that day, always staying about five steps behind.

"My mother was an art teacher, and she took me to museums all over the country. Her encouragement was very demanding and sometimes hard to take, but it helped me find myself in art. All kinds of art. I don't remember ever deciding that I would make pictures, I just always have. These two women had much to do with how I see the world. Later, the most exciting part of my adult education came from an informal apprenticeship with two very different fine artists who helped me learn to describe and express that world. My education took me all over. I studied stone sculpture in Japan; paintings, prints, and drawings in Austria and Germany and England; and I was an English major at the State University of New York in New Paltz.

"I love telling stories, and I am very interested in what words and pictures can do together that they can't do separately. There is a 'third thing' that occurs. It's a space where you are perceiving that which is suggested by both the images and the text, but it remains un-named by either. And it can be emotional, or a logi-

Courtesy of Bonnie To Yee

Jon J Muth
July 28, 1960–

cal story point, or intellectual. This space seems to be as flexible as either words or pictures. It's a dance between the two. Exploring this began in my work in comic books, which have traditionally been a forum for expressions of angst and questioning one's place in the universe. My work in children's books really grew out of a desire to explore what I was feeling as a new father. With the births of my son Nikolai and my daughter Adelaine there was a kind of seismic shift in where my work seemed appropriate. In 1995 I created the comic *Imaginary Magnitude* for Kodansha, a Japanese publisher, and that was where my work began to express the real joy I find in being a parent.

"The magic of those flights around the tree tops has circled back into my life through my children. They are a reminder that I don't always know what the leaves are up to and that I still, sometimes, believe that trees make the wind blow."

❄ ❄ ❄

Jon J Muth's career before 1999 was mostly involved in fine art and graphic novels. He had his first solo exhibit of paintings and drawings at the age of eighteen, and two books have featured his fine artwork: *Koan* and *Vanitas: Paintings, Drawings, and Ideas*. His award-winning comic books and graphic novels have been published extensively in the United States and Japan. He worked on the art for such characters as Sandman and the Silver Surfer and created his own adaptation of Bram Stoker's *Dracula*, which was subtitled, "A Symphony in Moonlight and Nightmares." Later he would adapt the characterization of a comic-book hero for the easy-reader children's book about the boyhood of Bruce Wayne, *Batman's Dark Secret*.

Muth entered the field of children's books with a very distinct style that seemed like a breath of fresh air; his gentle watercolor washes depicted scenes that hovered between reality and dream in Karen Hesse's picture book story of a summer rainstorm in a sweltering city. *Come On, Rain!* received a Gold Medal from the Society of Illustrators and was named a Blue Ribbon book by the *Bulletin of the Center for Children's Books*. When Eric Kimmel's story for the Jewish New Year, *Gershon's Monster*, became an ALA Notable Children's Book and won the Sydney Taylor Award, Muth's reputation as a picture book artist was firmly established. *Our Gracie Aunt*, a gentle story of family foster care written by Jacqueline Woodson, was cited as a Notable Social Studies Trade Book for Young People; Muth's watercolors for this story reflected many aspects of the children's plight that were not mentioned in the spare text and perfectly captured the complex emotions involved.

Themes of intergenerational relationships, friendship, and philosophical questions are prevalent in many of the books Muth has illustrated, and they all come together in his own adaptation of a Leo Tolstoy short story, *The Three Questions*. Changing Tolstoy's characters to a boy and his various animal friends and men-

"I love telling stories, and I am very interested in what words and pictures can do together that they can't do separately."

Courtesy of Scholastic Press

tors, he has created a child's morality fable that gently conveys the message of the Russian writer's adult story. *The Three Questions* received high praise when the *New York Times* called it "quietly life-changing." It was named a Notable Social Studies Trade Book and also won the 2002 Time of Wonder Award given annually by the Maine Discovery Museum to a book that "captures the sense of wonder and imagination of the most enduring children's literature." The illustrations reflect an Asian influence in the use of panels and open space, an influence that is echoed in Muth's adaptation of a European folk tale, *Stone Soup*. He sets the story in China and changes the soldier characters to three wandering monks. In this book once again the artist imparts an important life message to children—the meaning of true cooperation—through the vehicle of story and art. *Stone Soup* was included in the CCBC Choices list for 2003.

Jon J Muth lives with his family in upstate New York. The "J" in his name is not an initial; so like the "S" in Harry S Truman, it doesn't have a period. His children regularly model for the characters in his books. His son Nikolai is the model for the main character in *The Three Questions* who bears his name.

SELECTED WORKS WRITTEN AND ILLUSTRATED: *Imaginary Magnitude*, 1996, 2005; *The Three Questions*, 2002; *Stone Soup*, 2003.

SELECTED WORKS ILLUSTRATED: *Come On, Rain!*, by Karen Hesse, 1999; *Gershon's Monster: A Story for the Jewish New Year*, by Eric Kimmel, 2000; *Why I Will Never Ever Ever Ever Have Enough Time to Read This Book*, by Remy Charlip,

2000; *Batman's Dark Secret* (Hello Reader series), by Kelley Puckett, 2000; *Our Gracie Aunt*, by Jacqueline Woodson, 2002; *Old Turtle and the Broken Truth*, by Douglas Wood, 2003; *Mr. George Baker*, by Amy Hest, 2004; *No Dogs Allowed!*, by Sonia Manzano, 2004.

SUGGESTED READING: Duncan, Andrew, "Interview with Jon J Muth," May 26, 2003, *www.booksense.com/people/archive/m/muthjonj.jsp*; Hopkinson, Deborah, "Something Old, Something New: Jon J Muth's Magical Role As Storyteller," Interview, May 2003, *www.bookpage.com/0305bp/jon_muth.html*.

Courtesy of Scholastic Press

Christopher Myers

October 17, 1974–

"**M**y mother taught me to paint. My father is a writer, and I watched him working as an author while I was growing up. I think that creative work, both writing and visual art, is the greatest job in the world. I think images are very important, and that it is my job to create images that contribute to the betterment of the world around me. I've done a bunch of books in the last 10 years. I also make sculpture and write plays and poems. I'm working on a novel. I feel like I have a lot of work to do; there's never enough time in the day.

"I want my work to make black kids, around the world, look in the mirror and like what they see. I want my work to open the eyes of those who come in contact with it to the beauty of the world around them. My goals are simple and they will last a lifetime, which is why this is the greatest job in the world. (Plus the fact that I don't have to dress up to go to work.)

"These are the important things about me, but there are other details. The point of biographies, I guess, is to get to know the person who you are reading about. So these lists are another way of getting to know me.

"Things I want to learn how to do well: Swimming, Archery, Knitting.

"People I would like to have played a friendly game of basketball with: Akhenaton, Buster Keaton, Ida B. Wells, Frederick Douglass.

"Things I learned from my father about being an artist: Be disciplined; Do a little bit every day; Finish what you start; Do research; It's better than having a real job; Teach yourself to fall in love with the work; Plan your work carefully before you start.

"Why I love New York City: The subway is like a zoo, except you get to stare at people instead of animals; You can walk anywhere; There are places where you can hear 17 languages being spoken on one city block; At night the rivers sing the city to sleep; The world is at your fingertips, only a museum or a library away; You can ride your bike anywhere; So many musicians and dancers and theater artists come here to perform; Harlem is in New York City.

"Adult books every children's book author should read: *Muse and Drudge*, by Harryette Mullen; *Autobiography of Red*, by Anne Carson; *Platero y yo / Platero and I*, by Juan Ramón Jiménez; *The Tunnel*, by Russell Edson; *The Summer of Black Widows*, by Sherman Alexie; *Family Ties*, by Clarice Lispector; *Lyrics of a Lowly Life*, by Paul Laurence Dunbar; *Supposed to Fly*, by Miroslaw Holub; *A Good Man Is Hard to Find*, by Flannery O'Connor.

"Cities in Africa I want to visit within the next 10 years: Dar-Es-Salaam, Lagos, Nairobi, Mombassa, Mogadishu, Cairo (return trip), Johannesburg, Brooklyn.

"Some of my favorite Kung Fu movies: *Legend of Zu*, *The East Is Red*, *Enter the Dragon*, *The God of Cookery*.

"Good albums to illustrate by: *Reality of My Surroundings*, by Fishbone; *Buhloone Mind State*, by De La Soul; *Up for the Down Stroke*, by Parliament; *Greatest Hits*, by Johnny Cash; *Blowback*, by Tricky; *Rid of Me*, by P. J. Harvey; *Inspiration Information*, by Shuggie Otis; *Racines*, by Bisso Na Bisso; *Die Dreigroschenoper*, by Kurt Weill and Bertolt Brecht; *In Search of . . .*, by NERD.

"Cool things I have done this past year: Book signings at the NBA All-Star Game and Finals; Started playing tennis; Breakfast at the White House; Show at PS1 Contemporary Art Museum at MOMA; Demonstration at the National Gallery in Washington, DC; Wrote a 20-page poem.

"Nice to meet you, anyone who is reading this."

❃   ❃   ❃

> *"I think that creative work, both writing and visual art, is the greatest job in the world."*

The son of celebrated writer Walter Dean Myers, Christopher Myers has carved his own niche in the world of children's books with his distinctive art techniques and his own picture book stories. Chris was born in New York City and grew up just across the Hudson River in Jersey City, New Jersey. His parents encouraged his early tendency toward artistic creation and still treasure a photograph of toddler Chris standing in his Pampers beside an elaborate and intricate castle he had built with his blocks and toys. As early as age 13 Chris was attending the Art Students League and honing his skills in classes with much older students. He graduated from Brown University in 1995 with majors in American Civilization and art semiotics and completed the Whitney Museum of American Art Independent Studio Program in 1996.

blues journey

by Walter Dean Myers
illustrated by Christopher Myers

Courtesy of Holiday House

Chris Myers's illustrations first appeared in a young adult fantasy novel written by his father, *Shadow of the Red Moon*. The evocative jacket art of a boy huddled in a bleak landscape was a harbinger of his later work of deep emotional imagery. In 1997 Myers teamed with his father to create *Harlem*, a picture book poem that celebrates the vibrant life and history of this heart of black culture in New York City. While the words drum out the rhythms and sights of a distinctive lifestyle, the illustrations explode with color, texture, and emotional intensity to provide a total experience of the place that is Harlem. Using found materials, textured paper, photographs, textiles, and paint put together in an organic collage technique, Chris Myers grounded his art for this book in the everyday materials of city life, earning both a Caldecott Honor Award and a Coretta Scott King Honor Award. Harlem was also named an ALA Notable Children's Book and a Notable Children's Trade Book in the Field of Social Studies. In a very different collaboration, Chris created a unique half-jacket cover design for his father's evocative novel *Monster*, winner of the Michael Printz Award for Young Adult Literature.

About his first solo book, *Black Cat*, for which he won a second Coretta Scott King Honor Award, Myers says it is a "songbook about urban architecture and how much I love inner cities, no matter what they say in the newspaper." Again using the photo-collage technique enhanced with ink and gouache that was so successful in *Harlem*, he introduces the reader to a dramatic nighttime cityscape through the eyes of a street-smart feline prowler. The rap-like rhythm of the text perfectly complements the visceral feel of the illustrations as the artist, through the persona of the cat, introduces readers to the city he loves. *Black Cat* was named an ALA Notable Children's Book, a *School Library Journal* Best Book, and a Blue Ribbon title for the *Bulletin of the Center for Children's Books*. Turning to human characters for *Wings*, another ALA Notable Children's Book, Myers tells a metaphorical tale of how imagination and friendship can overcome the hardship and isolation of a lonely child's life. Showing growth in the depth of his writing as well his art, *Wings* earned Myers a Charlotte Zolotow Honor Award for picture book writing.

Using a more subdued style and a more limited palette in *Blues Journey*, Chris Myers once again demonstrated his uncanny ability to match his art to the mood of the words. The text by Walter Dean Myers, explaining the Blues by providing examples of the art form, takes the reader on a journey through time and space, through the history of the African American culture out of which Blues music arose. With tones of blue and white paint, black ink, and brown paper bag textures, Chris Myers complements the poetry of the words with remarkably evocative images that document the past and illuminate the present. Blues Journey was named an ALA Notable Children's Book, a *Bulletin* Blue Ribbon title, and a *Horn Book* Fanfare title. Most notably, it won a Picture Book Honor for the *Boston Globe–Horn Book* Award.

In addition to illustration, Christopher Myers creates sculpture and art for special exhibits, such as "Off the Record," a show at the Skylight Gallery in Brooklyn in 2003 where artists were invited to contribute an embodiment of a fantasy hero and one critic called Myers's work "part tribal mask, part *Clockwork Orange*." He has also exhibited at the Akron Art Museum and been artist-in-residence at the Family Academy, a school in Harlem. A line in *Harlem* exemplifies his creative work: " . . . the artist looking into a mirror / Painting a portrait of his own heart." Christopher Myers lives and works in Brooklyn, New York.

SELECTED WORKS WRITTEN AND ILLUSTRATED: *Black Cat*, 1999; *Wings*, 2000; *Fly*, 2001.

SELECTED WORKS ILLUSTRATED: *Shadow of the Red Moon*, by Walter Dean Myers, 1995; *Harlem: A Poem*, by Walter Dean Myers, 1997; *This I Know: Poetry Across Black Cultures*, sel. by Arlene Harris Mitchell and Darwin L. Henderson, 1998; *Monster*, by Walter Dean Myers, 1999; *A Time to Love: Stories from the Old Testament*, by Walter Dean Myers, 2003; *Blues Journey*, by Walter Dean Myers, 2003.

SUGGESTED READING: Bishop, Rudine Sims, "Following in Their Father's Paths: African American Children's Book Illustrators," *The Horn Book*, March/April 1998; Emberley, Michael, "Not Like Other Boys," *New York Times Book Review*, November 19, 2000.

A profile of Christopher Myers's father, Walter Dean Myers, appeared in *Fifth Book of Junior Authors and Illustrators* (1983).

Courtesy of Peter Belamarich

Keiko Narahashi

January 20, 1959–

"Sometimes I think that there are two kinds of people in the world, those who think in words and those who think in pictures (and a lucky few who are fluent in both). Images from childhood come to me of the shiny tin washtub in the yard that I spent hot days splashing in, the field of flowering yellow mustard greens across the street, the silhouette of my mother sitting by our futons while my brother and I fell asleep, the three of us under the mosquito netting in the twilight.

"I've always loved to draw, and my favorite topic was beautiful ladies. I copied them out of English fairy-tale books, which had the most elaborate illustrations. But my very favorites were in the Japanese picture books, which had simpler drawings. They really fascinated me—the drawings looked so clear and direct, but were full of interesting information. How did the artist get so much detail and expression into a simple brushstroke or pencil line? This is something which still interests me today. In my own illustrations, I like to keep things simple with just a few details that can reveal the whole story. I've found that you don't really need a lot to show a lot.

"I was born in Tokyo, Japan, and spent my childhood in North Carolina. My father was a scientist at Duke University. My classmates were always debating which was better, Duke or University of North Carolina. I assumed all their fathers were scientists working in universities—I didn't know they were talking about basketball teams! I had a lot to learn about America, beginning with learning how to speak English. I remember my first grade teacher holding a box of Crayolas, pointing to them and saying the colors, 'Red, blue, yellow . . .,' and my repeating them slowly after her. I was fine until we got to purple. I just couldn't figure out how to say that word—my tongue would not cooperate! I got into a lot of trouble that year at school. The other children would sometimes taunt me; they had never seen a Japanese kid before. I was frustrated that I couldn't speak English, that I couldn't use words to fight back. So I would sometimes use my hands and feet instead, which my teacher did not approve of. I got an 'F' in conduct that year for being so loud and disruptive.

My father wanted to know how I could be so loud when I couldn't even speak English!

"Things got better when my teacher discovered that I liked to draw and paint. She encouraged me to express myself through art, and she put my pictures up in the hallways. My classmates were impressed and asked me to draw pictures for them. They started to stick up for me when children from other classes tried to pick on me. I finally began speaking English, and most importantly, I learned how to read in English. My elementary school was very old, and some of the books in the library were from the early 1900s. I think I read almost every book in that library. Some of those books had the creepiest stories you could ever imagine. Of course, I loved them.

"Even though, growing up, I drew practically every day of my life, I never thought that I would be an artist. It took me a while to figure out that it was possible. I went to two colleges before I even thought to give art school a try, but once I did, I knew I was doing the right thing. Funny, I thought it would be easier than a regular school—draw pictures all day? I could do that! But it turned out to be the most difficult school I'd ever been to. I worked harder than I had ever worked before, maybe because I cared about it so much. I had drawing classes every day where we drew from a model (naked!), plus painting classes, art history classes, even a class just about color. I took one class in children's book illustration, but I have to admit that I didn't imagine that I would actually do that for a living some day.

"It wasn't until I had graduated and was married and at home with a baby that I thought about children's books again. Maybe it was having my very own baby that brought back childhood memories. I started to think about the times I spent on my own, wandering around the neighborhood daydreaming, and those memories became my first picture book. It's no accident that I'm an artist today even though it took me a while to get here. All those pictures and memories inside my head have a place to go now. How lucky for me that there's such a job as 'children's book illustrator'!"

"Sometimes I think that there are two kinds of people in the world, those who think in words and those who think in pictures (and a lucky few who are fluent in both)."

❄ ❄ ❄

Keiko Narahashi integrates her two worlds in her art, often using the expressive lines of Japanese brush work and glowing watercolors to create soft-focused scenes of childhood. Her scientist father and potter mother brought her to Durham, North Carolina, when she was quite young and she spent much of her childhood trying to conform to her American surroundings rather than celebrating her Japanese heritage. That changed as she grew older and began studying the work of Japanese and Chinese artists, especially the brush painting of Chinese monks. She graduated from high school at the North Carolina School for the Arts in Winston-Salem. After attending Oberlin College for one year, she eventually found her niche at the Parsons School of

By Nancy Minchella • *Illustrated By* Keiko Narahashi

Courtesy of Scholastic Press

Design in New York City, where she earned her B.F.A. in 1988. Narahashi married Peter Belamarich, a pediatrician, in 1982 and they have two children, Micah and Joy. They live in New York City.

In 1987, Narahashi wrote and illustrated her first picture book, the story of a young boy's discovery of, and fascination for, his own shadow. *I Have a Friend* received a Parents' Choice Award and reviews that appreciated her use of warm, soft colors and reassuring round shapes in this child-centered story. In the next few years, she illustrated texts by authors Mary Serfozo, Melanie Scheller, and Yoshiko Uchida, among others. *What's What?*, an original concept book written by Serfozo and illustrated by Narahashi, was named to the CCBC Choices list in 1996.

Narahashi's sensitive, comforting pencil and muted watercolors accompany Melanie Scheller's *My Grandfather's Hat*, a story about a boy missing his much-loved grandfather and remembering him by wearing and carrying his hat. In the art for Norma Farber's *Without Wings, Mother, How Can I Fly?*, published after the poet's death, Narahashi captures the animal-filled world of a child in the country and the many ways his mother suggests he can imitate what the animals do. In 1994 her own story *Is That Josie?* explored a child's imagination and cozy relationship with her mother. Asian-American Josie pretends to be a fox in its den, a possum swinging on its mother's tail, a kangaroo with a baby in her pouch, and, after several more transformations throughout the day and evening, becomes herself to be hugged good night. *Two Girls Can!* is an exuberant depiction of what two friends can do together, ranging from flying kites to digging holes to settling down to read. And in her illustrations for Nancy Minchella's story, *Mama Will Be Home Soon*, Keiko Narahashi gave visual depth to a child's fear and anxiety about separation from her mother.

SELECTED WORKS WRITTEN AND ILLUSTRATED: *I Have a Friend*, 1987; *Is That Josie?*, 1994; *Two Girls Can!*, 2000; *Ouch!*, 2004.

SELECTED WORKS ILLUSTRATED: *Who Said Red?*, by Mary Serfozo, 1988; *Who Wants One?*, by Mary Serfozo, 1989; *Rain Talk*, by Mary Serfozo, 1990; *The Little Band*, by James Sage, 1991; *My Grandfather's Hat*, by Melanie Scheller, 1992; *The Magic Purse*, by Yoshiko Uchida, 1993; *Do Not Feed the Table*, by Dee Lillegard, 1993; *What's What? A Guessing Game*, by Mary Serfozo, 1996; *Happy Birthday, Mrs. Boedecker*, by Marcia Vaughan, 1996; *Without Wings, Mother, How Can I*

Fly?, by Norma Farber, 1997; *A Is for Amos*, by Deborah Chandra, 1999; *Fawn in the Grass*, by Joanne Ryder, 2001; *Here Comes the Year*, by Eileen Spinelli, 2002; *Mama Will Be Home Soon*, by Nancy Minchella, 2003.

SUGGESTED READING: *Contemporary Authors*, vol. 186, 2000; Cummings, Pat, *Talking with Artists*, vol. 3, 1999; *Something About the Author*, vol. 115, 2000.

"I grew up in Gloucester, Massachusetts, during the 1950s and 1960s, a serendipitous, even magical, combination of time and place. Cape Ann was a lively ferment of painters, sculptors, designers, musicians, authors, and illustrators; added to this creative mix was a vibrant community of Finns, Greeks, Italians, Portuguese, and long-settled Yankees. Television and mass culture hadn't yet emerged as a strong influence; for entertainment, people got together to sing and play music; parties had an old-country feel with accordions and fiddles playing accompaniment to Finn hops and polkas and Greek three-man reels.

"My father, Robert Natti, was a teacher and principal in the Gloucester schools; at home he was a masterful storyteller, humorist, and all-around wise man. My mother, Lee Kingman, was an accomplished editor and author of children's books, who adored literature and classic children's books. My little brother Peter and I were read to, often, and as much as I loved the stories, I loved the illustrations even more. I can remember how the illustrations made me feel completely absorbed in a created world. Favorite illustrators of mine then, and now, are Maurice Sendak, Garth Williams, Lynd Ward, Erik Blegvad, Virginia Lee Burton . . . each one so different and so familiar to me.

"It seems almost inevitable that I became an illustrator of children's books, growing up in a house with a gleeful father recounting family tales and a mother providing a background soundtrack of her manual typewriter clickety-clacking out a story. At age 8, I decided that I wanted to draw pictures for books when I grew up. My parents encouraged my drawing, and when I was 10 I began attending a summer figure-drawing class, taught by a gifted teacher and sculptor named George Demetrios. That first summer I was the only child taking the class, which I found quite thrilling. The lessons had a profound influence on the course of my career. The quick gesture drawings we

Courtesy of Ivan Shovelhead

Susanna Natti

October 19, 1948–

always did at the start of class led to an interest in capturing body language and facial expressions, which I still find the most exciting part of drawing.

"I majored in art history at Smith College and then studied art and illustration, first at Montserrat School of Visual Art in Beverly, Massachusetts, and then at the Rhode Island School of Design. Landing my first illustration job took two more years; the book was *The Downtown Fairy Godmother* by Charlotte Pomerantz (Addison-Wesley), published in 1978, and I was, of course, almost beside myself with nervousness and excitement. I took time off from my typing job and went home to Gloucester, where I set up a desk in an old shed. In the morning my father would stoke the wood-burning stove, and I would spend the day out there facing the blank white page, terrified, until I started drawing. Getting over the hump of making the first line was always the hard part; once started, hours would pass unnoticed. Even today, when I no longer suffer 'nervous nellies' as I begin an illustration, I find that the calmest moments of my life are at my desk, drawing.

"I love illustrating for many reasons. Of course, the first is that I love to draw. I love to respond to a text and think about how I can help shape the book it will become by filling in detail and expression. I love working on pacing the rhythm of the book as I lay out the text and decide what scenes to illustrate. I love the creative moments of sketching out ideas. Being an illustrator offers the chance to work independently; I make my own hours and I am my own boss. I can balance the other parts of my life with my work with great flexibility. I love waking up in the morning and thinking, 'What am I going to do today? Why, I guess I'll go draw.'"

"The quick gesture drawings we always did at the start of class led to an interest in capturing body language and facial expressions, which I still find the most exciting part of drawing."

❊　❊　❊

After graduating from Smith College in 1970, Susanna Natti supported herself as a secretary and technical typist at the Massachusetts Institute of Technology until 1978. During this time she attended the Montserrat School of Visual Design (1972–1973) and the Rhode Island School of Design (1973–1975) and established her freelance career. In 1980 she married Alan Willsky; their two daughters, Lydia and Kate, are now nearly grown. All four family members have appeared in illustrations that Natti has created in her books. Jim, their Welsh Pembroke Corgi, has yet to make his appearance, but no doubt will in the future. Children's books are a family affair for Natti, and two of her published books have been collaborations with her writer mother, Lee Kingman: *Catch the Baby!* and *The Best Christmas*.

Success and recognition came early in Natti's career as an illustrator. In 1979 her book *Frederick's Alligator*, written by Esther Allen Peterson, was awarded a Christopher Medal. *Today Was a Terrible Day*, written by Patricia Reilly Giff, was named a Children's Choice by the IRA/CBC joint committee. In a sense, all of Natti's illustrated novels are children's choices because she has illustrated so many popular early chapter books for children who are just developing proficiency in reading. All 23 (to date) books in David Adler's Cam Jansen mystery series, about the young sleuth with a photographic memory, have been graced by Natti's engaging artwork, as well as the Young Cam Jansen stories for the easy-reader group. Her illustrations for series books by Patricia Reilly Giff (Ronald Morgan), Stephen Krensky (Lionel), Betsy Duffey (Pet Patrol), and Susan Wojciechowski (Beany) have enhanced these stories of realistic fiction and humor with great expressiveness and a breezy style that perfectly matches the text. In addition, she has illustrated single volumes by such luminous authors as Jane Yolen, Louise Fitzhugh, and Jim Murphy. Working hard to find just the right balance between text and art, carefully choosing which scenes to illustrate, and creating a flow for the pictures throughout the story are the challenges that face Natti in each project; and every book meets that challenge beautifully.

Courtesy of PenguinPutnam Books

Susanna Natti lives with her family in Bedford, Massachusetts, where she works at home in a studio on the top floor of her house. Her original work for *Frederick's Alligator* is deposited with the de Grummond collection at the University of Southern Mississippi.

SELECTED WORKS ILLUSTRATED: *The Downtown Fairy Godmother*, by Charlotte Pomerantz, 1978; *Dinosaurs and Beasts of Yore: Poems/Verses*, sel. by William Cole, 1979; *Frederick's Alligator*, by Esther Allen Peterson, 1979; *Midnight Moon*, by Clyde Watson, 1979; *The Mystery on Bleeker Street*, by William H. Hooks, 1980; *Today Was a Terrible Day*, by Patricia Reilly Giff, 1980; *Harold Thinks Big*, by Jim Murphy, 1980; *Cam Jansen and the Mystery of the Stolen Diamonds*, by David Adler, 1980 (and others in the series); *The Acorn Quest*, by Jane Yolen, 1981; *I Am Three*, by Louise Fitzhugh, 1982; *Penelope Gets Wheels*, by Esther Allen Peterson, 1982; *Helpful Hattie*, by Janet Quin-Harkin, 1983; *The Almost Awful Play*, by Patricia Reilly Giff, 1985; *Watch Out, Ronald Morgan!*, by Patricia Reilly Giff, 1985; *Lionel at Large*, by Stephen Krensky, 1986; *Happy Birthday, Ronald Morgan!*, by Patricia Reilly Giff, 1986; *Lionel in the Fall*, by Stephen Krensky, 1987; *Ronald Morgan Goes to Bat*, by Patricia Reilly Giff, 1988; *Lionel in the Spring*, by Stephen Krensky, 1990;

Puppy Love, by Betsy Duffey, 1992; *Lionel and Louise*, by Stephen Krensky, 1992; *It's My Money: A Kid's Guide to the Green Stuff*, by Ann Banks, 1993; *Throwaway Pets*, by Betsy Duffey, 1993; *Wild Things*, by Betsy Duffey, 1993; *Catch the Baby!*, by Lee Kingman, 1993; *Lionel in the Winter*, by Stephen Krensky, 1994; *School Daze: Jokes Your Teacher Will Hate*, by Louis Phillips, 1994; *Don't Call Me Beanhead!*, by Susan Wojciechowski, 1994; *Ronald Morgan Goes to Camp*, by Patricia Reilly Giff, 1995; *Good Luck, Ronald Morgan*, by Patricia Reilly Giff, 1996; *Lionel and His Friends*, by Stephen Krensky, 1996; *Beany (not Beanhead) and the Magic Crystal*, by Susan Wojciechowski, 1997; *Lionel in the Summer*, by Stephen Krensky, 1998; *Louise Takes Charge*, by Stephen Krensky, 1998; *Louise Goes Wild*, by Stephen Krensky, 1999; *Lionel at School*, by Stephen Krensky, 2000; *Louise, Soccer Star?*, by Stephen Krensky, 2000; *Beany and the Dreaded Wedding*, by Susan Wojciechowski, 2000; *The Best Christmas*, by Lee Kingman, 2001; *Beany Goes to Camp*, by Susan Wojciechowski, 2002; *Lionel's Birthday*, by Stephen Krensky, 2003; *Cam Jansen and the Tennis Trophy Mystery*, by David A. Adler, 2003; *Young Cam Jansen and the New Girl Mystery*, by David A. Adler, 2004.

SUGGESTED READING: *Something About the Author*, vol. 125, 2002.

A profile of Susanna Natti's mother, Lee Kingman, appeared in *More Junior Authors* (1963).

Kadir Nelson

May 15, 1974–

"When I was a kid, I was like most kids. I played outside with my friends, threw paper airplanes, and played hide-and-go-seek. The only difference was, I was an artist. When I was finished playing, I would go up to my room, pull out a piece of paper, and start drawing. I remember when I was about three or four years old, sitting in my room trying to draw a picture of myself. I didn't think to grab a photo or a mirror, so needless to say, it wasn't working. I took the paper down to my mother and asked her to do it for me. My mother could draw as well. After a few minutes, she handed the drawing back to me and I looked at it. I looked at my mother and said, 'Mommy, this looks like Fat Albert, this doesn't look like me.' I didn't realize that I did have a little afro and big cheeks and most certainly could have been mistaken for that character if I was put in a cartoon lineup. So, I took the paper back and drew it for myself.

"At one time in my mother's life, she wanted to be an artist but was met with discouragement from her family and decided to become an engineer. She always regretted making that decision, and when she discovered that her little boy loved to draw and paint, she made up her mind to nourish and protect his gift rather than discourage it. She always gave me plenty of paper and pencils to work with, and when I was older, she sent me to see my uncle Mike, an artist and an art teacher, for formal instruction. Later on, after I learned to paint with acrylics, my uncle taught me how to paint with oils, which is what I still use today.

"Upon graduating from high school, I received an architecture scholarship to study at Pratt Institute, but later changed my major to illustration. I have to say that was one of the best decisions of my life. I wasn't sure if I could make a living being an artist and had decided to become an architect 'to pay the bills.' But after realizing that architecture was not for me, I made a vow that it wouldn't matter if I had to starve, I was going to be the artist that I had always been. Fortunately, I didn't go hungry. After graduating from Pratt, I quickly began doing freelance illustration for magazines, books, and CD covers. I also did visual development artwork for film and animation, and it was during that time that I was presented with the opportunity to illustrate a children's book. While working on the film *Amistad*, I met Debbie Allen, the dancer. She told me she was looking for an artist to illustrate a children's book she was planning to write. The book was based on a stage production called *Brothers of the Knight* she was producing at the Kennedy Center in Washington, DC. I wasn't really sure that I could do this type of work because it was so different from my previous work, but, unbeknownst to me, doing visual development artwork helped prepare me for illustrating children's books. It taught me about storytelling, lighting and designing environments according to the mood of a story. I immediately volunteered and created a dummy of the book to show her. She loved it and after sharing it with a few publishers, we landed a deal. I had such a great time working on the book that I wanted to illustrate other stories. And fortunately, that is what I have been able to do.

Courtesy of Kadir Nelson

"Children's publishing, I learned, is a world within itself. It allows an artist to have relative creative freedom and share his or her artwork with larger audiences. It is particularly wonderful if you have children of your own because you become something of a celebrity with the little people (ages 3 and up!). I have been blessed with a loving family and great memories of my childhood, which I draw upon for inspiration for my artwork. Illustrating children's books allows me to remember what it was like to be a kid. And that makes me feel great. It makes me feel alive and inspires me to continue to live life to the fullest. I feel it is the responsibility of adults to remember that feeling and share it with others—especially children. The best way I can do that on a large and small scale is with my art. That is why I illustrate children's books. My wish is that all children, young and old, respond to the youthful quality that I hope is present in my work."

✵ ✵ ✵

Kadir Nelson was born in Washington, DC, but grew up in Atlantic City, New Jersey, and then San Diego, California, where his family moved when he was 10 years old and where he resides today. The early encouragement and foundation training he received for his art from his uncle and his high school art teacher led to an art scholarship to study at the prestigious Pratt Institute in New York. There he received his B.F.A. in communications design with highest honors in 1996. After graduating from Pratt he moved back to California and from 1996 to 1999 worked at Dreamworks studios as a visual development artist for the feature films *Amistad* and *Arkansas*, and the animated feature *Spirit: Stallion of the Cimarron.*

"Children's publishing, I learned, is a world within itself. It allows an artist to have relative creative freedom and share his or her artwork with larger audiences."

Nelson's freelance art career has been studded with awards. The Society of Illustrators presented him with its Starr Foundation Award, and he has received a Jellybean Photographics Award, an Editorial Gold Medal, and an Advertising Silver Medal. His art has appeared in many aspects of the entertainment industry, from CD covers to advertising campaigns to major-league baseball programs. His editorial artwork has appeared in prestigious journals and newspapers, including the *New York Times*, the *New Yorker*, and *Sports Illustrated*, for which he created a series of paintings on baseball's Negro Leagues. He has exhibited his works in galleries and museums throughout the United States and abroad including the Simon Weisenthal Center's Museum of Tolerance and the Academy of Motion Picture Arts and Sciences in Los Angeles; the Museum of African American History in Detroit; the Negro League Baseball Museum in Kansas City; the Society of Illustrators and the Studio Museum in New York City; the Bristol Museum in England; the Citizen's Gallery of Yokohama, Japan; and the Center for Culture of Tijuana, Mexico. His paintings are also found in the private collections of major celebrities in the entertainment industry, and some of those personalities have become his collaborators on children's books.

In Kadir Nelson's debut children's book, *Brothers of the Knight*, Debbie Allen's modern-day retelling of the "Twelve Dancing Princesses," his illustrations burst with energy and individuality. The title characters of the original tale are recast as the 12 sons of Reverend Knight in Harlem, who secretly sneak out to dance each night at a lively ballroom. In *Just the Two of Us*, based on a rap song by Will Smith, Kadir Nelson created illustrations that celebrate the bond between a divorced father and his son. This title received an NAACP Image Award in Outstanding

Children's Literature and was designated a Notable Social Studies Trade Book for Young People. *Big Jabe*, Jerdine Nolen's folkloric story of slavery times in which Nelson's art animates the larger-than-life hero, received an Oppenheim Toy Portfolio Gold Award and was named a Blue Ribbon book by the *Bulletin of the Center for Children's Books*. *The Village That Vanished*, an affecting story by Ann Grifalconi about an African village that outwits slave traders, received a Parents' Choice Silver Award and was named an Honor Book for the Jane Addams Children's Book Award. In the year 2001 Kadir Nelson was presented with an unprecedented total of three awards for excellence in picture book illustration by the Children's Literature Council of Southern California for *Big Jabe*, *Dancing in the Wings*, and *Salt in His Shoes*.

Courtesy of Harcourt, Inc.

Nelson's artistic skills range from the exuberant and playful, as in Spike and Tonya Lee's *Please, Baby, Please*, to the quietly joyful celebration of family life in *Under the Tree*, a collection of Christmas poems by Nikki Grimes for which the artist received a Silver Medal in the Society of Illustrators Original Art exhibition in 2002. *Thunder Rose*, Jerdine Nolen's creation of a powerful new African American heroine of the Wild West, gave Kadir Nelson full range for his larger-than-life characterization and earned him a Coretta Scott King Illustrator Honor Award in 2004. Working in a variety of styles and moods in these books, Nelson always expresses a strong sense of character and identity, and strong emotions.

SELECTED WORKS: *Brothers of the Knight*, by Debbie Allen, 1999; *Dancing in the Wings*, by Debbie Allen, 2000; *Big Jabe*, by Jerdine Nolen, 2000; *Salt in His Shoes: Michael Jordan in Pursuit of a Dream*, by Deloris Jordan with Roslyn M. Jordan, 2000; *Just the Two of Us*, by Will Smith, 2001; *Under the Tree: Poems of Christmas*, by Nikki Grimes, 2002; *The Village That Vanished*, by Ann Grifalconi, 2002; *Please, Baby, Please*, by Spike Lee and Tonya Lewis Lee, 2002; *Ellington Was Not a Street*, by Ntozake Shange, 2003; *Thunder Rose*, by Jerdine Nolen, 2003.

SUGGESTED READING: Jones, Lynda, "The Lees Do the Write Thing," *Black Issues Book Review*, November/December 2002; "Old Wounds," *New Yorker*, November 17, 1997. "Profile: Drawing Attention," *San Diego Magazine*, October 2001; Roberts, Ozzie, "Artist Sketches a Dream," *San Diego Union-Tribune*, June 4, 2001; "San Diego's Own Kadir Nelson: Family Man/Award-winning Illustrator," *San Diego Family Magazine*, November 2001.

Courtesy of Fran Funk

Marilyn Nelson

Marilyn Nelson

April 26, 1946–

"I was a dreamy, bookish, and hypersensitive child. A child who read every book in the school library and begged for more, a child who curled up on the couch or in the attic with a book on rainy afternoons and read under the covers with a flashlight after bedtime. I could spend hours lying on my back in a clover meadow, listening to bees and watching clouds form and melt and form and melt again, or sit on a sidewalk watching ants go about their minuscule business in the sandy strip between two squares of cement, or daydream at the window as raindrops joined each other in a criss-cross race down the windowpane. When a sunset or a moonrise or a red-winged blackbird's song moved me to sudden tears, my mother explained to concerned grown-ups that 'Marilyn is very sensitive; she's our poet.' So I grew up thinking of myself as a poet long before I started to write poems.

"My father was a career air force officer; my mother an elementary school teacher. Although it was shadowed by the turbulence of the 1950s Civil Rights Movement and the ugly violence of the responses to Aframerican struggles for school integration and voting rights, my childhood was sheltered by my father's position in the military world and the respect my parents' education and careers won within that world. Like most military families, we were transients who moved frequently from one air force base to another. Only when we left the air force bases where we usually lived and entered the narrow-minded nearby small-town civilian world was I confronted by the overt racial threat or the subtle discrimination faced by most Aframerican children of my generation. I was encouraged to be proud, to believe that I could accomplish anything I could dream.

"At the age of 12, I fell in love with poetry by reading one of my father's old college textbooks, and I decided that I wanted to be a poet when I grew up (either that, or maybe a doctor. Or a scientist. Or maybe all three). At that point we were living in the civilian world, in a big old colonial house on the seashore in Kittery Point, Maine. My sixth grade teacher, Mrs. Dorothy Gray, made predictions on the last day of school, of what she foresaw for my classmates and myself. I don't remember what she predicted for my classmates, but I've never forgotten that she said I would someday be a famous poet for children.

"I was in ninth grade, and we were living in Sacramento, California, when my father retired from the air force. I graduated from high school there and attended the University of California at Davis. I had been writing all through my high school years, and I continued to write poems as a university student. I graduated from UC Davis in 1968 and went on to the University of Pennsylvania for graduate school. I completed a master's degree, then dropped out of school to get married, teach, and travel. For the next 10 years I did not write at all. Instead, I lived and traveled in Oregon, Denmark, Minnesota, Germany, Venezuela, Italy, Norway, and Sweden.

"I started writing again just as I completed work for my Ph.D. in English at the University of Minnesota. My first book of poems was published about a year later, in 1978. With some necessary interruptions, I have been writing ever since."

❄ ❄ ❄

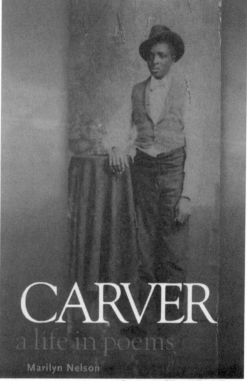

Courtesy of Front Street Press

Marilyn Nelson's spare and heartfelt poetic rendering of the life of George Washington Carver—*Carver: A Life in Poems*—made publishing history in 2001 when it captured a variety of awards. Named a Newbery Honor book and a Coretta Scott King Honor book, it also received the *Boston Globe–Horn Book* Award and was a National Book Award finalist. This lyrical account of one man's character and the events of his life in poetic vignettes also appeared on many important lists: It was named an ALA Notable Children's Book and a Best Book for Young Adults, a Notable Book for a Global Society, a *Bulletin of the Center for Children's Books* Blue Ribbon title, and a Notable Social Studies Trade Book for Young People. As Nelson stated in her acceptance speech for the *Boston Globe–Horn Book* Award, Carver's gentle humility and scientific achievements using the most basic resources to improve everyday life provide inspiring lessons for our own materialistic society.

Named the Connecticut State Poet Laureate in 2001, Marilyn Nelson has enjoyed great success with her published poems for the adult audience as well. *The Homeplace*, a series of poems that explore her family's history from the days of slavery to the present, won the Annisfield-Wolf Award in 1992 and was a finalist for the 1991 National Book Award. A reviewer in *Publishers Weekly* stated that *The Homeplace*, which was based largely on stories told to Nelson by her mother, "elevates personal history to universal experience." *The Fields of Praise* was also a finalist for the National Book Award and won the 1998 Poet's Prize.

Marilyn Nelson was born in Cleveland, Ohio, but spent her childhood in many different places. Married in 1970 to Erdmann Waniek, she was later divorced. She published under her married name—Marilyn Nelson Waniek—until 1995, when she dropped Waniek. In 1979 she married Roger Wilkenfeld, a university professor, and they have two children, Jacob and Dora. This marriage also ended in divorce. Nelson taught at the University of Connecticut from 1978–2002 and from 2002–2004 at the University of Delaware. She has established a reputation for providing strong support and encouragement to young writers and for giving poetry readings that are entertaining and inspiring. She has received two Creative Writing Fellowships from the National Endowment for the Arts, a Guggenheim Fellowship, and the Connecticut Arts Award.

SELECTED WORKS FOR YOUNG READERS: *The Cat Walked Through the Casserole and Other Poems for Children*, with Pamela Espeland, illus. by Trina Schart Hyman, et. al., 1984; *Carver: A Life in Poems*, 2001; *Fortune's Bones: The Manumission Requiem*, with notes by Pamela Espeland, 2004.

SELECTED WORKS FOR ADULTS: *For the Body: Poems*, 1978; *Mama's Promises: Poems*, 1985; *The Homeplace: Poems*, 1990; *Magnificat: Poems*, 1994; *The Fields of Praise: New and Selected Poems*, 1997.

SUGGESTED READING: *Contemporary Authors*, New Revision Series, vol. 51, 1996; *Dictionary of Literary Biography*, vol. 120, 1992; *Something About the Author*, vol. 151, 2004. Periodicals—Nelson, Marilyn, "Aborigine in the Citadel," *Hudson Review*, Winter 2001; Nelson, Marilyn, "Abracadabra, Alakazam, Paz, Salaam, Shalom, Amen" (*Boston Globe–Horn Book* Award Acceptance), *The Horn Book*, January/February 2002.

WEB SITE: *web.uconn.edu/mnelson/mainframe/index.html*

S. D. Nelson

January 25, 1950–

"On the prairies of Dakota there is only earth and sky. All is grass and clouds, forever. It is a land of brutal beauty, where terrible battles were fought—hand to hand—and where at twilight, the song of Sister Meadowlark will make your heart cry. When I was a boy, my mother told me coyote stories about Iktomi, the Trickster. I learned that the stars were the spirits of my ancestors, that my great-great-grandfather, Flying Cloud, still rode his snorting horse along the White Road of the Milky Way. If I looked carefully, Mom said, I would see the Great Bear and the Star That Did Not Turn—the North Star. She told me the Life Force or the Great Mystery is named *Wakan Tanka*; that all of creation—the four-legged beings, the tall standing trees, even the wind—has a spirit and is alive.

"I remember one particular summer night . . . cricket song filled my ears. Then, shimmering overhead, the Northern Lights came dancing, pale green at first, then in ethereal robes of red and gold, spiraling ever upward. Colors vanishing, only to reappear. Although I was staring directly into the heavens, from the corner of my eye I saw *something*. I was only a boy, but I was seeing in a *Wakan* manner, in a sacred way.

"My mother, who was a quarter-blood Sioux Indian, taught me at an early age to see the world with both the curious eyes of a child and the wistful eyes of an old man. I learned that morning is the most beautiful time. For at dawn the world is born anew. It is the time when the little flying creatures make their song. The little green growing things are covered in precious dewdrops. At dawn, all is golden. All is beautiful.

"I have not forgotten those long-ago teachings . . . *Walk with your vision in your heart*. The boy with the eyes of an artist was given a gift—to see things in a *Wakan* manner. In turn, I became a painter and a teller of stories. In the process of teaching art to middle school students, I was challenged to view the principles and elements of Art from every imaginable vantage point. As a teacher, I received an unexpected revelation—to view the Art process in the fresh and immediate way that a 12-year-old experiences it. I taught my students to reach for their personal dreams. So, all the while I was teaching I pursued my personal passion to paint.

"My path to publishing children's books began with T-shirt designs, logos, and program covers for local organization and charities. In time I realized that reproductions of my art looked pretty good. So I submitted my work to magazines and greeting card companies. The initial rejections made me even more determined, and eventually

Courtesy of Robin Nelson

my work gained acceptance. I was delighted when my art first appeared on book covers and CD jackets. One thing led to another—like individual steps up a mountain trail. Today I find it validating to receive a phone call from a publisher requesting my talents on a book project. People often say my art has a magical quality. I like hearing that, for art is magical. My advice to aspiring illustrators is *paint what you love and love what you paint*."

✿ ✿ ✿

S. D. Nelson is of Norwegian and Lakota descent and is a member of the Standing Rock Sioux Tribe in the Dakotas. His father was a career army officer, and his family moved often during his childhood. Born in Kentucky, by the age of 12 he had lived in 13 different places, including Kansas, Ohio, Missouri, and Germany. Fortunately, his mother's ties to her home were strong, and almost every summer his family would return to the reservation in western North Dakota. On the prairies Nelson made a personal connection to the land, a connection that can be seen today in his painting and in the books he has created for children.

Graduated from North High School in Fargo, North Dakota, in 1968, Nelson earned a B.S. degree at Minnesota State University, Moorhead, in 1972. As a middle-school art teacher for nearly 30 years, he taught Hispanic, Native American, and Anglo students in Flagstaff, Arizona. He speaks at conferences and seminars on the numerous ways the art experience can help minority students preserve their ethnic heritage even as they grow into "mainstream" society, introducing his talk with a slide show he calls "I'm Just a Kid Lost in the 21st Century." An avid outdoorsman, Nelson is an accomplished landscape and wildlife artist, and his paintings are included in many public and private collections. His artwork also appears on book jackets, CD covers, and greeting cards.

In 1999 Nelson published his first children's book, *Gift Horse: A Lakota Story*, which won a Parents' Choice Award and tells the coming-of-age story of Flying Cloud, his own great-great-grandfather. Steeped in the traditions of the 19th-century Lakota world, before the arrival of European settlers, this powerful story gives readers an understanding of that culture through both the text and the art—acrylics painted on wood panels with brightly colored, simplified, and strikingly angular figures. Nelson again employed this style, which is heavily influenced by the "ledger book" art of the Plains Indians, to illustrate Joseph Bruchac's *Crazy Horse's Vision*, about the youth of the great Lakota warrior. Named an ALA Notable Children's Book, an IRA Teachers' Choice, and a Notable Social Studies Trade Book, this evocative picture book also won a Parents' Choice Gold Award, a Parents' Guide to Children's Media Award, and a Reading Magic Award from *Parenting* magazine. Critics hailed Nelson as a highly talented interpreter of the Lakota experience. His third book, *The Star People: A Lakota Story*, an Oppenheim Toy Portfolio Gold Award–winner and recipient of the Spur Award from the Western Writers of America, shows the powerful connection to the natural world of a pair of children lost on the prairie and guided home by the spirits of the stars. The many traditional symbols, geometric designs, and stylized figures of Lakota art that give Nelson's illustrations a two-dimensional feel are balanced by his arresting perspectives and use of textures (created variously by brush, sponge, atomizer, spray bottle, and clear plastic wrap).

"My mother, who was a quarter-blood Sioux Indian, taught me at an early age to see the world with both the curious eyes of a child and the wistful eyes of an old man. I learned that morning is the most beautiful time. For at dawn the world is born anew."

In a second collaboration with author Bruchac, Nelson departed from his ledger book style to create a more representational depiction of the early life of a great 20th-century athlete in *Jim Thorpe's Bright Path*. Here the protagonist seems to leap off the page as he runs away from boarding school, bounds over hurdles, and hurtles down a football field. The artist's textured and earth-toned illustrations represent the legendary star's heritage and connection to his Indian roots. Today S. D. Nelson is a full-time artist, living with his wife in Chandler, Arizona.

SELECTED WORKS WRITTEN AND ILLUSTRATED: *Gift Horse: A Lakota Story*, 1999; *The Star People*, 2003.

SELECTED WORKS ILLUSTRATED: *Spider Spins a Story*, by Jill Max, 1997; *Crazy Horse's Vision*, by Joseph Bruchac, 2000; *Jim Thorpe's Bright Path*, by Joseph Bruchac, 2004.

Crazy Horse's Vision
BY JOSEPH BRUCHAC • ILLUSTRATED BY S.D. NELSON

Courtesy of Lee & Low Books, Inc.

Jenny Nimmo
January 15, 1944–

"One of my earliest memories is of a very tall man holding out a book. Perhaps this is significant. I don't know. The man was my father. He was a scientist and worked all hours, even on a Saturday. But nearly every weekend he would come home with a book for me. The first one was Beatrix Potter's *The Tale of Peter Rabbit*. Other Beatrix Potter books followed, and then *Winnie the Pooh* and *The Story of Babar* and *Orlando the Marmalade Cat*. Once the stories had been read to me I could 'read' them to myself, just by looking at the pictures. When I was five my father died and the books stopped coming. My mother became very ill, and by the time I was six our home had gone. Because there was no one to look after me, I was sent away to boarding school.

"In the long, cold dormitories our most precious possessions were kept in tuck-boxes under our beds, and that's where I kept my slightly shabby, well-thumbed, treasured books. We weren't allowed to read after 'Lights Out,' and so I would make up stories in my head. This always helped me to sleep. Soon I began to tell my stories aloud, and got into trouble for it. I didn't care. Other children in the dormitory were always begging for stories from me, and I was only too happy to oblige.

"My second school specialized in music, art, and drama. Although I enjoyed all these subjects, I was told that I would be an actor. I sort of accepted this. My exercise books were full of plays and stories, but no one suggested that I should write for a living. I imagined that it was something I would always do, but that it would never be my profession.

"After achieving unexpectedly high grades in my exams I was urged to go to university, but I rebelled. Teachers and relatives ranted at me, but I felt I had missed out on life and was determined to do something different. So, when I was seventeen, I joined a repertory theatre company as a working student. Theatre was an extension of the fantasy world I loved so much. Every week I could lay claim to a new home: a cottage by the sea, a castle, a church, an apartment, even a garden. My job was to find props and dress the set. I graduated to walk-on parts and then to major roles. I stayed up all night, devouring Eugene O'Neill, Tennessee Williams, and Arthur Miller. I began to write plays of my own, but I wasn't confident enough to show them to anyone.

Courtesy of David Wynn Millward

"When it became apparent that my acting career was going nowhere, I left the theatre and took a working holiday in Italy. I stayed three months, made copious notes, and on my return to Britain began a novel set in Sicily. This stayed in my files until I found work with the BBC as an adaptor/director of children's programmes. It was my producer on one of these programmes who suggested I finish the story I had begun in Italy. I took her advice and worked on *The Bronze Trumpeter* every evening after work.

"By day I would be searching out children's books and adapting them for television. Often I had to research legends and folktales from other lands, to find suitable material. On one memorable occasion I worked with a Welsh actor on a Celtic legend that was probably a thousand years old. After the programme had been recorded I read all the Welsh legends in a collection called *The Mabinogion*. In this treasure trove of magical beasts, fantastic forests, giants, witches, and vanishing castles, the characters were surprisingly complex. My favourite was Gwydion, the magician, and I resolved one day to put him into a novel of my own.

"I had developed a fascination for all things Welsh, and when I met the Welsh painter, David Wynn Millward, naturally I married him. Our first child was born in London, but then we headed back to the converted watermill in Wales that David had inherited from his father. There we raised our three children, and for eight years I had no time for writing. I was too involved with babies and growing children. When my youngest child started nursery school I began to think of Gwydion again. Now I lived in the landscape of the Welsh legends and could hardly wait to put all I saw into a book. My children helped me to find the title for *The Snow Spider*. I called my hero Gwyn, and I used a style of writing that I hoped would echo the lilting and poetic Welsh language. There were two sequels to *The Snow Spider* and many children wanted me to continue the series, but I felt that Gwyn's story had ended.

"During this time we discovered that two of our children were dyslexic. Their problems cause a great deal of heartache, and I couldn't help channeling my love and my fears for them into my work. I tried to focus on the positive aspects of being different, and I found fantasy an excellent way of setting my troubled characters free. Our children have since left university, where they were more successful than we could have dreamt, and now that they are leading happy and successful lives, I have returned to my original theme of a boy battling with an unusual talent. But my hero in *Midnight for Charlie Bone* is free from the restraints that burdened Gwyn. He has problems, of course—all heroes have problems—but he tackles them with vigour and enjoyment. Like my own children, he can have fun!"

❉   ❉   ❉

Jenny Nimmo is a writer of extraordinary power and expressiveness; her books for young readers are influenced by her own childhood experiences and her affinity for the legends and landscape of her adopted home, Wales. She was born in Windsor, England, with her early childhood spent in Chobham, living on the edge of her uncle's chicken farm. The years she spent in boarding schools, after her father's death, provided background for the fictional Bloor's Academy of her Charlie Bone books; memories of freezing cold dormitories, a nasty matron, and mysterious grounds helped her create a realistic setting for the magical happenings in the series.

Magic is often an important ingredient in Jenny Nimmo's books, and the landscape of the Welsh countryside where she now resides brings that magic into her own everyday world. When she integrated into her children's books the Welsh legends that had caught her imagination, the response was immediate. *The Snow Spider*, in which a boy named Gwyn calls on ancestral power from legendary Welsh heroes, won both the Smarties Prize and the Tir Na n'Og Award of the Welsh Books Council. All three books in this series—it continued with *Emlyn's Moon* (published in the United States as *Orchard of the Crescent Moon*) and *The Chestnut Soldier*—were made into a successful television series in England. The magical happenings in the Snow Spider trilogy relate directly to the stories of *The Mabinogion*, an ancient cycle of Welsh legends. In her later books, Nimmo has created her own forms of magic. In *Griffin's Castle*, 11-year-old Dinah calls on mythic stone animals to help her combat loneliness and the tensions between her and her mother's boyfriend. This powerful story was shortlisted for many

"In the long, cold dormitories our most precious possessions were kept in tuck-boxes under our beds, and that's where I kept my slightly shabby, well-thumbed, treasured books."

Courtesy of Scholastic Press

of the top book prizes in England, including the Carnegie Medal and the Whitbread Award. The Charlie Bone series, know collectively as "The Children of the Red King," also uses a mythology of Nimmo's own creation. All the children in the story who have extraordinary powers are descended from a legendary Red King; some use their powers for good and others for evil.

Nimmo's books have continued to garner awards over the years. *The Stone Mouse* and *The Rinaldi Ring* have been commended for the Carnegie Medal, and *The Owl Tree* won the Smarties Gold Medal in the ages 6–8 category, showing that she is equally adept at writing for younger children. Her writing has had great success in translation as well. Her first book, *The Bronze Trumpeter*, translated into German in 1982, won the Preis der Leiseratten, awarded by the Austrian Ministry of Culture. *The Witches and the Singing Mice* was given the Rattenfanger Literatur Preis, presented by the City of Hameln in Germany in 1994. Jenny Nimmo lives with her Welsh artist husband in a very old converted watermill near Welshpool. They have three grown children.

SELECTED WORKS (Dates are for British editions; American editions are shown in parentheses): *The Bronze Trumpeter*, 1974; *Tatty Apple*, 1984; *The Snow Spider*, 1986 (1987); *Emlyn's Moon*, 1987 (published in the United States as *Orchard of the Crescent Moon*, 1989); *The Chestnut Soldier*, 1989 (1991); *The Red Secret*, 1989; *Jupiter Boots*, 1990; *Ultramarine*, 1990 (1992); *The Bears Will Get You!*, 1990; *Delilah and the Dogspell*, 1991; *Rainbow and Mr. Zed*, 1992 (1994); *The Starlight Cloak*, illus. by Justin Todd, 1992 (1993); *The Witches and the Singing Mice*, illus. by Angela Barrett, 1993 (1993); *The Stone Mouse*, illus. by Helen Craig, 1994; *Griffin's Castle*, 1994 (1997); *The Breadwitch*, 1993; *Granny Grimm's Gruesome Glasses*, 1995; *Wilfred's Wolf*, illus. by David Wynn Millward, 1995; *Ronnie and the Giant Millipede*, 1995; *The Witch's Tears*, 1996; *Alien on the 99th Floor*, 1996; *Gwion and the Witch* (Legends from Wales), illus. by Jac Jones, 1996; *Branwen* (Legends from Wales), illus. by Jac Jones, 1997; *Delilah Alone*, 1997; *Hot Dog, Cool Cat*, illus. by David Wynn Millward, 1997; *Seth and the Strangers*, illus. by Peter Melynczuk, 1997; *The Dragon's Child*, 1997; *The Owl Tree*, illus. by Anthony Lewis, 1997; *The Rinaldi Ring*, 1999; *Toby in the Dark*, 1999; *The Dog*

Star, illus. by Terry Milne, 2000; *Esmeralda and the Children Next Door*, illus. by Paul Howard, 2000; *Something Wonderful*, illus. by Debbie Boon, 2001; *Midnight for Charlie Bone*, 2002 (2003); *Pig on a Swing*, illus. by Caroline Uff, 2003; *The Night of the Unicorn*, 2003; *Charlie Bone and the Time Twister*, 2003 (published in England as *The Time Twister*, 2003); *Charlie Bone and the Invisible Boy*, 2004 (published in England as *The Blue Boa*, 2004).

SUGGESTED READING: *Children's Literature Review*, vol. 44, 1997; Cooling, Wendy. *Telling Tales: An Interview with Jenny Nimmo*, 1999; *Something About the Author*, vol. 144, 2004; *Twentieth-Century Children's Writers*, 4th edition, 1995.

"**I** was born in Birmingham, Alabama, but I moved to New York with my family nine months later. I was the fourth of five children, and although most of my childhood years were spent living in the northeastern part of the country I spent most of my vacations down South where all of my relatives lived. Despite our northeastern surroundings my parents were still southerners, so we ate plenty of grits, attended church regularly, and heard lots and lots of stories about our kinfolk. I had one aunt in particular who loved to tell the family stories, and it is often her fast-paced southern voice I hear when I'm telling my own stories.

"My elementary school years were the hardest years for me. I was too full of spirit to settle my mind on school. I started off on the wrong foot almost from day one in kindergarten and continued to stumble until the sixth grade, when we had our first creative writing assignment. I had been telling stories and writing them down almost as soon as I could write. I loved to create my own stories, and often I would begin to read a book and fall in love with the setting on the first page and decide I needed to write my own story. This happened so often when I picked up the book, *A Tree Grows in Brooklyn*, that I never got farther than the first few pages in it until I was all grown up.

"Although I got lots of praise from my parents for the stories I wrote, it wasn't until that sixth grade year that anyone outside the family read and praised my creations. Mrs. Green gave us stories to write and had us keep a journal. I was so excited about this since I had been writing in a journal ever since I read *Harri-*

Courtesy of Brian Nolan

Han Nolan

August 25, 1956–

et the Spy two years earlier. I felt like an old pro at the process. With Mrs. Green's encouragement I started to feel smart in school and even a little special. My grades improved in all of my subjects after that, so that by high school I was an 'A' student.

"I wrote more stories in high school and in the back of my mind I thought about becoming a writer but, since I didn't know how one went about becoming one, I didn't take that dream seriously. It was just something I held in my heart.

"I had another love besides writing, though, and that was dance. All that energy I had as a child finally had some direction when I began my first dance lessons at thirteen, and—surprise, surprise—I was good at it! By the time I got to college I decided that majoring in dance would be a wonderful way to spend four

Courtesy of Harcourt, Inc.

years. I enjoyed it so much, in fact, that I continued on to get my master's degree in dance at Ohio State. It was there that I met my husband, and it was my husband who, when I told him of my dream of becoming a writer, bought me the *Writer's Market* book one day. That's what set me on the road to becoming an author. It was his constant support and encouragement, and later the support of my wonderful children, that kept me working toward my dream. Even though my first two stories got rejected, I had learned through my struggles to do well in school, to never give up. At last my third story was accepted and became the book *If I Should Die Before I Wake*.

"I believe that I have always loved to write stories because it helps me to understand better the world around me. By getting into the minds and hearts of people so different from myself, I get a new perspective on this great world, and that has helped me become a more compassionate and tolerant person."

❁ ❁ ❁

Han Nolan was born Helen Harris, which she found difficult to pronounce when she was young and called herself "Hannah Hollis." The name was shortened to various nicknames, but the one that stuck was the name she uses now, Han, which rhymes with "man." Although her own childhood and teen years were happy and she had a close, loving relationship with her parents and siblings, many of the characters in Nolan's novels lead unhappy lives, are disconnected from their families, or live with foster families. Nolan's own three children were adopted, and the adoption process made her aware of how many children do slip through the cracks. It is these children she writes about in her books.

Nolan drew on her own small-town experiences for *Send Me Down a Miracle*, which was nominated for the National Book Award in 1996 and received the 1999 Alabama Library Association Author Award. In this story, an artist who claims to have seen Jesus seated in a chair causes havoc in a small Alabama town, and a preacher's daughter must learn to reconcile her religious upbringing with the human shortcomings she sees in her family and community. In the office where she writes, Nolan has a small chair that was made by her great grandfather and served as the model for the Jesus chair in this book.

Her next book, *Dancing on the Edge*, which won the National Book Award and was an ALA Best Book for Young Adults, is about a journey to the edge of insanity and finally to recovery. Miracle is told by her grandmother, who constantly tells her half-truths, that she was born from a dead mother. Her reclusive father disappears when she is ten, and Miracle internalizes the blame for all her family's problems. She creates an alternate reality and only after a life-threatening crisis does she finds someone who might be able to help her. In 2001, the Alabama Library Association Author Award went to Han Nolan for *A Face in Every Window*, a story about a teenager who is resistant to the changes he must face. The son of an impractical, fragile mother and a mentally disabled father, J.P. loses the grandmother who was able to hold the family together. In the process of finding a new role in his reinvented family, J.P. also discovers a capacity for tolerance and compassion, qualities Nolan feels are nurtured in herself by writing her characters' stories.

Are children doomed to repeat their parents' mistakes? This is the question at the heart of *Born Blue*, named an ALA Best Book for Young Adults as well as a *School Library Journal* Best Book of the Year. The answer remains uncertain in this dark tale of a young white singer, whose first memory is of almost drowning at the hands of her heroin-addicted mother. Renaming herself Leshaya, Janie becomes a singer with big dreams. The memories of her childhood, however, prevent her from bonding with others. Despite trying to be different from her mother, she repeats her mother's mistakes by using drugs and becoming pregnant at age thirteen. In all of her books, Nolan writes of teens coming face to face with difficult life situations; the decisions they make will determine their futures as adults.

SELECTED WORKS: *If I Should Die Before I Wake*, 1994; *Send Me Down a Miracle*, 1996; *Dancing on the Edge*, 1997; *A Face in Every Window*, 1999; *Born Blue*, 2001; *When We Were Saints*, 2003.

SUGGESTED READING: *Something About the Author*, vol. 109, 2000.

WEB SITES: *www.hannolan.com*

Courtesy of Bill Wagner

Margie Palatini

*November 25,
1950–*

"When I was in third grade something wonderful happened to me. Actually, it was a somebody wonderful. My teacher, Mrs. Farwell. She was a tall, handsome woman with auburn hair pulled back in a bun. (Oh, how I wanted a bun. Very 'Lucy Ricardo-ish,' actually.) I remember her in long, straight skirts and turtleneck sweaters, with sleeves pushed up to the elbows. She wore chunky jewelry and had lots of noisy, clanking bracelets. Her white teeth gleamed through her big smile surrounded by red lipstick. And she wore high heels. You couldn't miss hearing Mrs. Farwell come down the hall with her click, click, click. But she would kick off those fancy shoes and slip on a pair of ballerina flats when she played the piano. Yes. Piano. We had a piano right in our classroom, and Mrs. Farwell always started the day off with a medley of songs. We put on elaborate musical productions for the whole school. Yup. It was quite grand. And she made learning fun. Even math. (And for me that was very difficult to do!)

"But I think the most incredibly special gift she gave to all of us was when she read aloud every afternoon. She would tell us to get comfy. Relax. We were allowed to put our heads down on our desks if we wanted. Then she put on her reading glasses that hung from her neck on a chain and began reading. Mrs. Farwell read a book like nobody else. When she read dialogue . . . wow! it was like the characters were right there with us. She was way better than movies or TV. When she got to the end of a chapter and closed the cover of the book, there were audible groans. Nobody wanted her to stop.

"In a very real way, for me, she hasn't stopped. I can still hear her in my head—making those characters leap off the pages. But now they're my pages. She is with me when I'm writing. I am that third grader filled with wonder and imagination, and I feel her presence somewhere deep inside me through the journey of the creative process.

"One day, a few years ago, her image suddenly became very vivid to me. Mrs. Farwell. Hilda Farwell. Hilda. Hilda. Hilda. I felt a rush of—I don't know—I'll call it creativity, but maybe it was Mrs. Farwell whispering in my ear. All I know is that I was overwhelmed with an idea of a character named 'Hilda' and had to get it down on paper. Right then and there. The words just came spilling out. It took me about two hours to write my four pages starring 'Hilda Mae Heifer' and her lost, and not quite melodious, mi mi moo's. The book was *Moo Who?*. I dedicated it to Mrs. Farwell. It's not dedicated to her just because the main character's name is Hilda. Or that the fabulous illustrator Keith Graves gave our Hilda those auburn bangs and huge smile—without even knowing anything about Mrs. Farwell. No. It's much more than that. Even though that's way goose-pimply, if you ask me! It's a thank you. A thank you to someone who inspired an eight-year-old girl to be all that she could be. To stretch her creativity. Believe in her talents.

"As writers we all put so much of ourselves into our stories. I feel incredibly lucky that Mrs. Farwell is in mine."

❅ ❅ ❅

Margie Palatini grew up in Edison, New Jersey. Although she never thought about being a writer as a child, and rarely put ideas on paper, she did put on a lot of plays and puppet shows, making up characters and stories as she went along. She also sang, danced, acted, and imitated people's voices and mannerisms. She created scenes, settings, and dialogue all the time—but never on paper. She went on to produce and direct her first play as an extra-curricular project for school. But by fifth grade, she was required to start writing her ideas down, which didn't quite work for her, so her writing talent went into hiding. She became very serious.

Margie attended Moore College of Art and Design in Philadelphia, then became an art director, working in several advertising agencies. She married one of her bosses, Richard Palatini, and after her son, Jamie, was born, she lost her serious veneer and started making up funny stories again. *Piggie Pie*, which was named an ALA Notable Children's Book and a Notable Trade Book in the Language Arts, also won at least five state awards (Colorado, Kansas, Kentucky, Maryland, and Vermont). It was actually a book that had been written—and rejected—years earlier. Dusting it off, she read the story to her son about the hungry but nearsighted witch who tries in vain to find some piggies on Old MacDonald's farm to make herself a piggie pie. He found it so funny that she tried again to get it published, and this time met with success. After that, none of her stories were submitted for publication without getting the seal of approval—and some good giggles—from her son. Jamie became what she calls her "supreme giggle-tester."

Another Jamie-approved book was *Zak's Lunch*, which was named an IRA Children's Choice selection and won the 1998 Irma S. and James H. Black Award for Excellence in Children's Literature, awarded by Bank Street College of Education. *The Web Files* became a 2002 ALA Notable Children's Book. *Moosetache* was an American Booksellers Association Pick of the Lists and an IRA Children's Choice selection. While many of Margie's picture books are illustrated by other artists, she has used her own considerable artistic skill to create the illustrations as well as the text for two books about an endearing young hero-

"As writers we all put so much of ourselves into our stories. I feel incredibly lucky that Mrs. Farwell is in mine."

Courtesy of HarperCollins Children's Books

ine named Goldie; *Good As Goldie* was an IRA Children's Choice selection, and *Goldie Is Mad* was chosen as a Children's Book-of-the-Month Club alternate selection.

Margie, Jamie, and Richard Palatini all live together in a big old white house in Plainfield, New Jersey. Margie is not serious anymore. In fact, she's become dedicated to pure silliness. "Silliness," she says, "is serious business."

SELECTED WORKS WRITTEN AND ILLUSTRATED: *Good As Goldie*, 2000; *Goldie Is Mad*, 2001.

SELECTED WORKS WRITTEN: *Piggie Pie*, illus. by Howard Fine, 1995; *Moosetache*, illus. by Henry Cole, 1997; *Zak's Lunch*, illus. by Howard Fine, 1997; *Zoom Broom*, illus. by Howard Fine, 1998; *Ding Dong Ding Dong*, illus. by Howard Fine, 1999; *Lab Coat Girl in Cool Fuel*, 1999; *Lab Coat Girl and the Amazing Benjamin Bone*, 1999; *Lab Coat Girl in My Triple-Decker Hero*, 2000; *Mooseltoe*, illus. by Henry Cole, 2000; *Bedhead*, illus. by Jack E. Davis, 2000; *Tub-BooBoo*, illus. by Glin Dibley, 2001; *The Web Files*, illus. by Richard Egielski, 2001; *Earthquack!*, illus. by Barry Moser, 2002; *Broom-Mates*, illus. by Howard Fine, 2002; *Bad Boys*, illus. by Henry Cole, 2003; *Mary Had a Little Ham*, illus. by Guy Francis, 2003; *Moo Who?*, illus. by Keith Graves, 2004; *Mooskitos: A Moose Family Reunion*, illus. by Henry Cole, 2004; *Stinky, Smelly Feet: A Love Story*, illus. by Ethan Long, 2004; *Sweet Tooth*, illus. by Jack E. Davis, 2004.

SUGGESTED READING: *Something About the Author*, vol. 134, 2003.

WEB SITE: *www.margiepalatini.com*

"Ever since I was a child, books have been my anchors. They are what connects me to people around me, to times and events, to the world. An example: In 1971, when I was 11 years old, my mother took my younger sister and me on an extended visit to Asia—Japan, Korea, and Taiwan. My father gave me a paperback copy of *Gone with the Wind* to read on the trip. I read *GWTW* at least three times that summer. Now, when I think of the places I visited in the Far East or the people I met, they're intertwined with images of antebellum plantations and Atlanta burning; likewise, when I see or hear anything about the Civil War, I think of Korea and Taiwan.

"This may seem like a recipe for confusion, but for me it's a way of making sense of the world. In my first book, *Seesaw Girl*, I wrote about the circumscribed life of a girl from a noble family in 17th-century Korea. And while I was writing, I sometimes thought about the dreadful corsets Scarlett O'Hara had to wear. There was a connection between Chosun-era Korea and Civil War America in the way women's lives were restricted: Jade Blossom's movement outside the home was limited, Scarlett's very breathing was limited! Maybe Korea wasn't so very far away after all.

"I could give a million more examples like the one above. Reading makes the world a bigger, richer, more colorful, livelier place for me while at the same time making it smaller, more intimate, more personal. I've been writing almost since I could first read, so I no longer remember the initial impulse that made me want to put words to paper. But I would imagine it was the same then as it is now: When I get excited about something, I want to explore it further and think about it in depth. Writing forces me to clarify my thoughts, and once that happens, I want to share those thoughts with others.

"While researching my first two books, I read a lot of Korean history. I kept coming across the information—just a sentence or two every time—that in the 11th and 12th centuries, Korean pottery was considered the finest in the world. I wondered about this. What made Korean ceramics of that time so special? I got more books (mostly out of the library—I am a library fanatic) and learned more, and what I learned was fascinating. So fascinating that I felt compelled to share it—and the result was *A Single Shard*.

Courtesy of Klaus Pollmeiser

Linda Sue Park

March 25, 1960–

"For me, reading and writing are inseparable—two halves of the same whole. In reading, I discover things I want to write about. In writing, I realize how much more I have to learn—which sends me back to reading again.

"I feel so fortunate to live in a time when I will never run out of wonderful books to read. Hopefully, that also means I will never run out of things to write about!"

❀　❀　❀

Linda Sue Park's parents were both born in Korea and grew up in Seoul; they immigrated to the United States to attend college in the 1950s and settled in Urbana, Illinois, where Linda Sue was born in 1960. While she grew up with a great deal of Korean culture, she knew very little about the history of her parents' native land. Graduating from Stanford University in 1981 with a degree in English and creative writing, she took a job as a public relations writer for a major oil company. While this was not the kind of writing she wanted to do, the job did teach her to present her writing professionally. After two years, Linda Sue moved to Dublin, studied Anglo-Irish literature at Trinity College, and married Ben Dobbin, an Irish journalist, in 1984. For a time, the couple lived in London, where Linda Sue worked for an advertising agency, taught English as a second language, and worked as a food journalist; their two children, Sean and Anna, were born in London.

Courtesy of Clarion Books

In 1990, Park and her family moved back to the United States for her husband's work. She has continued to teach English to foreign students and all along has written poetry and stories, as she did when she was a child, but it was a desire to introduce her children to the Korean side of their heritage that led her to research and write about Korean history. Her first novel, *Seesaw Girl*, in which 12-year-old Jade Blossom tries to circumvent the restrictions placed on a Korean girl of the 17th century, was included on New York Public Library's list 100 Titles for Reading and Sharing. *The Kite Fighters*, set in 15th-century Seoul and illustrated by the author's father, became a Junior Library Guild selection and was named to the IRA Teachers' Choice list, as well as the list called Notable Books for a Global Society. *A Single Shard*, which sprang from Linda Sue Park's curiosity about the unique quality of Korean pottery in the 12th century, tells the story of Tree-Ear, an orphan with a longing to create true art. This heartfelt and beautifully rendered tale was included on many "best of the year" lists, was named an ALA Notable Children's Book and captured the Newbery Medal in 2002 for the most distinguished writing for young people. In her acceptance speech for the award, the author credited her father as a major influence in her life, taking her to the library every week as a child and requesting the "best" books from the librarian. Many of those books were Newbery Award winners, including one of her favorites, *I, Juan de Pareja*, another story of an orphan, an outsider in a very different culture, who desperately longs to be an artist.

Drawing on her parents' memories of living in Korea under the Japanese occupation, Park next wrote *When My Name Was Keoko*, which became a *School Library Journal* Best Book, an Honor Book for the Jane Addams Children's Book Award, an ALA Notable Children's Book and an ALA Best Book for Young Adults. A strong novel for older readers, the story is told in alternating voices by a brother and a sister, representing different perspectives of the Korean population's response to that difficult time.

Linda Sue Park lives at present with her husband and two children in upstate New York.

SELECTED WORKS: *Seesaw Girl*, illus. by Jean and Mou-Sien Tseng, 1999; *The Kite Fighters*, illus. by Eung Won Park, 2000; *A Single Shard*, 2001; *When My Name Was Keoko: A Novel of Korea in World War II*, 2002; *The Firekeeper's Son*, illus. by Julie Downing, 2004; *Mung-Mung*, illus. by Diane Bigda, 2004.

SUGGESTED READING: *Children's Literature Review*, vol. 84; *Contemporary Authors*, vol. 197, 2002; *Current Biography*, June 2002; *Something About the Author*, vol. 127, 2002. Periodicals—Cindrich, Sharon, "Finding Her Roots," *Writer*, October 2002; Horning, Kathleen T., "Discovering Linda Sue Park," *School Library Journal*, July 2002; Johnson, Nancy, "Interview with the 2002 Newbery Medal Winner, Linda Sue Park," *Reading Teacher*, December 2002; Park, Linda Sue, "Newbery Medal Acceptance," *The Horn Book*, July/August 2002; Park, Linda Sue, "Staying on Past Canal Street: Reflections on Asian Identity," *Booklist*, January 1, 2002; Stern, Karen, "Linda Sue Park," *The Horn Book*, July/August 2002.

WEB SITE: *www.lspark.com*

Elizabeth Partridge

October 1, 1951–

" At first I didn't realize how different my family was. My grandmother, Imogen Cunningham, was a photographer, and my grandfather, Roi Partridge, an etcher. When my father, Rondal Partridge, was a teenager, he decided he wanted to be a photographer and Imogen sent him to work with her friend, Dorothea Lange. They developed a lifelong relationship— Dorothea was part teacher, part mother, part colleague. As my dad married and the five of us kids were born, we were blended into Dorothea's family.

"When I was eight years old my parents bought a huge, ramshackle house in Berkeley, California. Interesting people were always in and out, many of them artists—photographers, painters, writers, and dancers. Some evenings my father would smoke a gigantic turkey in a 55 gallon drum and invite over a group of friends who played chamber music. My mother would bustle around making salad and delicious side dishes. After dinner the musicians would play in the living room, and I'd go to sleep listening to violins and cellos playing Mozart.

"Most evenings I read in bed till late at night. I loved feeling that the world had gone to sleep and I was deliciously, privately, entranced in another time and place. My mother knew I was reading but never tried to stop me, even though she must have been frustrated trying to get me up in the mornings. In grammar school I was regularly sent to the principal's office for being tardy. It didn't do much good. Saturdays I'd sleep in, take a stack of books back to the library and check out another pile.

Courtesy of Tom Ratcliff

Elizabeth Partridge

"Artists don't usually make much money, and my parents were no exception. We were dressed in hand-me-downs, which I hated, especially because my next older sibling was a brother. His black and white high-top shoes weren't very feminine. In the fifth grade I realized how different, in fact, how weird my family was. I longed to have a father who would put on a suit and go to work with the other fathers. I wished my mother would throw out her handmade sandals (made by a big, roaring bear of a man named Guido with a huge beard) and put on pumps, take her hair out of a ponytail, and start wearing a bra. I wished they'd go to PTA meetings like the other parents.

"It never happened.

"What did happen was they'd throw the five of us kids and the two dogs in the back of my father's 1949 Cadillac limousine—which he had spray-painted a bright, shiny gold—and we'd wander around the United States on camping trips. Twice my parents decided to go all the way to New York City, lazily returning via the South and Southwest. At some point (maybe late September) my mother would realize we were missing school. She'd call and ask them to save places for all of us. We were allowed to collect pets the way some people collect rocks or stamps. We had cats and dogs, chickens and chameleons, tortoises, even a tarantula. Any project was considered a great idea. All phone numbers were written right on the wall next to the phone in an ever-increasing spiral. Spaghetti thrown on the kitchen wall to test for done-ness (whose idea was that, anyway?) was allowed to stay. Shoes were only considered necessary for school and camping.

"Growing up in such an unusual family gave me a chance to see the world differently than many people. I was taught to keep my eyes and ears and heart open to the world. I was also given a healthy disrespect for the social constraints and rules that govern most of our lives. Both blessings. I still check books out of the library every week and read late into the night. I love having a pile of books next to my bed, waiting to be read. Such possibilities!"

☀ ☀ ☀

In 1974, Elizabeth Partridge was the first student to graduate with a degree in women's studies from the University of California at Berkeley. Every quarter she had to have the dean approve her class list because her major course of study was unique, and every time he reluctantly signed he would say "You're wasting your education." Time, of course, has proven him wrong. There are now women's studies programs in colleges and universities across America, but in the early 1970s it was a very new idea. A year after graduation Elizabeth Partridge went to Great Britain to study Chinese medicine and qualified for a Licentiate of Acupuncture in 1978. Returning to the San Francisco Bay Area, she practiced acupuncture and herbal medicine, married, and started a family.

"In the fifth grade I realized how different, in fact, how weird my family was."

In the early 1990s, enchanted by the books she had discovered for her sons, she began writing books for young readers as well as practicing medicine. She is fascinated by the wide array of genres within the field of children's books and especially enjoys writing biographies, historical fiction, and picture books. In 2000 she closed her medical practice to write full time. While she has published a number of fine picture books with great success, she has gained the highest recognition for her insightful biographies. Her family connections to pioneering photographers lent a personal dimension to her well-researched biography of Dorothea Lange, *Restless Spirit*, which was named both a Notable Children's Book and a Best Book for Young Adults by the American Library Association.

This Land Was Made for You and Me, her excellent biography of the folksinger and activist Woody Guthrie, received the *Boston Globe–Horn Book* Award and the Golden Kite Award for nonfiction, and was one of five semi-finalists for the National Book Award in 2002. It was also listed in every major Best Book list in the country, including the ALA Notable Children's Books and Best Books for Young Adults. In this biography Partridge created a fully realized portrait of an important figure in American song and social history, describing Guthrie's rough beginnings in Oklahoma, the series of family tragedies that stalked

Courtesy of Viking Children's Books

him throughout his life, his empathy with downtrodden and displaced workers during the Depression years and beyond, the heartfelt "Dust Bowl Ballads" that first brought him fame, and his well-loved composition "This Land Is Your Land," a song that many call America's unofficial national anthem.

Elizabeth Partridge lives in the San Francisco Bay Area with her husband, Tom Ratcliff—who sings and plays a variety of instruments—and an assortment of dogs, cats, and chickens. They have two grown sons, Will and Felix, who took up the guitar and the mandolin, respectively, while their mother was writing about Woody Guthrie.

SELECTED WORKS FOR YOUNG READERS: *Clara and the Hoodoo Man*, 1996; *Restless Spirit: The Life and Work of Dorothea Lange*, 1998; *Pig's Eggs*, illus. by Martha Weston, 2000; *Oranges on Golden Mountain*, illus. by Aki Sogabe, 2001; *Annie and Bo and the Big Surprise*, illus. by Martha Weston, 2002; *This Land Was Made for You and Me: The Life and Songs of Woody Guthrie*, 2002; *Moon Glowing*, illus. by Joan Paley, 2002; *Whistling*, illus. by Anna Grossnickle Hines, 2003; *Kogi's Mysterious Journey*, illus by Aki Sogabe, 2003.

SELECTED WORKS FOR ADULTS: *Dorothea Lange: A Visual Life*, as editor, 1993; *Quizzical Eye: The Photography of Rondal Partridge*, with Sally Stein, 2002.

SUGGESTED READING: *Something About the Author*, vol. 134, 2003. Periodicals—Partridge, Elizabeth, "*Boston Globe–Horn Book* Award Acceptance Speech," *The Horn Book*, January/February 2003; Partridge, Elizabeth, "Open Questions: Why No Words?" *The Horn Book*, November/December 2002; Partridge, Elizabeth, "The Creative Life: A Biographer Strives to Connect Today's Teens with Artists from the Past," *School Library Journal*, October 2002.

Rodman Philbrick

January 22, 1951–

"I grew up in Rye Beach, a small town on the coast of New Hampshire where my father's family had lived for many generations. My grandfather had built summer rental cottages and a dance hall on the beach in the 1920s. That's also where my dad built a house (with the help of the G.I. Bill) in the early 1950s, and where he and my mom raised their family. I'm the oldest of four brothers, all of us quite close in age, and the beach was our playground. In those days no other families lived at the beach year-round, so for 10 months out of the year we had the place to ourselves. It was like having an empty stage to populate with players—pirates, sea monsters, ghosts from the past. Both of my parents were devoted readers, and I inherited their love of books and storytelling. In the sixth grade I began writing short stories and sending them out to magazines. No takers, unfortunately. While in high school I finished my first novel, but that, too, was rejected. After a few semesters at the University of New Hampshire, I left to write another novel. When that one was rejected, I sought employment as a longshoreman, carpenter, and later as a boat builder, writing whenever and wherever I could.

"It wasn't until my late twenties, having written eight or nine rejected novels, that I decided to try my hand at commercial fiction (my early efforts had all been 'serious' literary works) and finally taught myself how to write saleable mystery and detective novels. It was while writing a detective novel that I stumbled on the idea for a story intended for young readers—although it would take me years to realize it. My desk faced a window, and one afternoon I noticed two kids passing by on the sidewalk below. One was quite ruggedly built. The other was much smaller and had trouble walking. To solve this dilemma, the bigger kid hoisted the smaller boy up on his shoulders and strode away. I didn't think much of it at the time, but soon my wife and I became friends with the smaller boy's mother, and later with the boy himself. He was a brainy, brilliant kid who suffered from a rare condition called Morquio Syndrome, which meant that he would never grow to be much more than three feet tall. He had a highly active imagination and loved both science fiction and the Arthurian legends. When he died unexpectedly it seemed to me that a unique and compelling voice had been silenced.

Courtesy of Andrew Edgar

"In 1992, a year or so after his tragic death, I was driving home from a trip to New York when an opening sentence came to mind: 'I never had a brain until Freak came along and let me borrow his for a while, and that's the truth, the whole truth.' My wife took over the drive and I frantically made notes, hardly able to keep up with the outpouring of ideas, images, and characters. The voice of Max seemed to flow quite naturally, and I knew the story would be about a small, badly handicapped boy with a brilliant mind, and his larger, much slower friend, who would narrate the story of 'Freak the Mighty.' It wouldn't be a mystery, but it would involve suspense and help keep young readers turning the pages. Once home, I put aside a thriller that was due later that year, and for six weeks in the summer of 1992 I let Max do the talking. Along the way I discovered that I felt very comfortable inhabiting the mind of a 12-year-old—a fact that didn't surprise my wife in the least!

"That first sentence, spoken by Max, got me thinking and writing about ideas and stories with young protagonists. I realized I had a lot to say on the subject of growing up—how difficult it can be, and how exciting and thrilling it can be, too. So at the age of 41 I began a second career, one that I thoroughly enjoy, seeing the world through the eyes of a 12-year-old. I still write novels for adults—I like the longer and more complex form—but writing for adults is hard work. Writing for kids is something else again. Part exhilarating, part excruciating, part surprising. It comes down to this: Every page reminds me of why I originally wanted to be a writer, all those years ago."

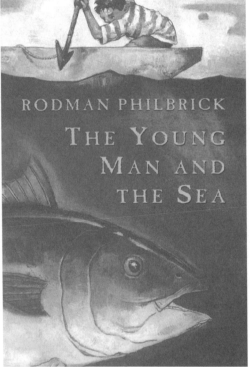

Courtesy of Blue Sky Press/Scholastic, Inc.

❅ ❅ ❅

Rodman Philbrick had published over a dozen novels for adults before he wrote his first book for young readers, *Freak the Mighty*, in 1993. Since then, he has won numerous awards and honors, including the California Young Reader's Medal, the Arizona Young Reader's Award, and the New York State "Charlotte" Award. A sequel, *Max the Mighty*, was published in 1998. *Freak the Mighty* has been translated into many languages and was made into a feature film, *The Mighty*, with Sharon Stone in the role of Kevin's mother, Eldon Henson as Max, and Kieran Culkin as Kevin.

Philbrick also collaborates on young adult books with his wife, Lynn Harnett. When working together, they will discuss and develop an idea; then Philbrick does an outline and Harnett does the actual writing. Their first series was a haunted-house trilogy, The House on Cherry Street. The couple also partnered on the three-volume Werewolf Chronicles and Visitors series, as well as the sci-fi novel *Abduction*.

The Private Eye Writers of America selected Philbrick's *Brothers & Sinners* for the Shamus Award as Best Detective Novel of 1993. Books he's written under the pen name William R. Dantz have delved into high-tech subjects such as genetic engineering and brain control.

Although Rodman Philbrick was born in Boston, his family roots on the New Hampshire coast go back generations, and that is where he was raised. A number of his books are set in that locale, including *Freak the Mighty* and *The Young Man and the*

Sea, which pays homage in plot to one of Philbrick's favorite writers, Ernest Hemingway. *The Young Man and the Sea* was named to *School Library Journal*'s Best Books list for 2004. Today Philbrick divides his time between Kittery, Maine, and the Florida Keys and, in addition to his fiction writing, he reviews movies for the *New Hampshire Gazette*.

SELECTED WORKS: *Freak the Mighty*, 1993; *The Fire Pony*, 1996; *Max the Mighty*, 1998; *The Last Book in the Universe*, 2000; *REM World*, 2000; *The Journal of Douglas Allen Deeds: The Donner Party Expedition*, 2002; *The Young Man and the Sea*, 2004.

SELECTED WORKS (with Lynn Harnett): The House on Cherry Street (*The Haunting, The Horror, The Final Nightmare*), 1995; The Werewolf Chronicles (*Night Creature, Children of the Wolf, Wereing*), 1996; Visitors (*Strange Invaders, Things, Brain Stealers*), 1997; *Abduction*, 1998.

SUGGESTED READING: *Contemporary Authors*, New Revision Series, vol. 100, 2002; Hipple, Ted. *Writers for Young Adults*, 2000; *Something About the Author*, vol. 122, 2001. Periodicals—"Finding a Voice," *ALAN Review*, Spring 1996.

Neil Philip

May 8, 1955–

"At school, I was always being told off for 'dreaming.' Looking back, I can see it was annoying for my teachers that I preferred to think my own thoughts rather than listen to what they were saying. But I understood very early that the daydreaming part of my brain was more vital to me than the knowledge-storing part. Anyway, the things I wanted to know I seemed to know without trying; the things I didn't want to know I couldn't learn if you paid me.

"Apart from a few poems in anthologies, I didn't read the work of the poet William Blake until my late teens. When I did, he seemed to be speaking directly to me when he wrote, 'This world of Imagination is the world of Eternity.'

"Although I loved stories and poems, reading came slowly to me. My class had 50 children, and I was about the slowest. The teacher taught us from a reading scheme called 'Janet and John.' You had to read each book aloud to her before going on to the next. The 'Janet and John' books were written in a flat, featureless style. There was no hint in them of the world of imagination, or the world of eternity. I just couldn't see the point.

"Then the first pupils in my class finished the final book in the scheme. Suddenly, a bookcase appeared in the classroom, with real books, to which these lucky children had free access. Next time I had a chance to read to the teacher, I read all the way through the first 'Janet and John' book. And the second. And the third. And the fourth. All the way to the end. And so the magical world of books was opened to me. From that time on, I always had my nose in a book. At bedtime, I would plead to just finish the page, and then read on, entranced, until forcibly stopped. There was always another page to finish.

"I began to read books from the adult section of the library. One, I remember, was a historical novel set in the Peninsular War, entitled *The Flying Ensign* (an ensign is a military flag, and also the rank of a junior officer in the British army). I wrote a report on it for my teacher. She returned it with the word 'ensign' crossed out and replaced by 'engine.'

"My reading was voracious and random. Some books I read quickly and then forgot. Others somehow sank deep into my mind. One such book was *Sentimental Tommy* by J. M. Barrie, the first book I ever read about a boy who lives in his imagination, as I did. An unremarkable book of adventure stories contained Rudyard Kipling's haunting short story 'The Strange Ride of Morrowby Jukes,' about a man trapped in the deadly sands

Courtesy of Jamie Pinto

of his own mind. And C. S. Lewis's *The Lion, the Witch, and the Wardrobe* showed me how the everyday world could be transformed by the imagination into the world of eternity.

"By the time I went to high school I was reading pretty much anything that took my fancy. I always carried a book with me to read in the five minutes between classes. As soon as I opened the pages, I was back in the writer's spell, and I wouldn't have noticed if a riot had broken out around me, which it sometimes did. When asked what I wanted to do when I grew up, I could not reply. But I knew what I wanted to do; I wanted to read.

"While studying English language and literature at Oxford University, I became interested in children's literature, especially the work of modern writers such as Alan Garner, William Mayne, and Ursula K. LeGuin. I made a special study of their work in my Ph.D. thesis on 'Myth and Folklore in Children's Literature,' and one chapter of this became the basis for my first book, *A Fine Anger*. My headmaster at school once told my mother, 'Neil is myth-mad.' Much of my own work has its roots in my passion for myths and folktales, married to my love of poetry and words. In exploring that love and that passion, I have found a way to make my living by reading, and it is reading that has turned me into a writer."

❈ ❈ ❈

Neil Philip was born in the city of York in the north of England and took his first degree in English language and literature at Brasenose College, Oxford. He studied for his Ph.D. at the University of London. While he was at Oxford, he met his wife,

Emma, and today they live in the Cotswolds, deep in the English countryside. Their house is one of only 30 in a village that has no shop, restaurant, or post office, but does have a church that dates back to Norman times. It seems that Neil Philip has found a way to live within the world he loves to write about, the world of myth and folklore.

Since beginning his writing career, Philip has published works of literary journalism and critical essays as well as poetry, a stage play, documentary dramas for the radio, scripts for documentary films, and even recipes for *Time-Life* cookery books. In 1984 his wife left her job in publishing to start a book-packaging company, the Albion Press Ltd., and they still run that enterprise together. Neil Philip's writing career and Albion's publishing history have intertwined: Some of his books, such as the various myth and fairy-tale titles, are written directly for a publisher, while others, such as *War and the Pity of War* and his Native American titles, are created by Albion, benefiting from Emma's beautiful sense of design.

Touching on many areas of folktale and myth, Philip has retold, adapted, and edited stories of Grimm, Andersen, Kipling, Wilde, and the Arabian Nights, as well as British and Irish legends and the stories of Greek and Norse mythology. Because of his fascination with the song-poems of oral traditions, he developed a keen interest in Native American culture and has collected about 700 books on the subject in his personal library. This interest has led to his creating his own books, and often the research for one book will lead to another—*In a Sacred Manner I Live* explored the tradition of Native American oratory he discovered while researching the poems, chants, and songs collected in *Earth Always Endures*, while *A Braid of Lives* delved into the tradition of Native American autobiography he found while compiling the writings and speeches that constituted *In a Sacred Manner I Live*. These titles have been well received in America. *In a Sacred Manner I Live* was named an ALA Best Book for Young Adults and a *New York Times* Notable Book of the Year. *Earth Always Endures* became an ALA Notable Children's Book, and both these titles were cited as Notable Children's Trade Books in the Field of Social Studies.

Singing America, an anthology edited by Philip of poems that define American character, was also named a Notable Social Studies Trade Book, as were several of his collections of folktales: *Celtic Fairy Tales*, *The Illustrated Book of World Myths*, and *The Illustrated Book of Fairy Tales*. In *Stockings of Buttermilk* he collected folktales that are found in many areas of the United States but are of European origin. This book earned him an Aesop Award Accolade from the American Folklore Society, and in 2003 he won an Aesop Award for *Horse Hooves and Chicken Feet*, a selection of Mexican folktales that was also named an ALA Notable Children's Book. This British born-and-bred folklorist keeps returning, over and over again, to his fasci-

> *"My reading was voracious and random. Some books I read quickly and then forgot. Others somehow sank deep into my mind."*

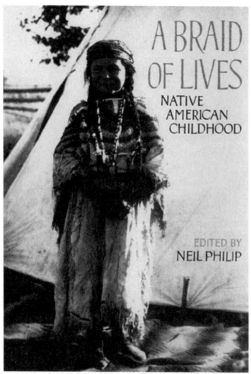

A BRAID OF LIVES

NATIVE AMERICAN CHILDHOOD

EDITED BY
NEIL PHILIP

Courtesy of Clarion Books

nation with the oral tradition in America, believing that his position of looking at American folk culture from outside gives him a unique perspective.

An anthology of war poetry edited by Philip, *War and the Pity of War*, was included in the "White Ravens," an annual list of books chosen for special merit by the International Youth Library in Munich, and was one of only 20 titles picked out for Special Mention on that list in the year 2000. The books chosen for this distinction are those that are considered of international interest and deserving of wide reception because of their universal themes and innovative style and design. In America, *War and the Pity of War* received a Blue Ribbon citation from the *Bulletin of the Center for Children's Books* and was chosen as an ALA Best Book for Young Adults. Recently Neil Philip has started writing and publishing his own poems and is currently at work on a fantasy trilogy. Known for many years as a gifted anthologist, scholar, and reteller of folk stories, he expects his future to be more of a balance between editing, retelling, and creative writing.

SELECTED WORKS: *A Fine Anger: A Critical Introduction to the Work of Alan Garner*, 1981; *Drakestail Visits the King: A Magic Lantern Fairy Tale*, illus. by Henry Underhill, 1986; *Guleesh and the King of France's Daughter: A Magic Lantern Fairy Tale*, illus. by Henry Underhill, 1986; *The Tale of Sir Gawain*, illus. by Charles Keeping, 1987; *The Snow Queen: A Story in Seven Parts*, by Hans Christian Andersen, illus. by Sally Holmes, 1989; *The Cinderella Story*, 1989; *Fairy Tales of Ireland*, by W. B. Yeats, illus. by P. J. Lynch, 1990; *A New Treasury of Poetry*, illus. by John Lawrence, 1990; *The Book of Christmas*, illus. by Sally Holmes, 1991; *Fairy Tales of Eastern Europe*, illus. by Larry Wilkes, 1991; *The Penguin Book of English Folktales*, 1992; *The Complete Just So Stories*, by Rudyard Kipling, illus. by Isabelle Brent, 1993; *The Arabian Nights*, illus. by Sheila Moxley, 1994; *A World of Fairy Tales*, by Andrew Lang, illus. by Henry Justice Ford, 1994; *King Midas*, illus. by Isabelle Brent, 1994; *The Fairy Tales of Oscar Wilde*, illus. by Isabelle Brent, 1994; *The Golden Bird, Retold from the Brothers Grimm*, illus. by Isabelle Brent, 1995; *Songs Are Thoughts: Poems of the Inuit*, illus. by Maryclare Foa, 1995; *Fairy Tales of Hans Christian Andersen*, illus. by Isabelle Brent, 1995; *The Penguin Book of Scottish Folktales*, 1995; *Poems for Christmas*, illus. by John

Lawrence, 1995; *Singing America*, illus. by Michael McCurdy, 1995; *Illustrated Book of Myths: Tales and Legends of the World*, illus. by Nilesh Mistry, 1995; *Odin's Family: Myths of the Vikings*, illus. by Maryclare Foa, 1996; *The New Oxford Book Of Children's Verse*, 1996; *American Fairy Tales: From Rip Van Winkle to the Rootabaga Stories*, illus. by Michael McCurdy, 1996; *Christmas Fairy Tales*, illus. by Isabelle Brent, 1996; *Earth Always Endures: Native American Poems*, photos. by Edward S. Curtis, 1996; *Robin Hood*, illus. by Nick Harris, 1997; *The Illustrated Book of Fairy Tales: Spellbinding Stories from Around the World*, illus. by Nilesh Mistry, 1997; *Fairy Tales of the Brothers Grimm*, illus. by Isabelle Brent, 1997; *The Adventures of Odysseus*, illus. by Peter Malone, 1997; *In a Sacred Manner I Live: Native American Wisdom*, 1997; *War and the Pity of War*, illus. by Michael McCurdy, 1998; *The Little Mermaid and Other Fairy Tales of Hans Christian Andersen*, illus. by Isabelle Brent, 1998; *Illustrated Dictionary of Mythology: Heroes, Heroines, Gods, and Goddesses from Around the World*, 1998; *Celtic Fairy Tales*, illus. by Isabelle Brent, 1999; *Stockings of Buttermilk: American Folktales*, illus. by Jacqueline Mair, 1999; *A Braid of Lives: Native American Childhood*, 2000; *It's a Woman's World: A Century of Women's Voices in Poetry*, 2000; *Weave Little Stars into My Sleep: Native American Lullabies*, photos. by Edward S. Curtis, 2001; *The Great Mystery: Myths of Native America*, 2001; *Noah and the Devil: A Legend of Noah's Ark from Romania*, illus. by Isabelle Brent, 2001; *Prince Zucchini*, illus. by Veronica Rooney, 2002; *The Fish Is Me: Bathtime Rhymes*, illus. by Claire Henley, 2002; *The Little People: Stories of Fairies, Pixies, and Other Small Folk*, 2002; *Horse Hooves and Chicken Feet: Mexican Folktales*, illus. by Jacqueline Mair, 2003; *In the House of Happiness: A Book of Prayers and Praise*, illus. by Isabelle Brent, 2003; *Hot Potato: Mealtime Rhymes*, illus. by Claire Henley, 2004; *Mythology of the World*, 2004.

SUGGESTED READING: Cart, Michael, "Carte Blanche," *Booklist*, December 15, 1996.

Giselle Potter

May 28, 1970–

"I drew a lot as a child because that is what everyone around me did. Both my grandparents were painters. My grandfather was an abstract expressionist and he always invited other people to add to his paintings. I loved having silent conversations of paint strokes with him.

"From about six years old until we were teenagers, my sister Chloe and I traveled and performed around the United States and Europe with our parents' puppet theater company, The Mystic Paper Beasts. Mystic because we were from Mystic, Connecticut, and Paper Beasts because the puppets and masks were made of papier-mâché. I mostly remember being in a panda costume, which was a panda head over mine with tiny holes that I could barely see through and an old-fashioned man's bathing suit stuffed with a pillow. As performers, we got to have an insider view of new places. We saw the backstage of countries, staying in other people's homes or sleeping in our truck by the gypsy camps. I brought my familiar world with me though; playing paper dolls in the back set while we drove through the Swiss Alps or drawing pictures on the table cloth instead of trying strange foods. I missed some school but kept journals of drawings, language, and tokens from the foreign places I went, and my parents kept me up with the multiplication table and cursive letters, so I didn't fall too far behind. At the time I think both my sister and I sometimes resented our untraditional upbringing, but after a few years of letting our experiences seep in, I look back with so much nostalgia to the exciting times we had and they inspire me constantly. *The Year I Didn't Go to School* is about those experiences; I used my journal for the endpapers of the book and to remember how it all was through my seven-year-old eyes.

Courtesy of Giselle Potter

"I always knew I loved to draw, but when I took a year off from college and went to Indonesia to study traditional Balinese miniature paintings, I became more focused. I decided to go to Rhode Island School of Design. I spent my last year of RISD in Rome, where there was a lot of independent study and freedom, which was great practice for the self-disciplined life of a freelance illustrator. I painted lots of pictures of saints there, and when I returned I published them along with their stories in *Lucy's Eyes and Margaret's Dragon: Lives of the Virgin Saints* with Chronicle Books.

"After carrying my portfolio around New York and feeling a little discouraged, I got my first illustration job from the *New Yorker* magazine. They sent me to a Shakespeare in the Park production of *Two Gentlemen of Verona*, and my picture of it was due the next day. I was so nervous and excited, I think I tried to fit everything about the play into one very busy illustration, but I guess they liked it because I did many more for them.

"Anne Schwartz from Atheneum Books saw one of my *New Yorker* illustrations and offered me my first children's book, *Mr. Semolina-Semolinus: A Greek Folktale*, and I have illustrated 14 other children's books since then.

"I've also continued other venues of illustration: magazines, catalogues, CD covers, and an ad campaign for Persil laundry soap in the United Kingdom, which included animated TV ads. But I always feel the happiest doing books. I have fun deciding who the characters are and how they look, and I like being left alone to paint for a few months without anyone over my shoulder.

"I live in the Hudson Valley with my husband, Kier, growing many vegetables and fruits that we enjoy eating."

✿　✿　✿

Giselle Potter was born in Mystic, Connecticut. She spent most of her early years there and in nearby Stonington when she wasn't traveling around Europe and the United States with her family. Fortunately, the private school she attended was very understanding about the school days she missed, and with the help of her parents, she kept up with the work. After attending Sarah Lawrence College for a year, she left college to spend a year in Bali, studying art. She graduated from the Rhode Island School of Design in 1994.

Courtesy of Atheneum Books for Young Readers

Festive, whimsical, playful, and homey are just a few of the words that reviewers have used to describe Potter's signature watercolor and ink illustrations, which often include wacky angles and offbeat perspectives. The influence of her background in puppetry and theater may be seen in the facial expressions and costumes of her illustrated characters. While her first book, *Lucy's Eyes and Margaret's Dragon: Lives of the Virgin Saints* was intended for an adult audience, she made an auspicious beginning in the field of children's literature when her first book for children, *Mr. Semolina-Semolinus: A Greek Folktale*, was named an ALA Notable Children's Book.

Of the books she has illustrated subsequently, *Gabriella's Song*, *Three Cheers for Catherine the Great!*, and *Kate and the Beanstalk* have also been named ALA Notable Children's Books. *The Honest-to-Goodness Truth*, *Shrinking Violet*, *Gabriella's Song*, and *Kate and the Beanstalk* were all cited as *School Library Journal* Best Books of the Year, and *Kate and the Beanstalk* was also on the New York Public Library's 100 Titles for Reading and Sharing. The Swedish edition of *Three Cheers for Catherine the Great!*, which is entitled *Hipp, Hurra för Mormor!*, received the Peter Pan Award in Sweden, and the reward for Potter, along with author Cari Best, was to be a trip to the Göteborg International Book Fair to present a seminar on September 14, 2001. Unfortunately, the disruption of air travel after September 11 that year prevented the two from making the trip.

Giselle Potter and Kieran Kinsella were married in June of 2001. They have a daughter named Pia, born in January 2003, and live in upstate New York.

SELECTED WORKS WRITTEN AND ILLUSTRATED: *Lucy's Eyes and Margaret's Dragon: Lives of the Virgin Saints*, 1997; *The Year I Didn't Go to School*, 2002; *Chloe's Birthday . . . and Me*, 2004.

SELECTED WORKS ILLUSTRATED: *Mr. Semolina-Semolinus: A Greek Folktale*, retold by Anthony Manna and Christodoula Mitakidou, 1997; *Gabriella's Song*, by Candace Fleming, 1997; *When Agnes Caws*, by Candace Fleming, 1999; *Three Cheers for Catherine the Great!*, by Cari Best, 1999; *The Big Box*, by Toni Morrison, 1999; *The Honest-to-Goodness Truth*, by Patricia McKissack, 2000; *Kate and the Beanstalk*, by Mary Pope Osborne, 2000; *Shrinking Violet*, by Cari Best, 2001; *Ghost Wings*, by Barbara Joosse, 2001; *The Brave Little Seamstress*, by Mary Pope Osborne, 2002; *Quentin Fenton Herter III*, by Amy MacDonald, 2002; *Trudi & Pia*, by Ursula Hegi, 2003.

SUGGESTED READING: "Flying Starts," *Publishers Weekly*, June 30, 1997.

Alice and Martin Provensen

Alice Provensen:
August 14, 1918–

Martin Provensen:
July 10, 1916–
March 27, 1987

Alice Provensen writes: "I suppose, like every other child given paper and a box of crayons, I drew many childish pictures. I hope my pictures were as good as the children's pictures I see now—those wonderful portraits of unknown people and large families, those huge forests of trees that look like lollipops, those hundreds of cars in small parking lots, or ships pitching and rolling on monstrous waves in the wind and rain—things that the average professional artist would be unlikely even to attempt.

"The first picture of my own that I really recall was painted when I was 10 years old. I had skipped 5th grade, not because I was clever, but because I was too tall—and even so, I towered over my classmates. I can still remember my 6th grade teacher's name, even though it was nearly 75 years ago! I loved Mrs. Lino. She seated me in the first row of desks where I could see and hear better than in the back where I had always had to sit before. One morning, Mrs. Lino brought in a bunch of purple irises, which we called 'flags' then. Our class's assignment that day was for each of us to paint a picture of the flowers in the vase. I though my picture was pretty good. I guess Mrs. Lino did too. She sent it to the committee that was choosing young children from the public schools to study at the Art Institute of Chicago. To my delight, I won a scholarship to the museum's innovative new program, and I suddenly wanted to be an artist.

"Each Saturday in spring and five days a week in summer, I rode the elevated train from the North Side of Chicago, where I lived, all the way downtown to the 'Loop' station closest to the museum. (I don't think a child of 10 would be allowed to make that trip alone these days.) When the train, after about an hour's trip, crossed the Chicago River, the smells from a nearby coffee-roasting plant always made me throw up, and I arrived pale but undaunted, ready for class. We young students attended lectures by and about famous artists. We toured the museum's galleries of paintings and marble statues of naked Greek and Roman warriors, all with clay fig leaves covering their private parts. We sawed and carved and painted wooden pull-toys of imaginary animals with wooden wheels. That winter, I particularly remember two things—the landscapes of George Inness and the unbelievably delicious mashed potatoes of the museum's cafeteria.

"In the summertime, we trooped outside to the back of the building and drew the Chicago skyline. One day, my instructor started to draw on my picture, I suppose to show me how to do it. She drew for so long that I got bored and wandered away to see what everyone else was doing. When I returned, I was harshly reprimanded. I never let anyone ever again draw on my drawings until I began my collaboration with my husband, Martin. But, by then, I got to draw on his, too!

"I don't think I did much drawing in junior high school. There seemed to be so many distractions. My mother, an interior decorator, approved of all things 'artistic,' as she called them. I took ballet lessons, but never learned to dance. I took piano lessons, but never learned to play. Jealous and in competition with my brother who played trumpet in the school band, I saved my allowances and bought myself a bugle, an instrument with which I can still make a lot

Courtesy of Susan Fowler-Gallagher

Alice Provensen

of noise. My mother also saw to it that I had private painting lessons. A woman, whose name I have forgotten, showed up once in a while with a basket of miscellaneous objects and a portable oil painting kit. She set up a 'still life' and we both sat down to paint it. I do remember that picture. It was of an ornamental box placed on a drape of red velvet. A string of faux pearls drooped over the edge of the box. My teacher said my pearls looked like steel BB shots, but I thought they were great. My mother had the picture framed to please and encourage me.

"In high school, during the depths of the Depression, I made a poster for the Community Chest's money-raising event. I designed a decorative panel out of the number '1' intertwined with the number '3.' The caption was: 'One out of three is jobless—Give!' I got an Honorable Mention for it and a picture in the newspaper of me standing with all the other 'also-rans' behind the 1st, 2nd, and 3rd place winners. But I liked school—I liked history and English and math and science. My last year of high school, I remember making a diagram of a flush toilet—how the handle lifted a ball on a chain to release the water and dropped down again to shut it off. The drawing had decorative colored arrows and symbols explaining the mechanism. I was quite proud of it, and it may well have influenced my decision to take a course in engineering drawing at UCLA. I still love T-squares and triangles.

"Looking back on this early part of my life, I realize that I have had very little formal training, except for a brief time when I studied lithography at the Art Students League in New York City. But I did always seem to be drawing something. I worked for a while in New York on 7th Avenue making sketches of dresses and accessories. I worked for a company that manufactured bar stools. I drew pictures of their possible installations and the decor surrounding them. I did drawings for my mother's drapery designs and attached swatches of suggested fabrics to them—my first collages! My education became a sort of 'learn while you earn' existence.

"In my spare time, I worked as a monitor in the studio of a quite well-known artist (you don't hear much about him anymore). 'Monitor' means, in this case, doing all the dirty work (for no pay)—opening the studio in the morning, cleaning it, and picking up after the paying students. I closed down the studio at night, long after the *maitre* had left for the day. I was rewarded with lessons which taught me to paint like he did (not exactly what I wanted to do) and his friendship.

"It wasn't until the start of World War II that jobs began to open up for women. We were hired to replace drafted servicemen. I got work in a shipyard making drawings of miscellaneous missing inventory parts, checking blueprints, and making safety posters. After that I got a job in the animated cartoon business, where I did my first drawings for children. I was working at the Walter Lantz Studio (where the Woody Woodpecker cartoons were produced) when I met my future husband and partner, Martin. Prior to his enlisting in the navy, he had worked for several years doing storyboards for Walt Disney. He was reassigned by the navy to Lantz's to make training films. When he was recalled to Washington, I followed him, and we were married there in 1944.

"The rest, as they say, is history. After the war, we had decided not to go back to cartooning but to try our hand at children's books, a new field for both of us. We moved to New York City

"That winter, I particularly remember two things—the landscapes of George Inness and the unbelievably delicious mashed potatoes of the museum's cafeteria."

and later to our farm in Dutchess County, New York, where we raised our daughter, Karen. We loved each other and worked together there for 43 years. When Martin died in 1987, I didn't think I would ever be able to work again—but with the support of my dear daughter and the encouragement of my former editor and good friend Linda Zuckerman, who begged and bullied me, I sent off a 'dummy' for a new book. *The Buck Stops Here* was a success, got great reviews, brought me a lot of attention and made me some money. I have published several books since then and am now working on another."

※　※　※

A husband and wife team creating books together is a rarity in children's literature, though there are several notable pairs. For over 40 years, Alice and Martin Provensen were personally and professionally the epitome of cooperative teamwork, in their marriage and in their work. There is a fascinating similarity in their lives as they grew up and began their careers; in fact, they actually traveled almost parallel paths. Both were born in Chicago; both their families moved cross-country town by town during the Depression. Alice has said, "No matter where we moved or how often, the libraries were safe havens for both of us." Both won scholarships to the Art Institute of Chicago; both transferred to the University of California—Alice in Los Angeles and Martin in Berkeley; both worked in the animation industry—Alice at the Walter Lantz Studios and Martin at Walt Disney, where he created storyboards and contributed to the feature animated films *Fantasia* and *Dumbo*.

Yet in all that time they never met until they both worked at the Walter Lantz studio. They moved to New York in 1945 when they began working as children's book illustrators. Two years later, in 1947, their first book was published—*The Fireside Book of Folksongs*—for which they did over 500 illustrations. This remarkable volume is still a family favorite in many homes today. Extensive travels in Europe in the early 1950s, including a three-month stay in Greece to prepare for illustrating *The Iliad* and *The Odyssey*, provided the Provensens with a collection of material and sketchbooks that became the creative foundation for future illustrated books. When they returned to the United States, they bought a farm near Staatsburg, New York, converting the barn into a studio. There the animals and pastoral setting provided the inspiration for many more books: *The Year at Maple Hill Farm*, *An Owl and Three Pussycats*, and *Town and Country*, to name a few.

Their training in animation contributed to the Provensens' style, which involved unique perspectives, creative hand-lettering, and strong design. That experience also gave them the skill to treat serious subjects with warmth and humor. Their deceptively simple, sometimes primitive-looking style, with crisp shapes, soft colors, and remarkable visual continuity could be

"I was working at the Walter Lantz Studio (where the Woody Woodpecker cartoons were produced) when I met my future husband and partner, Martin."

© Hilary Masters

Alice and Martin Provensen in 1983.

adapted to convey a strong sense of each text they illustrated. Recognition of the Provensens' distinctive shared style came early in their career. Among the many awards and accolades they received together were seven citations from the *New York Times*, for books listed among the Ten Best Illustrated of the Year: *The Animal Fair* in 1952, *The Golden Bible* in 1953, *The First Noel* in 1959, *Karen's Curiosity* in 1963, *The Charge of the Light Brigade* in 1964, *The Mother Goose Book* in 1976, and *A Peaceable Kingdom: The Shaker Abecedarius* in 1978. Their *Treasury of Myths and Legends* received a Gold Medal in 1960 at the Society of Illustrators Second Annual Exhibition.

In 1982 the Provensens were awarded a Caldecott Honor citation for their illustrations in *A Visit to William Blake's Inn: Poems for Innocent and Experienced Travelers*. A groundbreaking title in many ways, it was the first book to carry two award stickers on the cover: a Caldecott Honor for the illustrators and a Newbery Award for the author. It was also the first book of poetry to receive the Newbery Medal. As Nancy Willard's magical poems were written in the spirit of William Blake, so the captivating, imaginative illustrations by the Provensens flawlessly captured the whimsy of the imaginary 18th-century inn and its unusual visitors.

Then in 1984 Alice and Martin Provensen received the Caldecott Medal for *The Glorious Flight Across the Channel with Louis Blériot, July 25, 1909*, a book for which they also wrote the text. Based on a true event that occurred in France in the early 1900s, it stemmed from their own fascination with early flying machines, which they described in their acceptance speech for the award. Illustrated with scenes of shifting perspectives that evoke the excitement and danger of early aviation, the story also provides a witty, humorous portrait of Blériot's family. The skillful hands of the Provensens turned the facts of the historic event into a story of personal adventure, creating a convincing sense of air and space. The reader seems to experience the thrill of what it must have felt like to be up in the air in those early planes. The richly detailed paintings in this picture-book biography illuminate, both literally and figuratively, Blériot's tale of his triumphant flight across the English Channel.

After Martin's death from a heart attack in 1987, Alice was faced with tackling children's books on her own for the first time. But her artistic eye and deft hand held true when *The Buck*

Stops Here: Presidents of the United States was published in 1990. Her first solo venture continued the pair's tradition of strong design, solid facts, and a playful sense of humor. She immersed herself in researching American history, acquiring the necessary sensitivity to politics and the portrayal of politicians; and she then achieved a light-hearted, informative view of American presidents told in a crisp rhyming text. The book was hailed for its charm, originality, and humor.

In 1991 Alice triumphed once again on her own by winning another *New York Times* Best Illustrated Book of the Year citation for *Punch in New York*. Two of her more recent titles have been designated as Notable Social Studies Trade Books for Young People: *My Fellow Americans* and *The Master Swordsman and the Magic Doorway*, which recounts two tales from ancient China. *A Day in the Life of Murphy*, a picture book that is a charming slice of a dog's life, returns to a theme Alice and Martin explored together for so many years. Set on a farm, the story takes the reader inside the thoughts and feelings of a farm animal and was named a best book of the year by both *School Library Journal* and the *Bulletin of the Center for Children's Books*.

The Clinton Library in Dutchess County, New York, declared September 29, 2003, Alice Provensen Day to honor the town's most famous resident. Appreciation was expressed for her work that day by local, state, and national political figures, as well as art and literature specialists. In her remarks Alice said, "Art-

TWO LEGENDS FROM ANCIENT CHINA
Retold and Illustrated by ALICE PROVENSEN

Courtesy of Simon & Schuster Books for Young Readers

ists become artists by looking at art, not from first-hand observation; writers are readers, their inspiration comes from reading." The New York Library Association presented her in 2004 with the Empire State Award for Excellence in Literature for Young Readers, and a retrospective exhibit of her work and Martin's is scheduled for the Eric Carle Museum of Picture Book Art in the fall of 2005. From the charming and captivating style in her collaborative work with her husband to the wry, energetic depictions in her own volumes, Alice Provensen's books ring with authenticity of detail, careful research, and affection without sentimentality, always engaging their readers, both young and old.

SELECTED WORKS ILLUSTRATED BY ALICE AND MARTIN PROVENSEN: *The Fireside Book of Folksongs*, ed. by Margaret Bradford Boni, 1947; *The Golden Mother Goose: 367 Childhood Favorites*,

THE GLORIOUS FLIGHT
ACROSS THE CHANNEL WITH LOUIS BLÉRIOT
BY ALICE AND MARTIN PROVENSEN

Courtesy of Viking Children's Books

sel. by Jane Werner, 1948; *The Color Kittens*, by Margaret Wise Brown, 1949, 2000; *The Fuzzy Duckling*, by Jane Werner, 1949, 1997; *The Little Fat Policeman*, by Margaret Wise Brown and Edith Thacher Hurd, 1950; *A Child's Garden of Verses*, by Robert Louis Stevenson, 1951; *The Golden Bible for Children: The New Testament*, 1953; *The Iliad and the Odyssey*, adapted by Jan Werner Watson, 1956; *A Treasury of Myths and Legends*, by Anne Terry White, 1959; *The First Noel: The Birth of Christ from the Gospel According to St. Luke*, 1959; *An Introduction to the Instruments of the Orchestra*, by Jane Bunche, 1962; *The Charge of the Light Brigade*, by Alfred Lord Tennyson, 1964; *Aesop's Fables*, adapt. by Louis Untermeyer, 1965; *Tales from the Ballet*, adapt. by Louis Untermeyer, 1968; *The Golden Book of Fun and Nonsense*, ed. by Louis Untermeyer, 1970; *The Mother Goose Book*, 1976; *Old Mother Hubbard*, by Sarah Catherine Martin, 1977; *The Golden Serpent*, by Walter Dean Myers, 1980; *A Visit to William Blake's Inn: Poems for Innocent and Experienced Travelers*, by Nancy Willard, 1981; *Birds, Beasts, and the Third Thing: Poems*, by D. H. Lawrence, 1982; *The Voyage of Ludgate Hill: Travels with Robert Louis Stevenson*, by Nancy Willard, 1987.

SELECTED WORKS WRITTEN AND ILLUSTRATED BY ALICE AND MARTIN PROVENSEN: *The Animal Fair*, 1952; *Karen's Curiosity*, 1963; *Karen's Opposites*, 1963; *Who's in the Egg*, 1968; *The Provensen Book of Fairy Tales*, 1971; *Play on Words*, 1972; *My Little Hen*, 1973; *Our Animal Friends at Maple Hill*

Farm, 1974; *A Book of Seasons*, 1976; *The Year at Maple Hill Farm*, 1978; A *Peaceable Kingdom: The Shaker Abecedarius*, 1978; *A Horse and a Hound, a Goat and a Gander*, 1980; *An Owl and Three Pussycats*, 1981; *The Glorious Flight: Across the Channel with Louis Blériot, July 25, 1909*, 1983; *Leonardo da Vinci: The Artist, Inventor, Scientist in Three-Dimensional, Movable Pictures*, 1984; *Town and Country*, 1984, 1994; *Shaker Lane*, 1987.

SELECTED WORKS WRITTEN AND ILLUSTRATED BY ALICE PROVENSEN: *The Buck Stops Here: The Presidents of the United States*, 1990; *Punch in New York*, 1991; *My Fellow Americans: A Family Album*, 1995; *The Master Swordsman and the Magic Doorway: Two Legends from Ancient China*, 2001; *A Day in the Life of Murphy*, 2003.

SUGGESTED READING: *Children's Literature Review*, vol. 4, 1982; Cummins, Julie. *Children's Book Illustration and Design*, vol. 1, 1992; Cullinan, Bernice, and Diane Person. *The Continuum Encyclopedia of Children's Literature*, 2001; Marcus, Leonard S. *Side by Side: Five Favorite Picture-Book Teams Go to Work*, 2001; Silvey, Anita. ed. *Children's Books and Their Creators*, 1995; *Something About the Author*, vol. 70, 1993; vol. 147, 2004; *Twentieth-Century Children's Writers*, 1978. Periodicals—Provensen, Alice and Martin, "Caldecott Acceptance Speech," *The Horn Book*, August 1984; *San Francisco Chronicle*, March 30, 1987 (Obituary of Martin Provensen).

An earlier profile of Alice and Martin Provensen appeared in *Third Book of Junior Authors* (1963).

Vladimir Radunsky

March 1, 1954–

"It has been 15 years since I've been coming up with stories and pictures for small children. This occupation continually gives me immense pleasure, although it would be difficult to call it a serious profession—inventing absurd stories and drawing pictures that are filled with anatomically incorrect people, cats, dogs, trees, as well as strange hats, shoes, houses, etc. It is difficult to explain what in my childhood or later on in my youth nudged me towards this peculiar 'profession.' Now, if I had a really important profession—a doctor for example—oh, then I could really write volumes! I could write how as a little boy I had a calling. My imagination takes me so far that I can even see clearly my imaginary grandfather—yes, a humble country doctor—and how I often visited him in the summer and even helped him with his patients: a farmer, who broke all his front teeth trying to crack a nut, or the farmer's wife, who got pecked by a chicken. Or even something like this: I see myself as a young doctor performing my first operation. Imagine, a lion bit off the head of his trainer, and it is up to me to sew it back on and save the life of this great artist! And so the operation is a success, my colleagues are congratulating me, but their voices are coming to me as if from a distance; I am smiling weakly, all weary and sweaty. No kidding, such a complicated surgery! That would really be something! But unfortunately I am not a doctor.

"I don't ever recall that as a child I was excessively fond of drawing or made up any stories or even wrote poetry. I did read a lot, and I liked to watch my older brother draw—he really drew amazingly well. As for me, I never drew anything then and only started to do so much later, maybe at 18. I always loved to ride my bicycle, or better to say wander around the city on my bicycle. To tell the truth, I still do it to this day. I often thought that it would be a nice profession—a wandering cyclist. People would ask me, 'What is your profession?' And I would answer, 'I am a Senior Cyclist.' Or even 'I am the Managing Cyclist.' Or maybe even, 'I am a Senior Executive Cyclist,' and so on. When I was a young man, I was bitterly disappointed when I realized that I could not pursue a career of a 'wandering cyclist' and decided to strike a compromise and find myself a more or less serious profession.

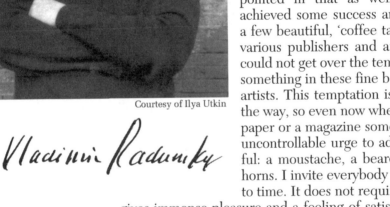

Courtesy of Ilya Utkin

"I began to study architecture and almost became an architect, when I suddenly understood that nobody was going to build my 'anatomically incorrect' houses. Then I decided to try my hand at graphic design, in particular book design, but I became disappointed in that as well. I had already achieved some success and even designed a few beautiful, 'coffee table' art books for various publishers and art galleries, but I could not get over the temptation to doodle something in these fine books by these fine artists. This temptation is still with me, by the way, so even now when I see in a newspaper or a magazine some mug, I have this uncontrollable urge to add something useful: a moustache, a beard, or maybe even horns. I invite everybody to do it from time to time. It does not require a lot of skill but gives immense pleasure and a feeling of satisfaction.

"Having realized that even such a respected occupation as graphic design does not provide me with enough freedom, I started thinking seriously about some useful profession, when all of a sudden I discovered—better say re-discovered—children's books. Children's books comprise all the things that I have always loved and enjoyed: literature, art, design, and humor. Different genres (high and low)—theater, classical art, and pop art—all come together in the most natural way. Besides, creating and drawing children's books finally gave me a legitimate reason to add moustaches, beards, horns, and anything else that comes into my head. And nobody can ever say to me, 'Stop drawing this silly nonsense! Go and find something serious to do.'

"My discovery of children's books and in particular picture books was to me similar to the discovery of gold in the Klondike. I found a number of wonderful books and a number of wonderful authors and artists—each one unlike the others. All of a sudden I understood that these small books play an irreplaceable role in the lives of children, 3–8 years old, because they serve as guides into their future interests: reading, art, etc. For the majority of the children, it is truly their first step towards education. That is precisely why I do not limit myself to any particular kind of art technique and, on the contrary, always work in an eclectic manner. I don't pick the medium I work in, but rather it just happens. If in order to visually interpret the story I feel that fine art technique is more appropriate, I paint. If photography is called for, I photograph. Or I draw or make a collage, etc., etc. Just at this moment, having thought about all this, I unexpectedly came to the following conclusion. The making of picture books is not just a demonstration of the mastery one has achieved in one or the other of the many different art techniques, although I admire many of the authors who do precisely that. The real goal is to express the literary idea using any means that are appropriate. That is why I think that anybody (especially the parents)—even if they cannot draw—can create children's book masterpieces, using manicure scissors, glue, paper, pencils, and pictures from magazines. It is even better when the children participate.

"These curious, homemade books often become the most treasured possessions that the already-grown children keep on their bookshelves throughout their whole life. Recently, I came across a story 'Godfather's Album' by Hans Christian Andersen. In it I found this thought that pretty closely resembles my work principle. These words were written more than 150 years ago: 'Ah. . . . Godfather could really tell fairy tales—they were long and plentiful. And at Christmastime he would take a thick, blank album and paste in it pictures that he cut out of books and newspapers. When he could not find a picture that would fit the story, he would draw one.' "

"Children's books comprise all the things that I have always loved and enjoyed: literature, art, design, and humor. Different genres (high and low)—theater, classical art, and pop art—all come together in the most natural way."

❊　❊　❊

Vladimir Radunsky grew up in Moscow, where he studied fine art, design, and architecture. Settling in New York City in 1982, he began designing art books for various publishers. Radunsky's first book for children, created together with his friend Robert Rayevsky, was a Catalan tale called *The Riddle*, published in 1987. After this first book, very quickly the main distinguishing characteristic of Radunsky's work became apparent. Extremely varied subjects, both in prose and poetry, provoke Radunsky to use very different techniques and styles, ranging from realistic painting (stylized in the manner of commercial posters of the

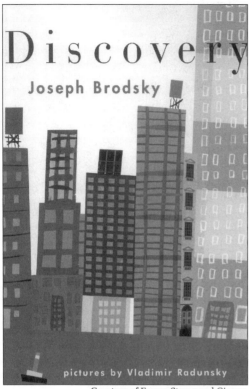

Courtesy of Farrar, Straus and Giroux

1930s) to abstract collages. In his own words, "The technique and style I choose in every new book depends entirely on its subject. I don't draw pictures, I create books. And these two things are entirely different art genres."

He quickly proved his concept with *The Pup Grew Up!* and *Hail to Mail*, both translations of stories first published in Russia in 1926 by Samuel Marshak. After that, a collaboration with the well-known writer Bill Martin Jr. led to the Children's Television Workshop animated short film based on the art for their book, *The Maestro Plays*. The film was shown on *Sesame Street* and later internationally syndicated on PBS.

For three picture-book editions of Woody Guthrie's children's songs, Radunsky used the peculiar mix of painting and collage that was undoubtedly inspired by Guthrie's own original collages, drawings, and even doodles, which have survived in the Woody Guthrie Foundation archives. Radunsky is constantly fascinated by very different types of books: from board books of shapes for the very young—*Square, Triangle, Round, Skinny* (a set of four books shaped the way their titles suggest)—to *Discovery*, a lyrical poem by Nobel Prize–winner Joseph Brodsky about the discovery of America. In his most recent book, *What Does Peace Feel Like?*, the text was culled out of conversations with children during school visits in America and Europe.

Vladimir Radunsky became an American citizen in 1989. He has received numerous awards for his books, and his artwork has been exhibited in the United States, Italy, France, and Japan. For the past two years, Radunsky and his family (wife, twin daughters, and a springer spaniel) have divided their time between New York and Rome, where he has been organizing an international art festival of children's book authors and illustrators.

SELECTED WORKS WRITTEN AND ILLUSTRATED: *Table Manners: The Edifying Story of Two Friends Whose Discovery of Good Manners Promises Them a Glorious Future* (with Chris Raschka), 2001; *10 (ten)*, 2002; *Mannekin Pis: A Simple Story of a Boy Who Peed on a War*, 2002; *Square, Triangle, Round, Skinny*, 2002; *#1 (one)*, 2003; *The Mighty Asparagus*, 2004; *What Does Peace Feel Like?*, 2004.

SELECTED WORKS ILLUSTRATED: *The Riddle* (with Robert Rayevsky), retold by Adele Vernon, 1987; *The Pup Grew Up!*, by Samuel Marshak, trans. by Richard Pevear, 1989; *Hail to Mail*, by Samuel Marshak, trans. by Richard Pevear, 1990; *The Story of a Boy Named Will*, by Daniil Kharms, trans. by Jamey Gambrell, 1993; *The Maestro Plays*, by Bill Martin Jr., 1994; *Telephone*, adapted and trans. by Jamey Gambrell, 1996; *Yucka Drucka Droni*, by Eugenia Radunsky, 1998; *An Edward Lear Alphabet*, by Edward Lear, 1999; *Discovery*, by Joseph Brodsky, 1999; *Bling Blang*, by Woody Guthrie, 2000; *Howdi Do*, by Woody Guthrie, 2000; *My Dolly*, by Woody Guthrie, 2001; *The Transmogrification of Roscoe Wizzle*, by David Elliott, 2001.

SUGGESTED READING: Cummins, Julie, ed. *Children's Book Illustration and Design*, vol. II, 1996. Periodicals—"About Our Cover Artist," *Publishers Weekly*, February 16, 1998.

"I didn't start reading for pleasure until I started writing, which was when I was about 20. *The Catcher in the Rye* had the greatest impact on me in high school. I'm sure both these facts have had an influence on how I write for young adults.

"My novels always start with the voice. I've never successfully written in the third person. If there's a rhythm or a musicality that interests me, I become obsessed with the character. I just have a need to spend time with him or her. Sometimes I'll be in the park or on the street or in a cab, and I'll hear someone say something I've never heard before. Listening to the nuances and rhythms of language in the unique tones and cadences of overheard conversations helps me imagine the tones and cadences of my characters. In some of my work, discovering a world and developing a language indigenous to that world is just as important as the voice. The language itself constructs the world of the story. With the novel, there's a lot of opportunity to explore the relationship between the world of the story and the character's voice.

"The characters are created in my head, and I follow them around inside myself listening to their voices. But I suppose there are bits and pieces of myself in my books, too. I write from very personal places, so from time to time, there's a random geographic or emotional fact about me that you might recognize. I was a late bloomer in high school and felt too different from all

Courtesy of Amelia Warner

Adam Rapp

June 15, 1968–

the other adolescents around me, plus I was separated from my family at age 11 and again at 14, so some themes of isolation and alienation come up in my stories. But my books are not autobiographical because I make so much up in order to move the story along.

"Writing plays is different than writing novels in that playwriting forces you to organize information into a compressed story. You only have two hours or so to tell it, and the story itself may be one that spans weeks, months, or even years. With playwriting, there are so many, so many factors that differ from writing a novel. Can it be spoken? How can I tell the story through hard action? Do I want to deal with the egos of actors, directors, and literary managers? Do I want to sit in an audience and bear witness to something that might fail? I love the solitude and meditative part of writing a novel. Novels involve many months and seasons and different kinds of weather. I tend to write plays in strange little fits. They seem to burst out of me. I tend to take a break from the novel I'm working on to write a play. Afterward, I return to the novel with a kind of recovered peace. The theater is hard on playwrights. There's very little money and so few slots for new work. Writing novels has kept me sane. Writing plays makes me go a little crazy. There are benefits to both."

Courtesy of HarperCollins Publishers

Born and raised in Chicago, Illinois, Adam Rapp attended high school at St. John's Military Academy in Delafield, Wisconsin. He went to college on a basketball scholarship at Clarke College in Dubuque, Iowa, where he was captain of the basketball team and studied fiction writing and psychology. He also completed a two-year Lila Acheson Wallace Playwriting Fellowship at the Juilliard School in New York.

In his first novel, *Missing the Piano*, he drew on his own background as a teenage boy in a military academy setting. The young sophomore makes the best of a bad situation by learning to confront diversity and prejudice as well as grasp the value of friendship, responsibility, and love. *Missing the Piano* was named a 1995 Best Book for Young Adults and a Quick Pick for Reluctant Young Adult Readers by the American Library Association. With his inventive use of language, Rapp created a gritty, surrealistic world in his second novel, *The Buffalo Tree*, about a juvenile detention center inmate who manages to transcend the brutality of his environment. This novel, a National Book Award nominee that was cited as a Best Book of the Year by *School Library Journal*, echoes with perceptions from a time when Rapp, at age 11, was sent to Glenwood School for Boys, a military-style reform school near the Illinois-Indiana state line. In *The Copper Elephant*, also a National Book Award nominee, Rapp continued to experiment with language, creating a disturbing post-apocalyptic environment in which the heroine relies on inner strengths and new friendships to find a way to look at her world and overcome the devastation around her.

Adam Rapp is a playwright as well as a novelist. He has received two Lincoln Center Lecomte du Nouy Awards, the 1999 Princess Grace Award for Playwriting, a 2000 Roger L. Stevens Award from the Kennedy Center Fund for New American Plays, and the 2001 Helen Merrill Award. His plays have been produced in London, New York City, Chicago, Los Angeles, and Washington, DC, among other cities. Some of the gritty realism and lyrical, musical language that make his novels distinctive can also be found in his theatrical works. *Nocturne* is a one-man play about a man trying to come to terms with the fact that he accidentally killed his sister in a car accident when he was a teenager. Rapp's actor brother, Anthony Rapp, who originated the role of Mark in the Broadway play *Rent*, starred in this tense, unnerving drama that critics applauded for its stunning confrontation with one man's truth. For several years, the two Rapp brothers were roommates in the East Village in New York City. They also have an older sister, Anne, who lives in the Chicago area with her family.

Recently Rapp has turned his attention to screenwriting and film directing. He wrote the screenplay for *Winter Passing*, a dramatic comedy about the fractious reunion of an estranged father and daughter in a literary family. The film is scheduled to be released in March 2005 and will feature Ed Harris, Will Ferrell, and Zooey Deschanel. Currently dividing his time between New York, Los Angeles, and the various cities where his plays are in production, Rapp makes his permanent home in New York City with singer-songwriter Dawn Landes.

SELECTED WORKS FOR THE THEATER: *The Ghost in the Cottonwoods*, 1996; *Trueblinka*, 1997; *Finer Noble Gases*, 2001; *Blackbird*, 2001; *Nocturne: A Play*, 2001; *Gompers*, 2003; *Stone Cold Dead Serious and Other Plays*, 2004.

SELECTED WORKS FOR YOUNG ADULTS: *Missing the Piano*, 1994; *The Buffalo Tree*, 1997; *The Copper Elephant*, 1999; *Little Chicago*, 2002; *33 Snowfish*, 2003; *Under the Wolf, Under the Dog*, 2004.

SUGGESTED READING: *Something About the Author*, vol. 148, 2004. Periodicals—Angel, Ann, "E-view with Adam Rapp," *ALAN Review*, vol. 28, no. 1, 2000.

Courtesy of McLouis Robinet

Harriette Gillem Robinet

(RO-bi-nay)

July 14, 1931–

Born and raised in Washington, DC, Harriette Gillem Robinet spent most of her childhood summers in nearby Arlington, Virginia. Steeped in the history of the area, she learned that her ancestors had been slaves there before the Civil War. After graduating from the College of New Rochelle in New York State with a B.S. degree in 1953, Robinet continued her education with graduate studies in microbiology at Catholic University in Washington. She received a Ph.D. in 1963 and enjoyed a full career as a bacteriologist, working at Children's Hospital, Walter Reed Army Medical Center, and the U.S. Army Quartermaster's Corps. Her first two books—stories for elementary grades about physically challenged children—were inspired by one of her sons, who had been born with cerebral palsy, and the variously challenged children and adults she met through him.

In the 1990s Robinet turned to writing historical fiction that would highlight the experiences of African Americans at different times and places in U.S. history. The Great Chicago Fire, the War of 1812, the Depression years in the American South, and the Civil War period have all provided backdrops for Robinet's stories. *Mississippi Chariot*, named a Notable Children's Trade Book in the Field of Social Studies, takes place in the Mississippi Delta during the 1930s. A 12-year-old boy plots to help his father escape the chain gang, and in consequence his whole family must run for their lives to a (hopefully) better life in the north. The story vividly evokes the violence of racial bigotry and its effects.

In *Forty Acres and Maybe a Mule* Robinet focuses on the heartbreaking era of Reconstruction after the Civil War. With the promises of emancipation a 12-year-old orphan named Pascal and his older brother set out to create a better life for themselves, working with others to create a true community on a farm in Georgia. Forced from their land by the changes instituted by President Andrew Johnson, successor to Lincoln, Pascal and Gideon head for the Georgia Sea Islands to find another way to succeed. Through meticulous research and well-drawn characters, Robinet illuminates this dark aftermath of the war in a novel that is fast-moving and heartfelt. *Forty Acres and Maybe a Mule* was also named a Notable Trade Book in social studies and received the Scott O'Dell Award for historical fiction. Her newest book *Twenty Travelers, Twenty Horses*, combines many historical elements: the 1860 presidential election, the Pony Express, westward expansion, and California gold with the hope for freedom growing strong in the hearts of her enslaved main characters.

Harriette Robinet firmly believes that books have the power to alter attitudes and change prejudices by introducing children to those who are different, whether those differences are in skin color, religion, economic status, or physical abilities. She is committed to reclaiming for young readers the forgotten people of history and often includes elements of mystery in her stories. *Walking to the Bus-Rider Blues*, set during the Montgomery bus boycott in 1956, is an evocative blending of history, adventure, and mystery and was nominated for the Edgar Award by the Mystery Writers of America. Robinet lives today in Oak Park, Illinois, with her husband, McLouis Robinet. They have six children and four grandchildren.

Courtesy of Atheneum Books for Young Readers

SELECTED WORKS: *Jay and the Marigold*, illus. by Trudy Scott, 1976; *Ride the Red Cycle*, illus. by David Brown, 1980; *Children of the Fire*, 1991; *Mississippi Chariot*, 1994; *If You Please, President Lincoln*, 1995; *Washington City Is Burning*, 1996; *The Twins, the Pirates, and the Battle of New Orleans*, 1997; *Forty Acres and Maybe a Mule*, 1998; *Walking to the Bus-Rider Blues*, 2000; *Missing from Haymarket Square*, 2001; *Twelve Travelers, Twenty Horses*, 2003.

SUGGESTED READING: *Children's Literature Review*, vol. 64, 2000; *Contemporary Authors*, New Revision Series, vol. 42, 1994; *Something About the Author*, vol. 104, 1999.

WEB SITE: *www.midlandauthors.com//robinet.html*

"'When are we going home?' I whispered and tugged on my Mom's smock. Huddled underneath her easel, I impatiently waited for her painting class to be over. It was a familiar place, the old train station in Cannondale, Connecticut. The smell of oil paint and turpentine, the laughter and ease of 'the girls,' my Mom's painting buddies. The quieting down as the model took the pose for the morning. The sound of stiff brushes sketching across canvas. The soft-spoken way of the instructor, Sam Brown, who was a former student of Robert Henri. At five years old, this was a pretty boring scene (ARGHH, how I wish I were there now!), so I spent most of my time drawing under that old metal easel. I drew bugs, dinosaurs, aliens, and horses— how I loved horses! They were my favorite thing to draw. I drew

Jacqueline Rogers

July 17, 1958–

them in every position I could think of—in all kinds of outfits, in all seasons, on figure skates and skateboards, at summer camp, school, and even in the army. I begged my parents for horseback riding lessons. When they finally said yes, I was beside myself with joy. But it didn't last long. My teacher wanted me to use a crop on an old school horse who was deathly afraid of even the sight of a crop. I decided that it was just too cruel a thing to do, so I dismounted and never went back. As an adult, I did go back to riding lessons, and even leased a horse for a couple of years. My passion for horses has never faded. To me they are an incredible, soulful animal, full of beauty and personality.

"Another beloved creature from my childhood, who is full of beauty and personality, is my dear brother Martin. I am the youngest of six children, and he is two years older. Martin was the brilliant creator of other worlds, from toothpick colonies jutting out of the bark of our terrific gingko tree, to clay civilizations from Mars, spread out across the vast plains of the kitchen table. Growing up with Martin was never dull. Of course, being the older brother, he could bully and tease with a vengeance, and I am sure that I was no angel either!

Courtesy of Jacqueline Rogers

"All of my siblings and both our parents were gifted in the arts. It was as though our whole family was exploring visual art. There were always plenty of art supplies, books, walls filled with paintings, and my mom's fabulous studio. Lots of people piled in and out of our big old house; there was always plenty of activity. Mentors in art were a very important part of my growing up. Starting with my mother and all my siblings, the list goes on and on. I always was under somebody's wing. My mentors continued right through college, where I studied at the Rhode Island School of Design. I graduated in 1981, with a B.F.A. in illustration. Out of school I tried many different types of illustration, including magazine, newspaper, advertising, and even store window. I decided to focus on children's books in 1984 because it was the most fun. I have spent the last 20 years engulfed in children's books and have *loved* my career. I would like to spend the next 20 years writing and illustrating my own stories, as well as painting, drawing, creating sculpture, making pottery, playing guitar and piano, gardening, hiking, and camping. And one more thing I would really love to do is paint my way around the world!"

✲ ✲ ✲

Jacqueline Rogers is equally adept at illustrating realistic stories and fanciful tales, in both picture books and chapter books. Her expressive art has appeared in a wide variety of children's literature, nonfiction as well as fiction. Known for a whimsical outlook in her artwork, Jackie often seems to focus on the most common human foibles and the most human aspects of our common experiences, and bring them completely to life in her work. The facial expressions and body postures of characters in her realistic drawings on book jackets invite readers to learn more by reading the story. A perfect example is Junior Blossom, poised in homemade wings on the barn roof on the cover of Betsy Byars's *The Not-Just-Anybody Family*, a humorous and heartwarming story of an unconventional family that was named an ALA Notable Children's Book. Throughout the last 20 years, Jackie has contributed art for some of the best-loved books of elementary grades: Paula Danziger's Amber Brown series, S. E. Hinton's *The Puppy Sister*, Stephen Roos's *Pet Lovers Club*, and easy-to-read versions of tales about The Littles, as well as jacket designs for paperback editions of these stories about miniature people.

In picture books, Jackie Rogers always tells more in her illustrations than is actually mentioned in the text. In her own *The Christmas Pageant*, the text is a retelling of the Nativity, while in the illustrations a group of children prepare and act out the story in a country barn over the course of an afternoon and evening. Each actor shows his or her own part in the production, from the children first arriving with their angel wings to the baby sucking a pacifier in the manger to the arrival of the 'Wise Men' carrying their unwieldy cardboard camel through the snow. While most of Jackie's illustration work has been for fictional stories, she has occasionally worked on informational books. In Connie Wooldridge's *When Esther Morris Headed West*, she rendered boisterous art to complement this chronicle of a remarkable woman in the Wyoming Territory in 1869, who eventually became the first female to hold public office in America. This title was cited as a Notable Social Studies Trade Book for Young People in 2002.

Jackie Rogers enjoys the fantastic side of children's imaginings as well, and she has rendered deliciously spooky art for Angela Shelf Medearis's *The Ghost of Sifty-Sifty Sam* and two volumes of Robert D. San Souci's Short and Shivery tales. Several books of poems, such as *Monster Soup*, compiled by Dilys Evans, have provided Rogers with ample room for her imagination to illustrate fairies, goblins, and monsters of all sorts. For *Weird Pet Poems*, she created inventive jacket art in which each letter of the title represents a feature of one of the 'pets,' and won the merit award for best jacket at the New York Book Show. This book was also an ALA Notable Children's Book and a Bank Street College Book of the Year. Perhaps her best-known animal art, though, is an entirely realistic rendering—the cover design

"All of my siblings and both our parents were gifted in the arts. It was as though our whole family was exploring visual art."

on *Wanted—Mud Blossom,* showing the very contrite family mutt in Betsy Byars's final volume of the Blossom family saga, which was an ALA Notable Children's Book and a *School Library Journal* Best Book.

Working now on writing the texts of her own picture books as well as illustrating, Jacqueline Rogers has created several vibrant stories about kindergarten experiences. She lives in upstate New York with her two teenage daughters, teaches art to private students, and works with local schools as an artist-in-residence. She also directs mural projects.

SELECTED WORKS WRITTEN AND ILLUSTRATED: *The Christmas Pageant,* 1989; *Best Friends Sleep Over,* 1993; *Tiptoe into Kindergarten,* 1999; *Kindergarten ABC,* 2002; *Kindergarten Count to 100,* 2004.

SELECTED WORKS ILLUSTRATED: *The Not-Just-Anybody Family,* by Betsy Byars, 1986; *The Blossoms Meet the Vulture Lady,* by Betsy Byars, 1986; *How a Weirdo and a Ghost Can Change Your Entire Life,* by Patricia Windsor, 1986; *A Blossom Promise,* by Betsy Byars, 1987; *The Blossoms and the Green Phantom,* by Betsy Byars, 1987; *Don't Call Me Toad!,* by Mary Francis Shura, 1987; *The Saddest Time,* by Norma Simon, 1987; *The Little Rabbit Who Wanted Red Wings,* by Carolyn Sherwin Bailey, 1988, 2001; *Getting Rid of Krista,* by Amy Hest, 1988; *The Prince and the Princess: A Bohemian Fairy Tale,* by Marianna Mayer, 1989; *Willy Is My Brother,* by Peggy Parish, 1989; *Wanted—Mud Blossom,* by Betsy Byars, 1991; *Dancing the Breeze,* by George Shannon, 1991; *The Pet Lovers Club: Love Me, Love My Werewolf,* by Stephen Roos, 1991; *The Pet Lovers Club: The Cottontail Caper,* by Stephen Roos, 1992; *Monster Soup and Other Spooky Poems,* comp. by Dilys Evans, 1992; *The Pet Lovers Club: Crocodile Christmas,* by Stephen Roos, 1992; *Monkey See, Monkey Do,* by Marc Gave, 1993; *Winter Wonderland,* by Dick Smith, music by Felix Bernard, 1993; *Footprints in the Snow,* by Cynthia Benjamin, 1994; *Five Live Bongos,* by George Ella Lyon, 1994; *Patrick's Day,* by Elizabeth Lee O'Donnell, 1994; *More Short & Shivery: Thirty Terrifying Tales,* retold by Robert D. San Souci, illus. with Katherine Coville, 1994; *Snow Angel,* by Jean Marzollo, 1995; *A Boy Named Boomer,* by Boomer Esiason, 1995; *Walk with Me,* by Naomi Danis, 1995; *The Puppy Sister,* by S. E. Hinton, 1995; *Nothing but Trouble,* by Betty Ren Wright, 1995; *We Eat Dinner in the Bathtub,* by Angela Shelf Medearis, 1996; *Weird Pet Poems,* comp. by Dilys Evans,

1997; *Once Upon a Springtime*, by Jean Marzollo, 1997; *The Ghost of Sifty-Sifty Sam*, by Angela Shelf Medearis, 1997; *Even More Short & Shivery: Thirty Spine-Tingling Stories*, retold by Robert D. San Souci, 1997; *Friends in Deed Save the Manatee*, by Alison Friesinger, 1998; *There Goes Lowell's Party!*, by Esther Hershenhorn, 1998; *The Stars Are Waiting*, by Marjorie Dennis Murray, 1998; *The Ghost in Room 11*, by Betty Ren Wright, 1998; *Private Lily*, by Sally Warner, 1998; *Ballerina Dreams*, by Diana White, 1998; *Sweet and Sour Lily*, by Sally Warner, 1998; *Footprints in the Sand*, by Cynthia Benjamin, 1999; *The Promise*, by Jackie French Koller, 1999; *Love Your Neighbor: Stories of Values and Virtues*, by Arthur Dobrin, 1999; *Accidental Lily*, by Sally Warner, 1999; *Leftover Lily*, by Sally Warner, 1999; *Fairies, Trolls & Goblins Galore: Poems about Fantastic Creatures*, comp. by Dilys Evans, 2000; *The Perfect Pony*, by Corinne Demas, 2000; *Story Time for Little Porcupine*, by Joseph Slate, 2000; *Good Luck Glasses*, by Sara London, 2000; *The Littles Make a Friend*, adapted by Teddy Slater from *The Littles* by John Peterson, 2000; *The Littles Go Around the World*, adapted by Teddy Slater from *The Littles Go to School*, by John Peterson, 2000; *A Big, Spooky House*, by Donna Washington, 2000; *When Esther Morris Headed West: Women, Wyoming, and the Right to Vote*, by Connie Nordhielm Wooldridge, 2001; *I Want to Say I Love You*, by Caralyn Buehner, 2001; *The Littles and the Big Blizzard*, adapted by Teddy Slater from *The Littles to the Rescue*, by John Peterson, 2001; *The Littles and the Secret Letter*, adapted by Teddy Slater from *The Littles Take a Trip*, by John Peterson, 2001; *"Wait for me!" said Maggie McGee*, by Jean Van Leeuwen, 2001; *The Littles and the Summer Storm*, adapted by

Courtesy of Random House, Inc.

Teddy Slater from *The Littles and the Big Storm*, by John Peterson, 2002; *Goosed!*, by Bill Wallace, 2002; *The Littles Go on a Hike*, adapted by Teddy Slater from *The Littles Take a Trip*, by John Peterson, 2002; *Little Scraggly Hair: A Dog on Noah's Ark*, by Lynn Cullen, 2003; *The Night Before Christmas: A Goblin Tale*, by Clement C. Moore, 2003; *Dodi's Prince*, by Vaughn Michaels, 2003; *Cars*, by Nancy Smiler Levinson, 2004; *Perfectly Chelsea*, by Claudia Mills, 2004.

Courtesy of Doug Nicholas

Gillian Rubinstein

Gillian Rubinstein

August 29, 1942–

"I was born in England in August 1942, the turning point of the Second World War (not that I had much to do with that!). I have one older sister whom I adored and fought with; we had a typical country childhood with a great deal of freedom and a succession of pets, most of which met untimely ends. I had a stick insect which miraculously produced an offspring after it was dead. I can still remember my amazement when the tiny creature emerged from what I'd thought was a lifeless egg. I was mad about horses and rode my friend Christine's ponies whenever I could, paying her sixpence an hour—hours which stretched into half a day as we explored the countryside on Buster and Trooper or in summer took them to swim in the river.

"I wanted to be a rider and my most exciting moment was when a friend said to me, 'That was a lovely pony you rode in that magazine.' I though that somehow a photographer from *Horse and Hound* had spotted me cantering round the field on Trooper and had seen my natural talent. What she really said was 'That was a lovely poem you wrote'—in the school magazine! I did write lovely poems, and stories too; everyone was always telling me that. Storytelling came so naturally to me I was not in the least impressed by it. I definitely did not want to be a writer.

"If I couldn't be a rider, I would be a reader. When it was too wet to go outside (a large part of the time in England) or if I had quarreled with Christine (I was a stormy child and fought with everyone, not only my sister), I read books. In those days reading was considered less admirable than it is now, and I was always being told, 'Get your nose out of that book and do something useful!' But I was addicted to reading. I read through all the disruptions of my early teens (divorced parents, boarding school, my father's tragic death). Books were my escape and my consolation. When I ran out of books to read I made up stories, on-going sagas of danger and romance in worlds that I created.

"I think I was quite a disturbed teenager, but it was the 1950s and nobody noticed. In the end I grew up, went to university, where I studied Spanish and French, had various different jobs, got married (twice), immigrated to Australia with my second husband, and had three children. All the time I was both refusing to be a writer and unable to stop writing: poems, plays, novels, none of which was ever finished. I was in my forties and my third child had just started school when I decided that I had to think about what I was going to do with my life (out of all late developers I must have been one of the latest). The only things I was any good at were reading and making up stories. In desperation I gave myself three months to see if I could write a novel. It took a lot more than three months, of course, but two years later that novel, *Space Demons*, was published."

☼ ☼ ☼

Gillian Rubinstein was born Gillian Margaret Hanson at Potten End, Berkhamstead, in the county of Hertfordshire, England. She received a B.A. with honors from Lady Margaret Hall, Oxford University, in 1964 and a postgraduate certificate in education from Stockwell College, London, in 1973. She worked at various jobs through those years—as a research assistant, editor, journalist, administrative officer, and film critic. After her marriage to Philip Rubinstein in 1973, she immigrated with her husband to Australia, where their three children were born: Matt in 1974, Tessa in 1977, and Susannah in 1979.

Courtesy of Simon & Schuster Books for Young Readers

Rubinstein achieved immediate success as a writer for young people when *Space Demons*, her first book, was named an Honor Book by the Children's Book Council of Australia in 1987. Hailed as a groundbreaking novel, *Space Demons* shows the influence of Gillian's reading of Ray Bradbury, Philip K. Dick, and Kurt Vonnegut; but her own blend of science fiction with the realities of children's video games and true-to-life emotions provided a new kind of fiction for children of the 1980s. Since that auspicious beginning, Gillian Rubinstein has gone on to win the Children's Book Council of Australia's Book of the Year award twice, for *Beyond the Labyrinth* and *Foxspell*, as well as several other Honor Book citations. She was presented with the Festival Award given by the government of South Australia for *Space Demons* and *Beyond the Labyrinth* and the New South Wales Premier's Award for *Answers to Brut*. In 1998 she received the South Australia Great Award for Literature. Two sequels to her first groundbreaking book have appeared—*Skymaze* in 1989 and *Shinkei* in 1996—creating the Computer Trilogy.

Rubinstein is equally adept and successful at writing picture book texts, many of which have been shortlisted for the Australian Children's Book Council Book of the Year award. *Dog In, Cat Out* received a Parents' Choice Award, and *Mr. Plunkett's Pool* received the Australian Multicultural Children's Book

Award. In 1999 she visited Japan on an Asialink Fellowship. Out of that residency and her longstanding interest in Japan, Rubinstein developed what would become known as the Otori Trilogy. A fantasy saga based on feudal Japan, these three books were published under the pseudonym Lian Hearn, a name created by combining her childhood nickname (the last four letters of Gillian) with the last name of Lafcadio Hearn, an American writer who settled in Japan in the late 1800s and did much to make Japanese stories popular in the West. Only after the initial success of *Across the Nightingale Floor*—and after it had been sold to publishers in many other countries and optioned for film rights too—did Gillian Rubinstein let it be known that she was the real author. She had wanted her first adult book to be judged on its merits and not pigeonholed as a book by a children's writer. *Across the Nightingale Floor* was named one of the Best Adult Books for High School Students by *School Library Journal* in 2002.

Gillian Rubinstein lives today in Goolwa, South Australia, with her husband. Their children are all grown and living in Sydney.

SELECTED WORKS (Australian publication dates are listed first; U.S. publication dates are in parentheses): *Space Demons*, 1986 (1988); *Answers to Brut*, 1988; *Beyond the Labyrinth*, 1988 (1990); *Melanie and the Night Animal*, 1988 (1989); *Skymaze*, 1989 (1991); *Flashback: The Amazing Adventures of a Film Horse*, 1990; *Dog In, Cat Out*, illus. by Ann James, 1991 (1993); *Squawk and Screech*, illus. by Craig Smith, 1991; *Galax-Arena*, 1992 (1993); *Mr. Plunkett's Pool*, illus. by Terry Denton, 1992; *The Giant's Tooth*, illus. by Craig Smith, 1993; *Foxspell*, 1996; *Sharon, Keep Your Hair On*, illus. by David Mackintosh, 1996; *Shinkei*, 1996; *Under the Cat's Eye*, 1997 (1998); *Pure Chance*, 1998; *Hooray for the Kafe Karaoke!*, illus. by David Mackintosh, 1998; *The Pirate's Ship*, illus. by Craig Smith, 1998; *Each Beach*, illus. by Mark Sofilas, 1998; *Ducky's Nest*, illus. by Terry Denton, 1999; *Prue Theroux, the Cool Librarian*, illus. by David Mackintosh, 2000; *The Whale's Child*, 2002.

SELECTED WORKS (as Lian Hearn): *Across the Nightingale Floor: Tales of the Otori, Book One*, 2002; *Grass for His Pillow: Tales of the Otori, Book Two*, 2003; *Brilliance of the Moon: Tales of the Otori, Book Three*, 2004.

SUGGESTED READING: *Something About the Author*, vol. 105, 1999.

"I have always wanted to be a children's book writer and illustrator. When I was a kid I was fascinated with children's picture books and thought that one day I would tell stories with pictures and words. But the dreams of an 11-year-old sometimes get lost along the way. When I was 46, after years of being a university teacher and a maker of handmade books, I met a retired librarian and storyteller named Harriett Oberhaus, who took a deep look inside me and simply asked, 'Aren't you ever going to write a children's book?'

"The question was a surprise, and I answered, 'No.'

"'Why not?'

"'Because I don't have any ideas.'

"'Sure you do. Everybody has ideas. Give me one.'

"I don't know why or how but before I knew it I was telling her a story about a Chinese grandfather and his grandson and how they made clouds. 'That's the best story I've ever heard.' Harriett said. 'Come on, Harriett. It can't be.' After all, I thought, she had heard thousands of stories in her career.

"'No, it is. Now write it down.'

"I didn't want to, but she insisted. In an hour I handed her a scribbled story. She read it and declared, 'That is the best story I have ever read! Now draw some pictures for it.'

"'I haven't drawn pictures since I was a kid.'

"'Anybody can draw. You have a pencil and paper, don't you?'

"'Yeah, but . . . .'

"'But what?'

"After a week of crumpling paper and wondering who I was kidding, I stood before Harriett, childishly holding an 'okay' drawing behind my back. 'Can I see it?' asked Harriett.

"I showed her. 'Jim, that's the best drawing I have ever seen!'

"'No, it can't be.'

"'Yes, it is. Now draw more.'

"Encouraged, I kept on.

"'You know,' she said weeks later, 'you need to color your drawings.'

"'Harriett, I don't know anything about color.'

"'Sure you do. Everybody does. Do you have crayons?'

"'No, but my son does.'

"'Well, borrow them.'

"When I showed her some crayoned pictures a week later, she was ecstatic. 'Jim, these are the best pictures I have ever seen! Draw more.' I knew that my pictures weren't that good, but

Courtesy of Brigitte Visser

James Rumford

August 13, 1948–

somehow, with the right words and her radiant *joie de vivre*, Harriett shepherded me, over that summer of 1994, from crude pictures in crayon to my first illustrations in watercolor.

"'What are you going to do with your 'book?'" Harriett asked when the pictures and the story were finished. I had no answer. Harriett's encouragement had gotten me this far, but I couldn't take the final step. Months passed. 'Do you have three dollars?' my wife asked. 'Yeah, what for?'

"'For postage. You're going to send your story to a publisher.' Two months after I took that 'final step,' I received a long letter from a young editor at Houghton Mifflin named Amy Thrall (now Flynn). When my astounded brain finally decoded the message, I phoned my wife. Then I phoned Harriett. Harriett had to sit down. My manuscript was to be published.

"It took four more years and three more books before I really understood what was happening. I was in a third grade class. I had just finished telling my 'Harriett Story' about how I got started and sharing with the students my plans for new books. A boy raised his hand. 'Mr. Rumford, did you always want to be a children's book writer and illustrator?' I was speechless. Then I remembered what I had hidden or forgotten. 'Yes,' I said. 'Always.'

"Harriett Oberhaus, now close to 80, remains my inspiration. I send her all my ideas. We chat on the phone. I visit her whenever I can. I never tire of hearing, with each new manuscript I give her, 'Jim, that's the best story I have ever heard!'"

❁   ❁   ❁

"When I was 46, after years of being a university teacher and a maker of handmade books, I met a retired librarian and storyteller named Harriett Oberhaus, who took a deep look inside me and simply asked, 'Aren't you ever going to write a children's book?'"

James Rumford grew up in Long Beach, California, and graduated from the University of California at Irvine in 1970 with a B.A. in French literature. Married in 1969 to Carol Drollinger, he served in the Peace Corps from 1971 to 1975. The first three years were spent in Chad teaching English as a foreign language in a rural middle school in Kelo, then two years as a lecturer in English at the University of Chad in Ndjamena. With his wife, he wrote a book on Chadian Arabic, traveling also to Nigeria, Cameroon, and Kenya. His Peace Corps tour finished in Afghanistan, heading the English program for Ariana Afghan Airlines in Kabul and traveling extensively in the Far East. From 1977 to 1981 Rumford chaired the English Department at the National University of Rwanda as a Fulbright-Hays teacher and wrote a book on the Rwandan language. Since 1976 he has called Honolulu his home, and it was there that his son Jonathan was born in 1982, but one more sojourn abroad took the family to a Saudi Arabian air force base in Jeddah, to teach in the English program for Litton Industries from 1984 to 1986.

Settling back in Honolulu, Jim Rumford founded Mānoa Press in 1986 to publish handmade books. In order to understand every aspect of the production of fine books, he has become a papermaker, letterpress printer, and bookbinder as well as author and illustrator. He has studied more than a dozen lan-

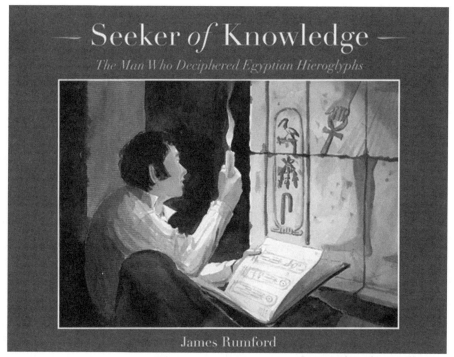

Courtesy of Houghton Mifflin, Inc.

guages in the course of his travels and researchs; he translated his own book, *Seeker of Knowledge*, into French in 2002. When he started to compose books for young readers, he called on all his interests and experiences with travel and languages, as well as his love of history. *The Cloudmakers* is a narrative explanation of how the art of papermaking might have traveled from its origins in China to the Western world. *The Island-below-the-Star*, written in the style of a chant, tells how five Polynesian brothers discover the islands of Hawaii, paralleling the journey of the unknown Polynesian peoples whose actual travels are not recorded by history. This book was named one of the *New York Times* Ten Best Illustrated Books in 1998.

Turning to a true historical figure in *Seeker of Knowledge*, Rumford relates the amazing story of Jean-François Champollion, the French amateur scholar who first deciphered Egyptian hieroglyphs in the early 19th century. This title was named a Notable Social Studies Trade Book for Young People and received the Bookbuilders Award from New England publishers and book manufacturers. In each of Rumford's books, the story is told as much through his remarkably evocative watercolors as by his clear, concise texts. Perhaps his finest achievement to date is *Traveling Man: The Journey of Ibn Battuta, 1325–1354*, in which he turns his art to the exquisite rendering of Arabic calligraphy and maps as well as representational pictures. Ibn Battuta's journey took him from one end of the 14th-century Muslim world to the other, from Morocco through the Russian steppes to China, India, and Asia Minor before he returned home 29 years and 75,000 miles later. *Traveling Man* was designated an ALA Notable Children's Book and a Notable Social Studies Trade Book for its artistic merit and its rich depiction of an era and culture with which many are unfamiliar. For contributing to knowledge and understanding about that part of the world, the book also received the Middle East Book Award from the Middle East Outreach Council. In 2001 Rumford received the Hawaii-based Cades Senior Literary Award for the body of his work. His book *Calabash Cat and His Amazing Journey* was featured on the cover of the New York Public Library's 100 Titles for Reading and Sharing list for 2003 and received an Honor Book citation for the Charlotte Zolotow Award. His picture book biography, *Sequoyah: The Man Who Gave His People Writing*, was named a *School Library Journal* Best Book.

SELECTED WORKS WRITTEN AND ILLUSTRATED: *The Cloudmakers*, 1996; *When Silver Needles Swam, the Story of Tutu's Quilt, ke kui ihe o tutu*, illus. by Leslie Lang, 1998; *The Island-below-the-Star*, 1998; *Seeker of Knowledge: The Man Who Deciphered Egyptian Hieroglyphs*, 2000; *Traveling Man: The Journey of Ibn Battuta, 1325–1354*, 2001; *Ka-hala-o-puna, ka u'i o Mānoa: The Beauty of Mānoa*, 2001; *There's a Monster in the Alphabet*, 2002; *Nine Animals and the Well*, 2003; *Calabash Cat and His Amazing Journey*, 2003; *Dog-of-the-Sea-Waves*, 2004; *Sequoyah: The Man Who Gave His People Writing*, 2004.

SUGGESTED READING: *Contemporary Authors*, vol. 188, 2001; *Something About the Author*, vol. 116, 2000.

Pam Muñoz Ryan

December 25, 1951–

" As a schoolgirl, I never kept a journal, made a book in class, or had an author visit my school. Curriculum was different then, and I never knew that a writer was something I could be someday. People ask me, 'Did you write as a child?' and the answer is, 'Not exactly.' But I could imagine just about anything. I was a benevolent queen, an explorer, or a doctor saving people from precarious deaths. It never occurred to me to write a story on paper, but I pretended many, right in my own backyard in Bakersfield, California.

"My background is an ethnic smorgasbord: Spanish, Mexican, Basque, Italian, and Oklahoman. When I was with one grandmother, I ate enchiladas, rice, and beans. When I was with the other, I ate black-eyed peas, fried okra, and peach cobblers. I spent a lot of time at my Mexican grandmother's house where there weren't many toys, so I often had to draw on my own curiosity and resources to entertain myself. She did have an old, weathered line-up of encyclopedias. I would tip each volume out of its space and look at the top of the book to see if there was a section printed in color. If I saw the definitive stripe, I'd take it out and go to that spot in the book. I studied the illustrated anatomy pages with the plastic overlays and the botanical plates that were pretty but not enticing to me. Once I found the illustrated Greek myths, however, I never went any farther. Looking back, I now realize how those stories were riddled with violence and torment. Prometheus's liver was eaten by an eagle. Echo was destined to never speak for herself but to only repeat the words of others. Pan became the cause of sudden unexplained anxiety. And glorious Pandora unleashed the world's misery. Horrible. Frightening. How I loved them!

"When I was in the fifth grade, my family moved across town. I was the new kid at school who didn't fit in, and that's when I discovered the East Bakersfield branch library. It became my refuge. There I could get out of myself and my immediate situation and, even better, read in air-conditioning. Books took me away, temporarily, from tallness, big feet, hot weather, cold weather, younger sisters, and a town that a late-night talk show host called, 'The armpit of the world.' (It wasn't.) When I read, I felt privy to the story. I felt a sense of ownership over what I was reading because I was reading for the love and sake of the book and nothing more. I've often wondered if the reason I have remained a book lover is because my early reading experiences were so joyful and un-choreographed.

"In junior high school, I joined the staff of the newspaper and wrote stories about sports events. The next year, I became the editor of the *Washington Bee*. I wish I could tell you that this was an incredible literary experience, but all I remember was getting out of class to run copies on the mimeograph machine in the school office. I also wish that I could report that I continued with journalism or creative writing in high school, but I didn't. Instead, I discovered football games, high school dances, and all the trappings of being a teenager. As I approached college, I looked away instead

Courtesy of Bill Keanne, Keanne Studios

of within. I wanted to be somewhere else, anywhere but Bakersfield, California. It wasn't until years later that I looked within, examined my beginnings and belongings, and began to write.

"I was married and a mom with four young children when I went back to school to get my master's degree in education. After reading some of my assignments, a professor asked me if I'd ever done any professional writing. The seed was planted, so that when a friend asked me to help her write a book for adults, I didn't hesitate, and after that I knew what I wanted to do when I grew up. I wanted to write for children.

"The most wonderful thing about writing has been that I can 'try on' many lives that might be different from my own. When I write, I can be as determined as Charlotte in *Riding Freedom*, as adventurous as Eleanor Roosevelt and Amelia Earhart in *Amelia and Eleanor Go for a Ride*, and as courageous as Marian Anderson in *When Marian Sang*. Or even as remarkable as my own grandmother, Esperanza, in *Esperanza Rising*, which is based loosely on her riches-to-rags story. Part of the enchantment of writing (and reading, too) is the well of strengths, weaknesses, and idiosyncrasies that I can sample and then keep, discard, or consider for my characters, and ultimately for myself. Today I write full time. I live in north San Diego County near the Pacific Ocean with my husband. We have four children and two dogs."

❁   ❁   ❁

"When I was with one grandmother, I ate enchiladas, rice, and beans. When I was with the other, I ate black-eyed peas, fried okra, and peach cobblers."

Pam Muñoz was born and raised in Bakersfield, in California's San Joaquin Valley, and grew up with a large extended family nearby. She graduated from San Diego State University with a bachelor's degree in 1974 and in 1975 married James Ryan. While raising their four children—Marcy, Anne, Matthew, and Tyler—she returned to San Diego State for graduate work, receiving her master's degree in 1991.

Pam Muñoz Ryan's grandparents on her mother's side came to the United States from Mexico in the 1930s, and it is her grandmother, Esperanza Ortega, on whose life she based the story in her award-winning novel, *Esperanza Rising*. The real Esperanza did grow up on a large ranch in Aguascalientes, Mexico, with servants and great wealth. Esperanza fell in love with her father's mechanic, who was the model for Miguel in the story. They married and moved to the United States, to Arvin, California, where they lived in the Mexican camp. Ryan made the character younger in the story as she was writing for a young audience. *Esperanza Rising* was awarded the Pura Belpré Medal and the Jane Addams Peace Award as well as being named one of the top 10 of ALA's Best Books for Young Adults and a Notable Social Studies Trade Book for Young People.

Some of the subjects Ryan has chosen for her historical books are well known, but others are less familiar. Her novel based on the life of Charlotte Parkhurst, *Riding Freedom*, which won the California Young Reader Medal and the Willa Cather Award, recounts the story of a young woman who lived disguised as a man and cast her ballot 50 years before women gained the right to vote. Ryan's picture books featuring Eleanor Roosevelt, Amelia Earhart, and Marian Anderson have also received many awards. Three of Ryan's books have been named ALA Notable Children's Books—*Mice and Beans*, *Amelia and Eleanor Go for a Ride*, and *When Marian Sang*. *Amelia and Eleanor Go for a Ride* was an ABA Pick of the Lists, named an IRA Teachers' Choice, and one of the New York Public Library's 100 Titles for Reading and Sharing; it was also named a Notable Trade Book in the Field of Social Studies. When *Marian Sang* was an Honor Book for the Robert F. Sibert Award for informational books, a *Booklist* Editors' Choice, and one of *School Library Journal's* Best Books of 2002.

SELECTED WORKS: *The Flag We Love*, illus. by Ralph Masiello, 1996; *The Crayon Counting Book*, 1996; *A Pinky Is a Baby Mouse: And Other Baby Animal Names*, illus. by Diane De Groat, 1997; *California Here We Come!*, illus. by Kay Salem, 1997; *One Hundred Is a Family*, illus. by Benrei Huang, 1998; *Riding Freedom*, illus. by Brian Selznick, 1998; *Amelia and Eleanor Go for a Ride: Based on a True Story*, illus. by Brian Selznick, 1999; *Esperanza Rising*, 2000; *Hello Ocean*, illus. by Mark Astrella, 2001; *Mice and Beans*, illus. by Joe Cepeda, 2001; *Mud Is Cake*, illus. by David M. McPhail, 2002; *When Marian Sang: The True Recital of Marian Anderson*, illus. by Brian Selznick, 2002; *How Do You Raise a Raisin*, illus. by Craig McFarland Brown, 2003; *Becoming Naomi León*, 2004.

SUGGESTED READING: "2002 Pura Belpré Acceptance Speech," *Journal of Youth Services in Libraries*, Summer 2002.

Courtesy of Scholastic Press

"I was born in St. Paul, Minnesota, and lived there until I was five years old, when my family moved to Moline, Illinois (another city along the Mississippi River). During my pre-teen years, I spent much of my time out-of-doors and developed a keen interest in wild and domestic animals. My mother was very relaxed about the number of stray dogs, baby birds, injured owls, squirrels, and rabbits that I brought home to nurture. During my youth, children had more freedom to roam about on their own than they do today. I loved to hike by myself, walk right out of town to the Rock River—a tributary that feeds into the Mississippi. Meandering along its banks, I pretended to be an Indian child, a member of Black Hawk's tribe. The Black Hawk State Park and Museum (which contains the tribe's artifacts) is situated beside the river, and this inspired my imagination. Every summer my family traveled to northern Wisconsin, where we had a cabin on a lake. There my interest in wildlife was heightened by the presence of loons, deer, skunks, snapping turtles, eagles, and even wolves.

Hope Ryden

"In the fifth grade I began writing poems about the natural world, and my teacher encouraged this effort. She permitted me to summarize geography lessons in verse rather than answer the standard questions at the end of every chapter. She even wrote one of my poems on the blackboard and had my classmates copy it. This did not make me popular, and I learned from that experience to keep my poetry a secret.

"In due course, I graduated from Moline High School and attended Augustana College and the University of Iowa, where I earned a B.A. degree. After graduation, I moved to New York City and took courses in photography in the New School for Social Research. I also took graduate courses in experimental psychology at Columbia University. This latter study was interrupted by an opportunity to travel, and I visited countries in Western Europe, Africa, and parts of Asia and South America. During that period of my life, I filed an occasional travel story with a newspaper syndicate, and upon returning to New York, I became a documentary filmmaker. As such, I wrote, directed, and produced films on many subjects, first for Drew Associates, and later for the CBS and ABC networks. My favorite film was made in Surinam, South America, and was named *Operation Gwamba*. It documented the rescue of hundreds of wild animals from a flooded jungle. While making that film, I also helped in the rescue operation itself, and in the rehabilitation of the injured animals we kept in our jungle camp.

Courtesy of Vito Forelli

"A few years later, I made another film on animals. It was a short news report on wild horses, and the subject so intrigued me that I left my staff job at ABC Evening News to research and photograph mustangs in the West in order to write a book about them. I found that experience so fulfilling that I never again returned to my staff job as a full-time film producer but continued to study animals in the wild. Watching animals is what I was born to do. After the publication of my first book on wild horses (for adult readers), I set off to study coyotes. The National Geographic Society helped finance both my horse and my coyote ventures and then published my photos and findings in their magazine. After coyotes, I went looking for bobcats, then eagles, then key deer, then beavers, and so on and on.

"Since then, I have published 23 books—five for adult readers and 18 for children, with two more works now in progress. When people ask me what I plan to do next, I can't be specific. All I know is that something will capture my attention and I will not be able to do otherwise than follow my bliss."

❁ ❁ ❁

Hope Ryden's field research and study of animals in the wild has taken her to many remote places for long stretches of time: The Pryor Mountains Wild Horse Range in Montana, the Sonora Desert in Arizona, and Wyoming's Yellowstone Park are just a few of the wilderness areas she has trekked. It was her groundbreaking book for adults, *America's Last Wild Horses*, published in 1970, that started her on a career devoted to tracking, photographing, and writing about animals in the wild; this work was reissued in a 30th anniversary edition, a testament to its enduring impact. A version for younger readers, *Wild Horses I Have Known*, was named a *Booklist* Editors' Choice and a Junior Library Guild selection.

A lifelong interest in wild canines prompted Ryden to spend two and a half years in the field tracking and studying coyotes, an endeavor that led to her adult book *God's Dog*, as well as *The Wild Pups: The True Story of a Coyote Family* for younger readers. She has published books for both adults and children on bobcats, beavers, red squirrels, and bald eagles. Her photographic study of an endangered species, *The Little Deer of the Florida Keys*, was named an ALA Notable Children's Book as well as an Outstanding Science Trade Book and a Notable Children's Trade Book in the Field of Social Studies. Equally adept at writing fiction, Ryden has also drawn on her experiences to publish an adventure story, *Wild Horse Summer*, which has been translated into several other languages. Her intense concern for animals in the wild led her to research wildlife rescue and to explore that and related issues in a fictional story for children, *Backyard Rescue*, as well as a nonfiction book, *Out of the Wild: The Story of Domesticated Animals*. *Backyard Rescue* received both the Young Hoosier Book Award in Indiana and the Sunshine State Young Readers Award in Florida. For the very young Ryden has created an alphabet book, *ABC of Crawlers and Flyers*, with blown-up, colorful photos of all sorts of common backyard insects. All of Ryden's book are illustrated with her own remarkable photographs.

Ryden's work has garnered many awards and support from prestigious organizations, such as the National Geographic Society. In 1979 she was named Humanitarian of the Year by the American Horse Protection Association; in 1981 she received the Joseph Wood Krutch Award from the Humane Society of the United States; and in 2002 she was presented with an Art and Literary Award by the New York State Outdoor Education Association. Her latest title, *Wildflowers Around the Year*, truly a book for all ages, was named an Outstanding Science Trade Book for Children as well as being included on New York Public Library's Books for the Teen Age list. A prize-winning journalist, photographer, and filmmaker, Hope Ryden has published numerous articles about animals and their habitats in periodicals

"My mother was very relaxed about the number of stray dogs, baby birds, injured owls, squirrels, and rabbits that I brought home to nurture."

Courtesy of Clarion Books

ranging from *Smithsonian* to *Science Digest* to *Ranger Rick*. She and her husband divide their time between New York City and Wolf Lake, in upstate New York.

SELECTED WORKS WRITTEN FOR ADULTS: *America's Last Wild Horses*, 1970, reissued 1999; *Mustangs: A Return to the Wild*, 1972; *God's Dog: A Celebration of the North American Coyote*, 1979; *Bobcat Year*, 1981; *Lily Pond: Four Years with a Family of Beavers*, 1989.

SELECTED WORKS WRITTEN FOR YOUNG READERS: *The Wild Colt: The Life of a Young Mustang*, 1972; *The Wild Pups: The True Story of a Coyote Family*, 1975; *Bobcat*, 1983; *America's Bald Eagle*, 1985; *Little Deer of the Florida Keys*, 1986; *The Beaver*, 1986; *Wild Animals of America ABC*, 1988; *Wild Animals of Africa ABC*, 1989; *The Raggedy Red Squirrel*, 1992; *Your Cat's Wild Cousins*, 1992; *Backyard Rescue*, illus. by Ted Rand, 1994; *Your Dog's Wild Cousins*, 1994; *Joey: The Story of a Baby Kangaroo*, 1994; *Out of the Wild: The Story of Domesticated Animals*, 1995; *ABC of Crawlers and Flyers*, 1996; *Wild Horse Summer*, 1997; *Wild Horses I Have Known*, 1999; *Wildflowers Around the Year*, 2001.

SUGGESTED READING: *Contemporary Authors*, New Revision Series, vol. 59, 1998; *Something About the Author*, vol. 91, 1997.

"When I was five years old I knew that I wanted to be an artist. Like most children, I loved to draw and color. But unlike many, I looked at my work seriously as a career choice, even though it would be almost 40 years before it could become my full-time profession, coupled with my writing. I don't have a clear memory of when writing caught hold of me as well, but I did have my first column in my junior high school newspaper, and I also wrote for the school paper in high school.

"I was born in Los Angeles, California, and first lived in the Bronx, New York, when I was two years old. At six years old I moved with my family back to Los Angeles, where if asked, I would answer that I was from New York, with my very thick accent. I was very disappointed when my mother busted my exotic bubble by telling me that I was actually born in Los Angeles. At 18, another move, and I was back in New York again until the age of 23. So I say that I spent my wonder years of growth in New York, two to six and 18 to 23. In fact, I even sold my first commissioned painting in New York at the age of 20, and many commissions followed for apartments, homes, and offices. Most of these commissions came directly from people on my full-time job, as accounts-receivable clerk for a mortgage insurance company. Our offices were directly across the street from St. Patrick's Cathedral in Manhattan.

"Those first paintings ranged from tremendous abstracts to small impressionistic paintings of French landscapes. Now why would this make sense? Well, my all-time favorite classic movie was, and still is, *Moulin Rouge*. The movie was primarily about the artist Henri de Toulouse-Lautrec and was one of the first technicolor films ever made. This movie made me determined to, in my lifetime, take care of myself as an artist and take good care of my health, so that I would live well past my thirties (Toulouse-Lautrec and Van Gogh both died young).

"I'm a self-taught artist, and I've had jobs that include accounting, publicity and promotion for record companies, advertising, modeling, and acting, as well as my own tax preparation and consulting company. All of these jobs have played a significant role in helping me to manage my own art business, Atelier SAINT JAMES. I have had the opportunity, so far, to write and/or illustrate 13 children's picture books, illustrate three children's activity books, write several books of poetry and prose, a cookbook, and a gift book. I've been fortunate enough to have

Courtesy of Leroy Hamilton

Synthia Saint James

February 11, 1949–

been commissioned to design a 150-foot ceramic tile mural for an airport and six large (9 x 4 foot) elevator doors for an office complex, etched into metal. I'm hoping soon to have the opportunity to design stained glass windows or doors. I also license some of my art images for merchandise, such as note cards, calendars, prints, and posters.

"I'm working on other book projects as well: more poetry and affirmations, short stories, and who knows, I may have a novel or two in me. I'm also a keynote speaker, and I conduct seminars, in addition to my many exhibitions and continued painting schedule. As for other pleasures in my life, I love reading good books, traveling and experiencing other cultures of the world. Both reading and travel have given me great inspiration for my work as well as for my love of life and friends and for the gifts of sharing. The islands of Tahiti, St. Lucia, St. Martin, and Fiji are some of my favorite places to indulge in relaxation and nature. My favorite feline friend is Kiku Saint James, a constant companion when I'm at home. She helps me work."

Courtesy of Holiday House

✿ ✿ ✿

Synthia Saint James's list of credits is an impressive and varied one. Her distinctive and colorful art has graced the walls of airports, the dust jackets of adult books, greeting cards, postage stamps, galleries, and private collections in the United States and abroad. The award-winning U.S. postage stamp she designed to honor the celebration of Kwanzaa has been reissued, as postal rates have increased, and is many people's favorite holiday stamp. Her commissioned painting entitled *In Unity* honors the 12 black firefighters lost in the World Trade Center terrorist attacks of September 11, 2001.

Refecting her many interests, from folklore and holidays to music and personal growth, Saint James's picture books for children have been widely acclaimed for their bold colors, joyful feeling, and strong affirmation. *Sunday*, a celebration of family life that she both wrote and illustrated, was named a Parents' Choice Silver Honor Book in 1996. *Neeny Coming . . . Neeny Going*, a family story by Karen English of changing times and clashing cultures, received a Coretta Scott King Illustrator Honor the following year. Her bright and lively paintings for *To Dinner, for Dinner*, Tololwa Mollel's Tanzanian folktale, won an Oppenheim Gold Award. This tale of Juhudi the rabbit outwitting a predatory leopard by appealing to his vanity was also named a Notable Social Studies Trade Book for Young People.

In recognition of her multiple talents, Saint James has received a YWCA Silver Achievement Award in the Creative Arts, a Women of Vision Award from Black Women Lawyers, Inc., and a NAPPA Gold Award from the National Association of Parenting Publications for her song, "Happy, Happy Kwanzaa." Synthia Saint James maintains her studio, Atelier SAINT JAMES, in Los Angeles and continues to explore new media and venues for the artistic expression of positive values and creative teaching.

SELECTED WORKS WRITTEN AND ILLUSTRATED: *Gifts of Kwanzaa*, 1994; *Sunday*, 1996; *It's Kwanzaa Time*, 2001.

SELECTED WORKS ILLUSTRATED: *Tukama Tootles the Flute*, by Phillis Gershator, 1994; *Snow on Snow on Snow*, by Cheryl Chapman, 1994; *How Mr. Monkey Saw the Whole World*, by Walter Dean Myers, 1996; *Neeny Coming . . . Neeny Going*, by Karen English, 1996; *Greetings, Sun*, by Phillis and David Gershator, 1998; *No Mirrors in My Nana's House*, by Ysaye Barnwell, 1999; *Girls Together*, by Sherley Anne Williams, 1999; *Hallelujah!: A Christmas Celebration*, by W. Nikola-Lisa, 2000; *To Dinner, for Dinner*, by Tololwa M. Mollel, 2000; *Alphabet Affirmations*, by Bunny Hull, 2000; *Peace in Our Land*, by Bunny Hull, 2002; *Enduring Wisdom: Sayings from Native Americans*, sel. by Virginia Driving Hawk Sneve, 2003.

SUGGESTED READING: *Something About the Author*, vol. 84, 1996.

Enrique O. Sánchez

(En-REE-kay SAN-chez)

March 24, 1942–

"I was born in Santo Domingo, Dominican Republic, where my father was director of the Columbus Museum and my mother was a music teacher. I had a sister who grew up to be a concert pianist.

"From an early age, I loved to draw the cathedral and other Spanish colonial buildings in the city where I lived. I especially enjoyed drawing the 500-year-old house I was raised in next door to my uncle, the cardinal of Santo Domingo. I studied at the Art Lyceum and the Institute of Bellas Artes, then studied architecture at Santo Domingo University and painted backdrops for theatrical and television productions.

"In 1962 I moved to New York to escape the political turmoil in the Dominican Republic and to further my education in art. In New York, I worked in many different aspects of the art world, and in 1982 I began to illustrate children's books.

"I like to illustrate stories that relate to my own personal experiences; not the same situations, of course, but stories that stimulate similar feelings. My memories may influence the color scheme or the way I pose a character. Remembered feelings may affect the way I draw a facial expression, the tilt of a head or a hand. Some of those experiences are unhappy ones. I remember the anguish I felt when I was separated from my elderly grandfather in a crowd while I was caring for him. I recall my fingers trembling with nervousness while playing clarinet solos in school recitals. I get flashbacks of how lonely I was when I moved far away to the United States and left my family and friends behind. I still feel sadness over my father's sudden and tragic death.

"Of course it goes without saying, my happy memories are important influences, too. I draw on the sweet days when my wife, Joan, and I first met and how incredibly happy I was when she first told me that she loved me. I remember my extreme delight when I saw our son, Aron, being born. All my memories of him growing up go into the children I illustrate. The beauty we have found in our lives in Maine and Vermont comes out in my art as well. And last, but not least, is all the joy I have had with the dogs of my life: Diana, Snejinka, Sabrina, Sienna, Misha, and Keeko."

❊   ❊   ❊

Courtesy of Joan Sanchez

Enrique O. Sánchez

Enrique O. Sánchez is a multifaceted artist whose talent has been seen in many different venues. After immigrating to the United States in 1962 he studied at the Pels School of Art, where he later taught painting and illustration. He also took courses at the Lester Polakoff School of Scenic Design and the Germain and RCA Schools for film and television design. In addition to his painting and illustration work, he has created storyboards, done animation for film and television, and worked as a theatrical designer and scenic painter. He was also a graphic designer for the *Sesame Street* television program in its early years.

The first children's book illustrated by Enrique Sánchez received wide acclaim: *Abuela's Weave* was named a Notable Book by *Smithsonian* magazine, received an Honor citation from Parents' Choice, and was included in the Cooperative Children's Book Center Choices list. *Confetti* and *When This World Was New* were also named CCBC Choices, and *Confetti* was included on the list of Notable Books for a Global Society by the International Reading Association. Two titles—*Lupe and Me* and *A Is for the Americas*—have been chosen as Notable Children's Trade Books in the Field of Social Studies. In 1998, Enrique Sánchez received a Pura Belpré Honor Award for the illustrations in *The Golden Flower*, a Taino creation story from Puerto Rico. The glowing colors and warm relationships pictured in these books reflect the artist's love of his Latino origins as well as his adopted country.

In *When This World Was New* he perfectly captures the apprehension, confusion, and excitement of a child caught between two cultures, learning to adapt to his new environment.

Enrique and his wife, Joan, also an artist, moved to the coast of Maine in 1971 to seek a slower pace and to pursue his passion to paint exclusively. For many years they made their home on Mount Desert Island, where they lived off their artwork. There they raised their son, Aron, who is now an artist and musician in New York. In 2000, Enrique and Joan moved to Vermont's Northeast Kingdom, where he continues to paint and illustrate. His paintings are included in many private collections.

In their spare time Enrique and Joan enjoy cross-country skiing, snowshoeing, kayaking, and hiking. Their dogs—Misha, a vizsla, and Keeko, a springer spaniel—accompany them on all their outings. Another of Enrique's joys has always been playing percussion instruments with various jazz musician friends.

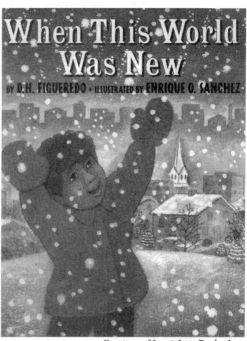

Courtesy of Lee & Low Books, Inc.

SELECTED WORKS: *Abuela's Weave*, by Omar S. Castañeda, 1993; *Amelia's Road*, by Linda Jacobs Altman, 1993; *Saturday Market*, by Patricia Grossman, 1994; *Maria Molina and the Days of the Dead*, by Kathleen Krull, 1994; *Lupe and Me*, by Elizabeth Spurr, 1995; *Golden Flower: A Taino Myth from Puerto Rico*, by Nina Jaffe, 1996; *Confetti: Poems for Children*, by Pat Mora, 1996; *Palampam Day*, by David and Phillis Gershator, 1997; *Big Enough/Bastante Grande*, by Ofelia Dumas Lachtman, 1998; *A Is for the Americas*, by Cynthia Chin-Lee and Terri de la Peña, 1999; *When This World Was New*, by D. H. Figueredo, 1999; *Speak English for Us, Marisol!*, by Karen English, 2000; *Estella's Swap*, by Alexis O'Neill, 2002.

"When I was a little girl, I picked flowers, collected leaves, watched bugs, read books, and wrote little poems and stories. Today I do the same thing, but now it's part of my job. I am a full-time author, writing children's books, mostly about nature.

"I was born in Greenville, South Carolina. I graduated from Duke University with a degree in biology, focused on primatology. I worked at the National Wildlife Federation and the National Geographic Society. Eventually, I became a freelance author. Recently I went back to school to earn my master's in fine

April Pulley Sayre

April 11, 1966–

arts in creative writing from Vermont College. I love my job. I like researching: reading books and magazines, calling people on the phone, and visiting museums, parks, and aquariums. The writing is satisfying, too. Recently I've been doing a lot of school visits, which has really enriched my life and my writing. Kids love animals, so we always have something to talk about. We also make a bit of noise because my area of special interest is sound—animal calls, in particular.

"Those animal sounds kept cropping up in my books, such as *Crocodile Listens* and *Army Ant Parade*. So I finally wrote a middle grade science book about the subject: *Secrets of Sound: Studying the Calls and Songs of Whales, Elephants, and Birds.* I loved interviewing the scientists for that book. The scientists

Courtesy of Harriet Hamblin

were so passionate about their work, so engaged in their lives. It doesn't matter whether someone studies whales or houseflies. If they love their subject, it spills over into their voice and you can hear their joy. Sound is important in other parts of my life too. My husband is an ecologist, birder, and native plant expert. So we travel to rain forests, deserts, seashores, and other wild areas. We lead ecotours. When my husband and I walk into a rain forest, we find a lot of animals by sound. We listen for barks, hoots, clicks, buzzes, scratching, and other signs that creatures are there. We point out the animals, and it seems as if we found them by magic. But really, we can find them because we have trained ourselves to listen. And we have begun to learn the meaning of sounds, and where certain kinds of animals live.

"Our trips to Ecuador, Madagascar, Panama, Alaska, Arizona, and other places are also the source of some of my books. We first saw army ant swarms in Panama. We hiked through a misty rain forest. When I saw an antbird, with its blue-ringed eyes, my heart squeezed. I was nervous and excited. For seven years I had been researching about these creatures, and finally I was seeing them! In my book *Army Ant Parade*, I tried to let readers know how it feels to see this marvelous natural event. *Dig, Wait, Listen: A Desert Toad's Tale* began in the desert near Tucson, Arizona. We visited the desert after rain and saw puddles full of spadefoot toad tadpoles. We heard the toads calling in the desert. How could toads, who need water, survive in a desert year-round? I knew this was a story that needed to be told.

"Not all of my work is about nature. I love being silly and making puns. I got to do that in the book *Noodle Man: The Pasta Superhero*, which began as a silly conversation after a spaghetti dinner. I like to write both fiction and nonfiction. When I am writing, I feel a rush of excitement as the words pour onto the page. At times, all I have to do is be there, to catch them as they fall. But not all of my writing pours out so smoothly. Sometimes, writing is more like playing with cookie dough. I pick up the words and pluck them, shape them, mash them, and rearrange them until they read just right. There are also times when writing is just plain hard work. Finding the right word can be like trying to pick up a rice grain with your toes.

"I hope to keep writing and exploring the natural world. I've been pecked on the head by an Arctic tern, pooped on by a toad, swarmed by army ants, peed on by a lemur, charged by a sea lion, and rejected by countless editors. But that hasn't made me want to stop exploring or writing. I hope that everyone out there who wants to write will hug that dream hard and keep going even through the tough times. It's worth it. By writing you can share something you care about with the rest of the world."

❊   ❊   ❊

A woman whose passion for nature and for words makes her the ideal author of books filled with fascinating facts for young people, April Pulley Sayre has been investigating the natural world with particular delight since she was born. Daughter of David Clarence Pulley, a university professor, and Elizabeth Richardson, an entrepreneur, Sayre received a B.A. from Duke University in 1987 and an M.F.A. in creative writing from Vermont College in 2000. After an internship at the National Geographic Society in 1988, Sayre worked as an associate editor of school programs for the National Wildlife Federation from 1988 to 1991. She married Jeffrey Peter Sayre, an ecologist and native plant expert, in 1989.

The author of over 50 books, plus poems, articles, and stories published in *Ranger Rick* and other magazines, Sayre pleases children and reviewers alike with her precise wording and clear science. Her books convey her own excitement about each subject while her style combines scientific knowledge with creative, upbeat writing. *If You Should Hear a Honey Guide* was a *School Library Journal* Best Book, a *Smithsonian* Notable Book for Children, and a Notable Children's Trade Book in the Field of Social Studies. *Secrets of Sound* was a *Booklist* Editors' Choice, and *Splish Splash* was named an IRA/CBC Children's Choice title. *Home at Last* and *Dig, Wait, Listen* were both designated Outstanding Science Trade Books for Children. *One Is a Snail, Ten Is a Crab*, which she co-authored with her husband, was named an ALA Notable Children's Book in 2004.

"I've been pecked on the head by an Arctic tern, pooped on by a toad, swarmed by army ants, peed on by a lemur, charged by a sea lion, and rejected by countless editors. But that hasn't made me want to stop exploring or writing."

Courtesy of Candlewick Press

Sayre has also written science books in series that are highly praised: for middle school students in the Seven Continents series and Exploring Earth's Biomes; and for primary grades in the Our Amazing Continents series, which includes *G'Day Australia* and *Hooray for Antarctica*. Members of the National Audubon Society, the Nature Conservancy, and the American Birding Association, Sayre and her husband are avid birders and inveterate travelers. Together they have run ecotours to Panama's rain forest and other regions. They collaborated on a book for adults about hummingbirds, and recently they have started collaborating on books for children.

SELECTED WORKS: *If You Should Hear a Honey Guide*, illus. by S. D. Schindler, 1995; *Hummingbirds: The Sun Catchers*, with Jeff Sayre, 1996; *Put on Some Antlers and Walk Like a Moose: How Scientists Find, Follow, and Study Wild Animals*, 1997; *Temperate Deciduous Forest*, 1997; *Desert*, 1997; *Tundra*, 1997; *Grassland*, 1997; *Seashore*, 1997; *Taiga*, 1997; *Ocean*, 1997; *River and Stream*, 1997; *Wetland*, 1997; *Coral Reef*, 1997; *Lake and Pond*, 1997; *Endangered Birds of North America*, 1997; *Tropical Rain Forest*, 1997; *Home at Last: A Song of Migration*, illus. by Alix Berenzy, 1998; *North America*, 1998; *Europe*, 1998; *Australia*, 1998; *Antarctica*, 1998; *South America*, 1999; *Africa*, 1999; *Asia*, 1999; *The Seven Continents*, 2000; *Turtle, Turtle, Watch Out!*, illus. by Lee Christiansen, 2000; *Splish! Splash! Animal Baths*, 2000; *El Niño and La Niña: Weather in the Headlines*, 2000; *Inside Government*, 2000; *Dig, Wait, Listen: A Desert Toad's Tale*, illus. by Barbara Bash, 2001; *It's My City!: A Singing Map*, illus. by Denis Roche, 2001; *The Hungry Hummingbird*, illus. by Gay W. Holland, 2001; *Crocodile Listens*, photos. by Joellen McAllister Stammen, 2001; *Noodle Man: The Pasta Superhero*, illus. by Stephen Costanza, 2002; *Shadows*, illus. by Harvey Stevenson, 2002; *Secrets of Sound: Studying the Calls of Whales, Elephants, and Birds*, 2002; *Army Ant Parade*, illus. by Rick Chrustowski, 2002; *Greetings, Asia*, 2003; *South America, Surprise*, 2003; *Welcome to North America*, 2003; *G'Day, Australia*, 2003; *Tropical Rain Forest*, 2003; *Good Morning, Africa*, 2003; *Hello, Europe*, 2003; *Hooray for Antarctica*, 2003; *One Is a Snail, Ten Is a Crab*, with Jeff Sayre, illus. by Randy Cecil, 2003; *Trout, Trout, Trout!: A Fish Chant*, illus. by Trip Park, 2004.

SUGGESTED READING: *Contemporary Authors*, vol. 152, 1997; *Something About the Author*, vol. 88, 1997. Periodicals—"Rising Star: April Pulley Sayre," *Bulletin of the Center for Children's Books*, April 2002.

"So I guess it's my grandmother's fault. Well, actually it's my grandmother's maid's fault. At least that's what my family says. When I was little and we visited my grandmother, her maid, Bertie, would give me tinfoil to keep me out of trouble. She showed me that you can sculpt with tinfoil by bending it and twisting it, and soon I was making tinfoil flowers and dinosaurs and the hours went by and I was hooked. I suppose she was my first art teacher.

"I can't remember a time when I was not drawing and making things. In kindergarten, the teacher used to draw our assignments on big pieces of paper in the front of the class and we would have to copy the drawings onto our own papers. I clearly remember drawing a seal with a ball on its nose and, best of all, I remember all the other kids gathering around me to see what a good job I had done. (I recently found my kindergarten report card and it says right on the bottom: 'Brian is a good artist.') Of course, I also remember them gathering around me because I was the only kid who could touch his eyeball. That was later though, in fifth grade, and by that time I was pretty well established as the class artist.

Courtesy of Scholastics, Inc.

Brian O. Selznick

July 14, 1966–

"I think being an artist kept me from being beaten up sometimes, because everyone, even the bullies, respected the fact that I could draw. I painted a mural on our fifth grade classroom wall, a dinosaur with circles in his body representing each of the topics we studied in school. It was a big hit. That was around the same time that I got glasses and realized that the world was far less fuzzy than I had thought. The first thing I saw when I came home with my new glasses was my little brother's red plastic elephant in the dining room. I'll never forget how sharp and clear and beautiful it was.

"I've been lucky because I had good art teachers who have been very supportive. I even had the first one-man art show ever held at my junior high school. By high school I was painting skulls on the football helmets of all the tough kids and taking classes outside of school with a wonderful artist named Eileen Raucher-Sutton. She taught me how to paint and encouraged me to really look at things. I still remember the first thing she ever taught me . . . . I showed her a pastel drawing I had done of an Eskimo woman and she pointed out that I had not drawn any reflections in the eyes. When I added those two little white dots, the whole face came to life. I think of her every time I draw those reflections in people's eyes.

"I was often told that I should go into children's books when I was in high school, which I think is why I decided not to go into children's books. Off I went to Rhode Island School of Design, where lots of great children's book illustrators teach, and what did I do? I didn't take classes with any of them. It wasn't until after I had graduated that I decided to become an illustrator. Oy! How could I learn about children's books now that I was out of school? A very smart friend suggested I get a job at a children's bookstore, and I did just that at what turned out to be one of the best children's bookstores in the country—Eeyore's Books for Children in New York City. The manager of the store took me under his wing and sent me home every night with bags of his favorite books. Working with him became my real education in children's books. My first book was published because of Eeyore's, and many of the people whom I worked with at that store (including Steve Geck, the manager) are now colleagues in the children's book publishing world. The influence of Eeyore's is a part of my life every day, and though I don't know what happened to my grandmother's maid who started it all, as my father recently said, 'Goodnight Bertie, wherever you are!' "

❋   ❋   ❋

Brian Selznick was born and raised in New Jersey and graduated from East Brunswick High School. He earned his bachelor's degree in illustration from the Rhode Island School of Design in 1988. From 1989 to 1992 he sold books and painted window displays for Eeyore's Books for Children in New York City before becoming a full-time artist and illustrator. He has also de-

---

"I think being an artist kept me from being beaten up sometimes, because everyone, even the bullies, respected the fact that I could draw."

---

signed theater sets and is a professional puppeteer. Occasionally his work in puppetry is related to his children's books, but often it is entirely separate, as when he performs in *Symphonie Fantastique* (an underwater abstract puppet show) and *Petrushka* (based on the ballet), both shows created by Basil Twist for an adult audience. In these shows he works with other puppeteers, dressed in black clothing and hoods, with puppets up to three feet tall. Selznick has also created his own puppetry pieces based on his work as an illustrator. He used the genre of toy theater to evoke the story of *The Dinosaurs of Waterhouse Hawkins*. The show takes place on an antique desk situated on a pile of dirt. The desk is covered with books and cabinets that open by themselves to reveal scenes from the history of paleontology and from Waterhouse's life. Selznick is the sole performer in this show, with the action timed carefully to music.

Courtesy of Scholastic Press

Brian Selznick's debut in children's books was auspicious and grew out of an art assignment at RISD. *The Houdini Box*, based on secrets the famous magician might have shared with a young fan, is an illustrated story that proved very popular with young readers and captured the 1993 Texas Bluebonnet Award. His illustrations for *Frindle,* Andrew Clements's extraordinarily successful novel, enhanced a story that captured many, many state-sponsored children's choice awards as well as a Christopher Medal, a Parents' Choice Award, and a *Horn Book* Fanfare citation.

Four of Selznick's books to date have been named ALA Notable Children's Books, including one illustrated novel—*The Doll People*, by Ann M. Martin and Laura Godwin—and three biographical picture books—*Amelia and Eleanor Go for a Ride* and *When Marian Sang*, both written by Pam Muñoz Ryan, and *The Dinosaurs of Waterhouse Hawkins*, written by Barbara Kerley. Selznick's richly saturated colors and dramatic rendering of scenes from Hawkins's 19th-century world earned him a Caldecott Honor Award in 2002. In many of his illustrations, Selznick's interest in the theater is evident, and especially in the life of this dinosaur impressario, whose flair for drama led him to host a dinner party for leading scientists inside his huge model of an Iguandodon.

Selznick and Kerley teamed again to create a compelling picture book biography of another important 19th-century figure in *Walt Whitman: Words for America*, which follows the poet through his early career and his compassionate work with soldiers during the Civil War. Selznick's evocative illustrations earned this title a citation as one of the *New York Times* Best Illustrated Books of 2004. In creating both picture books and longer illustrated stories, Brian Selznick has developed a fine ability to match art to text in works both fanciful and factual. He lives and works in Brooklyn, New York.

SELECTED WORKS WRITTEN AND ILLUSTRATED: *The Houdini Box*, 1991, reissued 2001; *The Robot King*, 1995; *The Boy of a Thousand Faces*, 2000.

SELECTED WORKS ILLUSTRATED: *Dollface Has a Party!*, by Pam Conrad, 1994; *Frindle*, by Andrew Clements, 1996; *The Boy Who Longed for a Lift*, by Norma Farber, 1997; *Riding Freedom*, by Pam Muñoz Ryan, 1998; *Amelia and Eleanor Go for a Ride*, by Pam Muñoz Ryan, 1999; *The Doll People*, by Ann M. Martin and Laura Godwin, 2000; *Barnyard Prayers*, by Laura Godwin, 2000; *The School Story*, by Andrew Clements, 2001; *The Dinosaurs of Waterhouse Hawkins*, by Barbara Kerley, 2001; *When Marian Sang: The True Recital of Marian Anderson*, by Pam Muñoz Ryan, 2002; *The Dulcimer Boy*, by Tor Seidler, 2002; *Wingwalker*, by Rosemary Wells, 2002; *The Meanest Doll in the World*, by Ann M. Martin and Laura Godwin, 2003; *Walt Whitman: Words for America*, by Barbara Kerley, 2004.

SUGGESTED READING: "From Scrapbook to Picture Book," *Book Links*, February/March 2002.

Barbara Seuling

(SOO-ling)

July 22, 1937–

"I grew up in the days of radio, when we would sit around the living room listening to stories. Some were mysteries, some were fairy tales, some were great dramas. I loved them all. I went to the movies, too, and the library, to take out all the books I could carry, so stories were very much a part of my childhood. It never occurred to me then that I might one day write stories of my own—but I drew pictures. People commented on my artistic skills, and so I thought of myself from a very early age as an artist. I was so happy to know I had this talent and became so identified with it that it wasn't until I was a grown woman that I entertained the thought of writing as well.

"I was born in Brooklyn and moved to the big city—New York—when I went to college. It was just a ride by subway across the river, but it was a huge new world, and I began exploring it, as well as exploring what I could do with my life. After several jobs—they were good, but I was bored—I invariably kept coming back to books, children's books in particular. This led to a job in publishing, where I worked in adult paperback reprints, then children's books. I wanted to learn more about illustrating children's books, but there were no courses available, so I took the next best thing: a course in writing children's books.

"With weekly writing assignments and lots of discussion about craft, I was bitten by the writing bug that had been lying dormant for years. I discovered that I could still draw, and perhaps illustrate, and I could write, too, although my confidence was pretty shaky at first. Fortunately, before I started sending out manuscripts, I wrote dozens of assignments and stories for my own amusement, all the time learning my craft.

"I continued to study writing, with Mina Lewiton, William Lipkind, Margaret Gabel, and others. Eventually, I found a couple of courses in illustrating with Robert Quackenbush and Caldecott winner Uri Shulevitz and took them both. With newfound skills and insights, I was lucky enough to illustrate my first books, and then to write one that I illustrated myself. I was still a full-time children's book editor, so I was totally immersed in the world I wanted for my own. I've been there ever since, loving what I do and the people I've met along the way.

Courtesy of Winnette Galsgow

"Today I have dozens of books behind me and, I hope, many new ones ahead. I often use my own childhood experiences in Brooklyn as a resource, but bring them into the present, because so much about growing up is common to children anywhere, in any time period. I have a strong sense of family, an appreciation of discovery through the eyes of a child, and a good sense of humor—all of which I hope are evident in the work that I do.

"When I'm not writing, I teach others what I know about the field of children's books and the craft of writing. Writing is a tough game. You're always having to prove yourself, and you can never take the next success for granted. Knowing that I can make the road a little easier for someone else coming along gives me pleasure. I will probably always be found somewhere around the edges of this wonderful profession."

❖   ❖   ❖

Author, illustrator, writing teacher, and consultant Barbara Seuling was born in the Bensonhurst section of Brooklyn, the daughter of Kaspar Joseph Seuling, a postman, and his wife, Helen Veronica. She attended Hunter College and Columbia University from 1955 to 1959, then took courses in writing and illustrating. As a children's book editor at Dell Publishing Company from 1965 to 1971, she helped establish the Yearling reprint line before moving on to work for several years at the J. B.

Lippincott Company. She has been a freelance writer and illustrator of children's books since 1975.

Seuling has taught courses in writing and illustrating for children at the Bank Street College of Education and the Center for the Arts in New York as well as the Institute of Children's Literature in West Redding, Connecticut. She also runs her own manuscript workshops in New York and Vermont. For several years she oversaw the annual conference of the Society of Children's Book Writers in New York City and has also served on its Board of Directors. In 2001 she traveled to Moscow on a grant and taught picture-book writing to students from 26 East European countries.

Always a lover of intriguing facts and humor, from the time she read *Ripley's Believe It or Not* as a child, Seuling developed her own Freaky Facts series, with intriguing titles such as *You Can't Eat Peanuts in Church and Other Little-Known Laws* and *You Can't Sneeze with Your Eyes Open and Other Freaky Facts About the Human Body*. Over the years she has continued that concept, accompanying the nuggets of information she researches with lighthearted illustrations. Deciding to retell and illustrate an old English folktale, *The Teeny Tiny Woman*, Seuling debuted in the picture book field with much praise for her writing, as well as her soft pencil drawings and hand-lettering, which earned an award from the American Institute of Graphic Artists. Her next picture book, *The Great Big Elephant and the Very Small Elephant*, executed in ink and watercolor, involved two friends as different as day and night who find a way to celebrate each other.

Seuling has written nonfiction about a wide variety of subjects as well as picture books and early readers. Her popular series about a boy named Robert (*Robert and the Weird & Wacky Facts* and similar titles) engages early readers with true-to-life third-grade woes and triumphs. Barbara Seuling divides her time between winters in Manhattan and summers in her cottage in southern Vermont.

> "With weekly writing assignments and lots of discussion about craft, I was bitten by the writing bug that had been lying dormant for years."

SELECTED WORKS WRITTEN AND ILLUSTRATED: *You Can't Eat Peanuts in Church and Other Little-Known Laws*, 1975; *The Teeny Tiny Woman: An Old English Ghost Story*, 1976; *The Loudest Screen Kiss and Other Little-Known Facts about the Movies*, 1976; *The Great Big Elephant and the Very Small Elephant*, 1977; *The Last Cow on the White House Lawn and Other Little-Known Facts About the Presidency*, 1978; *You Can't Count a Billion Dollars and Other Little-Known Facts About Money*, 1979; *Elephants Can't Jump and Other Freaky Facts about Animals*, 1984; *You Can't Sneeze with Your Eyes Open and Other Freaky Facts About the Human Body*, 1986.

SELECTED WORKS WRITTEN: *How to Write a Children's Book and Get It Published*, 1984, rev. and expanded, 1991 (for adults); *To Be a Writer: A Guide for Young People Who Want to Write and Publish*, 1997; *Winter Lullaby*, illus. by Greg

Newbold, 1998; *Drip! Drop! How Water Gets to Your Tap*, illus. by Nancy Tobin, 2000; *Spring Song*, illus. by Greg Newbold, 2001; *Robert and the Great Pepperoni*, illus. by Paul Brewer, 2001; *Robert and the Weird & Wacky Facts*, illus. by Paul Brewer, 2002; *From Head to Toe: The Amazing Human Body*, illus. by Edward Miller, 2002; *Robert and the Attack of the Giant Tarantula*, illus. by Paul Brewer; *Robert and the Back-to-School Special*, illus. by Paul Brewer, 2002; *Robert and the Lemming Problem*, illus. by Paul Brewer, 2003; *Whose House?*, illus. by Kay Chorao, 2004.

Courtesy of Harcourt, Inc.

SELECTED WORKS ILLUSTRATED: *That Barbara!* by Wilma Thompson, 1969; *Tarr of Belway Smith*, by Nan Hayden Agle, 1969; *Break a Leg!* by Stella Pevsner, 1969; *The Affair of the Rockerbye Baby*, by Antonia Barber, 1970; *Footsteps on the Stairs*, by Stella Pevsner, 1970; *The Ostrich Chase*, by Moses Howard, 1974; *Bembelman's Bakery*, by Melinda Green, 1978.

SUGGESTED READING: *Contemporary Authors*, vol. 52, 1996; *Something About the Author*, vol. 145, 2004; *Something About the Author Autobiography Series*, vol. 24, 1997. Periodicals—"Meet the Author," *Ladybug*, October 1996.

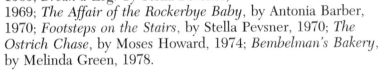

"I was born in Warsaw, Poland. When the Warsaw blitz occurred I was four years old. I still remember streets caving in, buildings burning, people carrying water from the Vistula. We fled Warsaw. Years of wandering followed. In 1947 we arrived in Paris. I was fascinated by the city, especially by the Quais de la Seine, where I spent countless hours browsing in the bookstalls. At that time I also developed a passion for films and comic books. I began drawing my own, and a friend wrote the words. At the age of 12 I won first prize in a drawing competition held among all the grammar schools in my district.

"In 1949 my parents, my baby brother, and I settled in Israel. From the age of 15 to 17 I went to high school at night and worked during the day at various jobs. I was apprentice to a rubber-stamp maker; then I worked as a house painter, a carpenter, and I issued dog licenses at Tel Aviv City Hall (where I also had time for reading and my first attempts at writing).

"It has been my great luck that my first art teacher was the great Israeli painter Yehezkel Streichman, who taught me oil painting when I was 15 years old. At that age I was the youngest to exhibit at the Tel Aviv Museum of Art in a drawing exhibition for artists under 35 years of age. Later I studied at the Art Insti-

Uri Shulevitz

February 27, 1935–

tute of Tel Aviv. Among my teachers was Marcel Janco, co-founder of the Dada movement. I studied watercolor with Avigdor Stematsky.

"In 1959 I came to New York to study painting at the Brooklyn Museum Art School with Reuben Tam. Later I studied at the Provincetown Workshop, in Provincetown, Massachusetts, with Leo Manso and Victor Candell. Last, but not least, was my teacher and friend, the painter Peter Hopkins, who taught me the techniques of the old masters.

"In 1963 *The Moon in My Room*, my first book (preceded by many unsatisfactory attempts) was published by Harper & Row. When it was suggested to me that I write my own book, my first reaction was that this was impossible, since I was not a writer and my English left a lot to be desired. 'Writing,' I later came to realize, has less to do with language than one might think. First, one has to have something to say. This may appear in one's mind in pictures, not necessarily in words, very much as in a film or comic strip. As I was to discover, the picture book is a medium in which words and pictures complement each other without repetition.

Courtesy of Mel Adelglass

"I've spent much time teaching and giving lectures throughout the United States. The most common question that my colleagues and I have been asked has been: 'Where do ideas come from?' My ideas have come from varied and unexpected sources, but they always have one thing in common—they're subjects or themes that I love. *One Monday Morning* was an elaboration and adaptation of a little French folk song I loved as a kid. One evening I thought I heard the sound of rain, and a series of words and images flooded my mind, which I jotted down; but when I looked out the window, the skies were clear—and there I had the idea for *Rain Rain Rivers* almost in its entirety. *Dawn* had its genesis in four lines of a 9th-century Chinese poem, followed by my own observation and experience of a sunrise by a lake in the country. *Snow* was born on a snowy day during a New York winter of 16 snowfalls. The idea came to me as I was looking out the window observing snowflakes falling gently on a dark roof across the street. More recently I've written stories based on my childhood memories.

"Contrary to common notions, the difficulty is not in getting ideas. I have notebooks full of story ideas. The difficulty lies in developing those ideas into books. I have been asked many times why my books look so different from each other. I believe that style and technique should be an organic outgrowth of the story. And since not all stories are alike, it stands to reason that books would look different from one another as well. *The Treasure* was done with pen and ink and watercolor, whereas *What Is a Wise Bird Like You Doing in a Silly Tale Like This?* with pen and ink, watercolor, colored pencils, and collage (mixed media).

"When I began making children's books and felt inexperienced, I wished there was a book to help and guide me. Later, when I taught others how to write and illustrate children's books, I missed not having such a book that could be used as a textbook in my workshops. And so I embarked on a journey of over 10 years to write the kind of book I wished I had when I began my career in children's books. The result was *Writing with Pictures*, a visual approach to creating picture books.

"One of the most moving and rewarding times of my career was when, following a talk I gave, a woman approached me and told me that she, her husband, and her young children were held hostage at the U.S. embassy in Tehran in a dark room, and what a comfort it was for their children to recite by heart the texts of my picture books *Dawn* and *Rain Rain Rivers* during those endless days as hostages.

"I have been fascinated by the concept of traveling, having covered many miles myself. In *The Moon in My Room*, my first book, a little boy 'travels' in his room, discovering the different worlds that make up his own. The journey theme has continued with *The Treasure*, in which a man travels far in search of a treasure only to discover it was all along in his own home. The journey culminates with my newest book, *The Travels of Benjamin of Tudela*, about the greatest Jewish traveler of the Middle Ages. Over 100 years before Marco Polo he was the first European to reveal the existence of a mysterious, faraway land called China. Thanks to a Guggenheim Fellowship, I was able to follow in Benjamin's footsteps a small part of the way from his native Tudela in northern Spain, through southern France, to Italy, Istanbul (Turkey), Jerusalem, and Cairo (Egypt).

"Now I no longer need to travel. My books in translation travel, on my behalf, far and wide."

"'Writing,' I later came to realize, has less to do with language than one might think. First, one has to have something to say. This may appear in one's mind in pictures, not necessarily in words, very much as in a film or comic strip."

❁ ❁ ❁

Uri Shulevitz's childhood was far from carefree, growing up in Warsaw during World War II when the city was being bombed by the German military. Memories from age four of a bomb crashing through the apartment building where he lived and of walking across a plank that bridged the abyss where the stairs had once been remain with him today, but they didn't overshadow his creative inclination in those days. The long journey to becoming an illustrator began when his artistic sensitivities were awakened in Paris and continued when his family moved to Israel, where he studied art and served in the Israeli army. Establishing a career at age 24 when he came to New York

City was difficult for a young man who spoke five languages but only a smattering of English. He worked as a graphic artist and substitute teacher while studying painting at the Brooklyn Museum Art School and illustrating for a publisher of Hebrew books for children.

One day while talking on the telephone, he noticed his doodles had a spontaneous look, totally different from the style of artwork that he had been doing. The discovery was the beginning of a new approach to illustrating. Fate and determination brought him to a fortuitous meeting with editor Susan Hirschman, then at Harper & Row. She suggested he write and illustrate a children's book. Four years later his first book, *The Moon in My Room*, was published. The year was 1963.

Today he has over 35 books to his credit. Many of them were written by others, but it is often the stories that he has written and illustrated himself that stand out as award winners. His wonderful palette of colors, evocative scenes, quirky lines and perspectives, rakish characters, and strong composition have graced many books of folklore, and his more contemporary stories all have a touch of folk whimsy. Shulevitz's eclectic style truly shapes his stories.

> *"I believe that style and technique should be an organic outgrowth of the story. And since not all stories are alike, it stands to reason that books would look different from one another as well."*

Topping his many awards and recognitions for excellence is the prestigious Caldecott Medal, awarded in 1969 for *The Fool of the World and the Flying Ship*, a Russian folktale retold by Arthur Ransome. He has since won two Caldecott Honor Book citations for books with his own texts: *The Treasure* in 1980 and *Snow* in 1999. For each book he has developed an artistic style suited to the story itself as well as to its geographical and cultural context. This is typified in the panoramic views and atmospheric backgrounds of *The Fool of the World* expressing the expanse of the Russian landscape. In *The Treasure*, an East European rendition of a folktale that has been told in many cultures, Shulevitz's gentle, earthy watercolor renderings of a rural landscape enhance the theme of finding true "treasure" in the most unexpected places. *Snow*, in which a boy's imagination soars as the first flakes come down, was created in response to a winter in which his neighborhood saw sixteen snowfalls. By the last page, the predominant blues and grays of the cityscape have been covered by the soft white blanket of snow. *Snow* was highly praised for both the art and the writing; in addition to the Caldecott Honor Award and a Golden Kite Award for illustration, it received the Charlotte Zolotow Award for picture book text. It also received an award as the Best Picture Book in Translation in Japan. To date *Snow* has been translated into French, Danish, Korean, Italian, and Chinese as well as Japanese.

Without a doubt, the difficult circumstances of Uri's childhood have influenced the underlying ideals of his books, especially those that recount stories of common folk who triumph over the powerful figures of the world. What adds the unique Shulevitz panache is the touch of puckishness in his characters, similar to his own charming smile and unassuming manner. As words in his titles suggest, he reaches out to the fool and dreamer in everyone, captivating readers in the same way that drawing captured his imagination. Three of his works have been cited by the *New York Times* as among the Best Illustrated Books of the Year: *Hanukah Money*, by Shalom Aleichem, in 1978; his own *The Treasure* in 1978; and *Hosni the Dreamer: An Arabian Tale*, by Ehud Ben-Ezer, in 1997. Each of these stories exemplifies the simple dignity of the common man, unaffected by the self-importance of those around him. Each is illustrated in a style appropriate to the tale, for example, the dominant desert gold in the illustrations for *Hosni the Dreamer*.

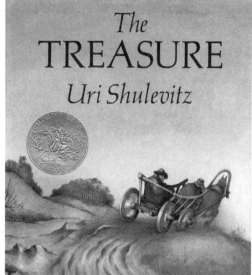

Courtesy of Farrar, Straus and Giroux

His evocative work in *Dawn* and *Rain Rain Rivers* led to both of those titles being named ALA Notable Children's Books, and the subjects here reflect his belief in the healing qualities of nature and the beauty of the natural world. In 1999 Shulevitz won a Guggenheim Fellowship to support his work and research for a book about the medieval traveler Benjamin of Tudela. Shulevitz's own *Writing with Pictures: How to Write and Illustrate Children's Books* has become an essential manual for aspiring illustrators as well as for those who evaluate children's literature. Uri Shulevitz divides his time between New York City and a small town in upstate New York.

SELECTED WORKS WRITTEN AND ILLUSTRATED: *The Moon in My Room*, 1963, 2003; *One Monday Morning*, 1967, 2003; *Oh What a Noise!*, 1971; *Rain Rain Rivers*, 1969; Dawn, 1974; *The Treasure*, 1979; *The Strange and Exciting Adventures of Jeremiah Hush*, 1986; *Toddlecreek Post Office*, 1990; *The Secret Room*, 1993; Snow, 1998; *What Is a Wise Bird like You Doing In a Silly Tale like This?*, 2000; *The Travels of Benjamin of Tudela Through Three Continents in the Twelfth Century*, 2005.

SELECTED WORKS ILLUSTRATED: *A Rose, a Bridge, and a Wild Black Horse*, by Charlotte Zolotow, 1964; *The Mystery of the Woods*, by Mary Stolz, 1964; *Charley Sang a Song*, by H. R. Hays and Daniel Hays, 1964; *The Second Witch*, by Jack Sendak, 1965; *Maximilian's World*, by Mary Stolz, 1966; *The Carpet of Solomon*, by Shulamith Ish-Kishor, 1966; *The Twelve Dancing Princesses*, by the Brothers Grimm, trans. by Elizabeth Shub, 1966; *The Silkspinners*, by Jean Russell Larson, 1967; *The Month Brothers*, by Dorothy Nathan, 1967; *Runaway Jonah*, by Jan Wahl, 1968; *The Fool of the World and the Flying Ship*, retold by Arthur Ransome, 1968; *The*

Courtesy of Farrar, Straus and Giroux

Wonderful Kite, by Jan Wahl, 1971; *Soldier and Tsar in the Forest: A Russian Tale*, by Afanasyev, trans. by Richard Lourie, 1972; *The Fools of Chelm and Their History*, by Isaac Bashevis Singer, 1973; *The Magician*, by I. L. Peretz, 1973; *The Touchstone: A Fable*, by Robert Louis Stevenson, 1976; *Hanukah Money*, by Shalom Aleichem, trans. and adapt. by Uri Shulevitz and Elizabeth Shub, 1978; *The Lost Kingdom of Karnica*, by Richard Kennedy, 1979; *The Golem*, by Isaac Bashevis Singer, 1982; *Lilith's Cave: Jewish Tales of the Supernatural*, by Howard Schwartz, 1988; *The Diamond Tree: Jewish Tales from Around the World*, sel. and retold by Howard Schwartz and Barbara Rush, 1991; *The Golden Goose*, by the Brothers Grimm, 1995; *Hosni the Dreamer: An Arabian Tale*, by Ehud Ben-Ezer, 1997; *Daughters of Fire: Heroines of the Bible*, by Fran Manushkin, 2001.

SUGGESTED READING: Cullinan, Bernice, and Diane Person, eds. *The Continuum Encyclopedia of Children's Literature*, 2001; Cummins, Julie, ed. *Children's Book Illustration and Design*, vol. 1, 1992; Hopkins, Lee Bennett. *Pauses: Autobiographical Reflections of 101 Creators of Children's Books*, 1995; Shulevitz, Uri. *Writing with Pictures: How to Write and Illustrate Children's Books*, 1985; Silvey, Anita, ed. *Children's Books and Their Creators*, 1995. Periodicals—Shulevitz, Uri, "Within the Margins of the Picture Book," *The Horn Book*, June 1971; Shulevitz, Uri, "Caldecott Acceptance Speech," *The Horn Book*, August 1969.

An earlier profile of Uri Shulevitz, with another first-person sketch, appeared in *Third Book of Junior Authors* (1972).

Courtesy of Laurie Gaboardi

Marc Simont

November 23, 1915–

"I was born in Paris in 1915 of Spanish parents. My father was an illustrator on the staff of *L'Illustration*. At the end of World War I he made an exploratory trip to the United States. He liked what he saw and welcomed the prospect of his children being brought up with both European and American influences. Meanwhile, newly imposed immigration laws prevented us from joining him for another five years. My mother and two sisters and I lived in Barcelona with my grandfather during that time.

"During my school years, I was always drawing and was more concerned with what a teacher looked like than what he said, which didn't do my grades any good. In 1927 the family was finally reunited in New York City. I spent as much time as possible in my father's studio, where I could work from models. In teaching me to draw he gave me the tools of what was to be my trade. In 1932 my family moved back to Paris, where I studied art full-time. I attended various schools, among them the Académie Julian, Académie Ranson, and the André Lhote School.

"I left the comforts of home in 1935 and came to the United States. I enrolled in the New York National Academy of Design, and on that day I sold a portrait-drawing for $35. I telegraphed my father to discontinue my allowance. It was a long stretch before I found regular work. My first real job was in 1939, illustrating a book titled *The Pirate of Chatham Square* by Emma Gelders Sterne. Following that, I worked as assistant to mural painters (F. S. Bradford and E. Winter). Working on such a large scale was a refreshing change from books, and later it was just as refreshing going back to books.

"From 1942 to 1945 I was in service with the army at Fort Bragg, designing visual aids in a training aid shop. It was during that time that I married Sara Dalton, a social worker with the U.S.O.-T.A. And we later had a son, Marc Dalton Simont.

"In its early days *Sports Illustrated* often used artists' depiction of professional sports, giving an extra dimension to the sporting scene. During a period of 10 years I covered such assignments as horseracing, yachting, bullfighting, auto racing, etc. My special beat was baseball, a sport where players bring their quirks and foibles into the game.

"As long as I can remember I have been drawing and caricaturing people. On Memorial Day in my town's fund-raising fair, I take a spot between the bullfrog jumping and the hotdog stand and put up my sign: 'Portrait Sketch While U Wait.'

"The bulk of my work has been in children's books, a field that is a wonderful mix of editors, teachers, librarians, artists, and writers, all dedicated to satisfying the curiosity of brand-new human beings . . . the children."

☼ ☼ ☼

Marc Simont is known internationally for his lively, humorous, and tender art, which has graced nearly 100 picture books. A master of line, movement, and expression, he has worked in the field of children's books for close to 70 years.

Though he was born in Paris, France, his parents—Josep Simont, an illustrator, and Dolors Baste Simont—were from the Catalonian region of northern Spain. They moved several times in Marc's childhood, which he claims did little for his formal education but improved his capacity to observe the world around him. Never graduating from high school, he was fluent in French, Spanish, English, and Catalan, and says he sketched bullfighters in Barcelona as a youngster. He claims his father was his first and greatest teacher, as well as his inspiration for making his living as an artist. His father, though, wasn't the only artist among Marc's relatives; two of his uncles and a sister were full-time artists as well. He calls art the "family trade."

After moving to New York, Simont studied at the National Academy of Design from 1935 to 1937. During that time he carried a sketchbook around with him wherever he went and, as he related in a recent *Horn Book* article, he "drew in subways, bars, and other public places around town where . . . it was possible to work unnoticed, like a 'bug in a fold in the curtain.' Sketching in this way became a lifelong habit." It was also in these student days that Simont formed a close friendship with illustrator Robert McCloskey, with whom he shared a studio.

His first job in children's books was to illustrate *The Castle in the Silver Woods*, a collection of Scandinavian fairy tales by Ruth Bryan Owens in 1939. In 1950 he captured his first Caldecott Honor Book award for Ruth Krauss's *The Happy Day*. His charcoal drawings of rounded, winter-snuggled animals awakening to the first scents of spring have lasting appeal. Over the year he illustrated several of James Thurber's humorous and ironic classics, first *The Thirteen Clocks* and later *The Wonderful "O."* Simont's rendition of the characters—shifty, innocent, or burdened—complements the spirit of both tales with just the right tongue-in-cheek humor. But it is his romantic watercolors for a new edition of Thurber's *Many Moons*, published in 1990, that shine with special splendor. Their dreamy grace and whimsicality bring the much-loved story to a new generation of children, providing counterpoint to Thurber's ebullient language. In 1955,

"During my school years, I was always drawing and was more concerned with what a teacher looked like than what he said, which didn't do my grades any good."

Simont received the Caldecott Medal for Janice Udry's *A Tree Is Nice*, alternating spreads of watercolor with black-and-white line drawings. The art is open, details sketched, making ample room—just as the simple but poetic text does—for each child's imagination to fill in his or her sense of trees.

Many well-known authors have had their words graced with illustrations by Marc Simont, among them Margaret Wise Brown, Jean Fritz, Charlotte Zolotow, Faith McNulty, David McCord, and Franklyn Branley. He seemed to be equally at ease with fictional whimsy and factual exposition. Over a period of 25 years, he illustrated Marjorie Weinman Sharmat's popular Nate the Great series, garnering several prizes for individual titles. Karla Kuskin's delightful and unexpected *The Philharmonic Gets Dressed*, with its 105 members of an orchestra in various stages of undress and preparation for a concert provided Simont with a chance to show the range of his expressive line drawings. He produced musicians tall and short, thin and broad, tired and twinkling, confident and less than confident with great humor and sympathy. In Kuskin's *The Dallas Titans Get Ready for Bed*, he portrayed a football team after a winning game, giving him even more room for play, his cartoon-like style managing to convey a wealth of detail and personality.

Among the books he's written himself, *The Goose That Almost Got Cooked*, with its witty adventurous goose, and *The Stray Dog* have both been praised for economical texts and illustrations filled with extra story details. *The Stray Dog*, a heart-warming story of a family's last-minute rescue and adoption of an irresistible stray dog, received both a *Boston Globe–Horn Book* Honor Book citation and a Caldecott Honor Award. To win such honors for this delightfully traditional and vibrant story over 50 years after first receiving a Caldecott Honor is a fine tribute to a long, successful career.

The recipient of many awards for excellence over the years, in this country and others, Marc Simont is particularly proud of being named the 1997 Illustrator of the Year by the Professional Association of Illustrators in his native Catalonia. The introduction to a booklet, *Marc Simont at the Library of Congress*, summarizes the appeal of this artist in a very special way: "Marc has a child's basic view of his world: open, fresh, and innately questioning. All his work since he first set pencil to paper in studying drawing with his father shows this engaging quality as well as the endless watching and seeing that creates the artist." He lives in West Cornwall, Connecticut, where he continues to work and enjoy the small-town life of his adopted country.

SELECTED WORKS WRITTEN AND ILLUSTRATED: *Polly's Oats*, 1951, 1994; *The Lovely Summer*, 1952, 1992; *Mimi*, 1954; *The Plumber Out of the Sea*, 1955; *The Contest at Paca*, 1959; *How Come Elephants?*; 1965; *The Goose That Almost Got Cooked*, 1997; *The Stray Dog: From a True Story by Reiko Sassa*, 2001.

> *"As long as I can remember I have been drawing and caricaturing people."*

Courtesy of HarperCollins Children's Books

SELECTED WORKS ILLUSTRATED (Nate the Great series, all by Marjorie Weinman Sharmat): *Nate the Great*, 1972; *Nate the Great Goes Undercover*, 1974; *Nate the Great and the Lost List*, 1975; *Nate the Great and the Phony Clue*, 1977; *Nate the Great and the Sticky Case*, 1978; *Nate the Great and the Missing Key*, 1981; *Nate the Great and the Snowy Trail*, 1982; *Nate the Great and the Fishy Prize*, 1985; *Nate the Great and the Boring Beach Bag*, 1987; *Nate the Great Stalks Stupidweed*, 1987; *Nate the Great Goes Down in the Dumps*, 1989; *Nate the Great and the Halloween Hunt*, 1989; *Nate the Great and the Musical Note*, 1990; *Nate the Great and the Stolen Base*, 1992; *Nate the Great and the Pillowcase*, 1993; *Nate the Great and the Mushy Valentine*, 1994; *Nate the Great and the Tardy Tortoise*, 1995; *Nate the Great and the Crunchy Christmas*, 1996; *Nate the Great Saves the King of Sweden*, 1997; *Nate the Great and Me: The Case of the Fleeing Fang*, 1998.

SELECTED WORKS ILLUSTRATED: *The Castle in the Silver Woods*, by Ruth Bryan Owens, 1939; *The Pirate of Chatham Square: A Story of Old New York*, by Emma G. Sterne, 1939; *Men of Power*, by Albert Carr, 1940; *Isabella, Young Queen of Spain*, by Mildred Cross, 1941; *Sarah Deborah's Day*, by Charlotte Jackson, 1941; *All Aboard the Whale*, by Richard Hatch, 1942; *Billy and the Unhappy Bull*, by Meindert DeJong, 1946; *The First Story*, by Margaret Wise Brown, 1947; *Flying Ebony*, by Iris Vinton, 1947; *The First Christmas*, by Robbie Trent, 1948, 1990; *The Red Fairy Book*, ed. by Andrew Lang, 1948; *The Happy Day*, by Ruth Krauss, 1949, 1992; *The Big World and the Little House*, by Ruth Krauss, 1949; *Good Luck Duck*, by Meindert DeJong, 1950; *The Backward Day*, by Ruth Krauss, 1950; *The Thirteen Clocks*, by James Thurber, 1951; *Timmy and the Tiger*, by Marjorie B. Paradis, 1952; *Christmas Eve*, by Alistair Cooke, 1952; *Jareb*, by Miriam Powell, 1952; *The American Riddle Book*, by Carl Withers and Sula Benet, 1954; *Deer Mountain Hideaway*, by E. H. Lansing, 1954; *Fish Head*, by Jean Fritz, 1954; *Deer River Raft*, by Elizabeth H. Lansing, 1955; *The Trail-Driving Rooster*, by Fred Gipson, 1955; *Now I Know*, by Julius Schwartz, 1955; *A Tree Is Nice*, by Janice May Udry, 1955; *I Know a Magic House*, by Julius Schwartz, 1956; *Pigeon Fly Home*, by Thomas Liggett, 1956; *Nellie and Her Flying Crocodile*, by Chad Walsh, 1956; *The Wonderful "O,"* by James Thurber, 1957; *The Rainbow Book of American Folk*

Tales and Legends, by Maria Leach, 1958; *The Seal That Couldn't Swim*, by Alexis Ladas, 1959; *The Duckfooted Hound*, by James A. Kjelgaard, 1960; *A Good Man and His Wife*, by Ruth Krauss, 1962; *The Earth Is Your Spaceship*, by Julius Schwartz, 1963; *Every Time I Climb a Tree*, by David McCord, 1967, 1999; *What to Do When There's Nothing to Do*, by members of the staff of Boston Children's Medical Center, 1967; *Down Boy, Down, Blast You!*, by Charlton Ogburn Jr., 1967; *Wolfie*, by Janet Chenery, 1969; *Glenda*, by Janice May Udry, 1969; *Belts On, Buttons Down*, by Edward Fales Jr., 1971; *A Child's Eye View of the World*, by members of the staff of the Boston Children's Medical Center, 1972; *The Star in the Pail*, by David McCord, 1975; *The Contests at Cowlick*, by Richard Kennedy, 1975; *Robert Louis Stevenson, Teller of Tales*, by Eulalie Osgood Grover, 1975; *The Beetle Bush*, by Beverly Keller, 1976; *A Space Story*, by Karla Kuskin, 1978; *Danger in Dinosaur Valley*, by Joan Lowery Nixon, 1978; *Mouse and Tim*, by Faith McNulty, 1978; *How to Dig a Hole to the Other Side of the World*, by Faith McNulty, 1979; *Ten Copycats in a Boat, and Other Riddles*, by Alvin Schwartz, 1979; *The Elephant Who Couldn't Forget*, by Faith McNulty, 1979; *Reddy Rattler and Easy Eagle*, by Mitchell Sharmat, 1979; *Speak Up: More Rhymes of the Never Was and Always Is*, by David McCord, 1980; *If You Listen*, by Charlotte Zolotow, 1980; *Chasing After Annie*, by Marjorie Weinman Sharmat, 1981; *No More Monsters for Me!*, by Peggy Parish, 1981; *The Philharmonic Gets Dressed*, by Karla Kuskin, 1982; *My Uncle Nikos*, by Julie Delton, 1983; *The Knight of the Golden Plain*, by Mollie Hunter, 1983; *Bruno the Pretzel Man*, by Edward Davis, 1984; *The Year of the Boar and Jackie Robinson*, by Bette Bao Lord, 1984; *Martin's Hats*, by Joan W. Blos, 1984; *Top Secret*, by John Reynolds Gardiner, 1984; *Volcanoes*, by Franklyn M. Branley, 1985; *The Three-Day Enchantment*, by Mollie Hunter, 1985; *The Dallas Titans Get Ready for Bed*, by Karla Kuskin, 1986; *Journey into a Black Hole*, by Franklyn M. Branley, 1986; *Glaciers*, by Wendell V. Tangborn, 1988; *Sing a Song of Popcorn*, (contributor) 1988; *The Quiet Mother and the Noisy Little Boy*, by Charlotte Zolotow, 1989; *What Happened to the Dinosaurs?*, by

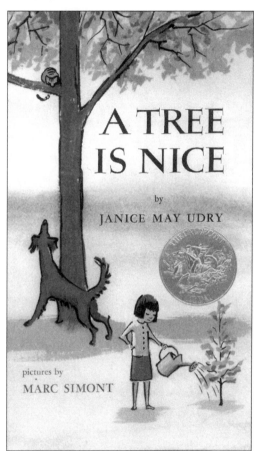

Courtesy of HarperCollins Publishsers

Franklyn M. Branley, 1989; *Many Moons*, by James Thurber, 1990; *Playing Right Field*, by Willy Welch, 1995; *My Brother Ant*, by Betsy Cromer Byars, 1996; *Ant Plays Bear*, by Betsy Cromer Byars, 1997; *Glenda Glinka, Witch-at-Large*, by Janice May Udry, 1997.

SUGGESTED READING: *Contemporary Authors*, New Revision Series, vol. 106, 2002; Hopkins, Lee Bennett. *Books Are by People: Interviews with 104 Authors and Illustrators of Books for Young Children*, 1969; Jagusch, Sybille, ed. *Marc Simont at the Library of Congress: A Lecture for International Children's Book Day, Presented on May 8, 1992*, 1995; Kingman, Lee, ed. *Caldecott Medal Books: 1938–1957*, 1957; Kingman, Lee, ed. *Newbery and Caldecott Medal Books: 1956–1965*, 1965; Silvey, Anita, ed. *Children's Books and Their Creators*, 1995; *Something About the Author*, vol. 126, 2002. Periodicals—Marcus, Leonard S., and Marc Simont, "Marc Simont's Sketchbooks: The Art Academy Years," *The Horn Book*, March/April 2004. Online—"Marc Simont," Meet the Author/Illustrator Archives, Children's Book Council, *www.cbcbooks.org/html/marc_simont.html*.

WEB SITE: *www.MarcSimont.com*

An earlier profile of Marc Simont appeared in *More Junior Authors* (1963).

"Lemony Snicket"

"The news that I am to be included in the *Ninth Book of Junior Authors and Illustrators* has filled my heart with astonishment, dismay, and the vague feeling that I should leave the room in the next few hours. Never in my career as a writer have I strived to give a moment's pleasure to any of my readers, and I always believed that I had succeeded in this modest if crucial goal. Inclusion in such a worthy volume of talent makes me realize that either I am a dismal failure or the victim of a cruel practical joke, or possibly both. Therefore, in an effort to save myself from further accusations, I will hastily write a few words here describing my as-yet-unfinished life and philosophy regarding literature.

"It was during my early years at the Academy that I first realized the elegant importance and dire limitations of the written word, when I looked up at the blackboard and saw something there which I believed to be false. I pointed this out to my instructor, who was not appreciative and offered me, in sarcastic terms, the opportunity to walk down the hallway to the library and prove her wrong. In retrospect I realize that this was probably meant to be some sort of punishment, but I have always had a tendency to take things literally, and so for the first time I entered a library unaccompanied, armed only with a specific purpose and shivering sense of injustice, two things which have guided me for much of my life.

"The sheer, implausible freedom of a library—in which one is free to peruse any book one could find, for any reason one can dream up—struck me that afternoon with all the force of a bag of frozen peas, dropped from a great height, and it is this same icy shiver which I experience whenever I enter a library to this day. That paginated afternoon I reveled in such pleasures, traveling from book to book by the very same route as the sputtering epiphanies of my brain. From poison—I was still angry at my teacher—to spiders, from spiders to African folktales, from African folktales to poltergeists, from poltergeists to cannibalism (I was growing hungry), and finally from cannibalism to the Egyptological question which had sent me to the library in the first place. I put my feet up on the underfunded, battered wooden tables and read until I found what I was looking for. Then, with the librarian's help, I copied it carefully onto a small index card, along with the correct bibliographical citation, and returned triumphantly to my classroom to read it out loud. The idea that books might contain secrets—hidden, like all worthwhile things, in obvious but unthinkable places—which could help set the world back on its proper axis is an idea that has never left me. It is eternal, faithful, and tough, this idea, unlike books themselves, which are vulnerable to fire, flood, age, defenestration, plagiarism, and, on the occasional dare, intestinal consumption.

Courtesy of Meredith Heuer

"Speaking of the digestive process, my instructor, predictably, reprimanded me for showing off and refused to change what was written on the blackboard, which of course is the other great lesson of literature: However compelling, a story doesn't change the sorry fact of who is holding the chalk. My own chronicles of the Baudelaire orphans decry Count Olaf and, allegorists may deduce, similar wicked, greedy, and unhygienic people, but I cannot help but notice that such people still walk the streets, and the Baudelaires themselves often find important secrets embedded in the literature they stumble upon, but it does not change their circumstances.

"What does change—as it did that day in the Academy's bridge parlor, where my classmates consoled me with vows of solidarity and a glass of brandy—is that the secret became less secretive, because the proper people were made aware of it, and thus I learned that the stain of injustice, which has fallen on every page of every worthwhile story, fades just a tad with every well-researched and well-told tale. Each real book helps with this immeasureable task, each book which lays bare a larger truth even under the murky and sometimes depressing guise of fiction, and that is why, one vital if overly windy evening, I vowed to become a writer or to die trying, and I have done one of those things and fully expect to do the other. In closing, readers of this volume may find it useful to learn that the nose of the Sphinx, despite persistent rumors to the contrary, was not shot off by Napoleon's soldiers for target practice."

❊   ❊   ❊

In 1999, "Lemony Snicket" burst upon the literary scene in children's book publishing with a flourish of theatricality and an ominous title—*The Bad Beginning*—that would become the first of a projected 13 volumes in his Series of Unfortunate Events. Since that auspicious start, the inimitable "Mr. Snicket" has continued to chronicle the fortunes of the hapless Baudelaire siblings, who lose their parents, their home, and their security in the very first chapter of the first book. It all goes downhill from there. Readers have responded to these dastardly circumstances by catapulting the books onto bestseller lists around the country, usually several titles at once. Millions of copies are now in print, and the books have been translated into 39 languages.

> "The idea that books might contain secrets—hidden, like all worthwhile things, in obvious but unthinkable places—which could help set the world back on its proper axis is an idea that has never left me."

The identity of the elusive "Mr. Snicket" is supposedly shrouded in as much mystery as the plots of his ubiquitous books. However, perceptive members of the large audiences he commands at bookstore appearances all seem to reach the conclusion that "Snicket" and Daniel Handler, the rather clean-cut, good-looking "representative" he sends when he is (as always) indisposed, are actually one and the same person. Handler explains to his audiences that "Mr. Snicket" is unable to appear because of a bite on his armpit by a huge black bug at a picnic the day before, a bug that he proceeds to pass around the room in a small box. He further admonishes the gathered throng of largely 9- to 12-year-olds to be cautious about raising their arms in class to answer questions, lest the same fate befall them. The audience loves it.

Daniel Handler was born and raised in San Francisco. His father worked as an accountant and his mother was a college dean. As a child he preferred reading books on the darker side of humor, those of Roald Dahl and Edward Gorey, and the novels of Zilpha Keatley Snyder, which he has called "creepy, but nonsupernatural." He didn't care for cheery stories with happy endings or fantasy or sports. After graduating from Wesleyan University, Handler lived in New York City. He had completed two adult novels (published under his own name), but at the suggestion of his editor, Susan Rich, he turned to writing a book for young readers. He decided to use the pseudonym "Lemony Snicket," a name he had invented in order to do some surreptitious online research for his first adult novel. Armed with an alter ego, Handler set out to write the books he would have enjoyed reading when he was young, but even the author could not have envisioned the enormous success those books would enjoy. Apparently there are hordes of young readers looking for antidotes to "cheery" books. They are devouring every dastardly turn of events faced by the unfortunate orphans, Violet, Klaus, and Sunny Baudelaire, in spite of all the author's protests that they should not read each volume and should indeed, among other things, "throw this awful book to the ground and run as far away from it as possible."

Against all better judgment, in fact, *The Bad Beginning* was voted a winner of the 2003 Colorado Children's Book Award and Hawaii's Nene Award. Mr. Handler continues to travel miles each year in a futile attempt to warn readers away from the frightening events chronicled in each new volume, but despite (or perhaps because of) these heroic efforts, the latest title invariably appears on the *New York Times* bestseller list. Indeed, readers seem to be drawn to these stories precisely because they prey on their darkest fears of abandonment, separation, and persecution in situations that, like old-time movie serials, al-

THE HOSTILE HOSPITAL
Courtesy of HarperCollins Children's Books

ways have an escape hatch. Along the way readers are also enlightened by "Mr. Snicket's" explanations of deliciously obscure words and phrases and delighted by his alliterative titles, authorial asides, and tongue-in-cheek character and place names (Heimlich Hospital, Pruefrock Preparatory School, and Vice Principal Nero, to mention just a few). To further disturb the universe, a feature-length film containing plot elements of the first three books is due to appear in theaters across the country "just in time to ruin Christmas" in December 2004.

After living for five years in New York, Daniel Handler moved back to San Francisco with his wife, Lisa Brown, in 2000.

SELECTED WORKS (all illus. by Brett Helquist): *The Bad Beginning*, 1999; *The Reptile Room*, 1999; *The Wide Window*, 2000; *The Miserable Mill*, 2000; *The Austere Academy*, 2000; *The Ersatz Elevator*, 2001; *The Vile Village*, 2001; *The Hostile Hospital*, 2001; *The Carnivorous Carnival*, 2002; *The Slippery Slope*, 2003; *The Grim Grotto*, 2004.

SELECTED WORKS (not illus. by Brett Helquist): *Lemony Snicket: The Unauthorized Autobiography*, 2002.

SUGGESTED READING: *Children's Literature Review*, vol. 79, 2002; *Contemporary Authors*, vol. 195; *Something About the Author*, vol. 126, 2002. Periodicals—Boodman, Sandra G., "In Troubled Times, Kids Go for the Feary Tales," *Washington Post*, December 3, 2001; Hepperman, Christine, "Angel

Wings and Hard Knocks," *The Horn Book*, March/April 2001; Merkin, Daphne, "Lemony Snicket Says, 'Don't Read My Books!'" *New York Times Magazine*, April 29, 2001.

WEB SITE: *www.lemonysnicket.com*

Courtesy of Allan Manham

Meilo So

October 24, 1963–

"I was born in Hong Kong. I had two brothers and one sister and many cousins. When we all met, at New Year or at other festivals, we played games that involved a lot of drawing. Battle games, guessing games, character invention games, fantastic animals and monsters. I was surprised to find that everyone drew very well. I think it was because all our lives centered around my grandfather's mannequin shop. We all watched him painting eyes and mouths and nails on the fiberglass models which he sold. We children could have a go now and again. It was a great game we all shared. Drawing is still very much a game to me. It has its rules, of course, but they can be bent a lot and sometimes even ignored. With a bit of luck, one can even then win through.

"My father was a history lecturer at Hong Kong Chinese University, and this allowed him to afford to send me abroad to be educated. It was so competitive in Hong Kong schools and one had to be so brilliant at all subjects to pass on to higher education that I would have stood no chance, so I went to a school in Oxford, England, mainly to study music. One of the other subject choices was either home economics or art. I chose art.

"My first art teacher was a very good figurative artist and draftsman, and that was when I got seriously interested in drawing. Instead of just doodling around the page margins of schoolbooks I could not understand, I was encouraged to draw on large sheets of paper. I decided to go to art school, but I faced a lot of doubt and soul-searching. My education was costing so much that I should really study a subject with a guaranteed financial future, a profession like an accountant, an engineer, an architect, medicine, the law. Could I really waste my father's money to study 'art'? The guilt associated with my decision I carried around with me for years, even after I had become a professional illustrator and had some success! It was only with the birth of my daughter Ming and observing her thirst for knowledge and understanding, for information and entertainment, as she began to grow into a person, that I realised that my work was in fact real work, useful work, not frivolous and vain at all. I could say to myself 'I have important work to do, for the children!'

"I can feel very distant from my drawings and paintings, as if someone else has done them for me. When, by what seems luck, everything comes together and a picture 'works,' I thank the magic hand that helped me. My husband is a fine draftsman and has helped me greatly by passing on to me skills and rules which allow me to make the magic happen on a more regular basis, to learn from my mistakes, to learn from other good artists of all kinds, and to take my own ability seriously.

"Origin in China, made in Hong Kong, packaged in England and domiciled in the Shetland Isles! What a tangled history! Yet this imparts a kind of freedom; many cultures are parts of me. I am a citizen of the world. It also reflects upon my attitudes to work. I am no purist, I change methods and media wherever it suits the work in hand. Whatever I make and however I make it, I believe it is still 'me'—whether a pen-and-ink or brush drawing, a watercolour, a linocut, or a little sketch from my life."

✤   ✤   ✤

Meilo So attended the School of St. Helen and St. Katherine in Oxford, England, before taking an art foundation course at Oxford Polytechnic. She received her B.A. with honors from Brighton College of Art in 1987. After some time traveling in Europe with her sketchbook, she worked as a freelance illustrator and taught part-time at Hong Kong Polytechnic. In 1994 she married her British husband, Ron Sandford, a freelance artist who had been her tutor at Brighton College of Art. For a while the couple lived in the south of England, but soon after the birth of their daughter, Ming, in 2000, they moved to the island of Yell in the Shetland Islands off the north coast of Scotland.

Meilo So's graceful and whimsical watercolors have enhanced many books for children since the early 1990s. Her art is especially well suited to illustrating poetry and folklore, and has been widely appreciated. For a collection of animal poems, *Beauty of the Beast: Poems from the Animal Kingdom*, selected by Jack Prelutsky, Meilo created illustrations for 200 poems about many types of animals, from the lowly earthworm to the lumbering elephant. Each illustration captures the essence of its subject and the many moods of these creatures with quick brush strokes, splashy color, and vibrant tones. This volume was named a Notable Children's Book by the American Library Association and a Blue Ribbon title by the *Bulletin of the Center for Children's Books*.

For *Tasty Baby Belly Buttons*, Judy Sierra's adaptation of a popular Japanese folktale, Meilo's artwork captures the humor as well as the horror of the evil *oni*'s search for victims and its defeat at the hands of tiny Uriko, the girl born in a melon. A Parents' Choice Silver Honor winner, this was also an ALA Notable Children's Book, a *Bulletin* Blue Ribbon title, and the recipient

"When, by what seems luck, everything comes together and a picture 'works,' I thank the magic hand that helped me."

Courtesy of Alfred A. Knopf, Inc.

of the Irma S. and James H. Black Award of the Bank Street College of Education. *White Swan Express*, in which Meilo rendered a more realistic setting with her characteristic whimsy and light touch, is the story of four North American families who travel to China to adopt four orphan babies. The heartwarming account is based on the experience of one of the co-authors, Elaine Aoki, and was named a Notable Social Studies Trade Book for Young People. *Footprints on the Roof*, in which Meilo illustrated poems by Marilyn Singer, was chosen as a *Riverbank Review* Book of Distinction in 2003.

SELECTED WORKS WRITTEN AND ILLUSTRATED: *The Emperor and the Nightingale*, retold from Hans Christian Andersen, 1992; *Gobble, Gobble, Slip, Slop: A Tale of a Very Greedy Cat*, 2004.

SELECTED WORKS ILLUSTRATED: *Wishbones: A Folk Tale from China*, retold by Barbara Ker Wilson, 1993; *The Monkey and the Panda*, by Antonia Barber, 1995; *Beauty of the Beast: Poems from the Animal Kingdom*, sel. by Jack Prelutsky, 1997; *The 20th Century Children's Poetry Treasury*, sel. by Jack Prelutsky, 1999; *The Tale of the Heaven Tree*, by Mary Joslin, 1999; *Tasty Baby Belly Buttons: A Japanese Folktale*, retold by Judy Sierra, 1999; *The Ugly Duckling*, retold by Kevin Crossley-Holland, from Hans Christian Andersen, 2001; *The Merchant Enticed by the Pearl of Great Price*, by Mary Joslin, 2001; *It's Simple, Said Simon*, by Mary Ann Hoberman, 2001; *White Swan Express: A Story About Adoption*, by Jean Davies Okimoto and Elaine M. Aoki, 2002; *Countdown to Spring: An Animal Counting Book*, by Janet Schulman, 2002; *Moonbeams, Dumplings & Dragon Boats: A Treasury of Chinese Holiday Tales, Activities & Recipes*, by Nina Simonds, Leslie Swartz, and the Children's Museum of Boston, 2002; *Footprints on the Roof: Poems About the Earth*, by Marilyn Singer, 2002; *How to Cross a Pond: Poems About Water*, by Marilyn Singer, 2003; *A Bunny for All Seasons*, by Janet Schulman, 2003.

SUGGESTED READING: *Book Trusted News*, Spring 2003.

"I was born in Aarhus, Denmark. In the summertime we lived south of the city near the beach. One of my first and strongest recollections is of sitting at the beach in the morning and watching the sunrise and the fishing boats passing by. My parents and I both recall that I did that every summer. I still have the feeling of joy when I hear the sounds of fishing boats, and I am sure that my love for the changing of light in nature was established at that time.

"In the city, I lived very close to the Art Museum. I went there once or twice a week to look at the works from the golden age of Danish painting, which I admired very much. I think that my interest in naturalism and impressionism was formed at that time. When I was a teenager, I was more interested in the non-figurative, abstract expression, but later my interest in naturalism reappeared.

"I knew that I couldn't live as a naturalistic artist in Denmark because it was considered very old-fashioned. So after school I was educated as a glazier in my father's company, and later I worked in another company for some years. In my spare time, I always painted. I decided to study art history and went to college and university. During my studies at the university, I found more and more pleasure in painting and less in the theoretical studies, so instead of teaching art history, I decided to paint. I studied three years at the Art Academy. I had a lot of pleasure painting every day and calling it my job. My main interest then, as now, was naturalistic/impressionistic painting. After finishing at the academy, I worked in a film company where I made graphics and models, but mostly studied studio lighting. At that time I discovered that there was a market for my kind of art in advertising and publishing, and so I started working as a freelance illustrator in 1985.

"In 1993 I moved to New York City. Even though New York is exciting, I missed having contact with nature, and I moved back to Denmark. Now I live near the beach again, and I often go down there. Unfortunately there aren't many fishing boats left, but the sound of the waves and the change of light are, as I recall, still the same."

Courtesy of Henri Sorensen

Henri Sørensen

February 28, 1950–

❈ ❈ ❈

Henri Sørensen's love of naturalistic painting and impressionistic art is apparent in his work in children's books. His illustrations are warm and gentle, with an air of nostalgia that heightens the historic settings of stories he has written himself and also in his collaborations with other writers. His subjects are the natural world, the emotions of childhood, family ties, and intergenerational relationships. In *New Hope* he tells the story of a boy who visits his grandfather and hears the story of how his Danish immigrant ancestor founded the town of New Hope in the Midwestern United States. For Jean Van Leeuwen's *A Fourth of July on the Plains*, Sørensen created the same softly realistic paintings to illustrate an impromptu celebration along the Oregon Trail in the 19th century. Other titles, such as Jonathan London's *Hurricane!*, illustrate forces of nature and seasonal changes. *Hurricane!*, *A Fourth of July on the Plains*, and *The Yellow Star* have all been named Notable Social Studies Trade Books for Young People.

Perhaps Sørensen's best-known work to date is the artwork he created for Carmen Agra Deedy's *The Yellow Star*, which recounts the legend of King Christian X of Denmark. Committed to protecting his subjects during the dark days of the Nazi occupation in the 1940s, the king, legend has it, wore the yellow star that was required of Jewish citizens himself when he rode his horse through the streets of Copenhagen. The legend epitomizes an individual act of courage that was actually replicated throughout Denmark many times over as the Danish people managed to conduct 7,000 of their Jewish neighbors to safety from the Nazi threat. Among its many accolades *The Yellow Star* received a Christopher Award, a Parents' Choice Gold Award, and the Bologna Children's Book Fair Ragazzi Award and was named a Jane Addams Peace Association Honor Book and an IRA Teachers' Choice.

Courtesy of Peachtree Publishers

Henry Sørensen attended the University of Aarhus, 1974–1980, and received a degree from the Academy of Fine Arts in 1983. He is married to Lisa Winther, a college teacher. They have two children, Mathilde Therese and Alexandra Beatrice, and live in Risskov, Denmark.

SELECTED WORKS WRITTEN AND ILLUSTRATED: *New Hope*, 1995; *Your First Step*, 1996.

SELECTED WORKS ILLUSTRATED: *Sun Up*, by Alvin Tesselt, 1991; *When the Rain Stops*, by Sheila Cole, 1991; *The Gift of the Tree*, by Alvin Tesselt, 1992; *Footprints and Shadows*, by Anne Wescott Dodd, 1992; *Granddaddy's Highway*, by Harriett Diller, 1992; *Mommy's Lap*, by Ruth Horowitz, 1992; *I Love You as Much*, by Laura Krauss Melmed, 1992; *I Know a Bridge*, by Jeff Sheppard, 1992; *What Does the Rain Play?*, by Nancy White Carlstrom, 1993; *Robert Frost*, ed. by Gary D. Schmidt, 1994; *River Day*, by Jane B. Mason, 1994; *Prince*

Nautilus, by Laura Krauss Melmed, 1994; *Deep River*, by Elaine Moore, 1994; *My Grandfather's House*, by Bruce Coville, 1996; *Daddy Played Music for the Cows*, by Maryann Weidt, 1996; *A Fourth of July on the Plains*, by Jean Van Leeuwen, 1997; *Hurricane!*, by Jonathan London, 1998; *A Book About God*, by Florence Mary Fitch, 1998; *Jumbo's Lullaby*, by Laura Krauss Melmed, 1999; *The Yellow Star: The Legend of King Christian X of Denmark*, by Carmen Agra Deedy, 2000; *The Cat Who Loved Mozart*, by Patricia Austin, 2001; *The Printer*, by Myron Uhlberg, 2002; *Wishes for You*, by Tobi Tobias, 2003.

SUGGESTED READING: *Something About the Author*, vol. 115, 2000.

WEB SITE: *www.illustrations.dk/index.htm*

"The first time I visited a public library (Sellers Memorial in Upper Darby, Pennsylvania), I was five years old. It was a summer Saturday afternoon. My mother took me. We walked. It felt far and adventurous. Along the way we stopped at a bakery for a cookie. Then at my grandparents' house for a drink. And three or four times to tie my shoes. Finally, we reached the library—a big white house with shutters and a heavy front door. The children's room was on the second floor. I climbed up the steps and into a wonderland! Books everywhere! Books about bears and bees and bunnies. Books about trees and trucks and triangles. Books with pictures. Books with poems. I didn't know which book to grab first. It made no difference to me that I couldn't read.

"That year, I visited the Sellers Library every Saturday with my mother. The following year, I was allowed to go with my friend Gladys. She was two years older. Gladys liked pickles better than cookies, so we always stopped at the deli to buy a pickle apiece. We stopped at my grandparents' house for a drink. By then I had learned how to make my shoestrings stay tied, and I had learned to read. And I had learned something else: What I wanted most of all was to become a writer.

"My father gave me his old black manual typewriter. The Z key stuck. Fine, I would not write stories about zebras or zippers. My father made me a desk from an orange crate. My mother filled a box with paper. And that's how I began, at my orange-

Courtesy of Jerry Spinelli

Eileen Spinelli

August 16, 1942–

crate desk in my tiny back bedroom. Two-fingered typing. Letters into words. Words into sentences. Sentences into stories. And poems. In high school I nearly failed geometry. But I won first prize for my poetry—a check for $50. I bought myself a new used typewriter, with a perfectly working Z key. I also bought a pair of red high heels. I won a dance contest wearing those shoes. But it was writing, not dancing, that stole my heart.

"After high school, I worked at an assortment of jobs. I was a waitress at a local diner. A secretary (still typing two fingers) in the city. I sold coffee and donuts on a trolley zipping between Philadelphia and Norristown, Pennsylvania. I answered the phone at an airplane factory. I filled subscription cards for the publisher of a department store magazine. I wrote on the bus going to work. I wrote on my lunch break. Sometimes I even— shhhh—wrote behind the counter or at my desk at work. I married. Had children. And continued to write. At the laundromat. In the grocery line. At home when the children were asleep. Long into the night I wrote. My husband, Jerry, was writing too. We had met at the department store magazine. We were drawn to each other by our love of words, our dreams of becoming published writers. We encouraged each other. Critiqued each other. Shared ideas. Rooted for each other. When Jerry got a rejection, I'd bake him a chocolate cake. When I got a rejection, he took me to the Village Porch for a hot fudge sundae.

"One day—a miracle—a manuscript of mine was accepted for publication, and the hot fudge sundae became a celebration instead of a consolation. And soon, so did the chocolate cake. Our dreams had come true. I love my writing life. My office is on the second floor of our house. It's cozy and warm. Plants at windows. My desk, our old dining room table. A teddy bear. Photos of my favorite people. An overstuffed rocking chair from Ikea. An electric typewriter (no, I don't use a computer). I write longhand, then type the manuscripts. Two fingers, just as I did when I was six. I'm faster now. Sometimes I'm so eager to get to work that I don't take time to get dressed in the morning. I just run upstairs in my flannel nightie or long tee-shirt. I sit in my overstuffed rocker, pen and paper tucked into clipboard, and the ideas flow. Sometimes.

"Sometimes there's no idea at all. I might as well be picking lint off the drapes or leaves off the spider plant. But I try to stay with it, stay in the chair. When the writing angel comes, she knows where to find me. My writing life is just a part of me. When I'm not writing you might find me hanging out with our grandkids (there are 16 of them—so far). Or heading for the beach with the family (we especially like Ocean City and Cape May, New Jersey). Or tending my herb garden, where I grow mint, parsley, sage, basil, thyme, oregano, rosemary, tarragon, cilantro, and bay leaf. Or browsing in a bookstore or library (poetry, biographies, novels, travel books, cookbooks, picture books; one is never too old for a hug or a picture book). Or walking to

> "I climbed up the steps and into a wonderland! Books everywhere!"

the pond (hoping to see the great blue heron). Or watching old movies, especially musicals. Or rummaging through thrift shops (any old teapots?). Or dancing in the hallway with my husband (high heels long gone, flat shoes now). Or baking (Jerry still likes chocolate cake). Or fixing dinner for friends (Italian my specialty). Or collecting river rocks (keeping a sharp eye out for heart-shaped ones). Or planning a trip to Venice (my favorite city of all).

"Or . . . well, you get the idea. So many things to do. As many things to do as there are things to write about. As there were things to read about when I was five years old at the Sellers Memorial Library, standing at the threshold of a wonderful world of books."

Courtesy of HarperCollins Children's Books

❀　❀　❀

Born in Philadelphia and raised in Upper Darby and Secane, Pennsylvania, Eileen Spinelli held various jobs after high school, all the while continuing to write poetry for adults. In 1977, she married writer Jerry Spinelli, and together they have raised six children.

Eileen's poems and stories for young people have appeared in *Highlights for Children* and other magazines. Her short story "Mannerly Moose" won the *Highlights* fiction contest in 1990. Her first picture book, *Thanksgiving at the Tappletons'*, was published in 1982 and reissued 10 years later with new illustrations. *Somebody Loves You, Mr. Hatch* received a 1991 Christopher Award, which recognizes books that affirm the "highest values of the human spirit." Spinelli also won the Society of Children's Book Writers and Illustrators Magazine Merit Award for fiction in 1990. *Sophie's Masterpiece* was an honor book for the 2003 Great Lakes Book Award.

Spinelli credits her early interest in poetry to a librarian, Miss Armstrong, who seemed to delight in words and books and passed that delight on to the future author. When she isn't writing, Spinelli enjoys gardening, traveling, and shopping at flea markets. She lives with her husband in West Chester, Pennsylvania.

SELECTED WORKS: *The Giggle and Cry Book*, illus. by Lisa Atherton, 1981; *Thanksgiving at the Tappletons'*, illus. by Maryann Cocca-Leffler, 1982 (illus. by Megan Lloyd, 1992); *If You Want to Find Golden*, illus. by Stacey Schuett, 1993; *Animals of the North*, illus. by Laura D'Argo, 1990; *Somebody Loves You, Mr. Hatch*, illus. by Paul Yalowitz, 1991; *Boy, Can He Dance*, illus. by Paul Yalowitz, 1993; *Lizzie Logan Wears*

Purple Sunglasses, illus. by Melanie Hope Greenberg, 1995; *Naptime, Laptime*, illus. by Melissa Sweet, 1995; *Where Is the Night Train Going: Bedtime Poems*, illus. by Cyd Moore, 1996; *Lizzie Logan Gets Married*, 1997; *Lizzie Logan, Second Banana*, 1998; *Tea Party Poems*, 1998; *Sophie's Masterpiece*, illus. by Jane Dyer, 1998; *When Mama Comes Home Tonight*, illus. by Jane Dyer, 1998; *Coming Through the Blizzard: A Christmas Story*, illus. by Jenny Tylden-Wright, 1999; *Six Hogs on a Scooter*, illus. by Scott Nash, 2000; *Night Shift Daddy*, illus. by Melissa Iwai, 2000; *Song for the Whooping Crane*, illus. by Elsa Warnick, 2000; *In My New Yellow Shirt*, illus. by Hideko Takahashi, 2001; *Wanda's Monster*, illus. by Nancy Hayashi, 2002; *Here Comes the Year*, illus. by Keiko Narahashi, 2002; *Rise the Moon*, illus. by Raúl Colón, 2003; *Three Pebbles and a Song*, illus. by S. D. Schindler, 2003; *Feathers: Poems About Birds*, illus. by Lisa McCue, 2004; *Do You Have a Hat?*, illus. by Geraldo Valério, 2004.

SUGGESTED READING: *Contemporary Authors*, vol. 107, 1983; *Something About the Author*, vol. 150, 2004; Spinelli, Eileen. "Life's Small Moments," in *Speaking of Journals*, ed. by Paula Graham, 1999.

A profile of Eileen Spinelli's husband, Jerry, appeared in *Sixth Book of Junior Authors and Illustrators* (1989).

Nancy Springer

July 5, 1948–

"My father's rule was: If it was daytime, children were to be outside getting 'fresh air and exercise.' No staying inside and reading a book unless it was pouring down rain. No books at the dinner table, either! I loved books, and I would sneak a flashlight to bed so that I could read under the covers. But daytime, I spent my happiest hours running like a little blonde collie dog through the woods and fields near my home along the Passaic River in New Jersey. I knew the grove of white trees deep in the forest, where the great horned owls perched. I knew the meadows where buttercups bloomed and where quail and pheasants hid their chicks. I knew where to find wild strawberries. I knew the raspberry patches where the raccoon feasted. I knew the green and yellow garter snake who lived in the rocks. I knew every frog in the little brook that ran down to the marsh. And oh, the marsh. I spent hours knee-deep in that wetland, fascinated by the snails on the rocks, the duck nests in the reeds, the muskrats, green herons and great blue herons and red-tailed hawks and water snakes and snapping turtles. At night, I fell asleep to the chiming of spring peepers, or a cicada chorus, or the faraway soprano voices of foxes. A butterfly perching on my finger, toads in the garden, a sparrow hawk flying, all these marvels were my joy and my refuge—especially from school, where I was a misfit, too shy, too smart, too skinny. But away from school, I had my favorite books—*Black Beauty*, *The Black Stallion*, tales of Robin Hood, many others. I had my father, who liked to walk the freshly plowed fields with me searching for Iroquois arrowheads. I had my mother, who painted wonderful pictures in her studio while she showed me the blue jays on the hickory tree outside the window. And above all, I had wrens in the maples and possums in the woods. I lived in my own garden of Eden, lovely, wide, wild, rife with life.

"But Eden disappeared when I turned 13. My family moved away, and when we came back to visit a year later, the fields were a housing development, the woods were being bulldozed for a military installation, the brook was in a culvert, and the marsh was being filled for an expressway. In my family, we didn't cry, but I wanted to. All my life since, I've felt a sense of deep loss, Eden lost, and that heartache has found its way into some of my stories.

"My new home was in Gettysburg, Pennsylvania, site of the climactic battle of the Civil War. My father had left his business career behind to buy a small motel in partnership with my mother, and I spent my teen years helping to make beds and clean rooms. There was a river, Marsh Creek, and there were fields, and sometimes I still got to run like a collie, and sometimes I even got to ride horses. But most of the time my father and mother needed me. I ran errands, swept, mowed grass, shoveled snow, waited on customers. Being useful helped me get over being shy. When I was fifteen, I ran the motel myself for a weekend while my parents traveled back to New Jersey to attend a funeral. I was still skinny, but in my new school it was okay to be smart, even though in history class we seemed to learn mostly about the Battle of Gettysburg. Anyway, I made good grades and won several small scholarships which enabled me to attend Gettysburg College, where I majored in English literature.

Courtesy of Jamie Pinto

Nancy Springer

"I'm not sure when I decided I wanted to write. My parents wanted me to be a schoolteacher or a librarian, but I sensed that wasn't for me. Yet to say I wanted to be a novelist was way over the top, because novelists were like gods in my universe, gods named Hemingway, Steinbeck, Faulkner. Perhaps because I had no idea what to do with me, I married while I was still in college, but no sudden-happiness Cinderella transformation took place. Yearning for something I couldn't even name, I spent hours lying in bed, daydreaming. After graduation I took pay-the-rent jobs and kept trying to think what to write, but with no confidence. Hemingway had shot lions and been to war, but I'd never done anything like that. Faulkner had gone fox-hunting on horseback, gotten drunk, and been in fights. Steinbeck had traveled across the country on his own. But all I'd ever done was be a girl, a motel maid and waitress; how could I possibly write anything good? In my college classes we hadn't studied a single female author aside from Jane Austen, who was all about getting married, and Charlotte Brontë, who was all about getting dead. I had never heard of Virginia Woolf, Sylvia Plath, Anne Sexton, Maya Angelou, Shirley Jackson, Flannery O'Conner, Marge Piercy, Margaret Atwood, Toni Morrison. I had no sense of women's authority to write *literature*.

"I have since learned how many other women writers have faced the same vacuum, the same lack of role models, and have arrived at the same solution. I gave up trying to write the Great American Novel, and instead I wrote fantasy novels based on my perpetual daydreams. They did so well that I was able to have two children and buy myself a horse. Then I started writing horse stories like the ones I'd loved when I was a girl. And after a while I found myself writing realistic books about young people, and mystery novels, and humor, and novels based on the legends of King Arthur, then a series about the daughter of Robin Hood. I write all kinds of books, and I love it. Maybe someday I'll write the Great American Novel without even knowing it. Maybe not. It doesn't matter. I've learned that good writing comes from emotion in the heart, not from ambition in the head.

"And my heart is still yearning for Eden. So I live in a house by a lake now, and when I'm not writing, I'm out there wading along the rocky shore and watching the little brown minks, the ducks and herons, the water snakes, the fish and the frogs."

❈ ❈ ❈

Nancy Springer was born in Livingston, New Jersey. Her father, Harry Connor, had emigrated from southern Ireland when he was a young man; her mother was an artist. When Nancy was thirteen, the family moved to Gettysburg, Pennsylvania, where they ran a motel business. Nancy attended nearby Gettysburg College, where in 1969 she married Joel Springer, a ministerial student. After graduating with a B.A. from Gettysburg College in 1970, Springer taught at the Delone Catholic High School in McSherrystown, Pennsylvania, for a year. She began her writing career in 1972, combining it with various jobs at colleges and universities that involved personal development, professional growth, and communications. The Springers had two children, Jonathan and Nora, and after 27 years of marriage, they were divorced. In 1995 Nancy Springer became a creative writing instructor at the York College of Pennsylvania and in 1997 joined the faculty at Seton Hill College in the master's degree program in popular fiction. She lives in East Berlin, PA.

Springer has written many fantasy, science fiction, and realistic novels for adults and for teens as well as prize-winning short stories and poetry. Her adult books *Apocalypse* and *Larque on*

> "In my college classes we hadn't studied a single female author aside from Jane Austen, who was all about getting married, and Charlotte Brontë, who was all about getting dead."

the Wing received Nebula Award nominations, while *Fair Peril* was a 1997 Mythopoeic Fantasy Award nominee.

Horses have played major roles in Springer's writing for young people. She says she "fulfilled a childhood dream," when, at the age of 33, she bought a horse. Her first children's book, *A Horse to Love*, shows the importance of a horse to a shy, uncertain girl and was an IRA/CBC Children's Choice Book. *Colt* won the Joan Fassler Memorial Book Award in 1992, was an IRA/CBC Children's Choice Book and a New York Public Library Book for the Teen Age. *Boy on a Black Horse* was an ALA Recommended Book for Reluctant Young Adult Readers. *Toughing It*, a realistic novel for young adults, was named an ALA Best Book for Young Adults, an ALA Recommended Book for Reluctant Young Adult Readers, a Carolyn W. Field Honor Book and an American Booksellers Association Pick of the Lists. Both *Toughing It* and *Looking for Jamie Bridger* won Edgar Awards in the Youth category from the Mystery Writers of America.

Courtesy of Holiday House

The Hex Witch of Seldom was an ALA Best Book for Young Adults and a New York Public Library Book for the Teen Age. In *I Am Mordred*, the author portrays the fateful son of King Arthur in a new light, garnering an ALA Best Books for Young Adults citation, a Carolyn W. Field Award, and inclusion in *Booklist*'s Top Ten Fantasy list. Developing another folkloric figure, Springer wrote *Rowan Hood: Outlaw Girl of Sherwood Forest* about a feisty daughter of Robin Hood who comes to be heralded for her own brand of courage and for her skill in healing arts.

SELECTED WORKS FOR CHILDREN AND YOUNG ADULTS: *A Horse to Love*, 1987; *Not on a White Horse*, 1988; *The Hex Witch of Seldom*, 1988; *They're All Named Wildfire*, 1989; *Red Wizard*, 1990; *Colt*, 1991; *The Friendship Song*, 1992; *The Great Pony Hassle*, 1993; *Music of Their Hooves*, 1993; *The Boy on a Black Horse*, 1994; *Toughing It*, 1994; *Looking for Jamie Bridger*, 1995; *Secret Star*, 1997; *I Am Mordred: A Tale from Camelot*, 1998; *Sky Rider*, 1999; *Rowan Hood: Outlaw Girl of Sherwood Forest*, 2001; *Separate Sisters*, 2001; *Lionclaw: A Tale of Rowan Hood*, 2002; *Wild Boy: A Tale of Rowan Hood*, 2004.

SELECTED WORKS FOR ADULTS: *The Book of Suns*, 1977; *The White Hart*, 1979; *The Sable Moon*, 1982; *The Black Beast*, 1982; *The Golden Swan*, 1983; *Wings of Flame*, 1985; *Chains of*

Gold, 1986; *Madbond*, 1987; *Chance: And Other Gestures of the Hand of Fate*, 1987; *Mindbond*, 1987; *Godbond*, 1988; *Apocalypse*, 1989; *Damnbanna*, 1992; *Stardark Songs*, 1993; *Metal Angel*, 1994; *The Blind God Is Watching*, 1994; *Fair Peril*, 1997; *Plumage*, 1999.

SUGGESTED READING: *Authors and Artists for Young Adults*, vol. 32, 2000; *Contemporary Authors*, vol. 106, 2002; *Something About the Author*, vol. 110, 2000; *St. James Guide to Fantasy Writers*, 1996; *St. James Guide to Science-Fiction Writers*, 4th ed., 1996.

Courtesy of Annie Hall

William Steig

(Rhymes with the first syllable of "tiger")

November 14, 1907–October 3, 2003

Many children's authors would feel that having their name on more than 30 books constituted a lifetime achievement. For William Steig, what is remarkable about the 30-plus books that he created is that he didn't write and illustrate his first until he was 61 years old. A latecomer to the field, this prominent figure in 20th-century children's literature was a noteworthy cartoonist, having produced more than 1,600 drawings and cartoons as well as 117 covers for the *New Yorker* magazine. For "The King of Cartoons," as he was called, the changeover was serendipitous. A colleague at the magazine, Robert Kraus, who had become a successful children's author/illustrator, suggested that Steig try doing a children's book, and presto! he found a new outlet for his skills, as well as immediate success.

William Steig started painting at an early age. He grew up in the Bronx in creative surroundings with parents who were both artists; when he exhibited an intense interest himself in painting, his eldest brother Irwin, a professional artist, gave him his first lessons. He was influenced by Grimms' fairy tales, Charlie Chaplin movies, the Katzenjammer Kids comics, the opera *Hansel and Gretel*, and especially Carlo Collodi's *Pinocchio*. In high school he found an outlet for his talent by creating cartoons for the school newspaper. After graduation, he attended City College in New York for two years, spent three years at the National Academy of Design, and then five days at the Yale School of Fine Art, because he was more interested in swimming and playing football. During the Depression when his father, a house painter by trade, couldn't find work, Steig supported the family by selling cartoons to the *New Yorker* and other magazines starting in 1930. From age 23 on, he viewed the world through eyes that observed human foibles, which his drawings immortalized with wit and satire. In the 1940s Steig began carving in wood; his sculptures are owned by several museums.

With the publication in 1968 of a letter-puzzle called *C D B!*, Steig launched his new career in children's books. In the same year *Roland, the Minstrel Pig* appeared, the beginning of a sequence of stories about pigs, dogs, donkeys, and other creatures began. He peopled his books with animals because they allowed him to bring the same tongue-in-cheek insouciance to children's books that made his adult work so popular. His third book, *Sylvester and the Magic Pebble,* earned him the Caldecott Medal in 1970 and was also nominated for the National Book Award. Though the book was adored by readers everywhere, Steig's tongue-in-cheek humor got him into trouble with one group: police associations across the country took umbrage over his portrayal of the animal police officer on one page of the story as a uniformed pig. At the time when protest and political unrest were raging, and "pig" was a notorious derogatory term for cop, Steig's illustration caused a hullabaloo that resulted in national headlines, but the controversy boosted sales. At the height of the uproar, Steig told *Time* magazine that he viewed pigs as good symbols for all mankind.

His next book, *Amos and Boris*, was also nominated for the National Book Award and was designated a *New York Times* Best Illustrated Book in 1971. In 1972 he turned his hand to a novel about a dog hero, *Dominic,* which earned another nomination for a National Book Award and won the Christopher Award in 1973. A year later, he wrote *The Real Thief,* acknowledging his fascination with King Arthur and quest literature by naming the goose hero Gawain. In 1977 his novel *Abel's Island,* about a proper Edwardian mouse who is stranded on an island in true Robinson Crusoe fashion and must use his wits to survive, was given a Newbery Honor Award. That same year Steig received a Caldecott Honor Award for *The Amazing Bone*, featuring his first female protagonist. His inimitable combination of a rich vocabulary and forthright style of writing with consistently humorous and poignant illustrations also earned him two U.S. nominations for the Hans Christian Andersen Award; one for writing in 1988 and one for illustration in 1982, rare recognition of a unique talent that could be expressed visually or verbally, with equal success.

ABEL'S ISLAND ○ *William Steig*

FARRAR / STRAUS / GIROUX

Courtesy of Farrar, Straus and Giroux

Steig's signature style of thick, sketchy black lines with loosely applied watercolors, often including patterns of stripes, polka dots, and flowers on clothing or backgrounds, evolved from and reflected his talent for cartooning. Whether portraying a mouse dentist or a donkey holding a magic pebble, his humor came from believable situations and characteristics that readers recognized. The problems were universal, the settings familiar, and the emotions recognizable by all. *Caleb and Kate*, published in 1977, was the first of his stories with characters in human form. Most of his later books focused on people and their interactions, as in *The Toy Brother* and *Pete's a Pizza*.

His honors were many, including numerous ALA Notable Children's Books citations, and in 1983 he received a second Newbery Honor Award for *Doctor DeSoto*, as well as the American Book Award. It was noteworthy that this picture book was cited for the writing rather than the illustrations, for Steig's art was often recognized for its excellence. Four of his books were cited by the *New York Times* as Best Illustrated books of their year; in addition to *Amos and Boris*, the honor was bestowed on *Gorky Rises* in 1980, *Brave Irene* in 1986, and *A Handful of Beans* in 1998. In the month after Steig's death his last book, *When Everybody Wore a Hat*, became the fifth work of his to be so honored. His picture book *Shrek!* inspired the blockbuster animated film that was nominated for an Academy Award for best screenplay based on a book. Though the film was very different from the book, Steig was said to have enjoyed the way Dreamworks Studios had adapted his short tale.

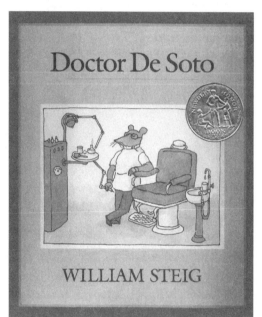

Courtesy of Farrar, Straus and Giroux

In an interview in 1992 with children's book critic Anita Silvey, Steig said: "The child is the hope of humanity. If they are going to change the world, they have to start off optimistically. I wouldn't consider writing a depressing book for children." William Steig helped refine and change the world of children's literature by creating witty, humorous books that celebrate the powers of imagination, language, and nature. Delightfully ironic with positive themes and heroic characters, they never lose sight of the ingenuity and resilience of the young.

SELECTED WORKS WRITTEN AND ILLUSTRATED: *C D B!*, 1968; *Roland, the Minstrel Pig*, 1968; *Sylvester and the Magic Pebble*, 1969; *Amos and Boris*, 1971; *Dominic*, 1972; *The Real Thief*, 1973; *Farmer Palmer's Wagon Ride*, 1974; *Abel's Island*, 1976; *The Amazing Bone*, 1976; *Caleb and Kate*, 1977; *Drawings*, 1979; *Gorky Rises*, 1980; *Doctor DeSoto*, 1982; *Yellow and Pink,*

1984; *Solomon and the Rusty Nail*, 1985; *Brave Irene*, 1986; *Spinky Sulks*, 1988; *Doctor DeSoto Goes to Africa*, 1992; *Shrek!*, 1993; *Zeke Pippin*, 1994; *Grownups Get to Do All the Driving*, 1995; *The Toy Brother*, 1996; *Pete's a Pizza*, 1998; *Toby, Where Are You?*, 2001; *Potch and Polly*, 2002; *When Everybody Wore a Hat*, 2003.

SELECTED WORKS ILLUSTRATED: *Consider the Lemming*, by Jeanne Steig, 1988; *Alpha Beta Chowder*, by Jeanne Steig, 1992; *A Handful of Beans: Six Fairy Tales*, retold by Jeanne Steig, 1998; *The Flying Latke*, by Arthur Yorinks, 1999.

SUGGESTED READING: Cott, Jonathan. "William Steig and His Path," in *Pipers at the Gates of Dawn: The Wisdom of Children's Literature*, 1983; Cullinan, Bernice, and Diane Person, eds. *The Continuum Encyclopedia of Children's Literature*, 2001; Lanes, Selma. *Down the Rabbit Hole: Adventures and Misadventures in the Realm of Children's Literature*, 1971; Lorenz, Lee. *The World of William Steig*, 1998; Marcus, Leonard. *Ways of Telling: Conversations on the Art of the Picture Book*, 2002; Silvey, Anita, ed. *Children's Books and Their Creators*, 1995; *Something About the Author*, vol. 111, 2000; Townsend, John Rowe. *Written for Children: An Outline of English Language Children's Literature*, rev. ed., 1974. Periodicals—Allender, David, "William Steig at 80," *Publishers Weekly*, July 24, 1987; Angell, Roger, "The Minstrel Steig," *New Yorker*, February 20, 1995; Heppermann, Christine, "William Steig," *Riverbank Review*, Summer 2002; Jones, Malcolm, "The King of Cartoons," *Newsweek*, May 15, 1995; *New York Times*, October 6, 2003 (obituary); Steig, William, "Caldecott Acceptance Speech," *The Horn Book*, August 1970.

WEB SITE: *www.williamsteig.com*

An earlier profile of William Steig appeared in *Third Book of Junior Authors* (1972).

"My family lived in northern New Jersey, not far from New York City. It was a typical suburban neighborhood with small ranch houses and sidewalks lining the streets. My two brothers and I were part of a big neighborhood filled with kids of all ages. Afternoons during school and in the summer we were on our bikes all over town. I have a memory of screen doors slamming up and down the street, as we were free to come and go. Nearly every day we rode our bikes down our street to Percy's store for penny candy and *Archie and Veronica* comic books. On summer nights we played games like kick-the-can and sardines well into the darkness with fireflies everywhere. It seemed unfair when our parents called us in for bed.

Melissa Sweet

April 19, 1956–

"I had a third grade teacher, Mrs. Blockburger, an enormous woman in size and spirit. I was always—and still am—a small person, and she called me her "wee lassie." In my hazy and distant memory of that year with her, I got a lot of attention for being pretty good at drawing. At home my folks were always making things. My mom sewed clothes for me and knit tiny doll sweaters. My dad built us a playhouse and did construction around the house. There were projects going on all the time.

"In school I did okay, but I had trouble sitting still all day, and I was not an avid reader. I always thought I'd be an artist—there was never any question for me. When I got to high school I wanted to be a potter, and at the time I had my own potter's wheel. During my first year in art school I really fell in love with drawing and painting. My roommate had brought several children's books with her, and one was *Little Bear,* with illustrations by Maurice Sendak. My dad had read that book to us as kids. When I saw Sendak's art again I became really interested in book illustration and thought my style of art might work in children's books.

"After a few years at college I ended up taking classes in whatever interested me. I noticed one of the things that drew me to art was the process—learning how to use tools, keeping sketchbooks, figuring out how different materials work. I took classes in welding, blacksmithing, calligraphy, and papermaking. I loved learning all kinds of things, but books remained my primary interest. Hoping to eventually illustrate books, I began making greeting cards and hand-made books, which got me drawing every day. Finally around 1985, I put together a portfolio and went to New York City to talk to art directors about getting published. During that trip I acquired my first job—illustrating the Pinky and Rex series by James Howe. It was incredibly exciting to illustrate my first books for such a fantastic author.

Courtesy of Annie Highbee/Imagewright

Melissa Sweet

"I find that each book calls for something different, and I spend a lot of time trying to figure exactly how I'm going to do my art and what materials I'm going to use. When I received the manuscript for *Moonlight: The Halloween Cat* by Cynthia Rylant, I knew I wanted the artwork to be in acrylics so I could get the deep, rich colors of a moonlit night. I kept the art simple by using a big brush for painting. Another book, *Giggle-Wiggle Wake-Up* by Nancy White Carlson, is about a preschooler getting ready to go to school. I used old notebook paper in the collages to help give it the feeling of being in a school classroom.

If I can, I like to travel to do the research for the nonfiction books. I traveled to Egypt to see the pyramids and research tombs for *The 5,000 Year Old Puzzle* by Claudia Logan. Recently I went to Kentucky and Pennsylvania for a book about John James Audubon, *The Boy Who Drew Birds* by Jacqueline Davies. I keep journals and collect a ton of stuff along the way because I never know what I might use in the books. Even after working on all sorts of projects, I still find it's the designing, research, and experimenting that is the most exciting part of making children's books.

"Now I live with my husband, Mark, and step-daughter, Emily, in a small coastal Maine village near a working harbor. Above my drafting table there's a quote from the poet Mary Oliver: 'To pay attention, this is our endless and proper work.' That's good, because I often find myself taking walks, gardening, or biking, but I'm taking in everything I experience, and it somehow shows up in my books. We have a dog, Rufus, who plays a major role in a book I just finished, *Carmine: A Little More Red*, about Little Red Riding Hood. This is the first book I've written and illustrated. Now that I'm writing my own stories I feel like I'm starting all over again. It's been 20 years, and I still can't wait to get into my studio every morning."

"I noticed one of the things that drew me to art was the process— learning how to use tools, keeping sketchbooks, figuring out how different materials work."

Born and raised in suburban Wyckoff, New Jersey, Melissa Sweet (whose maiden name was Melissa Vogels) received an associate's degree from Endicott Junior College in Beverly, Massachusetts, in 1976, and studied art at the Kansas City Art Institute in 1977. Working at a summer job in Maine in 1978, she met her first husband, and they lived in Boston, where he worked as a chimney sweep. They divorced in 1996 and Melissa moved to Maine, where they had spent many summers. She lives today in Rockport, married to Mark Holden, a boat builder who works for the Department of Environmental Protection.

Melissa has been a freelance artist for her entire career. In addition to children's books, she has worked at various types of commercial art, including illustrating maps for *Martha Stewart Living, Travel and Leisure*, and *Yankee* magazines. She has contributed illustrations to the *New York Times* and *Nick Jr.* magazine, made posters, designed greeting cards for Recycled Paper Products and Renaissance Greeting Cards, and created one-of-a-kind handmade books. Her work designing toys for Eeboo earned her several Parents' Choice Awards.

Since entering the world of children's books by creating illustrations for the first of James Howe's Pinky and Rex easy-to-read chapter books in 1990, she has published over 60 titles. Her lighthearted, gentle cartoon illustrations have graced a wide range of children's books from board books to series fiction to more serious nonfiction subjects, all with equal success. Sweet's signature style of whimsical watercolors is often enhanced by

Courtesy of Alfred A. Knopf/Random House, Inc.

collage art when she finds objects and details that are appropriate to the story. The light, joyous quality of her work and the technical skill in its execution have led to many of her books being chosen for awards. One of her very first books, *The Talking Pot*, was named an American Booksellers Association Pick of the Lists. *Llama in Pajamas* received a Parents' Choice Award, and *Bouncing Time* garnered an Oppenheim Toy Portfolio Gold Award. *The Dirty Laundry Pile* won a Texas Bluebonnet Award and was named a Children's Book of Distinction by the *Riverbank Review*.

For Catherine Thimmesh's *The Sky's the Limit: Stories of Discoveries by Women*, Melissa created a notebook-like effect with watercolors and collage over lined paper to simulate the notes of a working researcher or naturalist. The result is a book in which the design perfectly matches the text, and this title was included on lists of both Notable Social Studies Trade Books and Outstanding Science Trade Books, as well as winning the 2003 Minnesota Book Award for juvenile nonfiction. Two other nonfiction titles were named Outstanding Science Trade Books: *The 5,000 Year Old Puzzle* and *Girls Think of Everything*. *Leaving Vietnam*, written by Sarah Kilborne, is a Ready-to-Read book about the harrowing experiences of Vietnamese boat people; in preparing the illustrations, Sweet chose watercolors to emphasize the tender family bonds of the desperate refugees even while they are coping with extreme situations. This book was also named a Notable Social Studies Trade Book for Young People.

SELECTED WORKS WRITTEN AND ILLUSTRATED: *Carmine: A Little More Red*, 2005.

SELECTED WORKS ILLUSTRATED (Pinky and Rex series, all by James Howe): *Pinky and Rex*, 1990; *Pinky and Rex Get Married*, 1990; *Pinky and Rex and the Spelling Bee*, 1991; *Pinky and Rex Go to Camp*, 1992; *Pinky and Rex and the New Baby*, 1994; *Pinky and Rex and the Double-Dad Weekend*, 1995; *Pinky and Rex and the Bully*, 1996; *Pinky and Rex and the Perfect Pumpkin*, 1998; *Pinky and Rex and the Mean Old Witch*, 1999; *Pinky and Rex and the Just-right Pet*, 2001.

SELECTED WORKS ILLUSTRATED: *The Talking Pot: A Danish Folktale*, retold by Virginia Haviland, 1990; *Fiddle-i-fee: A Farmyard Song for the Very Young*, adapted by *Melissa Sweet*, 1992, 2002; *Snippets: A Gathering of Poems, Pictures, and Possibilities*, by Charlotte Zolotow, 1993; *A House by the*

Sea, by Joanne Ryder, 1994; *Llama in Pajamas*, by Gisela Voss, 1994; *Blast Off!*, by Lee Bennett Hopkins, 1995; *Naptime, Laptime*, by Eileen Spinelli, 1995; *The Bat Jamboree*, by Kathi Appelt, 1996: *Monsters in Cyberspace*, by Dian Curtis Regan, 1996; *Monsters and My One True Love*, by Dian Curtis Regan, 1998; *Bats on Parade*, by Kathi Appelt, 1999; *Love and Kisses*, by Sarah William, 1999; *Leaving Vietnam: The Journey of Tuan Ngo, a Boat Boy*, by Sarah S. Kilborne, 1999; *Bouncing Time*, by Patricia Hubbell, 2000; *Girls Think of Everything, Stories of Ingenious Inventions by Women*, by Catherine Thimmesh, 2000; *Bats Around the Clock*, by Kathi Appelt, 2000; *Charlotte in Giverny*, by Joan MacPhail Knight, 2000; *Dirty Laundry Pile: Poems in Different Voices*, ed. by Paul Janeczko, 2001; *Good for You!: Toddler Rhymes for Toddler Times*, by Stephanie Calmenson, 2001; *Now What Can I Do?*, by Margaret Park Bridges, 2001; *The 5,000 Year-Old Puzzle: Solving a Mystery of Ancient Egypt*, by Claudia Logan, 2002; *The Sky's the Limit: Stories of Discoveries by Women*, by Catherine Thimmesh, 2002; *Welcome Baby!: Baby Rhymes for Baby Times*, by Stephanie Calmenson, 2002; *Charlotte in Paris*, by Joan MacPhail Knight, 2003; *My Grandma Is Coming to Town*, by Anna Grossnickle Hines, 2003; *Giggle-Wiggle, WakeUp!*, by Nancy White Carlstrom, 2003; *Moonlight: The Halloween Cat*, by Cynthia Rylant, 2003; *Peek-a-Book*, by Lee Wardlaw, 2003; *Spring Is Here: A Barnyard Counting Book*, by Pamela Jane, 2004; *The Boy Who Drew Birds: A Story of John James Audubon*, by Jacqueline Davies, 2004; *Won't You Be My Kissaroo?*, by Joanne Ryder, 2004.

WEB SITE: *www.melissasweet.net*

Shelley Tanaka

June 28, 1950–

"As a kid I loved to read, and I kept lots of journals and wrote many poems and stories that were very sentimental and derivative (two things I still have to watch out for when I write). But I never intended to become a writer. I wanted to be a dancer or a musician or a florist.

"After university I got a job working in book publishing, and eventually I became a children's book editor. I worked with some amazingly gifted and creative fiction writers, and I knew that I could never do what they did. However, I did know how to put together a sentence. I was very organized and methodical and a good speller. And I was extremely curious and could become interested in just about anything.

"I slipped into writing gradually, through editing children's nonfiction. I started by writing the texts for a couple of day-books—*The Anne of Green Gables Diary, The Horse-Lover's Diary*. I rewrote a couple of manuscripts that had been written by other people. I co-wrote a few books. Then I was given the chance to write a full-length manuscript myself (*Disaster of the*

Hindenburg). This eventually led to writing *On Board the Titanic* and other books in the 'I Was There' series. I love writing these books because they are more than information books. They focus on the people behind historical events. The books are full of facts but also allow you to imagine how it felt when the *Titanic* sank, when Vesuvius exploded, when the Spaniards entered Mexico City, when the bombs fell on Pearl Harbor.

"When I'm writing a book, the work is very intense. I read and research and write and rewrite, and one day the book is finished and I have a wonderful souvenir (all the books I've worked on have been beautifully designed and illustrated). Then I move on to something else! It reminds me of going to school—reading, studying, working on a project or essay and handing it in, and then clearing off your desk and gettting ready to start work on something completely fresh.

"When I began to write books I was suddenly on the receiving end of the editorial process, and that was a big eye-opener. Now I understood how it felt to hover by the phone waiting to hear whether or not a publisher liked your manuscript. I knew what it was like to receive a manuscript back from an editor that was bleeding with comments and deletions and changes. How difficult it was to rewrite something for the umpteenth time long after you thought you had finished. How insecure and crazy a writer could get. I also saw that editors could be wrong.

"Writing books has made me a better editor. It keeps me on my toes. Each book is a different kind of adventure—a new group of people to learn about, a new deadline, new questions, a new section of the library to discover."

Courtesy of Gill Foss

Shelley Tanaka

❀ ❀ ❀

Shelley Tanaka was born and raised in Don Mills, which was at that time a brand new suburb of Toronto. Her parents had lived through Japanese internment camps in the interior of Canada during World War II and moved to Toronto from British Columbia after the war. She spent much of her childhood building forts in the woods, since the area was full of wide open spaces and ravines. When not playing in the woods, Shelley took piano lessons, ballet lessons, and swimming lessons and went to Brownies.

In 1973 she graduated with honors from Queen's University in Kingston, Ontario, where she majored in both English and German. She has found her knowledge of different languages extraordinarily useful in her writing. She was able to read, in the original German, Werner Franz's account of his experiences as a cabin boy on the *Hindenburg*, and claims that if she had not read the Franz account, she could never have written *The Disaster of the Hindenburg*, which is a tale of the last hours on the dirigible from the perspectives of two teenagers, one a passenger and the other a cabin boy. She also believes that only after immersing herself in the original account of Sir William Marshal (in rhymed medieval French) was she prepared to write *In the Time of the Knights: The Real-Life History of History's Greatest Knight*.

On Board the Titanic, The Disaster of the Hindenburg, Lost Temple of the Aztecs, and Secrets of the Mummies have all been named Notable Children's Trade Books in the Field of Social Studies. The International Reading Association named *On Board the Titanic* a Young Adult Choice; it was also an ALA Quick Pick for Reluctant Young Adult Readers and an ALA Notable Children's Book. *Lost Temple of the Aztecs* and *Discovering the Iceman* were also ALA Quick Picks for Reluctant Young Adult Readers. *Graveyards of the Dinosaurs* was named a *School Library Journal* Best Book of the Year and an IRA/CBC Children's Choice.

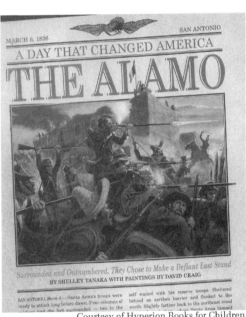

Courtesy of Hyperion Books for Children

Tanaka earned an M.A. in comparative literature from the University of Toronto in 1975. She has been a writer and book editor since 1975 and the fiction editor for Groundwood Books of Toronto since 1984. She also edits cookbooks because she loves to cook. Her two daughters are both at university now and are sometimes her most ruthless critics when she asks them to read a work in progress.

SELECTED WORKS: *The Heat Is On: Facing Our Energy Problem*, illus. by Steven Beinicke, 1991; *The Disaster of the Hindenburg: The Last Flight of the Greatest Airship Ever Built*, illus. by Donna Gordon, Ken Marschall, Jack McMaster, and Margo Stahl, 1993; *A Great Round Wonder: My Book of the World*, illus. by Debi Perna, 1993; *Discovering the Iceman: What Was It Like to Find a 5,300-Year-Old Mummy?*, illus. by Laurie McGaw, 1996; *On Board the Titanic: What It Was Like When the Great Liner Sank*, illus. by Ken Marschall, 1996; *The Illustrated Father Goose*, illus. by Laurie McGaw, 1996; *The Buried City of Pompeii: What It Was Like When Vesuvius Exploded*, illus. by Greg Ruhl, photos. by Peter Christopher, 1997; *One More Border: The True Story of One Family's Escape from Wartorn Europe*, with William Kaplan, illus. by Stephen Taylor, 1998; *The Lost Temple of the Aztecs: What It Was Like When the Spaniards Invaded Mexico*, illus. by Greg Ruhl, 1998; *Graveyards of the Dinosaurs: What It's Like to Discover Prehistoric Creatures*, illus. by Alan Barnard, 1998; *In the Time of Knights: The Real-life Story of History's Greatest Knight*, illus. by Greg Ruhl, 2000; *Footnotes: Dancing the World's Best-loved Ballets*, with Frank Augustyn, 2001; *Attack on Pearl Harbor: The True Story of the Day America Entered World War II*, paintings by David Craig, 2001; *New Dinos: The Latest Finds! The Coolest Dinosaur Discoveries!*, illus. by Alan Barnard, 2003; *The Alamo: Surrounded and Outnumbered, They Chose to Make a Defiant Last Stand*, illus. by David Craig, 2003; *D-Day: They Fought to Free Europe from Hitler's Tyranny*, illus. by David Craig, 2004.

SUGGESTED READING: *Contemporary Authors*, vol. 183, 2000; *Something About the Author*, vol. 136, 2003.

Courtesy of Theresa Dimenno

Tricia Tusa

July 19, 1960–

"By the age of five I had decided I wanted to write and illustrate books for children. I loved to draw, and I loved stories—those in my head and those in books. I have not changed. I was particularly taken with *Little Red Riding Hood* back then, wanting it read to me repeatedly. My mother could not bear yet another reading, and so I had to find another way. Not yet able to read, I would re-create the story. I would begin at the story's ending and move backwards. I would reinvent personalities for each character. Sometimes the wolf was depicted as a misunderstood, lonely animal all alone in the woods, or the grandmother as madly in love with the woodsman, or Red Riding Hood as very mischievous and into wearing various disguises (like a wolf costume).

"Around that same age, it was all I could do not to move my crayons and pencils across that vast expanse of white wall above my small bed. I knew I would get into trouble, and yet I had to see what it would look and feel like, doing it.

"My love of expressing what I was seeing and feeling inside myself through art and story-making was acknowledged by loving teachers and nuns in the first grade. This support and encouragement continued to be gently fostered throughout my school days.

"I received a B.F.A. in painting and sculpture from the University of Texas in Austin. I moved to New York City right after college, having been accepted into graduate studies at the Studio School. I decided, instead, to put a portfolio of illustrations together to take around to various publishing companies. Meanwhile, I had several jobs in order to pay for the rent. I freelanced at Estée Lauder and at D.C. Comics. I taught children art at a small art school. I acted as a personal assistant to an elderly woman. My last two years in New York were spent at graduate school at NYU studying art therapy.

"Many of the art directors who viewed my portfolio encouraged me to write stories behind the art. And so I did. I wrote a simple, somewhat autobiographical story about a little girl who gets her first pair of glasses. Holiday House published it. Hence my lifelong dream and career began.

"I have written and illustrated about 10 books. Within the last few years I have enjoyed illustrating others' books, equaling about 15 in number. I do a lot of freelance illustration as well, including book jacket covers, magazine illustrations, posters, etc.

"My hobbies are similar to my occupation. I paint, and create characters out of clay, and design and sew dolls. A lot of my time is spent with my six-year-old daughter making worlds out of cereal boxes and whatever else we have around the house. I love doing art with children in general; especially those having difficulties at school or in life. My husband is an architect who builds homes for people—sculptural houses that sometimes resemble tree houses or boats. Spaces full of light and whimsy.

"I am grateful for my entire life, the choices I have made, and for those I may have had nothing to do with."

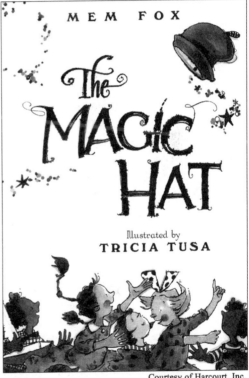

Courtesy of Harcourt, Inc.

❊   ❊   ❊

Born in Houston, Texas, Tricia Tusa studied art in Paris and Texas (B.F.A, University of Texas, 1982), art therapy in New York (M.A., New York University, 1989) and now brings together her interest in children, art, stories, and family relationships in her children's books. Her first picture book written and illustrated by herself was *Libby's New Glasses*, a gentle story about a girl getting used to wearing glasses who meets an ostrich hiding his beautiful bespectacled head. Her artwork won immediate attention for its humorous, "scratchy" line drawings and her characters' on-the-mark expressions. A year later, *Miranda*, the story of a young pianist with a sudden passion for boogie-woogie, was named an IRA/CBC Children's Choice. Tusa's exaggerated, comical illustrations convey the lively and intense feelings of her musical heroine. *Maebelle's Suitcase*, an American Booksellers Association Pick of the Lists, stars a zany and lovable 108-year-old woman who lives in a tree house to be close to her friends the birds while she makes very unusual hats.

A champion of outsiders, Tusa has created a group of quirky characters, young and old, who have (or grow into) the courage of their convictions along with an artist's desire to express themselves. In *Stay Away from the Junkyard!* her friendly heroine, Theo, discovers that the newcomer everyone in town has been avoiding is a sculptor in junk extraordinaire with a wonderful pet pig. *Miranda, Maebelle's Suitcase*, and *Stay Away from the Junkyard!* were all *Reading Rainbow* selections in 1989. *Bunnies in My Head* introduces a child artist who cannot stop filling the world with her paintings—they hang on clotheslines, embellish her kite, and decorate her room. The paintings were actually created by young patients at the M. D. Anderson Cancer Center in Houston where Tusa has worked as an art therapist.

Now living once again in her hometown of Houston, Tusa has recently been illustrating a number of picture books authored by others. *The Ballad of Valentine*, by Alison Jackson with Tusa's illustrations, was a *New York Times* best-seller. A member of the American Art Therapy Association and Southwest Writers, Tricia Tusa has demonstrated throughout her career that she is in touch with a child's real world, with all the fear and wonder that might entail.

SELECTED WORKS WRITTEN AND ILLUSTRATED: *Libby's New Glasses*, 1984; *Miranda*, 1985; *Chicken*, 1986; *Maebelle's Suitcase*, 1987; *Stay Away from the Junkyard!* 1988; *Sherman and Pearl*, 1989; *Camilla's New Hairdo*, 1992; *The Family Reunion*, 1993; *Sisters*, 1995; *Bunnies in My Head*, 1998.

SELECTED WORKS ILLUSTRATED: *Loose Tooth*, by Steven Kroll, 1984; *Lo-Jack and the Pirates*, by William H. Hooks, 1991; *Witches' Holiday*, by Alice Low, 1996; *Lemonade for Sale*, by Stuart J. Murphy, 1998; *Seal Island School*, by Susan Bartlett Weber, 1999; *Mrs. Spitzer's Garden*, by Edith Pattou, 2000; *The Magic Hat*, by Mem Fox, 2002; *The Ballad of Valentine*, by Alison Jackson, 2002; *A Long Way*, by Katherine Ayres, 2003; *The End of the Beginning*, by Avi, 2004; *Treasure Map*, by Stuart J. Murphy, 2004.

SUGGESTED READING: *Contemporary Authors*, vol. 182, 2000; *Something About the Author*, vol. 111, 2000.

"One of the most vivid and memorable impressions from my childhood in the north of Russia was a colorfully illustrated book that I received from my father on my birthday. The book was a Russian folktale called *Masha and the Bear*. My father used to read it to me out loud: '. . . the Bear walked through the fields and through the woods,' and in my mind I saw images of marvelous plants, animals, and birds from the illustrations contained in the book. I wanted to be able to capture the images from my own imagination on paper, and so I started to learn how to draw by copying illustrations from my favorite books.

"My attraction to the visual world of storytelling did not disappear as I grew older. At the age of 14 I began to study drawing and painting at a specialized school of art, where I remained for four years. During those years I also became a very active participant in sports. There were even times when I felt that a sport, not art, could be my true calling. At the nationwide exhibition of art from art schools held in Moscow, I received the first prize and graduated with honors. I was inspired and had a sense of security in my abilities, which allowed me to continue on my way to becoming an artist.

"I received my first job as an illustrator while I was studying design and illustration at the art institute in Moscow. I illustrated a children's book about insects, and observing the lives of those creatures still is one of my hobbies. I enjoyed the project immensely. The book was a success, and I began working on another children's book.

"In college, besides working on projects that directly related to my envisioned career as an illustrator, I became involved with singing in a jazz ensemble. One night after a performance I was approached by a director of a music studio. He asked if I wished to study singing seriously with his voice teachers, and I gladly agreed. Soon, art-related studies became second priority because voice lessons and performances occupied most of my time. But this change was not a permanent one. A teacher from the conservatory who was eager to find 'young talent' once listened to me sing and, contrary to my expectations, found nothing extraordinary in my voice. That was the end of my career as a singer. I was 25 years old, and once again the art of illustration became my main focus.

"Soon after graduation from the art institute, I became the art director in a publishing house in Moscow. I worked there for many years and continued to illustrate books as well. When my

Courtesy of Galina Vagin

Vladimir Vagin

March 9, 1937–

daughter, Anastasia, was born, I could not have had a more grateful listener for the improvised fairy tales that I narrated to her every night before bedtime for many years. The first sketches of my interpretations appeared at that time.

"My first encounter with American writers and illustrators of children's books took place in 1986, during the first Soviet-American Symposium on Children's Literature in Middlebury, Vermont. Frank Asch, one of the American authors whom I met there, saw my illustrations and expressed an interest in working with me on a children's book. We communicated by mail, sending sketches and letters back and forth, as I was living in Moscow and Frank was living in Vermont. Our book, *Here Comes the Cat*, was published in 1988 in New York as well as in Moscow. It was the first Soviet-American collaboration in the field of children's books.

Coutesy of HarperCollins Children's Books

"My second collaboration was with the American author Katherine Paterson, who wrote *The King's Equal* especially for me to illustrate after we met at the second Soviet-American Symposium on Children's Literature in Lithuania in 1987. In 1990 Frank Asch and I began to collaborate on our second book. That is when I visited the United States with my family. Since then I have illustrated many books by different authors as well as books based on my own interpretations while living in the beautiful state of Vermont."

❀ ❀ ❀

Prize-winning illustrator Vladimir Vagin was raised in Archangelsk in Russia. He graduated from the art institute in Moscow in 1963. In 1974 he married his wife, Galia, a pianist. Working as chief art director of the Moscow publishing house Sovremennik, Vagin designed and illustrated over 50 books and publications. Among numerous awards, he received the Soviet National Gold Medal for his illustration of *Russian Folk Tales* in 1989, and in that same year was named Distinguished Artist of the Russian Federated Socialist Republic. He also won an Honorable Mention and two Bronze Medals at the Annual Leipzig International Book Fair in Germany. Some of his work may be found in the collections in the Metropolitan Museum of Art, Johnson & Johnson's Art Gallery, the Weston Woods Art Collection, and the Mazza Collection Galleria. He was a member of the Russian Society of Miniaturists.

Here Comes the Cat, Vagin's groundbreaking collaboration with Frank Asch, is an almost wordless book expressing the exaggerated fears and misunderstanding of mice when they hear the cat is coming; the cat is actually bringing a great wheel of cheese. The story is considered by adults to be a political allegory on the Cold War, but it reaches all ages with its lively illustrations and surprise ending. Vagin has illustrated several more books written by Asch, becoming a close friend in the process. *Dear Brother* addresses sibling rivalry, and *The Flower Faerie* concerns the environment and humanity's relationship to nature; Vagin's art reflects his interest in Italian Renaissance settings. For Katherine Paterson's *The King's Equal*, the artist produced a detailed series of luminous paintings balancing between courtly formality and sly wit to match the story about a prince so vain he can't possibly find a princess to equal him. In Jane Yolen's retelling of *The Firebird*, Vagin combined lush, dramatic scenes from the story with panels of an actual performance of the ballet.

Since coming to the United States, Vagin has begun writing texts for his own work, beginning with a sumptuous presentation of *The Nutcracker Ballet*. His retelling of a folktale, *The Enormous Carrot*, was named a Notable Children's Trade Book in the Field of Social Studies. Russian themes are prominent in many of his books: *The Twelve Days of Christmas* combines exuberant winter scenes from both old Russia and Vermont in detailed watercolors. Russian folktales, such as the legend of Baba Yaga (*The Flying Witch*), retold by Jane Yolen, and Vagin's own version of Prokofiev's musical tale, *Peter and the Wolf*, are enriched by his unique visions of his homeland. Vladimir Vagin and his wife presently live in Vermont, while taking frequent trips to Russia. Their only daughter, Anastasia, also lives in the United States.

SELECTED WORKS WRITTEN AND ILLUSTRATED: *The Nutcracker Ballet*, 1995; *The Enormous Carrot*, 1998; *The Twelve Days of Christmas*, 1999; *Peter and the Wolf*, 2000.

SELECTED WORKS ILLUSTRATED: *Here Comes the Cat*, by Frank Asch, 1988; *Dear Brother*, by Frank Asch, 1992; *The King's Equal*, by Katherine Paterson, 1992; *The Flower Faerie*, by Frank Asch, 1993; *Insects from Outer Space*, by Frank Asch, 1995; *Celia and the Sweet, Sweet Water*, by Katherine Paterson, 1998; *The Wide-Awake Princess*, by Katherine Paterson, 2000; *The Circus Surprise*, by Ralph Fletcher, 2001; *The Firebird*, by Jane Yolen, 2002; *The Flying Witch*, by Jane Yolen, 2003.

Will Weaver

January 19, 1950–

"I grew up on a small dairy farm in northern Minnesota. I was raised in a 'plain style' religious manner (no television, the occasional movie). Having no television likely made me a better reader, and that, in turn, probably contributed to me becoming a writer. However, I had no inkling of becoming a writer until I was well into college.

"I met my wife-to-be at the University of Minnesota in a Shakespeare class when we were both 21; the stars were right, for we have been married ever since. Following graduation, we headed west to California, and it was there I began to write seriously, for the first time, about the Midwest. A story of deer hunting and family tension got me into the prestigious Stanford Writing Program, where I worked with Raymond Carver and John L'Heureux. It was at that time that I met Terry Davis (*Vision Quest*) and his good pal from Washington State, Chris Crutcher. We have stayed in touch ever since.

"Eventually my wife and I returned to the Midwest, where I began to publish short stories. My first story was 'A Gravestone Made of Wheat,' which got a good deal of attention and was eventually produced by National Public Radio. It later became the title story in a collection of short stories. My first book, however, was the novel *Red Earth, White Earth*. Focusing on the continuing culture clash between Native Americans and whites, it became a made-for-television movie for CBS.

"Following those two successes, I turned to writing for younger readers. This was because of my own two children. Their stories of school and sports reminded me of my own, and I published *Striking Out*, a novel about a farm kid pitcher with lots of family baggage. I followed with a sequel, *Farm Team*, and a third in the series, *Hard Ball*. Not wanting to be pigeonholed as a sports writer, I then wrote *Memory Boy*, a science fiction novel about environmental collapse, and *Claws*, about a family's collapse due to divorce. In addition to these young adult novels, I've also published several short stories for young readers in various anthologies."

Courtesy of Rosalie Weaver

❋ ❋ ❋

Will Weaver's full name is William Weller Weaver, but he uses "Will" for a pen name so as not to be confused with a renowned translator of Italian literature, William Weaver. Growing up on a dairy farm in northern Minnesota, he lived just a few miles from the White Earth Indian Reservation. He attended high school in Park Rapids and started college at Saint Cloud State, finishing his B.A. degree in English in 1972 at the University of Minnesota in Minneapolis. He worked as a technical writer for a few years before earning a master's degree in English and creative writing at Stanford University in California. He returned to run his family's farm for about two years when his father retired. At present, Weaver holds a position as professor of English and creative writing at Bemidji State University in Bemidji, Minnesota. His first novel, *Red Earth, White Earth*, was written for adults and tackled the ongoing problems between whites and Indians over reservation lands in the Midwest. The book was very successful, and a film version appeared on television in 1989.

Will Weaver turned to writing young adult books when he realized that it was a way to combine elements of his own life with his writing. As a father of teenagers, a baseball coach for youth, and one who remembered all too well his own years as a high school student from farm country, he created a memorable character in Billy Baggs. All three books in the Billy Baggs series— *Striking Out*, *Farm Team*, and *Hard Ball*—have been named ALA Best Books for Young Adults and included on the New York Public Library's Books for the Teen Age list. *Striking Out* was also an American Booksellers Association Pick of the Lists, and *Farm Team* was named a Distinguished Book for Young Adults by the International Reading Association. Praised for his ability to express true emotional depth in his characters and his gritty, unsentimental descriptions of farm life, Weaver puts his characters through grueling growth experiences both on and off the ballfield. Several memorable short stories followed, including "The Photograph" and "WWJD." These have been published in short story anthologies edited by Don Gallo. Weaver then wrote *Memory Boy*, a fast-paced survival story in which a boy helps save his family after volcanic fall-out has ravaged the landscape and destroyed the equilibrium of the country. Inspired by the Mount St. Helen's eruption, Weaver imagined a more enveloping disaster that would cause a family to flee their home and attempt to survive in the wilderness. *Memory Boy* was chosen as a Junior Library Guild selection and made the Top Ten in ALA's Best Books for Young Adults list.

Courtesy of HarperCollins Publishers

Living in northern Minnesota, Will and his family are all outdoors people. He enjoys fishing, canoeing, hiking, and hunting as well as winter sports such as skiing and snowshoeing. Nearly every summer he and his son join some other "Dads and lads" for a mountain hiking trip in the West.

SELECTED WORKS FOR ADULTS: *Red Earth, White Earth*, 1986; *A Gravestone Made of Wheat*, 1989.

SELECTED WORKS FOR YOUNG ADULTS: *Striking Out*, 1993; *Farm Team*, 1995; "Stealing for Girls," in *Ultimate Sports: Short Stories by Outstanding Writers for Young Adults*, ed. by Donald R. Gallo, 1995; "The Photograph," in *No Easy Answers: Short Stories About Teenagers Making Tough*

Choices, ed. by Donald R. Gallo, 1997; *Hard Ball*, 1998; "Bootleg Summer," in *Time Capsule: Short Stories about Teenagers Throughout the Twentieth Century*, ed. by Donald R. Gallo, 1999; "WWJD," in *On the Fringe: Stories of Alienation*, ed. by Donald R. Gallo, 2001; *Memory Boy*, 2001; "Bad Blood," in *Destination Unexpected*, ed. by Donald R. Gallo, 2003; *Claws*, 2003.

SUGGESTED READING: *Authors and Artists for Young Adults*, vol. 30, 1999; Hipple, Ted. *Writers for Young Adults*, Supplement, 2000; *Something About the Author*, vol. 109, 2000.

WEB SITES: *www.intraart.com/willweaver*; *www.authors4teens.com*

Courtesy of Harry Werlin

Nancy Werlin

October 29, 1961–

"One day, in my seventh grade English class, the girl who sat in front of me turned and picked up the book I was reading. (It was *Frederica*, a romance by Georgette Heyer, and I was reading it for the third or fourth time.) She examined it, asked me if it was good, and when I said yes, she sort of shrugged and said: 'I hate reading.' I gaped at her. It was as if she'd told me that she hated to breathe. I thought she had to be lying.

"Before that moment, I hadn't realized how I felt about reading. To me, books were like air; something you used constantly but took for granted. Of course, I knew that not everyone read as much as I did—a dozen books per week, toted home from the library—but I'd assumed that everyone understood how intoxicating, how pleasurable, any particular book might be. You opened a book and you were off on an adventure into other worlds, other minds, other hearts. I wasn't limited to being Nancy Werlin; I could be Jane Eyre, or Frodo, or Ponyboy, or Frederica. There were no limits. It was a terrible and wonderful freedom; it opened the world and made it mine.

"I realized at that moment that I loved reading.

"For me, then, it was entirely natural to dream about one day creating books that would be to others what the books I read were to me. During that seventh grade year I wrote some stories and some half-stories (including, I remember, a couple of mysteries), and so began to understand more about who I might become as a writer. I also took a creative writing class during eleventh grade and wrote some stories then (including, I remember, a suspense piece). That was all I wrote for a long time. And yet, in the years that followed, I continued reading, reading, reading, and I never lost sight of the fact that I wanted, eventually, to write fiction of my own. Finally, in my late twenties, I was ready to start.

"Now, I was and am a reader in just about every genre, but mysteries and suspense have long been among my favorites—along with science fiction, historical fiction, young adult fiction [of course], and the regular 'contemporary realistic' novel. Maybe, because I am a cross-genre reader, it's not so surprising that I ended up writing books that also attempt to cross genres. I've come to realize that the suspense thriller—a structurally demanding yet very flexible literary form—meshes powerfully with the themes of the traditional young adult 'coming of age' novel. I speculate that this is because growing up, coming into maturity, is often a dangerous business.

"Think about it. The world of the teenager often feels as if it's filled with deadly peril, and sometimes it really is. There are ordinary horrors: the daily gray misery of the school outcast, social pressures to conform, bullying, academic stress, agonies of love and sex. Many teenagers also deal with serious personal terrors—abuse, poverty, injustice, powerlessness. It's always possible someone will shoot you, too. Best years of your life? I hope not. In addition, the teenage years are a vital period of personal growth. The choices teenagers make, and the self-knowledge they acquire, have huge influence over the entire course of their lives—and, often, there isn't a lot of guidance available. What could be more terrifying? Or important?

"What I try to do in my books, I think, is use the dramatic threats involved in a suspense plot—killers, kidnappers, whatever—as metaphors for the terrors of adolescent life. If I do my job properly, external danger will force my characters across the rickety bridge to adulthood and into the self-knowledge that they need for the rest of their lives. They learn, in short, how to survive. And I hope readers will experience that process right along with them. The end result of this 'hybrid novel'—again, if I've done my work properly—is a book that offers escape and adventure with one hand, and psychological and moral depth with the other."

"To me, books were like air; something you used constantly but took for granted."

❄ ❄ ❄

Born and raised in Peabody, Massachusetts, Nancy Werlin attended Yale University and received her B.A. in 1983. She worked for various companies as a software technical writer from 1983 to 1987, which included 18 months living in Germany. For the next 10 years, she stayed with Thomson Investment Software, and it was during this time that she began writing her own fiction. She now works for Cognistar Corporation part time and makes her home near Boston, Massachusetts.

THE KILLER'S COUSIN

NANCY WERLIN

Courtesy of Delacourte Press

Werlin's first novel, *Are You Alone on Purpose?*, featured the distinct alternating voices of two protagonists whose relationship begins in hostility and evolves through friendship to deep caring for one another. Alison's life has always been shadowed by her twin brother's autism; when her nemesis Harry, the rabbi's son, is injured in a diving accident, Alison discovers some of the pain he has been hiding and begins to reach out to him. *Are You Alone on Purpose?* earned Werlin a spot in the *Publishers Weekly* "Flying Starts" column and was named to the New York Public Library's Books for the Teen Age list as well as the ALA's Quick Picks and Popular Paperbacks lists for teens. *The Killer's Cousin*, a thriller about teen homicide, was a *Booklist* Editors' Choice, a *Bulletin of the Center for Children's Books* Blue Ribbon title, and an ALA Best Book for Young Adults. In addition to accolades in the library community, *The Killer's Cousin* won the Edgar Award for best young adult mystery from the Mystery Writers of America and has been the recipient of many state-sponsored awards for teens.

Locked Inside was an Edgar nominee and listed on the Capitol Choices list of noteworthy books of the year. A taut drama involving kidnapping, a lonely and alienated teen's obsession with computer gaming, and the intriguing relationship that results, *Locked Inside* continued Werlin's competent blending of mystery elements with psychological coming-of-age stories. *Locked Inside* has appeared on many state-sponsored teen reading lists, as has *Black Mirror*. Another suspense thriller in which an angst-ridden teen is forced to shake off her own psychological difficulties to face the danger at hand, *Black Mirror* was named to the ALA Best Books for Young Adults list as well as New York Public Library's Books for the Teen Age. In 2004 *Double Helix*, a novel that explores bioethical issues, was named one of *School Library Journal's* Best Books of the Year.

SELECTED WORKS: *Are You Alone on Purpose?*, 1994; *The Killer's Cousin*, 1998; *Locked Inside*, 2000; *Black Mirror*, illus. by Cliff Nielsen, 2001; *Double Helix*, 2004.

SUGGESTED READING: *Authors and Artists for Young Adults*, vol. 35, 2000; *Contemporary Authors*, New Revision Series, vol. 97, 2001; *Something About the Author*, vol. 119, 2001. Periodicals—"Flying Starts," *Publishers Weekly*, December 19, 1994; Werlin, Nancy, "Experimental YA Fiction," *Booklist*, October 1, 1998; Werlin, Nancy, "Get Rid of the Parents?"

Booklist, July 1999. Online—"Interview with Nancy Werlin," *www.cynthialeitichsmith.com/auth-illNancyWerlin.htm* (August 2001).

WEB SITE: *www.nancywerlin.com*

M artha Weston was born Martha Hairston in Asheville, North Carolina, and grew up in Ann Arbor, Michigan. She loved to draw as a child, and was frequently reprimanded by her teachers for doodling instead of attending to her lessons. She knew from the beginning that she was going to draw for her living, finding it impossible to imagine any other kind of work. Her parents were supportive and encouraged her by praising her work. Martha attended the University of North Carolina, then the University of Michigan, where she obtained her bachelor's degree in fine arts in 1969.

After graduation, she began work in a design studio in New York, later moving to San Fransisco, where she worked as a freelance artist and created animation cels for the television show *Sesame Street*. Eventually she settled in Fairfax, California, where she married and raised her two children.

Weston was a prolific writer and illustrator, with over 60 books to her credit in her 30-year career. Eleven of those titles she wrote as well as illustrated. Many of the books she illustrated were award-winning nonfiction titles. *The Book of Think; or, How to Solve a Problem Twice Your Size*, with text by Marilyn Burns, was selected for the Children's Book Showcase in 1977, celebrating the great care taken with the design of the book. *Bet You Can't!: Science Impossibilities to Fool You*, by Vicki Cobb and Kathy Darling, won the New York Academy of Sciences Children's Science Book Award in the Younger Category, as did *The Sierra Club Wayfinding Book* by Vicki McVey some years later. One of the first books illustrated by Weston in the Brown Paper School series, *The I Hate Mathematics! Book*, with text by Marilyn Burns, was a groundbreaking title at a time when most nonfiction books were basically dry and humorless. Taking a light-hearted and more child-friendly approach to serious subjects, the Brown Paper School books appealed to children and adults alike. Burns and Weston teamed together for a number of titles in the series, and after 30 years the *I Hate Mathematics! Book* remains in print, a rarity in today's highly competitive publishing industry. *The Hanukkah Book*, also written by Marilyn Burns, was select-

Courtesy of Clarion Books

Martha Weston

January 16, 1947–
September 4, 2003

ed as a Notable Children's Trade Book in the Field of Social Studies.

Weston's illustrations were playful and full of fun. She was well known for adapting her style to the particular author in each book and for using her skill to honor famous illustrators of earlier books. In *Cora and the Elephants*, a little girl's elephant foster parents are shown as gentle giants reminiscent of the classic Babar and his family. In some books she actually imitated the style of a former illustrator, to maintain continuity for her readers. For Marjorie Sharmat's Nate the Great books, she adopted the style of the original illustrator, Marc Simont, so that the later books would be in keeping with the rest of the series. In 2001 Weston was chosen by Houghton Mifflin to illustrate new versions of the Curious George series, and she created the art for the new stories in keeping with the 60-year-old classics about the mischievous monkey originally created by Margret and H. A. Rey.

Weston did, of course, have her very own lively and amusing style, which graced other titles with wit and gentle humor. *Tuck in the Pool* introduces a funny chubby-cheeked little pig who overcomes his fear of the water with the help of his lucky rubber spider. In all of Weston's books her delightful sense of humor is evident; she enjoyed the offbeat, the quirky, the amusing side of life. For years she collaborated with author Lissa Rovetch to create the Kate 'n' Toady stories in *Spider* magazine, contributing over 100 stories. When she began illustrating, with the exception of cover illustrations for which she used color pencils, she used only black-and-white pen images in the body of her work, for a very good reason. Martha Weston was colorblind. Once she decided to add color to her work, she delighted in outwitting nature and consistently produced successful hand-colored illustrations even though she could not distinguish the colors naturally. She schooled herself in the technical details of color interaction, labeled all her paints and palette, and had others check her work. The first book she both authored and illustrated, *Peony's Rainbow*, published in 1981, was illustrated in pen-and-ink with only the rainbow painted in watercolors. It was reissued in 1989 as *If I Only Had a Rainbow*.

Courtesy of Delacorte Press/Random House, Inc.

Toward the end of her life, Weston was branching into other areas of children's literature and was pleased to have published her first novel, *Act I, Act II, Act Normal*, a book inspired by her son Charley's experiences in middle-school drama programs.

She found just the right voice for the story, and this book was included in the 2004 IRA/CBC Children's Choices list. She was busy working on a second novel when she died of heart disease at the age of 56. At the time of her sudden and tragic death, Martha was living in Fairfax, just north of San Francisco, with her husband, Richard Weston, a hospital consultant, and her son, Charley. Her daughter, Dory, lives currently in New York City. An endlessly creative, charismatic woman with a generous spirit who made many lasting friendships among other authors and illustrators, Weston will long be remembered as a dedicated artist, a hardworking mother, and a source of inspiration to her colleagues. Just as surely, her work will be enjoyed for many years to come by children and their caregivers everywhere, as they discover her unique, humorous, and lively books.

SELECTED WORKS WRITTEN AND ILLUSTRATED: *Peony's Rainbow*, 1981, reissued as *If I Only Had a Rainbow*, 1989; *Bea's 4 Bears*, 1992; *Apple Juice Tea*, 1994; *Tuck in the Pool*, 1995; *Bad Baby Brother*, 1997; *Cats Are Like That*, 1999; *Space Guys*, 2000; *Act I, Act II, Act Normal*, 2003.

SELECTED WORKS ILLUSTRATED: *The I Hate Mathematics! Book*, by Marilyn Burns, 1975; *The Book of Think; or, How to Solve a Problem Twice Your Size*, by Marilyn Burns, 1977; *I Am Not a Short Adult! Getting Good at Being a Kid*, by Marilyn Burns, 1977; *My Garden Companion: A Complete Guide for the Beginner*, by Jamie Jobb, 1977; *This Book Is About Time*, by Marilyn Burns, 1978; *The Long Ago Lake: A Child's Book of Nature Lore and Crafts*, by Marne Wilkins, 1978, 1989; *Bet You Can't!: Science Impossibilities to Fool You*, by Vicki Cobb and Kathy Darling, 1980; *Lucky Porcupine!*, by Miriam Schlein, 1980; *The Hink Pink Book; or What Do You Call a Magician's Extra Bunny?*, by Marilyn Burns, 1981; *The Hoople's Haunted House*, by Stephen Manes, 1981; *Honestly, Myron*, by Dean Hughes, 1981; *The Hanukkah Book*, by Marilyn Burns, 1981; *Math for Smarty Pants; or, Who Says Mathematicians Have Little Pig Eyes?*, by Marilyn Burns, 1982; *Should You Shut Your Eyes When You Kiss? or, How to Survive "The Best Years of Your Life,"* by Carol M. Wallace, 1983; *Brain Power!: Secrets of a Winning Team*, by Pat Sharp, 1984; *Word Works: Why the Alphabet Is a Kid's Best Friend*, by Catherine B. Kaye, 1985; *Lizzie and Harold*, by Elizabeth Winthrop, 1986; *Something for Mom*, by Norma Jean Sawicki, 1987; *Happy Valentine's Day*, by Carol Barkin and Elizabeth James, 1988; *Making Cents: Every Kid's Guide to Money*, by Elizabeth Wilson, 1989; *The Sierra Club Wayfinding Book*, by Vicki McVey, 1989; *Do You Wanna Bet?: Your Chance to Find Out about Probability*, by Jean Cushman, 1991; *Eenie Meenie Miney Math!: Math Play for You and Your Preschooler*, by Linda Allison, 1993; *Wordsaroni: Word Play for You and Your Preschooler*, by Linda Allison, 1993; *Pint-Size Science: Finding-Out Fun for*

You and Your Young Child, by Linda Allison, 1994; *The New Complete Babysitter's Handbook*, by Carol Barkin and Elizabeth James, 1995; *Cora and the Elephants*, by Lissa Rovetch, 1995; *Did You See What I Saw?: Poems About School*, by Kay Winters, 1996; *Owen Foote, Soccer Star*, by Stephanie Greene, 1998; *Owen Foote, Frontiersman*, by Stephanie Greene, 1999; *Nate the Great and the Monster*, by Marjorie Weinman Sharmat, 1999; *How Will the Easter Bunny Know?*, by Kay Winters, 1999; *Pig's Eggs*, by Elizabeth Partridge, 2000; *Owen Foote, Money Man*, by Stephanie Greene, 2000; *Nate the Great, San Francisco Detective*, by Marjorie Weinman Sharmat, 2000; *Owen Foote, Super Spy*, by Stephanie Greene, 2001.

SUGGESTED READING: *Something About the Author*, vol. 119, 2001.

Courtesy of Andrew Vracin

Terry Widener

December 15, 1950–

"I grew up in Sand Springs, Oklahoma. It is a small town just west of Tulsa. In school I liked to play football and baseball, and I liked to draw. In the sixth grade I started taking oil painting lessons after school from an elderly lady named Mrs. Homer. She taught me how to use pastels and oil paints. Her home was filled with all sorts of interesting objects to draw and paint. We would choose a different subject at each lesson. At the end of the lesson all of us in the class would draw straws and the winner would receive a prize for the day. It could be anything from a new paintbrush to a homemade pie.

"I took art classes and played golf all through high school and ended up going to the University of Tulsa on a golf scholarship and majoring in art. After I graduated I went to work at a graphic design studio. Every chance I got, I would include an illustration in whatever project I was working on at the time. Eventually I pursued illustration full time and went into business for myself.

"A big influence in my paintings has been the regionalist painters of the 1930s. Alexander Hogue and Thomas Hart Benton are among a number of artists from this era that I admire. I also like the works of Paul Davis, Seymour Chwast, and Milton Glaser, who gained prominence in the late 1950s and still do wonderful work today.

"Sports subjects are of great interest to me. Each year I do a poster for the Mickey Mantle World Series that is held here in the town where I live. It is a baseball tournament for 15- and 16-year-old boys from all over the country. I like doing the research for sports subjects, like old uniforms and stadiums and equipment.

"I enjoy going to schools and speaking to groups of students about what it is like to be an illustrator. I like hearing what they feel and think about the work I do. Their opinions and ideas really matter to me, since my work is for them."

❁　❁　❁

Terry Widener's debut in children's books was an exciting one. His illustrations for *Lou Gehrig: The Luckiest Man*, written by David Adler, illuminated the story of one of baseball's all-time greats and helped the book win numerous awards. Named a *Boston Globe–Horn Book* Honor Book, it was also included on ALA's Notable Children's Books list, the *Horn Book* Fanfare roster, and the *Bulletin of the Center for Children's Books* Blue Ribbon list. His stylized portrayals of the ballplayers lend a nostalgic air to the book that recalls the WPA mural art of the 1930s, perfectly in keeping with this story of a gentle, dedicated man who simply loved the game of baseball. Widener's love of sport is also apparent in his paintings for another Adler title, *The Babe and I*, which was named a Notable Children's Trade Book in the Field of Social Studies. Turning to a lesser-known sports legend, Adler and Widener created a vibrant picture book about Gertrude Ederle, the first woman to swim the English Channel. The strength of Ederle's muscular body and the triumph of her achievement against enormous odds are brought to life by Widener's acrylic renderings of events in her life. From her baths in the kitchen sink as a baby to the powerfully-felt threat of the stormy Channel in her historic swim, Widener creates a true heroine in his art. The reader seems to be beside her throughout the ordeal of the swim and the following celebrations. *America's Champion Swimmer* became an Orbis Pictus Honor Book and was named an ALA Notable Children's Book, a *School Library Journal* Best Book, a *Bulletin* Blue Ribbon title, and a Notable Social Studies Trade Book for Young People.

Sport is not the only theme that Widener has illustrated. A folk tale from the Caribbean retold by Robert D. San Souci, *The Twins and the Bird of Darkness*, added another type of hero story to his work and was named a Notable Social Studies Trade Book for Young People. Widener's bold, simple images for Gary Soto's *If the Shoe Fits* perfectly convey the frustration of a boy who always wears hand-me-downs and the sensible conclusion to a dilemma he faces. The rounded shapes and intense emotion of the images in *The Christmas Cobwebs*, a Junior Library Guild selection with text by storyteller Odds Bodkin, bring that gentle tale of family love fully to life with grace and joy.

"A big influence in my paintings has been the regionalist painters of the 1930s."

Courtesy of Harcourt, Inc.

Terry Widener received his B.F.A. from the University of Tulsa in 1974 and married art director Leslie Stall in 1977. The couple live in McKinney, Texas, and have three children: Kate, Kellee, and Michael. Since 1981, Widener has been a freelance illustrator and has also taught as an adjunct professor at Texas A&M University. Today his boldly colored illustrations are immediately recognizable, and each title he creates conveys a powerful message.

SELECTED WORKS: *Lou Gehrig: The Luckiest Man*, by David A. Adler, 1997; *The Babe and I*, by David A. Adler, 1999; *Tambourine Moon*, by Joy Jones, 1999; *America's Champion Swimmer: Gertrude Ederle*, by David A. Adler, 2000; *Shoe Magic*, by Nikki Grimes, 2000; *Peg and the Whale*, by Kenneth Oppel, 2000; *The Christmas Cobwebs*, by Odds Bodkin, 2001; *The Twins and the Bird of Darkness: A Hero Tale from the Caribbean*, by Robert D. San Souci, 2002; *If the Shoe Fits*, by Gary Soto, 2002; *Girl Wonder: A Baseball Story in Nine Innings*, by Deborah Hopkinson, 2003; *When the Fireflies Come*, by Jonathan London, 2003; *The Firefighters' Thanksgiving*, by Maribeth Boelts, 2004; *Let's Go Play Basketball*, by Charles R. Smith Jr., 2004; *Nonna's Porch*, by Rita Gray, 2004; *Roy Makes a Car*, by Mary E. Lyons, 2005.

SUGGESTED READING: *Something About the Author*, vol. 105, 1999. Periodicals—"The Big Picture," *Bulletin of the Center for Children's Books*, April 2000.

WEB SITE: *www.new-work.com*

"I was born in Muskogee, Oklahoma, where I grew up like most boys playing hard, fighting sleep, reading comic books, and dreaming. Thanks to my very active imagination and the physical development handed down to me through my grandfather, I was able to chase and sometimes catch many of my dreams—dreams that included one day winning a bodybuilding championship, being a football star, or living the adventures of my favorite literary characters like King Arthur, Robin Hood, or a salty high seas privateer. My art development, with the help of comic books and boys' adventure stories, was well nourished and supplied by my parents, who themselves had no knowledge or understanding of such talents. But, in their own words, 'It kept him active, out of trouble, and above all, quiet.'

"Without formal education or training I naively set out for studies at the University of Oklahoma, where the opportunity availed itself to work with Don Ivan Punchatz at his famous Sketch Pad Studio in Arlington, Texas. Working as an apprentice for two and a half years, I learned the business end of illustrating while also learning the painting techniques and working methods of many of the local Dallas illustrators. Afterwards I moved back to Norman, Oklahoma, so that my wife and childhood sweetheart, Carmelita, could finish her studies in early childhood education, and I could set up my studio to begin my life as an illustrator and artist.

"My career started out slowly, but it wasn't long before my portfolio was full and the workday busy. Most of my clients were local at first, but after a whirlwind tour of New York I began working more on a national scale and began taking on a broader audience.

"My workday starts early. I arise, get the kids off to school, and then sit down with a hot cup of tea and a little reading . . . a new manuscript, the latest murder mystery, or catching up on some correspondence. It gets me in a creative frame of mind. Then it's off to work on one of the many and diverse projects that course through the studio, such as creating the new 'Kinder and Gentler' Mr. Clean, the colorful and proud Simba on Pride Rock for the *Lion King* soundtrack packaging, and the large historical murals commissioned to be hung in the Oklahoma Capitol Building. I am constantly talking with clients throughout the day about upcoming deadlines or changes called for by anxious editors. I have worked for some of the largest corporations in the

Courtesy of Gordon Trice

Mike Wimmer

March 22, 1961–

world, such as American Airlines, Procter & Gamble, Reader's Digest, Disney, Kimberly Clark, Southwestern Bell, AT&T, as well as just about every major publisher in the United States. The list goes on and on, but I find my greatest pleasure as an artist creating images for children's books and fine art prints. They allow me to have the final word in the creative process. It is still very much like being that little boy lying on the floor with an empty drawing pad and a box full of crayons.

"My goals have stayed pretty much the same throughout my career. The details help tell the story. Those details are not just the ones found in my paintings, but are also those details in my life as a husband and father. If I could paint the perfect picture it would look pretty much like my life. My palette is full, but each color is lovingly applied with the tender touch of someone who really loves his work and his life."

❖   ❖   ❖

Courtesy of Penguin Putnam Books for Young Readers

Mike Wimmer spent much of his early years drawing and dreaming. His mother, a schoolteacher, brought home art supplies for him to use and taught him to read early, fostering his love of adventure and fantasy. But he was strong and healthy, and as he grew older, friends of the family began asking him to help on their farms when the season came around. He knows what it's like to bale hay and cut and dehorn cattle. He attended schools in Muskogee, graduating from high school in 1979. His teachers recognized his talent and gave him special art projects to work on for various organizations. Wimmer went on to study at the University of Oklahoma and graduated in 1983. He had been commissioned by the university to do the artwork for the diploma that he received the following spring, when he participated in graduation ceremonies.

Wimmer is a versatile artist who draws and paints in several mediums. His commissions have included advertising work for many major corporations, historical murals for the Oklahoma State Capitol Building, and portraiture work. But he finds his greatest satisfaction creating illustrations for children's books. He likes to use his own children in his paintings, and you can find both his son, Eli, and his daughter, Lauren, in the illustrations for Patricia MacLachlan's *All the Places to Love*, a Notable Children's Trade Book in the Field of Social Studies that also won the Oklahoma Book Award for Best Illustrated Children's Book for 1995. *Train Song*, written by Diane Siebert, and *Summertime: From Porgy and Bess* were also named Notable Social Studies Trade Books. *Flight: The Journey of Charles Lindbergh*, with text by Robert Burleigh, was the winner of the Orbis Pictus Award for Outstanding Nonfiction for Children in 1990 as well as being an ALA Notable Children's Book and a Notable Trade Book in the Field of Social Studies. Wimmer's second book with Burleigh, *Home Run: The Story of Babe Ruth*, was also named an ALA Notable Children's Book.

Mike Wimmer lives in Norman, Oklahoma, with his wife (his childhood sweetheart, Carmelita) and their two children.

SELECTED WORKS ILLUSTRATED: *Staying Nine*, by Pam Conrad, 1988; *Flight: The Journey of Charles Lindbergh*, by Robert Burleigh, 1990; *Train Song*, by Diane Siebert, 1991; *Bully for You, Teddy Roosevelt*, by Jean Fritz, 1991; *All the Places to Love*, by Patricia MacLachlan, 1994; *Home Run: The Story of Babe Ruth*, by Robert Burleigh, 1997; *Summertime: From Porgy and Bess*, by George Gershwin, Dubose Heyward, Dorothy Heyward, Ira Gershwin, 1999; *Will Rogers*, by Frank Keating, 2002.

SUGGESTED READING: *Something About the Author*, vol. 70, 1993.

"**I** can't remember a time when I didn't want to be an artist of some kind. I wanted a romantic life of exotic travel, while I painted pictures and wrote my poems. My mother looked askance at these aspirations, saying, 'You didn't inherit those grand ideas from me.' She never had to say who she thought I had inherited them from; that was obvious.

"Most of my family was quite happy living in Belleville, Illinois, a small and (I thought) unexciting place. All except my mother's younger brother, my Uncle Walt; he was a musician who traveled all over the country playing the trombone with dance bands. Every now and then, he'd show up on my grandmother's doorstep, carrying his trombone case and an old valise. The outside world came into our house on his shoulders; I loved listening to his stories of odd characters he'd bumped into on the road, not to mention the famous and semi-famous people he'd met on the big-band circuit.

"Uncle Walt was the person who opened up the world for me. He let me see that it was possible to live a different kind of life than the nine-to-five sort that was valued by my parents. You could live a life of art. Of course I didn't realize then exactly what that meant. Just wanting to be an artist wouldn't make me one—I would have to

Courtesy of Morgan Pritchard

Ellen Wittlinger

Ellen Wittlinger

October 21, 1948–

work a long time to develop my art. Although I majored in painting in college, I soon realized writing was my strength. Before long it became my passion.

"The idea that art can take you out of your small world is a statement that a number of my books make. In *Lombardo's Law*, Justine and Mike make a video together; main characters in both *Noticing Paradise* and *Razzle* are photographers; in *Hard Love*, Marisol and John are writers, as is O'Neill in *What's in a Name*. It may be overstating the case to say that art saved me, but I certainly believe it can save people. Art is the religion my characters seem always to turn to.

"Why did I need to make art so badly? Who knows what makes up the stew of a person's soul? I was an only child in a family heavy with elderly folks. Both my parents worked, and I spent a lot of time with my grandmothers and great-aunts. I imagine that reading, writing, and drawing were my escape into a larger world and imaginary life. I was never lonely as long as I had a book, a pencil, or a crayon in hand. Over the years I've written many different kinds of things. I began by writing poetry, and then for many years I wrote plays and short stories for adults. Before long I found myself working as a children's librarian, surrounded by a world of books I'd never read before: young adult novels. The best part of that job was reading so many wonderful novels, and they inspired me to write one myself. When *Lombardo's Law* was published in 1993 I knew this was the kind of writing I wanted to do forever.

Courtesy of Simon & Schuster Books for Young Readers

"I've never regretted my choice to make art a career, even though there were times it would have been more lucrative to work the cash register in the supermarket. I'm thankful that Uncle Walt put those grand ideas in my head. Now, even my mother is proud of them."

✿　✿　✿

Ellen Wittlinger earned a bachelor's degree from Millikin University in Decatur, Illinois, in 1970. Interested in a career in writing, she enrolled in the University of Iowa Writer's Workshop and received her M.F.A. in creative writing there in 1973. In addition to earning her degree, Wittlinger also learned to take herself seriously as a writer and to look at writing as a serious profession. After her marriage to David Pritchard, a reference editor, the couple moved to Swampscott, Massachusetts, where they raised two children.

Wittlinger had worked in the University of Iowa library while doing her M.F.A., then as a cataloging assistant at the Tufts University library for two years. She devoted much of her time in the 1970s and 1980s to writing adult fiction, poetry, and plays. When she was hired as a children's librarian at her local library in Swampscott, working there from 1990 to 1993, Wittlinger started to read YA novels as part of her job. It was a revelation. The genre became her passion, in part because she believes the teenage years are so important and so fascinating. Wittlinger's work often portrays the role art can play as a release and refuge for troubled teens. She has won critical praise for the subjects she tackles (such as the homosexuality of the protagonist in *Hard Love*) and the way her characters ring true to life. She credits her playwriting experience for the ease with which she handles dialogue and characterization.

Hard Love received many accolades, was named a Printz Award Honor Book and received a Lambda Literary Award. *Lombardo's Law*, *What's in a Name?*, *Razzle*, and *Zig Zag* have been included on ALA's Best Books for Young Adults list as well as the New York Public Library's Books for the Teen Age. *What's in a Name?* and *Hard Love* were named Blue Ribbon Books by the *Bulletin of the Center for Children's Books*. *What's in a Name?*, *Gracie's Girl*, and *Razzle* were all Junior Library Guild selections.

SELECTED WORKS: *Lombardo's Law*, 1993, 2002; *Noticing Paradise*, 1995; *Hard Love*, 1999; *What's in a Name?*, 2000; *Gracie's Girl*, 2000; *Razzle*, 2001; *The Long Night of Leo and Bree*, 2002; *Heart on My Sleeve*, 2004.

SUGGESTED READING: *Authors and Artists for Young Adults*, vol. 36, 2001; *Contemporary Authors*, New Revision Series, vol. 100, 2002; *Something About the Author*, vol. 122, 2001; *Something About the Author Autobiography Series*, vol. 25, 1998.

Janet S. Wong

September 30, 1962–

"When I was a child, I never thought I would be a writer. The idea never crossed my mind. Unlike most professional writers, I did not read a lot when I was growing up. I checked books out of the library, but often I didn't finish them. Or if I did read them, it was because I had a book report due. I knew I should've kept a journal, but I never kept one for more than a week. I worked hard on my school assignments, though, knowing that my parents expected good grades from me, and so—luckily—I learned how to write well. Wait: let me back up. I did read a lot, actually, but not books. I used to read our cereal boxes. I used to love to read the *TV Guide*. I used to read the words printed on the label of the seat belt in the car. I guess I have always liked words, but my mind jumped around too much for reading whole books. I am still this way, sort of, just a little bit better. Maybe this is why I mainly write poetry.

"Up until I was 14 or so, I liked to spend my free time watching TV, looking at books with photos of different breeds of dogs and horses, 'designing' clothes (which I never made), and playing with my friends. Until I was seven, we lived in an apartment building smack in the middle of the city of Los Angeles, the kind of neighborhood filled with apartment buildings and long sidewalks and mini-marts and tiny patches of lawn and lots of kids and old people and broken glass in the gutters and ants everywhere. When we lived there, I used to love to pluck the leaves off the jade plants under our living room window. Jade plants are succulents, with round, fleshy, waxy leaves. If you snap a leaf in half, you can use it to draw on the sidewalk. The neat thing about that is you can draw something really ugly and it's OK, the image will last only a half-hour before it dries up and fades back into the concrete. I also used to ride my skateboard a lot, up and down the sidewalk—until I fell off, split my chin open, and had to get 13 stitches. They took my first-grade school picture the next day with a huge Band-Aid on my chin.

Courtesy of Glenn Schroeder

"When I was seven, we moved from Los Angeles to San Anselmo. Even though it was close to San Francisco, San Anselmo seemed hundreds of miles away from city life. After school, kids liked to run like wild down steep dirt trails, splash in little creeks, and catch lizards. We lived in San Anselmo for just four years, but those were my favorite years. I wrote *Minn and Jake* thinking about the things my friend Jenny (the Minn character) and I (the Jake character) used to do—silly things, dumb dares (like kissing a dog on the mouth). I was incredibly stupid sometimes.

"What turned me into a writer? In my last job before becoming a writer, I was director of labor relations at Universal Studios Hollywood. I was earning a lot of money (and I love to spend money). My parents were very proud of me for having graduated from Yale Law School and for ending up in such a good job. But I was unhappy. Some lawyers do good work, but I thought I was becoming a mean person. I used to have to fire people, and the worst part is that it was starting not to bother me. One day I was browsing in a children's bookstore, looking for a gift for my young cousin. The next thing I knew, my arms were full of picture books for the very young, books like *Goodnight Moon*, that I wanted to buy . . . for myself. I fell in love with so many books, and the idea hit me: Somebody wrote those books. Why couldn't I be one of those people? I decided to quit my law job to write. I told my husband that I was giving myself a deadline of a year. If, by the end of the year, I had sold a book, then I would keep writing. If not, then I would return to the law.

"At the end of the year, I had received a pile of rejection letters for a couple of dozen picture book manuscripts. I felt like a failure. I was ready to pick up the phone and call my old boss, asking for my old job back. But then I remembered what my husband had said, the night before I quit my law job: Why don't you do it for a year, and if you love it, then keep on writing? I did love writing. I do love writing. I love the way you can create a whole new world in a book."

✿   ✿   ✿

Janet S. Wong was born in Los Angeles, California. Her father, who emigrated from China to the United States when he was 12, met her mother when he was stationed in Korea with the U.S. Army. Wong often writes about the experience of a first-generation American-born child of Asian heritage in her award-winning picture books and poetry for children and teens. Her favorite subjects in high school were French and German, and as part of her undergraduate program at UCLA, she spent her junior year in France, becoming fluent in French, studying art history at the University of Bordeaux, and traveling throughout Europe. Returning to Los Angeles, she founded the UCLA Immigrant Children's Art Project, which taught refugee children how to express themselves through art. After graduating from UCLA, summa cum laude, with a B.A. in history, Janet decided to go to law school and obtained her J.D. from Yale Law School in 1987.

Janet practiced corporate and labor law for GTE and Universal Studios Hollywood before making a dramatic career change. After leaving her job and collecting rejection letters for more than a year, she studied with poet Myra Cohn Livingston. Mrs. Livingston introduced Janet's work to her longtime editor, Margaret McElderry, and shortly thereafter Janet's first book, *Good Luck Gold*, was published. Her successful switch from law to children's literature has been the subject of several articles and television programs, most notably an *O Magazine* article and a "Remembering Your Spirit" segment on the *Oprah Winfrey Show*, both in 2001, and the Fine Living Channel's *Radical Sabbatical* in November 2002. While Janet's poems and stories have been featured in many textbooks and anthologies, they have also appeared in public venues. Poems from *Behind the Wheel* have been performed on the radio show *Car Talk*. "Albert J. Bell" from *A Suitcase of Seaweed* was selected to appear on 5,000 subway and bus posters as part of the New York City Metropolitan Transit Authority's Poetry in Motion program. In April 2003, Janet was invited to read her book *Apple Pie 4th of July* at the White House Easter Egg Roll.

"I guess I have always liked words, but my mind jumped around too much for reading whole books. I am still this way, sort of, just a little bit better. Maybe this is why I mainly write poetry."

Courtesy of Margert K. McElderry Books

Janet Wong has received numerous awards and honors, including the International Reading Association's Celebrate Literacy Award for exemplary service in the promotion of literacy. *A Suitcase of Seaweed* was listed on New York Public Library's Books for the Teen Age and named a Notable Children's Trade Book in the Field of Social Studies. *Behind the Wheel* was named an ALA Quick Pick for Reluctant Young Adult Readers. *Rainbow Hand* received a Lee Bennett Hopkins Honor Book award from Penn State University, and *Night Garden* was cited as a Notable Book by the National Council of Teachers of English. Both *Grump* and *Apple Pie 4th of July* were Highly Commended titles for the Charlotte Zolotow Award, while *Buzz* was cited by both *School Library Journal* and the *Los Angeles Times* as a Best Book of the Year. *Minn and Jake*, a Junior Library Guild selection, also made the Blue Ribbon list of the *Bulletin of the Center for Children's Books*. *Knock on Wood* was named by the Bank Street College as one of its Best Books of 2003.

As an indication of her commitment to literacy issues, Janet has been appointed to two terms on the Commission on Literature of the National Council of Teachers of English (NCTE) and one term on the NCTE Excellence in Poetry Committee. She currently resides in Medina, Washington, a suburb of Seattle, with her husband, Glenn, and her son, Andrew.

SELECTED WORKS: *Good Luck Gold and Other Poems*, 1994; *A Suitcase of Seaweed and Other Poems*, 1996; *The Rainbow Hand: Poems About Mothers and Children*, illus. by Jennifer Hewitson, 1999; *Behind the Wheel: Poems About Driving*, 1999; *Night Garden: Poems from the World of Dreams*, illus. by Julie Paschkis, 2000; *Buzz*, illus. by Margaret Chodos-Irvine, 2000; *This Next New Year*, illus. by Yangsook Choi, 2000; *The Trip Back Home*, illus. by Bo Jia, 2000; *Grump*, illus. by John Wallace, 2001; *Apple Pie 4th of July*, illus. by Margaret Chodos-Irvine, 2002; *You Have to Write*, illus. by Teresa Flavin, 2002; *Minn and Jake*, illus. by Genevieve Cote, 2003; *Knock on Wood: Poems about Superstitions*, illus. by Julie Paschkis, 2003; *Alex and the Wednesday Chess Club*, illus. by Stacy Schuett, 2004.

SUGGESTED READING: *Something About the Author*, vol. 148, 2004. Periodicals—"Are You Listening to Your Life?" *O Magazine*, January 2001; Odean, Kathleen, "Unanimous Verdict: For These Lawyers, the Decision's In: Kids Are a More Rewarding Audience than Jurors," *Book*, July/August

2003; Wong, Janet S., "Moon Soup: My Lunar New Year," *Instructor*, January/February 1997.

WEB SITE: *www.janetwong.com*

"I fell into children's books by accident. It seems strange to me now not to have pursued it sooner. I've always been very keen on telling stories and making pictures, but I never really considered writing and illustrating children's books until I met an editor in 1992. At that time, I was churning out dozens of editorial illustrations for a variety of known and (mostly) unknown magazines just trying to make a living. This editor asked me if I had any ideas for children's books. I didn't, so I immediately and most confidently said I did. The following day I left to visit a friend in California and by the time my plane landed I had a pile of drawings and most of the manuscript for what would be my first children's book, *Big Brother Mike*. It was a cinch to write since it was about my childhood and my relationship with my older brother.

"Since then, I've written and illustrated over 30 books for children, created and produced *Oswald*, an animated television series for preschoolers, and written and illustrated a novel for young adults, *Where the Four Winds Blow*. My childhood was filled with old monster movies, comics, and yes, even a few children's books. My parents enrolled me in an oil painting class when I was about seven years old and, a few years later, a cartooning class since I had a serious interest in drawing crazy animals, robots, and aliens. Even at that tender age, I possessed the characteristics of a workaholic. I kept to a strict production schedule and manufactured comic after comic.

"While in college, I was introduced to a whole new world of fine art, theater, and music. When I graduated in 1987, I was determined to take myself and my art more seriously. No longer would I draw goofy pictures of monsters. I left that behind to pursue more serious endeavors. I was an *artiste*!

"I started presenting my portfolio at the most prestigious places in New York. But soon reality hit, and I was hustling my portfolio around, trying to get any illustration assignment I could. I did get some small assignments from newspapers and magazines and, after a few years, did quite well for myself. The images that I created were a bit dark and very conceptual. Then I did my first children's book.

Courtesy of Greg Miller

dan yaccarino

Dan Yaccarino

May 20, 1965–

"After this training of coming up with images that tell a story and working fast to meet the deadlines, I immediately took a shine to children's books. In fact, I started to like doing the books even more than the other assignments I was getting. I'd been doing illustrations about computers, the economy, and a variety of other mind-numbingly dull subjects for what seemed like forever. Now, I'm back to doing what I truly enjoy: telling stories and making pictures of crazy animals, robots, and aliens!"

❊   ❊   ❊

Dan Yaccarino, a native of Montclair, New Jersey, enjoyed art all through his childhood: writing and illustrating handmade comic books, making short films with friends, and writing and performing comic routines and plays on audiocassette. Yaccarino majored in illustration at New York City's Parsons School of Design and graduated with a B.F.A. in 1987. He then spent several years teaching art—at Parsons, at the School of Visual Arts in New York City, and at Montclair State University in New Jersey. At the same time, he began to develop his successful career as an illustrator and commercial artist.

by Andrea Zimmerman and David Clemesha

Illustrated by Dan Yaccarino

Courtesy of HarperCollins Publishers

Yaccarino's work has appeared in publications such as *Business Week*, the *New York Times*, *New York Magazine*, *Rolling Stone*, and *Time* magazine. He has created images for advertising campaigns and has worked extensively for Japanese companies such as Sony and Nikkei. His work has been exhibited in galleries in New York, Tokyo, and Rome, among other cities; his designs have appeared in animated television commercials, plush toys, children's apparel, stationary, CD covers, and children's bedding.

In 1999 he produced a pilot for his animated preschool television series *Oswald* and over the next two years produced 26 half-hour episodes, many of which he also wrote. The series premiered on the Nickelodeon network in 2001.

In illustrating children's books, Yaccarino's bold and energetic style is varied to suit the subject in each of the stories, and his illustrations are always characterized by a robust energy. In *Trashy Town*, for example, he employs bold colors and geometric shapes to match the simplicity of the story line and the staccato text. *Trashy Town* was included on many best lists of the year 1999 and named an ALA Notable Children's Book. Yaccarino has also occasionally illustrated longer works of fiction very effectively. In *Surviving Brick Johnson*, a chapter book about a bully, which also received an ALA Notable citation, his art strongly enhances Laurie Myers's story line.

Dan Yaccarino makes his home in New York City with his wife, Susan, and their two children, Michael and Lucy.

SELECTED WORKS WRITTEN AND ILLUSTRATED: *Big Brother Mike*, 1993; *If I Had a Robot*, 1996; *Zoom Zoom Zoom!*, 1997; *Good Night, Mr. Night*, 1997; *An Octopus Followed Me Home*, 1997; *Five Little Pumpkins*, 1998; *Deep in the Jungle*, 2000; *Unlovable*, 2001; *Blast Off Boy and Blorp—The Big Science Fair*, 2002; *I Met a Bear*, 2002; *Where the Four Winds Blow*, 2003; *Dan Yaccarino's Mother Goose*, 2004.

SELECTED WORKS ILLUSTRATED: *The Sawfin Stickleback—A Very Fishy Story*, by Catherine Friend, 1994; *Bam Bam Bam*, by Eve Merriam, 1995; *Carnival*, by M. C. Helldorfer, 1996; *One Hole in the Road*, by W. Nikola-Lisa, 1996; *Little White Dog*, by Laura Godwin, 1998; *Circle Dogs*, by Kevin Henkes, 1998; *Trashy Town*, by Andrea Griffing Zimmerman and David Clemesha, 1999; *Come with Me: Poems for a Journey*, by Naomi Shihab Nye, 2000; *Surviving Brick Johnson*, by Laurie Myers, 2000; *The Good Little Bad Little Pig*, by Margaret Wise Brown, 2002; *Halloween Countdown*, by Jack Prelutsky, 2002; *Bittle*, by Patricia and Emily MacLachlan, 2004.

SELECTED WORKS WRITTEN: *The Lima Bean Monster*, illus. by Adam McCauley, 2002.

SUGGESTED READING: *Contemporary Authors*, vol. 174, 1999.

Ed Young

November 28, 1931–

"'Eddy, I wonder what is to become of you.' This sentence still rings clearly in my ears, when my mother would glance up from my uncomely report card for some 10 of my academic years in China. The glance, though concerned, had a touch of warmth and amusement to it. Somehow I knew that she knew my formal schooling was secondary to my dreams and everything would be all right in the end.

"I was born, near Peking, in a coal-mining town called Tienstin two months after the Manchurian invasion. Three years later, when northern China was under renewed threat, my family moved southward to the mouth of the Yangtze River, a cosmopolitan city called Shanghai. The city was divided under the jurisdiction of many European countries which, for a while, ironically guarded us against much of the new intruder's insensibility. It was there that I grew up. The war restricted many material things, but my family learned to develop great tenacity and flexibility so as to enjoy life under the most adverse circumstances. At one time my father held three jobs and my mother attempted many small enterprises to keep the household running. We had five children in the family and often it increased to seven or eight when our friends came and decided to stay for a while. We played unceasingly by ourselves, with friends and relatives and occasionally with several families.

"When I was alone I daydreamed, and many of my dreams were manifested in the form of plays or drawings. They were shown to loving friends of the family, and I knew no matter what I did in life it would have to be first and foremost related to art. Since my father was a structural engineer it was hoped that I might develop into an architect. When the Communists took Shanghai, I went to Hong Kong to continue high school. Two and a half years later I was able to come to the United States and start my schooling in architecture, which took three years to reveal itself as a mistaken profession.

"In 1954 I entered Art Center College in Los Angeles and

Courtesy of Sean Kerman

graduated in another three years as an illustrator. The forces of opportunity drew me to New York City and there I accepted work in an advertising studio until it folded in 1961. While there I did studies of movements on my own, especially those of animals. Upon the suggestion of friends I showed them to Ursula Nordstrom of Harper & Row, who asked if I would try a book called *The Mean Mouse and Other Mean Stories*. It was then merely fun to bring back for a moment the long forgotten childhood days when animals behaved like human beings. However, the book took root, and it was followed by many others. It is to my amusement now to be called a children's book artist. Somehow, 'Eddy, I wonder what is to become of you' still rings in my ears.

"We book lovers have always had a common goal to nurture young people by sharing what we had loved as children and by helping them grow into a world that we envision for them. In recent years, however, we are losing that dream to profit-making businesses. I have been fortunate in my life, as the 1990 Caldecott Award for *Lon Po Po* allowed me to introduce the lesser-known Chinese tales to the West. What was surprising was that my 1990 *Boston Globe–Horn Book* Award acceptance speech led to a book called *Voices of the Heart*. Its popularity, in turn, made possible yet another book on Chinese symbolic pictograms and nature-writing called *Beyond the Great Mountains*, which represents for me a fresh direction for a new century."

❋   ❋   ❋

One of the most versatile and honored children's book creators of the present day, Ed Young began his career by sketching animals in the Central Park Zoo during lunch hours when he worked for a New York advertising firm. He shares the distinction, with many other artists and authors, of having been "discovered" by the legendary editor Ursula Nordstrom; she published his first illustrations in a book by Janice May Udry, *The Mean Mouse and Other Mean Stories,* in 1962. That first book won an award from the American Institute of Graphic Arts, a distinction that convinced Young to continue working in children's books. Further recognition came when he won a Caldecott Honor Award in 1968 for his evocative cut-paper illustrations in *The Emperor and the Kite,* a story written by Jane Yolen. This book was called a perfect blend of art and words; it also afforded Ed Young his first opportunity to illustrate a story set in his homeland.

A native of China, Young incorporates many motifs and styles from his cultural background in his work and cites the philosophy of Chinese painting as a main source of inspiration. Like the picture books he illustrates, traditional Chinese paintings are often accompanied by complementary words that expand the understanding of the images, as the pictures expand the understanding of the words. A longtime practitioner of the ancient Chinese physical discipline of Tai Chi Chuan, he has also been an instructor in that form for many years. Young has also mastered the art of Chinese calligraphy, which can be seen most notably in his very personal book, *Voices of the Heart,* in which he explores the meaning of 26 ideograms, each an emotional concept and each containing the symbol for the heart. Each word is written in its Chinese form and then interpreted by intricate collages that expand the connotations of the word by their artistic rendering. *Voices of the Heart* was named a Notable Children's Trade Book in the Field of Social Studies.

In a career that has spanned more than 40 years, Ed Young has illustrated many stories and poetry books written by others, but it was his own adaptation of a Chinese folktale—*Lon Po Po*—for which he won both the Caldecott Medal and the *Boston Globe–Horn Book* Award in 1990. A story similar to the Western "Little Red Riding Hood," the tale is notable for the resourcefulness of the youngest sister in tricking the wolf. Young's illustrations echoed Chinese panel paintings, divided into sections on many pages. Each page contains an image of the wolf, sometimes hidden in the impressionistic landscape of the story. Young's deep respect for the animal world is evident in the wording of his dedication for this book: "To all the wolves of the world for lending their good name as a tangible symbol for our darkness." Three years later he won a Caldecott Honor Award and captured the *Boston Globe–Horn Book* Award as well for *Seven Blind Mice,* a book executed in a vastly different style. Distinctive collage cut-outs in bright colors against a stark black background

"When I was alone I daydreamed, and many of my dreams were manifested in the form of plays or drawings."

illustrate this version of the old fable of "The Blind Men and the Elephant." The story doubles as a concept book, teaching counting, colors, and the days of the week, as well as the moral that wisdom requires seeing the whole, not just the parts.

Ed Young's prolific body of work encompasses stories from other parts of the world, including many of Native American origin and the mythology of the ancient world. He has specialized in depicting animals in many moods and incarnations. His illustrations for Nancy Larrick's anthology of cat poems, *Cats Are Cats,* earned him a spot on the *New York Times* Ten Best Illustrated list in 1988. His pencil drawings for Priscilla Jaquith's *Bo Rabbit Smart for True* enliven the distinctive voice of African stories collected in the Georgia Sea Islands. Creating illustrations for favorite novels of the past has provided another outlet for Young's talent. Elizabeth Foreman Lewis's 1933 Newbery Medal winner, *Young Fu of the Upper Yangtze,* received new life with his illustrations in 1973; Jack London's *White Fang* and Oscar Wilde's *The Happy Prince* have also benefited by his interpretations. In 1995 Young's own adaptation of Carlo Collodi's classic novel, *Pinocchio,* gave a fresh approach to the story through an abridged text and large, evocative collage illustrations. Poetry is especially suitable for Young's interpretative art, and he has illustrated picture-book editions of Robert Frost's *Birches* as well as Coleridge's *The Rime of the Ancient Mariner.*

"We book lovers have always had a common goal to nurture young people by sharing what we had loved as children and by helping them grow into a world that we envision for them."

Many of Ed Young's books have been named ALA Notable Children's Books over the years. His softly focused pastels for a picture-book edition of Eleanor Coerr's touching story, *Sadako,* were adapted to the book from his film version of this story of a Japanese girl who succumbs to leukemia years after the bombing of Hiroshima. Blending the imagery of the crane figures that Sadako and her friends created in origami with the events of the story, Young created remarkably evocative illustrations to convey the mood of hope in the midst of tragedy. His pastel and gouace renderings on an earthy brown background for Mary Casanova's retelling of *The Hunter,* an ALA Notable Children's Book in 2001, convey the nobility of sacrifice that is at the heart of many Chinese folktales.

What characterizes Ed Young's work above all else is variety and integrity. For each project, he adapts his style to the needs and moods of the story, poem, or concept he is illustrating. He has mastered many techniques and mediums—from papercutting and collage to impressionistic painting in pastel and gouache to exquisite drawing in charcoal and pencil—and employs each with fine skill that is honed to the particular story. His newest book *Beyond the Great Mountains* combines a love for his native land and its language with beautiful torn-paper and ink illustrations that recall the rice paper paintings of Chinese tradition. A spare line of text on each of the stepped pages celebrates the natural beauty of China.

Courtesy of Philomel Books

Young was an instructor at Pratt Institute from 1960 to 1966 and has taught at various times at Yale University, Sarah Lawrence College, and the University of California at Santa Cruz. In 1995 he received the Empire State Award for the body of his work. He lives with his family in Hastings-on-Hudson, New York.

SELECTED WORKS WRITTEN AND ILLUSTRATED: *Bird from the Sea*, 1970; *The Lion and the Mouse: An Aesop Fable*, 1979; *High on a Hill: A Book of Chinese Riddles*, 1980; *Up a Tree*, 1983; *The Other Bone*, 1984; *Lon Po Po: A Red-Riding Hood Story from China*, 1989; *Seven Blind Mice*, 1992; *Moon Mother: A Native American Creation Tale*, 1993; *Red Thread*, 1993; *Little Plum*, 1994; *Donkey Trouble*, 1995; *Cat and Rat: The Legend of the Chinese Zodiac*, 1995; *Night Visitors*, 1995; *Pinocchio*, adapt. from C. Collodi, 1995; *Mouse Match: A Chinese Folktale*, 1997; *Genesis*, adapt. from the King James Version, 1997; *Voices of the Heart*, 1997; *The Lost Horse: A Chinese Folktale*, 1998; *Monkey King*, 2001; *What About Me?*, 2002; *I, Doka: The Tale of a Basket*, 2004; *The Sons of the Dragon King: A Chinese Legend*, 2004; *Beyond the Great Mountains*, 2005.

SELECTED WORKS ILLUSTRATED: *The Mean Mouse and Other Mean Stories*, by Janice May Udry, 1962; *Poetry for Young Scientists*, comp. by Leland B. Jacobs and Sally Nohelty, 1964; *The Yellow Boat*, by Margaret Hillert, 1966; *The Emperor and the Kite*, by Jane Yolen, 1967, 1988; *Chinese Mother Goose Rhymes / Ju tzu ko t'u*, sel. by Robert

Wyndham, 1968, 1982; *The Tiniest Sound*, by Mel Evans, 1969; *Golden Swans: A Picture Story from Thailand*, retold by Kermit Krueger, 1969; *The Seventh Mandarin*, by Jane Yolen, 1970; *The Girl Who Loved the Wind*, by Jane Yolen, 1972; *8,000 Stones: A Chinese Folktale*, told by Diane Wolkstein, 1972; *Young Fu of the Upper Yangtze*, by Elizabeth Foreman Lewis, 1973; *The Red Lion: A Tale of Ancient Persia*, retold by Diane Wolkstein, 1977; *Cricket Boy: A Chinese Tale*, by Feenie Ziner, 1977; *Tales from the Arabian Nights*, retold from the original Arabic by N. J. Dawood, 1978; *White Wave: A Chinese Tale*, retold by Diane Wolkstein, 1979, 1996; *Bo Rabbit Smart for True: Folktales from the Gullah*, retold by Priscilla Jaquith, 1981, 1995; *Yeh-Shen: A Cinderella Story from China*, retold by AiLing Louie, 1982; *Bicycle Rider*, by Mary Scioscia, 1983; *The Double Life of Pocahontas*, by Jean Fritz, 1983; *Foolish Rabbit's Big Mistake*, by Rafe Martin, 1985; *Moon Tiger*, by Phyllis Root, 1985; *I Wish I Were a Butterfly*, by James Howe, 1987; *Whale Song*, by Tony Johnston, 1987; *Eyes of the Dragon*, by Margaret Leaf, 1987; *Who-Paddled-Backward-with-Trout*, by Howard Norman, 1987; *Cats Are Cats: Poems*, comp. by Nancy Larrick, 1988; *Birches*, by Robert Frost, 1988; *In the Night, Still Dark*, by Richard Lewis, 1988; *The Voice of the Great Bell*, by Lafcadio Hearn, retold by Margaret Hodges, 1989; *High in the Mountains*, by Ruth Yaffe Radin, 1989; *Oscar Wilde's The Happy Prince*, by Oscar Wilde, 1989; *Mice Are Nice*, comp. by Nancy Larrick, 1990; *Goodbye, Geese*, by Nancy White Carlstrom, 1991; *All of You Was Singing*, by Richard Lewis, 1991; *While I Sleep*, by Mary Calhoun, 1992; *The Rime of the Ancient Mariner*, by Samuel Taylor Coleridge, 1992; *What Comes in Spring?*, by Barbara Savadge Horton, 1992; *Dreamcatcher*, by Audrey Osofsky, 1992; *The First Song Ever Sung*, by Laura Krauss Melmed, 1993; *Sadako*, by Eleanor Coerr, 1993; *Bitter Bananas*, by Isaac Olaleye, 1994; *Iblis*, retold by Shulamith Levey Oppenheim, 1994; *The Turkey Girl: A Zuni Cinderella Story*, retold by Penny Pollock, 1995; *October Smiled Back*, by Lisa Westberg Peters, 1996; *The Hunter, A Chinese Folktale*, retold by Mary Casanova, 2000; *Desert Song*, by Tony Johnston, 2000; *White Fang*, by Jack London, 2000; *A Pup Just for Me: A Boy Just for Me*, by Dorothea P. Seeber, 2000; *Tai Chi Morning*, by Nikki Grimes, 2004.

Courtesy of Philomel Books

SUGGESTED READING: *Children's Literature Review*, vol. 27, 1992; Pendergast, Tom. *St. James Guide to Children's Writers*, 5th ed., 1999; Silvey, Anita, ed. *Children's Books and Their Creators*, 1995; *Something About the Author*, vol. 122, 2001. Periodicals—Brainard, Dulcy, "Ed Young," *Publishers Weekly*, February 24, 1989; Young, Ed, "Boston Globe–Horn *Book* Acceptance Speech," *The Horn Book*, January/February 1991; Young, Ed, "*Boston Globe–Horn Book* Acceptance Speech," *The Horn Book*, January/February 1993; Young, Ed, "Caldecott Acceptance Speech," *The Horn Book*, July/August 1990.

WEB SITE: *www.nccil.org/young.html*

An earlier profile of Ed Young appeared in *Third Book of Junior Authors* (1972).

"**M**y very first memory is of a visit to Hokkaido when I was about one and a half years old. Hokkaido is a large island in northern Japan. Although the winters are cold and harsh, the land is blessed with virgin forests, jewel-like lakes, and majestic mountains. It is also my father's native land. In this memory, I see the laughing faces of my grandparents and parents from where I sit on horseback at my grandparents' home. Suddenly frightened, I begin to cry and someone reaches up and takes me into their arms.

"I now spend half the year in Tokyo and the other half in Hokkaido. A horseback riding school happened to open in the neighborhood where I stay when I am in Hokkaido, and I have started riding. Horses have become special friends that I regard with respect and admiration. They also inspired me to write another story.

"An immense distance seems to lie between who I am today and the person I was 30, 20, or even 10 years ago. Yet I still feel a strong connection between my childhood memories and my present self. Memories do not belong to the past. At times, they are mirrors reflecting the future. Even more so, they form part of me now, the person remembering. Although I do not write directly about my own limited memories, when I read what I have written I can see how it expresses in a different form the road my life has traveled.

"I was born and raised in Tokyo, the largest city in Japan, yet when I was a child, the outskirts where I lived were still country-like. On the way to school, I often passed through a small wood

Courtesy of Shoichiro Hattori

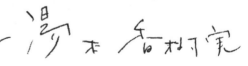

Kazumi Yumoto

1959–

all by myself. People today would probably condemn this as shockingly dangerous. Looking back on my childhood, though, I think the luxury of being alone in the woods, home to the birds, field mice, and other creatures, was the greatest blessing. I was an awkward child, and consequently I rarely felt at ease or carefree at school or at home. Walking on my own, smelling the fragrance of the foliage, and sensing the presence of little animals were things I enjoyed from the heart. Not that I was thinking of anything particularly grand or profound at the time. But suddenly I would be startled into awareness of the mystery of myself as a thinking being. I will never forget the wonder of such moments. Today I continue this search for wonder." [Translated from the Japanese by Cathy Hirano.]

❉ ❉ ❉

"An immense distance seems to lie between who I am today and the person I was 30, 20, or even 10 years ago. Yet I still feel a strong connection between my childhood memories and my present self."

Kazumi Yumoto's *The Friends*, a sensitive and perceptive story of three boys who stalk an old man so they can experience the meaning of death in his passing, made a strong impact on American readers when it was published in English translation in 1996. Awarded the *Boston Globe–Horn Book* prize for fiction, it was also named an ALA Notable Children's Book and a Notable Children's Trade Book in the Field of Social Studies. The publisher, Farrar, Straus, Giroux, received the Mildred A. Batchelder Award, which is presented to the publisher of a book that was originally issued in a foreign language and subsequently published in the United States in translation.

This was an auspicious beginning for a writer who started her career creating scripts for operas while attending Tokyo University of Music. After graduation she decided to draw on her childhood remembrances of a sense of wonder and mystery to create a book for young readers. With her deft style and strong sense of connection to the mind of a child, her books have been applauded by children and critics alike in her home country and abroad. In her own country *The Friends* won the Recommended Book Prize from the Japan School Library Book Club. In her acceptance speech for the *Boston Globe–Horn Book* Award, Yumoto shared her concerns about issues facing children that seemed to have grown ever more serious in the five years between the Japanese publication of *The Friends* and its American translation. She talked of the increase in bullying, suicide, and juvenile crime, and suggested that one aspect of the helplessness, despair, and lack of connection felt by troubled children is the fact that over the course of a generation they have become less likely to experience death as a part of the natural world and to share the last moments of life with elderly people who are dear to them. It is a curiosity about death that drives the plot of *The Friends*, but in the course of the story the three boys learn more about life and love and caring as their lives become intertwined with the old man's. In the end they are immeasurably enriched by the experience.

Yumoto continued to probe the theme of death and grief in her novel *The Letters*. For an older audience than *The Friends*, this story explores both past and present griefs in the life of Chiaki as she attends the funeral of a former landlady. Mrs. Yanagi had helped Chiaki cope with the death of her father when she was six years old by urging her to write letters, which the old woman promised to deliver to him when she herself died. Attending the funeral years later, as a young woman grieving the loss of a lover and an unborn child, Chiaki finally is able to unravel the mystery surrounding her father's death and move beyond her present despair to new hope. *The Spring Tone* confronts the issues that face a young girl who is reluctant to grow up and once again demonstrates the importance of inter-generational relationships that relieve a child's feelings of loneliness, guilt, and fear. All of Yumoto's books that have been published in English have received sensitive and lyrical translations by Cathy Hirano, a Canadian woman who lives in Japan with her Japanese husband and two children, and who has a fine understanding for the nuances of translating from one language to another.

Courtesy of Farrar, Straus and Giroux

SELECTED WORKS (all translated by Cathy Hirano; U.S. publication dates): *The Friends*, 1996; *The Spring Tone*, 1999; *The Letters*, 2002.

SUGGESTED READING: Hirano, Cathy, "Eight Ways to Say 'You': The Challenges of Translation," *The Horn Book*, January/February 1999; "*Boston Globe–Horn Book* Award Acceptance Speech," *The Horn Book*, January/February 1998.

Awards and Honors
(cited in this volume)

Aesop Prize
The Children's Folklore Section of the American Folklore Society presents this award to the book for children or young adults that best incorporates folklore into its text and illustrations. English language books published in the year of the award or the year previous are eligible; in some years two books have shared the award. An annual roster of exceptional books from among the prize nominees constitutes the Aesop Accolade list. See *www.afsnet.org/sections/children/*.

ALA Best Books for Young Adults
Chosen by a committee of the Young Adult Library Services Association, a division of the American Library Association, this list is compiled annually to present the books deemed most worthy for readers aged 12–18 from among those published in the previous year. Available on the ALA Web site: *www.ala.org/yalsa*.

ALA Notable Children's Books
An annual list of distinguished books for children from infancy through age 14, compiled by a committee of the Association for Library Service to Children, a division of the American Library Association. Available on the ALA Web site: *www.ala.org/alsc*.

American Booksellers Association Pick of the Lists
Chosen twice a year from publishers' spring and fall offerings, these are the books that booksellers feel will be most popular with their patrons; Pick of the Lists appears in the spring and fall issues of *Bookselling This Week*.

Américas Award
Given in recognition of U.S. works of fiction, poetry, folklore, or selected nonfiction (from picture books to works for young adults) published in the previous year in English or Spanish that authentically and engagingly portray Latin America, the Caribbean, or Latinos in the United States. The award is sponsored by the national Consortium of Latin American Studies Programs (CLASP): *www.unwn/edu/Dept/CLACS/outreach/americas.html*.

Booklist Editors' Choice List
Published each January in ALA *Booklist*, a reviewing journal of the American Library Association, this list cites 40–60 titles chosen by the journal's editors as the outstanding books of the previous year.

Boston Globe–Horn Book Awards
Given annually since 1967 for the year's best fiction/poetry, nonfiction, and picture books, these awards are conferred by a committee of three experts and announced in *The Horn Book* magazine. The awards are presented at a special ceremony in the fall, and the acceptance speeches are subsequently printed later in *The Horn Book*. See *www.hbook.com/bghbabout.shtml*.

Bulletin of the Center for Children's Books Blue Ribbon List

The reviewing journal of the Center for Children's Books, an extensive reference collection of contemporary children's literature at the Graduate School of Library and Information Science at the University of Illinois at Urbana-Champaign, the *Bulletin* publishes an annual list of top titles of the year chosen by the editors and reviewers of the journal. See *www.lis.uiuc.edu/puboff/bccb/blueindex*.

Caldecott Medal and Honor Awards

Announced annually at the Midwinter Conference of the American Library Association, the Caldecott Medal is presented by the Association for Library Service to Children to the illustrator of the most distinguished picture book for children (from infancy through age 14) published in the United States in the preceding year. Other books worthy of notice may also be cited. In 1971 the term *runners-up* was officially changed to *honor books* for these additional titles. The award is presented and an acceptance speech is made by the winner at a banquet during the annual conference of the association in early summer. See *www.ala.org/ala/alsc*.

Canadian Library Association Book of the Year for Children Award

Established in 1947 and administered by the Canadian Association of Children's Librarians, this award is sponsored by the National Book Service and presented annually to an author who is a Canadian citizen or permanent resident in Canada. Any work of creative writing is eligible. The association also presents the Amelia Frances Howard-Gibbon Illustrator's Award and the Young Adult Canadian Book Award. See *www.cla.ca*.

Carnegie Medal

This medal has been awarded every year since 1936 to the writer of an outstanding book for young people that was first published in the United Kingdom (or co-published elsewhere within a three-month time lapse). All categories of books are eligible. The award is administered by a committee of the Youth Libraries Group, a division of CILIP, the Chartered Institute of Library and Information Professionals in the United Kingdom. The winner receives a gold medal as well as £500 worth of books to donate to libraries. See *www.carnegiegreenaway.org.uk*.

CCBC Choices

The Cooperative Children's Book Center (CCBC) at the University of Wisconsin-Madison, a children's and young adult literature reference library, publishes an annual list of about 250 outstanding books, annotated and arranged by subject area and genre. See *www.soemadison.wisc.edu/ccbc/*.

Charlotte Zolotow Award

Established in 1998 and administered by the Cooperative Children's Book Center, a children's literature library at the School of Education, University of Wisconsin-Madison, this award honors the author of the best picture book text published in the United States in the preceding year. See *www.soemadison.wisc.edu/ccbc/zolotow.htm*.

Children's Book Committee at Bank Street College of Education

The Bank Street College of Education in New York City publishes an annual list, the Best Children's Books of the Year, chosen by a committee that includes educators, librarians, authors, parents, and psychologists, with input from young reviewers across the country. Books are chosen for literary quality, excellence of presentation, and potential emotional impact on young readers. In addition, the committee gives three annual awards: for fiction, for nonfiction, and for poetry. See *www.bankstreet.edu/bookcom*.

Children's Book Council (CBC)

The Children's Book Council, Inc., is a not-for-profit organization of publishers and packagers of trade books for children and young adults, located in New York City. Its goals include enhancing public perception of the importance of children's reading and working with other professional groups to increase awareness of children's books. For further information see the CBC Web site at *www.cbcbooks.org*.

Christopher Awards

The Christopher Awards are presented to producers, directors, and writers of books, motion pictures, and television specials that affirm the highest values of the human spirit. Presented by the Christophers, a lay religious organization headquartered in New York City. See *www.christophers.org*.

Coretta Scott King Award

Since 1970 this annual award has recognized the creative work of African American authors whose books are deemed outstanding, educational, and inspiring; a parallel award, established in 1974, honors African American illustrators. From 1970 to 2003 the awards were sponsored by the Social Responsibilities Roundtable of the American Library Association; they are now administered by the Coretta Scott King Task Force of ALA's Ethnic Multicultural Information Exchange Round Table. See *www.ala.org/ala/ emiert/corettascottkingbookawards/corettascott.htm*.

Golden Kite Awards

Presented annually by the Society of Children's Book Writers and Illustrators, these four awards—for fiction, nonfiction, picture book text, and picture book illustration—are given to authors and artists selected by their fellow creators of children's books. The awards are announced in April of every year. See *www.scbwi.org*.

Horn Book Fanfare

This annual compilation of 20–30 titles recognizes outstanding books of the previous year. The titles are chosen by the review staff of *The Horn Book* magazine, which publishes the list in its first issue every year. See *www.hbook.com*.

IRA/CBC Children's Choices

A joint project of the International Reading Association and the Children's Book Council, these books are chosen by children polled in schools around the country. The list appears in the October issue of the *Reading Teacher*, a publication of the International Reading Association, at the CBC Web site *www.cbcbooks.org/childrens_choices/ booklists*, and at the IRA Web site *www.reading.org/choices*.

International Reading Association (IRA) Teachers' Choices

This is an annual list of trade books that teachers have found to be exceptional for classroom use. The titles are selected by teams of teachers throughout the country and published in the November issue of the *Reading Teacher*, with annotations and suggestions for use in the curriculum. See *www.reading.org/choices/tcfacts*.

International Reading Association Young Adults' Choices

Begun in 1987, this compilation of approximately 30 titles of new books chosen by students in grades 7 to 12 from different areas of the country is published in the November issue of the IRA's *Journal of Adolescent & Adult Literacy*. See *www.reading.org/choices/yacfacts*.

Irma Simonton Black and James H. Black Award

Administered since 1973 by Bank Street College of Education, this award goes to an outstanding book in which text and illustrations are inseparable. Presented solely in Irma's name until 1992, when James Black's name was added. Children pick the winning book from a list compiled by librarians, writers, and educators. See *streetcat.bnkst.edu/html/isb.html*.

Jane Addams Children's Book Award

Presented annually since 1953 by the Women's International League for Peace and Freedom and the Jane Addams Peace Association, this award is given to the children's book of the preceding year that most effectively promotes the cause of peace, social justice, and world community. See *www.janeaddamspeace.org*.

Junior Library Guild

The Junior Library Guild is a service that reviews books in manuscript form and selects 12 books a year for each of nine reading levels. Subscribers receive the books at a reduced price. The JLG editorial staff consistently chooses books that later win awards and appear on "Best" lists. Headquarters are in Worthington, Ohio. See *www.juniorlibraryguild.com*.

Kate Greenaway Medal

This medal is awarded annually to an artist for excellence in illustrating a children's book published in the United Kingdom. The award was established in 1955 and is administered by a committee of the Youth Libraries Group, a division of CILIP, the Chartered Institute of Library and Information Professionals in the United Kingdom. A short list of candidates is announced in April or early May from books published in the previous year; the winner is announced at an awards ceremony in July. See *www.carnegiegreenaway.org.uk*.

Michael L. Printz Award

Conferred annually since 2000 by a committee of the Young Adult Library Services Association, a division of the American Library Association, this award honors a book that exemplifies literary excellence in young adult literature published for ages 12–18. A winning book can be either fiction, nonfiction, or poetry, or an anthology. See *www.ala.org/ala/yalsa*.

Mildred L. Batchelder Award

Established in 1966 and presented by the Association for Library Service to Children, this award is named for a former executive director of the association. It is presented to an American publisher for the most outstanding book of the preceding year originally published in a foreign language and subsequently translated into English and published in the United States. Beginning in 1994, honor books were named as well. See *www.ala.org/ala/alsc*.

National Book Awards: Young People's Literature

Sponsored by the National Book Foundation, a consortium of publishers, and presented each year in November, this award honors a full-length original work of fiction, poetry, or nonfiction by an American author. A panel of judges chooses from among a short list of five titles. The winning author receives $10,000 and shortlisted authors receive $1,000 apiece. National Book Awards for adult literature were initiated in 1954; awards for young people's books were given annually from 1969 to 1983 and then reinstated in 1996. See *www.nationalbook.org*.

Nestlé Smarties Book Prize

Administered by Booktrust, an independent charity that promotes books and reading, this British award is presented for a work of fiction or poetry written by a citizen or resident of the United Kingdom. Gold, Silver, and Bronze awards are given in each of three age categories (under 5, 6–8, and 9–11). A panel of adult judges chooses a short list, and school classes compete to become Young Judges, who determine the winners.

Newbery Medal and Honor Awards

Announced annually at the Midwinter Conference of the American Library Association, the Newbery Medal is presented by the Association for Library Service to Children to the author of the most distinguished contribution to literature for children (from infancy through age 14) published in the United States in the preceding year. Other books worthy of notice may also be cited; in 1971 the term *runners-up* was officially changed to *honor books* for these additional titles. The award is presented and an acceptance speech is made by the winner at a banquet during the annual conference of the association in early summer. See *www.ala.org/ala/alsc*.

New York Public Library: 100 Titles for Reading and Sharing

An annual list of distinguished books of the year, published in an attractive booklet by the Office of Children's Services of the New York Public Library each November. Copies are available for a fee from the Office of Branch Services, New York Public Library, 455 Fifth Avenue, New York, NY 10016. See *www.nypl.org/publications/children.cfm*.

New York Public Library: Books for the Teen Age

This is a comprehensive and retrospective list of titles for teens, published each year by the Office of Young Adult Services of the NYPL. Copies are available for a fee from the Office of Branch Services, New York Public Library, 455 Fifth Avenue, New York, NY 10016. See *www.nypl.org/publications/children.cfm*.

Notable Social Studies Trade Books for Young People

This fully annotated list of books intended for grades K–8, published in the previous calendar year, is compiled by a committee of the National Council for the Social Studies in cooperation with the Children's Book Council. To be listed, books must emphasize human relations, represent a diversity of groups, and be sensitive to a broad range of cultural experiences. The list is published in the April/May issue of *Social Education* and is available as a brochure from the CBC: *www.cbcbooks.org*. (Before 1999, known as Notable Children's Trade Books in the Field of Social Studies.) See *www.ncss.org/resources/notable*.

NSK Neustadt Prize for Children's Literature

This new award to promote writing that contributes to the quality of children's lives has been made possible through the generosity of Nancy Barcelo, Susan Neustadt Schwartz, and Kathy Neustadt Hankin. It is administered by the University of Oklahoma and its quarterly publication, *World Literature Today*, and is presented every other year, beginning in 2003, to a living writer for significant achievement, either over a lifetime or in a particular publication. All nominations come from jury members; the prize is $25,000. See *www.ou.edu/worldlit/neustadt*.

Oppenheim Toy Portfolio

Founded in 1989 as the only independent consumer review of children's media, this group publishes a quarterly newsletter and field-tests products with families from all walks of life. It is administered by Joanne Oppenheim, an authority on child development and education, Stephanie Oppenheim, an attorney and a leading consumer authority on children's media, and James Oppenheim, attorney and computer consultant.

Orbis Pictus Award for Outstanding Nonfiction

Given annually since 1990 by the National Council of Teachers of English to an informational children's book published in the preceding year, this award is named for the book *Orbis Pictus* published by Johan Amos Comenius in 1659 and generally considered to be the first book created exclusively for children. See *www.ncte.org/elem/awards/orbispictus*.

Outstanding Science Trade Books for Students

This is a fully annotated list of books published in the previous calendar year, compiled by a committee of the National Science Teachers Association in cooperation with the Children's Book Council. The committee uses rigorous guidelines for content and presentation, accuracy and appropriateness for age level. The list is published in *Science and Children* in the spring and is also available as a brochure from the CBC. From 1973 to 2001 this list was known as Outstanding Science Trade Books for Children and covered grades K–8. Since 2002 books for grades 9–12 have been included. See *www.nsta.org/ostbc*.

Parents' Choice Awards

Established in 1978, the Parents' Choice Foundation is a not-for-profit evaluator of books and other media to help parents make informed choices. These awards are given to books, toys, videos, computer programs, etc., that are judged to be the best and most appealing products in their genre and to have a unique, individual quality. See *www.parents-choice.org*.

Pura Belpré Awards

Co-sponsored by the Association for Library Service to Children and the National Association to Promote Library Services to the Spanish Speaking (REFORMA), these awards were first presented in 1996 and are given biennially to a Latino/Latina writer and an illustrator whose works affirm and celebrate the Latino experience. Named for the first Latina librarian in the New York Public Library. See *www.ala.org/ala/alsc*.

Robert F. Sibert Informational Book Award

Established in 2001, the Sibert Award is presented annually to the author of the most distinguished informational book published in the United States in the preceding year. Chosen by a committee of the Association for Library Service to Children, a division of the American Library Association. See *www.ala.org/alsc*.

School Library Journal Best Books of the Year

Published annually in the December issue, this list of 50–60 outstanding titles is compiled by the editors of *School Library Journal* from over 4,000 books reviewed throughout that year. See *www.schoollibraryjournal.com*.

Scott O'Dell Award for Historical Fiction

Established by author Scott O'Dell and awarded annually since 1984 to a book of historical fiction that is set in the New World (North American, Central America, or South America) and written by an American author: *www.scottodell.com/sosoaward.html*.

State Awards

Most of the 50 states now sponsor children's choice awards through a state library association or educational media association. These awards are typically chosen from lists of 10–20 titles prepared by adults and then voted on by children.

Whitbread Book Awards

Established in 1971, this prestigious British award is given in five categories, including children's books. Winners are chosen by a three-judge panel generally consisting of a bookseller, a journalist, and an author. Eligible authors are those who have been residents of the United Kingdom or Ireland for at least six months of the previous three years. See *www.whitbread-bookawards.co.uk*.

Note: This is a sampling of the awards and lists that are cited most frequently in this volume. Other awards are explained in the context of profiles in this book. There are many ways in which children's book authors and illustrators are honored each year, an indication of the growth of the field and recognition of the excellence found in a wide variety of children's books today. An extensive and continually updated compilation of children's literature awards and honors is available by subscription from the Children's Book Council: *www.cbcbooks.org*.

Authors and Illustrators Included in This Series

The following list indicates the volume in which each person may be found:

J—*The Junior Book of Authors*, second edition (1951)
M—*More Junior Authors* (1963)
3—*Third Book of Junior Authors* (1972)
4—*Fourth Book of Junior Authors and Illustrators* (1978)
5—*Fifth Book of Junior Authors and Illustrators* (1983)
6—*Sixth Book of Junior Authors and Illustrators* (1989)
7—*Seventh Book of Junior Authors and Illustrators* (1996)
8—*Eighth Book of Junior Authors and Illustrators* (2000)
9—*Ninth Book of Junior Authors and Illustrators* (2004)

Aruego, Ariane
  See Dewey, Ariane—**4**
Aruego, José—**4**
Arundel, Honor—**4**
Asch, Frank—**4**
Ashabranner, Brent—**6**
Asher, Sandy—**7**
Ashmun, Margaret—**J**
Asimov, Isaac—**3**
Atwater, Florence Hasseltine
  Carroll—**M**
Atwater, Montgomery Meigs
  —**M**
Atwater, Richard Tupper—
  M
Atwood, Ann—**4**
Auch, Mary Jane—**8**
Aulaire, Edgar Parin d'—**J**
Aulaire, Ingri Parin d'—**J**
Austin, Margot—**M**
Averill, Esther—**J**
Avery, Gillian—**4**
Avi—**5**
Ayer, Jacqueline—**3**
Ayer, Margaret—**M**
Aylesworth, Jim—**7**
Azarian, Mary—**8**

"Babbis, Eleanor"
  See Friis-Baastad, Bab-
  bis—**3**
Babbitt, Natalie—**4**
Bach, Alice—**5**
Bagnold, Enid—**4**
Bailey, Carolyn Sherwin—**J**
Baity, Elizabeth Chesley—**M**
Baker, Alan—**8**
Baker, Betty—**3**
Baker, Jeannie—**7**
Baker, Keith—**7**
Baker, Leslie—**7**
Baker, Margaret **J**.—**M**
Baker, Margaret—**J**
Baker, Mary—**J**
Baker, Nina Brown—**J**
Baker, Olaf—**J**
Baker, Rachel—**M**
Balch, Glenn—**M**
Balderson, Margaret—**4**
Baldwin, James—**J**
Balet, Jan—**3**
Balian, Lorna—**5**
"Ball, Zachary"—**4**
"Bancroft, Laura"
  See Baum, L. Frank—**3**

Bang, Betsy Garrett—**5**
Bang, Molly Garrett—**5**
Banks, Kate—**9**
Banks, Lynne Reid—**6**
Bannerman, Helen—**J**
Bannon, Laura—**M**
Barbour, Ralph Henry—**J**
Barne, Kitty—**J**
Barracca, Debra—**7**
Barracca, Sal—**7**
Barrett, Judi—**6**
Barrett, Ron—**6**
Barron, T.A.—**8**
Bartoletti, Susan Camp-
  bell—**9**
Barton, Byron—**5**
Bartos-Höppner, Barbara—
  4
Base, Graeme Rowland—**7**
Bash, Barbara—**7**
Baskin, Leonard—**5**
Baudouy, Michel-Aimé—**3**
Bauer, Joan—**8**
Bauer, Marion Dane—**5**
Baum, L. Frank—**3**
Baumann, Hans—**3**
Bawden, Nina—**4**
Bayley, Nicola—**6**
Baylor, Byrd—**4**
Baynes, Ernest Harold—**J**
Baynes, Pauline—**3**
"BB"—**3**
"Beach, Webb"
  See Butterworth, W. E.—**5**
Beatty, Hetty Burlingame—
  M
Beatty, John—**3**
Beatty, Patricia—**3**
Becerra de Jenkins, Lyll
  See Jenkins, Lyll Becerra
  de—**7**
Beckman, Gunnel—**4**
Bedard, Michael—**7**
"Beddows, Eric"—**7**
Beeler, Nelson F.—**M**
Begay, Shonto—**7**
Behn, Harry—**M**
Behrens, June—**8**
Beim, Jarrold—**J**
Beim, Lorraine—**J**
Beisner, Monika—**6**
Bell, Anthea—**7**
Bell, Corydon—**3**
Bell, Margaret E.—**M**
Bell, Thelma—**3**

Bellairs, John—**5**
Belpré, Pura—**4**
Belting, Natalia Maree—**3**
Bemelmans, Ludwig—**M**
Benary-Isbert, Margot—**M**
Benchley, Nathaniel—**4**
Bendick, Jeanne—**M**
Bendick, Robert—**M**
Bennett, Jay—**6**
Bennett, John—**J**
Bennett, Rainey—**4**
Bennett, Richard—**J**
Benét, Laura—**J**
Berenstain, Jan—**5**
Berenstain, Stan—**5**
Berg, Björn—**4**
Berger, Barbara Helen—**6**
Berger, Melvin—**5**
Berna, Paul—**3**
"Bernadette"
  See Watts, Bernadette—**7**
"Berry, Erick"—**J**
Berry, James—**7**
Berson, Harold—**4**
Beskow, Elsa—**J**
Bess, Clayton—**6**
Best, Cari—**9**
Best, Herbert—**J**
Beston, Henry—**J**
Bethancourt, T. Ernesto—**5**
"Bettina"—**M**
Betz, Betty—**M**
Bial, Raymond—**8**
Bialk, Elisa—**M**
Bianco, Margery Williams—
  J
Bianco, Pamela
  See Bianco, Margery Will-
  iams—**J**
Bierhorst, John—**5**
Bileck, Marvin—**4**
Bill, Alfred H.—**J**
Billings, Henry—**M**
Billingsley, Franny—**9**
Binch, Caroline—**7**
Bing, Christopher—**9**
Birch, Reginald—**J**
Birdseye, Tom—**8**
Bischoff, Ilse—**M**
Bishop, Claire Huchet—**J**
Bishop, Elizabeth—**4**
Björk, Christina—**8**
"Blacklin, Malcolm"
  See Chambers, Aidan—**6**
Blades, Ann—**9**

Calhoun, Mary—**3**
Callen, Larry—**5**
Calmenson, Stephanie—**8**
Calvert, Patricia—**6**
Cameron, Ann—**7**
Cameron, Eleanor—**3**
Cameron, Polly—**4**
Camp, Walter—**J**
"Campbell, Bruce"
    See Epstein, Samuel—**M**
Cannon, Janell—**8**
Carbone, Elisa Lynn—**9**
Carigiet, Alois—**3**
Carle, Eric—**4**, **8**
Carlson, Nancy—**8**
Carlson, Natalie Savage—**M**
Carlstrom, Nancy White—**6**
Carpenter, Frances—**M**
Carr, Harriett H.—**M**
Carr, Mary Jane—**J**
Carrick, Carol—**4**
Carrick, Donald—**4**
Carrick, Valery—**J**
Carris, Joan—**7**
"Carroll, Jenny"
    See Cabot, Meg—**9**
Carroll, Latrobe—**M**
Carroll, Ruth—**M**
Carter, Alden—**7**
Carter, Helene—**M**
Caseley, Judith—**7**
Cassedy, Sylvia—**6**
Casserley, Anne—**J**
Catalanotto, Peter—**7**
Caudill, Rebecca—**M**
Cauley, Lorinda Bryan—**6**
Cavanah, Frances—**M**
Cavanna, Betty—**M**
Cazet, Denys—**7**
Cepeda, Joe—**9**
Chaikin, Miriam—**6**
Chalmers, Mary—**3**
Chambers, Aidan—**6**
"Chambers, Catherine E."
    See Johnston, Norma—**5**
"Chance, Stephen"
    See Turner, Philip—**4**
"Chapman, Walker"
    See Silverberg, Robert—**3**
Chappell, Warren—**3**
"Charles, Nicholas"
    See Kuskin, Karla—**3**
Charlip, Remy—**3**
Charlot, Jean—**M**

"Chase, Alice Elizabeth"
    See McHargue, Geor-
    gess—**5**
Chase, Mary Ellen—**4**
Chase, Richard—**M**
Chastain, Madye Lee—**M**
Chauncy, Nan—**3**
Chen, Tony—**5**
Cherry, Lynne—**7**
Chess, Victoria—**6**
Chetwin, Grace—**7**
Chew, Ruth—**6**
Childress, Alice—**5**
Chipperfield, Joseph E.—**M**
Chocolate, Debbi—**8**
Choi, Sook Nyul—**8**
Choi, Yangsook—**9**
Chorao, Kay—**4**
Chrisman, Arthur Bowie—**J**
Christelow, Eileen—**7**
Christie, R. Gregory—**9**
"Christopher, John"—**4**
Christopher, Matt—**5**
Church, Alfred J.—**J**
Church, Richard—**M**
Chute, B. J.—**M**
Chute, Marchette—**M**
Chwast, Jacqueline—**4**
Chwast, Seymour—**4**
Chönz, Selina—**4**
Ciardi, John—**3**
Clapp, Patricia—**5**
"Clare, Helen"
    See Clarke, Pauline—**3**
Clark, Ann Nolan—**J**
Clark, Emma Chichester—**7**
Clark, Mavis Thorpe—**4**
Clarke, Arthur C.—**4**
Clarke, Pauline—**3**
Cleary, Beverly—**M**, **8**
Cleaver, Bill—**4**
Cleaver, Elizabeth—**4**
Cleaver, Vera—**4**
Clements, Andrew—**8**
Clements, Bruce—**5**
Clifford, Eth—**6**
Clifton, Lucille—**5**
Climo, Shirley—**7**
Cline-Ransome, Lesa—**9**
Clymer, Eleanor—**4**
Coatsworth, Elizabeth—**J**
Cobb, Vicki—**5**
Cober, Alan E.—**4**
Coblentz, Catherine Cate—**J**
Coerr, Eleanor—**6**

Coggins, Jack—**M**
Cohen, Barbara—**5**
Cohen, Daniel—**6**
Cohen, Miriam—**5**
Colby, Carroll B.—**M**
Cole, Babette—**7**
Cole, Brock—**6**
Cole, Joanna—**5**
Cole, William—**4**
Coleman, Evelyn—**9**
"Colin, Ann"
    See Ure, Jean—**6**
Collier, Christopher—**5**
Collier, James Lincoln—**5**
Collington, Peter—**7**
"Collodi, C."—**J**
Colman, Hila—**3**
Colón, Raúl—**9**
Colum, Padraic—**J**
Coman, Carolyn—**8**
Cone, Molly—**3**
Conford, Ellen—**5**
Conklin, Gladys—**4**
Conly, Jane Leslie—**7**
Conover, Chris—**6**
Conrad, Pam—**6**
Conroy, Robert
    See Goldston, Robert Con-
    roy—**4**
"Cook, John Estes"
    See Baum, L. Frank—**3**
Coolidge, Olivia E.—**M**
Coombs, Patricia—**5**
Cooney, Barbara—**M**, **9**
Cooney, Caroline B.—**8**
Cooper, Elizabeth K.—**4**
Cooper, Floyd—**7**
Cooper, Helen—**9**
Cooper, Ilene—**8**
"Cooper, Melrose"
    See Kroll, Virginia—**8**
Cooper, Susan—**4**, **8**
Corbett, Scott—**4**
Corbin, William—**M**
Corcoran, Barbara—**5**
Cormack, Maribelle—**J**
Cormier, Robert—**5**
Cosgrave, John O'Hara, II—
    M
Cosgrove, Margaret—**4**
Cottrell, Leonard—**4**
Couloumbis, Audrey—**9**
Courlander, Harold—**M**
Cousins, Lucy—**8**
Coville, Bruce—**7**

Duvoisin, Roger—**J**
Dyer, Jane—**7**
Dygard, Thomas **J**.—**6**

Eager, Edward—**M**
Earle, Olive L.—**M**
Eastman, Charles A.—**J**
Eaton, Jeanette—**J**
Eberle, Irmengarde—**J**
Eckert, Allan W.—**4**
Edmonds, Walter
    Dumaux—**M**
Egan, Tim—**9**
Egielski, Richard—**6**
Ehlert, Lois—**7**
Ehrlich, Amy—**7**
Eichenberg, Fritz—**M**
Eipper, Paul—**J**
Eitan, Ora—**9**
Elkin, Benjamin—**4**
Ellis, Ella—**5**
Ellis, Sarah—**7**
Ellsberg, Commander
    Edward—**J**
Els, Betty Vander
    See Vander Els, Betty—**6**
Elting, Mary—**M**
Emberley, Barbara—**3**
Emberley, Ed—**3**
Emberley, Michael—**9**
Emberley, Rebecca—**8**
Emery, Ann—**M**
Engdahl, Sylvia Louise—**4**
English, Karen—**9**
Enright, Elizabeth—**J**
Epstein, Beryl Williams—**M**
Epstein, Samuel—**M**
Erdman, Loula Grace—**M**
Ernst, Lisa Campbell—**7**
Esbensen, Barbara Juster—**8**
Estes, Eleanor—**J**
"Estoril, Jean"
    See Allen, Mabel Esther—
    6
Ets, Marie Hall—**J**
Evans, Eva Knox—**M**
Evans, Shane—**9**
"Every, Philip Cochrane"
    See Burnford, Sheila—**4**
Eyerly, Jeannette—**5**
Eyre, Katherine Wigmore—
    M

Fabre, Jean-Henri—**J**
Facklam, Margery—**8**

Falconer, Ian—**9**
"Fall, Thomas"—**4**
Falls, C. B.—**J**
Falwell, Cathryn—**9**
Farber, Norma—**5**
Farjeon, Eleanor—**J**
Farley, Carol—**5**
Farley, Walter—**J**
Farmer, Nancy—**7**
Farmer, Penelope—**4**
Fatio, Louise—**M**
"Faulkner, Anne Irvin"
    See Faulkner, Nancy
Faulkner, Nancy—**4**
Feagles, Anita MacRae—**4**
Feelings, Muriel—**4**
Feelings, Tom—**3**, **8**
Feiffer, Jules—**9**
Felsen, Gregor—**J**
Felton, Harold W.—**M**
Fenner, Carol—**8**
Fenton, Carroll Lane—**M**
Fenton, Edward—**3**
Fenton, Mildred Adams—**M**
Ferris, Helen—**J**
Feydy, Anne Lindbergh
    See Lindbergh, Anne—**6**
Field, Rachel—**J**
Fife, Dale—**4**
Fillmore, Parker—**J**
Fine, Anne—**7**
Fine, Howard—**9**
Fischer, Hans Erich—**M**
Fisher, Aileen—**M**
Fisher, Leonard Everett—**3**,
    8
Fitch, Florence Mary—**M**
"Fitzgerald, Captain Hugh"
    See Baum, L. Frank—**3**
Fitzgerald, John D.—**5**
Fitzhugh, Louise—**3**
Flack, Marjorie—**J**
Flake, Sharon—**9**
Fleischman, Paul—**5**
Fleischman, Sid—**3**, **9**
Fleming, Denise—**7**
Fleming, Ian—**5**
Fletcher, Ralph—**8**
Fletcher, Susan—**9**
Flinn, Alex—**9**
Floca, Brian—**9**
Floethe, Richard—**M**
Floherty, John J.—**J**
Flora, James—**3**
Florian, Douglas—**6**

Forberg, Ati—**4**
Forbes, Esther—**M**
Foreman, Michael—**6**
Forman, James—**3**
Fortnum, Peggy—**4**
Foster, Genevieve—**J**
Fox, Mem—**6**
Fox, Paula—**4**
Fradin, Dennis Brindell—**8**
Frampton, David—**9**
Franchere, Ruth—**4**
"Francis, Dee"
    See Haas, Dorothy—**6**
Franklin, George Cory—**M**
François, André—**3**
"Françoise"—**M**
Frascino, Edward—**5**
Frasconi, Antonio—**3**
Fraser, Claud Lovat—**J**
Frazee, Marla—**9**
"Freedman, Peter J."
    See Calvert, Patricia—**6**
Freedman, Russell—**6**
Freeman, Don—**M**
Freeman, Ira Maximilian—
    M
Freeman, Lydia—**M**
Freeman, Mae Blacker—**M**
Freeman, Suzanne—**8**
French, Allen—**J**
French, Fiona—**7**
"French, Paul"
    See Asimov, Isaac—**3**
Freschet, Berniece—**4**
Friedman, Frieda—**M**
Friermood, Elisabeth
    Hamilton —**M**
"Friis, Babbis"
    See Friis-Baastad, Bab-
    bis—**3**
Friis-Baastad, Babbis—**3**
Fritz, Jean—**3**, **8**
Froman, Robert—**4**
Frost, Frances—**M**
Fry, Rosalie K.—**3**
Fuchs, Erich—**4**
Fujikawa, Gyo—**4**
Fyleman, Rose—**J**

Gackenbach, Dick—**5**
Gaer, Joseph—**M**
"Gage, Wilson"—**3**
Galdone, Paul—**3**
Gall, Alice Crew—**J**
Gallant, Roy A.—**5**

Harkins, Philip—**M**
Harness, Cheryl—**8**
Harnett, Cynthia—**3**
Harris, Christie—**4**
"Harris, Lavinia"
  See Johnston, Norma—**5**
Harris, Robie H.—**9**
Harris, Rosemary—**4**
Harrison, Ted—**8**
Harshman, Marc—**9**
Hartman, Gertrude—**J**
Harvey, Brett—**6**
Haseley, Dennis—**7**
Haskell, Helen Eggleston—**J**
"Haskins, James"
  See Haskins, Jim—**6**
Haskins, Jim—**6**
Hastings, Selina—**8**
Haugaard, Erik Christian—**3**
Hautzig, Deborah—**5**
Hautzig, Esther—**3**
Havighurst, Marion—**M**
Havighurst, Walter—**M**
Haviland, Virginia—**4**
Havill, Juanita—**7**
Hawkes, Kevin—**7**
Hawkinson, John—**4**
Hawthorne, Hildegarde—**J**
Hays, Michael—**8**
Hays, Wilma Pitchford—**3**
Haywood, Carolyn—**J**
Hazen, Barbara Shook—**6**
Headley, Elizabeth
  See Cavanna, Betty—**M**
"Hearn, Lian"
  See Rubinstein, Gillian—**9**
Hearne, Betsy—**6**
Heide, Florence Parry—**4**
Heine, Helme—**6**
Heinlein, Robert A.—**M**
Heller, Ruth—**7**
Hendershot, Judith—**6**
Henderson, Le Grand
  See "Le Grand"—**J**
Henkes, Kevin—**6**
Hennessy, B. G.—**7**
Henry, Marguerite—**J**
Henstra, Friso—**4**
Hentoff, Nat—**3**
Heo, Yumi—**9**
Herald, Kathleen
  See Peyton, K. M.—**3**
Herman, Charlotte—**7**
Hermes, Patricia—**6**
Hess, Fjeril—**J**

Hess, Lilo—**5**
Hesse, Karen—**8**
Hest, Amy—**7**
Hewes, Agnes Danforth—**J**
Heyliger, William—**J**
Hightower, Florence—**3**
Highwater, Jamake—**5**
Hildick, E. W.—**4**
Hill, Douglas—**6**
Hill, Eric—**6**
Hillenbrand, Will—**8**
"Hillman, Martin"
  See Hill, Douglas—**6**
Hillyer, V. M.—**J**
Himler, Ronald—**6**
Hine, Al—**3**
Hines, Anna Grossnickle—**6**
Hinton, S. E.—**4**
"Hippopotamus, Eugene H."
  See Kraus, Robert—**3**
Hirsch, S. Carl—**3**
Hirschi, Ron—**8**
Hirsh, Marilyn—**5**
"Hitz, Demi"
  See Demi—**6**
Ho, Minfong—**7**
Hoban, Lillian—**3**
Hoban, Russell—**3**
Hoban, Tana—**4**
Hobbs, Will—**7**
Hoberman, Mary Ann—**6**
Hodges, C. Walter—**3**
Hodges, Margaret Moore—**4**
Hoff, Syd—**3**
Hoffman, Mary—**7**
Hoffman, Rosekrans—**7**
Hoffmann, Felix—**3**
Hofsinde, Robert—**3**
Hogan, Inez—**M**
Hogner, Dorothy—**J**
Hogner, Nils—**J**
Hogrogian, Nonny—**3**
Holabird, Katharine—**8**
Holberg, Richard A.—**J**
Holberg, Ruth—**J**
Holbrook, Stewart—**3**
Holland, Isabelle—**5**
Holland, Kevin Crossley-
  See Crossley-Holland,
  Kevin—**4**
Holland, Rupert Sargent—**J**
Holling, H. C.—**J**
Holling, Lucille W.
  See Holling, H. C.—**J**

Holm, Anne—**4**
Holm, Jennifer—**9**
Holman, Felice—**4**
Holt, Kimberly Willis—**9**
Hoobler, Thomas & Dor-
  othy—**8**
Hooks, William H.—**6**
Hoover, Helen M.—**5**
Hopkins, Lee Bennett—**5**
Hopkinson, Deborah—**9**
Höppner, Barbara Bartos-
  See Bartos-Höppner, Bar-
  bara—**5**
Horvath, Polly—**9**
Hosford, Dorothy—**M**
Hotze, Sollace—**7**
Houston, Gloria—**7**
Houston, James A.—**4**
Howard, Elizabeth Fitzger-
  ald—**7**
Howard, Elizabeth—**M**
Howard, Ellen—**7**
Howe, Deborah—**6**
Howe, James—**6**
Howker, Janni—**6**
Hoyt-Goldsmith, Diane—**7**
Hudson, Cheryl Willis—**8**
Hudson, Jan—**7**
Hudson, Wade—**8**
Hughes, Dean—**6**
"Hughes, Eden"
  See Butterworth, W. E.—**5**
Hughes, Langston—**4**
Hughes, Monica—**6**
Hughes, Shirley—**5**
Hunt, Clara Whitehill—**J**
Hunt, Irene—**3**
Hunt, Mabel Leigh—**J**
Hunter, Kristin—**4**
Hunter, Mollie—**3**
Huntington, Harriet E.—**M**
Hurd, Clement—**M**
Hurd, Edith Thacher—**M**
Hurd, Thacher—**6**
Hürlimann, Bettina—**3**
Hurmence, Belinda—**6**
Hurwitz, Johanna—**6**
Hutchins, Pat—**4**
Hutchins, Ross E.—**3**
Hutton, Warwick—**6**
Hyde, Margaret O.—**3**
Hyman, Trina Schart—**4, 8**

Ibbotson, Eva—**9**
Ichikawa, Satomi—**7**

"Ilin, M."—**J**
Ingpen, Robert—**7**
Ipcar, Dahlov—**3**
"Irving, Robert"
See Adler, Irving—**3**
Irwin, Annabelle Bowen
See "Irwin, Hadley"—**6**
"Irwin, Hadley"—**6**
Isaacs, Anne—**8**
Isadora, Rachel—**5**
Isbert, Margot Benary-
See Benary-Isbert, Mar-
got—**M**
Ish-Kishor, Sulamith—**5**
Iterson, S. R., van—**4**

"J Marks"
See Highwater, Jamake—**5**
Jackson, Jacqueline—**4**
Jacques, Brian—**7**
Jacques, Robin—**3**
Jaffe, Nina—**8**
Jagendorf, Moritz Adolf—**M**
Jakobsen, Kathy—**9**
"James, Dynely"
See Mayne, William—**3**
James, Synthia Saint
See Saint James, Synthia—
9
James, Will—**J**
Janeczko, Paul B.—**6**
"Janosch"—**4**
Jansson, Tove—**3**
Jardin, Rosamond du
See du Jardin,
Rosamond—**M**
Jarrell, Randall—**3**
Jasperson, Willliam—**7**
Jauss, Anne Marie—**4**
Jeffers, Susan—**4**
Jenkins, Lyll Becerra de—**7**
Jenkins, Steve—**8**
Jeschke, Susan—**5**
Jewett, Eleanore M.—**M**
Jiménez, Francisco—**9**
Johnson, Angela—**7**
Johnson, Annabel—**3**
"Johnson, Crockett"—**3**
Johnson, D. B.—**9**
Johnson, Dolores—**8**
Johnson, Edgar—**3**
Johnson, Gerald W.—**3**
Johnson, **J.** Rosamond
See Johnson, James Wel-
don—**4**

Johnson, James Weldon—**4**
Johnson, Margaret Sweet—**J**
Johnson, Paul Brett—**9**
Johnson, Siddie Joe—**J**
Johnson, Steven T.—**8**
Johnston, Johanna—**4**
Johnston, Norma—**5**
Johnston, Tony—**6**
Jonas, Ann—**7**
Jones, Adrienne—**5**
Jones, Diana Wynne—**5**
Jones, Elizabeth Orton—**J**
Jones, Harold—**3**
Jones, Jessie Orton—**5**
Jones, Marcia Thornton—**8**
Jones, Mary Alice—**M**
Jones, Rebecca C.—**7**
Jones, Tim Wynne-
See Wynne-Jones, Tim—**8**
Jones, Weyman B.—**4**
Jong, Dola de
See de Jong, Dola—**M**
Joose, Barbara M.—**7**
Jordan, June—**4**
Jordan, Sandra—**9**
"Jorgenson, Ivar"
See Silverberg, Robert—**3**
Joslin, Sesyle—**3**
Joyce, William—**6**
Judson, Clara Ingram—**J**
Jukes, Mavis—**6**
Juster, Norton—**4**
Justus, May—**J**

Kahl, Virginia—**M**
Kalashnikoff, Nicholas—**M**
Kalman, Maira—**7**
Karas, G. Brian—**8**
Karl, Jean E—**5**
Kasza, Keiko—**7**
Kaye, Marilyn—**7**
Keats, Ezra Jack—**M**
Keeping, Charles—**3**
Kehret, Peg—**8**
Keith, Eros—**4**
Keith, Harold—**M**
Keller, Beverly—**7**
Keller, Holly—**9**
Kelley, True—**8**
Kellogg, Steven—**4**, **9**
Kelly, Eric P.—**J**
Kelsey, Alice Geer—**M**
Kendall, Carol—**3**

"Kendall, Lace"
See Stoutenburg, Adrien—
3
Kennaway, Adrienne—**7**
Kennedy, Richard—**5**
Kennedy, X. J.—**6**
Kent, Jack—**5**
Kent, Louise Andrews—**J**
Kepes, Juliet—**3**
Ker Wilson, Barbara—**4**
Kerr, Judith—**5**
"Kerr, M. E."—**4**
"Kerry, Lois"
See "Duncan, Lois"—**5**
Kessler, Ethel—**5**
Kessler, Leonard—**5**
Kettelkamp, Larry—**3**
Khalsa, Dayal Kaur—**7**
Kherdian, David—**5**
Kimmel, Elizabeth Cody—**9**
Kimmel, Eric A.—**7**
"Kincaid, Beth"
See Applegate,
Katherine—**9**
Kindl, Patrice—**8**
King-Smith, Dick—**6**
Kingman, Lee—**M**
"Kinsey, Elizabeth"
See Clymer, Eleanor—**4**
Kinsey-Warnock, Natalie—**8**
"Kirtland, G. B."
See Hine, Al & Joslin,
Sesyle—**3**
Kitamura, Satoshi—**8**
Kitchen, Bert—**7**
Kjelgaard, Jim—**J**
Klass, Sheila Solomon—**8**
Klause, Annette Curtis—**7**
Klein, Norma—**5**
Kleven, Elisa—**7**
Kline, Suzy—**7**
Knight, Eric—**4**
Knight, Hilary—**4**
Knight, Kathryn Lasky
See Lasky, Kathryn—**6**
Knight, Ruth Adams—**M**
Knipe, Alden Arthur—**J**
Knipe, Emilie Benson—**J**
"Knox, Calvin M."
See Silverberg, Robert—**3**
Knox, Rose B.—**J**
Knudson, R. R.—**6**
Koehn, Ilse—**5**
Koering, Ursula—**M**
Koertge, Ron—**7**

Koller, Jackie French—9
Komaiko, Leah—8
Konigsburg, E. L.—3, 8
Korman, Gordon—7
Krahn, Fernando—4
Krasilovsky, Phyllis—M
Kraus, Robert—3
Krauss, Ruth—M
Kredel, Fritz—M
Krementz, Jill—5
Krensky, Stephen—6
Kroeger, Mary Kay—9
Kroll, Steven—5
Kroll, Virginia—8
Krull, Kathleen—7
Krumgold, Joseph—M
Krush, Beth—M
Krush, Joe—M
Krüss, James—3
Kudlinski, Kathleen V.—9
Kuklin, Susan—7
Kullman, Harry—5
Kurelek, William—5
Kurtz, Jane—8
Kuskin, Karla—3
Kvasnosky, Laura McGee—9
Kyle, Anne D.—J
"Kyle, Elisabeth"—M
Kästner, Erich—3

"L'Engle, Madeleine"—M, 9
La Mare, Walter De
    See De La Mare, Walter—J
Laan, Nancy Van
    See Van Laan, Nancy—8
Laboulaye, Édouard—J
LaMarche, Jim—9
Lamb, Harold—J
Lambert, Janet—3
Lamorisse, Albert—4
Lampman, Evelyn Sibley—M
Lamprey, Louise—J
Landau, Elaine—8
Langstaff, John—3
Langton, Jane—5
Lansing, Marion Florence—J
Larrick, Nancy—8
Lasker, Joe—5
Laskowski, Jerzy—3
Lasky, Kathryn—6
Latham, Jean Lee—M

Lathrop, Dorothy P.—J
Lattimore, Deborah Nourse—7
Lattimore, Eleanor Frances—J
Lauber, Patricia—3
Laut, Agnes C.—J
Lavies, Bianca—7
Lawlor, Laurie—9
Lawrence, Iain—9
Lawrence, Jacob—4
Lawrence, Louise—6
Lawrence, Mildred—M
Lawson, Don—6
Lawson, Marie Abrams
    See Lawson, Robert—J
Lawson, Robert—J
Le Cain, Errol—6
"Le Grand"—J
Le Guin, Ursula K.—4, 9
Le Sueur, Meridel—M
Le Tord, Bijou—6
Leach, Maria—4
Leaf, Munro—J
Lee, Dennis—7
Lee, Dom—8
Lee, Jeanne M.—8
Lee, Manning de V.—M
Lee, Marie G.—8
Lee, Mildred—3
Lee, Tina—M
Leedy, Loreen—7
Leeming, Joseph—J
Leeuw, Adèle de
    See de Leeuw, Adèle—J
Leeuwen, Jean Van
    See Van Leeuwen, Jean—5
Leighton, Margaret—M
Lenski, Lois—J
Lent, Blair—3
Lent, Henry B.—J
"Leodhas, Sorche Nic"
    See "Nic Leodhas, Sorche"—3
Lerner, Carol—6
Leroe, Ellen W.—7
Lessac, Frané—8
Lester, Alison—8
Lester, Helen—8
Lester, Julius—4, 8
Levin, Betty—6
Levine, Ellen—7
Levine, Gail Carson—8
Levinson, Riki—6

Levitin, Sonia—5
Levoy, Myron—5
Levy, Elizabeth—5
Lewellen, John—M
Lewin, Betsy—8
Lewin, Ted—7
Lewis, C. S.—M
Lewis, E. B.—8
Lewis, Elizabeth Foreman—J
Lewis, J. Patrick—7
Lewis, Richard—7
Lewiton, Mina—M
Lexau, Joan M.—4
Ley, Willy—3
Lifton, Betty Jean—3
Lindbergh, Anne—6
Lindbergh, Reeve—7
Linde, Gunnel—4
Lindenbaum, Pija—7
Linderman, Frank B.—J
Lindgren, Astrid—M
Lindgren, Barbro—6
Lindman, Maj—J
Lindquist, Jennie D.—M
Lindquist, Willis—M
Lingard, Joan—5
Lionni, Leo—3
Lipkind, William—M
Lippincott, Joseph Wharton—M
Lipsyte, Robert—5
Lisle, Janet Taylor—6
Little, Jean—4
Lively, Penelope—4
Livingston, Myra Cohn—4
Lloyd, Megan—8
Lobel, Anita—3
Lobel, Arnold—3, 9
Locke, Robert
    See Bess, Clayton—6
Locker, Thomas—6
Lofting, Hugh—J
London, Jonathan—8
Long, Sylvia—9
Longstreth, T. Morris—M
Look, Lenore—9
Lord, Beman—4
Lord, Bette Bao—6
"Lord, Nancy"
    See Titus, Eve—3
Lorraine, Walter—4
Lottridge, Celia Barker—9
Lovelace, Maud Hart—J
Low, Alice—6

Minarik, Else—**3**
"Minier, Nelson"
   See Stoutenburg, Adrien—
   3
Minor, Wendell—**8**
Mitchell, Margaree King—**9**
Mizumura, Kazue—**3**
Mochizuki, Ken—**8**
Modell, Frank—**5**
Moeri, Louise—**5**
Mohr, Nicholasa—**5**
Mollel, Tololwa M.—**8**
Monjo, F. N.—**5**
Montgomery, Rutherford—
   M
Montresor, Beni—**3**
Monvel, Boutet de
   See Boutet de Monvel—**J**
Moon, Carl—**J**
Moon, Grace—**J**
Moore, Anne Carroll—**J**
Moore, Lilian—**4**
Moore, Patrick—**4**
Mora, Pat—**8**
Moray Williams, Ursula—**4**
Mordvinoff, Nicolas—**M**
"More, Caroline"
   See Cone, Molly—**3**
Morey, Walt—**3**
Morgan, Alfred P.—**M**
Morgenstern, Susie—**9**
Morin, Paul—**9**
Morpurgo, Michael—**9**
Morris, Ann—**8**
Morris, Gerald—**9**
Morrison, Lillian—**6**
Mosel, Arlene—**5**
Moser, Barry—**6**
Moss, Marissa—**9**
Most, Bernard—**7**
Mowat, Farley—**3**
Mullins, Patricia—**8**
Munari, Bruno—**3**
Munro, Roxie—**6**
Munsch, Robert—**8**
Munsinger, Lynn—**7**
Murphy, Jill—**6**
Murphy, Jim—**7**
Murphy, Robert W.—**4**
Murphy, Shirley Rousseau—
   6
Murphy, Stuart J.—**8**
Muth, Jon J—**9**
Myers, Christopher—**9**
Myers, Walter Dean—**5**

Müller, Jörg—**6**

Naidoo, Beverly—**7**
Namioka, Lensey—**7**
Napoli, Donna Jo—**8**
Narahashi, Keiko—**9**
Nash, Ogden—**4**
Natti, Susanna—**9**
Naylor, Phyllis Reynolds—**5**
Nelson, Kadir—**9**
Nelson, Marilyn—**9**
Nelson, S. D.—**9**
Nelson, Theresa—**7**
Nesbit, E.—**M**
Ness, Evaline—**3**
Neufeld, John—**8**
Neville, Emily—**3**
Newberry, Clare—**J**
Newcomb, Covell—**J**
Newell, Crosby
   See Bonsall, Crosby New-
   ell—**3**
Newell, Hope—**M**
Newman, Robert—**6**
Newton, Suzanne—**6**
Ney, John—**5**
"Nic Leodhas, Sorche"—**3**
Nichols, Ruth—**4**
Nicolay, Helen—**J**
Nimmo, Jenny—**9**
Nixon, Joan Lowery—**5**
Noble, Trinka Hakes—**6**
"Nodset, Joan L."
   See Lexau, Joan **M.**—**4**
Nolan, Han—**9**
Nolan, Jeannette Covert—**J**
North, Sterling—**3**
"Norton, Andre"—**M**
Norton, Mary—**3**
Novak, Matt—**8**
Numeroff, Laura (Joffe)—**7**
Nutt, Ken
   See "Beddows, Eric"—**7**
Nye, Naomi Shihab—**7**
Nöstlinger, Christine—**5**

O'Brien, Anne Sibley—**8**
O'Brien, Jack—**M**
"O'Brien, Robert C."—**4**
O'Dell, Scott—**M**
O'Kelly, Mattie Lou—**7**
O'Malley, Kevin—**8**
O'Neill, Mary—**3**
Oakley, Graham—**5**
Olcott, Frances Jenkins—**J**

Olcott, Virginia—**J**
Olsen, Ib Spang—**3**
"Oneal, Zibby"—**6**
Orgel, Doris—**4**
Orlev, Uri—**7**
Ormerod, Jan—**6**
Ormondroyd, Edward—**3**
Orton, Helen Fuller—**J**
"Osborne, David"
   See Silverberg, Robert—**3**
Osborne, Mary Pope—**8**
Otfinoski, Steven—**8**
"Otis, James"—**J**
Ottley, Reginald—**4**
Owens, Gail—**6**
Oxenbury, Helen—**3**

"Page, Eleanor"
   See Coerr, Eleanor—**6**
"Paisley, Tom"
   See Bethancourt, T.
   Ernesto—**5**
Palatini, Margie—**9**
Palazzo, Tony—**3**
Paola, Tomie de-
   See dePaola, Tomie—**5**
Paradis, Adrian A.—**M**
Parish, Peggy—**4**
Park, Barbara—**6**
Park, Linda Sue—**9**
Park, Ruth—**6**
Parker, Bertha M.—**M**
Parker, Dorothy D.—**4**
Parker, Edgar—**3**
Parker, Nancy Winslow—**5**
Parker, Robert Andrew—**4**
Parker, Steve—**8**
Parnall, Peter—**3**
Parrish, Maxfield—**J**
Parton, Ethel—**J**
Partridge, Elizabeth—**9**
Pascal, Francine—**5**
Patch, Edith M.—**J**
Patent, Dorothy Hinshaw—
   6
Paterson, Diane—**6**
Paterson, Katherine—**5**
Paton Walsh, Jill—**4**
Paull, Grace A.—**J**
Paulsen, Gary—**6**
Paxton,Tom—**8**
Pearce, Philippa—**3**
Peare, Catherine Owens—**M**
Pearson, Kit—**7**
Pearson, Susan—**7**

Pearson, Tracey Campbell—
7
Pease, Howard—**J**
Peck, Anne Merriman—**J**
Peck, Richard—**5**
Peck, Robert Newton—**5**
Peet, Bill—**3**
Pellowski, Anne—**5**
"Penn, Ruth Bonn"
    See Clifford, Eth—**6**
Peppé, Rodney—**5**
Perkins, Lucy Fitch—**J**
Perl, Lila—**6**
Petersen, P. J.—**6**
Petersham, Maud—**J**
Petersham, Miska—**J**
Peterson, Hans—**4**
Petry, Ann—**3**
Pevsner, Stella—**5**
Peyton, K. M.—**3**
Peyton, Michael
    See Peyton, K. M.—**3**
Pfeffer, Susan Beth—**6**
Pfister, Marcus—**8**
Philbrick, Rodman—**9**
Philip, Neil—**9**
Phillips, Ethel Calvert—**J**
"Phipson, Joan"—**3**
Piatti, Celestino—**3**
Picard, Barbara Leonie—**3**
Pienkowski, Jan—**4**
Pier, Arthur Stanwood—**J**
Pierce, Meredith Ann—**6**
Pierce, Tamora—**7**
"Pilgrim, Anne"
    See Allen, Mabel Esther—
    6
Pilkey, Dav—**7**
Pincus, Harriet—**4**
Pinkney, Andrea Davis—**8**
Pinkney, Brian—**7**
Pinkney, Gloria Jean—**8**
Pinkney, J. Brian
    See Pinkney, Brian—**7**
Pinkney, Jerry—**6**
Pinkwater, Daniel Manus—**5**
"Piper, Watty"
    See Bragg, Mabel Caro-
    line—**4**
Pitz, Henry C.—**M**
Platt, Kin—**5**
Plotz, Helen—**6**
"Plumb, A. R."
    See Applegate,
    Katherine—**9**

Plume, Ilse—**5**
Pogány, Willy—**J**
Polacco, Patricia—**7**
Politi, Leo—**J**
Polland, Madeleine—**3**
"Pollari, Pat"
    See Applegate,
    Katherine—**9**
Polushkin, Maria—**6**
Pomerantz, Charlotte—**6**
Poole, Lynn—**M**
Pope, Elizabeth Marie—**5**
Portal, Colette—**4**
Porte, Barbara Ann—**6**
Porter, Connie—**8**
Porter, Sheena—**3**
Potter, Beatrix—**J**
Potter, Giselle—**9**
Poulsson, Emilie—**J**
Prelutsky, Jack—**5**
Preussler, Otfried—**4**
Price, Christine—**M**
Price, Edith Ballinger—**J**
Price, Susan—**7**
Priceman, Marjorie—**8**
Primavera, Elise—**6**
Pringle, Laurence—**4**
Proudfit, Isabel—**M**
Provensen, Alice—**3, 9**
Provensen, Martin—**3, 9**
Pryor, Bonnie—**8**
Pullman, Philip—**6**
Pyle, Katharine—**J**
Pène du Bois, William
    See du Bois, William
    Pène—**J**

Quackenbush, Robert—**4**
Quennell, Charles Henry
    Bourne—**M**
Quennell, Marjorie—**M**

Rabe, Berniece—**5**
Rackham, Arthur—**J**
Radunsky, Vladimir—**9**
Raffi—**6**
Rahn, Joan Elma—**6**
Rand, Anne (or Ann)—**3**
Rand, Gloria—**8**
Rand, Paul—**3**
Rand, Ted—**6**
Randall, Florence Engel—**6**
"Randall, Robert"
    See Silverberg, Robert—**3**
Rankin, Louise S.—**M**

Ransome, Arthur—**J**
Ransome, James E.—**7**
Ransome, Lesa Cline-
    See Cline-Ransome,
    Lesa—**9**
Raphael, Elaine
    See Bolognese, Don &
    Elaine Raphael—**4**
Rapp, Adam—**9**
Rappaport, Doreen—**7**
Raschka, Chris—**7**
Raskin, Ellen—**3**
Rathmann, Peggy—**8**
Ravielli, Anthony—**3**
Rawlings, Marjorie Kin-
    nan—**3**
Rawls, Wilson—**6**
Ray, Deborah Kogan—**6**
Ray, Jane—**7**
Raynor, Mary—**5**
Reed, Philip—**3**
Reed, W. Maxwell—**J**
Reeder, Carolyn—**7**
Rees, David—**5**
Reeves, James—**3**
Regniers, Beatrice Schenk
    de
    See de Regniers, Beatrice
    Schenk—**M**
Reiser, Lynn—**8**
Reiss, Johanna—**5**
Rendina, Laura Cooper—**M**
Renick, Marion—**M**
Rey, H. A.—**J**
Rey, Lester del
    See del Rey, Lester—**3**
"Rhine, Richard"
    See Silverstein, Virginia
    B.—**5**
"Rhue, Morton"
    See Strasser, Todd—**6**
Ribbons, Ian—**4**
Rice, Eve—**5**
Richard, Adrienne—**5**
Richter, Hans Peter—**4**
"Rigg, Sharon"
    See Creech, Sharon—**7**
Ringgold, Faith—**7**
Ringi, Kjell—**4**
Robbins, Ruth—**3**
Roberts, Willo Davis—**5**
Robertson, Keith—**M**
Robinet, Harriette Gillem—
    9
Robinson, Barbara—**5**

Robinson, Charles—**6**
Robinson, Irene B.—**J**
Robinson, Mabel Louise—**J**
Robinson, Tom—**J**
Robinson, W. W.—**J**
Rochman, Hazel—**7**
Rockwell, Anne F.—**5**
Rockwell, Harlow—**5**
Rockwell, Thomas—**5**
Rodgers, Mary—**5**
Rodowsky, Colby—**6**
Rogers, Fred McFreeley
   See "Rogers, Mister"—**7**
Rogers, Jacqueline—**9**
"Rogers, Mister"—**7**
Rohmann, Eric—**8**
Rojankovsky, Feodor—**J**
Rolt-Wheeler, Francis—**J**
Roop, Peter & Connie—**8**
Roos, Ann—**M**
Roos, Stephen—**6**
Root, Barry—**8**
Root, Kimberly Bulcken—**8**
Root, Phyllis—**8**
Rose, Elizabeth—**3**
Rose, Gerald—**3**
Rosen, Michael J.—**8**
"Rosenberg, Ethel"
   See Clifford, Eth—**6**
Ross, Gayle—**8**
Ross, Pat—**7**
Ross, Tony—**6**
Rostkowski, Margaret—**6**
Roth, Susan L.—**7**
Rounds, Glen—**J**
Rourke, Constance—**M**
Rowe, Dorothy—**J**
Rowling, J. K.—**8**
Rubel, Nicole—**5**
Rubinstein, Gillian—**9**
Ruby, Lois—**6**
Ruckman, Ivy—**6**
Ruffins, Reynold
   See Sarnoff, Jane & Rey-
   nold Ruffins—**5**
Rugh, Belle Dorman—**3**
Rumford, James—**9**
Russo, Marisabina—**7**
Ryan, Cheli Durán—**5**
Ryan, Pam Muñoz—**9**
Ryden, Hope—**9**
Ryder, Joanne—**6**
Rylant, Cynthia—**6**

S., Svend Otto—**6**

Sabin, Edwin L.—**J**
Sabuda, Robert—**8**
Sachar, Louis—**7**
Sachs, Marilyn—**4**
Sadler, Marilyn—**8**
Saint James, Synthia—**9**
Saint-Exupéry, Antoine de—
   4
Salassi, Otto R.—**6**
Salisbury, Graham—**8**
Samuels, Barbara—**7**
San Souci, Daniel—**7**
San Souci, Robert D.—**7**
Sánchez, Enrique O.—**9**
Sandberg, Inger—**3**
Sandberg, Lasse—**3**
Sandburg, Helga—**3**
Sanders, Scott Russell—**7**
Sandin, Joan—**6**
Sandoz, Mari—**3**
Sanfield, Steve—**8**
Sarg, Tony—**J**
Sargent, Pamela—**6**
Sargent, Sarah—**6**
Sarnoff, Jane—**5**
Sasek, Miroslav—**3**
Sattler, Helen Roney—**6**
Sauer, Julia L.—**M**
Savage, Deborah—**7**
Savage, Katharine—**4**
Savery, Constance—**J**
Savitz, Harriet May—**5**
Sawyer, Ruth—**J**
Say, Allen—**6**
Sayers, Frances Clarke—**J**
Sayre, April Pulley—**9**
Scarry, Richard—**3**
Schaefer, Jack—**3**
Schami, Rafik—**7**
Schechter, Betty—**4**
Scheele, William E.—**3**
Schertle, Alice—**8**
Schick, Eleanor—**5**
Schindelman, Joseph—**3**
Schindler, S. D.—**7**
Schlee, Ann—**5**
Schlein, Miriam—**M**
Schmid, Eleonore—**4**
"Schneider, Elisa"
   See Kleven, Elisa—**7**
Schneider, Herman—**M**
Schneider, Nina—**M**
Schnur, Steven—**8**
Schoenherr, John—**4**

"Scholefield, Edmund O."
   See Butterworth, W. E.—**5**
Scholz, Jackson V.—**M**
Schoonover, Frank—**M**
Schroeder, Alan—**8**
Schultz, James Willard—**J**
Schulz, Charles—**3**
Schwartz, Alvin—**5**
Schwartz, Amy—**6**
Schwartz, David M.—**6**
Schweninger, Ann—**7**
Scieszka, Jon—**7**
Scoppettone, Sandra—**5**
Scott, Ann Herbert—**4**
Scott, Jack Denton—**6**
Scoville, Samuel, Jr.—**J**
Seabrooke, Brenda—**7**
Seaman, Augusta Huiell—**J**
"Sebastian, Lee"
   See Silverberg, Robert—**3**
Sebestyen, Ouida—**5**
"Sefton, Catherine"
   See Waddell, Martin—**7**
Segal, Lore—**4**
Segawa, Yasuo—**4**
Seidler, Tor—**6**
Selden, George—**4**
Selsam, Millicent E.—**M**
Selznick, Brian—**9**
Sendak, Maurice—**M**
Seredy, Kate—**J**
Serraillier, Ian—**3**
Service, Pamela F.—**7**
Seuling, Barbara—**9**
"Seuss, Dr."—**M**
Sewell, Helen—**J**
Sewell, Marcia—**5**
Seymour, Tres—**8**
Shannon, David—**8**
Shannon, George—**6**
Shannon, Monica—**J**
Shapiro, Irwin—**J**
Sharmat, Marjorie Wein-
   man—**5**
Sharmat, Mitchell—**6**
Sharp, Margery—**3**
Shaw, Nancy—**7**
Shecter, Ben—**3**
Shelby, Anne—**8**
Shepard, Ernest—**M**
Sherburne, Zoa Morin—**4**
Shimin, Symeon—**3**
Shippen, Katherine B.—**M**
Shotwell, Louisa R.—**3**
Showers, Paul C.—**4**

Wier, Ester—**3**
Wiese, Kurt—**J**
Wiesner, David—**7**
Wijngaard, Juan—**8**
Wikland, Ilon—**4**
Wilder, Laura Ingalls—**J**
Wildsmith, Brian—**3**
Wilkinson, Barry—**4**
Wilkinson, Brenda—**5**
Willard, Barbara—**4**
Willard, Nancy—**5**
Willey, Margaret—**7**
"William, Kate"
   See Armstrong, Jennifer—**8**
Williams, Barbara—**6**
"Williams, Charles"
   See Collier, James Lincoln—**5**
Williams, Garth—**M**
Williams, Jay—**4**
Williams, Karen Lynn—**8**
"Williams, Patrick J."
   See Butterworth, W. E.—**5**
Williams, Sherley Anne—**7**
Williams, Ursula Moray
   See Moray Williams, Ursula—**4**
Williams, Vera B.—**5**
Williams-Garcia, Rita—**8**
Williamson, Joanne S.—**3**
Wilson, Barbara Ker
   See Ker Wilson, Barbara—**4**
Wilson, Budge—**7**
Wimmer, Mike—**9**
Windsor, Patricia—**5**
"Winfield, Julia"
   See Armstrong, Jennifer—**8**
Winter, Jeannette—**7**

Winter, Paula—**6**
Winterfeld, Henry—**3**
Winthrop, Elizabeth—**5**
Wiseman, David—**5**
Wisler, G. Clifton—**7**
Wisniewski, David—**7**
Wittlinger, Ellen—**9**
Woerkom, Dorothy Van
   See Van Woerkom, Dorothy—**5**
Wojciechowska, Maia—**3**
Wolf, Bernard—**5**
Wolff, Ashley—**6**
"Wolff, Sonia"
   See Levitin, Sonia—**5**
Wolff, Virginia Euwer—**7**
Wolitzer, Hilma—**5**
Wolkstein, Diane—**5**
"Wolny, P."
   See Janeczko, Paul B.—**6**
Wondriska, William—**3**
Wong, Janet S.—**9**
Wood, Audrey—**6**
Wood, Don—**6**
Wood, Esther—**J**
Wood, James Playsted—**4**
Woodruff, Elvira—**8**
Woodson, Jacqueline—**8**
Woody, Regina J.—**M**
Woolley, Catherine—**M**
Worth, Kathryn—**J**
Worth, Valerie—**5**
Wrede, Patricia C.—**7**
Wright, Betty Ren—**6**
Wrightson, Patricia—**4**
Wuorio, Eva-Lis—**3**
Wyeth, N. C.—**J**
Wyler, Rose
   See Ames, Gerald & Rose Wyler—**3**
Wyndham, Lee—**M**

Wynne-Jones, Tim—**8**

Yaccarino, Dan—**9**
Yamaguchi, Marianne—**3**
Yamaguchi, Tohr—**3**
Yarbrough, Camille—**7**
Yashima, Taro—**M**
Yates, Elizabeth—**J**
Yates, Raymond F.—**M**
Yee, Paul Richard—**7**
Yep, Laurence—**5**
"Ylla"—**M**
Yolen, Jane—**4**
Yorinks, Arthur—**6**
York, Carol Beach—**5**
Youd, Samuel
   See "Christopher, John"—**4**
Young, Ed—**3**, **9**
Young, Ella—**J**
Yumoto, Kazumi—**9**

Zalben, Jane Breskin—**5**
Zarchy, Harry—**M**
Zei, Alki—**4**
Zelinsky, Paul O.—**6**
Zemach, Harve & Margot—**3**
Ziefert, Harriet—**7**
Zim, Herbert S.—**J**
Zimmer, Dirk—**6**
Zimnik, Reiner—**3**
Zindel, Paul—**5**
Zion, Gene—**M**
Zollinger, Gulielma—**J**
Zolotow, Charlotte—**M**, **8**
Zwerger, Lisbeth—**6**
Zwilgmeyer, Dikken—**J**

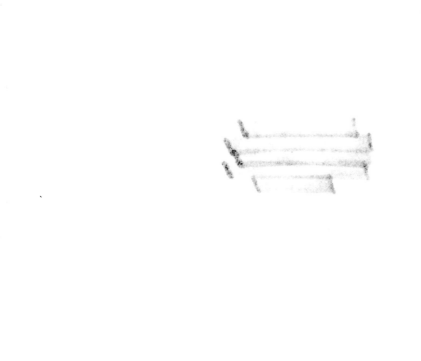

j920 W748 2004

Ninth book of junior authors
and illustrators